THE HISTORY OF
MARKETING THOUGHT

THE HISTORY OF
MARKETING THOUGHT
Third Edition

BY
ROBERT BARTELS, Ph.D.
Professor Emeritus of Marketing and International Business
The Ohio State University

Publishing Horizons, Inc.

©COPYRIGHT 1988, PUBLISHING HORIZONS, INC.
2950 North High Street P.O. Box 02190
Columbus, Ohio 43202

Originally published by Richard D. Irwin, Inc. (1962)
as *The Development of Marketing Thought*.

Printed in the United States.

1 2 3 4   8 7 6 5

Library of Congress Cataloging-in-Publication Data

Bartels, Robert, 1913–
    The history of marketing thought.

    Includes index.
    1. Marketing—History.   I. Title.
HF5415.B36   1988   658.8′009   87-20702
ISBN 0-942280-44-X

TABLE OF CONTENTS

1920s. Integration of Credit Thought in the 1920s. Credit Thought — 1930 to 1950. Continuing Revision of Credit Thought. Credit Thought in the 1950s. Credit thought since 1960. Contributions of Credit Literature to Marketing Thought.

Environment of the Sales Literature. Selling and Salesmanship: Subjective Selling. Preparation for Selling. Selling, a Part of Marketing. Salesmanship — Science or Art. Inside Salesmen. Integration of Sales Thought. Scientific Selling. Development of Sales Thought — 1950 to 1960. Sales Thought Since 1960. Sales Management. Supervisory Sales Management. Sales Work Analysis. Sales Organization. Sales Management, a Marketing Function. Strategy in Marketing Management. Integration of Sales Management Thought. Sales Management Thought — 1950 to 1960. Sales Management Thought since 1960. Contributions of Literature On Selling and Sales Management To Marketing Thought.

Contributions of Paul H. Nystrom. "The Retailing Series." Contributions From Other Sources: Retailing Manuals. Retail Buying. Retail Selling. Retail Credit. Retail Accounting. Organization and Personnel. Principles of Retailing. Retailing Problems. Retailing Thought in the 1950's: Changes in the Environment of Retailing. Changes in Stores and Merchandising. New Concepts in Retailing Thought. Retailing Thought since 1960. Standard Texts Updated. Retailing Folklore. Specialized Technical Studies. Broader Views of Retailing. Contributions of Retailing Literature to Marketing Thought.

Conditions Inducing the Study of Wholesaling. Initial Conception of Wholesaling. Wholesaling in Transition. Other Works on Wholesaling. Wholesaling Thought in the 1950s. Wholesaling Thought Since 1960. Contributions of Wholesaling Literature to Marketing Thought.

Factors Influencing Development of Marketing Research. Beginnings of Marketing Research. Evolving Concept of Research in Marketing. Contributions to Marketing Research: Qualitative Determination of Markets. Measurability of Markets. Market Surveys. Marketing and Distribution Research. Sales Research. Consumer Research. Statistical Research. Developments of Thought After 1950. Marketing Research Thought Since 1960. Contributions of Research Literature To Marketing Thought.

Concept of Marketing. Holistic Approach. Managerial Marketing. Consumer Problem Solving. Projected Development Of Marketing Thought. The Development of Thought Since 1960. The Issue of Science. The Issue of Theory. The Issue of Definition.

Introduction. Early Influences. Beginnings of Conceptual Change. Reevaluation in the 1950s. New Concepts Appearing. Upgrading Through Quantification. Consumer Behavior. New Dimensions. Special Interest Areas. Conclusions.

APPENDIXES

PREFACE

In the first edition of this book (1962), the formation of marketing thought after 1900 was traced in analysis of extant literature and in a survey of writers' self-perception of subjective influences upon their involvement in marketing. In the second edition (1976), new literature of the fourteen-year interim was read to observe changes in thought as expressed in writings. In the third edition (1987), changes since 1950 were again sought in subjective factors which contributors reported as influencing their marketing scholarship and writing.

The surveyed authors were asked to relate: (1) what subjective factors had incited and influenced their creative perceptions brought to the study of marketing; (2) how this had affected their writings and other professional production; and (3) how their thoughts and writings had fitted into or changed the course of marketing thought.

Of twenty-five leaders to whom requests were sent, twenty responded appropriately, and their replies constitute the substance of this revision. In the final chapter, the relation of influences to writings, 1950–1987, is presented. Additional information in the reports relating mainly to the formation of the scholarly and cultured intellect is presented in the Appendix, Section B, "Contributors to Marketing Thought, 1950–1987," there added to the comparable letters written in 1940.

ROBERT BARTELS

Columbus, Ohio
1987

THE MEANING
OF MARKETING

There are periods of such rapid social evolution in the annals of human history that one can scarcely tell which has had more effect upon the other: changes in thinking or changes in the environment. The years since 1900 have been such a period.

For much of the world this has been a period of slow progress and destructive warfare. In countries where industrialization was advanced, the establishment of a market economy wrought marked changes in the social and economic structure. In the United States, not only did the market economy develop, but a new attitude toward business revolutionized the economy of the country and gradually affected the whole world. That revolutionary element was identified by the term "marketing."

The development of marketing was a result of circumstances. Environmental conditions focused attention on market practices. Industrial production was expanding; inventions created new products; population, education, and personal income were on the increase; social values exalted financial success; and new and widening markets offered unlimited opportunity for initiative and innovation. At the same time, the manner in which people regarded the market and practices also changed. Increased attention was given to the market, to its institutions, to its social role, and to the improvement of the practices of those who were engaged in market undertakings. In those circumstances early concepts of marketing were formulated, and the modern practice of marketing was begun.

Those same circumstances gave birth also to the body of marketing thought that has since been developed. This thought consists of the accumulated understandings of marketing: the facts of our markets, rules of operation, principles of marketing behavior, and theories advanced for the achievement of certain marketing objectives. This thought has found expression in both periodical and book literature.

The influence of this body of thought during this century has been inestimable. It has given guidance to millions of businessmen and has been the chart for planning the structure of our marketing institution. It has been the voice of a new philosophy extolling and extending the role of sales promotion in the economy. The literature of this new body of thought has been read by college students of business. It has been the backbone of business teacher training programs on the graduate level. Even in secondary and vocational education, sometimes diluted and distorted, it has molded values, standards, and motivations of our society. Seldom has a literature been so influential or a society so receptive to the influence of a new body of thought.

SURVEY OF MARKETING THOUGHT

Marketing thought, through most of this period, has been developed as a spontaneous and voluntary contribution of those who were concerned with solving problems of the market place. Objective regard for this body of knowledge did not develop along with the thought itself, and it was not until the 1930s that much interest in the scientific character of this knowledge was expressed. Interest in application of scientific standards to marketing research and management was amply manifested earlier, but concern for whether the body of marketing thought approximated, or had the potential of, a "science," or why it developed in the manner in which it did, was not so soon forthcoming.

In recent years such consideration of the body of marketing thought has grown as a result of several factors. First, within the field of marketing have evolved new concepts, new explanations of marketing, which challenged those which had become accepted as basic marketing knowledge. Those who believed in the "rightness" of the marketing principles and theories evolved during the first half of this century grew to accommodate newer ideas. In the process, however, more objective scrutiny and appraisal of all marketing thought was required. Both the older and the newer elements in marketing thought came to be seen as understandings produced by the circumstances of the times. Thought that was produced in past decades took on new meaning when oriented in the economic and intellectual environment in which it was conceived. As marketing methods are a function or variable of a marketing objective, so marketing thought itself is dependent upon the factors that impell such thought at any given time.

Second, appraisal of the state of marketing thought has been impelled in recent years by upheaval in academic circles over the content of the marketing curriculum. Most marketing programs, until 1950, were based upon the structure of marketing knowledge devised up to that time. Increasing demand for education of students of business in broader management capacities turned attention from traditional to less orthodox concepts of marketing and thought structures. This development, too, has emphasized the relativity of marketing thought − its relativity to the problems to be solved in our economy and to the specific use to be made of it. Re-examination of marketing knowledge has been impelled by the effort to shape scholastic offerings to the present needs of our business and social community.

A third impulsion to the present growing interest in marketing thought springs from a broadening concept of marketing. Heretofore, marketing has been looked upon primarily as a technical business activity. It has been regarded also as an economic activity. More recently, however, it has been viewed as a social activity or institution − the activity of society providing for its material needs. Consequently, the structure of thought that had served the former, more narrow purpose and concept of marketing has yielded to a broader concept, with the result that marketing thought has been appraised from the standpoint of other social sciences. Interdisciplination, or the interrelating of marketing with other social studies, has contributed to marketing knowledge a number of concepts and methods of research. It is increasingly providing a social viewpoint that, by way of formulating new objectives for marketing, has caused restructuring and reappraisal of marketing thought.

EMERGENCE OF MARKETING

If marketing thought is an expression of what is known about "marketing," it follows that the beginnings of marketing thought would be traceable to the beginnings of marketing. If, as is commonly claimed, the beginnings of marketing are lost in antiquity, the beginnings of marketing thought would be equally ancient. That this cannot be taken for granted, however, is clear because the beginnings of marketing thought are associated with events following the turn of the present century. The problem posed by this inconsistency is simply this: *Has marketing always existed?*

Historical accounts of trade lead one to conclude that marketing *has* always existed. Six thousand years of recorded history shows the roots of both Western and Eastern civilization to have included various forms of trade. This is not conclusive evidence, however, that *marketing* has always existed. The issue relates to whether marketing is a *concept* or a *percept*.

Was the original use of the term "marketing" merely an application of a new name to an old practice? Or did it represent the discovery of something new, which demanded also a new name? It is believed that the term "marketing" was first used as a noun, in contrast to its earlier use as a verb, between 1906 and 1911. Could it be said that that was when marketing *began?* Or did it *exist* before? This is in part a question of semantics and and etymology, but it is an important question, for what marketing *is* must be understood before the nature of marketing *thought* can be ascertained.

Two philosophic theories concerning the origin of language are interestingly discussed by Richard Chenevix Trench, in a series of lectures given in 1851.[1] One theory, he says, is that language is an invention of man, an adornment, something he might create or not create, as his pleasure might direct. If that were the case, there might be found primitive people who had no language. But human beings who did not use language to communicate have never been found.

The other explanation of the origin of language is that it is inseparable from reason and is a spiritual faculty of expression, apart from man's ability to think. Man's *word* and his *reason* are essentially one and the same; the Greek language had one word for both. Accordingly, man's language has developed as his thoughts have developed. New ideas find expression in new words.

Emphasizing the indigenousness of words to a people's thinking, Trench wrote that the manner in which people become aware of thought deficiencies is by comparing their own language with another.

> Compelled by such comparisons through having undertaken to transfer treasures of (another) language into their own, they become conscious (that) . . . another language has found no voice in their own . . . Men are so little accustomed, indeed so little able, to contemplate things . . . except through the invention and by the machinery of words . . . that the absence of words from a language almost necessarily brings with it the absence of any sense of that absence.

This is simply to say that thoughts find expression in words, that realities await discovery and naming, and that new thoughts – and thoughts are "things" – take new words.

The significance of this theory of language to the study of marketing thought lies in the fact that the term "marketing" was not used until early in this century and that even yet there is in other languages no equivalent for the word "marketing." The French, for example, use the term *"le marketing,"* and in other languages also the English term is used to represent an idea that is not indigenous to their thinking or their vocabulary. The inference is that the *idea* that the term "marketing" represents has *not* always existed. If, therefore, the *idea* that "marketing" represents has not always existed, can it be said that *marketing* has always existed? No single change in distributive practice in the early twentieth century so abruptly impelled the use of a new name. But the confluence of ideas producing a new conception of distributive practice did produce that result and led to the initial use of the term "marketing." Marketing must therefore be regarded not simply as a *practice* but as a *conception – a concept of a practice.*

According to Trench, a problem in the development of thought is the use of a single term to designate a variety of concepts. This problem has been experienced in the development of marketing thought, for not only did "marketing" represent something different from "trade" or "selling" but throughout the usage of the term "marketing" it has been employed to represent a variety of slightly differentiated ideas.

By "marketing" was first meant that combination of factors which had to be taken into consideration prior to the undertaking of certain selling or promotional activities. The essence of "marketing" was the *combination* of factors. Blindness to and ignorance of that *combination* of factors is the reason for the absence of terms equivalent to "marketing" in other languages. In the development of marketing thought even in the United States, the conceptual, rather than the perceptual, nature of marketing has been too little appreciated, with the result that structures of marketing thought have not always included clearly defined concepts of the subject. In general, however, it has been treated as a business activity, a technical function, a practice, a trade phenomenon.

MARKETING AND SOCIAL SCIENCE

Thought about marketing reveals it to be more than simply a business activity. Economists have regarded it as a type of economic activity. But more than that, sociological research has shown increasingly that the institution of the market, and therefore perhaps marketing and marketing thought, is primarily a *social* rather than merely an *economic* institution.

Polyanyi is an exponent of this idea; his writings[2] lift the traditional subject of marketing out of the realm simply of business thought and place it in a much broader social context. From his viewpoint, marketing must be regarded not merely as a business practice but as a social institution. Marketing is essentially a means of meeting and satisfying certain needs of people. It is a highly developed and refined system of thought and practice characteristic of a period in the development of market economy.

Market economy, according to Polanyi, is a social system that has been developed mainly since the sixteenth century. In it economic factors have superseded other social institutions that were previously paramount. Assumptions made concerning man's behavior in the market, both as seller and as buyer, have been foremost determinants of economic and social practices. Marketing thought has been part of the superstructure built mainly upon economists' premises during this period, some of which Polanyi holds to be fallacious. By his timetable, not only marketing but also the market economy is new, for before the past few hundred years there had never existed a social or economic system similar to the market economy in which we are now operating. This is a system in which the market regulates and runs society rather than society's holding the economy subordinate to social interests. According to Polanyi, this autonomous market economy has risen to its zenith and is already in a declining stage, evidenced by the restoration to society of some of its social, moral, and ethical values with which the market economy has been in conflict.

A latent presumption in the practice of marketing has been that marketing gives to society more than society gives to it. The fact is that marketing is but one of several *means* of accomplishing a social *objective*. Polanyi explains that this objective is accomplished by societies in different ways: by reciprocity, redistribution, economy, trade, and the market.

Reciprocity, according to sociologists, is a social system wherein material needs are met through exchange carried on between individuals and groups in the form of gift-giving. Usually, surplus goods are given to those lacking such goods. Through a concept of symmetry, or duality, individuals or groups are paired for reciprocal giving. Rules govern the practice, requiring the exchange of equivalencies, although not of numerically equated offerings. No records or administration is involved, and there is no concept of "truck and barter." When carried on extensively, this system is said to involve intricacies the accounting for which modern record systems would be inadequate.

Redistribution is a social system involving the assembling of goods at a point from which they are redistributed by a duly constituted authority. An extended family, a tribe, or even a larger political group may be a unit carrying out this concept of centricity. This system provides for the needs of all by a type of rationing, providing also for those who do not contribute physical products but who serve the community in other ways, as well as those who are unable to make a contribution to the community.

Householding, or *oeconomia,* to use the Greek term, is a third social system accomplishing what marketing does in our society. Autarchy is an essential feature of the household economy. It involves production for use, not for exchange. The unit of self-sufficiency is a closed social group. There is no need for trade or markets, although some goods are sold, despite the fact that production is for use rather than for gain. Householding was the system prevailing at the time of Aristotle, who recognized in the early markets then beginning to appear new concepts and new implications.

In these three systems individual motives are disciplined by the general principles of behavior for the society, and the motive of gain is not present in any of them. Adam Smith's presumption of man's innate propensity to "truck and barter" was unfounded in sociological fact. Stemming from economic theory based upon that hypothesis, which did not even appear valid until after the Industrial Revolution, marketing thought had at the outset a variance from other social sciences with which it only lately has begun to become reconciled.

A fourth system of supplying society's needs is that of trade — marketless trade. Trade is a form of exchange which may be carried on in the absence of markets. Historically, it involved prices, in the form of equivalencies, determined by treaty or administrative decision and not by behavior in a market place.

Trade was generally conducted between countries or groups and not between individuals. Products were produced for trade. Functionaries having status as traders performed the necessary activities. Trade was documented, but it was risk free, in regard to both price and debtors' insolvency.

The market is the fifth type of social system supplying society's material needs. Originally, the market was a local institution. It was entirely separate from the trade carried on outside the country, and there was no such thing as a "national" market. The market supplied the common people with daily provisions. It was conducted mainly by women, and in definite parts of the cities, often in the open, sometimes in shops. It was separately administered, and it was governed by such social customs and practices as guaranteed the "peace of the market."

With the Industrial Revolution, changes occurred in many of these concepts. The motives of trucking and bartering, which before had not existed, were then assumed to be inherent. The sociologist explains, however, that these are not inherent tendencies but "effects of highly artificial stimulants administered to the body social in order to meet a situation which was created by the no less artificial phenomenon of the machine."[3] In other words, the Industrial Revolution, with the machine and its mass production, was the beginning of a change to the market economy. In that change, the local markets were of little significance. Long-distance or export markets were also of little significance to the development of economic thought because they functioned mainly outside the economy. Internal or national markets were the product of the Industrial Revolution.

It is in this context that the necessity for improving distributive practice impelled the conception of marketing and the development of marketing thought. Thus, in social history and in comparative social organizations, the system of behavior called "marketing" has a highly specialized position.

The same circumstances that created national markets for products required that, for the accomplishment of the potentialities of "free trade," land, labor, and money be dealt with as marketable commodities. The presumption of the marketability of these three factors, however, conflicted with the innate dignity and importance of individuals as social entities and in the course of years destroyed social values by subserving them to economic interests. The extreme extent of this dominance of economic over social interests, beginning in the late nineteenth century, evoked state regulation counteracting and modifying basic concepts of the market economy.

What Polanyi terms the "rise and fall of market economy" is relevant to the history of marketing, inasmuch as the study of marketing, and therefore the development of marketing thought, has coincided somewhat with the rising interest in social welfare with which he associates the "decline" of the market economy. It seems particularly significant that, from the start, the assumption of the paramount importance of consumption has been fundamental to marketing thought. Moreover, throughout the history of marketing during this century, and the development of marketing thought, interest not only in consumption but in consumers has continually increased. In recent years, marketers have had recourse more generally to studies that voice social interests and values.

In this perspective, therefore, marketing thought cannot be regarded merely as part of the system of business or business thought but rather as an interpretation of an institution in our particular social structure.

MARKETING AND HUMAN DEVELOPMENT

Explanation of the appearance of marketing on the surface of the world's time and space is more difficult than the mere identification of marketing with a social system or a business philosophy. Nevertheless, conjecture as to "why" is as important as analysis of "how" marketing thought has developed. Such speculation presumes causes, and causal interpretations of social developments are yet taken to be hypothetical and undemonstrable. Nevertheless, there are theories of determinism based upon a number of points of view.

Perhaps the most familiar to students of business is the theory of economic determinism, whereby the evolution of a marketing order is traceable to economic development. It might be said that in the natural course of the economic development society progresses through predatory, hunting, pastoral, agricultural, craft, manufacturing, and marketing stages. This is the outline of economic history; it arrays the stages through which underdeveloped economies even today seem to evolve. Marketing is associated with that stage of economic affluence which emphasizes distribution, consumer-oriented product innovation, service, etc. Thus, according to economic determinism, is explained the emergency of marketing in this era.

There are likewise other deterministic explanations of the evolution of the social and economic order:

1. *The biological*—whereby evolution is attributed to development of the species of man, his intellectual capacity, his physical strength, etc.

2. *The technological*—whereby progress is attributed to man's developing ability to use such instruments and forces as the wheel, the lever, fire, the plane, mathematics, chronometers, microscopes, steam, standardization, and management.

3. *The astrological*—whereby human events are related to positions and relations of celestial bodies.

Many other concepts of determinism are expressed in the theories intended to aid in understanding the changes that occur in human society. Not the least provocative of them is the theory of spiritual determinism, whereby *human* progress is attributed to a *divine* influence. The foretold patterns of the advent of this influence are the subject of prophetic literature, which is found in many writings, ranging from those of ancient patriarchs to those of Free Masonry. The prophetic account of spiritual determinism known as The Revelation of Saint John the Divine has particular reference to what is now called marketing, and it is of special interest inasmuch as some exegetes link the fulfillment of his prophecies with the twentieth century.

According to John, throughout a period in history, trade is predominantly characterized by deception and fraud. Increasing spiritualization of mankind is accompanied by the fall of materialism, and that event is attended by the ineffectuality of merchants and tradesmen who practice the former deceptions. Trade then continues on a higher level of practice in expression of a more spiritual means by which the needs of mankind are met.

If the advent of marketing has meant anything, it represents just such transition of trade from domination of seller interests to a consideration of buyer or consumer interests. Throughout history, commerce and trade have been associated with base practices, even throughout the nineteenth century under the sanction of doctrines of *laissez faire* and the Protestant Ethic. The conception of marketing, however, introduced two new elements in trade: first, a more scientific character of management and, second, a primary service motive. As faintly as they have appeared at times, they nevertheless witness an unprecedented turn in the tides of trade.

The import of this observation is simply this: marketing thought can be regarded not less than as a portion of human intelligence and social development at this time. It is more than a business technique, more than an economic function, more than a social institution. Our way of thinking about marketing reflects our way of thinking about life.

The serious student of marketing may well consider what incites such an event as the conception or discovery of marketing and how it evolves. Do men make the times in which such an event occurs, or have the times made the men? Has the evolution of something more fundamental caused men to perceive and to divine a more basic occurrence *as* marketing? Could such an idea have been uttered before "its time"? Hindsight shows that certain things were not known to men in the past. Had not the time come for them to be uttered? Was human thought not ripe for the unfolding of certain ideas? Are these maturities surface evidences of something deeper in the growth of civilization? Is marketing a fundamental phenomenon, or a passing one, in the sum of human knowledge?

ENDNOTES

[1] Richard Chenevix Trench, *On the Study of Words* (New York: Macmillan Co., 1925), pp. 13-14, 206-7.

[2] Karl Polanyi, Conrad M. Arensberg, and Harry W. Pearson, *Trade and Market in the Early Empires* (Glencoe, Ill.: Free Press, 1957), and Karl Polanyi, *The Great Transformation* (Boston: Beacon Press, 1957).

[3] Polanyi, *The Great Transformation, op. cit.,* p. 57.

EARLIER THEORIES RELEVANT 2
TO MARKETING THOUGHT

The development of marketing thought began early in the twentieth century with the conception of marketing. It would be naive, however, to believe that marketing thought had no antecedents, for the period in which study of marketing began was rich in economic thought, which unquestionably influenced thinking about this new subject. To understand the evolution of marketing thought, some appreciation of the mental and environmental climate in which it dawned is necessary.

Like earlier economists, students of marketing were concerned with the practical problems of their day. Economists had undertaken to formulate theory to guide public policy. Over the years, as circumstances changed, new theories were forthcoming, based upon modified assumptions more in accord with prevailing conditions. By 1900, the body of economic thought consisted of many theories that had been developed in England, France, Austria, Germany, the United States, and other places. Their suitability to our own problems at that time was strongly debated.

The prevailing economic thought of their time was well known to early students of marketing, for they would have been exposed to the thinking of economists in their educational programs, and many were actually educated as economists. They were equipped, therefore, with a frame of reference when new problems of the market place came to their attention.

Unlike earlier economic theorists, who, although they brought forth divergent theories, remained in the ranks of theoretical economists, students of marketing evolved a body of thought that, by its nature, scope, and application, set them apart from the usual economists. Their studies were more empirical than theoretical, more practical than abstract, more descriptive than philosophical. They, too, were concerned with social and economic problems of the day, but from the standpoint of the business firm more than from that of public administration. Prevailing theories of value, exchange, price behavior, division of labor, and governmental regulation found new interpretation and expression through their work, in what has become the body of marketing thought.

The debt of early students of marketing to economic theory for guidance of their thinking should not be underestimated; yet the significance of the departure from theoretical economics that marketing thought represented cannot be overemphasized. For a proper appraisal, one must understand, first, the principal points in prevailing theory from which marketing thought departed as it developed and, second, the circumstances that impelled the new line of thinking.

In the remainder of this chapter these two areas of consideration are analyzed. First, a review is made of the contributions to thought made by Smith, Ricardo, John Stuart Mill, Marshall, the marginalists, and some more modern economists, to determine how a traditionally trained marketing economist around 1900 would have thought concerning the market, value, production, government and business, the consumer, the role of business, the nature of man, social philosophy, and the state of the economy. Second, an analysis is made of environmental conditions that were at variance with assumptions underlying accepted theory and whose accompanying problems impelled the study of marketing for the solution of them.

THE MARKET

As study began to yield knowledge of marketing, certain established concepts of the market needed to be re-examined.

One was the idea that demand originates in the creation of a supply. This concept had grown out of economic situations simpler than those existing in 1900. Marketable supply began to appear in the householding economy of the ancient Greeks; it was a prominent feature of the economy at the time of the Industrial Revolution. Wages earned by those who participated in production constituted the effectual demand of individuals who bought the varied supplies offered in the market. J. B. Say generalized the phenomenon, saying that supply creates demand.

By 1900, however, it was being found that demand consisted of more than simple purchasing power. It reflected desire as well as ability to purchase, and new experiences with advertising and salesmanship were proving that desire could be increased and molded by factors other than the mere existence of supply. Such a concept of demand was not found in prevailing economic theory because, until that time, incomes had not been to any great extent sufficiently above subsistence levels to permit men to be subject to "demand-creating" influences. The increase of spending power and discretionary spending led to new thoughts of the relation of demand and supply in the market, which were developed in marketing thought.

Another concept of the market concerned its capacity to adjust itself automatically to a harmonious equilibrium. It had long been held that competitive forces would normally, in the long run, dissipate tendencies of disequilibrium in the market. Adam Smith characterized this tendency of the market as the "guiding hand," which produced under the motivation of self-interest a generally harmonious consequence. This effect of competition continued in a measure through the nineteenth century, but, as competition diminished in some industries and trades, the assumptions found in traditional economic theory became increasingly invalid. Students of marketing found need for fuller explanation of short-run behavior in the market, and their explanations of this became a part of marketing thought.

A third idea of the market current in economic thought was that cost was the principal determinant of price, at least in the long run. Cost was held to consist of payments of wages, profit, rent, and interest. Some economists measured value in terms of labor or the "toil and trouble" of obtaining an item. With stimulus given to the analysis of demand by psychological studies of the late nineteenth century, demand came to occupy a more important position in price theory. Thus the concepts and work of the marginal utility analysts prepared the way for students of marketing who would find in the *market,* rather than in the *process of production,* explanations of price formation.

Prevailing concepts of the elasticity of demand were still another influence upon the thinking of early students of marketing. They were directly related to the theory that demand could be increased through promotional effort, while at the same time costs of production could be decreased as a result of larger scale of operation. The concept of eleasticity, however, was the result of a long development in economic thought. Adam Smith had recognized that demand was not a fixed amount at all prices. To him, "effectual" demand was willingness to pay the natural price. Malthus, on the other hand, had a better appreciation of some of the subjective character of demand and recognized what he called "intensity" of demand. Jevons and the Austrians expanded that idea into a theory of diminishing utility. Alfred Marshall later generalized it in the concept of elasticity. His interpretation of demand has long been used by marketing writers as a theoretical basis for selling, advertising, and the promotional work of marketing in general.

THE MEANING OF VALUE

Value theory was another area of economic thought relevant to early studies of marketing, but, because economists had dealt mainly with value in tangible goods created in processes of physical production, new concepts of value were required after 1900 to justify the growing distributive activity.

In their explanations of value, economists leaned heavily upon input factors, determining their relative quantities and prices. For them, however, value was a characteristic of wealth, and wealth consisted of salable, tangible, material goods. Services were not wealth, and economists were in disagreement as to whether services that did not alter the physical product contributed to wealth — created value. With distributive services growing in importance at the beginning of the century, the question of whether they were value-creating was an important one for students of marketing.

Smith held that distributive activities contributed to value, but only indirectly. They extended the market, thereby making opportunities for increased production and for greater specialization of labor in production. Therefore, the contribution of distribution was made through the labor engaged in physical production. Malthus and some of his predecessors had a greater appreciation of the direct productive contribution of distributive service to value, but their views were not in wide circulation when students of marketing undertook to interpret its economic contribution. Various economists had distinguished different types of utilities, and in due course marketing students identified time, place, and possession utilities as three for which distributive activity was directly responsible. It was not until after many years, however, that the concept of "value added by marketing" was set forth.

Economists also distinguished in their value theories value-in-use and value-in-exchange. The former consisted of the general total utility inherent in an item; the latter was the power of one item to command another in exchange. Both were important in the development of marketing thought, but neither was fully explained by economists. The concept of value-in-use gained credence as the marginal utility analysis was employed to explain demand behavior. The earliest students of marketing did not employ this neoclassical concept, but later ones found it helpful in interpreting marketing.

PRODUCTION

Early students of marketing had no particular intent to prove the productivity of marketing, although they began their studies at a time when in economic theory trade was generally held to be unproductive. Not only productivity but even respectability was lacking from trade. From the time of the ancient Greeks and Romans to the nineteenth century, tradesmen were not held in high esteem. In fact, even in this century tradesmen have been depicted as parasitic, their activities shrouded in the darkness of the market place.

The essence of this attitude was found in some of the earlier economic theories. In the eighteenth century, productivity was held by the physiocrats to be the production of a surplus over costs. Proprietors were the "productive" class; agriculturists were the instrumentality by which production was brought forth; merchants, artisans, and professional men were "non-productive"; laborers were considered passive and inconsequential. Such was the concept of productivity of the social classes identified in the *Tableau Economique*.

Productivity was defined not only in terms of the type of contributor but also in terms of what was produced. The physiocrats regarded as productive only that activity which yielded material goods; moreover, they held that production must result in a surplus above costs, which they called the *produit net*. Smith and his followers regarded production as any addition to value, yet excluded the performance of services on the ground that their value perished at the instant of production. No distinction was made between the production of consumer services and such business services as distributive activities.

Other concepts related to production, such as diminishing returns, marginal productivity, opportunity costs, and the representative firm, were included in economic theories of production, but in 1900 there was no clear concept of the justification of marketing as a productive activity or as a contribution to economic production. On the contrary, the popular impression was that the middleman added *cost* instead of *value*. Students of marketing, on the other hand, could see that distributive services did increase values, but the establishment of that fact in marketing thought was a long and gradual development.

GOVERNMENT

Another thread in the theoretical background against which students of marketing began the development of marketing thought concerned the relation of government to business. The attitudes of most people toward that lay somewhere between the extremes of governmental intervention and governmental nonintervention in business affairs. The twentieth century marked, in general, the transition in political philosophy from *laissez faire* to more positive governmental aid to and regulation of business.

Students of marketing would have been familiar with several concepts of *laissez faire*, and, being generally sympathetic with the interests of business, they would have placed great hope in the effectiveness of competition. Throughout the eighteenth and nineteenth centuries it was businessmen who were prominent in defining *laissez faire* for their periods. In the era of mercantilism, tradesmen advocated such governmental action as would foster and benefit trade, but they discouraged further intervention. In the time of Adam Smith, economic liberalists believed that all individuals in business should have equal opportunity but not the special privileges that they had enjoyed under mercantilism. The duty of the government was held to be the protection of society, the administration of justice, the establishment of public works, and the taxation of imports in order to make the nation self-sufficient. John Stuart Mill interpreted *laissez faire* to mean that the government should do no more than protect the general rights of citizens as individuals. In the latter part of the nineteenth century, businessmen took *laissez faire* to mean the absence of all reform legislation but the supplying by government of increasing services to the business community.

Against this background of thought, marketing writers attempted to describe the assistance that government organizations gave to marketing entrepreneurs, to interpret the regulations affecting marketing activity, and to encourage such competitive practices as would take full advantage of the opportunities open to business.

PHILOSOPHIC FRAMEWORK

The varied economic theories prevailing by 1900 embodied a variety of philosophic concepts, not the least of which pertained to the nature of man as a social individual and as an economic entity. They included widely divergent assumptions concerning the laws that governed individual and collective behavior. Adam Smith, for example, conceived man as the "economic man," bent upon a constant effort to better his condition. Each individual was regarded as his own best judge of what was good for him, and this self-interest was assumed to work for the general good. Smith assumed for the individual an innate propensity of "truck and barter," a trait that was held to be the basis of division of labor. Thus there was a *natural* basis for competition, and if these tendencies were expressed without hindrance, according to natural motivations, they would effect perfect competition. The harmonies of Smith's plan, however, were not so broad as they have sometimes been thought, for the unity of interests achieved was *within* economic groups and not *among* them.

An opposite assumption was held by Ricardo, who foresaw the uncertainties of an expanding economy. He saw conflicting interests — among landlords, labor, and businessmen. His new assumptions were warranted by changes which had taken place in economic conditions. He was less idealistic and more pessimistic than Smith, as he viewed the growing disparity of interests in the rising factory system.

The nineteenth century brought still another change in philosophy. Success of the factory system and prospects of prosperity revived again a faith in the economic harmonies. Once more free play of individual self-interest was believed most likely to result in harmonies and general welfare. The continual opening of geographic frontiers produced a concept of inevitable progress. Also, growing confidence in the practical application of scientific knowledge inspired confidence in man's ability to control the course of human affairs. Businessmen of wealth assumed positions of social and economic leadership, feeling themselves charged, as political aristocrats had felt before, with responsibility for bringing about the best state of society — as they saw it.

As economic activity underwent great expansion during that period, economic theory also manifested certain changes. The subject of "political economy" was narrowed down simply to "economics," indicating a shift from a motivation to formulate public policy to an interest in economics for the formulation of business decisions. Economists themselves tended to be more specialized in their areas of interest. Some of them adhered to traditional liberal views, emphasizing a free society, limited intervention, and free play. Others urged public control and enforced competition — competition unimpeded by the obstacles that monopolistic business itself had posed.

Marshall disavowed the "economic man." He denied that greedy, selfish competition was distinctive of free enterprise. He opposed both big business and socialism. And he perceived basic co-operation among all parties through the system of markets. His viewpoint, insofar as he emphasized the short run, tended to coincide with the interests of businessmen.

Thus at the outset of the twentieth century, students of marketing were equipped with a general philosophy of optimism, a vision of new frontiers of progress, a businessman's viewpoint of confidence in free play in the market, and widespread agreement that consumers acted rationally in the market.

THE CONSUMER

While much was said about buyer behavior in the market, relatively little was said of it from the viewpoint of the market or consumer. Nevertheless, the contention that consumption is the end and object of production had considerable influence upon the development of marketing thought, for, as the viewpoints from which marketing could be studied were developed, this economic concept became the basis for marketing writers' taking what they regarded to be the "consumers' viewpoint."

Not until the latter part of the nineteenth century, with the writings of the Austrians or marginal analysts, did real consideration of the consumer get into economic theory. Even then, analyses of the consumer tended to explain his operation as an *economic* unit in the market rather than as a *consuming* unit in the market, as businessmen have been inclined to view him. Thus, while economists' concepts of the consumer may not have aided much in making market analyses, their concepts of marginal utility, opportunity costs, subjective and objective value, abstinence, hedonism, "the marginal man," and rationalism were useful tools of thought available when students of marketing began their research into this new area of thought.

SOCIAL AND TECHNOLOGICAL CHANGE

The history of economic thought illustrates that, as changing conditions created new problems, new theories and schools of thought evolved. At the same time new technologies required different types of technical experts to solve their attendant problems. Consequently, as the economic problems involving public policy were followed by those of more technical managerial character in production, and ultimately in distribution, three types of theorists became identifiable in economic analysis: traditional theoretical economists, management engineers, and marketing analysts. Each was the product of the conditions and problems of his times.

The traditional economists, whose thoughts have already been discussed, directed themselves mainly toward the formulation of public and private policy. Adam Smith, for example, was interested in finding means of increasing England's commerce and trade for diplomatic, military, and security reasons. While he attempted to explain actual behavior patterns, he evidently did not aspire to present a fully integrated theory. Ricardo, on the other hand, was primarily concerned with the distribution of wealth, and he inquired into the laws of a competitive economy that controlled price and the distribution of income. Mill had still another objective: to explain all that was known about the whole subject of economics by the best experts. Marshall undertook to clarify some of the complex interrelationships of economic forces.

Toward the end of the nineteenth century, as industrialization progressed, interest in problems of a more technical production nature gave rise to a new type of "economist"; namely, engineers who concerned themselves with effecting business economies through the study of the causes and effects of good business administration. Their theories resulted in what became known as "scientific management." The growing size of business organizations presented the new problems of the day, problems which could be solved only by careful planning. Production processes, methods, and equipment became the immediate areas of study. Gradually distinction was drawn in the early 1900's between engineering and management as two separate and distinct functions.

A body of thought and literature dealing with this new branch of "economics" began to appear about 1880. Frederick W. Taylor, a leader in the development of that phase of business thought, began writing in 1895. In 1912 he defined "scientific management" (a term said to have originated with E. L. Gantt in 1910) as a complete mental revolution, both for workmen and for management, a new outlook toward the solution of worker and management problems. Education in management also began around 1910, and within fifteen years the subject had become well established in leading universities.[1]

Neither traditional economists nor leaders in scientific management, however, concerned themselves at the beginning of this century with the new problems of distribution and of the market place that were then increasing in importance. Economists dealt with business problems of broad scope and political significance. Management engineers dealt with internal problems of business organization, particularly those related to production processes. Problems in distribution and of the market remained to be handled by a new type of analyst, who evolved still another body of thought known as "marketing."

The emergence of this third type of economist – the scientific student and practitioner of marketing – was the result of the same forces that had produced successive and divergent economic theories: changing economic conditions, growing disparity between facts and assumptions underlying prevailing theory, and the rise of new technologies requiring original research and theorization. All these forces worked in the early part of this century to stimulate the beginnings of the new body of marketing thought. Most prominent among them were the enlargement of the size of the market, new conditions of production, new expansiveness of demand, the changing role of the middleman, new social conditions, and reinterpretation of *laissez faire*.

ENLARGEMENT OF THE MARKET

Never before in the history of mankind had markets been so large as they were in 1900. Classical economists had assumed markets to be local, wherein demanders and suppliers knew of each other's presence and this knowledge resulted in "perfect competition." With the Industrial Revolution that condition diminished somewhat, and by the last of the nineteenth century conditions in the vast market of the United States were quite different from those assumed in most accepted economic theories.

Between 1860 and 1900 the population of the United States had increased from 31.4 millions to 91.9 millions. In the 1860's, 21 per cent of the people in the United States lived in cities of over 2,500 population; in 1900, the figure was 40 per cent, and in 1920, 51 per cent. The size of the market, measured by per capita income, increased from $134 in 1859 to $185 in 1899, and $285 in 1914.

Those are but a few of the evidences of the economic changes that forced thinking along new lines. It could no longer be assumed that buyers and sellers were aware of the presence of each other in the market and that such knowledge would contribute to the automaticity with which the market wrought harmonies for all. New importance was attached to information, promotion, and the quest for satisfactory products. Extended markets gave opportunity for production on a scale larger than had ever before been undertaken. They also introduced new pricing factors, for, with the opportunity to sell in a number of markets, businessmen found new competition and developed new operating strategies.

NEW CONDITIONS OF PRODUCTION

As the Industrial Revolution in England had effected changes in economic theories there, so the industrialization in the United States in the last part of the nineteenth century impelled still further revision of thought. The rapid transition from an agricultural economy at the time of the Civil War to an industrial economy at the end of the century — notwithstanding the opening of vast agricultural territories of the West — poured into the market such quantities of products as to warrant the conclusion that a buyers' market was replacing a sellers' market.

Industrialization was encouraged by a number of factors: by progress in science; by use of interchangeable parts, standardization, and machine tools; by the development of food-preserving processes: by the replacement of charcoal with coke and the discovery of the Bessemer process in stell manufacturing; by the invention of steel rails and the Westinghouse air brake, electric light, and the automatic loom, etc. By 1914, 54 per cent of the value of all manufactured products was in the lines of food, textiles, iron and steel, and lumber. Production formerly carried on in the home was increasingly transferred to the factory. Capital was also more readily available for industrial expansion, as a result of personal savings, corporate savings, savings in trade and commerce, and foreign investments. Moreover, industry was stimulated by governmental action through the manner in which timber and mining lands were distributed, by the giving of free factory sites and tax favors, by weak enforcement of business regulations, by the use of regressive tax schedules, and by the inclination of politicians to represent big business.

In that transition, economists' assumptions that producers, at least in the long run, adjust their activities to the market became untenable. Increasingly, producers attempted to *adjust the market* to their production capacities and ambitions. Production was no longer carried on for an immediately available market but *in advance* of known markets and for unknown markets at great distances. The size of producing organizations increased to the point where communities became dependent upon their continuous operation, and the assumed mobility of the factors of production was no longer a reality.

MARKETS NOT DETERMINED BY SUPPLY

It had also long been a presumption of economic theorists that production was basic, that the value created by production was distributed among the factors contributing to it, and that those shares in the hands of individuals constituted the extent of their demand in the market. To the extent that a society has a static market condition, that may be true, but the American market of the late nineteenth and early twentieth centuries, motivated by the general emphasis placed upon improving one's lot, was anything but static. Growing use of credit in business, and later in personal consumption, augmented the growth of demand. Higher attainments in education, increased personal income, and more rapid communication created a market unlike those described by earlier theorists, a market requiring new analysis.

DYNAMIC SYSTEM OF MIDDLEMEN

When most of the classical theories were developed, the middlemen standing between producers and consumers were of incidental significance to the economies of those times. Individually they were necessary, but collectively they did not constitute what might be regarded as a distributive "system." They were passive and served producers neither as developers of markets nor as warehouses essential to the orderly flow of goods to the market. They were not the typical business organization in the economists' minds when they analyzed factors of production, creation of value, or even pricing policies.

By 1900 the significance of middlemen was changing; middlemen were performing functions which they formerly did not perform. The number of them was growing, and collectively they represented a distinct type of business activity. In the late 1900's they were becoming more diversified, and among department stores, mail order houses, and chain store organizations were firms as prominent in the national eye as some leading producers.

One challenge to assumptions underlying economic theory presented by the new distributive system concerned the concept of value. The idea of time, place, and possession utilities assumed new significance with the rise of specialists whose principal function was the creation of these forms of value. Services, excluded from production by earlier economists, had to be included if a consistent interpretation of the new economy was to be developed. Early students of marketing who perceived that made strong claims for the values contributed by distributors. Their conclusions, however, were sometimes weakened by empirical, inductive reasoning, which appeared to justify value by the performance of the distributor rather than justifying the distributor by the market's desired to have certain services performed.

Some concepts of pricing and price behavior had also to be altered with the advent of new factors in pricing. The concepts of price as market or natural price, and of price comprising the cost of factors of production, were insufficient to explain managed price in a distributive system. Price became less a matter of accountable costs entering into production and more a managed phenomenon. Distributive enterprises used price as a means to an end – low price to obtain high volume; high price with low volume to obtain maximum profit; psychological pricing, etc. Some types of pricing are technical and superficial; others represent new factors in pricing introduced by the distributive system.

The growth of the distributive system paralleled the rise of large producing organizations that, as has been pointed out, inspired the development of a professional class of business managers. Management of the mammoth producing firms was originally in the hands of the founding entrepreneurs of those companies. Among them were J. J. Hill, E. H. Harriman, Jay Gould, W. Vanderbilt, Andrew Carnegie, P. D. Armour, G. Swift, M. Cudahy, and J. P. Morgan, all with northern European backgrounds, all from our northern states, and none with a college education. Similarily, in distribution there were also creative entrepreneurs who represented new inventive management talent: John Wanamaker, Adam Gimble, Isador Straus, Marshall Field, Fred and Ralph Lazarus, F. W. Woolworth, S. S. Kresge, B. H. Kroger, G. H. Hartford, Richard W. Sears, and Aaron Montgomery Ward. The talent required for managing a factory, however, was different from that needed for the new distributive organizations. The development of such talent required a type of scientific or academic thought that no prevailing theories provided, and that it became the objective of marketing thought and marketing literature to supply.

NEW SOCIAL PROBLEMS

Transactions in the past have been dependent upon buyers and sellers' achieving mutual understanding and confidence, but the security that buyers found when sellers were small, local, and known to the market was diminished as markets grew larger. The insecurity of buyers was increased many fold in the nineteenth century, as haggling and bargaining, which expressed negotiational forces at work in the market and which represented equal knowledge of demand and supply and equal bargaining power, waned. Thus another assumption underlying economic thought deteriorated. In addition, the introduction of many new products, the interposition of an impersonal middleman between the producers and consumers, the use of new media for aggressive promotion in the market — all these factors contributed to the consumers' dilemma in the face of many new market problems. Vendor irresponsibility, the evaluation of new distributive services, the attitude of *caveat emptor,* and the loss of contact with the market's real needs also created problems that students of marketing sought to solve.

LASSEZ FAIRE AND THE NEW ORDER

Throughout the nineteenth century, businessmen largely determined the philosophical atmosphere in which business itself operated. They believed strongly in individualism, in a dominating class of business aristocracy, and in minimum governmental regulation but maximum governmental assistance to business. Business leaders believed firmly in the right of an individual to acquire and to hold property without restriction or interference by the state. They emphasized the right to property, the law of accumulation, and the law of competition, although competition in business was regarded by some as inefficient and wasteful. It was generally believed that thrift and hard work would be rewarded and that poverty came from laziness and shiftlessness. These convictions, strengthened by theological doctrines, supported concepts of economic liberalism, and upon them economic theorists based great hopes in market competition.

An opposite assumption, that general welfare was not best served by complete freedom in the market place, likewise gained considerable acceptance at the beginning of this century. At the same time, the notion, postulated by economic liberals, that problems created by new practices in the market were a result of natural law, was refuted. In 1901, Theodore Roosevelt was elected on a tide of movement for economic, social, and political reform of the evils which had grown out of advanced industrialism. The Progressive Party demanded government control of large industry and of financial and transportation companies and the enactment of pure food and drug legislation. Pools, trusts, mergers, and combinations were under continual legislative and judicial fire, indicating that the long-held assumption that competition should prevail in the market was being abandoned. There was growing opposition to *private* monopoly, even as after the Civil war there was opposition to *government-granted* monopoly. The opposition expressed the antagonism of agriculturists and labor groups to business and of the South to the industrial North. By 1890 fourteen states had constitutional provisions against monopoly and thirteen had antimonopoly laws; by 1900 these numbers had increased to twenty-seven and fifteen states, respectively.

The philosophic atmosphere of the late nineteenth century was a mixture of economic, sociological, and religious principles justifying *laissez faire.* But competition had progressed to such extremes that even competitors sought some protection from competition. The opponents of *laissez faire* advocated reforms that would bring about better working conditions. The achievement of the Kingdom of God on earth, it was believed, would remove monopoly and unearned income. Along with such thinking were introduced the concepts of Darwinism, which Herbert Spencer attempted to apply to human society and social relationships. The idea of the "survival of the fittest" encouraged optimism, sanctioned competition, and opposed welfare programs designed to help the poor. However, advocates of Social Darwinism conceived society as having already evolved — the fittest having survived. Proponents of Reform Darwinism saw existing society as only one stage in social evolution, with continuing reformation further to improve the lot of men.

Among leading thinkers of the period there was much disagreement on these issues. In general, it has been said that Reform Darwinism had little effect upon economists. On the other hand, R. T. Ely and others interested in reforms established the American Economic Association in 1885 as a protest against their conservative colleagues, who in general espoused the principles of *laissez faire.* At the same time, pragmatists such as William James and John Dewey furnished a logical basis of reforms in all fields. Veblen, in 1899, also rebelled, expressing his theory of the leisure class. Oliver Wendell Holmes and Louis Brandeis at the same time introduced economic and sociological data into court decisions.

Such were the conditions of the economy and economic thought at the time that changes were occurring in the market place and students of marketing were laying what was to become the groundwork for the structure of marketing thought.

ENDNOTE

[1] John F. Mee, *A History of Twentieth Century Management Thought* (unpublished dissertation, The Ohio State University, Columbus, 1959), p. 71.

BEGINNINGS OF MARKETING THOUGHT

3

New market problems at the beginning of this century did not of themselves produce a body of marketing thought. They impelled inquiry, resulting in teaching and writing and in gradual evolution of *thought,* involving new concepts, literature, educational programs, and business practices. Neither did the information provided by early studies constitute a *body* of thought. That developed only as thought about marketing attained structure, breadth, and maturity. Nevertheless, from the new circumstances, and from men's endeavor to make the best of them, has arisen in the name of marketing thought a significant body of social and economic knowledge.

As in recent years this accumulation of information and knowledge has been viewed objectively, interest in its origin and character has increased. There has been speculation as to whether the study of marketing has the status of a science, and why it has developed in the particular way that it has. Such questions relate to facts about the beginnings of the study of marketing that passing time is increasingly making obscure. They are facts, however, that are important to understand if one is to gain a correct appreciation of the influences that shaped marketing thought.

MARKETING THOUGHT AND THE ACADEMICIAN

As might be expected in the development of a body of scientific knowledge, universities and men engaged in academic pursuits have played a major role in the evolving of marketing thought. It was in response to social issues more than to business urgency that schools first began to offer courses in the distributive trades, for businessmen and others early in this century viewed dimly the profitability of such study. In keeping with progress, however, universities and academicians did foresee new lines along which the business economy was developing, and they gave expression to what they knew.

EARLIEST TEACHERS OF DISTRIBUTION

An early impulse to the formation of marketing thought lay in the decisions, by whomever they were made, to provide at several universities courses that dealt with what was then known as the "distributive industries." The first such courses on record were given between 1900 and 1910 as follows:

1902   University of Michigan, by E. D. Jones
1902   University of California, by Simon Litman
1902   University of Illinois, by George M. Fisk
1903   University of Pennsylvania, by W. E. Kreusi
1904   University of Pennsylvania, by H. S. Person
1905   The Ohio State University, by James E. Hagerty

1908	Northwestern University
1909	University of Pittsburgh
1909	Harvard University, by P. T. Cherington
1910	University of Wisconsin

The background of all those courses is not known,[1] but it appears that the idea for such a course did not always originate with the individual who taught it. Some were assigned to teach a course; others undertook it as a product of their research interest. In any case, the beginnings of thought were original, and there is no indication that any teacher prior to 1910 had any knowledge of anyone else working in this field.

According to James E. Hagerty, inductive research and descriptive findings characterized the studies he made among businessmen in Philadelphia, who were amazed that anyone should be objectively interested in their practices and curious as to what use could possibly be made of such information. He used for text purposes, after 1905, Volume 6 of the *Industrial Commission Reports* dealing with the distribution of farm products. He also had businessmen speak to his classes but found that he had to spend several hours with them showing what he wanted them to tell the class.

When Simon Litman was asked to teach a course called "The Technique of Trade and Commerce," he had never heard of such a subject. Moreover, he was unfamiliar with American business, for he had lived and been educated in Russia, France, and Germany. He assumed that "problems and methods do not differ in essentials from country to country" and that "fundamentals are the same irrespective of boundaries within which they are being applied."[2] For help in planning and organizing his course, he relied upon material obtained from treaties by three German writers: Cohn, Grunzel, and van der Borgt. Thus Litman brought to the study of marketing a viewpoint probably unlike that of anyone else at that time. He may have been justified in emphasizing similarities rather than differences among practices of various countries more then than later, for the practice of marketing had not yet wrought changes in American business that during ensuing years were to differentiate it from business elsewhere.

EARLY COURSES IN DISTRIBUTION

Notwithstanding the immaturity of concepts and thought during those early years, the content of courses offered shows them to have dealt substantially with the subjects that were later called "marketing." At that time, the course titles usually identified them with "distribution" rather than "marketing." Bulletins from two universities reveal the following content of their courses during the first years in which they were offered:

University of Michigan 1902	*The Ohio State University* 1906
"Distributive and Regulative Industries of the United States"	"The Distribution of Products"
This course will include a description of the various methods of marketing goods, of the classification,	This course considers mercantile organizations from points of view: (1) The evolution of mercantile organizations in the United States and

grade, brands employed, and of wholesale and retail trade. Attention will also be given to those private organizations, not connected with money and banking, which guide and control the industrial process, such as trade associations, boards of trade and chambers of commerce, etc.

their relation to each other; and origin and development of the various mercantile institutions with special reference to the economic conditions which brought them into existence and perpetuated them. The various methods of marketing goods, and the functions of the various distributors, manufacturers, manufacturers' agents, brokers, jobbers, traveling salesmen, etc. Advertising, its psychological laws, its economic importance and the changes it has introduced in selling goods. The work of stock and produce exchanges. (2) The internal or administrative organization of mercantile concerns. A study of the divisions and subdivisions of mercantile concerns and the relation of the various departments to each other and to the whole. The systems in use of recording and preserving data.

Following the initial offering of courses in distribution, marketing thought developed in specialized areas as courses and writings grew simultaneously. Frequently the necessity to teach a course in a particular subject impelled research and writing by the teacher; at other times the availability of writings encouraged the multiplication of courses in some phase of marketing. As an example of the growth of thought expressed in course offerings, the additions to the curriculum in marketing at The Ohio State University are cited:

1905 Spring. "Distribution of Products," offered for the first time.

1905-1906 The course was expanded into a year's work, two terms (Fall, 1905; Winter, 1906). It was titled "Distributive and Regulative Institutions"; in the Spring term, 1906, "Commercial Credit" was offered.

1906 Title of "Distributive and Regulative Institutions" was changed to "Mercantile Institutions."

1909-1910 "Commercial Credit" was dropped, but the subject was absorbed in the institutional course. Two courses were then in effect: "Mercantile Institutions in Domestic Trade," and "Foreign Markets and the Consular System."

1911 "Principles of Advertising" was added and it has been offered continuously since that time.

1915-1916 Title of "Mercantile Institutions" was changed to "Marketing."

1916-1917 "Salesmanship" was added.

1920-1921 "Wholesaling" and "Retailing" were added.

1921 The curriculum consisted of the following courses: "Business Communications"; "Marketing"; "Marketing Problems"; "Wholesaling"; "Retailing"; "Credits and Collections"; "Salesmanship";

"Advertising"; "Advertising Practice"; "Exporting and Importing"; "Research in Marketing."

1925 "Sales Management" was combined with "Salesmanship."

1927 "Marketing Problems" was omitted.

1940 "Credit Problems" was introduced.

1940 "Business Research" and "Market Research" became two courses.

1941 "Salesmanship" and "Sales Management" became two courses.

CONCEPTION OF "MARKETING"

During the earliest years of the study and teaching of distributive trade practices, no use was made of the word "marketing." Instead, "trade," "commerce," and "distribution" were the most common designations of the area to which thought was being given. Between 1900 and 1910, conceptual changes occurred that resulted in the adoption of the term "marketing" to identify this field.

As the study of "distribution" began simultaneously in several places, it is reasonable to think that several people may also have felt the necessity of finding a new term to designate the subject with which they were dealing. Ralph Starr Butler, then a professor at the University of Wisconsin, has told how he, for one, conceived "marketing."

In considering the whole field of selling, I developed the idea that personal salesmanship and advertising had to do simply with the final expression of the selling idea. My experience with the Procter & Gamble Company had convinced me that a manufacturer seeking to market a product had to consider and solve a large number of problems before he ever gave expression to the selling idea by sending a salesman on the road or inserting an advertisement in a publication.

I surveyed the very meager literature of business which was available at that time and was astonished to find that the particular field that I have very briefly described above had never been treated by any writer. I decided to prepare a correspondence course covering this phase of business activity.

In brief, the subject matter that I intended to treat was to include a study of everything that the promoter of a product has to do prior to his actual use of salesmen and of advertising. A name was needed for this field of business activity. I remember the diffiuclties I had in finding a suitable name, but I finally decided on the phrase "Marketing Methods."[3]

Recognition that the subject with which they were dealing was different from that designated by "distribution" or "trade," other men also used the term "marketing," and gradually it became accepted in both course and book titles, as is indicated by the following:

1902 University of Michigan Bulletin used the phrase "various methods of marketing goods" in the description of the course entitled "The Distributive and Regulative Industries of the United States."

1905 University of Pennsylvania offered a course entitled "The Marketing of Products," taught by W.E. Kreusi.

1909 University of Pittsburgh offered a course entitled "Marketing of Products."

1910 University of Wisconsin offered a course entitled "Marketing Methods," taught by Ralph Starr Butler, who also that year published six pamphlets with the same title.

1913 University of Wisconsin offered a course entitled "The Marketing of Farm Products," taught by Louis D. H. Weld.

1916 Weld published *The Marketing of Farm Products.*

1917 Butler published *Marketing Methods.*

EARLY CONTRIBUTORS TO MARKETING THOUGHT

In comparison to the number of men who were engaged in marketing practice early in this century, or even of those who taught and wrote of the subject, the number who made significant contributions to the development of marketing thought was small. Contributions consisted of a variety of undertakings: original research, new conceptions, fresh viewpoints, innovative writing or teaching, unprecedented analysis or synthesis of thought. Judged by their works and by concensus of men making contributions to marketing thought the following men[4] were leaders in the development of marketing:

1902	E. D. Jones		1914	P. W. Ivey
1902	S. Litman		1914	W. C. Weidler
1902	G. M. Fisk		1915	N. H. Comish
1904	W. E. Kreusi		1915	P. D. Converse
1905	J. E. Hagerty		1915	C. S. Duncan
1905	B. H. Hibbard		1919	F. L. Vaughan
1908	P. T. Cherington		1920	R. S. Alexander
1909	P. H. Nystrom		1920	H. H. Maynard
1910	R. S. Butler		1920	M. P. McNair
1910	A. W. Shaw		1920	H. R. Tosdal
1911	T. Macklin		1921	T. N. Beckman
1912	M. T. Copeland		1922	C. W. Barker
1913	H. E. Agnew		1922	N. H. Borden
1913	L. D. H. Weld		1923	R. S. Vaile
1914	F. E. Clark		1924	R. F. Breyer

The number of teachers contributing to marketing thought increased as the study of the subject gained momentum and scope. Among them there was remarkable stability of devotion to advancing knowledge of marketing. Having once taught in this field, most men remained in that occupation, and of those who were so engaged in teaching before 1920 a great many remained in that work into the 1930s. Some early teachers were drawn from marketing to other academic interests; others left teaching entirely; but the majority continued in that work. Few men remained long in their first teaching assignment. On the other hand, when once well established, they were little inclined to change schools, for they bore responsibilities for developing courses and programs upon which their reputations were to rest.

As writers, those men were equally impressive. To them may be traced roots not only of general writings on marketing but also of such specialized fields as agricultural marketing, advertising, retailing, commercial research, salesmanship, wholesaling, credits and collections, marketing of manufactured goods, and compilations of case and problem materials. It would be difficult to find elswhere such a small group to whom so much credit is due for the development of an important segment of human knowledge.

CENTERS OF INFLUENCE UPON MARKETING THOUGHT

As knowledge of marketing increased, it was influenced by characteristics of the men who produced it and by the environments in which they worked. The schools where the first four or five marketing courses were taught were not the ones whence emanated the foremost marketing scholars of the first two decades of the study of marketing. Preparation for original thought in that area was best achieved at established, advanced, and liberal centers of learning at that time. The University of Wisconsin and Harvard University were attended by more of the early marketing scholars, at some time in their careers, than were any other educational institutions. Those two institutions, therefore, were the original centers of intellectual influence upon marketing thought, whereas those at which the first courses in marketing were taught became important centers for the development of marketing education.

Wisconsin, at the turn of the century, was the residence of such economists as W.A. Scott, J.R. Commons, R.T. Ely, and H.C. Taylor, to whom were attracted such pioneer students of marketing as Jones, Hagerty, Hibbard, Macklin, Nystrom, Butler, Converse, Comish, and Vaughan. Among the contributions to marketing thought made at Wisconsin were the conception of the field as "marketing" and the offering of the first course in co-operative marketing of agricultural products. The contributions and influence of men who went out from that school to teach and write throughout the country were immeasurable.

Harvard not only was influential during the early years but, unlike Wisconsin, continued as a center of influence in the development of marketing thought and practice. To Harvard went such students as Cherington, Shaw, Copeland, Tosdal, Weidler, Maynard, McNair, Borden, and Vaile. Their contributions to marketing thought have included methodology for the analysis of problems of market distribution, methodology for teaching marketing by the use of problems, major works on advertising, merchandising, sales management, retailing, and general marketing.

The most pronounced influence upon the integrated and general development of marketing thought, however, centered not at Wisconsin or Harvard but at The Ohio State University, the University of Illinois, and Northwestern University — all Middle Western schools — whence flowed for a quarter of a century the writings and students of Maynard, Weidler, Beckman, Converse, and Clark, whose approach to marketing analysis and synthesis became traditional. Among the other Middle Westerners who made important contributions to marketing thought are Weld, Ivey, and C. S. Duncan.

The group from the Middle West made notable contributions to marketing thought in the decade following World War I. Whereas by 1910 the field of study was delineated by the new concept and term "marketing," by 1920 some of the *principles* of the subject were being postulated. Students at the beginning of the century explored the marketing practices of business in general. Those who developed the subject ten years later, particularly at Wisconsin, specialized in the commodity analysis of marketing. Those whose contributions appeared following World War I concentrated primarily on the functional aspects of marketing. Thus the middle-western group of writers contributed mainly to the integration of the study of marketing, emphasizing functions and principles and treating the subject with a form and fullness that has since characterized the central body of marketing thought.

Still another center of influence was in New York City, where at Columbia and New York Universities a group developed that made significant contributions to the institutional analyses of marketing. Among them were Nystrom, Agnew, Brisco, Wingate, Alexander. With an emphasis on practice, the work of those urban writers complemented that of others who were adding to marketing thought elsewhere.[5]

ASSOCIATIVE ACTIVITIES

Another facet of the development of marketing thought is reflected in the associative activities of the men who were engaged in this study. Although at the outset there was no awareness of what others were doing, that condition did not continue long. The work of students of marketing became known at meetings of professional associations, and eventually those engaged in the development of marketing thought organized their own professional association.

Louis D. H. Weld, in 1914, read before the American Economic Association a paper on "Market Distribution." To his knowledge,[6] that was "the first scientific presentation of the subject of marketing, as we know it today, before that Association." With the development of courses on marketing, articles on the subject began to appear.

H. E. Agnew has also chronicled[7] the development of the American Marketing Association, tracing it to 1915, when, at the invitation of Hotchkiss at the Chicago conference of the Associated Advertising Clubs of the World, twenty-eight men gathered to discuss the contents of an advertising course. At that meeting, W. D. Scott was elected president. Agnew said also that in 1917 three members of the group held further discussion at St. Louis.

Weld, on the other hand, wrote:

> ... in 1918 at a meeting of the American Economic Association in Richmond I was able to scrape together five or six men who were interested in marketing, and we had a dinner together. This group, which I assembled yearly at subsequent meetings of the American Economic Association, grew fairly rapidly, and was soon important enough to get a place on the Economic Association's program for round table discussions of marketing. This was the first associative effort among men interested in marketing as we know it today, and formed the nucleus out of which developed the Association of Teachers of Marketing.

It is thus apparent that between 1915 and 1918 interest in marketing, and the number of marketing-interested teachers, had increased to the point that they began to meet each other at meetings of other professional societies. It is conceivable that some men who would have attended a conference on advertising clubs would not have been at meetings of the American Economic Association. Notwithstanding, inasmuch as identification with the subject of marketing was increasing, the associative efforts also prospered.

After 1920, according to Agnew, teachers of marketing increasingly joined the American Economic Association. In 1924 the National Association of Teachers of Marketing and Advertising was formed, representing the expanding interest of the group organized in 1915 merely as the National Association of

CHART 1: LINES OF PERSONAL INFLUENCE IN THE DEVELOPMENT OF MARKETING THOUGHT

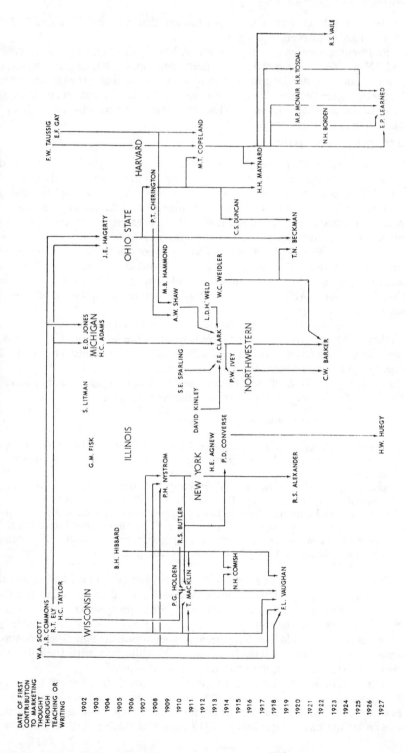

Teachers of Advertising. The second change in the name of this group occurred in 1933, when it became the National Association of Marketing Teachers.

Meanwhile, in 1930 the American Marketing Society had been organized, representing, in contrast to the Teachers Association, the practitioners' interest in marketing. The Society in 1934 published the *American Marketing Journal,* which in 1935 became the *National Marketing Review* and in 1936 the *Journal of Marketing,* which it has remained. In 1937 the teachers and the practitioners groups were merged to form the American Marketing Association.

CHARACTERISTICS OF MARKETING THOUGHT

From the beginnings of marketing thought has evolved a body of scientific knowledge that has some distinctive characteristics, determined by the motivations of writers, the scope of their interests, the progressive stages of thought, and the form, structure, and dimensions of its expression.

MOTIVATIONAL INFLUENCES ON MARKETING THOUGHT

One of the strong influences upon the development of marketing thought was the motivation of men who became interested in this subject. For one thing, they did not set out to produce a "body of thought." They were more concerned with developing practice than theory, and the fact that a structured, coherent, and unified thought resulted was secondary to the fact that information was provided for the solution of problems. "Contributions" were made for the purpose of describing, explaining, and justifying prevailing marketing practices and institutions, particularly newer ones. They were offered to clarify misconceptions held among the public, such as the belief that the wholesaler was parasitic and would disappear from the distributive system, fear of the annihilation of small stores by chain organizations, and dismay at the plight of consumers before the ruthless practices of vendors.

The development of marketing thought represented also an effort to compensate for the omissions of existing theory, but it did not represent a theoretical revolt. Economic theories dealt only generally with distributive problems and practices. They offered little assistance to the growing need for knowledge of "applied" economics. Early students of marketing picked no quarrel with prevailing economic theories; instead, they built upon concepts and assumptions provided by the economists. If marketing thought was more closely related to economics than to other social disciplines, it was because economics was the only one at that time that dealt with market phenomena.

THE SCOPE OF MARKETING THOUGHT

The character of marketing thought has been affected also by the focus and scope of the interests of men engaged in this study.

1. Associated with the Concept of Marketing. Their focal interest has been "Marketing," as conceived by Butler and others. Among those men has existed a relationship that has unified and identified both them and their works. Apart from them have been others, both precedent and contemporary, who have been concerned with distributive phenomena but whose writings could not be regarded as directly relevant to the body of marketing thought.

The scope of marketing thought is such as to include only contributors since 1900. An interesting case is made for the origination of marketing thought in writings of liberal economists of the late nineteenth century, such as Edward Atkinson, David Ames Wells, Arthur Farquhar, and Henry Farquhar.[8] Unquestionably the advanced thoughts of such economists regarding distribution antedated those so-called "marketing writers," and their writings were known to early marketing teachers and students. They wrote, however, not of "marketing" but of trade, distribution, wholesaling, and retailing. Their preoccupation was with public policy and economic effects rather than with the operational interests around which the beginnings of marketing thought took form.

2. *Produced by Men Committed to the Study of Marketing.* Not economists but students of marketing, not marketing practitioners but marketing teachers and theorists, produced the body of marketing thought. Others have provided concepts and findings, but the body of our knowledge of marketing has been the product of men giving their full time to this activity. Some, like Nystrom and Clark, were educated as economists, but they wrote as students of marketing. Others, like Weld and C. S. Duncan, went from teaching to business practice, whereafter, although they may have advanced marketing practice, they made no further contribution to marketing thought in published form.

3. *Common Professional Recognition.* Contributions to thought are not only *given* but *accepted,* and professional acceptance of writers has helped to determine the body of marketing thought. Men who have been identified with the subject through membership on marketing faculties or participation in activities of the American Marketing Association have been the acknowledged contributors to marketing thought. Again, contributions have been made by others in allied fields, but the interests of the fraternity of men professionally engaged in the advancement of marketing have mainly determined the character of marketing thought.

4. *Literary Interreference.* The scope and nature of marketing thought have been influenced also by the fact that writers tended to build upon foundations laid by their predecessors. When the structure of thought was framed, when concepts, definitions, principles, or exceptional facts were presented by one, they were often adopted and acknowledged by another. Thus the body of thought in both the general and the specialized fields developed with considerable interference, so that the contributors to thought were known not only by their own writings but by reference made to them by others.

DEVELOPMENTAL STAGES OF MARKETING THOUGHT

Progressive unfolding has characterized the development of marketing thought. Although there was much repetition of ideas once they were established, in succeeding periods new aspects of thought were forthcoming, so that the history of its first fifty years may be classifed as follows:

1900-1910–*Period of Discovery.* Initial teachers of marketing sought facts about the distributive trades. Theory was borrowed from economics relating to distribution, world trade, and commodity markets. The conception of "marketing" occurred, and a name was given to it.

1910-20–*Period of Conceptualization.* Many marketing concepts were initially developed. Concepts were classified, and terms were defined.

1920-30–*Period of Integration.* Principles of marketing were postulated, and the general body of thought was integrated for the first time.

1930-40—*Period of Development.* Specialized areas of marketing continued to be developed, hypothetical assumptions were verified and quantified, and some new approaches to the explanation of marketing were undertaken.

1940-50—*Period of Reappraisal.* The concept and traditional explanation of marketing was reappraised in terms of new needs for marketing knowledge. The scientific aspects of the subject were considered.

1950-60—*Period of Reconception.* Traditional approaches to the study of marketing were supplemented by increasing emphasis upon managerial decision making, the societal aspects of marketing, and quantitative marketing analysis. Many new concepts, some borrowed from the field of management and from other social sciences, were introduced into marketing

1960-1970—*Period of Differentiation.* As marketing thought became expanded, new concepts took on substantial identity as significant components of the total structure of thought. Among them were such elements as managerialism, holism, environmentalism, systems, and internationalism.

1970—*Period of Socialization.* Social issues and marketing became much more important, as the influence not of society upon marketing, but of marketing upon society became a focus of interest.

THE FORM OF MARKETING THOUGHT

Form is given to marketing thought by the medium in which it is expressed. A formal body of thought is more than just a stream of ideas. It is a composite of ideas, including both those currently in circulation and those of a historical nature. It exceeds the knowledge of any one person and includes the sum total of what is known about a subject. It is more than an aggregate of fragmentary ideas; rather it is a group of ideas centered upon a principle.

So conceived, a body of thought takes form over a long period in a literature. Some literary forms are periodic; others are more permanent. Each makes a distinct contribution to the form of thought developed therein. Periodicals in marketing are written mainly for trade purposes, to report new discoveries, to recount successful experiences, and to discuss problems and techniques of comparatively narrow scope. Journals and research reports, on the other hand, deal more abstractly with problems and investigations and usually contain substantial types of ideas. Books provide formal, conceptual, and integrated expression of thought. Some of them are very specialized, others general. Books of scientific character, particularly textbooks for academic use, usually represent an integration of thoughts that may have been presented in segregated fashion elsewhere, as in periodicals.

Thus, because in books the more considered, permanent, and integrated elements of a body of thought take form, it is in the books of the marketing literature that the body of marketing thought analyzed in this study has been sought.

DIMENSIONS OF MARKETING THOUGHT

To describe the content of the body of marketing thought is to perform a dissection that presupposes a concept of its anatomy. It cannot be stated of what this body of thought consists *as a whole,* for, while its subject matter is marketing, its content is as multiform as the prismatic refractions of a many-sided cut stone. The facets of marketing thought are multidimensional—not linear but qualitative, yet nonetheless definite and measurable. Like any body, the body of marketing thought is comprised of certain materials; it has members or components; it has foundation and superstructure; it has size, shape, proportion, and appearance; and it has orientation or external relationships. The dimensions, or lines for measurement, of marketing thought are, at least, structural, intellectual, temporal, spatial, interdisciplinary, and personal.

1. Structural Dimension. Structurally, marketing thought is divided topically, on the basis of literature areas. They correspond with the divisions of marketing initially made to distinguish areas of practice and areas of academic offerings. Later they became conceptually identified with the functional, institutional, and commodity approaches to the study of marketing. Thus the content of marketing thought may be said to consist of the separately developed thought areas: advertising, salesmanship, sales management, credit, market research, wholesaling, retailing, general marketing, and a miscellany of unclassified subjects. Writings and thought in each of these areas may also be classified as specialized and general. Thought content, in the form of books, has also a structural classification, describable as elementary or advanced, theoretical or practical, traditional or orthodox.

2. Intellectual Dimension. The intellectual dimension of marketing thought represents the extent to which it embraces the elements of a scientific discipline. Progress in the development of a discipline consists of its rising from factual and conceptual bases to higher levels of generalization and integration. By this criterion, it may be said that marketing thought has attained status in the intellectual dimension. Facts have been abundantly reported and kept up to date in successive publications. Together, they recount vividly an important segment of our business history. More than that, marketing and its environment have been appropriately conceptualized by students of the subject. This is evidence of intellectual stature and assurance of a foundation upon which constructive and critical thought may be built.

Generalizations deduced from those concepts have variously been called elements and principles. They have ranged from simple rules of action to interpretative generalizations of the marketing institution and to statements approximating economic principles. Of theories, at first they were few, and often implicit rather than explicit. The nearest approximation to early theory was the structure of thought steming from certain premises about the concept of marketing, its purpose, and responsibilities. Because of general unanimity among writers, there was but one "school of thought," or a common "theory" of marketing. On the other hand, writers emphasized marketing's economic role, its broader than technical management role, and its social responsibility. Such interpretations of marketing constituted in a sense its theories.

3. Temporal Dimension. The temporal dimension of marketing thought has been discussed previously as its "development." It need only be reiterated here that this development through time is a measurement of the progress made in the explanation of marketing, or in the explanation of social behavior made from a marketing viewpoint. With continued change in our environment, with changes in our marketing concepts, and with changes in our concept of marketing, the future holds further evolution for the body of marketing thought according to this dimension.

4. The Spatial Dimension. When the development of marketing thought is said to have occurred *in the United States,* a spatial orientation is given it, but two aspects of this dimensional orientation are sometimes overlooked by such a broad generalization. First, it conceals the fact that local interests in marketing have affected the development of thought along different lines. Agricultural interests of the Middle West produced studies of the marketing of farm products. Large-scale retailing interests in New York City produced studies of institutional management. This is evidence that marketing thought has mirrored problems and interests of the land in which it has grown.

Second, such a broad generalization, conceals that the marketing thought here developed is indigenous to the setting of the United States and may not be equally explicative of business systems of other countries. Growing recognition of this comparative or cultural dimension of marketing thought in recent years has tempered our presumptions that marketing is a universal business system rather than a cultural social system.

5. The Interdisciplinary Dimension. The interdisciplinary dimension is the extent to which marketing thought embraces ideas drawn from other social disciplines. The stuff of which marketing thought is made is not wholly from marketing experience or from the intellectual innovations of those who undertake its study. From economics, psychology, accounting, statistics, law, political science, and other social disciplines, concepts and ideas have been borrowed that, conjoined with marketing concepts, enrich the body of this thought. No social discipline develops in a vacuum, and the more integrated are the findings of all, the more nearly will our knowledge of society approximate a social science.

6. The Personal Dimension. The personal dimension is the extent to which the character of marketing thought has been determined not only by external problems inciting study but by the subjective factors that have influenced the viewpoints of men contributing to the development of thought. Personal traits, family backgrounds, academic training, occupational assignments, and business experience combine to influence the manner in which students of marketing have viewed and written of the subject.

PLAN OF ANALYSIS

In the following chapters analysis is made of marketing thought along the lines of its different dimensions. The body of thought is first classified topically, and separate attention is given to each of the structural members or literature areas. Within each, the development through time is traced so as to show the response of marketing students to changing environmental conditions. The progress from facts to concepts, to principles, and to broader generalizations is shown. Personal influences in the study of marketing are also considered. Finally, an appraisal is made of the contributions to the general body of marketing thought that have been made by students writing in each of the topical areas.

ENDNOTES

[1] Several early teachers have recounted their experiences: James E. Hagerty, "Experiences of Our Early Marketing Teachers," *Journal of Marketing*, I (July, 1936), 20; L. D. H. Weld, "Early Experiences in Teaching Courses in Marketing," *Journal of Marketing*, V (April, 1941), 380; Simon Litman, "The Beginnings of Teaching Marketing in American Universities," *Journal of Marketing*, XV (October, 1950), 220; H. H. Maynard, "Marketing Courses Prior to 1910," *Journal of Marketing*, V (April, 1941), 382.

[2] Litman, *op. cit.*, p. 380.

[3] Stated by Ralph Starr Butler in correspondence with the author, in 1940. See Appendix A.

[4] Arranged chronologically in the order of their first main contribution to marketing thought through teaching.

[5] Chart 1 shows lines of intellectual influence between teachers and students in the early development of marketing thought. This chart was included in the article by the author entitled "Influences on the Development of Marketing Thought," published in the *Journal of Marketing*, XVI (July, 1951), 1.

[6] Stated by Weld in correspondence with the author in 1941. See Appendix A.

[7] "The History of the American Marketing Association," *Journal of Marketing*, V (April, 1941), 374.

[8] Frank G. Coolsen, *Marketing Thought in the United States in the Late Nineteenth Century* (Lubbock, Tex.: Texas Tech Press, 1961).

ADVERTISING

4

Some of the earliest developments of marketing thought occurred in writings on advertising, resulting from a conjuncture of events early in the twentieth century that caused hope to be placed in advertising as a panacea for disposing of the products of industry. Use of advertising was increasing, owing to success experienced in its use, to growing circulation of newspapers and magazines, and to almost unbounded confidence in psychological discoveries of means of motivating and influencing human behavior in the market.

After 1903, the literature of advertising grew rapidly and passed through several stages significant to marketing thought. More than one hundred and thirty books on the subject were published before 1950. This number exceeded that of works written on other aspects of marketing, indicating the popularity of advertising from the standpoint of both readers and writers. The advertising literature was divided between trade books and textbooks, the latter being much more numerous. The former, written primarily for practitioners of advertising, were often not suitable for formal educational purposes, because of the scope of their coverage or the manner of their presentation. Textbooks, on the other hand, were of two types: those treating the whole subject of advertising and those dealing with specialized phases of it. The specialized works were the more numerous. Topically, the most often discussed subjects were advertising copy, layout, campaigns, principles and practices, economics, and psychology. The specialized books generally preceded the more general texts; the trade books appeared mainly during and after the late 1920s.

Scores of writers contributed to the advertising literature, but only a few of them stand out as principal contributors to advertising and marketing thought. Among them are Walter Dill Scott, Harry L. Hollingworth, S. R. Hall, H. W. Hess, Lloyd D. Herrold, Daniel Starch, George B. Hotchkiss, Otto Kleppner, A. J. Brewster and H. H. Palmer, Hugh E. Agnew, Neil H. Borden, Paul T. Cherington, C. H. Sandage, H. K. Nixon, and A. W. Frey. That group spans about the entire history of the advertising literature. Some of them maintained positions of eminence for many years, for revision of even the earliest books was common.

Thought in the advertising literature evolved through three stages: initial statement, integration, and specialization.

FORMATIVE STAGE OF ADVERTISING THOUGHT

Although writings on advertising appeared prior to 1900 — for example, a monumental work entitled *The History of Advertising,* was published in England in 1875 — none can be considered to have contributed to marketing thought in America until the beginning of the twentieth century. From then until 1920, thought in this field had a distinctive character that might be described as *formative*. The conception of advertising, the organization of thought, and the relation of it to marketing were without precedence. Original verbalizations of advertising partook of the viewpoints of writers, many of whom were psychologists. Advertising thought, therefore, in its initial stage was colored by a strong emphasis upon psychological or mental factors. Being a new body of thought, it was at first exploratory, tentative, ill-proportioned, incomplete. It nevertheless constituted the foundation for the superstructure that was to arise.

Prominent among the psychologists writing of advertising were Walter Dill Scott, director of the Psychological Laboratory at Northwestern University, Harry L. Hollingworth, instructor in psychology at Columbia University, and Henry F. Adams, professor of psychology at the University of Michigan. They undertook to state the principles of psychology related to advertising, to explain the mental processes that an advertisement was intended to affect, and to apply that understanding in the creation of advertisements.

Scott asserted that in his wide discussions and readings concerning advertising at that time (1903), he had never heard or seen a reference to anything except psychology that could furnish a stable foundation for a theory of advertising. He therefore introduced into the analysis of the subject such concepts as attention, association of ideas, suggestion, fusion, perception, apperception, illusions, and mental imagery. The psychological laws that he propounded were not new, but his application of them to this realm of business was. His ideas found expression in his books on the theory and psychology of advertising.[1]

Hollingworth's approach was also psychological. His chief concern was the use of psychological principles to get responses from advertisements, and he devoted himself mainly to devising methods of measuring appeals, memory, etc. He made no mention of marketing, economics, salesmanship, journalism, or advertising agencies in *Advertising and Selling*,[2] which was published in 1913.

Adams similarly concerned himself with setting forth psychological principles related to advertising. He believed that it was possible to break down advertisements into their elements and to show with mathematical accuracy their effectiveness. This was to be done by tests, and his theories were set forth in 1916 in his *Advertising and Its Mental Laws*.[3]

Those three writers were typical of a group that influenced the development of advertising and marketing thought in its early stage. They typified the close relationship that existed at that time between the business of advertising and the social science of psychology, a relationship that faded in later years as emphasis on technical knowledge of marketing increased. The relationship originally was due largely to the fact that before 1910 there were, strictly speaking, no marketing specialists. The scientific students of marketing were primarily psychologists, economists, sociologists, and some business practitioners.

The prominence of psychologists among the early contributors to marketing thought indicated also the awareness of those social scientists of the marketing problems of the day. Business was weighted with products for which there was no apparent market, and disposing of them was a problem. Advertising was being used with increasing success, and it was natural that this practice should arouse further interest in manipulation of consumer desires. Psychological methods appeared to furnish the solution to the problem, and proponents of psychological techniques found a market for their knowledge. Motivation was the subject of the day. The psychological steps in the selling process – attention, interest, desire, action – were a formula to be applied.

By 1915, knowledge of advertising, as well as knowledge of marketing in general, had increased to the point that other than psychologists were writing of advertising, and the literature took on some different characteristics. Economic and other business considerations relative to advertising were beginning to appear, and writers were increasingly men experienced in advertising agency practice or in the teaching business subjects. The approach, purpose, and content of the writings expressed a more comprehensive grasp of the meaning and role of advertising not only in business but in the business world.

The diversity of viewpoints that were being brought to bear upon the study of advertising was illustrated by the backgrounds of the authors of *Advertising: Its Principles and Practice:*[4] Harry Tipper, advertising manager of the Texas Company; Harry L. Hollingworth, psychologist at Columbia University; George B. Hotchkiss, business English professor at New York University; and Frank A. Parsons, on the faculty of the New York School of Fine and Applied Art. Thus they brought to bear upon the subject economic, psychological, technical, and artistic appraisal. Stating their objective, they wrote: "This book is an attempt to combine all the various arts and sciences that enter into the work of advertising and to give the fundamentals of each with reference to all the others."[5] They perceived, more deeply than their predecessors had expressed, the relation of advertising to the general distributive undertakings of a firm, saying that advertising was causing businessmen to analyze their distribution more carefully in order that the most possible good will be derived from the advertising. They viewed advertising – "this new force in marketing" – with much optimism, and they spoke of its economic advantages but not of its possible disadvantages. Advertising to them was the application to business of the force of publicity.

The gradual transition of advertising practice from the application of mere psychological principles to the application of an integrated group of principles was recognized at that time as a "great change" taking place in business practice. This was illustrated somewhat by developments of thought expressed by E. E. Calkins and R. Holden in 1905 in *Modern Advertising*[6] and in 1915 in the revision of that book entitled *The Business of Advertising.* Originally, advertising was defined as a "commercial force" and described as one of the factors breaking down the control that a manufacturer's salesman might have over the lines of trade. Outdoor advertising was discussed as "mural" advertising; general, retail, and mail order advertising, as well as the advertising manager and the advertising agency, were also topics of consideration. The revision, it was said, was made necessary because of the advances in the scientific development of advertising. Throughout, however, the viewpoint expressed by the authors was that of the manufacturer using advertising. The consumer interest was subordinated.

Herbert F. DeBower, vice-president of the Alexander Hamilton Institute, also attempted to treat the subject as more than a psychological phenomenon and to classify the principles on which the new "science" was founded.[7] He linked advertising with the creating of an economic utility, without which he said it would cease to exist. He regarded it as a type of business "insurance." Its function was to assist intelligent selection, improve quality of goods, educate the public, create new wants, and reduce price to customers. He criticized Webster's dictionary for failure in its definition of advertising to express the full significance of the term, but he did not offer a definition of his own. He was perhaps the first to discuss the legal restrictions then placed upon advertising.

Of the many others contributing to advertising literature in that formative period, only a few need be mentioned to indicate the stature that advertising thought attained during the first two decades of this century. H. W. Hess[8] covered the following subjects: psychology, typography, the English of advertising, economic implications, and a philosophical interpretation of the principles. His was somewhat a trade-school approach, with emphasis on the making of better ads. S. R. Hall[9] centered his attention on devices for attracting readers' interest and on the actual writing of the ads. E. H. Kastor drew from his own agency experience during twenty years the sales and merchandising approach he used in *Advertising*.[10] He evidenced a good grasp of the whole merchandising scheme and the relation of advertising to it. George H. Sheldon,[11] although taking what was claimed to be a merchandising point of view, dwelt heavily on media and gave descriptive treatment of other phases of the subject.

Thus in the earliest period of the development of advertising thought two stages are discernible: that in which psychological factors were emphasized and that in which the combined factors essential to the success of advertising were set forth. It was a period of gathering into focus ideas stemming from different viewpoints, a time for crystalizing concepts of what advertising is, what it does, and where it fits into the general business scheme of things. It was a period when experience was distilled in thought and thought was given expression.

CONTRIBUTIONS OF PAUL T. CHERINGTON

Although Paul T. Cherington is recognized for his contributions to the advancement of marketing thought in general, he is associated with the literature of advertising through his *Advertising as a Business Force* and *The Consumer Looks at Advertising*.[12] Prior to teaching at the Harvard Business School in 1908, he had served as editor of two business trade publications. Afterward, he was director of research at the J. Walter Thompson Company. Throughout, he was a creative and critical thinker concerning advertising. At a time when many of the pioneers in this field of investigation were producing highly specialized works and writing from a narrow point of view, Cherington dealt with advertising as a pervasive force in the distributive system.

His first book was mainly a compilation of articles gathered from leading advertising periodicals of the time: *Printers' Ink, System,* and *Advertising and Selling.* In it his contribution was found in the point of view that tied them together. He identified three factors in the distribution of goods that have a bearing on advertising: the article, the consumer, and the means by which the two are brought together. He considered the buying motives recognized by psychologists at that time, but his main consideration was the relation of advertising to physical distribution. To him the process of distribution, involving channels through wholesale and retail outlets, embodied a great deal of conflict. The advertiser, he believed, must deal effectively with this conflict if his job is to be well done. The effect that advertising has on the distributive process makes it "a business force." The existing system, in other words, was undergoing modifications through the use of advertising.

Whereas his first book was eclectic, his second was strikingly original, containing throughout not a single footnote, although a few references in the text were made to other sources. This work was philosophic rather than factual. Picking up the theme of his 1913 publication, he defended the use of advertising as a business force in distribution, and he defined the scope of advertising in the social and economic system. He held that the real task of business was to bring about more *enlightened* consumption rather than merely *increased* consumption.

By the time that viewpoint was set forth in 1928, the nation had been subjected to some years of the Consumer Movement, during which both distributive and advertising practices were roundly criticized. Cherington's interest, nevertheless, was not superficial; it went deep. He posed the question "Is advertising an economic waste?" which was not considered in advertising literature ten or fifteen years earlier. He discussed advertising not only as it was practiced but also as it might be used in connection with banking, law, medicine, and religion. In many respects the philosophy expressed in both his writings is worthy of consideration even today.

PERIOD OF INTEGRATION AND ESTABLISHMENT

Although some integration of viewpoints and findings in the study of advertising had been evident, it was not until after 1920 that general works on advertising appeared that established the structure of thought for years to come. Those were the writings of Otto Kleppner, president of the Kleppner Company and lecturer on marketing at New York University; George B. Hotchkiss, professor of marketing at New York University; Daniel Starch, professor of marketing at New York University; Daniel Starch, professor at the Harvard Business School; A. J. Brewster, head of the department of advertising; and H. H. Palmer, associate professor of business English and advertising, both of Syracuse University.

One of the evidences of maturity in advertising thought was the appearance in book titles of the word "principles." As early as 1908 the term had been used in *The Principles of Practical Publicity;* a few years later it was used in *The Principles of Advertising Arrangement;* in 1915 in *Advertising: Its Principles and Practices;* in 1917 in *Advertising Principles;* and in 1923 in *Principles of Advertising.* The tendency was for both the content and the presentation to become more comprehensive. It indicated the effort to present a complete and balanced concept of advertising useful to practitioners and scholars alike. It represented consolidation of thought concerning the techniques applicable to the work of advertising, the relation of advertising to other aspects of distribution, and the role of advertising in the economic and social structure of our culture. Books of this character served as texts in the increasing number of courses offered in advertising. Therefore, they were the mold that shaped the ideas about advertising for a generation of students.

The nature of the integration of thought that was taking place during the early 1920s — a time when the knowledge of marketing in general was attaining an integration — is illustrated in the thought set forth by Otto Kleppner.[13] In 1925 he gave a rather full treatment of the course of an advertisement in its creation, showing the inception and development of advertising ideas. By 1933 he had made a contribution to advertising thought in the concept of the "advertising spiral" and, in addition to discussing the procedures for preparing the advertisement and selecting media, had discussed control techniques and the historical development of marketing and advertising.

The "advertising spiral" was a concept that appeared to be original with Kleppner. It was a phrase used to express three stages in the advertising of a product. The *pioneering* stage is that in which the advertising of a product is designed to open new markets for it. The *competitive* stage is devoted to strengthening its competitive position. The *retentive* stage is that in which markets won are retained and guarded against appropriation by others. The "advertising spiral" set a practical and competitive background for discussing the advertising procedure in all Kleppner's revisions.

By 1941 Kleppner had refined his definition and classification of the concepts involved in the subject of advertising as a whole, and a comprehensive treatment was given this function. As environmental changes and new conceptual developments occurred, attention was given to copy, the media plan, radio and television advertising, campaigns, and the economic aspects of advertising.

As thought in the field of advertising developed, there was a good deal of cross fertilization among the prominent writers of the time. Kleppner's inspiration therefore came in part from other extant writings on the subject, and in his second edition he referred to works in both the general marketing and the advertising literature, including those of Hotchkiss, Starch, Hall, Osborne, Scott, and Hollingworth. In the third edition, the bibliography, then entitled "Reading Suggestions" mentioned books by Hotchkiss, Sandage, Goode, Larrabee, Agnew, Dygert, and others.

A somewhat different trend in the integration of advertising thought in the 1920s was represented by the development of case materials for teaching broad and comprehensive analysis of fundamental problems of advertising. Daniel Starch was one of the leading contributors to this trend while at the Harvard Business School, where he used the case method. His objective in his 1923 publication[14] was to develop scientific methods of dealing with fundamental advertising problems and to present information bearing upon the solution of those problems. His information was taken from experience, from experimentation, and from scientific and statistical sources. Actual advertising cases gathered from several advertising agencies were presented. So comprehensive was his coverage of the subject that his original edition included discussion of the history and development of advertising, sample investigation for a retail store, sample investigation among dealers and consumers, results of a complete series of advertisement tests, foreign advertising, and financial advertising.

The extent to which advertising thought was developed in the 1920s is further shown by the contributions of George B. Hotchkiss. As a professor of English and business correspondence, his view of advertising naturally differed from those of some of his contemporaries. According to the Preface of his *Advertising Copy,*[15] in 1924 he regarded the subject of copy writing as a "comparatively neglected field," notwithstanding the fact that in 1915 S. R. Hall had published *Writing an Advertisement,*[16] and many other writers had dealt at length with the subject in comprehensive treatises. Considering the art of writing advertising messages to be a branch of English composition, Hotchkiss thought that his treatment of the subject might be used in "cultural colleges" or as a text in "practical" English composition. Accordingly, he discussed such topics as the substance of reason-why copy, style of reason-why copy, descriptive copy, direct emotional appeals, good diction in copy, choice of words, etc. The art of writing advertising had never been more minutely treated!

In 1927, in collaboration with Hugh E. Agnew, Hotchkiss published *Advertising Principles*,[17] an undistinguished text even for its day. In 1933, writing alone, he published *An Outline of Advertising: Its Philosophy, Science, Art, and Strategy*,[18] a book that established Hotchkiss' position among advertising writers and became one of the classical works in the field. Hotchkiss saw advertising as a phenomenon with broad associations. Starting with general rather than particular conceptions, he dealt with it from the philosophical standpoint, showing its development throughout history, its relation to journalism, and its social and economic contribution. The "science" of advertising pertained to its modern procedures and practices, including research, selling, and the advertising department and agency. Its "art" related to copy, layout, and production. "Strategy" had to do with media selection, testing, etc.

In general, this pattern of integration in advertising thought became traditional and was accepted as satisfactory coverage of what related to this area of marketing. It consisted essentially of four elements:

1. Conception of advertising *as an institution* of the American culture, as having a historical background in both this country and abroad and as having discernible impact upon the economic and social structure of the culture.
2. Conception of advertising *as an element in marketing,* as one of the factors combined in varying proportions in different circumstances to produce the desired ends of business enterprise. Its relation to the whole distribution program is depicted, as well as its relation to the financial, production, personnel, and other aspects of the business.
3. Conception of advertising *as an area of management* decision itself, a system of functions or interrelated activities that demand science and artistry in their performance.
4. Conception of advertising *as a function* giving rise to organized and institutional bodies for the performance of it, including the media, agencies, departments, and service groups.

While the scope and pattern of general advertising thought was well established, writings originating in that area after 1935, while conforming to the accepted pattern, gained distinction mainly through the organization and emphasis of the component ideas. C. H. Sandage[19] approached an integrated statement of advertising principles via discussion of the social and economic setting of advertising and progressed toward technical considerations: research, preparation of advertisements, media, and testing. Institutional and budgetary matters were deferred until last. H. K. Nixon[20] described first the advertising organization, then its functions, including its economic and social functions, and finally the principles or rules for construction of advertisements. A. W. Frey,[21] on the other hand, took the viewpoint of management, beginning with the techniques for development of campaigns and advertisements, leaving economic and social considerations until last. Donald W. Davis,[22] after a historical introduction, dealt first with the preparation of the message. Next he took up the production of printed advertising, media, and, finally, the factors that determine the success of a campaign.

SPECIALIZED ADVERTISING THOUGHT

While there is a strong tendency in thought development for broader stages of generalization to be sought, specialized works on advertising continued to appear. A contrast is evident, however, between earlier and later specialized writings, insofar as their relation to the growing body of thought is concerned. Immediately after the turn of this century, advertising treaties were fragmentary and unrelated to a body of context, for a body of advertising thought had not yet been generalized. From whatever experiences they had, writers drew ideas concerning psychology, copy writing, advertising techniques, and the like. Variety characterized the inductive research that resulted in the statement of a general theory. When thought attained some degree of generalization, continued specialized studies served another purpose, namely, verification, elaboration, and penetration of the phenomenon of advertising. Such writings appeared throughout the decades following 1920, enlarging and enriching marketing thought.

Hugh E. Agnew made several contributions to the more specialized advertising thought. Having been interested in the business of advertising and selling from his early years, he was led to write articles about it because of a conviction that it was being handled in an unbusinesslike manner. He praised the writings of Scott, Calkins, and Cherington, regarding the latter's *Advertising as a Business Force* more as a book on marketing than on advertising. It was after 1920, however, while teaching at New York University, that Agnew made his principal contributions to the development of thought. One was an analysis of co-operative advertising practices prevalent in the mid-1920s,[23] made in the light of current government regulation of the advertising practices of trade associations. Another was the first comprehensive analysis of the advertising media, which established standards for judging and comparing media in the practice of space buying.[24] Still another was a detailed analysis of the outdoor advertising industry[25] and the setting forth of steps involved in the use of the outdoor medium. Its enduring principles have outlived its factual material.

Lloyd D. Herrold,[26] of Northwestern University, contributed to the understanding of copy writing through explanation and illustration of logical steps involved in the function, rather than through the study of examples of finished ads.

Two contributions were made in the mid-1920s to understanding the procedures and implications of the organized advertising campaign. Harry Tipper and George French,[27] and Bernard Lichtenberg and Bruce Barton[28] were writers in this highly specialized field, which added also to knowledge in the general field of selling.

Further writing was done in the psychology of advertising during the 1930s,[29] but unlike some of the earlier works, by which advertising was to be taught, that of Poffenberger presumed that the student had a knowledge of both advertising and psychology and that the text was to be used for a more advanced, specialized study of the subject.

Illustrative of other specialized contributions made to advertising thought were writings dealing with such subjects as retail advertising,[30] radio advertising,[31] dealer display advertising,[32] the advertising agency,[33] and advertising appropriations.[34]

Exceptional among the specialized works on advertising were the problem and case books prepared by Neil H. Borden. His *Problems in Advertising*[35] was a compilation drawn from files of the Harvard Business School, together with data from official sources and materials from other advertising texts. It covered such subjects as the appraisal of marketing and advertising possibilities, determination of the place of advertising in the sales program — for both consumer and industrial goods — use of research for determination of advertising policy, preparation of the product, determination of copy approach, and selection of media. His *Advertising: Text and Cases*[36] gives similar coverage.

SOCIAL AND ECONOMIC ASPECTS OF ADVERTISING

A dimension of advertising thought that is not general in the integrative sense or specialized in the technical sense relates to the appraisal of economic and social aspects of advertising. So long as advertising was regarded only as a business tool or as a business force, little interest was expressed in its broader implications. Also, so long as only the benefits of advertising to the economy were seen, its full measure was not taken. When the social and economic aspects of advertising came under consideration, few students of the subject were apparently either willing or able to cope with it. Projections of traditional economic thought provided some easy generalizations, but concrete factual evidence of the social and economic effects of advertising was hard to come by. Consequently, less than a handful of writers made original and substantial contributions in that area. Neil H. Borden is outstanding among them.

As early as the late 1920s some attention was directed to that subject, partly because advertising bore the condemnation of deceptions and exaggerations cited in the Consumer Movement. With the increase of quantitative marketing data and the exigencies of the depression, interest in the question grew.

One of the first writers to make a critical analysis was Floyd L. Vaughan.[37] His appraisal from a social and public standpoint, however, covered the whole distributive process and not merely advertising itself. Unimpressed with the profit return as a standard for the judgment of advertising, he analyzed the social cost and utility of advertising. His analysis was mainly theoretical, for at that time empirical data were not available for proving or disproving grand contentions concerning advertising. Vaughan's contribution to thought, therefore, was to furnish a type of introduction to the analysis of advertising. Being somewhat critical of advertising, his ideas had no popular appeal. Being theoretical, they did not fit into the "how to do it" trend of thought that was then in the ascendancy.

Roland S. Vaile[38] was another to undertake an analysis of the subject. His objective was to present a sympathetic and impartial review of advertising and its role in the development of a dynamic society. His analysis was realistic; it had a firm theoretical background. He discussed the relation of advertising to marketing research, to educational effects, to decreasing and overhead costs, to the business cycle, and to long-run effects on industry, all of which constituted a significant contribution to understanding the subject up to that time.

The most formidable analyses of economic aspects of advertising were those made by Neil H. Borden,[39] one a thousand-page tome, the other a three-hundred-page condensation thereof. While these studies did not change the prevailing concept of the role of advertising in our economy, they did validate many of the theoretical presumptions that had prevailed in the thoughts of both economists and students of marketing. Little more can be done here than to indicate something of the outline along which Borden developed his thought and to present a few of the general conclusions that he reached.

The first book was organized along the following lines: economic background of the development and use of advertising; its effects on demand, on costs, on prices, on the range of products, and on investment and volume of income; and ethical aspects of advertising.

From the summary chapter of the larger book, the following are some of the principal generalizations:

Advertising by itself serves not so much to increase demand for a product as to speed up the expansion of a demand that would come from favoring conditions, or to retard adverse demand trends due to unfavorable conditions [p. 843].

Demand for all products can increase only as income from production increases [p. 847].

It appears likely that for products whose demand is inherently inelastic, i.e., whose consumption by individuals is limited by the character of the products, advertising does not materially affect the elasticity of demand [p. 848].

One cannot be certain to what extent the increased distribution costs which have attended the growth of industrialism are attributable to advertising [p. 851].

The evidence indicates that in many industries advertising tends to impede quickly-acting price competition, but in no case does it prevent it ultimately [p. 860].

Advertising cannot be classed as an important causal factor in cyclical fluctuations, although . . . it has tended to aggravate cyclical fluctuations [p. 865].

Advertising's chief task from a social standpoint is that of encouraging the development of new products [p. 881].

Until more conclusive evidence comes into print, Borden's analysis stands more or less as the last word on the subject.

DEVELOPMENT OF THOUGHT, 1950–1960

Prior to 1950, advertising thought may be said to have developed along both general and specialized lines, attention being given to the advertising functions of both manufacturers and retailers and to social and economic as well as technical considerations. In the postwar years of the 1950s, a number of environmental technological factors wrought changes in advertising practice and ultimately in advertising thought.

Nine basic developments are identified as follows:

1. Changing emphasis in the American business community.
2. The general expansion of the American economy.
3. The changing character of the American market.
4. The increase in advertising volume.
5. The increase in the size and complexity of media.

6. The rise of television.
7. Shifts within media groups.
8. Important developments in media technology.
9. Changes in distribution concepts.[40]

The effects of these factors corresponded to many of the changes that were occurring in marketing thought in general during that decade, namely, improvement in scientific management in advertising and increased social consciousness in the appraisal of it.

ADVERTISING TECHNOLOGY

As has always been true in advertising thought, improvements in technology have been regarded as a means of improving advertising management. Two areas in which technological thought were advanced in writings of the period were in television and radio advertising management and in copy writing.

The writing of copy has engaged students of advertising from its inception, but no exposition has been more complete and scholarly than that given by Merrill DeVoe in 1956. He attempted "to bring into the basic literature of advertising copy the technical copy principles that gradually have been evolved through advertising copy research."[41] Thus approaching the subject in more scholarly, objective, and historical fashion than most writers, he undertook to deal with the general considerations pertinent to all kinds of copy. The following are some of the subjects with which he dealt, which indicate new concepts introduced into copy technology: appraising product interest, differentiating the undifferentiated brand, the concept of user benefits — motivation, advertising as communication, advertising objectives, and extraneous devices. Through works of this type, advertising thought gained depth and provided a more substantial basis for advertising practice.

Similarly, institutional management technology was enhanced by such works as those of Gene F. Seehafer and Jack W. Laemmar on radio and television advertising.[42] In each they dealt at length and in great detail with what might be regarded as the production and marketing of radio and television programs. Characteristics of the "product" were discussed, along with analysis of the broadcast market, institutions engaged in "distribution" of the programs, and relations with buyers of broadcasting service. Thus the general frame of marketing analysis was applied to the marketing management involved in a particular type of advertising service.

MANAGEMENT STRATEGIES IN ADVERTISING

Increasing objectivity in marketing thought produced a concept of "strategies," by which it is indicated that directed managerial efforts are made in terms of selected objectives. The means-end relationship has always been implicit in technological thought, but during the 1950s emphasis was given to it in expression of the decision function in business management. An interesting exposition of this idea was given by Lyndon O. Brown in his discussion of media. He held media selection to be an executive decision, and the strategy of media selection to be developed within the total marketing context. The determinants of media strategy are the market situation itself, the marketing policy of the firm, and all specific marketing strategies involved. Differences in media strategy result from dissimilar objectives in an over-all program, in different knowledge of existing facts, and in unequal judgment ability of those making decisions. The concept of strategies is as applicable to other advertising functions as to the selection and use of media.

ADVERTISING IN THE MARKETING MIX

While advertising has long been regarded as a form of sales promotion, a new management concept of it as one of the variables to be combined and integrated in the over-all marketing program gained acceptance during the 1950s. An overexaggerated regard for advertising or the creation of advertisements as "the solid foundation on which the entire business rests,"[43] has given way to viewing it as a factor subject to strategic deployment. This view is developed by Borden and Marshall, who said that "advertising is a selling tool whose effective and profitable use is inextricably intertwined with an understanding of the business and marketing operation of which it is but one part."[44] Thus the idea was advanced that advertising not only is a variable contingent upon the objective of the firm but also is a variable relative to other means that might be considered for accomplishing a given objective. Among the many factors to which it is related in the marketing mix, Borden mentions the following: brand policy, selling methods, variations in channels used, merchandising policies.[45] The role that advertising plays in the activities of any given firm is, therefore, a decision that not only must be made by management but must be made by management on different levels of responsibility. Top management integrates advertising with overall business objectives. Middle management integrates advertising with the other available promotional means. Technical operatives, even as in the writing of copy, integrate the advertising statement with product, brand differentiation, price policy, etc. Thus integration *in* advertising and *of* advertising has been one of the key concepts developed in thought during the 1950s.

ADVERTISING AS COMMUNICATION

While advertising has been regarded in many ways, mainly as a form of selling, during the 1950s it was increasingly viewed as a means of communication. The function of communication includes educating, informing, persuading, propagandizing, and brainwashing, and in recent years the relevance of each of these to advertising has been examined. Communication implies selection of idea symbols for imparting meaning, and effectiveness is affected by the climate of mass thinking, attitudes, receptivity, provincialism, and the like. It is recognized also that ideas are not transmitted but that images are built in the thought of perceivers, that motivation influences receptivity, and that communication is a two-way exchange through carriage and feedback of messages. These are some concepts of communication in terms of which advertising has recently been analyzed.

ADVERTISING AND SOCIAL CONSCIOUSNESS

Thought concerning advertising has, in its broader dimensions, always included a generous analysis of the economic and social consequences of that instrument. For the most part, appraisals have been made from the standpoint of the firm, of classical economists, or of analysts of imperfect competition. The prominence of sociological appraisal has grown since early in this century, with periods of accentuated criticism, as during the late 1920s and the 1950s. Yet as derogatory criticism has multiplied, so has appreciation of the constructive force that advertising constitutes in contemporary society.

Typical of the protestants are Mayer and Packard,[46] who depict advertising as a "culturally repulsive" institution in our midst, thriving on competition among manufacturers, causing insecurities and magnifying pains, creating wants instead of values, and embracing a delusion among businessmen that they are being "scientific" when actually they are only naive.

At the other extreme are the host of thinkers who support advertising as an institution that, although, like any institution, it is abused, nevertheless has contributed undeniably to the material progress of our society. They find among advertising men many who, with intelligent insight and capacity, are concerned with social responsibility, comply with laws, and use the medium with discretion and effectiveness. Both sides of this picture have been given much exposure during the decade of the 1950s.

ADVERTISING THOUGHT AFTER 1960

Advertising thought published during the 1960s represented a combination of the best carried on from former years and that which emerged anew from circumstantial and conceptual developments of the period. It was a period in which changes in values affected advertising practice perhaps more than changes in advertising techniques, and those new values were interpreted in print by many writers. Newcomers to advertising authorship as well as authors whose books had evolved through many editions all reflected the influences of the decade in shaping the body of contemporary advertising thought. The following are some of the circumstances which brought change to advertising thought during the 1960s.

ENVIRONMENTAL CHANGE

Circumstances external to advertisers directly affected advertising practice and the development of thought. They consisted largely of changes in social values concerning advertising. During this period the use of billboard advertising was curbed somewhat; likewise the use of radio and television for advertising hard liquors; and advertisements of cigarettes were required to include health warnings. Federal regulatory authorities required substantial proof of claims made by advertisers for product quality and performance, and advertisers were sometimes required in subsequent advertisements to correct misleading claims previously made. Such new demands upon advertising reflected the growing expectation that business be socially responsible. Writers had long discussed the influence of advertising upon the economy and society, and the reaction of the public thereto. During the 1960s, emphasis was turned to the influence of social valued *upon advertising,* and the reactions of *advertisers* thereto.

CRITICAL REPORTS OF BUSINESS EDUCATION

During the 1960s, widespread attention was given to the Gordon-Howell and Pierson studies of business school curricula, in which courses of low technical content were criticized, in contrast to "managerial" courses then increasingly in vogue. Kleppner in 1966 cited this as evidence of the changing philosophy which wrought changes in advertising courses and texts. Accordingly, whereas during the 1950s the term "management" did not appear in titles of advertising texts, during the following decade there did appear such titles as the following:

Advertising Techniques and Management (Zacher)

Advertising Management (Wedding)
The Management of Promotion (Brink)
Advertising Management (Boyd)
Management of International Advertising (Miracle)
Advertising Department Management (Nodar)
Successful Advertising Management (Obermeyer)

Although Obermeyer's book was not published until 1969, he believed that he taught the first course in advertising management in 1948. The need for such a course he attributed to the paucity of writing on the subject, to the rise of new areas of management specialization, and to the increased size of advertising expenditures. There was needed an integration of management knowledge, which previously had been specialized and fragmented.

CONCEPTUAL CHANGE

Increased emphasis on management reflected acceptance of a concept of management as a decision making process. Engel, Wales, and Warshaw[47] in *Promotional Strategy* undertook to analyze the management process in terms of the variables upon which decisions are made. They sought to avoid oversimplification and postulation of dogmatic rules. They saw freshness of management thought deriving from familiarity with new research in consumer behavior and from appreciation of the role of advertising in its larger environment both within and without the business firm.

Within the management context, advertising assumed new character as part of the promotional and total marketing process, or mix of variables employed for attaining marketing objectives. The manageable work of advertising was seen to be variously divisible among many institutions and agencies which linked themselves together in systems for the achievement of efficiency and economy. Conceived as a form of communication, advertising became explained more in psychological and sociological terms than as formerly in straight "sales jargon."

Still another development in marketing thought during the late 1960s was the visualization of marketing practice extended to the promotion of marketables other than physical products, as to services and noneconomic institutional ideas and offerings. Advertising played an increasing role in such promotion, and toward the end of the decade reference to this began to appear in advertising literature.

CHARACTER OF THE LITERATURE

The composition of advertising thought during the decade of the 1960s is indicated by the diversity of titles published. The 67 books listed in the Bibliography of Appendix B had titles indicating topics of interest as follows:

General advertising	19
Methodology, techniques, and testing	16
Management	9
Media	9
Specialized advertising	4
Principles of advertising	4
Economic and social issues	2
Miscellaneous	4

As has always been the case, the majority of publications during the decade had a life span of a single edition. Only six works appearing after 1960 were in a third edition or more. Of these, three had originally been published prior to 1959 and three after 1958. Longest lived was Kleppner's *Advertising Procedure*[48], and its sixth edition since originally published in 1925. *Advertising Theory and Practice*[49] by Sandage appeared in its eighth edition since 1936, and Burton's *Advertising Copywriting*[50] in its third edition since 1949. Three authors who initially published later than 1958, and who had multiple editions by 1973, were Kirkpatrick[51], Dirkensen[52], and Wright.[53]

The longevity of some earlier books and the popularity of later ones is no evidence of uniformity in the thought which they presented. Rather they show diversity in thought and continuity of ideas originally presented. While cognizant of environmental and conceptual changes occurring in advertising, both Kleppner and Sandage presented in later editions essentially the same structure of thought they did initially. Kleppner continued his emphasis of the "advertising spiral," and Sandage retained "the social consciousness of previous editions." On the other hand, although late comers to the field professed managerial, consumer, behavioral, or systems viewpoints, the body of a comprehensive treatment of advertising continued to include the role of advertising in its broader context, campaign planning, use of media, creative communication, management of functions, and response to social expectations.

CONTRIBUTIONS OF ADVERTISING LITERATURE TO MARKETING THOUGHT

The objective of reviewing the advertising literature so fully is to ascertain what contribution writers thereof have made to the developing body of marketing thought. That body, it must be remembered, is not merely a static aggregation of thoughts or ideas. It is a vital structure embracing a range from simple facts to broad theories, including all related concepts and principles. It is a framework that serves to guide action in marketing and for appraisal the world around. Writers on advertising have made a number of contributions to marketing thought.

1. A variety of *concepts of advertising,* which have influenced the scope and character of the thought developed, depicting it as follows:

As a business tool — a means of accomplishing some business end; a device by which selling may be accomplished more economically than otherwise; a "silent salesman"; a mass helper of personal salesmanship.

As a technical process — that of putting together elements or components of an advertisement, including copy, artwork, headlines, etc., and of placing the finished product in appropriate media.

As a psychological process — a means of manipulating the emotions and behavior of people, particularly in mass selling; the application of psychologists' methods and knowledge; the utilization of a mental process.

As a literature — a medium of expression, emphasizing the power of the written word and approached as any piece of formal writing would be.

As a business force — a force in business society, a compelling influence, a dynamism affecting relations of business with both its customers and other firms.

As an operating function — an activity managed within the business organization, to be budgeted, staffed, administered, and controlled.

As an element of the marketing mix — an element to be combined in different proportions, and with varying emphases, with other elements that contribute to the accomplishment of the marketing objective.

As a historical institution — a practice sanctioned by society as a means of communication, a stimulant, a guide to decision making.

As an economic function — a factor of production, a field of employment, a production and distribution function and cost, a creator of markets, an educational influence.

2. Many *technical concepts* useful in understanding advertising and in communicating thoughts about it:

Account executive	Campaign	Network
Advertising agency	Commission	Outdoor advertising
Advertising appropriation	Copy	Panel poster
Advertising media	Co-operative advertising	Point-of-sale advertising
Advertising spiral	Coverage	Protesting
Agate line	Demand creation	Production
Agency compensation	Depth of penetration	Reason-why copy
Appeal	Full position	Sponsor
Bait advertising	Gaze motion	Spot announcement
	Kinescope	Theme
	Layout	Visualization
	Media	
	National *vs.* Local rates	

3. Incorporation in marketing thought of *theory* borrowed from the field of psychology concerning the market behavior of consumers.

4. Development of some *research methodology,* such as methods for the testing of advertisements, which have contributed to the establishment of marketing on a more scientific basis.

5. Development of technical *principles* or rules as means for the achievement of selected ends, as in the production of advertisements or the selection of media.

6. Formulation of a critical frame of *judgment* of the ethical, social, and economic responsibilities inherent in marketing.

ENDNOTES

[1] Walter D. Scott, *The Theory of Advertising* (Boston: Small, Maynard & Co., 1903; rev., 1913), and *The Psychology of Advertisings,* (Boston: Small, Maynard & Co., 1908).
[2] Harry L. Hollingworth, *Advertising and Selling* (New York: D. Appleton — Century Co., Inc., 1913).
[3] Henry F. Adams, *Advertising and Its Mental Laws* (New York: Macmillan Co., 1916).
[4] Harry Tipper, Harry L. Hollingworth, George B. Hotchkiss, and Frank A. Parsons, *Advertising: Its Principles and Practices* (New York: Ronald Press Co., 1915).
[5] *Ibid.,* p. v.
[6] E. E. Calkins and R. Holden, *Modern Advertising* (New York: D. Appleton — Century Co., Inc., 1905); rev. by Calkins, 1915, as *The Business of Advertising.*
[7] DeBower, *Advertising Principles* (New York: Alexander Hamilton Institute, 1917).
[8] H. W. Hess, *Productive Advertising* (Philadelphia: J. B. Lippincott, 1915); rev. ed., 1931, as *Advertising: Its Economics, Philosophy, and Technique.*

[9] S. R. Hall, *Writing an Advertisement* (Boston: Houghton Mifflin Co., 1915).

[10] E. H. Kastor, *Advertising* (Chicago: La Salle Extension University, 1918).

[11] George H. Sheldon, *Advertising Elements and Principles* (New York: Harcourt, Brace & Co., 1925).

[12] Paul T. Cherington, *Advertising as a Business Force* (Garden City, New York: Doubleday, Page & Co., 1913), and *The Consumer Looks at Advertising* (New York: Harper & Bros., 1928).

[13] Otto Kleppner, *Advertising Procedure* (New York: Prentice-Hall, Inc., 1925; 2d ed., 1933; 3d ed., 1941; 4th ed., 1950; 5th ed., 1966; 6th ed., 1973).

[14] Daniel Starch, *Principles of Advertising* (New York: A. W. Shaw Co., 1923).

[15] George B. Hotchkiss, *Advertising Copy* (New York: Harper & Bros. 1924; 2d ed., 1936, 3d ed. 1949).

[16] S. R. Hall, *Writing an Advertisement* (Boston: Houghton Mifflin Co., 1915.)

[17] George B. Hotchkiss and Hugh E. Agnew, *Advertising Principles* (New York: Alexander Hamilton Institute, 1927).

[18] George B. Hotchkiss, *An Outline of Advertising: Its Philosophy, Science, Art, and Strategy* (New York: Macmillan Co., 1933; 2d ed., 1940; 3d ed., 1950.)

[19] C. H. Sandage, *Advertising Theory and Practice* (Chicago: Business Publications, Inc. 1936; 2d ed. Richard D. Irwin, Inc. 1939; 3d ed., 1948; 4th ed., 1953; 5th ed., 1958, with Vernon Fryburger; 6th ed., 1963; 7th ed., 1967; 8th ed. 1971).

[20] H. K. Nixon, *Principles of Advertising* (New York: McGraw-Hill Book Co., 1937).

[21] A. W. Frey, *Advertising* (New York: Ronald Press Co., 1947; 2d ed., 1953; 3d ed., 1961).

[22] Donald W. Davis, *Basic Text in Advertising* (New York: Printers' Ink Publishing Co., 1955).

[23] Hugh E. Agnew, *Cooperative Advertising by Competitors* (New York: Harper & Bros., 1926).

[24] Hugh E. Agnew, *Advertising Media* (New York: D. Van Nostrand Co. 1932; 2d ed. with Warren B. Dygert (New York: McGraw-Hill Book Co., Inc. 1938).

[25] Hugh E. Agnew, *Outdoor Advertising* (New York: McGraw-Hill Book Co., Inc. 1938).

[26] Lloyd D. Herrold, *Advertising Copy* (New York: A. W. Shaw Co., 1926), and *Advertising Copy, Principles and Practice* (New York: D. Van Nostrand Co., 1930).

[27] Harry Tipper and George French, *Advertising Campaign* (New York: D. Van Nostrand Co., 1925).

[28] Bernard Lichtenberg and Bruce Barton, *Advertising Campaigns* (New York: Alexander Hamilton Institute, 1926).

[29] Albert T. Poffenberger, *Psychology in Advertising* (Chicago and New York: A. W. Shaw Co., 1926; 2d ed., 1932); H. C. Link, *The New Psychology of Selling and Advertising* (New York: Macmillan Co., 1932); H. E. Burtt, *Psychology of Advertising* (New York: Houghton Mifflin Co., 1938).

[30] Lloyd D. Herrold, *Advertising for the Retailer* (New York: D. Appleton-Century Co., Inc. 1923).

[31] Herman S. Hettinger, *A Decade of Radio Advertising* (Chicago: University of Chicago Press, 1933).

[32] M. Gross, *Dealer Display Advertising* (New York: Ronald Press Co., 1936).

[33] A. E. Haase, L. C. Lockley, and I. W. Digges, *Advertising Agency Compensation in Theory, Law, and Practice* (New York: National Process Co., 1934).

[34] A. E. Haase, *The Advertising Appropriation* (New York: Harper & Bros., 1931).

[35] Neil H. Borden, *Problems in Advertising* (New York: A. W. Shaw Co., 1927; 2d ed., 1932; 3d ed., 1937).

[36] Neil H. Borden, *Advertising: Text and Cases.* (Chicago: Richard D. Irwin, Inc., 1949; revised, 1965).

[37] Floyd L. Vaughn, *Marketing and Advertising* (Princeton, N.J.: Princeton University Press, 1928).

[38] Roland S. Vaile, *Economics of Advertising* (New York: Ronald Press Co., 1927).

[39] Neil H. Borden, *The Economic Effects of Advertising* (Chicago: Richard D. Irwin, Inc. 1942), and *Advertising in Our Economy* (Chicago: Richard D. Irwin, Inc., 1945).

[40] Lyndon O. Brown, Richard D. Lessler, William M. Weilbacher, *Advertising Media* (New York: Ronald Press Co., 1957), p. 12.

52

[41] Merrill DeVoe, *Effective Advertising Copy* (New York: Macmillan Co., 1956), p. v.

[42] Gene F. Seehafer and Jack W. Laemmar, *Successful Radio and Television Advertising* (New York: McGraw-Hill Book Co., 1951), and *Successful Television and Radio Advertising* (New York: McGraw-Hill Book Co., 1959).

[43] Charles L. Whittier, *Creative Advertising* (New York: Henry Holt & Co., 1955), p. viii.

[44] Neil H. Borden and Martin V. Marshall, *Advertising Management* (Homewood, Ill.: Richard D. Irwin, Inc. 1959), p. vii.

[45] *Ibid.,* p. 166.

[46] Martin Mayer, *Madison Avenue, U.S.A.* (New York: Harper & Bros., 1958); Vance O. Packard, *The Hidden Persuaders* (New York: D. McKay Co., 1957).

[47] James F. Engel, Hugh G. Wales, and Martin R. Warshaw, *Promotional Strategy* (Homewood, Ill.: Richard D. Irwin, Inc., 1967; rev. ed., 1971).

[48] Otto Kleppner, *Advertising Procedure* (New York: Prentice-Hall, Inc., 1925; 6th ed., 1973).

[49] C. H. Sandage and Vernon Freyburger, *Advertising Theory and Practice* (Homewood, Ill.: Richard E. Irwin, Inc., 1936; 8th ed., 1971).

[50] Philip W. Burton and G. Bowman Kreer, *Advertising Copywriting* (Englewood Cliffs, N.J.: Prentice-Hall, Inc., 1949; 3d ed., 1974).

[51] C. A. Kirkpatrick and J. E. Littlefield, *Advertising: Mass Communication in Marketing* (Boston: Houghton Mifflin, 1959; 3d ed., 1970).

[52] C. J. Dirksen and A. Kroeger, *Advertising Principles and Problems* (Homewood, Ill.: Richard D. Irwin, Inc., 1960; 4th ed., 1973).

[53] John S. Wright, D. S. Warner, and W. L. Winter, Jr., *Advertising* (New York: McGraw Book Co., Inc., 1962; 3d ed., 1971).

Another fiber in marketing thought was spun by men concerned with credit. Unlike other aspects of marketing, early thought on credit was developed primarily by men who in all probability would have regarded themselves as students of finance rather than marketing. Nevertheless, because credit—particularly mercantile and retail credit—has been inseparable from distribution itself, and because market financing has universally been regarded as a marketing function, contributions to thought in that area may be regarded as contributions to marketing thought in general.

As with thought evolution in other fields, the understanding of credit unfolded from circumstances in the successive decades of this century. Its topical development was not uniform; rather, the literature was characterized by subjects of changing contemporary interest. Mercantile credit was the subject of interest from 1900 to 1920. Then retail credit was of ascending importance in the 1920s, and personal and sales financing in the 1930s. Credit in foreign trade received much attention immediately following World War I, and the economic implications of credit were widely discussed during the growth of instalment selling and during the depression of the 1930s. When thought became integrated, it was expressed in general books on the subject. Following 1940, thought developed mainly along lines already established.

FACTORS INDUCING STUDY OF CREDIT

The reasons for this study may be inferred from the early writings on credit. The practice of lending had pervaded history and ancient trade and was both an object of interest to economists and a subject for disputation by moralists and theologians. At the beginning of the nineteenth century, credit—or "credits," as the term was generally used to designate credit accounts and the management of them,—assumed a new role and new importance. Credit granting was increasing and had been for some years. Panics, crises, and business failures always accentuated interest in it, as did also the enactment of bankruptcy legislation in that period. Specialized credit institutions had developed during the nineteenth century, such as R. G. Dun and Company and Bradstreet's Improved Commercial Agency. In 1876 the Lyon Furniture Mercantile Agency was organized; in 1877 the Shoe & Leather Mercantile Agency, Inc.; in 1900 the National Credit Office; in 1901 the first mercantile credit bureau; in 1912 the central bureau for exchange of credit information, taken over by the National Association of Credit Men in 1917; and in 1914 the Federal Reserve Board was created. Such developments indicated the growing interest in mercantile credit. By 1914, it is said, difficulty was experienced in securing clerks for credit work. Consequently, lectures relating to credit work were sponsored by organizations such as the Y.M.C.A., and classes in "Commercial Credit" were offered at the university level.[1]

CREDIT PRACTICES AND PROBLEMS PRIOR TO 1920

During the first two decades of this century, a dozen books were published that described prevailing credit practices and constructed roughly the framework of credit thought. The writings dealt with mercantile credit practices, with the use of credit along with advertising and selling as an aid to distribution, and with collection procedures. The writings of William A. Prendergast and James E. Hagerty typified the credit thought of that period.

William A. Prendergast, LL.D., president of the New York and Honduras Mining Company, stroked with a broad brush[2] the outlines of credit as it was then recognized. The details of credit management or of credit thought had not yet been brought into focus. Credit was held to be one of the elements or branches of political economy, according to economic theory. Tracing the development of the use of credit from Roman times and quoting both classical and contemporary economists, Prendergast characterized credit as the exchange of tangible property for an intangible promise. He amplified that concept in different ways, with reiterated emphasis on the basis of confidence and the element of futurity in credit. He cited the effects of the use of credit on social and economic institutions. He explained the previous lack of credit study as resulting from failure to distinguish between mercantile and bank credit and the devotion of attention largely to the instruments of credit rather than to the confidence upon which the use of credit rests.

While credit, or the financing of the market and of marketing activity, has long been regarded as a marketing function, it was not primarily so regarded by Prendergast. To him it was, rather, a financial function and an administrative activity. That is evident in the topical outline that structured the thought in Prendergast's book. It included the following subjects: the functions and organization of credit; the primary divisions of credit, such as bank, capital, public, personal, and commercial credit; the credit department and its sources of credit information; credit office administration; and general considerations.

In the early years of credit study, numerous concepts were stated differently than they are today. For example, shares in incorporated companies were regarded as credit instruments. Financial statements were regarded primarily as a source of information concerning a company's net worth. Little attention was given to collection procedures. The individual who performed the credit work was called "the credit man." The safeguarding credits was a main responsibility of the credit office.

Prendergast justified credit as an economic function. His conception of it as something based upon confidence was conductive to the development of some management principles.

In 1913 James E. Hagerty, a sociologist with substantial economic training, brought out another significant work on credit.[3] It differed in some respects from Prendergast's. Prendergast gave no emphasis to credit instruments; in fact he deplored preoccupation with instruments rather than with confidence. Hagerty approached the study of credit through analysis of those instruments. That approach was generally used in works written thereafter. From a source named Hildebrand he got a concept that credit characterized the third of three periods of economic development, preceded by a barter period and a money period. While recognizing various kinds of credit, he believed that bank credit "sets the standards," that personal credit provides the basis for the level of mercantile credit.

Credit thought presented by Hagerty was organized along the following lines: theory and history; credit instruments; kinds of credit; mercantile credit; personal credit, including that extended to individual proprietors and partnerships as well as to consumers; the credit man; the credit office; sources of information; adjustment bureaus; collections; and bankruptcy. To the last topic he devoted five chapters, because of its importance at that time.

Hagerty's work represented an advance in credit thought; it was a fuller, better balanced treatment of the management of credit, from the point of view of the businessman, than had been made up to that time. His practical treatment of the subject advanced thought perhaps more than a general or theoretical analysis of it then would have.

Although several other books appeared between that of Hagerty in 1913 and that of Ettinger and Golieb in 1917, none made the contribution to thought that those two did. M. M. Kallam in 1914 published a series of fourteen lectures[4] that had been given by nonacademic men before Y.M.C.A. audiences. They consisted of success stories in credit work. In the same year, the A. W. Shaw Company published a similar book,[5] but it was unco-ordinated, loosely thought out, incomplete, and shallow. Moved by what he regarded to be "little literature on the subject" and by changes resulting in credit granting from the development of commercial agencies, trade bureaus, the National Association of Credit Men, and business laws, B. H. Blanton, a credit man for twenty years, in 1915 published still another work[6] which, too, was unbalanced, uncritical, overloaded with credit office forms, and overwhelmingly practical. The same may be said of the work of E. M. Skinner, R. S. White, and H. E. Kramer.[7]

A notable contribution to credit thought was made, however, by R. T. Ettinger and D. E. Golieb,[8] the former a lawyer and the latter a practical credit man, in consolidating and refining thought that had been developed up to that time. They followed the viewpoint and organization that by then had become traditional. They dealt mainly with mercantile credit, devoting only six pages to personal credit. They elaborated the three "C's" of credit — Character, Capacity, and Capital — as factors to be considered in appraising the credit risk, and they discussed the possibilities of formulating a credit equation. Actual credit granting had by then become somewhat routinized, and the authors undertook to state the rudiments of practice in an integrated fashion. Not until the concept of credit and credit practices themselves changed during the next decade, however, were significant changes made in the form and presentation of credit.

ADDITIONS TO CREDIT THOUGHT IN THE 1920s

As the postwar years evolved into economic recovery and expansion, new conditions and credit practices called for re-examination of the statement of credit thought. The Federal Reserve System had begun to function. Foreign trade was on the increase. The financial crisis of 1921 raised new problems for collection and legal settlement. Personal loan companies were being organized under state laws based on the Uniform Small Loan Act. Expanding production of automobiles and other durable goods created a market for instalment credit, and institutions engaged in sales financing became more numerous. These and other such conditions needed expression in the credit literature.

W. H. Steiner[9] was one whose writings early reflected these changing conditons. As acting chief, Division of Analysis and Research, Federal Reserve Board, who had done extensive research and writing in the fields of credit, money, and banking, he devoted himself primarily to analyzing the relative merits of the trade acceptance and the cash discount credit systems, a controversy which at that time was vigorous. Unconcerned with consumer credit or with collection problems, he investigated instead the factors affecting the use and role of terms involving acceptances and discounts. No less than sixteen chapters of his book were devoted to aspects of that subject!

In that work there were some interesting concepts. Steiner held that every stage in the economic process had its own credit and banking relationships and that businesses at the same stage or level, regardless of the products they handled, would manifest that relationship. He classified credit problems according to the stage of the economic process and the line of business.. He claimed that credit problems of businessmen are determined for them, not by them; that the length of time an article passing through the economic process remains in each stage fixes the upper limit of the time for which credit at that stage should be granted; that the fundamental factor in credit granting is the recipient of the credit and not the form in which credit is extended or the agency by which it is measured; and that credit terms lengthen and shorten in a wave-like movement in response to business conditions, varying with and parallel to the business cycle.

Another tack in the development of credit thought was taken by E. R. A. Seligman, professor of political economy, Columbia University, in his two-volume work *The Economics of Installment Selling.*[10] Writing to defend the science of economics against criticism that it was bankrupt because it did not attack instalment selling, he undertook to show the competence of the science of economics to deal with a fundamentally practical problem. He did that in part by setting forth a description of the nature and effects of instalment credit selling against its historical and statistical background. In addition, he presented in detail the findings of a series of studies relating consumers' and dealers' experiences in the use of instalment selling with regard to repossessions, merchandising practices, and depressions. The study was a pretentious undertaking, and the work gave a factual appraisal of instalment selling at a time when it was regarded as a disturbing phenomenon. Thought developed by Seligman was much built upon in subsequent writings.

While credit thought gained profundity through such works as that of Seligman, it gained little more than breadth of readership through some writings. James H. Picken's *Credits and Collections,*[11] one of a series of "Manuals of Business Management" written to help the beginner organize a collection department, illustrates the point. In it, thought that elsewhere had been expressed more profoundly was reduced to shibboleths, such as: "Credit should tend to liquidate itself"; "The merchant gives credit and gets nothing for it"; and "The right angle in collection is the sales angle." Such a turn of thought illustrates the dilution that occurred in most business literatures to accommodate a superficial audience of practitioners.

Another type of specialization that occurred during the 1920s focused attention on credit management in the distribution of industrial products.[12] Other specialization concentrated interest in retail credit operations. Among the men of that period who made contributions to that area of thought were Frederick W. Walter;[13] John T. Bartlett and Charles M. Reed;[14] and Norris A. Brisco.[15] All those men were intent upon improving credit management in the retail store. Their treatments of the subject were generally similar. That of Brisco served to indicate that the concept of retail credit was not so clear in that decade as was the idea of what mercantile credit encompassed. Brisco became diverted into a lengthy but irrelevant discussion of "standard money and subsidiary money" and of the minting of coins. He presented a standard organization chart for a retail credit department but did not explain the possibility of many satisfactory variations thereof. He gave a long history of Bradstreet's and Dun's services, despite an admission that little use of general mercantile agency information was used for "consumption" credit. He did, nevertheless, as was commonly done, distinguish three classes of credit: bank, mercantile, and retail. He conceived credit to be a representation of money, saying that when a person used credit he was spending his money—future money. He detailed the requisite mental qualities of credit managers for the effective discharge of their responsibilities to their businesses. He noted, further, that trading stamps were then given to credit customers who paid their bills promptly, as well as to cash customers. The entire "Retailing Series" edited by Brisco was dedicated to the use of research in retailing; his book on credit, however, did not represent very extensive research, even at that time.

Other developments in credit practice during that period also gave rise to new ventures in credit thought. They included the increase of credit granting in the expanding foreign trade,[16] the development of co-operative organizations in loan service,[17] the growing application of credit selling to durable goods,[18] and the professionalization of credit information management.[19]

INTEGRATION OF CREDIT THOUGHT IN THE 1920s

While credit thought during the 1920s was infused with details and specialization in management technique, it was, at the same time, also brought to a state of integration.

Theodore N. Beckman, one of Hagerty's students at The Ohio State University, dealt with the subject more broadly than his teacher had done and in 1924 published an analysis of credit not unlike that of Ettinger and Golieb, although incorporating evidence of the growing importance of retail credit.[20] Beckman was introduced to the field of credit through an assignment to teach the subject, and he began to write in the area because of an impression of the inadequacy of the literature on the subject. Never having had a course in credits and unimpressed with the available literature, he resorted to surveying the literature and supplementing his readings with firsthand observations in business, banks, and credit agencies. Conceptually, thought in his book was not unique; it was in accord with credit practice and was structured as other writers were presenting the subject at that time. It did bring the subject up to date, and throughout the development of credit thought, updating has constituted something of a contribution.

Because the term "principles" gained usage in marketing circles as a result of the integration of the subject in the early 1920s, Beckman referred in this book to the "principles" of credits and collections. In credit, however, as in marketing in general, principles had not been developed to the point where really significant and profound generalizations were being stated; consequently, so-called "principles" were often in the nature of descriptions of credit practices, institutions, and instruments. While few concepts and generalizations in Beckman's book were new, it was a comprehensive treatment of credit such as had not been achieved before.

Some of the same circumstances that induced Beckman to write also moved Ettinger and Golieb in 1926 to rethink their analysis of the subject in collaboration with H. W. Diamond. Changes in the credit picture required that consideration be given to the Federal Reserve Bank system; to use of the trade acceptance; to salesmen, attorneys, and banks as sources of credit information; to credit insurance and foreign credit; and to retail credit and collections. Notwithstanding additions made along these lines, Ettinger and Golieb continued to develop credit thought almost solely as it pertained to mercantile transactions.

When in 1929 A. F. Chapin published his book on credits and collections,[21] the integration of credit thought was well advanced, and one more book similar to those already published contributed little either to the content of thought or to the form in which it was presented. Ettinger and Golieb had first achieved the needed integration. Subsequent developments were added by Beckman. Chapin followed closely the outlines of the two earlier works. He made no conceptual contribution to credit thought, but his presentation of the subject nevertheless was influential in shaping the thinking of students of credit for years to come.

CREDIT THOUGHT — 1930 to 1950

Following the period in which the integration of "principles" was achieved, conceptual changes with regard to credit, its administration, or the teaching of it were few. The literature during the 1930s and the 1940s kept abreast of the times, and in successive revisions the "general" writings incorporated those changes in thought. At mid-century this field of marketing thought had attained "maturity."

Among the business and economic developments of that period to influence the evolution of credit thought were the following:

1. Problems of the depression, which emphasized functions of maintenance and collection of accounts receivable.[22]

2. Growth of the personal finance industry, which led to application of management and credit principles to that particular segment of market financing.[23]

3. Increased use of the retail charge account, which evoked renewed interest in the management of credit on the retail level.

Clyde W. Phelps made several contributions to the literature and thought in the third field. His first[24] was a discussion of what he regarded as the three fundamental functions of credit management: securing accounts, controlling accounts, and collection of accounts. A "practical treatise," it was designed to treat "those basic functions which every employee in the credit department should be expected to know."[25] He referred to credit as a "business force," and a "power" and, quoting a German economist of the old historical school, to the credit economy as a type following the natural or barter economy and the money economy in an order of economic development. Phelps saw credit also as a "balance against the antisocial policy of extreme sales and advertising pressure." That viewpoint regarded the credit manager as a restraining influence upon the seller and the buyer. Said Phelps: "He must develop a social consciousness and take into consideration the effects of his store's credit policy upon the lives of his customers as well as the effects on the store's balance sheet."[26]

In addition to that social view of the responsibilities of credit management, Phelps made a distinction between "potential credit" and "actual credit." He defined potential credit as the power to obtain present goods in exchange for a promise to render a future equivalent; actual credit he regarded to be a creditor-debtor relationship. He also classified credit as public, private, investment, banking, and consumer credit, and added a fourth "C," Conditions, which should be taken into consideration as influencing the three "C's" of Character, Capacity, and Capital.

Phelps also introduced the concept of temporary suspension of past-due accounts as a practice fair to both sellers and buyers. Suspension of past-due accounts until either payments were received, or agreements were obtained which would bring such accounts to terms, was set forth as "the heart of credit control" in the six principles of a controlled credit policy formulated by Phelps. While this concept of suspension did not gain immediate acceptance by retail credit granters generally, the principle of temporarily suspending credit privileges on past-due accounts was incorporated in wartime regulation in both Canada (beginning October 10, 1941) and the United States (Regulation W, as revised effective May 6, 1942). After World War II, this practice became more general on a voluntary basis.

A second book produced by Phelps,[27] was concerned with management level problems in retail credit operations. Emphasis was placed upon the scientific approach to problem solving, and principles of scientific management set forth by F. W. Taylor were quoted. Because Phelps regarded the personnel of the credit department as the basis of efficiency in credit operation, much attention was given to personnel selection, training, and organization. Credit department positions were distinguished, and job qualifications for each were set forth. However, regard for credit personnel as "non-selling" workers in retailing continued the concept of credit as an unproductive function, a concept that was later to yield to that of credit as a "sales supporting" function. According to the Preface of this second volume, Phelps envisioned publishing still another book, one dealing with the economic aspects and implications of credit. That has not yet been published.

In 1950 still another work on retail credit appeared, embodying new concepts and treatment of the subject. Integrating contributions of seventy-seven credit specialists, J. Gordon Dakins offered practical answers to credit problems of that day. Although many technical activities were viewed traditionally, a concept of five stages of the evolution of credit in the United States was advanced.[28]

1. Prior to 1912 — Credit extended to wealthy customers and those who were near to and known by the vendor.

2. 1912-1929 — Increased use of instalment credit.

3. 1930-1940 — Instalment credit extended to soft goods; repossession value considered of prime importance; rise of sales financing.

4. 1941-1947 — Period of Regulation W.

5. 1948 — Return to self-regulation; rise of revolving credit plans.

Dakins also gave extensive treatment to laws pertaining to credit as they related to contracts, legal capacity, husband's liability, liens, instalment contracts, collections, bad checks, false financial statements, and the like.

4. Economic fluctuations, which led to efforts to link the growing field of consumer credit to business cycles.[29] Throughout a number of writings prevailed a strong presumption that because consumer credit, particularly instalment credit, constituted a commitment of future income, economic imbalance was accentuated and accelerated by a large volume of outstanding consumer debt.

A quite different viewpoint was brought to bear upon the picture of consumer credit by Reavis Cox in *The Economics of Instalment Buying.*[30] Whereas most writers on consumer credit took the viewpoint of sellers, endeavoring to make credit selling more efficient and more effective, and economists looked from the standpoint of the economy as a whole, Cox concerned himself with broad aspects of credit's contribution to consumer satisfaction. He analyzed the instalment system as a device used by consumers for spending their income rather than as a device used by sellers for promotion. Instalment buying was held to be a means by which consumers accumulated investments. The credit system was regarded as the "supporting structure" of instalment buying. Cox's study was a pretentious and scholarly assembly of significant facts of instalment credit.

5. New developments in credit financing, which lead to a more detailed statement of the role played by different types of finance agencies. Saulnier and Jacoby were among those who wrote on this subject.[31] The most productive contributor to that field of thought was Clyde W. Phelps, whose writings spanned two decades. He dealt mainly with the functions of sales financing, accounts receivable financing, and factoring,[32] showing the histories of those methods of financing, their current practices, their advantages and disadvantages to users of their services, and costs and charges of their operations.

6. The rise of wartime credit problems which produced at least one work on that subject, by Roy A. Foulke.[33]

Throughout the 1940s there were also a number of miscellaneous additions to credit thought. Historical perspective was contributed by Foulke[34] and by Sprague.[35] The history of the development of credit had not been given much attention in other books on the subject, as Nystrom had incorporated the history of retailing into retailing management thought. Problems of instalment credit charges were also taken up by Milan V. Ayers in a study of instalment mathematics.[36]

Of the remaining notable additions to the credit literature one in particular may be singled out: *Credit Management Handbook.*[37] Sooner or later handbooks have been published in most areas of marketing thought. They are handy compendia of useful knowledge amassed concerning the subject. The *Credit Management Handbook,* however, includes not only digests of theories and descriptions of practices already written but also some new material. In a chapter entitled "The Basis for Dynamic Credit Management," psychological and philosophic considerations are discussed in their relation to credit management. In "Organization of the Credit Department" and "Manning the Credit Department," organizational structure and the descriptions and specifications for various credit management position levels are analyzed in greater detail than elsewhere in the literature. Both are based upon another publication prepared by the Credit Research Foundation in 1953 – *Analysis and Evaluation of Credit Management Functions.*[38] Valuable contributions have been made also in the sections dealing with training for credit management, the use of special financial techniques in credit analysis, the advisory capacity of the credit manager, credit department reports, and credit mathematics.

CONTINUING REVISION OF CREDIT THOUGHT

Trends in the expanding use of credit that found expression in many specialized credit writings shaped also the successive and frequent revisions of credit thought in more general writings. One function of contributors to marketing thought is to analyze, interpret, and record changing conditions and practices in the field. That has been the area in which credit writers have made their chief contributions. Another function is to develop new concepts and theory for business practice. In that activity credit writers have been somewhat less creative than have those in some other areas of marketing.

Prendergast made only one revision of the thought set forth in his 1906 publication. That was done in 1931 through a consolidation of his initial publication with that of W. H. Steiner published in 1922. It was, according to the authors, designed to incorporate developments in the field of credit, which, while they did not alter the basic principles of credit, did enrich and enlarge the understanding of credit principles and their varied applications.

Ettinger and Golieb twice updated and revised the thought originally set forth in 1917. Some changes in concepts occurred. For example, in the first publication stock certificates were classified as a form of credit instrument. In 1926 the statement was made that stock certificates are not "true credit instruments." In 1949 stock certificates were said to be not credit instruments but rather instruments of ownership. Developments in retail credit were incorporated into their treatment of the general subject. Retail collections, credit department operation, and instalment credit were three topics introduced as they loomed in management thought. Foreign credit was discussed only in 1926, credit limits only in 1949, and the Federal Reserve System in all but 1949.

Beckman made similar changes in his mold of general credit principles. In 1930 he included instalment credit, credit limits, mercantile agencies, and methods of controlling credits and collections. In 1938 the growing importance of consumer credit and the operations of finance companies reshaped the proportions of his writings. Changes made in the bankruptcy law in 1939 impelled further alterations of credit thought. In collaboration with Robert Bartels in 1949, he broadened the economic analysis of credit, reflecting somewhat the emphasis given this subject in wartime federal regulation of credit. In 1955 the authors attempted to alter the viewpoint from which credit thought was stated, emphasizing management of credit rather than merely the types of credit managed. Theodore N. Beckman also, in collaboration with Schuyler F. Otteson, prepared, in keeping with growing emphasis of managerial functions, a book entitled *Cases in Credits and Collections.*[39]

A late contributor to credit literature and thought was William J. Shultz, a professor at City College of New York. He was concerned primarily with mercantile credit, and the expression given his ideas[40] was one of the better guides to practical credit management in the literature of that period. He was unconcerned with credit as an economic or social institution, however, and his presentation is essentially descriptive. Shultz also, with H. Reinhart, published a book of problems in credit and collection management.[41]

CREDIT THOUGHT IN THE 1950s

During preceding decades, credit thought evolved mainly by introduction of changes brought about in credit practices; during the 1950s it was altered somewhat by the incorporation of new concepts adopted in marketing thought in general.

Notwithstanding such innovations, the core of credit thought continued to be based upon a concept of credit as a *business system.* Long regard for it as an operational activity consisting mainly of analysis of creditworthiness continued. So did strong emphasis upon mercantile credit. Even in 1960, Chapin and Hassett[42] devoted but one short chapter to "Retail, Consumer, and Instalment Credit."

For several decades, consumer credit had been playing an increasing role in credit thought. Its peculiarities had been pointed out, and the application of evaluation standards to consumer credit had been explained. In the 1950s revolving credit plans came to occupy a prominent place in most expositions of consumer credit, as did such newer credit forms as bank charge account plans and credit card services like the Diners' Club. The authors of one text[43] even extended credit thought to the point of including mortgage credit in their discussion of the subject.

Even with the introduction of new forms of credit, heavy emphasis, both in organization of thought and in the proportional space given it, continued to be given to the process of analyzing creditworthiness as one of the principle functions of credit management.

During this period, there was only slightly growing concern for the economic aspects of credit. The role of consumer credit in the economy had been a subject of interest in the depression years of the 1930s, and the administration of credit under Regulation W during the war years led to further economic appraisal of the use of such credit. The subject was dealt with in an exploratory fashion in many credit conferences during the decade. Relatively little of the macro-analysis of credit, however, appeared in the thought published in books during the period. Beckman and Bartels undertook to show behavior patterns[44] in the use of different forms of consumer credit and to point out the significant differences among consumer, business, and government with respect to their effects upon economic fluctuations. Because few data are available on the volume and behavior of all forms of business or mercantile credit, detailed evidence of the economic implications of that are generally meager. Cole also dealt briefly with economic aspects of credit, but in a general way and in terms of traditional economic theory. Not much progress was made during the decade in advancing the analysis of credit in the economy.

A new concept was introduced into credit, however, that did gain some acceptance and that gave promise of fresh views of credit management, namely, the idea that credit is a social institution. In this sense, it is more than a technique, more than an economic function; it is conceived as a phenomenon peculiar to our society with its particular set of values, attitudes, capacities, and other institutions. This approach explains credit as emerging from the social environment. It is the beginning of a market analysis approach to the study of credit, and as such it is consistent with the consumer-oriented concept of marketing in general that has gained acceptance in recent years.

The most fully developed presentation of the social orientation of credit has been presented by M. R. Neifeld.[45] He explained the role which credit now plays in our society in terms of the contemporary family unit, the church and its attitude toward usury, the law, the use of the automobile, and the institution of insurance. He related credit to the national income, to savings and investment, and to the social controls imposed upon it by federal and state governments. He interpreted findings of psychologists, as well as sociologists' concepts of standards of living, in his explanation of consumers' use of credit. Neifeld has also introduced a historical dimension into some of his explanations of various types of credit institutions. While his book is quite specialized, it is a valuable addition to credit thought.

Another incipient development in credit thought is evident in a growing interest expressed in the comparative costs of operating various types of credit service organizations and in the comparative rates charged for their respective services. This subject, however, is yet dealt with almost wholly in a descriptive fashion, without quantitative support because of the absence of comparable accounting data among credit institutions and because of a wide diversity of rates and forms of charges employed in the credit industry. It seems inevitable that thought should develop more in coming years along these lines.

Finally, into the concept of credit management has been introduced the distinction of several management levels. Whereas in the past the credit operation has been dealt with as an operational or supervisory function, in recent years it has been conceived as line, staff, and functional operations and as including top management level of policy making, intermediate administrative control, and routine operational activities. Such additions to credit thought are found in two publications of the National Association of Credit Management: *Analysis and Evaluation of Credit Management Functions* and *Credit Management Handbook.*

CREDIT THOUGHT SINCE 1960

Throughout its history, the development of credit thought has been influenced more by external developments than by conceptual innovations. During the decade of the 1960s, this continued to be the case, although some new concepts from the broadening concept and analysis of marketing were introduced into credit literature.

Among the new books published after 1960, several topics of contemporary interest were discussed. Attention to consumer credit increased appreciably as consumers' use of credit increased in the economy, but this took several forms. Credit cards, revolving credit, and credit insurance were included in titles of books. From the management side, score rating and computerization in operations were discussed, as, from the standpoint of institutional development, were credit unions and the services of the credit information reporting industry.

Of the longstanding, widely accepted, general works on credit, the 1969 eighth edition of *Credits and Collections*[46] by Beckman and Foster reflected incorporation of external influences without change in the conceptual structure of thought which the book represented. It continued to be a work dedicated to mercantile credit management, relatively little space yet devoted to consumer credit. Passing attention was given to residential mortgage credit, the concept of return on asset investment, electronic data processing in credit management, and to the "checkless" society. The book nevertheless continued to be the one-man tour de force which most general credit books have been, based minimally upon research, employing few footnotes, seldom referring to other authorities in the field, and providing no study references for the reader.

Two contrasts in the development of credit thought were offered in *Credit Management*[47] by Robert Bartels in 1967 and in *Consumer and Commercial Credit Management*[48] by Robert H. Cole, the fourth edition in 1972.

Bartels introduced into credit thought a concept of environmentalism which had been evolving in marketing theory. The institution of credit not only in the economy but rather in society was shown to be the effect or outcome of broad environmental factors of which makers of both public and management policy must be aware. Users of credit were identified as "markets" for credit service — segmented markets requiring an assortment of differentiated services. The credit service industry was analyzed as specialists in the performance of functions essential to credit service — specialists which were linked together as systems through which credit functions were channeled in the quest for economy, efficiency, and competitive advantage. Internal credit department management was held to occur within a broader framework, in which credit *management* is done not only by credit "managers" but also internally by others of management rank, and externally by a variety of functional credit specialists. Control of credit, therefore, must be viewed as a measurement of achievement in the firm providing credit service, in the market system, and in society in general. Because this book at its publication was conceptually innovative, it too is generally without references, for the innovations were without precedent in credit thought and the descriptive or common knowledge was without proprietary claim.

Cole, in his 1972 edition, impartially treating consumer and commercial credit management, incorporated influences of the Age of Consumerism and described the management function within the extant legal framework relating to credit. Thus the environment which he visualized was particularly the legislative, which reflects the social environment. Whereas Bartels treated the management functions of both consumer and business credit establishments as generic, and Beckman dealt with some as common and some as particular, Cole, taking the risk of some duplication, developed completely the management process for each field of credit business. Of special value in this work was the documentation of source material and the provision of references for further reading, which, nevertheless, reflecting the state of the credit literature, predominantly consisted of trade publication articles and monographs. An Appendix of Federal credit legislation was included.

Mention should also be made of the 1965 publication of the second edition of the *Credit Management Handbook* by the Credit Research Foundation of the National Association of Credit Management. Prepared by 123 contributors and editors, this compendium provided exhaustive coverage of every topic of interest to mercantile credit managers. In traditional fashion, it was concerned with the nuts and bolts elements of the internal operation, beginning with credit department organization and proceeding through credit analysis, department systems, financial instruments and miscellaneous credit services.

Normative standards for judging credit management have almost always related to the profitability of the performance, and little has been said in appraisal of its social and economic impact. Seligman explored the economics of instalment selling in 1926; several authors have spoken of the social benefits deriving from the general use of credit; and some have reported criticisms voiced in legislative hearings and other public forums. The negative aspects of credit, however, have generally been treated as faults of unscrupulous vendors and creditors individually and seldom attributed to the credit system as a whole. Thus it would seem that credit thought had advanced to a stage where efficient practice of it is accepted almost unquestionably as good for society in general. This is probably true, when all forms of credit including both public and private are considered, but another side of the macro-picture gained attention.

Griffin in *The Credit Jungle*[49] depicted credit management and the entire institution of credit from the viewpoint of a critic who sees a gullible public being oversold. Elimination of the abuses which he chronicled, however, would require recasting some accepted credit thought, or rather incorporating in it some missing social concepts. The book is of the "exposé" type which has appeared also in other periods of consumer emphasis, relating more often to advertising, selling, and general marketing policy. Written in journalistic style, reporting many brief, newsy case histories, the work is critical and provocative although not original in structure or conception. It presents the history of such popular forms of credit as credit cards, bank credit, and auto financing; it discusses the broadening uses and users of credit, as in land sales and among teenagers and the "poor"; and it expresses interest in practices of credit bureaus, collectors, and money lenders. Its contribution to credit thought lies in showing the need for broadening the concept of credit to include more of its social, as well as its economic and mangerial, aspects. The book dispells any illusion that "the last word" has been written about credit.

CONTRIBUTIONS OF CREDIT LITERATURE TO MARKETING THOUGHT

In the credit literature may be found a number of contributions to the body of marketing thought:

1. Several *concepts* of credit itself:

An Ability — "Potential credit," a power possessed by individuals with certain qualifications to obtain goods or services now in exchange for a promise to pay later.

A legal claim — debt, representative of the creditor's interest and viewpoint in a credit transaction.

Commercialized confidence — trustworthiness, faith as the basis of the credit promise.

A finance function inherent in marketing. — Success in marketing undertakings is partially dependent upon management of financial factors. The fact that credit literature, particularly general marketing literature, suggests that the concept of marketing management was an integrated view of more specialized forms of management.

A marketable service — Attention has been concentrated on goods and services bought *on credit,* to obscuration of the fact that *credit service itself* is a part of the value received. Failure to appreciate that has resulted from the fact that credit selling has been used mainly as a tool in the sale of merchandise, no charge being made for the "credit" — more specifically, the credit service — and no accounting of costs being kept in the performance of the credit operation. Circumstances of the past may not have demanded the making of this distinction, but clarification of it in the future may be more necessary.

2. A concept of *credit elasticity of demand.* It has been both hypothetically assumed and empirically verified that the availability of credit service affects the amount and intensity of demand for products sold on credit. Knowledge of this is of importance to vendors, but it had been important also to economists, who have sought to understand the relation of credit, credit terms, sales, and economic stability. Some of these relationships have been explored in the credit writings.

3. Illustration of the manner in which *literature follows* developments in practice. It would appear in retrospect that credit writers have not been particularly original or creative in their writings. Rather, one gets an impression that, in general, they have narrated and refined practices already existing in business. Though this be true, they have nevertheless made contributions to thought by conceptualizing practice, by perceiving relationships and principles, by interpreting currents in practice in terms of historical and prevailing circumstances.

4. Development of a body of *technique for management.* As in the study of retailing, a valuable and essential part of accumulated knowledge is that of operational procedures.

5. A concept of credit as an *institution.* Banking is generally regarded as one of our economic institutions. Credit, particularly when viewed from the standpoint of mercantile credit, is seldom thought of as an institution but simply as a business or management practice. On the other hand, consumer credit, perhaps because of its presumed influence upon social and economic behavior, has increasingly been regarded as an institution of our particular culture.

6. A concept of credit as a *calculated business risk.* Although it has sometimes been held that minimization of bad debt loss is the principal objective in credit management, increasingly emphasis is placed upon its use as a means toward achieving increased sales and profits. Distinction is made between mere risk and calculated risk involved in credit.

7. A concept of credit as *business force.* Advertising is almost universally recognized to be a type of business force, one of the dynamic, causative factors to be managed and controlled in a business undertaking. A long-standing passive regard for credit as "unproductive" is yielding to the conception of it, too, as a positive and contributing factor in business success. It is one of the interchangeable factors mixed and blended by management.

8. A *variety of concepts* that have entered into marketing thought to explain the phenomenon of credit:

Anticipation
Cash discount
Collection
Consumer credit
Credit information
Credit instrument
Credit institution
Credit agency
Credit insurance
Credit limit
Credit man
Credit manager
Credit risk
Credit spending
Credit systems
"C's" of credit
Cycle billing

Delinquency
Dun
Factoring
Instalment credit
Levels of credit management
Mercantile agencies
Mercantile credit
Open account credit
Personal financing
Rate of collectibility
Revolving credit
Sale credit
Sales financing
Self-liquidation credit
Time-sale price

ENDNOTES

[1] Such a course was offered by James E. Hagerty at The Ohio State University beginning in 1906.

[2] William A. Prendergast, *Credit and Its Uses* (New York: D. Appleton–Century Co., Inc., 1906).

[3] James E. Hagerty, *Mercantile Credit* (New York: Henry Holt & Co., 1913).

[4] M. M. Kallam et. al., *Mercantile Credits* (New York: Ronald Press Co., 1914).

[5] *Credits, Collections, and Finance* (New York: A. W. Shaw Co., 1914).

[6] B. H. Blanton, *Credits: Its Principles and Practices* (New York: Ronald Press Co., 1915).

[7] E. M. Skinner, R. S. White, and H. E. Kramer, *Credits and Collections* (Chicago: LaSalle Extension University, 1916).

[8] R. T. Ettinger and D. E. Golieb, *Credits and Collections* (New York: Prentice-Hall, Inc., 1917; 2d ed., 1926, 1937; 3d ed., 1949; 4th ed., 1956; 5th ed., 1962).

[9] W. H. Steiner, *The Mechanism of Commercial Credit* (New York: D. Appleton–Century Co., Inc. 1922).

[10] E. R. A. Seligman, *The Economics of Installment Selling* (New York: Harper & Bros., 1926).

[11] James H. Picken, *Credits and Collections* (New York: A. W. Shaw Co., 1929).

[12] Robert Young, *Industrial Credits* (New York: Harper & Bros., 1927).

[13] Frederick W. Walter, *The Retail Charge Account* (New York: Ronald Press Co., 1922).

[14] John T. Bartlett and Charles M. Reed, *Retail Credit Practice* (New York: Harper & Bros., 1928).

[15] Norris A. Brisco, *Retail Credit Procedure* (New York: Prentice-Hall, Inc., 1929).

[16] G. W. Edwards, *Foreign Commercial Credits* (New York: McGraw-Hill Book Co., Inc., 1922).

[17] E. L. Whitney, *Cooperative Credit Societies* (Washington, D.C.: U. S. Government Printing Office, 1922).

[18] B. W. Griffin, *Instalment Sales and Collections* (New York: Prentice-Hall, Inc., 1923).

[19] T. R. Truesdale, *Credit Bureau Management* (New York: Prentice-Hall, Inc. 1927).

[20] Theodore N. Beckman, *Credits and Collections in Theory and Practice* (New York: McGraw-Hill Book Co., Inc., 1924; 2d ed., 1930; 3d ed., 1938; 4th ed., 1939; 5th ed., 1949, with Robert Bartels; 6th ed., 1955; 7th ed. by Beckman, 1962; 8th ed. with R. S. Foster, 1969).

[21] A. F. Chapin, *Credits and Collection Principles and Practices* (New York: McGraw-Hill Book Co., Inc. 1929; 2d ed., 1935; 3d ed., 1940; 4th ed., 1941; 5th ed., 1947; 6th ed., 1953; 7th ed., 1960, with George E. Hassett).

68

[22] Morris Marks, *How To Correct Credit Abuses* (New York: Harper & Bros., 1930); Ed M. Gardner, *Effective Collection Methods* (New York: Ronald Press Co., 1932); Samuel W. Guggenheim, *How To Collect Instalment Accounts,* (Rochester, N. Y.: Credit Press, 1933).

[23] M. R. Neifeld, *The Personal Finance Business* (New York: Harper & Bros., 1933), and *Personal Finance Comes of Age* (New York: Harper & Bros., 1939).

[24] Clyde W. Phelps, *Retail Credit Fundamentals* (St. Louis: National Retail Credit Association, 1938; 2d ed., 1947; 3d ed., 1952; 4th ed., 1963)

[25] *Ibid.,* p. ix.

[26] *Ibid.,* p. 4.

[27] Clyde W. Phelps, *Retail Credit Management* (St. Louis: National Retail Credit Association, 1949).

[28] J. Gordon Dakins, *Retail Credit Manual* (New York: National Retail Credit Association, 1950), pp. 31-38.

[29] W. L. White and Dudley Gates, *Economic Effects of Instalment Credit* (New York: American Management Association, 1938); W. T. Foster, *Public Supervision of Consumer Credit* (Newton, Mass.: Pollack Foundation, 1939); Rolf Nugent, *Consumer Credit and Economic Stability* (New York: Russell Sage Foundation, 1939); Blanche Bernstein, *The Pattern of Consumer Debt* (New York: National Bureau of Economic Research, 1940); D. McC. Holthausen, M. L. Merriam, and Rolf Nugent, *The Volume of Consumer Instalment Credit* (New York: National Bureau of Economic Research, 1940).

[30] Reavis Cox, *The Economics of Instalment Buying* (New York: Ronald Press Co., 1948).

[31] R. J. Saulnier and Neil H. Jacoby, *Accounts Receivable Financing* (New York: National Bureau of Economic Research, 1943).

[32] Clyde W. Phelps, *The Role of the Sales Finance Companies in the American Economy* (Baltimore: Commercial Credit Co., 1952); *Instalment Sales Financing: Its Service to the Dealer* (Baltimore: Commercial Credit Co., 1953); *Financing the Instalment Purchases of the American Family* (Baltimore: Commercial Credit Co., 1954); *The Role of Factoring in Modern Business Fianance* (Baltimore: Commercial Credit Co., 1956); *Accounts Receeivable Financing as a Method of Business Finance* (Baltimore: Commercial Credit Co., 1957); and *Commercial Credit Insurance as a Management Tool* (Baltimore: Commercial Credit Co., 1961).

Also written by Phelps were a number of smaller booklets entitled: *More Profits from Charge Business: Bookkeeping for Credit Control: Accounts Receivable System for Small Stores; A Community Credit Policy; How To Understand Age Analysis of Charge Accounts; Making Prompt Paying Customers Out of Slow Accounts; Ten Hidden Losses in Slow Charge Accounts; Using Instalment Credit;* and *Important Steps in Retail Credit Operation.*

[33] Roy A. Foulke, *Credit Problems in a War Economy* (New York: Dun & Bradstreet, Inc., 1942).

[34] Roy A. Foulke, *The Sinews of American Commerce* (New York: Dun & Bradstreet, Inc., 1941).

[35] J. R. Sprague, *The Romance of Credit* (New York: D. Appleton–Century Co., Inc., 1943).

[36] Milan V. Ayres, *Instalment Mathematics Handbook* (New York: Ronald Press Co., 1946).

[37] *Credit Management Handbook* (Homewood, Ill.: Richard D. Irwin, Inc. 1958).

[38] *Analysis and Evaluation of Credit Management Functions* (New York: Credit Research Foundation, 1953).

[39] Theodore N. Beckman and Schuyler F. Otteson, *Cases in Credits and Collections* (New York: McGraw-Hill Book Co., Inc., 1949).

[40] William J. Shultz *Credit and Collection Management* (New York: Prentice-Hall, Inc., 1947; 2d ed., 1954, with H. Reinhart; 3d ed., 1962).

[41] William J. Shultz and H. Reinhardt, *Problems in Credits and Collections* (New York: Prentice-Hall, Inc., 1950).

[42] Albert F. Chapin and George E. Hassett, Jr., *Credit and Collection Principles and Practice* (New York: McGraw-Hill Book Co., Inc., 7th ed., 1960).

[43] Robert H. Cole and Robert S. Hancock, *Consumer and Commercial Credit Management* (Homewood, Ill,: Richard D. Irwin, Inc., 1960; 2d ed., 1964; 3d ed., 1965; 4th ed., by Cole, 1972; 5th ed., 1976).

[44] Theodore N. Beckman and Robert Bartels, *Credits and Collections in Theory and Practice* (New York: McGraw-Hill Book Co., Inc., 6th ed., 1955), chap. 3.

[45]M. R. Neifeld, *Neifeld's Manual on Consumer Credit* (Easton, Pa.: Mack Publishing Co., 1961).

[46]Theodore N. Beckman and Ronald S. Foster, *Credits and Collections: Management and Theory* (New York: McGraw-Hill Book Co., Inc. 1969).

[47]Robert Bartels, *Credit Management* (New York: Ronald Press Co., 1967).

[48]Robert H. Cole, *Consumer and Commercial Credit Management* (Homewood, Ill.: Richard D. Irwin, Inc., 4th ed., 1972).

[49]Al Griffin, *The Credit Jungle,* (Chicago: H. Regnery Co., 1971).

SALESMANSHIP AND SALES MANAGEMENT 6

From the beginning until the middle of this century, more than one hundred authors contributed to the development of marketing thought through writings on salesmanship and sales management. Their contribution was both to increase technical marketing efficiency and to broaden the concept of functional management in distribution.

ENVIRONMENT OF THE SALES LITERATURE

It has already been seen that development of marketing thought was prompted by circumstances of the times. One environmental influence upon development of sales thought was the tremendous growth of production facilities. Manufacturers grew in number and in size, and mergers further increased their capacity. The introduction of new products accentuated the need for improved selling. Whereas staples had moved smoothly through traditional channels, new specialty products needed more selling, more explanation. Demand had to be created for new products and for products of different kinds. Competitive representation increased.

Conventional sales practices were changed also by new circumstances among buyers. Buyers as well as sellers, grew larger, and consumer purchasing power expanded. Opportunities for selling and the rewards for effective selling were unprecedented. Salesmen became heroes of the business world. Salesmen, however, were not the sole cause of increasing business; they were supported by improved distribution, advertising, and planning. All those activities increasingly needed to be co-ordinated.

Into sales activity early in this century was introduced still another factor, which had far-reaching effects upon the development of sales thought, namely, the principles of scientific management, as presented by Frederick W. Taylor. The effects of Taylorism, however, were delayed by a persistent early regard for selling as an art, and therefore not subject to scientific analysis or application. Moreover, the manner in which many "sales" of that period were consummated invited no scientific analysis, for they were behind-the-scenes business deals.

Prior to 1930 strong confidence in prosperity prevaded the atmosphere in which sales thought was taking form. Not only was the country prosperous economically, but, according to the accepted Protestant Ethic, whoever worked hard and applied himself could be successful. That conviction promised great rewards for the agressive salesman and the well-managed sales organization.

The period of the 1930s, however, with economic reversals and consumer resistences, put to severe tests many easy sales philosophies. Fortunately, by then the scientific aspects of selling had been developed to the point where substantial contributions were made through sales literature to the body of marketing thought.

SELLING AND SALESMANSHIP

Thought on selling and salesmanship tended to develop along contrasting lines. One represented selling as a highly subjective activity; the other, as objective and subject to learning and teaching. One presented it as a solo performance; the other, as an integral part of a broader business activity. One depicted it as a popular pursuit; the other, as a field of economic, social, and philosophical consideration.

SUBJECTIVE SELLING

Regard for salesmanship as based upon highly subjective qualifications appeared early in works on the subject. William Maxwell expressed this concept as early as 1913 in a book entitled *Salesmanship.*[1] To him, selling was directed by rules-of-thumb, and he thought that it did not lend itself to analysis and interpretation. He believed that a salesman could not tell how he sold or what made him a success in the work. Maxwell did, nevertheless, recognize that in the process of selling there was a meeting of the minds, and he associated this with a procedural pattern involving attention, interest, belief, and resolution to do the thing asked. Such concepts at that time had been introduced into business thinking, particularly through advertising theory, by business psychologists.

Further evidence of the subjective nature of selling was shown in Maxwell's explanation of how the salesman undertook appraisal of his customer. This began, he claimed, with the salesman's analyzing himself. From that image he subtracted those of his characteristics that were not shared by a majority of his acquaintances and added to what was left the traits of other men. Thus viewing the customer in his mind's eye, the salesman was supposed to see "an average man." That not many salesmen were adept at doing this is indicated by Maxwell's objection to the prevalent unimaginative, stereotyped manner of selling. He gave expression to this opinion in a series of articles published in *Collier's Weekly,* which later formed the content of his book.

PREPARATION FOR SELLING

Despite the evidently widely held notion that selling was essentially subjective, which prevailed in some quarters before 1920, the necessity for better selling mothered a growing contrary conviction that salesmanship could be taught. Harold Whitehead was of that opinion and expressed the idea that, unless men could be taught to sell effectively, business firms would be unable to dispose of their mounting products.[2] He granted that some men may have an inborn aptitude for selling, but he was confident that through instruction the practice of selling could be taught.

His approach to presenting such instruction revealed his concept that selling pertained mainly to the individual or the salesman. The salesman's responsibility for improvement involved preparation to meet the customer, contact with the customer, sales follow-up and continuing education, and cultivation of his own character. Successful selling, he thought, depended principally upon this last point, thus showing a respect for genuine character in salesmen in contrast to the pseudo-, supersalesmanship that some theories espoused. Whitehead presented dialogues to illustrate selling at wholesale, specialty selling, and retail selling.

Variations of the idea that selling consisted of the mastery of an aggressive viewpoint and simple techniques are to be found throughout the literature on the subject. One proponent of this idea was Paul W. Ivey, who at least sold himself successfully to more than 100,000 people in lectures on selling known as "The Paul Ivey Salesmanship Institute." He continued to emphasize the selling personality,[3] hammering at the point that salesmanship is the persuading of the customer "to accept your viewpoint in the sale and purchase of goods." His thesis that "everyone is a salesman" was far removed from the notion held a decade earlier that salesmanship was the indefinable qualification of a few.

Even late in the 1930s loud-sounding explanations of simple selling techniques continued to appear. Such was one turned out by H. Simmons,[4] in which he sought to remove the subject of selling from the realm of theoretical discussion and to plant it on the most practical kind of working information and knowledge: that gained from actual selling experience and from the school of hard knocks. He presented more than seven hundred specific "brass tacks ideas, suggestions, talking points, and selling points" intended to stimulate mental activity and imagination. He called them "thinking points."

SELLING, A PART OF MARKETING

A broader view of selling related it to the larger subject of marketing. Both personal salesmanship and advertising were held to be parts of the over-all marketing plan. In that context was salesmanship discussed by John G. Jones and Raymond J. Comyns.[5] They took issue with the concept of selling as the imposition of the salesman's viewpoint upon the customer. They held that the prospect was not a victim of the transaction and should not be sold something he could not use. To them the sale was not merely a cold, scientific process but a warm, man-to-man affair. The best way to improve salesmanship, they believed, was to improve the salesman.

Jones and Comyns dealt also with the salesman as an employee, treating him as a unit of the selling organization. His valuable individual talent had to be integrated with the institutional performance of the distributive process. His co-operation with the house, the credit man, the sales manager, and the advertising manager was very important, not to speak of his co-operation with customers and the general public. Touching upon the relations of the salesman with the sales manager, the authors were concerned with such subjects as the demand and supply of salesmen, remuneration of salesmen, opportunities in salesmanship, and the universality of selling.

SALESMANSHIP – SCIENCE OR ART

Developing and unresolved in sales literature were the arguable parallel propositions that selling was a science and that it was an art. In the year 1919 Archer Wall Douglas dealt specifically with this issue, stating:

The science, as distinguished from the art of salesmanship, consists rather in the systematized direction and careful handling of the many details of the salesman's work. It is quite as necessary to successful salesmanship as the more intellectual and psychological methods of artistic persuasion. It is only within the last generation that there has come, even in the commercial world, a widespread realization of the true nature and importance of salesmanship.[6]

From long contact with traveling salesmen, Douglas spoke from experience of some phases of selling that relate the salesman to the distributive policy of his house. Among the facets of selling, he saw the meeting of arguments relating to changing channels of distribution, the importance of selling largely the profitable goods, the handling of claims and credits, and the establishment of agencies for certain lines of goods.

INSIDE SALESMEN

Whereas until 1920 most attention given to salesmanship related to outside selling, some thoughts concerning selling within retail establishments then began to appear. Norris A. Brisco was one of the first to develop the common ground that lay between "retailing" and "selling."[7] In three books, which were to be used together in schools and stores where courses in retail salesmanship were given, he presented principles of retail salesmanship, illustrations or readings relevant to selling, and a manual on the teaching of salesmanship.

A unique feature of Brisco's concept of the function of selling was the historical perspective in which he held it. He attributed the long neglect of distribution and improvements in selling to the ill repute in which the retailer or peddler had for centuries been held. He pointed to the Persians, who regarded all trade as dishonest, and to the Greeks, for whom the word for retail "trader" meant the same as "falsifier." Cicero stated that no one could be a successful merchant without lying. Brisco held that those qualities were no necessary part of retail salesmanship.

Further historical narration also pertained to the rise of commercial travelers in the United States. He said that the traveling employees whom wholesalers sent out to gather credit information and to collect bills due from retailers did not at first sell. Only gradually did they begin to book orders for future delivery, and in that way the modern traveling salesman came into being. The origin of a class of retail salespeople he attributed to the growth of specialty and department stores, wherein help was needed to care for stock and attend the needs of customers.

Brisco reflected also upon the changing viewpoint that had evolved concerning the relationship between salesmen and their customers. John Wanamaker in 1876 established a policy that his salesmen were not to importune customers to buy, thus rejecting the haggling and pressure selling that had long characterized retailing. This was one evidence of the "new retailing." Formerly, salesmanship was measured by one's ability to sell goods to people who did not need them; salesmanship then became identified with the ability to sell goods at a profit to the mutual benefit of buyers and sellers. Order fillers also were replaced by customer-interested salespeople. The day of systematic training in retail selling was at hand!

INTEGRATION OF SALES THOUGHT

Most of the varied aspects of selling and salesmanship that had developed up to 1924 were integrated by Frederic A. Russell in his *Textbook of Salesmanship.*[8] Throughout its successive revisions, the book combined the concept of different types of selling requiring different types of salesmen, buying motives considered in the light of new psychological findings, and growing emphasis on retail selling.

In view of the fact that Brisco had already given one explanation of the origin of traveling salesmen, it is interesting that Russell should have given another and different one. According to him, the origin of traveling salesmen lay in the practice by wholesalers of going to the local railway station to meet incoming merchant customers. Like summer resort "greeters" or "drummers," wholesalers sometimes encountered their competitors at the station for the same purpose. To avoid this situation, some wholesalers conceived the notion of meeting incoming trains at a station a few miles outside the city. Thus they could secure a firm hold on prospective buyers before rival drummers spied them. Competition ultimately drove sellers to greater distances until finally they called upon buyers rather than awaiting the buyers' visit.

Another integrative view of selling was set forth by E. E. Ferris and G. R. Collins,[9] who regarded the study of salesmanship as "an integral part of any thoroughgoing preparation for a business career, a complement to the student's work in production, management, finance, and accounting."[10] Accordingly, in their concept of selling they included the salesman's interest in pricing problems, advertising, wholesale selling to dealers and to consumers, house-to-house selling, and retail store selling. The customer of the wholesaler, although called "the user or ultimate consumer," was actually the industrial consumer. There apparently was at that time no conceptual distinction between household and business consumers, so far as these writers were concerned.

As sales thought became more integrated and inclusive, it also assumed characteristics of a more mature academic presentation. Experience alone was not the sole, or even the principal, source of ideas for the writers. Among the authorities on the subject quoted by Frederic Russell were E. St. Elmo Lewis, J. S. Knox, Paul W. Ivey, William Maxwell, Herbert N. Casson, W. W. Charters, Irving Bush, and others. He even cited Daniel Defoe's *The Complete English Tradesman,* published in 1726, on the thesis that a salesman must know his merchandise. At the same time, Ferris and Collins employed a number of technical features that helped to make their work a mature and advanced publication: divisions and subdivisions of the contents, and appendix containing three illustrative sales presentations and a list of supplementary readings from books and magazine articles; illustrations in the text; documented quotations; problems at the end of each chapter; italicized definitions; chapter subtitles, tabulations, outlines, and indentations made for emphasis; and illustrations of principles cited.

Still other elements of selling were brought into the integration by Harry R. Tosdal,[11] who in 1925 undertook to present the subject from the viewpoint of economics and its allied social sciences, to reconcile sound economics with practical business procedures. In addition to the usual topics, he dealt with ethics of personal selling and presented a history of personal selling, an analysis of market data, and a study of gross margin, expense, profit, and stock turnover ratios of various types of business.

Further effort to integrate selling with the allied social sciences was made by H. K. Nixon,[12] who attempted to combine the following:

The inspirational—formulas for quick success.
The psychological—motives and mental states of customers and salesmen.
The economic—selling as a part of the great business of making and
    distributing goods.
The personal—narratives of exceptional sales.
The sociological—social consequences of good and of inefficient selling.

Nixon tried to avoid the simple generalization sometimes called "principles," of which the average book contained many, and he adopted the concept of a principle as a guiding rule of sales conduct so universal as to be applicable to some degree in all selling. Such principles, he believed, had changed the concept of selling from exploitation to the art of helping people to buy.

SCIENTIFIC SELLING

As another stage through which sales thought evolved, the contributions of B. R. Canfield[13] along the lines of scientific selling might be cited. He epitomized the objective, research approach to selling. Mere sales experience was insufficient for basing theories about how salesmen do and should act. Instead, Canfield resorted to a variety of newer methods of studying the salesman's function. He used concealed microphones, he had investigators pose as buyers, he recorded salesmen's traveling time, and he measured their foot travel with pedometers. This was the antipode of early approaches to the development and statement of sales thought.

DEVELOPMENTS IN SALES THOUGHT — 1950 to 1960

Trends during the 1950s that wrought changes in marketing thought in general influenced thinking regarding selling in particular, and they were manifested in new concepts of salesmanship and sales management. One of the developments was a growing regard for the "problem-solving" requirements of salesmen. A far cry from the days when selling was thought to be merely self-expression, the memorization of canned presentations, or the mastery of simple product-market knowledge, this was recognition that salesmen have to think on their feet, make decisions, and work in the interests of each customer. This concept, which reflected increased emphasis on problem solving in marketing management, was presented by several writers. Wayland A. Tonning introduced it in the revision of Paul W. Ivey and Walter Horvath's *Successful Salesmanship*,[14] and S. J. Shaw and J. W. Thompson used it in their *Salesmanship*.[15] The latter termed this development a transition from "functional fixedness" to "situation management" for salesmen.

The concept of problem solving, however, depended upon another, which was equally new, namely, "consumer orientation" rather than "company orientation" of salesmen. Formerly it was expected that salesmen be familiar with customers' buying motives; now it was assumed that they have some acquaintance with the idea implicit in the "marketing concept." This was the idea that selling and all business functions logically begin with an understanding of the market and interprets this understanding into all activities of the business.

Preparation of salesmen with this new viewpoint or orientation required that they be made more familiar with contempory concepts of human behavior. Therefore findings drawn from psychology, sociology, anthropology, and other social sciences were increasingly introduced into the sales literature. Theories of "motivation" and "communication" supplanted concepts of "buying motives" and "sales appeals." Salesmen also were regarded as "channels" for the "feedback" of information to the sales organization, as well as carriers of the sales message.

Throughout the history of literature on selling, more attention has been devoted to non-retail than to retail selling. After World War II, non-retail selling was increasingly regarded specifically as "industrial selling," and it was singled out for particular attention on the ground of its growing complexity, the keener competition found in the industrial market, and the diversity of services that came to be associated with that type of selling.

Selling was also appraised in a broader dimension in relation to the whole promotional strategy of companies, rather than as merely the process of personal selling. Such was the viewpoint taken by Taylor W. Meloan and John M. Rathmell,[16] who, as editors of a book of readings on the subject, undertook to explain the composition of the sales mix. They brought into sales thought better than did others of that period the fact that the blending of different elements in the sales strategy — and therefore in selling — depends upon the circumstances of the market. Selling was also thereby linked to another concept that gained circulation in the 1950s, namely, "market segmentation," for it was understood that there are many markets, or segments of "the" market, to which selling strategy must be adapted.

A still broader dimension of sales thought was the appraisal of this function, not in terms of company strategy, but in terms of social significance. That analysis of selling is seldom found in the specialized sales literature, but more often — and then only in modest degree — in works on general marketing. Harry R. Tosdal undertook such an appraisal and in 1957 published *Selling in Our Economy*.[17] He saw selling not only as a business activity but as the means by which the standard of living in the United States had been achieved and maintained. Whereas Cherington had once written of advertising as a business force, Tosdal wrote of selling as a social force. Selling, he held, furnished "leadership-to-buying-action." The need for such leadership grew out of social conditions — out of our mass production and distribution facilities, the social habits of our people, and the irrationality as well as the rationality of their buying habits. He did not overlook the untruths and abuses found in selling, but he held that such excesses are found in any form of leadership and that the history of the past century shows that in selling they have been diminishing. He recognized that selling might be replaced by such leadership alternatives as initiative taken by consumers in seeking out what they need, or governmental planning or "production for use" programs, but he discarded them as unlikely to produce social or economic improvements over what we now have.

SALES THOUGHT SINCE 1960

During the 1960s, as during previous decades, expositions of selling ranged from "how to do it" literature to objective and scholarly treatises on the rendering of service by salesmen to customers and society. Some writers saw no difference in selling in the 1960s from that of earlier periods. Selling was selling! Others, perceptive of change, cast the selling process and the work of salesmen in a new light. Those changes were seen in both the external sales environment and ways in which selling was viewed.

The environmental changes identified in the literature consisted to a large extent of changes in the buying process. In industrial purchasing, more authority was being delegated to purchasing agents, while the complexity of equipment purchased placed new demands for knowledge and information upon salesmen. Household consumers, too, demanded more product information. This was one phase of Consumerism. Moreover, the buying process became more hedged about by laws and ethical codes outlining perimeters of the negotiatory process.

And the widening of the international market provided increased sales opportunities and increased sales competition. Such environmental changes changed selling, but apart from being mentioned in the literature they had relatively little effect upon what was written about selling.

More manifest influence was in the form of conceptual change, in the ways in which the sales process was conceived and in the perceived requirements of salesmen. It mirrored change occurring more generally in marketing as infusions from the behavioral disciplines described selling in psychological and sociological rather than merely economic terms. The consequence of this was the appearance in sales literature of such titles as the following:

The New Psychology of Selling (Hattwick)
Selling: a Behavioral Science Approach (Thompson)
Promotion: a Behavioral View (Boyd and Levy)
Effective Selling Through Psychology (Buzzotta)

Selling was also viewed more conceptually in other ways. Pederson and Wright[18], for example, presented not one but three theories of the buying process: the mental states theory, the buying decision theory, and the problem solving theory. Marketing thought came to embrace the ideas (1) that business strategy should be based upon consideration of market needs and wants; (2) that consumers have rights to protection, information, privacy, and equal treatment; (3) that interaction is a two-way process requiring comprehension as well as expression; (4) that business has civil as well as economic responsibilities to society; and (5) that intelligent business thought is increasingly cast in quantitative terms – if only requiring simple mathematics. As these ideas gained prominence in marketing thought, they also found expression in the sales literature.

The sales process had previously been described in terms of the selling of particular types of products, both at retail and at wholesale, but in the 1970s two works particularly reflected sales opportunities of the period. One was *Sales Engineering* by Black,[19] who defined sales engineering as the use of skills and knowledge inherent in engineering education to sell products and services to institutions. Because the subject was neglected in schools and texts, engineers, he thought, often knew little about selling, and ordinary salesmen knew little about engineering. This, then, was a case where special competence was required of salesmen, technical competence being added to acknowledged requisites of imagination, drive, and ability to communicate. In this very technical role, salesmen sometimes found themselves in a position where expectations concerning their loyalty to company and customer, respectively, were not known with certainty.

Also reflecting the times as Hanan's *Consultative Selling*.[20] He was concerned with the salesman, or "account consultant," who is responsible for developing and servicing his company's key accounts. Hanan emphasized that this is *not* product selling. Such a salesman is concerned with the sum total of his client's needs. He is a marketer in the broad sense, a manager of a personal service business, a business planner, an innovator, a problem solver. His success depends upon his ability to manage customer relations, to build his product into the customer's long-run plans, and to target profit improvement for his client. His responsibility goes beyond merely selling his product *to* the customer but extends to its projection *through* the customer's own business. Hanan's treatment of the subject is professional, conceptual, and analytic, employing matrix models and flow diagrams. The book elevates selling technique to a higher level of management thought and interaction.

Probably the most conceptually developed book of the sales literature is *Effective Selling Through Psychology*,[21] by Buzzotta and his collaborators. This is an ideally structured book built upon explicit premises and developed to the level of a theory consisting of sets of comprehensible and demonstrable generalizations. The authors review and discard the myths that salesmen "are born," that selling is either a mystery or an arbitrary set of rules, and that salesmen are "different." They regard selling as "applied behavioral science," and the sources of their concepts include psychology, sociology, social pyschology, economics, anthropology, linguistics, education, and political science.

The premise underlying their structure is that every person tends to be either warm or hostile, dominant or submissive. They arrange these variables in the following four-cell matrix:[22]

```
                          Dominant
                             |
      Dominant—              |          Dominant—
      Hostile                |          Warm
                 Q1          |    Q4
Hostile  --------------------+-------------------- Warm
                 Q2          |    Q3
      Hostile—               |          Submissive—
      Submissive             |          Warm
                             |
                        Submissive
```

These four quadrants represent states of buyers' mind, and in successive chapters the attributes of salesmen are matched with them. The Dominant-Warm salesman is deemed the best for dealing with the four types of customers. Sales managers and companies are likewise classified and analyzed.

The value of this book in the literature is that it represents a scholarly analytical approach to the subject, an incorporation of contemporary interdisciplinary thought, an original conceptualization of the selling process, and a development of thought to an exceptional level of theory in this area of marketing.

Whereas most of the sales literature eulogizes selling and the sales career, a single exception makes a positive contribution to thought by taking a diametrically opposite approach, namely, Susser's *The Truth About Selling*.[23] Long a salesman himself, he sees selling, in his words, as "a lousy way to make a living in this age." Because of the inexorable demands selling makes upon one, a man who stays at this work becomes "a nothing." He disclaims that there is anything "basic" about selling. Selling to him is an art which requires talent. With it you can *sell*. Without it you can't. It cannot be taught. Such a reversion to a long-tempered attitude about selling, and in the face of the more recent developments, may seem anachronistic. Without the preponderence of the more objective literature, it perhaps would be, but in context it is delightful and effective. Delightful because of the Jewish vernacular in which some of its salient points are made; effective because, being essentially true, it is a constructive complement to other more florid expositions.

SALES MANAGEMENT

Thought on sales management developed contemporaneously with that on selling and salesmanship. Some authors dealt with both subjects in the same book. For the most part, however, when management of sales was conceived to be distinct from selling itself, thought in the two areas developed apart but along parallel lines.

SUPERVISORY SALES MANAGEMENT

As the "old" type of salesman, who worked for himself and according to his own ideas, gave way to the "new" type, who accepted help from the house that employed him and co-operated with planners at headquarters, a growing need for supervision of salesmen was felt. This was the work of the sales manager, as he was described by C. W. Hoyt in 1913.[24] The sales manager was the link between the salesmen and the house. According to Hoyt, the sales manager's functions in the work of co-operating with salesmen and seeking to maximize their efficiency were as follows:

To standardize salesmen's arguments or sales talks.
To obtain complete business histories of candidates for sales positions; this to be done through the use of application blanks.
To talk common sense with the sales force, and to avoid "ginger" or "inspirational" talks.
To eliminate the idea that advertising is a substitute for salesmen.

Other duties of the sales manager included the holding of councils, meetings, and conventions for salesmen; the rating of salesmen through the use of contests; and the hiring, selecting, and supervising of salesmen. In general, Hoyt's approach to sales management was directly along the lines of general management then being laid down by Frederick W. Taylor.

SALES WORK ANALYSIS

Concepts of Taylorism relating to work analysis and scientific selection of salesmen received further attention from R. S. Butler, H. F. deBower, and J. G. Jones.[25] Convinced of the usefulness of the new studied methods of personnel analysis, they nevertheless recommended caution in their use with salesmen. Subjecting salesmen to sales management was in a sense bringing them under a yoke, they felt. Doubt was expressed, therefore, that experienced salesmen would be willing to work for a house that used tests for the selection and rating of salesmen — "new fangled ideas based entirely on theory." Yet they thought that rating charts, by directing attention to some things overlooked in the interview, could be used, but not with the knowledge of the applicants. This difference of responsibility, interest, viewpoint, and function between sales managers and salesmen led those writers to hold that the sales manager must be more than merely a successful salesman, particularly more than the "hail fellow — well met" type. This distinction was essential in the evolution of sales management thought.

A few years later, Frederic A. Russell[26] developed the opposite idea, namely, that salesmen can and do work into positions of sales management, and he wrote of sales management in a way intended to provide salesmen with insight that might aid them ultimately in coming "off the road." That was a practical objective, for notwithstanding the differences between the two types of work, the fact was that salesmen did become sales managers, and part of the development of management thought was for their education. However, despite the fact that Russell was well informed on many aspects of selling, he expressed amazing naivete, even for 1922, in objecting to salesmen's traveling by auto, on the ground that salesmen might seek bad companions in their free time and that the use of a car would provide them more free time!

SALES ORGANIZATION

More than mere sales supervision, and nothing less than sound organization for selling was regarded as the responsibility of sales managers by John G. Jones.[27] He saw the need for managing salesmen as "distinctly a present day problem," arising from the advent of specialty products, whose distribution did not follow the channels of staples. Efficient organization of sales alone, he felt, could meet the needs of sellers of specialties, and that was the responsibility of the sales manager. Organization appeared to him more important in selling than in other phases of business, for the management of salesmen determined to a great extent the volume of a business.

In connection with this concept of organization, Jones included the following as some of the responsibilities of sales managers: selection and training of salesmen, development of selling methods and equipment, planning of compensation and territories, maintenance of sales records, co-operation with salesmen, and organization of sales contests and conventions.

SALES MANAGEMENT, A MARKETING FUNCTION

As selling became recognized as an integral part of the broader activity of marketing, so sales management also gained that broader association. Whereas Jones saw the sales manager in relation to his sales organization, J. George Frederick[28] saw him in relation to the total marketing activity, even in relation to the entire business enterprise. He beheld him in an executive capacity, in a top-level position, contributing to the shaping of policies and responsible for the carrying-out of them, concerned with qualities of the product and conditions in the factory. In his mind, the sales manager had an interest in shaping products for the market, in synchronizing production and selling, in balancing standardization and the multiplicity of products. Frederick also had an embryonic concept of trading areas as a unit of territorial administration, and he recognized the dangers of pseudopsychology in the selection of salesmen. He was indeed a contributor to marketing thought!

STRATEGY IN MARKETING MANAGEMENT

Remarkable were two early conceptions of sales management as "marketing management." Leverett S. Lyon defined "marketing management" in 1926 as "the continuous task of re-planning the marketing activities of a business to meet the constantly changing conditions within and without the enterprise."[29] Harry R. Tosdal held marketing management to represent the administrative or executive officers' viewpoint of what businessmen generally called sales management.[30]

Lyon's concept of "marketing strategy" was drawn from an analogy made between marketing management and the responsibilities of military leadership. Both have responsibility for achievement of certain ends. In marketing, the ends are both general and specific and their choice is somewhat up to the discretion of the manager. Achievement of the desired ends depends to a large extent upon the "strategy" employed — upon the "instruments," or means, employed. Within the over-all strategy may be programs or campaigns of lesser scope. The "instruments" employed may include such factors as salesmen, advertising, credit terms, price, etc. — factors which in more recent years have been called elements of the marketing "mix." The "ammunition" of the marketing manager consists of the talking points that he presents through the various instruments.

After establishing the concept of the salesman as an instrument in the marketing strategy, Lyon dealt with the preparation, planning, operation, organization, and control of the sales force. His viewpoint was always broad, his approach objective, and his ideas verified by actual business experience. Combining analysis, philosophy, description, and "case" material, he developed a text intended for economists (to demonstrate to them how values are made), for university students, and for sales managers alike.

Lyon's contribution to thought in this book lies primarily in the breadth of his conception of the work of marketing management. He saw the marketing manager operating in "the economic-social order of our time," engaged with varying responsibility on the manufacturing, wholesale, or retail level of business. He saw him also circumscribed by internal characteristics of his business organization: physical restrictions, lack of materials, limited finances, or the co-operative relationship in which the business may be. That viewpoint reappeared in later years as the concept of the "marketing manager," in a position above sales management, consumer oriented, and having a sense of social responsibility.

INTEGRATION OF SALES MANAGEMENT THOUGHT

By the late 1930s, thought on sales management had attained a maturity that permitted an integration of the subject in books that for more than a decade were regarded as "basic" statements of the subject. Two writers who brought thought to a point of focus without contributing appreciably to its conceptual development were J. Russell Doubman and B. R. Canfield.[37]

Two others integrated into the body of thought new developments in research and accounting. They were Herman C. Nolen and Harold H. Maynard,[32] who undertook to introduce the changes in sales management that had come about since 1925, during a period when marketing research knowledge had progressed rapidly. Sales managers had come to base selling decisions on facts rather than on hunches, and the writers dealt with the bases of those fact-based decisions.

They distinguished between the sales manager's functions of personnel management and policy making. The sales manager, they believed, was in the middle position with respect to responsibilities upward in the line organization for making policies, and with responsibilities downward for co-ordinating and carrying out those policies.

The growing professionalization of sales management around 1950 was evident in the appointment to sales management and marketing management positions of men who were trained in psychology, accounting, statistics, and marketing – and who had not been active primarily in selling. That trend led to incorporation into sales management thought of new concepts and to reduction of emphasis upon others. Omitted or deemphasized thereafter were such matters as equipment, routing, conventions, and contests. Additional emphasis was given to price and service policies, choice of channels, use of distribution cost information in formulation of sales policies, and policies governing choice of products.

SALES MANAGEMENT THOUGHT – 1950 to 1960

The same circumstances that brought new views of salesmanship also altered sales management theory in postwar years. In general, the changes were expressed in a broadened concept of the sales or marketing function in business, evidenced in the emergence of the position of marketing manager that superseded or supplanted that of sales manager. This change in sales management theory involved the following new concepts:

that marketing management includes all activities embraced in a broad concept of marketing.

that marketing management begins with a knowledge and appreciation of the market.

that marketing management in a firm is responsible for interpreting the concept of the market – or the "marketing concept" – to all functional divisions of the firm: production, finance, personnel, warehousing, etc.

that marketing management is jointly responsible for formulation of top management policy.

that marketing management is responsible in line organization for planning the "mix" of marketing activities and for implementing this plan through sales personnel and other means.

Although the bulk of management literature in marketing during the 1950s dealt with these new concepts, traditonal theories of managing sales personnel continued to occupy a place in revisions of some earlier writings as well as in a few new books. That published by William J. Stanton and Richard H. Buskirk[33] illustrated the manner in which new ideas were introduced into sales thought without producing a complete departure from established thinking. The authors gave more emphasis to analysis and planning than had most former writers, whose concern had been mainly with the selection, training, and compensating of salesmen. They introduced also more of the concept of social responsibility, which sales executives should have as representatives not only of their company but of our sales economy. The social responsibility of sales executives was held to be fulfilled in several ways: by increasing the efficiency of the sales department, by interpreting consumer demand aright, by involvement in community affairs, and by understanding the impact that internal decisions would have upon environment.

Broader treatment of sales management was given by most writers during the decade, and, accordingly, numerous book titles included the term "marketing management" rather than "sales management." One of them was that of D. Maynard Phelps, who, with J. Howard Westing,[34] developed thought along lines of the increasing authority given to marketing executives of manufacturers in product planning, investigation of the market, pricing, inventory control, and production scheduling. They interpreted the growth of marketing management as resulting from concentration of production, the increasing cost of implementing marketing decisions, the enlarged number of non-staple products, and the control over marketing channels that is held by manufacturers.

Another approach to stating management theory was taken by John A. Howard,[35] who described his concept of the management of sales as "decision oriented" rather than "research oriented." Assuming profit to be the guiding criterion in marketing decision making, he interpreted marketing management as the making of decisions concerning products, channels, price, promotion, and locations. Such decisions are made with consideration given to competition, demand analysis, costs, distribution structure, and law. Concepts of cost allocation, marginal analysis, and recent developments from the behavioral sciences are all woven into his fabric of marketing management.

Most of the writers dealing with this subject around 1960 took the same point of view and discussed essentially the same subjects, although with varying degrees of emphasis placed upon the following: consumer orientation or the marketing concept, methods of decision making, tools of analysis for decision, conceptual classifications of traditional marketing institutions, activities, and policies, and organization and implementation of management for marketing. The philosophy of the period was summarized in Hector Lazo and Arnold Corbin's *Management in Marketing,* in the Foreword written by Peter Drucker. He wrote that one phase of marketing is the "management of marketing." Another phase is the viewing of the entire business as based upon contemplation of customer needs and wants. The marketing view, he held, puts "in its center the unique and specific purpose of business enterprise, the purpose of economic performance. . . . [Marketing is] a basic attitude and understanding that must prevade the entire business."[36]

Thus throughout the 1950s not only did *sales* management become *marketing* management but the managerial approach to marketing tended to displace the usual "general" approach to the study of marketing. That it actually did not is due to the perception of some students that the study of marketing is not exclusively for management purposes and that even management is not always best served by exclusive devotion to decision-making techniques. The developments of thought along this line are discussed later, in the section dealing with trends in general marketing thought during the 1950s.

SALES MANAGEMENT THOUGHT SINCE 1960

A bibliography of books on sales management since 1960 shows little innovation in titles, for the majority of them are simply Sales Management or Management of the Sales Force. Tendencies to straddle the gap between sales management and marketing management which had earlier appeared now seemed lost in a clearer distinction of what belonged to each field. Writings on sales management were generally confined to that management function, although its inseparability from the total marketing task was not forgotten. Notwithstanding this conceptual separation, not all works on sales management were equally broad. Among the more specialized titles were the following:

Marketing and the Sales Manager (Elsby)
Sales Management: Contemporary Perspectives (Barnhill)

The Arithmetic of Sales Management (Truitt)
From Selling to Managing (Brown)
The Human Side of Sales Management (Bigelow)
The Art of Persuasion for Sales Managers (Christensen)
Management of the Personal Selling Function (Goodman)

A survey of books of the period indicates little new or different about the management of selling. Elsby[37] identified the basic responsibilities of sales management as the following: (1) discovery and research, (2) formulation of policy, (3) planning operation of the sales force, (4) implementation, (5) control of sales force operations, and (6) warehousing and distribution management. Such functions were similarly itemized by other writers. Elsby recognized that through specialization and the division of labor, performance of some of these functions might be delegated to other than the sales manager. External developments of the 1960s did not appreciably affect the task of sales management.

What did affect the *performance* if not the *task* of sales management, however, was the changing perspective in which the work was held. Perspective changes originated in the new concepts being introduced into marketing thought in general.

One of the perceptions in which sales management was held was that the sales manager performed within the viewpoint and the organization of marketing. Dodge[38] saw him as a marketing technician, or manager of a marketing unit. The sales manager thus redefined from a marketing point of view was concerned with the relationship to field selling of all the marketing research, customer financing, customer service, and logistics.

Another viewpoint was that the sales manager was in a role position and that there were technical and behavioral expectations of him. Although not essentially a hehaviorist, DeVoe[39] viewed these expectations as demands for personal effectiveness in planning, decision making, managerial leadership, and communication. Still and Cundiff[40] recognized the demands for technical efficiency in recruiting, training, motivating, compensating, and evaluating the sales force, but they also saw the demand for interaction of the sales manager in his relations with not only the sales organization but with top management and with the distributive network.

In a third perspective, the sales manager was viewed as a decision maker. In this capacity he was presumed to possess ability to utilize information for the formulation of sales forecasts, sales budgets and cost analyses, sales territories, and quotas. He was expected to understand and apply technology for making rational decisions, for differentiating between programmable (delegatable) and non-programmable decisions, and for guiding group and organizational decision making.

Furthermore, with the competence of a behaviorist versed in concepts derived from several disciplines, the sales manager might be expected to act in accord with such concepts as the following discussed by Davis and Webster[41]:

Role	Group
Feedback	Group conflict
Message receiver	Gatekeeper
Sleeper effect of influence	Diffusion of innovation
Hierarchy of effects of	Communication network
communcation	Optimum allocation of
Salesman-prospect interaction	effort

Perceptions

Expectations

Critical path analysis

Operations research
technique

Territorial design

Still another perception of sales management emphasized the interaction of the sales manager with top management.[42] If personal selling be a part of the marketing mix, and if intelligence concerning the market gathered by the sales force be a significant factor in implementation of the marketing concept, a natural responsibility of the sales manager would be participation with top management, in the formulation of policy concerning the product line and quality, promotion and brand management, pricing, marketing channels, and the general coordination of the marketing mix.

CONTRIBUTIONS OF LITERATURE ON SELLING AND SALES MANAGEMENT TO MARKETING THOUGHT

The contributions to marketing thought that have been made by men writing in the field of the sales literature are as follows:

1. Concepts of Selling. Although the common activity of selling is readily recognizable, when conceived abstractly, selling, like other abstractions, has a wide range of meanings to different people. The following are some of the more important concepts:

As an Art. When held to be strictly a personal achievement, a mode of individual self-expression, a notion prevailed that "salesmen are born, not made." Ability to persuade is the measure of success in personal selling. Literature based upon this conception has consisted largely of success experiences, inspiring the willing, provoking the challenged. Most eloquently described, the sales personality has been depicted, not as the razzle-dazzle individual, but as the person with warmth and dignity, who looks and acts like the man worthy of being invited into an office or home. Character development, therefore, was held to be the key to the development of sales ability.

As a Formulated Process That Can Be Learned. Somewhat impersonalized, selling has been regarded as a process of complying with certain rules of sales behavior and of memorizing tested selling phrases. So effectively was that concept employed when most salesmen were unaggressive product representatives that many industrial organizations achieved sales success merely by having their salesmen memorize canned talks.

As a Process of Applied Analysis. Psychologists, who were among the first to be interested in describing the selling process, analyzed the function in terms of the steps through which the human mind is supposed to move in accepting a new idea: attention, interest, conviction, and action. Dormant and unconscious wants in the buyer's mind, it is reasoned, can be brought to the surface. This analytical approach to selling has inspired the hopes of many an aspiring salesman, for it appears to be practical; it has, therefore, structured the selling thought in many a book on the subject.

As a Meeting of Minds. Less objectionable and less aggressive was the concept of selling as a mutually satisfying transaction. It was a procedure in satisfying customers' wants, in helping buyers. It was not an imposition of the seller's will upon the buyer. Nystrom expressed this concept as "the fine art of presenting facts about goods, showing how the goods will serve the customer's needs, and guiding the mental adjustments of customers to satisfied purchases."

As a Businesslike Function. Not all selling occurs in the presence of the buyer. Selling is broader than the mere transaction, and it includes all that is expected of the salesman in his self-preparation, in his arrangement of the pre-approach, in the sales presentation, in his writing of reports, in co-operation with sales planners, and in taking general direction from the sales manager.

As a Marketing Function. Amplification has been given the meaning of selling as a marketing function. Actually, little reference is made in this literature to the "marketing functions," although the terms "marketing methods" and "distributive process" are used.

As an Economic Function. So conceived, selling is a macro-consideration. It is a force in the economy. It is an occupational classification of the gainfully employed. It is a service, performed at a cost, with value and price. It is a means of effecting economic exchange. This concept has been generally subordinated to the more practical aspects of selling in the literature.

As an Institution. Selling and salesmanship have been shown to be an institution of our society — a product of economic circumstances, of our philosophy of free enterprise, and of our psychological interpretations of human mentality and behavior.

As a Sociological Influence. Selling is an institution in our society. Not only does it condition our values and our standards of living, it introduces a unique element into our social structure. In no other society has the salesman occupied the social position that he does in the United States. In ancient cultures, women, servants, and slaves tended the local market institutions. Export trading was apart from domestic selling, and vendors lacked status because of their presumed unproductivity and their unscrupulous tactics. While even yet not comparable to a professional group, salesmen are a respected, productive, and influential class exerting a significant influence upon our society.

2. *Concepts of Sales Managements.* The concept of sales management is a twentieth-century development, following and paralleling the expanding concept of salesmanship. How one regards selling determines the responsibility of the manager of salesmen. With the increase of both marketing and management knowledge, sales management was recognized to include more than mere management of salesmen. The following are the principal concepts:

As a Supervisory Capacity. At first, the position of the sales manager was analogous to that of a foreman or job supervisor. So long as salesmen operated with the independence they initially had, there was little more to do than co-ordinate them, render them service, and maintain a liaison between them and the selling house.

As a Director of Promotions. To the sales manager, in this capacity, falls responsibility not only for personal selling but also for advertising and for development of all promotional undertakings.

As a Manager of Distribution. Responsibility for directing all activities and functions involved in the distribution of products and services, including not only promotions but also determination of channels, prices, market policies, etc.

As a Top Management Executive. Co-ordination of distribution functions with others in the total business operation. Responsibility for interpretation of market research to product designers, to production schedulers, to the financial officer responsible for financing inventories and accounts receivable, and to all other major functional divisions of an enterprise.

3. Development of New Viewpoints. Two viewpoints from which not only selling but marketing in general may be approached have been developed: the subjective versus the scientific, the self-centered versus the service centered.

4. Psychological Analysis of the Mentality and Motivation of the Market. Findings of psychologists were introduced also through the advertising literature, but in sales writings more attention was devoted to the explanation of mental behavior; in advertising writings more attention was given to advertising techniques related to the assumed behavior patterns.

5. Ratification of the Principle That the Customer's Interest Is Paramount in Marketing. This contradicted the idea of the limited and selfish objectives of salesmen; far-seeing merchants conceived selling as a performance of service.

6. Comparatively Low Level of Generalizations or Principles. Actually, few principles were set forth. Instead, descriptions, outlines, procedures, and rules of action were the general content of the writings on selling.

7. A History of Development of Salesmanship. Much of this is factual; part of it is interpretive.

8. A More Comprehensive Concept of the Application of Scientific Management to Marketing. Not only has organizational structure been discussed in more detail than is found in the literature on wholesaling, retailing, advertising, and credit, but also management of broad functional activities in selling.

9. Emphasis on Interrelationships within a Firm. Interrelationships within a business enterprise have been emphasized, particularly those that come to a focus in selling and are managed or administered through the position of the sales manager.

10. New Concepts and Terminology. A variety of *concepts* that aid in the statement and communication of marketing thought have been developed:

Buying fatigue	Sales budget
Dealer salesmen	Sales conference
Director of marketing	Sales contest
Drawing account	Sales convention
Functionalized operation	Sales engineering
Inspirational selling	Sales forecast
Marketing management	Sales planning
Marketing mix	Sales quota
Missionary salesmen	Sales strategy
Personal selling	Sales territory
Profile of salesman	Trading area

ENDNOTES

[1] William Maxwell, *Salesmanship* (Boston: Houghton Mifflin Co., 1913).

[2] Harold Whitehead, *Principles of Salesmanship* (New York: Ronald Press Co., 1917).

[3] Paul W. Ivey, *Salesmanship Applied* (New York: A. W. Shaw Co., 1925; 2d ed., 1937).

[4] H. Simmons, *A Practical Course in Successful Selling* (New York: Harper & Bros., 1939).

[5] John G. Jones and Raymond J. Comyns, *Salesmanship and Sales Management* (New York: Alexander Hamilton Institute, 1918).

[6] Archer Wall Douglas, *Traveling Salesmanship* (New York: Macmillan Co., 1919), p. 4.

[7] Norris A. Brisco, *Fundamentals of Salesmanship* (New York: D. Appleton-Century Co., Inc., 1916); *Retail Salesmanship* (New York: Ronald Press Co., 1920).

[8] Frederic A. Russell, *Textbook of Salesmanship* (New York: McGraw-Hill Book Co., Inc. 1924; 2d ed. 1933, with F. H. Beach; 3d ed., 1941; 4th ed., 1949; 5th ed., 1955; 6th ed., 1959).

[9] E. E. Ferris and G. R. Collins, *Salesmanship* (New York: Ronald Press Co., 1924; 2d ed., 1930; 3d ed., 1939; 4th ed., 1941).

[10] *Ibid.*, p. iv.

[11] Harry R. Tosdal, *Principles of Personal Selling* (New York: A. W. Shaw Co., 1925; rev. and abridged, 1927, as *Principles of Personal Salesmanship).*

[12] H. K. Nixon, *Principles of Selling* (New York: McGraw-Hill Book Co., Inc. 1931; 2d ed., 1942).

[13] B. R. Canfield, *Salesmanship Practices and Problems* (New York: McGraw-Hill Book Co., Inc., 1940; 2d ed., 1947; 3d ed., 1958).

[14] Paul W. Ivey and Walter Horvath, *Successful Salesmanship* (Englewood Cliffs, N.J.: Prentice-Hall, Inc., 4th ed., 1961).

[15] S. J. Shaw and J. W. Thompson, *Salesmanship* (New York: Henry Holt & Co., Inc., 1960).

[16] Taylor W. Meloan and John M. Rathwell, *Selling: Its Broader Dimensions* (New York: Macmillan Co., 1960).

[17] Harry R. Tosdal, *Selling in Our Economy* (Homewood, Ill.: Richard D. Irwin, Inc., 1957).

[18] C. A. Pederson and M. D. Wright *Salesmanship* (Homewood, Ill.: Richard D. Irwin, Inc., 1951; 2d ed., 1955; 3d ed., 1961; 4th ed., 1966; 5th ed., 1971).

[19] George Black, *Sales Engineering* (Houston: Gulf Publishing Co., 1973).

[20] Mack Hanan, *Consultative Selling* (New York: AMACOM, 1973).

[21] V. R. Buzzotta, et al., *Effective Selling Through Psychology* (New York: Wiley Interscience, 1972).

[22] *Ibid.*, p. 22.

[23] Samuel S. Susser, *The Truth About Selling* (New York: Paul S. Eriksson, Inc., 1973).

[24] C. W. Hoyt, *Scientific Sales Management* (New Haven, Conn.: G. B. Woolson & Co., 1913).

[25] R. S. Butler, H. F. deBower, and J. G. Jones, *Marketing Methods and Salesmanship* (New York: Alexander Hamilton Institute, 1914).

[26] Frederic A. Russell, *The Management of the Sales Organization* (New York: McGraw-Hill Book Co., Inc. 1922).

[27] John G. Jones, *Salesmanship and Sales Management* (New York: Alexander Hamilton Institute, 1918).

[28] J. George Frederick, *Modern Sales Management* (New York: D. Appleton–Century Co., Inc. 1919).

[29] Leverett S. Lyon, *Salesman in Marketing Strategy* (New York: Macmillan Co., 1926), p. 3.

[30] Harry R. Tosdal, *Problems in Sales Management* (New York: McGraw-Hill Book Co., Inc., 1921; 2d ed., 1925; 3d ed., 1931; 4th ed., 1939 [see 3d ed., p. 1]; *Introduction to Sales Management* (McGraw-Hill Book Co., Inc., 1933; 2d ed., 1940; 3d ed., 1950; 4th ed., 1957).

[31] J. Russell Doubman, *Fundamentals of Sales Management* (New York: F. S. Crofts & Co., 1937); B. R. Canfield, *Sales Administration: Principles and Problems* (New York: Prentice-Hall, Inc., 1939; 2d ed., 1947; 3d ed., 1954; 4th ed., 1961).

[32] Herman C. Nolen and Harold H. Maynard, *Sales Management* (New York: Ronald Press Co., 1940; 2d ed., 1950, by H. H. Maynard and H. C. Nolen; 3d ed., 1957 by H. H. Maynard and J. H. Davis).

[33] William J. Stanton and Richard H. Buskirk, *Management of the Sales Force* (Homewood, Ill.: Richard D. Irwin, Inc., 1959).

[34] D. Maynard Phelps and J. Howard Westing, *Sales Management: Policies and Procedures* (Homewood, Ill.; Richard D. Irwin, Inc., 1951; rev. ed., 1960, as *Marketing Management,* with J. H. Westing; 3d ed., 1968).

[35] John A. Howard, *Marketing Management: Analysis and Decision* (Homewood, Ill.: Richard D. Irwin, Inc., 1957).

[36] Hector Lazo and Arnold Corbin, *Management in Marketing* (New York: McGraw-Hill

90

Book Co., Inc., 1961), p. vi.

[37]F. H. Elsby, *Marketing and the Sales Manager* (Oxford, N.Y.: Pergamon Press, 1969).

[38]H. R. Dodge, *Field Sales Management: Text and Cases* (Dallas: Business Publications, 1973).

[39]M. DeVoe, *The Effective Sales Manager* (Lexington, Ky.: EMD Publications, 1968).

[40]R. R. Still and E. W. Cundiff, *Sales Management* (Englewood Cliffs, N.J.: Prentice-Hall, Inc., 2d ed., 1969).

[41]K. R. Davis and F. E. Webster, *Sales Force Management* (New York: The Ronald Press Co., 1968).

[42]Still and Cundiff, *Op. cit.*

The field of retailing is another from which important contributions to marketing thought have come. Literature in this area, while not so voluminous as in some other areas, nevertheless includes more than one hundred books published since 1914. Development of thought on retailing did not begin as early as in the functional fields of selling, credit, and advertising, but it preceded the study of wholesaling. Many writers have contributed to this segment of marketing thought, but a few are especially outstanding. Early contributors to retailing thought were chiefly men on the faculties of eastern schools: New York University, Columbia University, and the Harvard Business School. Those in New York had a unique influence upon the development of institutional aspects of marketing thought.

Contributions to marketing thought coming from works on retailing have been primarily of a technical nature. Comparatively little attention was given in this literature to the economic aspects of marketing, but much was given to institutional operating functions and techniques. A reason for this was the increasing need for technology in a period of rapidly changing conditions in retailing. The first years of this century witnessed the growth of department stores, mail order houses, and chain stores. That was a period, too, when a high rate of failures among retailers was dispelling the illusion that just *anyone* could "run" a retail store.

On the scene of this environment appeared a succession of men who brought into focus a broad view of both the structure of retailing establishments and the principles of retail store management.

CONTRIBUTIONS OF PAUL H. NYSTOM

For the initial conception and development of retailing thought, much credit is due Paul H. Nystrom. A native of Wisconsin, a teacher and principal in the high schools of that state, and a special investigator for the Wisconsin Tax Commission during the summers of 1906-8, Nystrom undertook his graduate education in economics at a mature stage in his own experience. While studying at the University of Wisconsin under some of the country's leading economists, his combined interest in tax problems and economic theory led him to study the problems of retail institutions. As a result of this, his Ph.D. dissertation was published under the title *The Economics of Retailing,*[1] a book that is one of the marketing classics. Meanwhile, however, he had also written *Retail Selling and Store Management,*[2] which he used in mimeographed form as early as 1911 for University extension classes. Following some years out of teaching and with the Associated Merchandising Corporation, upon returning to the university he wrote *Economics of Fashion*[3] and *Economic Principles of Consumption.*[4] Both the nature and the timing of his contributions to the field reflected the man himself.

Through Nystrom's work, retailing thought developed along two lines, one institutional and the other technical. Institutionally, he regarded retailing as one link in the distributive system. He chronicled the history of retailing up to that time, narrating not only the development of certain large retailing establishments, presenting pictures of the stores and their founders, but also the rise of other famous stores in foreign cities. He described the respective characters of department stores, chain store systems, and mail order houses, giving to this aspect of retailing an amount of attention unmatched by subsequent writers. He discussed also the theory of location and rent as applied to retail stores, identified some characteristics of consumers, and dealt with such topics as buying at "inside prices," the failure rate, the question of whether there were too many retail stores, price maintenance, public regulation, and the "ideal" retailing system. So vast was the quantity of information presented in this institutional study of retailing that it became the content of Volume I of *The Economics of Retailing* when the publication appeared in two volumes. That this portion of retailing thought was rarely treated more than summarily by other writers in the field was due partly to the thoroughness with which Nystrom had originally presented it and partly to the fact that extensive discussion of the institutional character of both retailing and wholesaling became traditionally included in works on general marketing.

The other line along which Nystrom developed retailing thought was more technical or managerial in nature. Believing that distribution had not received the attention it should and that the public regarded distributors as something of a necessary evil, he wrote of subjects that would increase the efficiency – solve the problems of retail store managers. The problems of small stores especially concerned him, although he thought that the operating principles applicable to retailing were applicable equally to all types of stores. Judged from the problems that confronted managers, and of which Nystrom wrote in 1913, the body of retailing thought embraced management practices related to locating a store, buying a business, organizing for operation, buying merchandise, accounting for business done, maintaining inventory records, selling, receiving, pricing, and hiring, paying, and training employees. Nystrom's active interest in retail personnel management caused him at that time to devote half of his book to the subject.

Although *Retail Selling and Store Management* was essentially an operating manual, it contained the structural elements upon which the body of retailing thought was hung by subsequent writers. Nystrom himself, in Volume II of *The Economics of Retailing,* further contributed to its refinement, incorporating developments in retailing during the 1920s, new retailing statistics that had become available, and the fruits of his own experiences with the Associated Merchandising Corporation. While maintaining a strong managerial viewpoint, Nystrom nevertheless made use, where applicable, of thought borrowed from economic theory, psychology, and sociology. In 1937 he imputed to retail managers six responsibilities or ethical obligations, namely, their obligations to owners of the business, to customers, to employees, to the community, to competitors, and to themselves and their families.[5]

Expressive of Nystrom's special retailing interests was the thought he developed on the subject of fashion. Much of his preparation for work in that area grew out of his experience with the resident buying office in New York City. Said he, "I was impressed by my observations that buyers of fashion goods had no idea of the real significance of fashion underlying the saleability of the goods they were handling. Indeed, they had no idea of the difference between style and fashion. It was my intention in the *Economics of Fashion* to explain the significance of fashion."[6] Further interpretation of his principles of fashion for the merchandising manager was given in *Fashion Merchandising,*[7] in which he expressed his opinion that consumers, not producers, made fashions, and that fashions could be measured and their trends determined. At that time he also set forth five principles that to him described and explained business and that characterized well the viewpoint he brought to the study of retailing:[8]

Free and equal opportunity should be accorded to all who enter business.
The prospect of profit is a great incentive.
Consumers and society are preserved against abuses from private lines and unreasonably high prices by maintenance of free and active competition.
Competition is encouraged by prohibition of monopoly.
In the long run, under free competition, net profits tend to decline.

Nystrom was an ardent and outspoken exponent of individual initiative and competition in business enterprise. While he was much concerned for the welfare of retail employees, he ralied against the restrictions imposed upon retail management by modern trends in labor organizations.

Nystrom's contributions to marketing literature and marketing thought are many. His study illustrated both the time and the space dimensions of marketing thought, in his accounts of retailing's historical development and of retailing abroad. He conceived and refined the structure of retailing thought, filling in details as environmental circumstances changed. He perceived the interests of consumers as keenly as he did those of business management; he dealt with the problems of buying and selling as well as with those of personnel management. For these reasons, Nystrom is one of the peers among contributors to marketing thought and possibly the most eminent single writer on retailing.

"THE RETAILING SERIES"

In the decade following Nystrom's first publication, in 1913, a few other men contributed to retailing thought by writing on store management, buying, and selling. It was not until 1924, however, that the volume of contributions appreciably increased. That development evidenced an accelerated turning of retail merchants, particularly large ones, to systematic study of their operating problems. Principles of scientific management were being applied in retail stores, and scientific methods of inductive research were increasing the knowledge of operating principles applicable to retailing. The 1920s were years of significant thought formation in this area of marketing.

So imbued were merchants and academicians with confidence in the potentialities of research for improving retail management that a number of New York businessmen and teachers dedicated themselves to advancing "the new retailing" — based upon research — through a program of study and writing. The

94

publications that issued from that undertaking were known as "The Retailing Series," sponsored by the New York University School of Retailing under the leadership of Dean Norris A. Brisco. The series, based largely upon experiences of large New York department stores, which constituted the laboratory for the studies, included analyses of buying, selling, credit, financing, personnel, record keeping, publicity, service, control, and merchandising in general.

Although regarded at that time as representing the "scientific" approach to retail management, the studies represented mainly those methods of science that relate to the gathering and classifying of data and to the drawing of generalizations therefrom. Yet, though largely descriptive of prevailing practices, "The Retailing Series" provided for ten or fifteen years the most authoritative and influential statement of retailing thought.

Contributors to and titles of writings regarded as part of the series, arranged in the order in which they were published, are as follows:

1925 James L. Fri, *Retail Merchandising, Planning, and Control.*
1925 Norris A. Brisco and John W. Wingate, *Retail Buying.*
1927 Norris A. Brisco, *Principles of Retailing.*
1929 Norris A. Brisco, *Retail Credit Procedure.*
1934 C. K. Lyans and Norris A. Brisco, *Retail Accounting.*
1935 Norris A. Brisco, *Retailing.*
1937 John W. Wingate and Norris A. Brisco, *Buying for Retail Stores.*
1938 O. P. Robinson and Norris B. Brisco, *Retail Store Organiza-tion and Management.*
1938 John W. Wingate and Norris A. Brisco, *Elements of Retail Merchandising.*
1940 O. P. Robinson, *Retail Personnel Relations.*
1941 Norris A. Brisco, G. Griffith, and O. P. Robinson, *Store Salesmanship.*
1942 Norris A. Brisco and Leon Arnowitt, *Introduction to Modern Retailing.*
1942 Norris A. Brisco and R. W. Severa, *Retail Credit.*
1944 John W. Wingate, E. O. Schaller, and I. Goldenthal, *Problems in Retail Merchandising.*
1950 John W. Wingate and E. O. Schaller, *Techniques in Retail Merchandising.*

CONTRIBUTIONS FROM OTHER SOURCES

Imposing as were the contributions from New York University, ideas appeared from other sources also at every stage of the development of retailing thought. As progress was made along different lines of retailing, the body of thought was structured topically rather than according to its source, and it is along topical lines that the analysis of thought in the remainder of this chapter is organized.

RETAILING MANUALS

One form in which retailing thought took shape was the manual, intended particularly as a guide or reference book. While several authors used this term loosely in connection with comparatively broad treatments of retailing, others designated by it the handbook type of thought usually associated with the term.

The "Merchandise Manuals for Retail Salespeople"[9] prepared and edited by W. W. Charters, Director of the Bureau of Research for Retail Training, University of Pittsburgh, typify the latter group. They consisted of a series of publications, each devoted to the description of a product and to the analysis of its features for sales purposes. Among the titles were the following: *Aprons and House Dresses; China and Glassware; Coats; Draperies; Dresses, Hosiery, Knit Underwear, and Gloves; Muslin Underwear and Petticoats; Sweaters and Bathing Suits;* etc. Studies of commodity marketing had been made previously, but never had such detailed studies been undertaken for specific goods. While no generalizations or principles of selling were drawn, the studies contributed to marketing-thought vocabulary for describing values, consideration of the customer's viewpoint in transactions, and an example of the extreme detail that characterized some phases of marketing research.

Scarcely less specialized was John W. Wingate's *Manual of Retail Terms,*[10] in which, instead of merchandise classes, he put into manual form retailing concepts and terminology. In doing so, he showed the growing interest at that time in clarification of marketing vocabulary. Wingate undertook not only to define terms, setting forth definitions in bold type and giving in some instances authority for the definitions, but he explained at length the concepts set forth. The work was in line with the interests that ultimated in 1937 in the appointment by the American Marketing Association of a committee asked to bring uniformity into an even wider array of marketing concepts. Wingate dealt with marketing organization, merchandising organization, merchandise control, packing and delivery, marking and storing, and credits and collections. The book was a landmark of a type in the development of marketing thought. Its usefulness diminished, however, as newer concepts and terms were introduced.

Broader in scope, although still meriting its title because of its encyclopedic character, was *The Merchant's Manual* edited by Lew Hahn and Percival White.[11] Believing that business had not yet been reduced to a set of standards and rules, they attempted "to put into writing some of the principles of store operation and management,"[12] and they claimed this to be the first treatise of its kind.

More significant than mere details, which they provided abundantly, were some of the concepts set forth by the writers. To them, retailing consisted of physical factors, store operation, store organization and management, merchandising, personnel, and special services. They interpreted the objectives of retail business in terms of the "merchant's responsibilities," as follows:

to the public:
   responsibility to distribute necessities and luxuries in a satisfactory manner and in a manner that minimized charge; to provide full assortment and the best combination of quality and price; to fulfill the "trust relationship" between the store and the public; and to tell the truth.
to employees:
   responsibility to pay at least the minimum wage; to hire the best workers available; and to endeavor to increase the individual's capacity.
to the business:
   responsibility to consider other responsibilities in the light of cost and law.

Other concepts employed by the authors in their exposition of retailing were the following:

> Classes of merchandise: impulse, convenience, necessity, utility, and luxury.
> 100 per cent locations.
> Reserve stocks versus forward stocks.
> Types of organization: military, functional, departmental.

RETAIL BUYING

Termed "manual" but, while in form related to retail manuals, related in content more to other writings on buying, James L. Fri's *The Buyer's Manual*[13] consisted of articles previously published by the National Retail Dry Goods Association. It reflected two opposite trends in buying. One was the growing concern of buyers with consumers' wants, resulting in part from consumer response to marketing practices, called in the early 1930s the "Consumer Movement." The other was an increased preoccupation with details of internal management of buying.

An extensive treatment of buying, made by Norris A. Brisco and John W. Wingate, was published under the titles *Retail Buying* and *Buying for Retail Stores*.[14] Imbued with the vision of the "new retailing," they aspired to help retail buying, through research, to become more professionalized. Professionalization of buying was held to depend upon consideration of the ethical aspects of buying – profits alone were regarded as an insufficient measure of the service rendered consumers. Assuming that customers knew what they wanted and that buyers were responsible for ascertaining this information from customers, they conceived retail buyers to be "purchasing agents" for customers rather than "manufacturers' outlets."

With the passing of years, as reflected in the works of Brisco and Wingate, the concept of the buying function was broadened. Originally, it consisted of the activities for which the buyer was responsible and of the processes of handling goods upon their arrival at the store. That concept of buying was elaborated into concern with what, when, where, and how to buy for the retail operation. Buying became increasingly dependent upon information and aids outside the business. Likewise, buying involved knowledge of services of various associations and of governmental regulations and studies. Ultimately, buying was held also to embrace organization for buying, the position of the buyer, what and how much to buy, where and how to buy, means of gathering data about consumers, sources of merchandise, legal limitations, and brands and labels.

RETAIL SELLING

Retail merchants have often subscribed to the maxim that "goods well bought are half sold." That attitude may account somewhat for the fact that writers on retailing devoted comparatively little attention to the selling function and more to buying. Selling was dealt with more by students of salesmanship per se than by men concerned with the complex of problems constituting retailing in general. The term "retail selling" has often carried a broader connotation of retail merchandising, of which salesmanship is but a part. Nystrom, Brisco, Ivey, Hall, and Wheeler are a few who gave thought to salesmanship on the retail level. The substance of their ideas has been presented in a previous chapter and needs no further elaboration here.

A possible exception to the generalization just made may be found in a small number of books on retailing that had a highly specialized purpose.[15] They were written for vocational guidance of young people who were to enter business through a retail selling career. Their approach, however, was to present the prospective salesperson with a picture of retailing as consisting of more than salesmanship alone.

The Leigh book was a non-technical beginner's textbook arranged in the order in which problems arise in the locating and starting of a retail store. Maynard and his collaborators claimed for their presentation the distinction of having the consumer's point of view. While it was useful for vocational education, it also was an indirect approach to consumer education, using the analysis of retail operations as a means of increasing consumer understanding and appreciation of the distributive process.

RETAIL CREDIT

The function of retail credit management is another that has been dealt with by writers in two fields: retailing and credit. This subject, also, is discussed in the chapter of this book concerned with that function rather than in this, pertaining to the institution. Interest in retail credit, suffice it to say, increased markedly during the 1920s with the growth of department-store selling and with the expanding sales of durable goods offered on installment credit terms. Before the end of that decade, only a few titles[16] among the credit prublications dealt specifically and exclusively with credit in retail stores. After that, the number increased appreciably, and increased attention was given to retail credit in the general works on credit management.

RETAIL ACCOUNTING

One facet of retailing thought, sometimes associated with the buying function, has to do with store records and accounting. Nowhere except in connection with institutional thought have ideas of this nature evolved, and, while the subject is treated in both wholesaling and retailing literature, far more attention is given to it in the latter.

Interest in this subject grew rapidly in the early 1920s, with the development among retail stores of new concepts of record keeping and accounting for merchandise control purposes, and in 1925 no less than four authors gave expression to their thoughts along this line: E. A. Filene,[17] James L. Fri,[18] Malcolm P. McNair,[19] and H. B. Wess.[20] A few years later, Filene published his concept of the model stock plan,[21] for which he has been renowned. In 1931 John W. Wingate, E. O. Schaller, and I. Goldenthal cast the subject in the form of a book of problems.[22] In 1934 C. K. Lyans and Norris A. Brisco added *Retail Accounting* to "The Retailing Series."[23] The ten years from 1925 to 1935 were the period in which the principal additions were made to this area of retailing thought.

Filene's model plan for stock was based upon the concept of maintaining three full price lines of merchandise. The objective of the buying administration being to provide the right goods, at the right time, in the right quantities, and at the right prices, the plan included policies concerning stock sizes, markdowns, buying and selling times, publicity, and bargains. Filene set forth this highly specialized structure of thought in handbook style.

At the same time, McNair pioneered in stating a method of determining accurately the merchandise profit earned during any period and arriving at a conservative cost valuation of merchandise remaining in stock. No one person actually invented that accounting method; it had been developing for years as an indispensable control device in the growing field of large retail establishments. McNair, Wingate, Filene, and others contributed to expansion of such thought. In 1961, McNair was still active in the development of accounting systems for retail stores.

Of similar nature was the 1931 contribution of Wingate, Schaller, and Goldenthal, a book designed to instruct students in the calculation of "open to buy," determination of markup percentages, classification and distribution of expenses, control of relationships between sales and stocks, and the analysis and application of statistical data. Their material was presented as a collection of problems, to which, when accepted methods were applied, definite answers would be obtained.

Lyans and Brisco undertook to describe what they regarded as good accounting practice for all sizes of retail stores. They applied, in other words, standard accounting principles to retail operations. Retail accounting, however, was complicated by the fact that retailing required the keeping of many special ledgers: sales and returned goods analysis; accounts receivable ledger; accounts payable ledger; departmental purchase journal; retail inventory stock ledger; expense ledger; department operating statement; etc. They discussed the techniques and forms involved in those ledgers.

ORGANIZATION AND PERSONNEL

While some students of retailing concerned themselves with functional and statistical problems, others developed retail management theory relating to organization structure and personnel. Paul M. Mazur was one who pioneered this field of thought. Having made a study for the National Retail Dry Goods Association, he wrote in *Principles of Organization Applied to Modern Retailing*[24] what he believed to be the first comprehensive analysis of retail organization. His experiences had shown him that, even among large stores at that time, there was lack of uniformity, system, and science in procedures and practices. Business leaders still regarded scientific organization as academic.

From his research experience in retailing, Mazur postulated thirteen principles of store organization and operation that gradually gained wide acceptance among retail merchants. He conceived the department store as an organization of personnel with interrelated duties. He regarded its organizational divisions as pertaining to merchandise, publicity, store management, and financial control — divisions that provided balances and checks upon each other. Manufacturers, he believed, could learn from retailers the importance of anticipating sales possibilities and of planning and control of inventories. The department store, to him, was an economically sound institution, whose growth reflected fundamental social conditions and business development. Other principles that he set forth are that organization must fit the personnel, each executive must have a complete circle of responsibility, and each department should specialize in a particular function.

Organization also interested Harold B. Wess, who in his *Profit Principles of Retailing*[25] set forth twenty principles upon which he regarded sound operations to be based. Some pertained to organization, some to methods. The following are typical:[26]

> *Organization* — Every important executive must have an assistant as capable as his boss — and both should be secure and happy.
> *Clientele* — A precise determination of the store's customers must be made and these characteristics must be known and understood by the personnel of the store.
> *Scientific Norms* — Scientific norms must be used to determine the size ratios, color ratios, fabric ratios, etc., according to which customers buy in your store.
> *New Methods* — New methods of operation must be introduced slowly and only when the entire organization is ready to receive them.

Both Mazur and Wess wrote independently and were concerned with a comparatively specialized segment of retailing thought. In that area, however, they both were creative and made contributions that became incorporated in the works of others who wrote following them. Additional concepts of organization continued to appear throughout the years that followed. O. P. Robinson and Norris B. Brisco introduced some of the new ideas into "The Retailing Series."[27] They conceived organization as a system of relationships between work, people, place, and equipment. They generalized that as the size of an organization increases, the components of the organization change: the functions of merchandising and operations change to merchandising, control, and store operations; to those are next added publicity and personnel. Recognition of that dispelled somehow the belief that the principles of retailing were equally applicable to both small and large stores.

PRINCIPLES OF RETAILING

The afore-mentioned writings were narrow and specialized in comparison to a number of works intended to present the general principles of retailing. Integration of thought has taken place in all areas of marketing thought, and the product has served for the basic orientation of students in the subject.

After Nystrom had published his general treatment of retailing in 1919, the next major integrated statement of thought was published in 1927 by Brisco.[28] Whereas others at that time were concentrating attention on organization, controls, and buying, Brisco undertook to give a general statement to the whole subject of retailing. His was a students' textbook, describing actual store practices and drawing principles or rules therefrom, rather than primarily a book for retailing practitioners. Inasmuch as the 1920s was a decade of the integration of marketing thought in general, some of the topics included were linked to related marketing principles. Originally, Brisco had given little attention even to retail advertising and personnel, and none to store insurance and fashion. Those topics were incorporated in his material in 1935, when thought along those lines had become a more important part of retailing thought.

By 1935 a new turn had been taken in the development of retailing thought. In that year C. W. Barker and I. D. Anderson, published *Principles of Retailing*,[29] the first major book on the subject to be written by men not residing in the East. Theretofore, retailing thought was framed mainly by men in New York and Boston. Actually, Barker and Anderson added to thought little that was new, from the standpoint of either fact or concept. They relied considerably upon secondary sources; among their referred-to sources were such names as Nystrom, McNair, Robinson, Brisco, and Wingate. Their principles of retailing were set forth in the nature of operating generalizations or rules of action, phrased sometimes as "should" and "should not" statements. No concern was shown for the social or economic implications of retailing, and the organization of management activities followed closely the traditional precedents. Such a book indicated that retailing thought had reached a plateau of maturity and was likely to be restated in a number of ways without much variation until new ideas came to the fore.

Further evidence of such maturity was indicated by the appearance of J. Russell Doubman's *Principles of Retail Merchandising,*[30] in 1936. In it the subject of retailing was covered in 206 pages, and its scope was not enlarged in the revision of the book thirteen years later, when it was published as one of the "College Outlines" books. The digest of retailing thought in this publication was comparable to that which had occurred in other literatures at an advanced stage. While one might not regret its brevity, inasmuch as there were other longer texts, it is lamentable that a book with such an opportunity for conveying important information was not of better quality.

By 1941 the study of retailing had been amplified, integrated, specialized, and simplified. There was not much more to say or to add from the same point of view. Fresh ideas were awaited. That is what D. J. Duncan and C. F. Phillips in some measure brought to the study of retailing. Both were established students, teachers, and authors in the field of general marketing before they turned their attention to writing about retailing. It was natural, therefore, that their approach should be broader than those of men whose complete preoccupation had been only with retailing. Consequently, their objectives included giving emphasis to the fact that the present-day retailer needed to know much more than merely how to "operate" a store. They attempted to bring small and medium-size stores into the retailing perspective and to set forth the qualifications requisite for success in a retailing undertaking.

The structure of thought in Duncan and Phillips' *Retailing: Principles and Methods*[31] included the retail field, the store and its organization, functions of buying, selling, operation personnel, control, and retail opportunities. In 1947 they gave greater emphasis to coordination of the store's activities as an obligation of both management and employees. The increasing attention then being given to personnel management caused the treatment of retail personnel problems to be enlarged. Finally, consideration was given to wartime and postwar governmental controls over retailing, and a shift of viewpoint replaced a discussion of store mortality with one of opportunities in retailing. Thus some breadth was added to the traditional analysis of retailing, enlarging the concept of retail management to include more than technical facility – even the orientation of retailing in the marketing system and in the entire business environment.

A final example of mid-century broadening influences in retailing thought is cited in another work, which was the product of post-World War II circumstances. Paul L. Brown and William R. Davidson,[32] rather than merely describing the operating practices of individual stores, conceived retailing as involving interinstitutional relationships – the relationship of stores with other stores, with suppliers, and with the markets to which they sold. They saw it also as comprising numerous activities that required planning, organizing, and control. A knowledge of retailing, they held, was essential not only for those making a career of retail merchandising but also for manufacturers and wholesalers of consumer goods, for suppliers of business goods and services bought by retailers, and for citizens in general. While taking into consideration those various interests in retailing, the authors presumed to present their thought from the view of retail management. They introduced also the concepts of retailing as creating "information utility" and of "value added" by retailing.

RETAILING PROBLEMS

The field of retailing thought has included more than the usual amount of problem materials because of the dependence of retail management upon control statistics, including inventory records, prices, sales, markups, and the like. Many books that were expository in nature included chapter-end problems to illustrate the principles of retailing. Other books of manual type furnished even more elaborate problems involving record forms and accounting procedures. All such problems, so long as they are primarily mathematical, have definite solution answers.

Another type of problem, sometimes distinguished as a "case," may have no single answer, because it is subject to judgment in retail management. It is situations of this type that have been presented in most of the "problems" books[33] prepared by the faculty of the Harvard Business School. Selecting locations for retail businesses, determining the store "image" that should be created, arbitrating cases of adjustment with customers, establishing price lines for merchandise, expansion into warehouse operations – these are illustrative of the types of problems found in these books.

The contributions of the problem literature to retailing thought were not conceptual or substantial but, rather, contributive to the development of managerial insight, rationale, and judgment.

RETAILING THOUGHT IN THE 1950s

The changes occurring in general marketing practice during the 1950s were so marked in the field of retailing as to cause them to be called a "revolution." These changes, in turn, impelled much fresh thinking about retailing in the effort to solve new problems. As a result, several new or revised concepts were introduced in retailing thought, and some important contributions were thus made to marketing theory.

CHANGES IN THE ENVIRONMENT OF RETAILING

The principal changes involved in this area related to the manner in which people choose to live. Following World War II and the reestablishment of our civilian economy, personal incomes continued to increase and a strong propensity to consume was manifested. Suburban housing developments attracted large numbers of people. Homeownership, better furnishings and appliances, and commuting to work became symbols of status in the American community. Living in outlying areas gave rise to a large demand for second cars and therefore for the credit service which they necessitated. Both living and entertaining were kept on an informal or even a casual basis, and various kinds of sporting goods, patio accessories, and casual clothing were sought. Electrical appliances were relied upon to provide assistance formerly supplied by servants, who no longer were needed, or even available in some areas. Convenience came to be defined in terms of accessibility by automobile, parking facilities, one-stop shopping for both related and unrelated items, and freedom of choice.

CHANGES IN STORES AND MERCHANDISING

These trends remolded to some extent our retailing system and resulted in many changes in policies and practices. In general, they forced reconsideration of the objectives of retail establishments, particularly those relating to customers, resources, competitors, employees, stockholders, the community, and the government, as well as to the means by which internal efficiency is achieved in the business operation.

The primary objective of retail businesses to serve their customers and prospective customers in the manner those customers preferred, was clarified by an effort to obtain a better understanding of the nature, extent, and motivation of the "market." Stores followed their customers to the suburbs with branch stores and a variety of other services and selling techniques. They catered to the desire for convenience through preselling, prepackaging, self-service, and impersonal relations. They attempted to group items for convenience in shopping and to employ space in a manner convenient to customers and profitable to themselves.

Changes in the relation of stores to all others than customers took a variety of forms. Contacts were established with new resources, often through new channels. Competitive relations among dealers in large-ticket durables were realigned by the advent of low-cost, low-price dealers, called "discount houses." Renewed attention was given to improving personnel administration and public relations. Stores co-operated with civic authorities in recognition of their responsibility for rehabilitating downtown shopping areas. They shouldered new obligations to the government in the form of new taxes.

The efficiency objectives of stores, or those relating to internal means for improving operations, involved the revamping of organization structures to provide a new alignment of buying and selling functions. Merchandise assortments became more diverse. Mechanical means were introduced to expedite the physical movement of merchandise. Electronic data processing supplanted other methods of record keeping in the larger stores, and central buying tended to increase as multiple-unit stores became the accepted pattern. New methods of pricing were employed to produce *sales* and *profits* rather than the customary *percentages of sales*. And new methods of allocating costs and determining profitability were adopted.

NEW CONCEPTS IN RETAILING THOUGHT

In a period when new thought is forming so rapidly, in different places and among a variety of contributors, it is risky to attribute new concepts to any one source or to attach significance to the initial appearance of an idea in published writings. At best it can be said that during this period certain terms, indicative of ideas in current circulation, are identifiable. Among those most prominent are the following:

1. "Package." In recent years, new meaning has been given to the term "product," defining it as not merely the physical commodity but the package, brand, service, and associations attached thereto. The "product" of a retail store has been recognized as that combination of physical commodities, customer services, convenience of location and layout, personal friendliness, store image, and the like that is characteristic of a particular institution. No two are alike. Collectively, such customer-satisfying characteristics constitute the "package" of values that a store sells. To place emphasis upon certain features competitively is to employ a policy of product differentiation, whereby aspects of similar product packages are emphasized as a means of attracting customers. To alter the components of the product package in consideration of market segment differences is to adopt a policy of market segmentation, whereby a store designs its offering to appeal to distinctive and selective market segments. The different combination of products and services offered by discount houses, in contrast to department stores, illustrates the concept of differing product "packages."

2. Merchandise "Mix." An element of the product package is the assortment or combination of commodities offered. The "mix" implies a blending or variation according to policy, a combination designed to contribute to the achievement of corporate objectives. The mixing of merchandise is a subject of management decision.

3. "Scrambled" Merchandise. An increasing postwar tendency has been the combining in a retail store of items not commonly regarded as part of the natural "line" carried by that type of store. Drugstores have added to their line items of toys, housewares, sporting goods, and the like; grocery stores have added to their line toiletries, pharmaceuticals, and soft goods; department stores have added to their lines nursery plants, garden equipment, and baked goods. The lines of these respective store types have become "scrambled." This has represented a twofold tendency to provide one-stop shopping convenience and to broaden the base of sales volume.

4. "Contribution." Efforts to restate pricing theory, which have been general among marketing students in recent years, have in retailing taken the form of "merchandise management accounting" and of "margin of profit contribution." As it became recognized that undue emphasis had been placed upon profit percentages, even to the neglect of dollar profits earned from operations, the relating of markon for specific products to the costs involved in the handling of those products led to reconsideration of what costs should actually be included. Before, indirect costs, allocated on some basis, were added to the direct costs of handling an item. The newer concept was that indirect costs should not be allocated to departments or items; rather, that income, or sales, *exceeding direct costs* should be regarded as the "contribution" of an item to the general costs of operating the store. While pros and cons of this theory have been argued, it has nevertheless been one of the prominent concepts evolved during the 1950s.

5. "Work Centers." Work centers are centers of functional activity serving various merchandise departments, whose costs have usually been allocated on some basis to departments. Work centers are regarded as units of activity meriting functional analysis and control in their own rights.

6. Organizational Concepts. Since the 1920s department store organization has traditionally followed the four-divisional plan. In recent years, three-divisional organization has been given some attention, and there has been considerable discussion of organizational means of separating buying and selling and of combining in one organizational unit all the promotional and selling activities.

7. *Shifting of Retail Functions.* While certain activities of retailing, such as advertising, credit granting, investment of funds, and providing of parking space, have been regarded as part of the entrepreneurial responsibility of the enterprise, it is increasingly a management decision whether some of such functions should be performed by the enterprise or shifted to functional specialists that have arisen to assume such responsibility. Advertising agencies, commercial banks with retail charge-account plans, and insurance companies offering lease-back arrangements for special purpose real estate investments are typical of the specialists to whom management is shifting some of its activities.

8. *Productivity.* The unequal rates of rise among prices, labor costs, and labor productivity in different industries and trades have accented the fact that worker productivity in retailing has not increased comparably to that elsewhere. Thus the very concept of productivity has impelled consideration of means whereby the output or input in retailing may be increased.

RETAILING THOUGHT SINCE 1960

The retailing literature was exceptionally representative of the changes occurring in marketing thought during the decade of the 1960s. While retailers coped with new environmental conditions which theorists sought to incorporate in their analyses of retailing, academics rose at the challenge of curriculum criticism to preserve the subject of retailing in the business school offering. "Retailing" was one of the fields of study designated by Gordon and Howell as unworthy of college status in the form which it existed in 1959. Fortunately for the field, there were scholars equal to the challenge, and developments in the general study of marketing which they could use to good advantage.

STANDARD TEXTS UPDATED

One group of literature of the 1960s consisted of revisions of well-established general works on retailing, as those by Wingate (1933), Richart (1937), Duncan (1941), Davidson (1952), McGregor (1953), and Jones (1957). The initial works of all of them had appeared while retailing was conceived as store operation, and management as the manipulation of certain internal economic variables. It was this interpretation of retailing, and the level of intelligence upon which it was presented, to which critics took exception. Consequently, their authors, most of whose frames of reference were cast in traditional molds of marketing thought, endeavored to adapt their texts to new demands and changed circumstances. These adaptations, however, were largely within the context of familiar economic and marketing concepts.

Duncan's 8th edition in 1972[34] listed such contemporary problems as inflation, curtailed buying power, uncertainty in fashion merchandising, and changes in consumer location, tastes, and shopping patterns, age-distribution, legislation, and electronic data processing. These circumstances imposed upon management reappraisal of plans, more stringent buying policies, reevaluation of suppliers, scrutiny of merchandise classifications, attention to stock shortages, control of the drain on operating revenue, and reappraisal of management and personnel. The revision consisted of incorporating discussion of these management problems and practices within the conventional framework dealing mainly with the store, organization, merchandise management, sales promotion, and accounting control.

Davidson and Doody[35] broadened their concept of retailing to include not only retailing done in retail stores but also by producers and wholesalers, and they gave greater emphasis to the relations of retail store managers with others in the distributive channel. This approach reflected the increasingly popular systems concept, and orientation of retailing in the larger context of marketing. The structure of their thought, however, remained conventional.

RETAILING FOLKLORE

From time to time, studies of personal experiences in retailing have been published, documenting the great name developments in the field, even as biographies of manufacturer barons have been in the field of production. Two such works appeared during the 1960s, by Mahony and by Reilly[36]. The latter narrated notable events in the lives and careers of 35 founders of leading department stores. The biographies were intended to show the importance, romance, and glamour of retailing. They detailed the backgrounds of the men, their character, and philosophies which led to success in merchandising, to mergers, and to attainment of a large volume of sales. All fields of marketing have their personal side, and a study of important practitioners illustrates ways in which theory — implicit or explicit — has been employed to achieve business objectives.

SPECIALIZED TECHNICAL STUDIES

Throughout the years, a variety of special studies of retailing have appeared, indicating to some extent the awareness of new developments and expressing the state of analytical concepts and techniques applied to retailing. From earliest years such studies have pertained to fashion merchandising, retail gravitation, trends toward statistical "mediocrity" in business, chain store retailing, standard ratios, and shopping centers. Since 1960, additional notable studies have pertained to careers for women in retailing, mass merchandising, mathematics of retailing, retail decentralization, merchandising decision models, multinational retailing, and retailing in other countries. Such studies are valuable additions to marketing thought because of both the factual information which they provide and the new theoretical elements which they contain.

One of the oldest empirical studies of a scientific nature made by marketing analysts is that designated "Reilly's Law of Retail Gravitation" (1929). Supplemented by Converse's work, Reilly's findings postulated a tendency of trade to gravitate toward metropolitan centers, proportionately to the distance involved. E.P. Cox and Erickson,[37] in 1967, attempting to extend the earlier works, observed a reverse tendency toward retail decentralization. Their analysis and reasoning as to the causes of this phenomenon constitute the body of their book.

Dalrymple[38] likewise applied fresh techniques to gain light on an old problem, namely, the effect upon profit of the following merchandising decision variables: sales, turnover, markup, markdown, contribution return, and price. By the application of methods for ascertaining coefficients of correlation, coefficients of determination, and stepwise regression, he sought to evaluate hypotheses developed in previous studies and to demonstrate further the superiority of sound reasoning over intuition and ill-formulated rules for optimizing the mix of merchandising control factors and maximizing the profits of individual departments. The study illustrates the increasing regard for control factors as "variables" and of quantitative techniques for testing the generalizations implicit in the relationships of variables.

Still another advance in retailing thought is represented by *Public Policy and Retailing* by Boddewyn and Hollander.[38] Employing concepts of variable factors and of environmental constraints, it constitutes a study in comparative retailing. As such, it stands on a level of thought above the merely descriptive studies of retailing in a few other countries which have been made. The book consists of articles on retailing in 20 countries, written largely by nationals of those countries. Its conceptual framework includes categories — actors, structures, processes, and functions — in terms of which retailing in each country is analyzed. These are variables the particular circumstances of which are deemed accountable for differences in retailing around the world. The authors had observed that most countries had sets of policies toward retailing but that they generally disclaimed that they had *a* policy. The "sets of policies" were observable in laws specifically regulating retailing during the past 40 years. The theoretical significance of this book lies in its orientation of retailing in its larger social environment, in its use of a common conceptual framework for analysis in dissimilar situations, and in its exploration of the interface between government policy and retailing.

BROADER VIEWS OF RETAILING

Hollander's eminence as a contributor to retailing thought is established not only by his collaboration with Duncan and Phillips in their management text and by his comparative analyses mentioned above, but also by his early representation of retailing from a social and behavioral point of view. This he undertook to do in 1959 in his *Explorations in Retailing*.[39]

The innovativeness of his approach can be appreciated in view of the fact that at that time the social and behavioral concept of marketing in general was relatively new. As has often been the case, when a new viewpoint was being explored, it was first expressed in a book of Readings rather than in an integrated text. Throughout the decade there were also other Readings, reflecting the changing times and management problems, but none attained the level of theorization of Hollander's. He particularly sought articles by academics rather than by businessmen, for the latter, he said, *used* theory but the former more often *formulated* theory and took pains to make explicit the theoretical framework underlying their analyses. Hollander sought to bring into clearer focus even the theory which was unexpressed or implicit. Consequently, by careful selection of articles which were *conceptually relevant* to the subject, he achieved a coherence more common to integrated texts than to Readings. Through them the reader views retailing in the context of changing economic environment; changing social values, costs, and gains; new social relationships among competitors and between retailers and their suppliers and labor; and in the context of operations theories about costs and margins, accounting, research, operations research, merchandising research, spatial and locational research, and organizational planning.

A decade later, Dalrymple, stating that he was building upon Hollander's

Explorations in Retailing, published *Retailing – an Economic View.*[40] Especially reacting to the Gordon-Howell criticism, he approached retailing from an economic analysis rather than from the traditional descriptive treatment, which he termed "managerial folklore." Specifically noting that he gave little attention to traditional personal selling, retail advertising, employee compensation, store layout, merchandise budgets, buying, and retail arithmetic, he intended his book as broad background material for readers who would later have on-the-job training, for manufacturers as well as retailers, and for students who had had prior courses in economics and marketing. He eschewed giving specific recommendations for operational techniques, but rather developed his thesis from the general to the specific, discussing the retail enterprise and its problems in an overview of retailing which showed the relation of the retail sector to the economy as a whole.

Classifiable either as "retailing" or as "international" literature, Hollander's *Multinational Retailing*[42] is a contribution to both. As a study of retailing, it reflects the addition to thought which arises from changing practice, rather than from the introduction of new concepts. It is an extensive study of institutional structure showing the channels of primary and auxiliary organizations engaged in commodities which ultimate in retail trade. The book is thus in contrast to most other international marketing books, which deal with wholesaling, either of wholesalers or producers. The book, however, is essentially descriptive, classifying institutions and identifying management variables which are a dependent function of differing social and economic conditions in the developed and developing countries into which the multinational retailing activities have been extended. While not conceptually innovative, the book is a substantive addition to the retailing literature and an example of management strategy adapted to the multinational corporation.

CONTRIBUTIONS OF RETAILING LITERATURE TO MARKETING THOUGHT

Enrichment of marketing thought has come through retailing thought in a number of ways:

1. It has contributed a variety of *concepts of retailing* itself, including the following:

As a distinct economic and business function.
As an institution adaptive to social and economic change.
As an internal management function.
As a stage in the distributive process.
As a level in the distributive channel.
As a service in the role of purchasing agent for consumers.
As an influence upon the standard of living.
As a means of supplying a standard of living.
As a means of creating additional value for a product.
As a distinct type of distributive organization.
As a social force.

2. It has brought to marketing thought, and therefore to the marketing vocabulary and terminology, many more or less *technical concepts,* which have become useful tools in understanding retailing and in communicating thoughts about it:

Adjustment policy	Markon	Reductions
Balance assortments	Markup	Retail method of inventory
Basic stock	Merchandise budget	Scrambled merchandising
Comparison shopping	Merchandising	Shopping center
Expense center accounting	Model stock	Shortage
Fad	Odd pricing	Size selection
Fashion	100 per cent location	Solo store
Fashion coordination	Open to buy	Stock balance
Fashion cycle	Overage	Stock control
Full line	Parasite store	Stock depth
Impulse goods	Percentage lease	Stock turnover
Maintained markup	Preretailing	String street
Markdown	Price line	Style
	Production unit accounting	Suburban store
	Push money	Variety
	Quota bonus	Visual front

3. It has clarified the concept of the *institutional structure* of marketing, whereby retailing establishments are distinguished from wholesaling establishments, and thereby various types of retailing institutions are designated and defined. Retail stores are recognized as a distinct and productive type of business institution.

4. It has shown the *adaptive nature* of the retailing portion of the marketing institution, whereby in response to social and economic changes new establishments, new techniques, and new problems evolve. All this in turn requires the development of managerial talent competent to make the necessary institutional changes and to keep abreast of the changing environment.

5. It has produced a thoroughly researched body of *techniques* for organization and operation of retailing establishments. Many of these techniques are as applicable to other types of business establishments as to retailing organizations.

6. It has evolved a concept of retailing as not merely an internal management function but rather as a stage in the distributive process, as a part of the economic function of society, as a level or unit in the distributive channel, or as a service in the role of purchasing agent for the consumer.

7. It has emphasized the importance of basing marketing activity upon the consumers' wants and needs and has shown the folly of the philosophy that unwanted fashions and items can be forced upon the market.

8. It has shown the reciprocal influences between society and the retailing structure in the creation of a standard of living and the supplying of that standard of living. What consumers want, retailers attempt to supply. On the other hand, retailers are constantly bringing to consumers' attention available items and services that they might consume with pleasure and profit.

9. It has introduced scientific methods of gathering and using information by managers, as in the data provided by retail methods of accounting and stock records.

10. It has shown the vocational opportunities in selling *at retail* on different levels of distribution.

11. It has developed marketing thought as operating rules of action, telling not only how to do it but explaining the independent variables upon which the rules are based. An important part of the body of marketing thought is its knowledge of how to perform, and the retailing literature has made a major contribution to this knowledge.

12. It has raised some ethical considerations as to the social obligations of not only retailing establishments but all marketing institutions.

13. It has contributed to the clarification of marketing terminology, particularly in the area of retailing.

14. It has produced a concept of the "new retailing" − the practice of marketing based upon research and scientific application of principles of management.

15. It has established centers of leadership and authority in the study of marketing, although in recent years important contributions to retailing thought are being made in several parts of the country.

16. It has shown, although too briefly, the comparative nature of retailing in different countries.

17. It has emphasized − almost overemphasized − the viewpoint of the merchant in the consideration of retailing, although in recent years even this viewpoint is broadening to the point that it embraces more than merely personal interests.

18. It has included some adaptation of the findings of psychologists, sociologists, and political scientists in the analysis and interpretation of marketing.

ENDNOTES

[1] Paul H. Nystrom, *The Economics of Retailing* (New York: Ronald Press Co., 1915); 2d ed., 1919; 3d ed.; 1930, Vols. 1 and 2; rev. ed., 1932, Vol. 2 only; 4th ed., 1937; as *Retail Store Operation.*

[2] Paul H. Nystrom, *Retail Selling and Store Management* (New York: D. Appleton − Century Co., Inc., 1913); republished, 1917, as *Retail Store Management.*

[3] Paul H. Nystrom, *Economics of Fashion* (New York: Ronald Press Co., 1928).

[4] Paul H. Nystrom, *Economic Principles of Consumption* (New York: Ronald Press Co., 1929, 1931).

[5] Paul H. Nystrom, *Retail Store Operation* (New York: Ronald Press Co., 1937), pp. 618-20.

[6] Stated in correspondence with the author, 1940. See Appendix A.

[7] Paul H. Nystrom, *Fashion Merchandising* (New York: Ronald Press Co., 1932).

[8] Op. Cit., pp. 16-17.

[9] W. W. Charters, ed., *"Merchandise Manuals for Retail Salespeople"* (New York: A. W. Shaw Co., 1924-25.)

[10] John W. Wingate, *Manual of Retail Terms* (New York: Prentice-Hall, Inc., 1931).

[11] Lew Hahn and Percival White, ed., *The Merchant's Manual* (New York: McGraw-Hill Book Co., Inc., 1924).

[12] Op. Cit., p. vii.

[13] James L. Fri, *The Buyer's Manual* (New York: National Retail Dry Goods Association, 1930; 2d ed., 1937; 3d ed., 1957).

[14] Norris A. Brisco and John W. Wingate, *Retail Buying* (New York: Prentice-Hall, Inc., 1925), and Wingate and Brisco, *Buying for Retail Stores* (New York: Prentice-Hall, Inc., 1937; 2d ed., 1946; 3d ed., 1953, by Wingate alone; rev. ed., with J. S. Freedlander, 1963).

[15] Ruth Leigh, *Elements of Retailing* (New York: D. Appleton − Century Co., Inc., 1936); Paul H. Nystrom, *Elements of Retail Selling* (New York: Ronald Press Co., 1936); Harold H. Maynard, K. Dameron, and C. J. Seigler, *Retail Marketing and Merchandising*

110

(New York: Ginn & Co., 1938); R. G. Walters and E. J. Rowse, *Fundamentals of Retail Selling* (Cincinnati: South-Western Publishing Co., 1931; 2d ed., 1938; 4th ed., 1951, as *Retail Merchandising;* 5th ed., 1957 by Wingate and J. D. Weiner).

[16]Dwight E. Beebe, *Retail Credits and Collections: Modern Principles and Practices* (New York: Harper & Bros., 1919); Frederick W. Walter, *The Retail Charge Account* (New York: Ronald Press Co., 1922); John T. Bartlett and Charles M. Reed, *Retail Credit Practice* (New York: Harper & Bros., 1928); Norris A. Brisco, *Retail Credit Procedure* (New York: Prentice-Hall, Inc., 1929).

[17]E. A. Filene, *More Profits from Merchandising* (New York: A. W. Shaw Co., 1925).

[18]James L. Fri, *Retail Merchandising, Planning, and Control* (New York: Prentice-Hall, Inc., 1925).

[19]Malcolm P. McNair, *The Retail Method of Inventory* (Chicago: A. W. Shaw Co., 1925).

[20]H. B. Wess *Merchandise Control* (New York: Dry Goods Economist, 1925).

[21]E. A. Filene, *The Model Stock Plan* (New York: McGraw-Hill Book Co., Inc., 1930).

[22]John Wingate, E. O. Schaller, and I. Goldenthal, *Problems in Retail Merchandising* (New York: Prentice-Hall, Inc., 1931); 2d ed., 1937; 3d ed., 1944; 4th ed., 1952; 5th ed., 1961; 6th ed., 1973).

[23]C. K. Lyans and Norris A. Brisco, *Retail Accounting* (New York: Prentice-Hall, Inc. 1934).

[24]Paul M. Mazur, *Principles of Organization Applied to Modern Retailing,* (New York: Harper & Bros., 1927).

[25]Harold B. Wess, *Profit Principles of Retailing* (New York: McGraw-Hill Book Co., Inc. 1931).

[26]Op. Cit., pp. 1-3.

[27]O. P. Robinson and Norris B. Brisco, *Retail Store Organization and Management* (New York: Prentice-Hall, Inc., 1938; rev. ed., 1949, as *Store Organization and Operation;* 2d ed., 1957, by O. P. Robinson, J. G. Robinson, M. P. Matthews. O. P. Robinson, *Retail Personnel Relations* (New York: Prentice-Hall, Inc., 1940).

[28]Norris A. Brisco, *Principles of Retailing* (New York: Prentice-Hall, Inc., 1927; 2d ed., 1935, as *Retailing;* 3d ed., 1947, by Norris B. Brisco).

[29]C. W. Barker and I. D. Anderson, *Principles of Retailing* (New York: McGraw-Hill Book Co., Inc., 1935; 2d ed., 1941; 3d ed., 1956, with J. D. Butterworth).

[30]J. Russell Doubman, *Principles of Retail Merchandizing* (New York: Longmans, Green & Co., 1936); rev. ed. as *Retail Merchandising: Principles and Practice* (New York: Littlefield, Adams, 1949).

[31]D. J. Duncan and C. F. Phillips, *Retailing: Principles and Methods* (Chicago: Richard D. Irwin, Inc., 1941; 2d ed., 1947; 3d ed., 1951; 4th ed., 1955; 5th ed., 1959; 6th ed., 1964; 7th ed., 1967; 8th ed., 1972 with S. C. Hollander, as *Modern Retailing Management – Basic Concepts and Practices).*

[32]Paul L. Brown and William R. Davidson, *Retailing Principles and Practices* (New York: Ronald Press Co., 1952; 2d ed., 1960, as *Retailing Management).*

[33]D. K. David, *Retail Store Management Problems* (Chicago: A. W. Shaw Co., 1922); D. K. David and M. P. McNair, *Problems in Retailing* (Chicago: A. W. Shaw Co., 1926); M. P. McNair and C. I. Gregg, *Problems in Retail Distribution* (New York: McGraw-Hill Book Co., 1930); and *Problems in Retail Store Management* (New York: McGraw-Hill Book Co., Inc., 1931); M. P. McNair, C. I. Gragg, and S. F. Teele, *Problems in Retailing* (New York: McGraw-Hill Book Co., Inc., 1937).

[34]D. J. Duncan, C. F. Phillips, and S. C. Hollander, *Modern Retailing Management – Basic Concepts and Practices* (Homewood, Ill.: Richard D. Irwin, Inc., 1972).

[35]W. R. Davidson and A. F. Doody, *Retailing Management* (N.Y.: Ronald Press Co., 3d ed., 1966).

[36]T. Mahoney, *The Great Merchants* (New York: Harper & Bros., 1966). Philip J. Reilly, *Old Masters of Retailing* (New York: Fairchild Publications, 1966).

[37]Eli P. Cox and L. G. Erickson, *Retail Decentralization* (East Lansing: Bureau of Business and Economic Research, Michigan State University, 1967).

[38]D. J. Dalrymple, *Merchandising Decision Models for Department Stores* (East Lansing, Michigan: Bureau of Business and Administration Research, Michigan State University, 1966).

[39]Jean J. Boddewyn and S. C. Hollander (eds.), *Public Policy and Retailing* (Lexington, Mass.: Lexington Books, 1972).

[40] S. C. Hollander, (ed.), *Explorations in Retailing* (East Lansing, Bureau of Business and Economic Research, Michigan State University, 1959).

[41] D. J. Dalrymple, *Retailing – an Economic View* (New York: Free Press, 1969).

[42] Stanley C. Hollander, *Multinational Retailing* (East Lansing: Michigan State University International Business and Economic Studies, 1970).

Of the several branches of the marketing literature, that dealing with wholesaling has two distinctive characteristics. First, it was comparatively late in being developed. Second, it consists of one of the smallest bibliographies in the marketing field.

CONDITIONS INDUCING THE STUDY OF WHOLESALING

An objective in the study of marketing in general and of its specialized areas in particular was to solve business problems that had become more acute around the beginning of the twentieth century. Thus it was expected that a knowledge of the principles of advertising or credit and the introduction of research into retail management would increase the efficiency and effectiveness of these undertakings. That objective, however, did not stimulate the study of wholesaling. In fact, very little attention was given to this subject until 1920, by which time an extensive body of literature had been developed in every other field of marketing thought and the treatment of marketing in general had reached a stage of some integration.

Rather than thinking that increased knowledge about wholesale operations would increase efficiency, it was thought that it would result in the elimination of the wholesaler, and with him also the wholesaling functions, for of all middlemen considered to be parasitic the wholesaler was the most accused. Since the beginning of the century, criticism made of "the middleman" rested most heavily on the wholesaler, and considered opinion was that he was passing out of the picture. Consequently, this was no field in which to undertake scientific research, and interest in studying wholesaling was discouraged.

Apart from that negative outlook, study of wholesaling was impeded also by a lack of perception of its essential character. The terms "wholesaling" and "retailing" were in common use, but to no one's vision was there an appreciable or significant difference between those two forms of marketing activity. Both were parts of marketing. Both were involved in the distribution of goods. Both were concerned with institutional management. That seemed to be reason enough for regarding them as a homogeneous activity.

The import of the distinction between wholesaling and retailing dawned slowly. Its rise was an interesting moment in the enlightenment of marketing thought. It required vision of a threefold distinction that was not apparent in common thought:

1. *Between Wholesalers and Retailers.* That distinction between institutions was commonly made.
2. *Between Wholesaling and Retailing.* As the concept of a function is more intangible than a visible institution, those generic activities were

not so widely identified. Wholesaling and retailing meant the specific activity of wholesalers and retailers, respectively, and were not thought of as abstractions.

3. *Between Wholesaling and Wholesalers, and between Retailing and Retailers.* Separation of a function from the institution commonly identified with that function is still more difficult, but it was essential to the evolution of wholesaling and marketing thought.

In 1920 those distinctions were not scientifically made, and initial perception of them met with vigorous and continuing resistance. Whereas other fields being written about in the marketing literature at that time could be described, analyzed, and theorized, wholesaling, if it was to be a field of investigation, had to begin as a new and controversial conception. It is little wonder that the study of wholesaling attracted so few people and that the initiator of this new undertaking should have had to bear the burden of carrying the conception through to its logical implications. Such were the circumstances when in 1919 Theodore N. Beckman undertook the study of wholesaling per se.

The environment in which crystallization of these concepts occurred was one in which the position of the wholesaler was increasingly criticized but in which marketing in general was becoming better understood. It was that period following World War I in which business was expanding, agriculture increasing, and new forms of retailing gained prominence. Nystrom's *The Economics of Retailing* was already in its second edition, and "The Retailing Series" of New York University had been started. Numerous specialized books in retailing had been published, and an integration of the field had been achieved by several authors. Writings on credit were in a similar stage, the books of Prendergast, Hagerty, Ettinger and Golieb, and others being available. Progress had been made even in the more general statement of marketing by Shaw, Weld, Cherington, Converse, Duncan, and Clark. In that environment of business change and developing thought the conception of wholesaling was born.

INITIAL CONCEPTION OF WHOLESALING

Nystrom, it will be recalled, introduced his study of retailing with an extensive history of the development of retailing. It was essentially descriptive. Beckman, on the other hand, in the preparation of his book on wholesaling,[1] took a more analytical approach. His intention being to show the stability of the wholesaler's position in distribution, he presented the concept of *wholesaling* as an *institution* and did not deal merely with the wholesaling institutions or establishments. That was a distinctive characteristic of his first book and one of its contributions to marketing thought. The unstructured state of thought about wholesaling at that time, however, is evident in the fact that the thirty-three topics discussed in as many chapters of the first edition of his book were ungrouped. Nevertheless, five chapters dealt with the concepts of wholesaling functions and institutions; the remaining chapters were concerned with managerial problems and practices.

Despite the fact that wholesalers were classed as a group and a general area of practice was referred to as wholesaling, no real distinction was made between wholesaling and wholesaler. Wholesaling was not defined — it could not have been, for the essential scope and character of that activity was not then perceived. Neither did the concept of "circumvention" exist although factors affecting the use of wholesalers were recognized, and the efforts of producers to distribute without the aid of wholesalers were discussed. Nor was there apparent a distinction between "merchant" and "functional" middlemen. Also, the aggregate of wholesale establishments was not regarded as a wholesaling "system," and the only classification of wholesalers was on the basis of lines handled.

Notwithstanding that conceptual immaturity, the treatment given wholesalers and wholesaling was important. It was the precedent for the conceptualization of types of wholesaling establishments and for discussion of them in the subsequent literature on wholesaling. The retailing literature, by contrast, did not usually embrace all forms of retailing establishments but was devoted to the problems and practices of the larger stores, particularly department stores. The retailing literature dealt almost wholly with retail managerial functions. The structure of the retailing system was treated in the general marketing books more than in those on retailing.

Wholesale management thought at the time of Beckman's first writing was concerned with location, layout, organization, pricing, planning, buying, receiving, stock control, administration, personnel, and credit. Topically, those functions resembled ones in retailing, but in practice their differences were marked. A few management problems that were also discussed found no parallel at that time in the retailing thought: private brands, exclusive representation, handling and filling of orders, traffic management, and packing, shipping, and billing.

WHOLESALING IN TRANSITION

During the 1930s, many changes in wholesaling practice and thought came about. The state of flux in wholesaling resulting from changes occurring both in retailing and production was not diminished. On the contrary, it was augmented by the further development of chains, voluntary chains, department-store branches, increased scale of manufacturing, and the use of manufacturers' sales branches. Extensive inquiry had also been made into the nature of wholesaling in numerous surveys and censuses of distribution. Beckman has been a principal participant with the Bureau of the Census in the development of concepts of wholesaling and wholesaling establishments, which were enumerated in the censuses. Scientific investigation of wholesaling, however, continued to be neglected. Only a handful of books had been published within the decade, and none treated the subject with the conceptual breadth and incisiveness needed for the advancement of wholesaling thought beyond the mere techniques of management. At the same time, increasing competition and government regulation of wholesaling made more urgent the clarification of essential concepts.

Beckman's revised exposition of wholesaling was made in collaboration with Nathanael H. Engle, expert in marketing with the Bureau of the Census, later assistant director of the Bureau of Foreign and Domestic Commerce. By 1937 it was more clearly evident that the activity of wholesaling was not confined to wholesalers and that the body of wholesaling thought was intended to serve not only wholesalers but also manufacturers, retailers, and industrial consumers with buying problems. Knowledge of wholesaling was vital for the effective conduct of business in general. Wholesaling was a segment of the modern business structure, and abundant statistical evidence had come to support this view.

As reflected in this 1937 publication, thought in wholesaling was beginning to be oriented to other social disciplines, history and economics, particularly. The incidence of wholesaling in ancient societies, as well as in some other contemporary cultures, was described, and its current economic role was discussed in a macro analysis. Concepts of wholesaling held by economists were cited. Wholesaling was related to its socioeconomic environment, especially as related to the political philosophy expressed through legislation that had then been enacted. New management practices had also developed and continued to form part of the body of wholesaling thought.

Since World War II wholesaling thought has been further refined. The concept of wholesaling has been elaborated, both in theory and in light of legislative developments often culminating in United States Supreme Court decisions. Processes of managerial decision making have been applied to wholesale operations. The orientation of the wholesaling institution and its organic structure as a phenomenon of the American economy have been detailed. The concept of "value added" by wholesaling has been introduced. Also discussed has been the philosophy of competition and enterprise that underlies numerous legislative and administrative actions of the government and that permeates the environment in which wholesaling — commonly regarded as "trade," in connection with "trade regulation" — operates.

OTHER WORKS ON WHOLESALING

While the Beckman books are not the sole works on wholesaling, they are the principal ones, and he has treated the subject as no other author has. Other writers have dealt primarily with the wholesaling of certain products, such as food or industrial goods, or they have dealt mainly with problems of cost analysis and control through accounting techniques. Illustrative of the former are works on the wholesale marketing of live poultry, fruits and vegetables, groceries, or drugs. Typical also are four books on industrial marketing by J. H. Frederick,[2] R. F. Elder,[3] B. Lester,[4] and V. D. Reed,[5] all appearing in the mid-1930s. The commodity approach to this subject obviously does not lend itself to consideration of the broadest principles of wholesaling; rather, it gives emphasis to techniques of performance. Even those on industrial distribution were narrow, in the sense that they corresponded somewhat to the treatment of distribution given in the retailing literature. Not enough new factual or conceptual material was included in them to make an important or lasting impression upon marketing thought.

WHOLESALING THOUGHT IN THE 1950s

Throughout the 1950s, publications on wholesaling seemed to reach the end of an era. A few books and monographs appeared dealing with wholesaling either in an area or in relation to the distribution of a type of goods. In 1959, Beckman updated his book with the assistance of Buzzell, and this was the last time that any then existing works on wholesaling were revised.

Beckman's revision purported to reflect the "dynamic changes" in wholesaling, the quickening tempo, and the growing awareness of need for professionalization of management in wholesaling. Having always presented both broad and operational views of wholesaling, he continued to do so, concepts of a descriptive, academic, or economic nature being used, with management implications. Economic, social, and legal environmental factors were shown not merely as molding the wholesaling system but as factors to which management must give heed in doing a first-rate job. Court decisions relevant to concepts and classifications of wholesale establishments were reviewed from a management viewpoint rather than merely from an academic standpoint.

Three new concepts were introduced in the revision: productivity and efficiency in wholesaling, and value added by wholesaling. These represented the continuing effort to deal with the age-old question of the contribution made by operators on the wholesale level. "Productivity" was defined as a ratio of output to input of economic resources in a business operation, during a given period of time; "efficiency," as the comparison of productivity with a supposedly ideal relationship of output and input. The concept of "value added" represented an attempt to reduce to quantitative terms, somewhat as in measures of "value added by manufacturing," the contribution of wholesaling to products as they pass through the wholesaling system.

At about the same time, *Industrial Marketing* was published by Alexander, Cross, and Cunningham.[6] Although the work is unique in several respects, it did not constitute any appreciable addition to wholesaling thought. It represented an effort to explain the marketing of industrial goods from the standpoint of the manufacturers of such products. It was also an expression of management viewpoint rather than a macro interpretation of wholesale marketing. It differed from general marketing treatises concerned predominantly with the marketing of consumer goods. It differed also from usual analyses of "wholesaling" which, in addition to including a systemic analysis, take the managerial viewpoint of distributive organizations rather than that of the manufacturers.

Industrial Marketing is mainly an application of existing thought structure to a specialized field of marketing. It does not deal with the whole subject of wholesaling or of marketing. It does illustrate the mid-century recognition of the growing importance of manufacturers' marketing decisions and of the managerial considerations that underlie them.

WHOLESALING THOUGHT SINCE 1960

With the beginning of the new decade, an era in the writing of wholesaling began, whose roots were already established, but whose development gave new direction to the field. One incentive for this, as for the renaissance in fields already discussed, was the criticism of the low level upon which texts and curricula dealt with wholesaling. That a turnabout took place is evident even statistically in the fact that whereas from 1920 to 1960 only twenty-four book titles were listed in the bibliography, from 1960 to 1972 twenty-two listings were included. The number of books published under some titles is as follows:

Wholesaling operations and management	6
Industrial goods distribution	5
Selling through wholesalers	3
Wholesaling in the marketing process	2
Wholesaling in other countries	2
Wholesaling of agricultural products	2

Several authors specifically commented on the paucity of writings on wholesaling at that time, and noted that little had been written about marketing industrial goods, in contrast to the marketing of consumer goods. As in the other areas, new developments called for explanation. Whereas until the 1930s wholesalers had been essentially warehouses, thus contributing to circumvention of merchant wholesalers by manufacturers, by 1960 changes had taken place which preserved this middleman. Among these changes were improved warehousing techniques, new merchandise handling procedures, better methods of internal operation, and replacement of "order taking" with more aggressive sales promotion.

Whereas most earlier books dealt with management of individual wholesale establishments, Warshaw[7] explored the means whereby manufacturers might, through reassessment of their own policies, achieve more cooperation from wholesalers and thus better balance their direct and indirect channels of distribution. Such cooperation, however, representing a mutually agreeable division of the distribution task, was an economic rather than a social concept of cooperation. Wholesalers were recognized to have a limited economic role, which should be used to the best advantage by manufacturers. Thus a small step was taken in the direction of the systems concept which was to be given fuller exposition by other writers.

A more radical departure from the traditional treatment of wholesaling was that of Revzan in *Wholesaling in Marketing Organization*[8] published in 1961. Revzan regarded Beckman to be the only one who covered the entire field of wholesaling. He proposed to do the same, but in a different way, namely, by a holistic approach, which had characterized his writing with Duddy even in 1947. Revzan intended to emphasize the managerial implications of this "whole" analysis.

Before setting forth his own concept of wholesaling, he cited those of some other writers:

The Beckman-Engle concepts of wholesaling as narrow, middle, and broad views of wholesaling.

The Fred E. Clark concepts of concentration, equalization, and dispersion.

The Wroe Alderson concepts of sorting out, accumulating, allocating, and assorting.

The Vaile-Grether-Cox concepts of collecting, sorting, and dispersing.

Revzan undertook also to explain the operation of the wholesaling system through the "funnel concept," whereby the marketing medium was likened to a series of composite and component funnels through which merchandise flows at rates dependent upon the following variables: the type of product, the physical volume of commodity flow, the monetary value of the physical flows, variations in types of middlemen found in the channels, varieties and levels of users, number of assortment combinations in which the product appears, and geographical variations in commodity flows, channel patterns, and types of users. Along with this were introduced also the concepts of "linkages," or the connections and relations among middlemen and other businessmen, and "blockages," or obstructions to the formation of linkages.

The linkage of middlemen in common or uncommon groups determines the orthodoxy or unorthodoxy of the channels formed. Much emphasis was given to channels by Revzan, for he saw them as the ground on which abstract concepts of competition are worked out and for the control of which manufacturers struggle. The implications of those concepts are elaborated throughout the remainder of his treatment of the subject.

Both Beckman and Revzan dealt with new developments in internal management. Attention was given to establishing the wholesale enterprise and financing it, to merchandising strategies, to control of costs and profits, and to salient features of legislation pertaining mainly to wholesaling activity.

As shown in the preceding tabulation, increased attention was given to the marketing of industrial goods in the 1960s. Several reasons for this were given. Whereas only *part* of the distribution of ultimate consumer goods involves the wholesaling process, *all* of the distribution of nonultimate consumer goods falls to the wholesaling system. Moreover, before the second World War marketing as a management function was not much developed in manufacturers of industrial goods. Marketing techniques were widely applied in the consumer goods field before in industrial goods. Marketing was overshadowed by production in the industrial goods field, and the very technical nature of those goods did not attract distribution studies. Nevertheless, the need for knowledge gave rise to courses in industrial marketing at a number of schools, including the Harvard Business School, where Corey[9] prepared a book of cases on the subject.

Throughout the decade, a variety of studies attempted to throw more light upon the process of wholesaling. One made by Diamond[10], who studied the gross margins provided to industrial distributors by manufacturers in their pricing policies, suggested the amount and value of services performed by that middleman for the manufacturer. Revzan also cast additional light upon the division of the task in the channel of distribution in an analysis of wholesale/retail sales ratios in various lines of goods.[11] Underlying his study was a concept of the marketing system as subdivided into wholesaling and retailing sectors between which the distributive task is allocated. The respective sales of each sector were given as evidence of this. Revzan studied the geographical patterns of the ratios, and the influences of products and locations upon the division of the task between the sectors. His approach was holistic, as it was in his book published ten years earlier. One value of the book is in its explaining the multiplicity of systems in distribution, which was the objective of much of the literature of the decade.

Of the entirely different character in the wholesaling literature was *Comparative Marketing: Wholesaling in Fifteen Countries,* edited by Bartels in 1963[12]. Whereas Beckman and Engle had presented *descriptions* of wholesaling in a few countries, this comparative work undertook to *analyze* a nation's wholesaling in terms of a conceptual framework of social environment. Thus showing wholesaling in *different circumstances* through the lens of a given frame of reference, some of the basic patterns of the role of wholesaling in marketing and in economic development became apparent. The changing relations of direct and indirect channels and the decline and restoration of merchant wholesalers were seen to be a phenomenon characteristic of stages of economic change, and not merely a product of capricious management strategy. The process called "wholesaling," however it may be conceived, is inherent in all forms and types of distribution, and under a variety of political and social systems. This was an innovative comparative study in wholesaling and a contribution along these lines to the development of marketing thought in general.

Whereas the comparative analysis of the Bartels book related the wholesaling system to spatially different environments at a given time, Bucklin in *Competition and Evolution in the Distributive Trades,*[13] similarly presented the environmental influences upon wholesaling systems in a given place at different times. Both studies make clear that neither time nor place alone, but rather the prevailing economic and social circumstances, are the determinants of distributive systems. Bucklin's book is not primarily a study of wholesaling *per se,* but rather of both the retailing and wholesaling sectors of the distributive trades. Nevertheless, his explication of the "metamorphosis" of wholesaling under the influence of time and change, and the attendant effects of this upon the distributive structure and upon the interaction of its component members, is a definite addition to wholesaling thought, as well as to the development of marketing thought in general.

CONTRIBUTIONS OF WHOLESALING LITERATURE TO MARKETING THOUGHT

Many contributions to marketing thought that have been made through the wholesaling literature are not always associated with this source because they have become accepted and incorporated in the body of marketing thought as presented in the general writings. So strong remains even yet the impression that wholesaling is the activity of wholesalers that students of marketing bypass the wholesaling literature on the presumption that it is analogous to the retailing literature, with which more people are familiar. The fact remains, nevertheless, that to the writings on wholesaling may be traced several important contributions to marketing thought:

1. A variety of *concepts of wholesaling* itself, including the following:

As a level in the distributive channel.
As the business done by wholesalers.
As the transacting of business with other than ultimate consumers.
As the selling in large quantities.
As the selling at a discount price.
As a distinct business and economic function.
As a business institution.
As an institution of an industrialized economy.

2. Many *concepts* useful in understanding wholesaling and in communicating thoughts about it:

Circumvention	Wholesale establishment
Functional middleman	Wholesale sale
Industrial distributor	Wholesaler
Merchant middleman	Wholesaling
Private brands	Wholesaling structure
Wholesale	

3. Distinction between *wholesaling functions* and *wholesaling institutions.* Gradually the idea has been clarified that wholesaling is a generic type of activity rather than being merely the functional operations of wholesale establishments. Distinction has also been made between business organizations that are

pre-eminently engaged in wholesaling and those that perform functions of wholesaling while being primarily otherwise occupied.

4. The concept of *organic structure* of an institutional system. As the fundamental characteristics of institutions became recognized, classification of business organizations into orderly categories was made possible. Thus was structured the wholesaling system.

5. Exploration of the *temporal and spatial dimensions* of wholesaling activity, as illustrated in the historical practice and recent development and in the conduct of wholesaling in other nations and societies.

6. The concept of *wholesale channels*. Recognition of the diverse courses by which commodities and their titles flow from producers to consumers depended upon clear-cut distinctions of institutions and their activities. Thus could be conceptualized not only as channels, and channels of different lengths, but also as "circumvention," or the bypassing of units in the regular channels.

7. *Definitions and terminology* relevant to wholesaling and wholesalers have been clarified.

8. The compilation and presentation of *statistical data* relating to wholesaling, although undertaken by the Bureau of the Census, has also been the product of contributors to wholesaling literature.

9. Principles of marketing in general have been developed and crystallized in this literature.

10. Management techniques have been presented and explained.

11. The relevance of law to marketing has been shown.

12. The concept of productivity in wholesaling, or of value added by wholesalers, has given justification for this middleman that has been sought throughout the fifty years that marketing has been studied.

13. The conceptual framework for comparative analysis of marketing from both a temporal and spatial standpoint.

ENDNOTES

[1] Theodore N. Beckman, *Wholesaling* (New York: Ronald Press Co., 1926; rev. ed., 1937, with N. H. Engle, as *Wholesaling: Principles and Practice;* 2d ed., 1949; 3d ed., 1959, with R. D. Buzzell).

[2] J. H. Frederick, *Industrial Marketing* (New York: Prentice-Hall, Inc., 1934).

[3] R. F. Elder, *Fundamentals of Industrial Marketing* (New York: McGraw-Hill Book Co., Inc., 1935).

[4] B. Lester, *Marketing Industrial Equipment* (New York: McGraw-Hill Book Co., Inc. 1935).

[5] V. D. Reed, *Advertising and Selling Industrial Goods* (New York: Ronald Press Co., 1936).

[6] Ralph S. Alexander, James S. Cross, and Ross M. Cunningham, *Industrial Marketing* (Homewood, Ill.: Richard D. Irwin, Inc., 1956).

[7] M. R. Warshaw, *Effective Selling Through Wholesalers* (Ann Arbor: University of Michigan Press, 1961).

[8] David A. Revzan, *Wholesaling In Marketing Organization* (New York: John Wiley & Sons, 1961).

[9] E. R. Corey, *Industrial Marketing* (Englewood Cliffs, N.J.: Prentice-Hall, Inc., 1962).

[10] W. M. Diamond, *Distribution Channels for Industrial Goods* (Columbus, O.: Ohio State University Bureau of Business Research, 1963).

[11] David A. Revzan, *The Marketing Significance of Geographical Variations in Wholesale/Retail Sales Ratios* (Berkeley: Institute of Business and Economic Research, University of California, 1966, 2d ed., 1972).

122

[12]Robert Bartels (ed.), *Comparative Marketing: Wholesaling in Fifteen Countriess* (Homewood, Ill.: Richard D. Irwin, Inc., 1963).

[13]Louis P. Bucklin, *Competition and Evolution in the Distributive Trades* (Englewood Cliffs, N.J.: Prentice-Hall, Inc., 1972).

The development of marketing thought was not without some self-consciousness concerning the manner in which that thought was being derived and developed. Simultaneously with writings analyzing marketing practice came also a literature pertaining to the methodology employed in ascertaining the facts about marketing. That literature contained the body of thought concerning marketing research, sometimes called "market analysis," "market research," or "distribution research." Its subject was *method,* not simply *marketing.* The practice of marketing research yielded knowledge of marketing, but the literature on marketing research was concerned with the methodology applicable to research practice.

The practice of marketing research was begun about 1910, at the time when the methods of science employed in industrial production were being discovered as applicable also to marketing. Writings on research, however, did not appear in book form until 1919, although a few articles on the subject appeared earlier. From then until 1960, approximately thirty-seven books on the subject had been published. Ten appeared during the 1920s, six during the following decade, eight during the 1940s, and thirteen were published between 1950 and 1956. There were almost as many different authors as there were books published.

FACTORS INFLUENCING DEVELOPMENT
OF MARKETING RESEARCH

The emergence and evolution of research thought were the result of a growing demand for accurate knowledge of marketing and of an increasing application of the methods of science to marketing management.

The need for precise knowledge inspired the study of marketing from the beginning. At first, however, knowledge of marketing practice alone was sought. Gradually, recognition grew that markets and the marketing establishments themselves were complex organizations that could be understood only by penetrating analysis. Contact that management had with business through direct observation, in small organizations, was lost as those organizations increased in size and complexity. Co-ordination of activities within the business depended upon the development of new probes for information and new measures of management control. The need was met by the development of methods of researching internal records and operations.

The need for co-ordinating business with its external environment was also accentuated following World War I. Expansion of agriculture and industry and changes in the habits of people altered the configuration of markets. The realignment of international relations changed also the pattern of world markets. In addition to those secular trends stimulated by postwar readjustment, the violent cyclical depressions of 1921 and 1932 also showed the need for more knowledge of business and its environment. Throughout those periods of economic change and business adjustment, marketing bore particularly the brunt of a general impression that distribution was wasteful, inefficient, and costly. Only research could prove or disprove the validity of such accusations.

As the need for better knowledge of marketing became apparent, confidence in the applicability of the methods of science to marketing problems inspired early students and writers. Shaw, Nystrom, Cherington, and C. S. Duncan linked marketing with systematic and scientific research. Many methods of science were drawn from studies of production management. Some came also from studies of government administration, where methods of budgetary planning and forecasting had been developed. Discoveries in psychological, sociological, and statistical analysis likewise contributed tools by which marketing research could be done.

Growing interest in marketing research following World War I increased the number and types of organizations conducting marketing research. Whereas originally such research was done mainly by governmental agencies, university bureaus of business research, advertising agencies, and the research departments of manufacturers and distributors, market research began to be offered by independent research organizations, media, trade associations, channels of communication, co-operative associations, independent consultants, and syndicated research services.

BEGINNINGS OF MARKETING RESEARCH

In no other marketing literature is the origin of an activity so generally referred to as that of marketing research in the writings pertaining to it. Numerous writers have pinpointed the beginning of marketing research at about 1910 and have attributed to Charles Coolidge Parlin the inception of this work. The manner in which he came to undertake market and marketing studies seems to be well known, and accounts of it appear in the marketing research literature.

In an address given in 1947, Ralph Starr Butler,[1] told that the idea of marketing research originated about 1910 with Stanley Latshaw, advertising representative in Boston for the Curtis Publishing Company. Latshaw was dissatisfied with the way in which advertising space was sold. Neither salesmen nor their customers knew much about markets, about the wants and habits of consumers and dealers. Neither were they certain what were the virtues and faults of the products being advertised. Salesmen talked about their publications, but they had no information with which they could show customers why advertising in a particular medium would help in marketing their goods. Latshaw's idea was that such information ought to be available to advertising salesmen and their customers. After selling his idea to Mr. Curtis, he hired a competent man who was turned loose with a roving commission to see what could be developed. Responsibility for that unusual and unprecedented assignment fell to Charles Coolidge Parlin, a schoolmaster from a small city in Wisconsin.

When in 1911 Parlin undertook to gather information useful to businessmen, the Bureau of the Census was collecting facts, but businessmen were unskilled in interpreting them. Parlin called his proposed operation "Commercial Research." His first study was one of the agricultural implement industry. It was based upon information taken from manufacturers' catalogues and gathered in talks with manufacturers, wholesalers, and retailers. It resulted in a 460-page report, which is credited with being the first marketing research study.[2] Questionnaire surveys are said to have been used as early as 1824 by some newspapers, and in 1879 N. W. Ayres and Company surveyed grain production by states for a client, but the work of Parlin was the first that developed into a continuing and organized research operation.

In 1912 Parlin visited all cities over 50,000 population to estimate the volume of business done in department stores, wholesale dry goods establishments, and principal merchant tailoring operations. That resulted in a second report — a four-volume study published that year entitled *Department Store Lines.* In that study Parlin contributed the concept of "convenience goods, emergency goods, and shopping goods," which, with modifications, became a basic marketing concept. He also stated in that study that "The Consumer is King" — a marketing interpretation of the economic principle that consumption is the end and object of production, which became a slogan throughout the period of the Consumer Movement.

Parlin's third study was, in a sense, the first census of distribution. It attempted to estimate the trading population of the cities over 50,000, and the volume of department store, dry goods, and ladies ready-to-wear business. In 1914, he published still another study, *Automobiles,* pointing out possible successful lines and prices. All those studies served Latshaw's purpose to provide advertisers with information to guide not only their advertising but their entire business practice.

The studies made by Parlin led to increased advertising in the *Saturday Evening Post,* they introduced science into fact-finding as well as into management, and they made commercial fact-finding a profession. Other research activities also began to develop about then. In 1916 the United States Rubber Company established a research department under the direction of Paul Nystrom. In 1917 Swift and Company hired L. D. H. Weld as economist and commissioned him to organize a commercial research department for that company. Such were the beginnings of marketing research.

EVOLVING CONCEPT OF RESEARCH IN MARKETING

The application of research to marketing did not begin with a full-blown body of methodology. Neither did the investigations conducted by Parlin and other pioneers suggest the scope that marketing research would ultimately attain. Beginning simply, marketing research has evolved in breadth and complexity *in keeping with the problems that needed to be researched.* In general, its progress has been related to the expanding concept of marketing. When marketing was regarded mainly as the process of distribution, simple techniques of observation and analysis sufficed. When marketing was regarded more as a process of locating and reaching markets, survey techniques became the principal subject of research. When marketing was regarded as a function of internal management, methods of gathering and utilizing sales, costs, inventory, and other internal records were developed. When marketing has been regarded as an area of decision making, methods and techniques appropriate to the need have been devised. The stages in the evolution of marketing research may be identified with periods of decades as follows:

Prior to 1910. Investigations into marketing practice conducted prior to 1910 can scarcely be considered marketing research. They were scientifically conducted investigations, but their objective was the gathering of information for teaching purposes rather than specifically for the solution of business problems. Inquiry into the findings of psychologists by advertisers was, in the strictest sense, not marketing research but a process of learning rather than researching. Psychologists' findings themselves were frequently based upon hypothetical and subjective analyses rather than upon external and objective research. Nevertheless, during that period the method of first-hand observation, which has always been important in marketing research, was explored and found productive of useful information.

1910-20. Between 1910 and 1920 the growing size of business establishments, particularly in the distributive trades, focused interest on measures of internal activity and encouraged research in operating statistics and other internal data. Studies of operating costs made by university bureaus of business research, as at Harvard and some other schools, illustrate a type of research conducted at that time. During World War I the use of questionnaires for military screening purposes increased familiarity with that research tool and led to its extensive use in opinion polls conducted by magazine publishers.

1920-30. Focus of attention on markets, resulting from the introduction of new products, growth of new types of marketing establishments, and the uncertainty of consumer buying habits in economically unstable periods, coupled with experience in the use of questionnaires, made the 1920s a period of surveys in the evolution of marketing research. Rising interests in the consumer led to extensive thought and writing on the proper use of the questionnaire tool.

1930-40. With the taking of censuses of business, interest in research turned to statistical methodology. Quantitative rather than qualitative information was emphasized, particularly for use in analysis of factors affecting sales and in the setting of sales quotas. Marketing research during the 1930s contributed perhaps more to scientific sales management than to any other part of the marketing task. That was also a period when many accounting techniques of cost analysis were adapted to the study of distribution costs. Methods of measuring correlation and problems of sampling also engaged the interests of some writers.

1940-50. The decade of 1940-50 is identified with the refinement of statistical techniques and with the growing interest in research methodology drawn from other social sciences. Attention was given to sampling theory and to multivariate and correlation methods. Keener awareness of the importance of hypotheses in marketing research was evident, and more was written of the securing of information on behavior, intentions, attitudes, habits, and "reasons why" through the use of panels, interview-roster methods, coincidental methods, mechanical devices, and other psychological testing techniques. Motivational and operations research was also dealt with in the research literature.

1950-60. In the decade of the 1950s, emphasis placed upon managerial decision making in marketing in general evoked in marketing research new analyses of consumer motivation and greater use of concepts developed in related behavioral sciences. Attention was also turned to quantitative analysis through use of advanced mathematical techniques.

CONTRIBUTIONS TO MARKETING RESEARCH

In the following pages some of the types of research to which attention has been given are discussed, and the principal contributors to the ideas are identified.

QUALITATIVE DETERMINATION OF MARKETS

In its earliest conception, market analysis consisted of qualitative determination of the markets for products. When writings on market research began to appear, systematic analysis of business practice was yet new, and earliest writers undertook little more than to set forth a conceptual framework for considering business problems. Market activity was not at first, however, a subject of separate consideration.

A. W. Shaw was one of the first to deal with market analysis, but he gave it only one chapter in his *An Approach to Business Problems.*[3] Approximately half the book was devoted to "The Problems of Distribution." His "approach" to the solution of business problems was a four-step procedure: (1) elimination of the personal element or subjective interest in the problem situation; (2) recognition of the fact that each problem is made up of a bundle of minor problems; (3) cognizance of all factors entering into the solution; and (4) a fresh look at the problem, divorced from traditional approaches to it.

Shaw believed that production, distribution, and administrative problems were essentially similar and could be approached alike. Analysts of production had abstracted five factors held to be basic to production problems: location of the plant, construction and equipment, materials, labor, and organization. While admitting that all the factors relating to distribution were not yet known, Shaw held that distribution problems required consideration of the same factors as did production problems.

To one type of distribution problem, namely, the analysis of markets, Shaw gave particular attention. Theretofore, knowledge of markets had been largely a trial and error effect; he saw the possibility of eliminating some uncertainties by systematic and conceptual consideration of the market. He regarded markets as made up of "strata" or as having segments distinguished by territorial distribution of customer, mental attitudes, climate, racial characteristics, density of population, and the like. Stratification of the market produced by economic and social factors created what he termed "market contours."[4] Anaylsis of the market was made by careful consideration of these strata factors for the purpose of determining who bought where; how often they came to the market; how much they were willing to pay; and the most effective agency by which those consumers could be reached.

Carson S. Duncan, another early writer, set forth some of the general principles underlying business research, which he called "commercial research," as had Parlin. He made a strong case for his belief that business problems could be solved by the use of facts. Because he felt that the problems of business enterprise are basically market problems, he recommended the application of scientific methods to the solution of them.

In his *Commercial Research*[5] he set forth a series of propositions expressing the logic underlying this form of research:

128

1. The immediate and primary need of business is for intelligent direction and control.
2. Intelligent control can be had only by a better knowledge of business principles.
3. A knowledge of business principles can be derived only from a careful and comprehensive survey of business facts.
4. The securing of business facts is a problem for business research.
5. Therefore, the immediate and primary need of business can be met only by business research.

Duncan did not limit commercial research to mere *use* of figures; he considered also the origin of those figures, the quality of thought that organized and presented the figures, and the subjects of commercial research that cannot be tabulated. He encouraged the use of both internal and external information in the commercial process of business, which he treated as an area of management. Among the types of researchable business facts that he held to be essential to management are the following: the commodity, trade organization, the market, population statistics, wealth statistics, wages and prices, per capita consumer income, standards of living, markets for special commodities, business habits, the will to buy, and potential markets.

Commercial Research was one of the first books of its kind, and it made several contributions to thought. It postulated general principles of research. It dealt with business problems and their solutions on a broad scale. It was challenging rather than definitive, expository rather than descriptive. It made no distinction, however, between market research and marketing research. Neither did it elaborate upon the techniques by which research was to be carried on. Among the bibliographical references found in the book are the following:

William Kent, *Investigating Industry*
S.O. Martin, "Scientific Study of Marketing," *The Annals,* May, 1915
E.N. Hurley, *The Awakening of Business*
Ernest J. P. Benn, *Trade as a Science*
M. P. Copeland, *Business Statistics*
J. R. Smith, *Industrial Management*
Harry Tipper, *The New Business*

MEASURABILITY OF MARKETS

After the general applicability of scientific research to the commercial problems had been discussed, its specific pertinence to marketing was introduced through the concept of measurability of markets.

Percival White was one of the earliest to develop this subject, saying in his *Market Analysis: Its Principles and Methods*[6] that markets are measurable and that the measurements of them serve to guide manufacturers, sales managers, engineers, advertising agencies, and others for whom understanding, discovery, and prediction of markets is important.

White thought of both domestic and foreign markets as measurable and capable of analysis. He encouraged research of customers, distribution, sales, and competition, as well as of the product and the company. The methodology by which he proposed making this analysis consisted mainly of securing data by interview and questionnaire — in other words, by the method of the market survey. What he said influenced the structure of thought for years. He was the first writer to publish a work on market analysis under that name. He was the first to build a set of general principles of marketing policies.

White's thought about research unfolded in response to changes in distribution occurring during the 1920s, and by 1925 he showed increasing concern with *marketing* research rather than with mere *market* analysis. He therefore included in his treatment of the subject organizations for market research, agency market research, industrial and commodity surveys, and newspaper surveys.

MARKET SURVEYS

A number of contributions to thought were made in the development of survey research. Survey methodology, however, has been developed not only by students of marketing but also by other social scientists.

William J. Reilly added to the knowledge of survey research in his *Marketing Investigations.*[7] When it was published in 1929, Reilly claimed that the available information about conducting field investigations was negligible. He dealt at length, therefore, with problems of interviewing and use of the questionnaire. He discussed the potentialities of retailers, consumers, jobbers, and marketing organizations as sources of information. More than others at that time, he expressed concern with the reliability and accuracy of samples. After discussing some of the ethical implications of research, he concluded his study with consideration of "What Is Most Needed," itemizing the following: development of the scientific method, training of marketing research men, organization of a clearing house, emphasis upon more fundamental surveys, arrangement for continual study of problems, and more work by impartial organizations. Reilly's work was one of the most comprehensive treatments of the marketing-field investigation.

Percival White also contributed to the understanding of survey research; in 1931 he published a manual for field workers, entitled *Marketing Research Technique.*[8] He covered thoroughly the nature, organization, and work involved in field research. To the questionnaire technique, which in earlier years had been regarded as the principal form of field investigation, he added analysis of personal interviewing, telephone interviewing, group interviewing, and field tests. He developed at length the pre-interview work required in field research, including the writing of instructions, local situation surveys, classification of respondents, information about respondents, memorizing the questionnaire, quotas, and rules of conduct. White visualized the marketing research organization on a level with market planning, marketing accounting, and merchandising. He related the history of field research up to that time, commenting that few if any recognized standards of practice had been developed in the work.

So widespread was interest in survey research during the 1930s that a Committee on Marketing Research Techniques was appointed by the American Marketing Association to prepare and present a series of charts of the best methods to be followed in markting research. The study of the Committee dealt at length with the use of the questionnaire method of gathering business information, and its charts and explanations thereof were published in 1937 under the title *The Technique of Marketing Research,* edited by Ferdinand C. Wheeler.[9] Notwithstanding its sponsorship, the book made no significant contribution to research thought. It so condensed and abbreviated prevailing knowledge of the subject that it was little more than a checklist of research procedure.

MARKETING AND DISTRIBUTION RESEARCH

Market analysis and survey research furnished only part of the assistance that scientific research could give, and throughout the 1930s increasing emphasis was given to marketing or distribution research rather than mere market studies. Lyndon O. Brown, in *Market Research and Analysis,*[10] made some contributions along this line. He dealt with topics not usually treated: quantitative analysis, sales analysis, market trends, advertising research, and product analysis. He represented the viewpoints that he thought combined to make the ideal analyst, namely, those of the psychologist, statistician, accountant, engineer, sociologist, and marketing man.

Brown contributed to the clarification of research concepts and terminology. *Market research* he defined as the scientific study of markets or marketing methods in a broad general way; *market analysis,* as the scientific study of markets or marketing methods for a specific product or service — for an individual firm. The basic *methods* of science he identified as historical, inductive, deductive, analytical, and experimental; the general *techniques* of research, as statistics, accounting, engineering, psychology, and sociology. The basic *marketing analysis methods* he listed as survey, observation, and experimentation; the types of *quantitative analysis methods,* as direct data, corollary data, arbitrary factors, family budget, consumption rate, and multiple correlation. Brown introduced more concepts and organization of thought to the subject of market research than had his predecessors. He also related the subject of research to science, to marketing, and to other fields of study.

Developments in research during the 1940s sprang from the employment of new methods of research and from the application of scientific research to an increasing variety of marketing problems. The structure of Brown's thought about research in 1949 was based largely upon the types of problems to be researched. Among those discussed were product and package research, brand position analysis, industrial and institutional marketing research, sales organization and operation research, sales record analysis, distribution cost research, opinion and public relations research, advertising copy testing, price and market trend analysis. Duncan had emphasized the business use of research findings; White, the types of organizations engaged in survey work; Reilly, problems involved in gathering and interpreting marketing data; Brown, the areas of marketing whose problems lent themselves to research.

Still another organization of thought was presented by Brown in the 1955 revision of his book. New emphasis was given to research methodology, and some of the newer developments were incorporated. In addition to an elaborated statement of survey procedure, he increased the attention given the planning and analysis of the sample. He also discussed techniques contributed by other specialized fields that were being used in marketing research, particularly motivational research and operations research.

SALES RESEARCH

While a large part of marketing research focused attention on factors external to a business enterprise, efforts were also made to utilize internal information. Statistics of retail store operations were collected and published by the Harvard Bureau of Business Research and by the National Retail Dry Goods Association prior to 1920. Not until somewhat later, however, did information that manufacturers possess concerning their sales become the material for marketing research. In the late 1920s and thereafter, as sales management became increasingly fact-based decision making, marketing research turned to supplying the needed facts from both external and internal sources.

Percival White was one of the first to write in this field, publishing *Sales Quotas*[11] in 1929, a sequel to his *Market Analysis*. Defining the sales quota as the share of the market that a company plans to appropriate, he amplified the concept of the quota as the goal set for the company, for the territory, or for the individual. Setting quotas required research. Markets were located on the basis of research into territorial factors. Sales opportunities were measured by indices of related factors. White made a stong case for research of this type as a basis of sales forcasting.

Donald R. G. Cowan also contributed to understanding the use of research for promotional purposes. His *Sales Analysis from the Managment Standpoint*[12] set forth standard research procedure and explained the conditions under which various types of research could be used. Rather than merely prescribing methods to be used, it stimulated the reader to consider applicability in terms of circumstances. Developed while the author was engaged in research work for Swift and Company, the book was actually an outgrowth of a doctoral dissertation and a series of articles published in the *Journal of Business*.

Whereas White's *Sales Quotas* dealt with sales forecasting on the basis of fairly simple internal and external data and Cowan's *Sales Analysis* illustrated a variety of sales problems and research techniques, R. Parker Eastwood's *Sales Control by Quantitative Methods*[13] was a highly specialized study of operations control through the use of internal data. Specialization in production was held to impose upon business a great need for control and co-ordination. The market place itself provided co-ordination among companies. Within firms co-ordination is accomplished by managerial techniques, sales forecasting being a crucial factor. Eastwood undertook to discuss the methods appropriate for controlling sales. That involved budgetary control, a concept of formally estimating future operations, which, according to Eastwood, began in the administration of governmental fiscal policies. Business managers adopted the concept. Whereas, in the government, he pointed out, estimated *costs* are the starting point of a budget, in business estimated *sales* are the starting point.

Eastwood regarded marketing research as a broad field subdivided into such activities as sales analysis, distribution cost analysis, market analysis, and advertising research. *Sales analysis,* which was generally based upon existing sales data, he thought to be most helpful in connection with products that are in general and continuing use. *Market analysis*, on the other hand, looking to the gathering of external data, he regarded as more applicable to the sale of goods purchased intermittently or irregularly. Sales analysis was based in part upon classifications of sales, on such bases as geographic area, customers, size of orders, products, selling units, sales outlets or channels, terms of sale, methods of delivery and advertising media. Eastwood did not present a study of distribution costs, but, because he wrote at a time when such cost studies were popular, his book would have been a complement to such studies and an aid in the establishment of distribution and promotional policies.

132

CONSUMER RESEARCH

When the use of questionnaires was first adopted by marketing researchers, it was mainly as a device for gathering and counting opinions. Questionnaire construction had been developed by psychologists and others than those who were engaged primarily in market research. However, with continuing progress made in behavior analysis by social scientists, survey research gradually took on a new dimension in marketing. It aimed at reaching greater depths of discovery, at ascertaining with more accuracy the subjective factors affecting consumption, upon which sound marketing plans could be based. The introduction into marketing thought of techniques that would accomplish this end was achieved in part by market researchers' gaining understanding of new psychological concepts and in part by psychologists' directing their research toward the solution of marketing problems.

Albert B. Blankenship, who was trained in psychology and was director of market research for N. W. Ayres and Sons, Inc., was one who contributed to marketing thought along lines of psychological research. He added to the research literature three books: *Consumer and Opinion Research,*[14] *How To Conduct Consumer and Opinion Research,*[15] and, with Myron S. Heidingsfield, *Market and Marketing Analysis.*[16]

Consumer and Opinion Research is perhaps one of the most authoritative writings on questionnaire construction, but while it *influenced* market research it did not pertain specifically to market research. It dealt with the questionnaire technique as that form of investigation might be used among the various social disciplines: sociology, psychology, marketing, advertising, political science, and statistics. Because of his business experience, Blankenship abundantly illustrated his theories with actual business cases.

A second book, written by numerous individuals, was edited by Blankenship. Its principal contribution was to show what research services were being offered by various types of organizations, including research organizations, syndicated services, specialized services, and general practitioners. The book was informative but nontechnical.

Blankenship incorporated much of his questionnaire research in his collaborated writing with Heidingsfield, but their work presented a broad, general, and simplified treatment of research. Convinced that most of the literature was written for professionals and graduate students, they undertook to prepare a book for beginners. With the intention of showing the use of internal data and external surveys, they included also the use of observation and panel methods and the study of comparative consolidated balance sheets and statements of income. Noteworthy is their distinction between concepts, defining *market analysis* as the procedure of evaluating the desire of a group of people, and *marketing analysis* as the study of the methods of marketing.

STATISTICAL RESEARCH

Knowledge of statistical methodology has always been of importance to market researchers, but treatment of that subject has occupied a minor place in market research literature. This has been due mainly to the highly technical nature of statistical theory. Consequently, the relevance of statistical techniques to market research has been dealt with but little, and only in the later years of the study of market research, as the solution of problems involving more statistical intricacies has been undertaken.

The closest approximation to a work devoted to statistical market research is that by Robert Ferber: *Statistical Techniques in Market Research*,[17] which actually is a book more on statistical techniques than on market research. Earliest writers on the survey made little if any mention of the statistical problems involved; their successors discussed sampling theory to some extent; Ferber wrote with considerable penetration of sampling and of multivariate and correlation methods. Even then, he admitted that his treatment was less technical than if intended for statisticians. Nevertheless, this was the more specialized refinement of the subject applied specifically to market research, and it had a continuing influence upon the development of marketing thought and the training of market researchers.

DEVELOPMENTS OF RESEARCH THOUGHT AFTER 1950

In the postwar years, and into the 1950s, developments in business had several effects upon the nature of marketing research. To begin with, there were an increasing number of marketing problems that were not being solved satisfactorily by the methods of research then employed. At the same time, the necessity of relying upon research in marketing increased. With the trend toward decentralization management, encouragement was given the establishment of marketing research departments acting in a staff capacity and the use of research consultants. Thus the need for research specialists trained and experienced in technical skills increased. Simultaneously with the growing conception of the function of top management as that of integrating and co-ordinating the diverse activities within an organization, the need for broader research into all aspects of business related to marketing became more apparent. Thus marketing research was expected to provide not only information descriptive of the market for the formulation of sales strategy but also information that would be useful in determining prices, product policies, geographic deployment of physical facilities, and proper utilization of invested capital for maximum return on marketing activity. The demand upon marketing research was for improved technical skills and for better use of researchable information in the co-ordinative function of management.

The deficiencies of prevailing methods of marketing research were stated by Robert Ferber and Hugh G. Wales[18] to be as follows:

1. Excessive dependence upon accumulated experience of business itself, upon the records which business has kept of its own activities. Not only are such bases of research static and tax-directed, they do not reflect the many complex marketing situations which cannot be reduced to statistical terms.

2. The time lag in gathering data external to the business which makes them available only after change in the market place has altered the conditions which they are intended to depict. This is true of both trade and government reports.

3. Unconscious but significant distortion of the judgment of department heads, employees, and others whose opinions are sought in survey research.

4. The limited usefulness of information gathered by means of questionnaires in connection with a random sample, because of public excitement concerning an issue, relevance of findings to peculiar local circumstances, and the unforeseen introduction of new variables into a situation.

It is said that the inadequacies of exiting marketing research methods became more apparent in 1949 and 1950, when businesses became uneasy about accumulating inventories and changes in consumer demands. To meet the needs of new marketing problems, new research methods had to be found.

One approach to improve research was by development of judgment skills in the use of research. In the 1950s attempts were made to provide this skill through the use of problems and case materials illustrating various research methods. The objectives of writers who supplemented text with cases were differently stated, but the general intent was to emphasize the making of decisions and the use of strategies by marketing managers in their blending of a marketing mix and in their adaptation of it to changing circumstances. Such emphasis of practice, in contrast to mere theory, was intended to bring the student to grips with actual problems and techniques, to show how research methodology in the social sciences is applicable to the solution of marketing problems, and to avoid the supposedly "too dry" traditional approach to the study of marketing research. Actually, the concept of research methodology presented by such writers did not differ much from those traditionally discussed in the preceding decades. A few exceptions are notable, however. Harper W. Boyd and Ralph Westfall[19] gave more than usual attention to the experimental methods, including "Before-After," "Before-After with Control Group," "Four-Group—Six-Study," "After Only with Control Group," and "Ex Post Facto Design." David E. Faville,[20] on the other hand, introduced thirteen cases based upon European research experiences.

A contrasting trend of thought, complementing the use of cases, was manifested in increasing incorporation in marketing research of methods and techniques borrowed from related social sciences. This represented a popularized concept of man, not merely as an economic mechanism or as a simple combination of urges and wants, but rather in terms of Gestalt psychology and psychoanalysis. The probing of the "why" of consumer behavior in the market developed along lines of indirect questioning, in contrast to the methods of direct interrogation formerly commonly employed in survey research. Some techniques were devised to study the unconscious or subconscious mind and to explore consumer goal-directed behavior; others related to the probing of so-called instinct drives, or of the unconscious motivation in quest of unrecognized goals.

From the fields of psychology and sociology were drawn for use in marketing research a number of concepts and techniques for motivation research, a subject which, as evidenced by book titles, had considerable impact upon marketing research thought in the 1950s. Among them were the following:

Word association	Symbolism
Sentence completion	Projective techniques
Rorschach tests	Depth interviews
Thematic apperception tests	Focused group interviewing
Role-playing	Error-choice techniques
Situational methods	Cartoon and picture devices
Chain interviews	Picture frustration

A third variation of research thought was represented by publications of readings or the republication of articles on a wide variety of research subjects. Typical of other fields of marketing in recent years, such readings were the contributions of many specialists and tended to give a breadth of treatment better than any one author could present at that time. In one of the more widely used of such publications, Robert Ferber and Hugh G. Wales[21] selected and organized their selections with the intent to dispell the notion that motivation in market behavior should be limited to such types of motivation as had constituted the inquiries of psychologists who more narrowly used that term.

A fourth trend in marketing research thought evidenced the increasing reliance upon mathematics and models for the solution of marketing problems. As articles on motivation appeared first in journals of psychology, so employment of mathematical concepts in marketing problems appeared first in journals of economics, statistics, and mathematics. A number of them were republished in a book edited by Frank M. Bass et al.[22] entitled *Mathematical Models and Methods in Marketing.* The editors saw the application of mathematical concepts and techniques to solve marketing problems to be one of the important current trends in marketing thought. Therefore, in order to make intelligible to students of marketing with both little and considerable mathematical knowledge, they have, on the one hand, translated the mathematical discussions into more simple English terminology and, on the other, elaborated in detail the mathematical analysis presented in more general and summary fashion in the articles themselves.

MARKETING RESEARCH THOUGHT SINCE 1960

Prior to 1960, the literature on Marketing Research generally included those terms in book titles. After that, titles increasingly featured new methodologies being introduced into marketing research. During the first half of the decade, much attention was given to attitude and consumer research; thereafter, titles often reflected content employing such concepts as decision theory, mathematical models, quantitative techniques, simulation, and experimentation. Some books still bore the traditional title of "marketing research," but few were concerned with *market* reseach.

Several distinctions might be made between the earlier and the later books. The former were generally descriptive; the latter, more analytical. Earlier works were concerned with assessment of the current status of marketing *operations;* more recent research investigated relationships *between* elements of the marketing process. Earlier writings presented techniques commensurate with the perceived marketing problems of that time; as the complexity of marketing increased, so did the problems and the analytical tools for solving them. In fact, the recognition of problems did not always precede the development of techniques. Contrariwise, as new techniques became available, problems were perceived where none had been seen before. New concepts and techniques were obtained from the fields of logic, mathematics, engineering, the behavioral sciences, and economics (econometrics). Moreover, as managers, who were the *users* of research, no longer possessed or needed capabilities for the *conduct* of research, markets for two distinct literatures and educational programs arose.

Evidence of the changing thought in this area is apparent in the revisions during the 1960s of books originally published earlier, such as those of Brown (1937), Ferber (1949), and Luck (1952). Having initially been dedicated to the survey type of research, such books continued this emphasis; yet the manner and extent to which they incorporated the new technologies indicated the nature of trends in the field.

Brown and Beik[23] enumerated the new developments to which they gave accommodation as follows: concepts of model building, improved techniques of problem definition, decision theory, experimental design, operations research, advances in logic and statistics, new methods of data definition incorporated from behavioral sciences, and computer analyses. Notwithstanding continuation of the survey techniques in which Brown had pioneered in the 1930s, the incorporation of the new material was impressive. Being of broad coverage, however, its usefulness to either decision makers or technicians was general.

Luck, Wales, and Taylor[24] likewise initially published when popularity of survey research was high and later adapted their book to the fact that readers were no longer "overwhelmingly interested in technical methods." They shifted their emphasis to conceptualizing decision making for integration with research design, and to organization and administration of marketing research. They nevertheless continued oriented to survey techniques and to market data analysis, and the minimal employment of new concepts was apparent in the absence from the index of such terms as operations research, multivariate analysis, decision tree, and systems concept. Bayesian analysis was given only a 6-line mention of a bibliographical reference.

The inferences drawable from both of these revisions of earlier research thought are (1) that there is a continued market for such collegiate introductions to the general field of research, (2) that it is very difficult to combine both managerial and technical levels of exposition, and (3) that the real development of the new lines of research required fuller treatment than could be given in the general text.

Books published for the first time after 1960 were generally divisible into two groups: those intended for decision makers who would *use* the information obtained from research, and those intended for the researchers themselves. Books addressed to users of research services and information were the less technical. Decision makers needed to know enough to lift the mystique from marketing research; to recognize information as an input equal in importance to investment of capital and other physical assets; and to weigh the value of additional information against the cost of obtaining it.

Books intended for the research practitioners presented in considerable detail the techniques of the new methodologies which were being introduced. The following were topics which were treated in detail as essential knowledge in research:

1. Defining problems and information needs.
2. Statistical decision theory
3. Bayesian theory, or the mathematical determination of probabilities in decision making
4. Regression analysis, or the analysis of relationships between dependent and independent variables
5. Model building, including linear, static forecasts, regression coefficients, time functions, difference equations, Markov chains, factor analysis
6. Experimentation, including completely randomized design, randomized block design, Latin square design, double change over design, and factorial design
7. Buyer behavior, including projective tests, depth interviews, and scaling techniques

Among the representative books of the later period were the following:

Marketing Research: Selected Readings and Analytical Commentaries (Barksdale and Weilmacher, eds,. 1966) purporting to integrate marketing research into marketing management, and falling between elementary descriptive books and advanced monographs.

Marketing Research (Boyd and Westfall, 1972), including new developments in decision theory, advanced statistical analysis procedures, and experimentation in marketing, while retaining original basic format or survey techniques and application of behavioral sciences.

Marketing Research and Information Systems: Text and Cases (Buzzell, Cox, and Brown, 1969) providing a basis for learning about problems involving the use of marketing information and some of the concepts and methods that can be used in solving these problems.

The Marketing Research Process (Cox and Enis, 1972) based upon a model of the information decision process, for guidance in the purchase of relevant information for decision making

Consumer Behavior (Engel, Kollat, and Blackwell, 1968) providing a basic conceptual model of consumer motivation and behavior stating variables that shape consumer action.

Marketing Decisions: a Bayesian Approach (Enis and Broome, 1971) analyzing probability in decision making.

A Manager's Guide to Marketing Research (Green and Frank, 1967) a survey of recent developments; a book for nonspecialists.

Research for Marketing Decisions (Green and Toll, 1972) a comprehensive coverage of latest developments in marketing research, including the use of a data bank case study throughout the book.

No sharp line can be drawn between writings of interest primarily for their content of marketing practice and problems and those of interest for their exposition and amplification of methodoloy and techniques. The books surveyed here are intended to be of the former group; some of those of the latter will be referred to later among the contributions from other disciplines.

CONTRIBUTIONS OF RESEARCH LITERATURE TO MARKETING THOUGHT

Appraisal of the contributions that the literature on marketing research has made to the body of marketing thought must take into account that this literature is as concerned with methodology as with the content of marketing thought and practice. From the outset, it drew heavily upon concepts and logic of other disciplines. Students of marketing were primarily adopters and adapters of methods and techniques, the theories behind them having been developed by others engaged in the disciplines of mathematics and the behavioral sciences, particularly. As marketing scholars have in recent years been more highly trained in these methods fields, they have done more original work. Nevertheless, what has been written has been mainly from the standpoint of marketing rather than for the methodology per se.

The following are some of the contributions that have been derived from the introduction of research ideas and concepts:

1. The character and identity of the consumer and of the market have been established through the information gathered from survey investigations and other statistical data.

2. The concept of what constitutes *facts* in marketing has been clarified. As the statement of the *problem* in marketing has called for

138

keener insights, so facts have become not merely simple observations and tangible evidences, but rates, ratios, relationships, and other intangibles.

3. Concepts have been developed for the analysis, measurement, and control of marketing activities. They have consisted of sampling, quality control, sales quotas, sales analyses, distribution cost analyses, correlation coefficients, variance, operating ratios, and the like.

4. The concepts and terminology of marketing thought have been enriched by the addition of such terms as market research, marketing research, analysis as contrasted with research, survey, field investigation, method, technique, internal data, external data, and a host of other terms drawn from statistics, psychology, and sociology.

5. Elevation of marketing thought to a higher level of theorization through employment of variable relationships, guides to clear logic, and more rigorous scientific methodology applied to marketing intelligence.

6. Introduction of forms of theory into marketing thought through various types of models.

ENDNOTES

[1] Donald M. Hobart, *Marketing Research Practice* (New York: Ronald Press Co., Inc., 1950), p. 34.

[2] *Ibid.,* pp. 3-9.

[3] A. W. Shaw, *An Approach to Business Problems* (Cambridge, Mass.: Harvard University Press, 1916).

[4] *Ibid.,* p. 223.

[5] Carson S. Duncan, *Commercial Research* (New York: Macmillan Co., 1919).

[6] Percival White, *Market Analysis: Its Principles and Methods* (New York: McGraw-Hill Book Co., Inc., 1921; 2d ed., 1925).

[7] William J. Reilly, *Marketing Investigations* (New York: Ronald Press Co., 1929).

[8] Percival White *Marketing Research Technique* (New York: Harper & Bros., 1931).

[9] Ferdinand C. Wheeler, (ed.), *The Technique of Marketing Research* (New York: McGraw-Hill Book Co., Inc., 1937).

[10] Lyndon D. Brown, *Market Research and Analysis* (New York: Ronald Press Co., 1937; 2d ed., 1949, as *Marketing and Distribution Research;* 3d ed., 1955; 4th ed., 1969, with L. L. Beik).

[11] Percival White, *Sales Quotas* (New York: Harper & Bros., 1929).

[12] Donald R. G. Cowan, *Sales Analysis from the Management Standpoint* (Chicago: University of Chicago Press, 1938).

[13] R. Parker Eastwood, *Sales Control by Quantitative Methods* (New York: Columbia University Press, 1940).

[14] Albert B. Blankenship, *Consumer and Opinion Research* (New York: Harper & Bros., 1943).

[15] Albert B. Blankenship, *How to Conduct Consumer and Opinion Research* (New York: Harper & Bros., 1946).

[16] Albert B. Blankenship and Myron S. Heidingsfield, *Market and Marketing Analysis* (New York: Henry Holt & Co., 1947).

[17] Robert Ferber, *Statistical Techniques in Market Reserach* (New York: McGraw-Hill Book Co., Inc., 1949; rev. ed., 1963, as *Market Research).*

[18] Robert Ferber and Hugh G. Wales, *Motivation and Market Behavior* (Homewood, Ill.: Richard D. Irwin, Inc., 1958).

[19] Harper W. Boyd and Ralph Westfall, *Marketing Research* (Homewood, Ill.: Richard D. Irwin, Inc., 1956; rev. ed., 1964; 3d ed., 1972).

[20] David E. Faville, *Selected Cases in Marketing Management* (Englewood Cliffs, N.J.: Prentice-Hall, Inc., 1961).

[21] *Op. cit.*

[22] Frank M. Bass, (ed.) *Mathematical Models and Methods in Marketing* (Homewood, Ill.: Richard D. Irwin, Inc., 1961).

[23]Lyndon O. Brown and L. L. Beik, *Marketing and Distribution Reserach* (New York: Ronald Press Co., 4th ed. 1969).

[24]D. G. Luck, H. G. Wales, and D. A. Taylor, *Marketing Research* (New York: Prentice Hall, 3d ed., 1970).

Seldom has a literature had so much influence upon a succession of generations as have the writings on the general subject of marketing. The swelling tide of opportunities and successful practice in marketing brought many people to the study of the subject for professional reasons. Students of other phases of business, if they made any contact with the area of marketing, touched it first — if not solely— through the general writings on the subject. Concepts from this field penetrated even secondary education through texts and teacher training. The general statement of marketing has furnished a picture of business and economic activity for a large part of our society to view and thereby appraise it.

The significance of the general literature in the development of marketing thought is also great. It is a distillation and integration of thought developed by those who practiced and wrote in the specialized areas. The general literature presents the area of thought in which marketing is most likely to be dealt with as a social institution rather than as a technical activity. In that literature, too, are found the best measures of marketing thought: its scientific character, its historical evolution, its social orientation, its philosophic, economic, and cultural characteristics.

The development of marketing thought in the general literature has been an evolution of a body of viewpoints, concepts, and principles. Between 1900 and 1960, one hundred books dealing with general marketing were published. More than eighty individuals contributed to those works.

The fifty years during which this body of literature and thought has taken shape may be divided into six decades, each representing a stage of its development:

> 1900-10 — The Period of Discovery
> 1910-20 — The Period of Conceptualization
> 1920-30 — The Period of Integration
> 1930-40 — The Period of Development
> 1940-50 — The Period of Reappraisal
> 1950-60 — The Period of Reconception
> 1960-70 — The Period of Differentiation
> 1970 — The Period of Socialization

1900-1910 — THE PERIOD OF DISCOVERY

The decade beginning in 1900 witnessed the inception of marketing thought and its initial appearance in a few collegiate courses and in such writings as those of Scott and Calkins in advertising and of Prendergast in credit. It was a period of awakening to a recognition of problems in distribution. The orderly gathering of market information began. Concepts were borrowed from established disciplines, such as economics, psychology, sociology, and scientific management, for the improvement of trade practice and management.

E. J. Jones, George M. Fisk, Simon Litman, and James E. Hagerty were four of the earliest teachers, but during that decade Butler, Nystrom, Hibbard, and others also taught marketing courses. Each gathered his own information. There were no formal texts for the subject, except a few of a specialized nature then appearing. Nevertheless, catalogue descriptions of early courses indicated that topics such as the following were discussed: mercantile institutions; organizations; systems; methods of marketing goods, particularly farm products; grading; and selling and advertising. By the end of that decade the entity of the subject was sufficiently recognized to be identified by the term "marketing."

Something of the discovery of ideas that occurred in those early years of this century is evident in one of the first of what might be called the "general" works on marketing: the report on the distribution of farm products prepared by John Franklin Crowell for the Industrial Commission.[1] It was a publication in which some of the prevailing ideas about marketing were set forth. A twofold problem gave rise to the report: the need for a description of the distributive system by which farm products went from producers to consumers and the need for some understanding of the portion of consumers' dollars in the purchase of farm products that went to producers and distributors, respectively.

Although the bulk of the report dealt with costs and factors affecting them in the distribution of farm products, and although the writer's concept of marketing as "speculative" was drawn from the susceptibility of farm products to price movements in agricultural markets, four general observations indicate the nature of the discovery that early students of distribution were beginning to experience:

1. The number and quality of people engaged in distribution were said to be a function of the opportunity, or lack of opportunity, for investing funds and talents elsewhere. Changes in rates of return on capital reflected the risks involved in distributive activity, it was held, and entrance into distributive activity was the result of rational appraisal of the opportunities seen therein. In accordance with the explanations of classical economists, attraction toward or away from trade activity was automatically a result of economic rationality.

2. The larger the volume of trade under a single control, the lower the rate of profit on each unit of farm product was likely to be. This observation was an interpretation of the advantages of large-scale activity in terms of distributive operations.

3. Improvements in communications tended to reduce dependence upon the "expensive" middlemen, whose service had been mainly the supplying of information that was otherwise unobtainable but that was now becoming more available. This generalization suggested the fluidity of the distributive structure, a concept that was not crystalized until some years later.

4. The "more expensive methods of distribution" were seen to be more persistent "where no storable visible supply exists because of their perishable nature."[2] Where no storage was available there was less large-scale handling of products.

Part of the significance of this publication lay in the fact that it served as a text in early marketing courses, even until about 1920.

1910-20 – THE PERIOD OF CONCEPTUALIZATION

In the second decade, many of the basic concepts of marketing were crystalized. The commodity, institutional, and functional approaches to the analysis were conceived, and a number of the marketing functions were identified. A degree of integration in the statement of marketing was also achieved. Arch W. Shaw, Ralph Starr Butler, Louis D. H. Weld, and Paul T. Cherington were the principal contributors to the body of general thought during that period.

The decade was one of outstanding economic, business, and intellectual attainments. It was a time of industrial growth and of increasing pre-eminence of both wholesale and retail distributors. Numerous new specialty goods appeared on the market, constituting challenges for advertising and salesmanship. The growth of large-scale enterprise disrupted traditional channels of distribution. Appearing simultaneously were books on advertising by Cherington, Hollingworth, Hess, and Hall; on salesmanship by Maxwell, Jones, Hess, and Douglas; on sales management by Hoyt, Jones, Frederick, and Butler; on credits and collections by Hagerty and Ettinger and Golieb; and on retailing by Nystrom.

EARLY CONCEPTS OF MARKETING

About 1910 the term "marketing" was added to the familiar terms "distribution," "trade," and "commerce." It was not merely another synonym, however. On the contrary, that it was meant to identify a new concept is clearly indicated by recollections of two of the men instrumental in initially stating this concept: Ralph Starr Butler and Arch W. Shaw.

Through his experience as sales manager with a large manufacturer, Butler had become familiar with the diverse activities entailed in personal selling and advertising. Apparently not until 1910, when he undertook to organize a course in selling at the University of Wisconsin, did he attempt to conceptualize what before had been only firsthand experience. He was impelled partly by the fact that there was a lack of written material on the subject. He knew from experience that a manufacturer seeking to market his product had to consider and solve a large number of problems before he ever gave expression to the selling idea by sending a salesman on the road or inserting an advertisement in a publication. Personal salesmanship and advertising were simply the final expression of the selling idea. It was Butler's intent to consider "the whole field of selling" – "everything that the promoter of a product has to do prior to his actual use of salesmen and of advertising."[3] In attempting to find a name to designate this "field of business activity," he hit upon the phrase "marketing methods." He then used that term in the title of a course consisting of six printed pamphlets published by the University in 1910, as the name of a course in residence in 1911, and as the title of his book published in 1914.

To Butler, what he called "marketing" was a *combination* of factors. It was more than selling, more than choice of channels, advertising, or the operation of wholesale and retail establishments. Marketing was a job of co-ordination, of planning – the "binding force" in marketing, of management of the complicated relations among the various "factors in trade" that must be considered first by the distributor who wishes to build his campaign with care.

Shaw's conception of marketing was comparable, although perhaps more

144

scholastic. He, too, through wide experience with many types of businesses, had perceived the uniformity of business procedures, and he was interested in the application of scientific management principles to their common distribution problems. While assisting in the reorganization of the Harvard Business School, he found it necessary to intellectualize his observations when asked to lecture on English middlemen for a class in English economic history. Thinking of what middlemen did, Shaw distinguished three basic operations in business: production, distribution, and facilitating functions or administration. In connection with that, he recalled a concept credited to Bohm-Bawerk, that business is concerned with "motion" of one sort or another – specifically, motion changing form, called "production," or motion changing place and ownership, called "distribution."[4] The motion of administration included financing, credits and collections, purchasing, employment, and accounting. Generalizing this concept, he conceived marketing as "matter in motion." Many of these ideas were incorporated in an article, "Some Problems in Market Distribution," published in the *Quarterly Journal of Economies,* August, 1912, which, with an added first chapter, was published in book form in 1915.

EARLY GENERALIZATIONS

With Butler and Shaw, some of the earliest generalizations concerning the over-all marketing process began to appear. Some of those stated by Shaw were of an economic nature, but for the most part they expressed the types of ideas that within a few years thereafter were called the "elements" of marketing, and in the early 1920s "principles." The following are illustrative:

1. Lost motions in distribution are a social waste, for which consumers pay.
2. Accepted systems of distribution at that time (in the nineteenth century) had been built for the selling of staples.
3. Progressive manufacturers differentiated their goods and, by branding, isolated them in the market.
4. The ideas about goods are the materials for demand creation.
5. Goods are sold in bulk by inspection, by sample, and by description. Sale by sample was considered best when distribution was made by direct saleman or by middlemen; description was involved in sale through advertising.
6. The basic functions of middlemen include sharing the risk, transporting, financing, selling, and assembling, sorting, and reshipping.
7. Middlemen include insurance agencies, transportation companies, and banks.
8. As responsibility for performance of these functions is shifted from middlemen to manufacturers, the middleman's margin should be diminished.
9. The market is characterized by "market contours," in contrast to a level plain, representing different economic and social strata in the market.
10. Despite the trend toward shorter channels of distribution, elimination of the middleman did not always make for the most economical distribution.

Butler's writings also contained a number of such generalizations:[5]

1. That the marketing function is universal in business.
2. That "factors in trade," which are considered in managerial decisions concerning the over-all marketing program, include (a) the goods to be sold, (b) the markets for those goods, and (c) methods reaching the markets. Reduced to such an analysis, the management decision appears to have been placed upon the "philosophy and principle at the heart of sound marketing procedure."
3. The predictions that chain stores would gain prominence in the sale of foods and drugs and that advertising would become a main force in selling.
4. Concepts indicating the interests of the period: bypassing the middleman, price fixing, and the private-brand problem.

INSTITUTIONAL ANALYSIS

Throughout the period 1910-20 three approaches to the analysis of marketing were developed: the commodity, the institutional, and the functional. The first was a study of the processes involved in the marketing of a product or group of products. The second was a descriptive analysis of the wholesale and retail institutions. The third was a study of marketing functions or activities. Normally, all three "approaches" were included in the traditional general work on marketing, and precedence for this was established by Louis D. H. Weld in his *Marketing of Farm Products,* in 1916.[6]

Originally a teacher of economics, Weld began his interest in marketing with a teaching and research assignment that required him to ascertain how Minnesota products were marketed. As a result of his firsthand investigation of the subject, he offered a course on the marketing of farm products — the first such course, according to him, in which "marketing" appeared in the name. Like others, when Weld began to teach marketing in 1913, he was impressed with the lack of literature on the subject. His investigations preparatory to his teaching led him to consider particularly practices of grain exchanges, price quotations, operations of co-operatives, and costs of marketing.

Weld's contributions to marketing thought were influenced by his training in economics and by his thorough habits of research. He regarded marketing as a part of production, since it is a part of the productive process, creating time, place, and possession utilities. Although centering his attention on the marketing of farm products, he actually emphasized the institutional approach to marketing concentrating his attention on wholesale middlemen engaged in agricultural marketing. He saw merchants as specialists in the handling of certain commodities — specialists in four successive stages between farmers and consumers: country shippers, transportation companies, wholesale dealers, and retail stores. He believed specialization to be desirable because it reduced costs. However, knowing that specialization can become excessive, he questioned whether there might be too many middlemen — too many successive steps, and too many middlemen in each class. The problem was that of finding the most economical combination of functions. Weld believed that produce exchanges represented the most efficient type of marketing, and retailing the most expensive. His interest in marketing was more than merely managerial, rather, it was in part an interest from the social point of view.

Although Weld gave some consideration to functions in his book, more attention was given them in his article "Marketing Functions and Mercantile Organizations, " [7] in which he identified seven functions of middlemen: assembling, storing, risk bearing, financing, rearrangement (sorting, packing, dividing), selling, and transporting. He discussed also the functions involved in marketing goods through different channels.

Weld's contributions were his analysis of marketing as an economic process, his concept of specialization among institutions of the marketing system, and his further clarification of thought concerning marketing functions.

MARKETING FUNCTIONS

With marketing institutions well described by Weld, Paul T. Cherington[8] developed more the concept of marketing functions. Almost all writers had been concerned with the activities performed by organizations engaged in marketing; some dealt with them as the "specialization" that justified the marketing establishments. Gradually, however, the concept became clearer that institutions arose to perform the functions that were inherent in the marketing task. This was the idea implicit in Cherington's treatment of marketing functions as the most fundamental aspect of marketing, for which "other aspects are used."

Cherington defined marketing as "the science involved in the distribution of merchandise from producer to consumer, excluding . . . alterations of form." That definition excluded from marketing changes in product form, an exclusion that was not made by some students of agricultural marketing at that time. Moreover, the definition represented a crystalizing concept of marketing as activities — activities between the producer and consumer — a definition that became almost universally accepted in the following years.

1920-30 — THE PERIOD OF INTEGRATION

Events in the third decade of this century gave great impetus to marketing activity. Industrial and agricultural production reached new peaks. New products appeared in the retail market. Agricultural producers' co-operatives flourished under governmental encouragement. Studies of the wholesaler gave justification to his role and position in distribution. Market research based upon surveys and censuses promised a new era of marketing. Prosperity in general was on the increase, although spokesmen for the consumer became vocal in criticism of neglect of the consumers' interest in the market. Metropolitan areas expanded with the influx of emigrants from farms. Department stores were thriving, and retail chains grew in size through mergers.

That decade was a fertile period in the writing of specialized marketing books. Knowledge in all areas was in a stage of integration, and basic or "principles" texts were produced in every field. General works on advertising were published by Keppner, Brewster, Starch, Hotchkiss, and Agnew. In salesmanship, books were written by Brisco, Russell, Tosdal, and Ivey, and in sales management by Russell. Important writings on credit appeared, such as Seligman's study of the economics of instalment selling and Young's work on industrial credit; the principal works in that field were the integrative writings of Steiner, Brisco, Beckman, and Chapin. "The Retailing Series" produced by New York University appeared during that decade, including writings by Brisco,

Wingate, Severa, and Fri. Beckman's *Wholesaling* was published in 1926. Thus, in addition to the stimulating environmental circumstances, marketing thought was attaining a richness, variety, and maturity that opened the way for important developments in the general statement of marketing.

During the ten years following 1920 the "principles of marketing" were first presented in book form, built upon foundations laid previously, integrating scattered concepts and tentative generalizations, and incorporating an abundance of new material then available. Clark, Converse, and Maynard, Weidler, and Beckman were the foremost writers of integrated marketing thought. Others during that decade were C. S. Duncan, Ivey, Hibbard, Macklin, and Moriarity.

COMMODITY ANALYSIS

Several of the integrative works appearing early in the 1920s were basically commodity studies of marketing. While they described the marketing of specific commodities, they illustrated, as had Weld's *Marketing,* the interrelations of commodity characteristics, functions, and institutions. C. S. Duncan, Theodore Macklin, and B. H. Hibbard were three who undertook such an integration of marketing thought at that time.

Duncan dealt with both agricultural and manufactured products[9] because his interest in marketing arose in connection with individual commodities. Actually, rather than "agricultural" commodities, Duncan spoke of "raw materials and foodstuffs." He analyzed the functions performed in the marketing of them. The marketing of manufactured goods he discussed from the standpoint of functions, institutions, economic analysis, and policies and procedures. It was his belief that the best scientific approach to commercial problems was through a combination of functional, institutional, and commodity approaches.

C. S. Duncan published his work on marketing the year after his *Commercial Research* has appeared and simultaneously with the preparation by Clark and Converse of their books. Duncan's interest in marketing was short lived. Previously he had been engaged in the study of English composition; ultimately he devoted himself to problems of transportation and wrote no more in the field of general marketing.

Macklin undertook through the study of agricultural marketing to answer the criticisms of marketing in general that were commonplace then. Having become interested in the marketing of agricultural products in 1911, he observed the ignorance of what transpired between farmers and consumers, which was depicted even in cartoons captioned "What happens in the dark?" He shed light on this question by showing the essentiality of certain services if consumers were to utilize the products of farms: assembling, grading and standardizing, packaging, processing, transporting, storing, financing, and distributing. He defined marketing as the rendering of those essential services.

Macklin's concept of marketing, however, was characterized by an element more common among students of agricultural marketing than of the marketing of manufactured products, namely, the inclusion in marketing of the creation of certain types of form utility. In fact, he regarded production as the rendering by farmers and middlemen of all those services essential to bringing into use the goods and services required to satisfy wants of consumers.[10] He identified five types of utilities: elementary, place, form, time, and possession utilities. The tendency to include processing of farm products in marketing has persisted even until today. While such a concept may have served the purpose of farmers and their economists, it has not been consistent with the evolving concept of marketing.

Edmund Brown, Jr., also employed the commodity analysis in his *Marketing,*[11] in which two-fifths of the book consisted of fourteen chapters describing the marketing of fourteen commodities. His work was descriptive and uncritical, based more upon his own practice and observations than upon contemporary developments in marketing thought. For that reason, perhaps, he conceived of consumer goods as staples and specialties, giving no heed to other classifications then in use.

"PRINCIPLES" OF MARKETING

When the commodity, functional, and institutional analyses of marketing had been sufficiently explored, and when the "elements" of marketing had been set forth, general marketing thought was integrated under the heading of "principles of marketing." Three or four such statements of marketing appeared in book form in a short succession of years.

Paul W. Ivey was the first to use the title *Principles of Marketing,*[12] although others had previously used "principles" in connection with advertising, retailing, and credit granting. Like some of his contemporaries, Ivey approached the subject from the standpoint of functions, which he called "functions of middlemen": assembling, grading, storing, transporting, risk bearing, financing, and selling. "All of them," he said "usually function to some extent in the marketing of goods,"[13] expressing a concept of the universality of such functions. He recognized, however, that the performance of functions was split between manufacturers and middlemen. Sometimes, on the other hand, manufacturers undertook to perform all but assembling, thus tending to eliminate both wholesaler and retailer. Ivey stated somewhat as a principle that "the middleman himself can be eliminated, but his functions cannot."

In his discussion of marketing institutions, Ivey recognized the essential character of different types and also the tendency of institutions to change their character by changing the functions they perform. He allayed criticism of wholesalers by enumerating the functions performed by that middleman for both manufacturers and retailers. Among the newer types of institutions then gaining attention were manufacturing wholesalers, retailers who took on wholesalers' functions, and wholesalers who sold on the retail level.

Much emphasis was given by Ivey to advertising and its costs. He was concerned with the fact that "getting the goods to the consumer has now become as important as the actual production of goods, and the costs are oftentimes as great."[14] He discussed at length the incidence of advertising costs, showing their significance in the case of goods produced under conditions of constant, increasing, and decreasing costs. The extent of his analysis of this subject was not equaled in any marketing book for fifteen years thereafter.

Ivey also introduced into the general analysis of marketing a concluding critique of the marketing system, giving a social evaluation not found in the purely technical treatises on marketing. Because Ivey never revised his book, apparently as a result of increasing preoccupation with the selling function, it was eventually replaced; by others soon to appear, and the impact of his contribution to the field was less than it might otherwise have been.

Of greatest influence upon the integration of general marketing thought were Paul D. Converse, Fred E. Clark, Harold H. Maynard, Walter C. Weidler, and Theodore N. Beckman, all of whom wrote "principles" texts during the 1920s. Their influence was measured not only by innovations introduced in structuring marketing thought but also by the fact that they, through repeated revision of their writings, continued for the next thirty or forty years to influence the manner in which marketing was conceived. There were always differences in the details of their presentations, but their uniformity was more significant than were their differences.

In general, under the influence of those men, threads of thought that had been forming through the work of Butler, Shaw, Weld, Cherington, Ivey, and others writing in the specialized fields were woven into a logical, coherent, and encompassing body of thought. The core of their presentation was the interrelated commodity, functional, institutional analyses, which were descriptive of prevailing practices, yet which depicted the marketing system in general rather than presenting operating rules for any one type of marketing activity. Some management viewpoint was introduced in the discussion of "marketing policy." The subject of marketing was introduced by consideration of "the market" and some aspects of consumer behavior; it was concluded by a social appraisal of marketing made mostly in terms of economic criteria.

Part of the distinctive character of the work contributed by the writers was due to the personal backgrounds of each. Converse flavored his work with practicality and gave much attention to the marketing of agricultural products. He had been reared in a religious but free-thinking family, and this somewhat tempered his idealism with realism. The guiding influence in business, he thought, were self-interest, moral percepts, and policemen. Instruction under Butler and teaching experience in a vocationally inclined school caused him to emphasize the occupational use of marketing knowledge. Use of Nystrom's *Economics of Retailing* as a text in his teaching influenced his emphasis on institutions in marketing. The fact that he was situated in rural Illinois drew his attention to problems of agricultural marketing. And the absence of vocational evening school classes where he taught allowed him to concentrate upon fundamentals and principles rather than upon mere techniques.

In his *Marketing Methods and Policies,*[15] Paul D. Converse distinguished between "functions of middlemen," or the marketing activities related to the individual firm, and "marketing functions," or the abstract, generalized activities that pervade marketing in general. His list of marketing functions included assembling, dividing, grading, transporting, storing, financing, risk, sorting, and packing.

His treatment of marketing institutions consisted mainly of a consideration of the advantages and disadvantages of each. He interpreted changes in retailing from a historical standpoint, showing the newer institutions that represented modification of wholesalers' service. Auctions, co-operative marketing and consumers' co-operatives also held his attention. In subsequent years he gave increasing emphasis to functional and commodity approaches and to the marketing of industrial goods and services.

Fred E. Clark, trained as an economist and reared and educated in farm states, combined these influences in his *Principles of Marketing.*[16] He defined marketing as those efforts which effect transfer in the ownership of goods and

150

care for their physical distribution. His list of functions corresponded closely to those given by Weld; and from Cherington he took his classification of functions as physical supply, exchange, and auxiliary or facilitating functions. The following concepts illustrate something of the substance of his thought and the status of marketing at that time.

A market: a point of concentration
The need for markets: an outgrowth of division of labor
The market structure: built around two processes — transfer of title; transfer of goods.
Channel: the course taken in transfer of title
Types of middlemen: merchant, functional (including advertising agencies — including banks and warehouses).
Classification of middlemen: based upon concentration and dispersion.
Classes of goods: personal goods, production goods, and equipment for use in production and distribution.
Marketing efficiency: a judgment from two viewpoints — private, appraising operating efficiency; public, appraising social significance.
A typical generalization: Middlemen will continue so long as they perform useful functions.

Clark was much concerned with the role and efficiency of marketing from a social point of view. Therefore, in a chapter on "Final Criticism" he dealt with a number of topics then being widely discussed. He defended advertising for its educational value and for sometimes providing a cheaper method of selling than would personal salesmanship. He placed hope in the chain store as an efficient method of merchandising. He advocated more standardization of consumer goods but questioned the desirability of branded staples.

Harold H. Maynard, Walter C. Weidler, and Theodore N. Beckman published their *Principle of Marketing*[17] when the concept of marketing and structure of analysis had been well established. They added few new ideas to the subject, but their objective in writing was to supply "suitable text material for our classes in marketing. We felt that our points of view were somewhat different from all but one of the existing textbooks. Our organization seemed more teachable, and we thought that we had had more practical experience than some of the writers, and therefore, could enrich the material with many more useful illustrations."[18]

The point of view referred to was the "consumers' viewpoint," in contrast to the entrepreneur's viewpoint, which characterized most of the marketing writings then. The effect of adopting this "viewpoint" was mainly the introduction at the beginning of their treatise of consideration of consumer buying motives. Neither the analysis nor the appraisal of marketing differed perceptibly from other existing texts.

Their second innovation, reflecting academic rather than business factors, was to discuss institutions in advance of functions, on the ground of proceeding from the tangible to the intangible, from the known to the unknown.

UNORTHODOX APPRAISALS OF MARKETING

The type of analysis presented by Maynard, Weidler, and Beckman in the *Principles* quickly became the accepted pattern for a general treatise on marketing. Their nicely structured, approving discourse, however, although satisfying to many readers, was not all that some writers wished to say about marketing. On the contrary, there were more critical appraisals of the subject, more penetrating analyses than the simple descriptions of marketing institutions and practices, which people wanted to present, and some of these observations got into print. Most of them made little impression upon marketing teachers and writers imbued with the "traditional" approach, but in the development of marketing thought they represent a divergent viewpoint that after the middle of the twentieth century found wider expression.

One of the atypical writings in the 1920s was W. D. Moriarity's *The Economics of Marketing and Advertising,*[19] in which the author undertook to interpret marketing phenomena in terms of classical economic doctrine. He took the point of view that marketing is largely an expression of economic theory. Therefore, in terms of standard economic analysis he discussed a great many marketing topics, such as the relationship of supply and demand in the marketing economy; the impossibility of overproduction so long as goods are marketed and sold; the contrast between general overproduction and overproduction of specific articles; the limitless possibilities of market development when production is co-ordinated with the capacity of the sales force; the possibility of "anticipated demand" through credit buying, which may cause market demand to exceed market supply; the reality of time and place utilities; the creation of new value through salesmanship creating consumer surplus or real income; and the relation of marginal buyers to market price.

Such an analysis had little to offer either economists or students of marketing at the time, for it neither improved upon prevailing economic theory nor met the needs for which the study of marketing had originally departed from traditional economic analysis. It did, nevertheless, represent a more theoretical approach that might be taken in the study of marketing.

Another unusual point of view was contributed by Percival White, an engineer by training, who was well informed on Taylor's scientific principles of management. In *Scientific Marketing Management: Its Principles and Methods,*[20] White exposed "abuses" of marketing as wastes of the distributive system and proposed a system of practice for the guidance of individual companies in their marketing activity. This was not a full treatment of the subject of marketing; it covered only a selected area from a particular point of view.

Floyd L. Vaughan was still another who, purporting to speak from a social or public standpoint rather than from that of the acquisitive businessman, criticized the increasing cost of marketing.[21] Some of the greater costs, he held, were justified in terms of changing market conditions, but many reflected competitive, wasteful, and harmful business practice. He proposed reducing the cost of marketing by giving less emphasis to quality, variety, style, service, and salesmanship, by closer relationship between production and consumption; by discontinuance of indirect subsidies; and by emphasis of functions rather than media. He advocated less advertising but better advertising. In general, Vaughan looked at the *cost* instead of the *value* of marketing; he appraised it from a conservative rather than a progressive viewpoint.

Roland S. Vaile and Peter L. Slagsvold gave still another emphasis to the subject in their *Marketing,*[22] published in 1929. They viewed the age as one of co-operative economic action. Self-sufficiency was superseded by specialization and exchange – in both domestic and international production and trade. In this milieu of exchange they were concerned with two types of understanding of marketing principles: (1) those of price, involving all the forces that affect supply and demand, and (2) those of production economics, involving questions as to the best size of marketing unit, the most efficient combination of production factors, and the most expeditious degree of specialization. They developed, therefore, exposition of the forces and institutions concerned with price making, contrasting those operating in the more competitive markets for agricultural goods with those in the manipulatable markets for manufactured goods. Their discussion of institutions showed not merely the operation of those institutions but also the manner in which they represented some degree of effectiveness in the combination of factors for the accomplishment of distributive objectives. Theirs was an economic analysis based upon a few basic propositions.

READINGS IN MARKETING

At the same time that "principles" of marketing were being written, several books of "readings" also appeared. Fred E. Clark,[23] I. Wright and C. E. Landon,[24] and E. L. Rhoades[25] were the contributors to this form of literature in the 1920s. The term "readings" did not thereafter appear in general marketing titles until 1949, when M. P. McNair and H. L. Hansen published *Readings in Marketing*.[26] These books played a small role in the development of marketing thought, but they are indicative of an interesting stage in its evolution.

Of his book, Clark said that the readings were designed to provide descriptive and supplementary material for use in the study of commodity marketing. They were intended to aid both student and teacher and to provide current material likely to be missing in the libraries of many schools where the *Principles* was used. The *Principles* and the *Readings* followed the same pattern of organization. The readings were digests of articles, pamphlets, monographs, texts, etc.

The compilation of readings by Wright and Landon was similar. In it they attempted to provide the student and teacher with the "best material" available relating to economics and marketing. Articles were arranged according to functions, institutions, and policies.

Rhoades, on the other hand, prepared readings to keep the principles of marketing from being mere "empty theories." He presented articles describing the marketing of fifty-nine specific commodities – the functions performed and the institutions involved. From this he expected the student to make a "comparative" study.

Whereas the earlier group of readings was mainly factual, supplementing theory or principles with detail, those appearing around the mid-century contained articles often more theoretically advanced than the prevailing general texts. During the later period similar books, not called readings, were also published, containing article digests, talks presented at special conferences, and the like.

PROBLEMS IN MARKETING

Throughout the 1920s *Marketing Problems*[27] by Melvin T. Copeland appeared in several revisions. Its objective was the same as for the general texts: to develop principles. After teaching from problems for three years, Copeland said in the 1923 edition that he found this to be the best way. On the whole, the problems were related to the same topics developed in the principles' texts. As changing circumstances required, new topics were added. In 1927 a section on the consumers' point of view was dropped and one on industrial goods added. In 1931 emphasis was placed on showing the interrelation of the various marketing activities.

1930-40 — THE PERIOD OF DEVELOPMENT

Following what might be regarded as the Golden Decade in the development of marketing thought, when its traditional integration and statement were achieved, the next ten years were characterized by revision and enlargement of thought. The "principles" texts were kept up to date, and a number of other writings appeared that were in different ways unlike the popular writings.

COMMODITY MARKETING

The interest that had long been shown in the marketing of specific commodities persisted, and two studies were forthcoming relating to non-agricultural products and manufactured goods. Ralph F. Breyer, in *Commodity Marketing*,[28] furnished an excellent example of illustrating marketing principles by the commodity approach. Feeling that too little attention had been given to other than agricultural products in marketing descriptions, Breyer devised a standard form of analysis, which he applied to the marketing of bituminous and anthracite coal, crude petroleum, iron ore, rolled steel, Portland cement, cotton textiles, passenger automobiles, and electricity and telephone service. For each he showed the conditons of demand and supply, major characteristics of the product, channels of distribution, agencies engaged, functions performed, pricing, distribution costs, trade practices, and association activities.

A second study, *Marketing of Manufactured Goods*,[29] was made by Newel H. Comish. As Weld in his study of farm products actually furnished a thorough analysis of the *institutions* engaged in the marketing of them, so Comish provided a highly specialized discussion of the institutions engaged in marketing manufactured goods. In great detail, he discussed thirteen channels through which products move, identifying each with a particular institution, such as the sales agency, the broker, the specialty store, etc. Their respective advantages and disadvantages were carefully considered. He was also concerned with a variety of special marketing problems related to specialty goods, prices, price maintenance, industrial recovery, and market research. The book was essentially a manual prepared for manufacturers.

SIMPLIFIED STATEMENTS OF MARKETING

A tendency evident in specialized marketing literatures characterized also the general writings, namely, the simplification of a substantial body of thought for elementary academic purposes. Whereas, in successive revisions the leading principles text became enlarged and more complex, a number of writers condensed and simplified the subject.

One example of this tendency is seen in *Outlines of Marketing*,[30] by H. E. Agnew, R. B. Jenkins, and J. C. Drury. Written for a freshman course in marketing, it followed somewhat the usual organization, but its proportions were unusual. Only six pages were given to the subject of chain stores, three to mail order houses, and nine to marketing functions, while fourteen pages were devoted to reproducing census data. The authors presented a glossary of marketing terms, expressive of the rising interest in uniformity of terminology, but even that feature could not have constituted a contribution to marketing thought in such a book.

C. W. Barker and N. Anshen presented another condensation of the usual treatment of marketing.[31] In 326 pages they presented a text intended for a one-course student with limited background or as an introduction to marketing "why" rather than the "what," but in that respect their book did not differ from others. Marketing was regarded as a fine art rather than as an exact science, thus permitting the emphasis they gave to the development of problem-solving ability — a concept then beginning to appear increasingly in management and marketing thought.

NEW STANDARD STUDIES

Throughout the 1930s a few efforts were made to duplicate or to better the general treatises on marketing contained in the principles texts by Converse, Clark, and Maynard, all of whom made periodic revisions of their works. Competition was too great, and no significantly new ideas threatening change in the concept of marketing seemed capable of assimilation into the traditional body of thought without altering it more than was then acceptable.

The single exception to this general failure of new writers to break into the popular field of general texts was Charles F. Phillips, whose *Marketing*[32] was published in 1938.

One of its distinctive characteristics was the light in which he held the consumer. This, of course, would have been a natural effect of the expressions of consumers' rights and interests made during the 1930s. Most of the general writers professed interest in the consumer, but Phillips went beyond mere statement of consumer buying motives and conditions affecting consumers. He was concerned with the part consumers take in guiding the economy, their problem in getting their money's worth, and the effects of consumers' poor buying effort.

Phillips also introduced into the general text more economic analysis than other authors had. His treatment of price policies and price behavior incorporated into the text analyses of marginal and average revenue and costs, as well as monopolistic-competitive pricing, which were popular among economists then. He also presented interesting historical interpretations of the evolution of marketing institutions.

UNORTHODOX STUDIES

As in the preceding decade, several contributions were made to marketing thought that were not cut to the accepted pattern. Ralph F. Breyer and H. B. Killough were two whose ideas were set in a frame of untraditional concepts and organization.

Breyer, in *The Marketing Institution*,[33] broke with the conventional economic concept of marketing by drawing concepts from physics, sociology, psychology, and other social sciences in his attempt to portray the functioning of the marketing system "as a whole." He saw marketing, viewed in its unity, as a continuous performance of each and all of the marketing functions. Rather than "functions," he used a concept of marketing "tasks": contactual, negotiatory, storage, measurement, quality determination, packing, transportation, payment, financing, and risk-bearing. Channels were conceived as analogous to electric circuits, through which "flows" move in both directions; i.e., merchandise flows in one direction, payments in the other. Time, space, and cost elements were fundamental factors in the explanation of channel choices. The latter portion of his book was devoted to the social effectiveness of marketing, particularly in relation to the New Deal, which was effective then.

At the time of its publication, Breyer's book was compared unfavorably with conventional works because the concepts he employed were foreign to the economic theory upon which traditional explanation of marketing was based. From the common viewpoint, Breyer may have been appraised as trying to say "the same thing" in a "different" way. Actually, however, he was attempting to rise above the mechanistic concept of marketing, whereby it was portrayed as separate or unrelated functions, and to present a *theory* of a compound operation. His effort failed to make much impression on the market for ideas at the time, yet it represented another expression of ideas of marketing that were struggling to be heard.

Another unorthodox analysis of marketing was offered by H. B. Killough in his *Economics of Marketing.*[34] Designed to provide an economic background against which to examine the evolution of marketing institutions and practices, it differed completely in organization and content from the usual works. Eight chapters dealt with the economic and geographic setting of American business, to show the continuing change taking place. Ten marketing functions were recognized, including accounting (usually a factory function) and estimating (more of a marketing function). He also thought that record keeping and figure analysis were as important marketing functions as storing and transporting. The subject of marketing agencies was dispensed with in twenty-three pages. More than two hundred pages, on the other hand, were devoted to marketing research, an extension of the scientific method applied to marketing. While there was merit in some of the innovations introduced by Killough, his concepts and terminology did not become a part of popular marketing thought.

1940-50 – THE PERIOD OF REAPPRAISAL

During the decade 1940-50 there were interruptions to the development of marketing thought, but following World War II the lines of thought that had been evolving were again carried forward. Revisions were made of the Converse, Maynard, and Phillips books, and a vast market was supplied with their type of presentation of marketing. Simultaneously, however, an increasing number of ideas – concepts and approaches – at variance with the traditional explanation of marketing found expression and acceptance. It was as though ideas given utterance by such men as Moriarity, Vaughan, Breyer, Killough, and others, during the preceding twenty years, were taking form with new meaning – not necessarily the same ideas or the same symbolism in the presentation of them, but a viewpoint expressing concepts that were not included in the usual interpretations of marketing. New emphasis was given to the management of marketing – as consisting of more than the application of simple rules or principles. More of the consumer viewpoint and of economic analysis were introduced. Repeated effort was made to deal with marketing as a "whole," and its aspects as an institution – a social institution – were interpreted.

The concept of marketing as a management function was basic to thought set forth in 1940 by Ralph S. Alexander, F. M. Surface, R. F. Elder, and Wroe Alderson in *Marketing.*[35] Unlike some authors, they disparaged the commodity approach and referred to specific commodities only to point out their essential characteristics as they affect the performance of marketing management. More than usual emphasis was given to the planning of marketing activities, to research, and to budgetary control. A number of management functions not provided for in the usual array of marketing functions were included in a ninth function — merchandising — which was defined as "the adjustment of merchandise produced or offered for sale to consumer demand." This consisted of product planning, simplification, grading, and packaging, all of which were areas of management. Separate chapters were devoted to such topics as the work of marketing, the business establishments that do the work of marketing, the problems of marketing management, the planning of marketing activities, and the consumer's stake in the marketing system. No final chapter on evaluation or critique of marketing was given, but merely one on the problems of consumers in the presence of the prevailing marketing systems.

Thus were incorporated into marketing thought new emphases on consumer interest in marketing and on marketing management functions. Increased attention to those two factors was also found in the later editions of *Marketing: Principles and Methods* by Phillips and D. J. Duncan. These changes and others were made when Duncan assumed co-authorship.

E. A. Duddy and D. A. Revzan took still a different tack in their analysis of marketing, having as their objective getting "the student to think of the marketing structure as an organic whole made up of interrelated parts, subject to growth and change and functioning in a process of distribution that is coordinated by economic and social forces."[36] Thus in taking the "institutional approach," they were concerned not merely with individual marketing establishments or the management of them, but with the entire marketing operation as a phenomenon and expression of our society.

Duddy and Revzan defined marketing as "the economic process by means of which goods and services are exchanged and their values determined in terms of money prices."[37] They classified markets as to place, time, theory, and function. They identified as possible approaches to the study of marketing the following: legal, commodity, theoretical, institutional, and functional. They saw functions giving rise to structural organizations — of agency, area, and price — all of which were co-ordinated through the instrumentalities of price, management, and the controlling and regulating power of government. Their interpretation of marketing was the analysis of the interrelationships of structures and their co-ordinating forces, particularly as they affect the performance of functions and the satisfaction of consumers.

Still another approach to marketing was taken by Roland S. Vaile, E. T. Grether, and Reavis Cox in *Marketing in the American Economy,*[38] in which they attempted to show "the transcendent importance of this social institution (marketing) as a vast and complex function of our free-enterprise economy." They conceived marketing as a process of allocating and directing the use of resources, the activities and organizations, collectively, by which all things are assembled simultaneously for consumption. The "core of marketing" was the exchange and movement of goods among areas and within and between regions.

They saw marketing as a dynamic process, and their explanation gave emphasis to sellers, particularly manufacturers, because, in taking the initiative in distribution, the promotional plans of manufacturers characterize marketing in the United States. Institutions, agencies, and channels were regarded as sequences and combinations of ownership. Processes of collecting, sorting, and dispersing give rise to specialization and integration of enterprises. Management of processes and institutions is conducted for the purpose of maximizing net income of the firm, but the marketing operation as a whole is appraised in terms of social growth.

Thus a number of explanations of marketing had an entirely different conceptual framework than did those which had been dominant for many years. Although these atypical approaches did not displace others or influence changes in the standard presentations, they were significant expressions of dissatisfaction with the inadequacy of the functional-institutional-commodity analysis of marketing. It was not expected that such different interpretations of marketing would serve the same purpose; rather, the newer ones expressed conviction of new needs in marketing education and training — need for education in the broader role that marketing plays among our social institutions and need for training in management of a more conceptual and theoretical nature. These varied ideas, which had been reaching for expression throughout several decades, after the middle of the century found wider outlet in emphasis of integrated marketing management, managerial problem solving and decision making, integration of marketing with the behavioral sciences, the case method of teaching marketing, and comparative marketing studies.

1950-60 — PERIOD OF RECONCEPTION

The distinction between the more or less untraditional writings of the 1940s and those of the following decade was thin, but as it became clarified it was apparent that the concept of marketing was being reformulated. The distinguishing factors in the literature of the two periods are the degree of concern with theoretical statement of marketing knowledge, reliance upon concepts from other social sciences for interpreting market behavior, and replacement of the commodity-function-institution classification of subject matter by one dealing with products, channels, prices, and promotional activities. The so-called management approach, which had been introduced into all areas of marketing thought and which had predominant expression in sales management literature, influenced also the general marketing writings. However, whereas in the works on "sales management" the managerial approach was used to develop management talent, in "general marketing" writings that approach was used to acquaint students, particularly the nonmarketing majors, with the types of problems and decisions faced by managers of marketing activity. On the whole, the trends of thought that marked the 1950s continued with increased elaboration and clarification into the 1960s.

The growing interest in theoretical aspects of marketing, for example, was shown in the selection by Cox and Alderson of the title *Theory in Marketing*[39] for a compilation of essays dealing with assorted aspects of marketing. Their selections were made to show the relations of marketing to economic theory, public policy, and other social disciplines. Concepts such as the following were presented by the writers represented: social physics, vector psychology, behavior systems, pluralistic competition, theory of economic opportunity, and regional and interregional trade. Many of the ideas therein presented were fragmentary, abbreviated, and personal. They nevertheless contained germs of thought that developed in following years.

Wroe Alderson gave fuller expression to what he called a "functional theory of marketing" in his *Marketing Behavior and Executive Action*.[40] That too represented an effort to show the relationships of marketing thought to knowledge developed in the other social sciences. His analysis proceeded from a concept of market behavior as group behavior and of individuals seeking to achieve their purposes through organized behavior systems. He regarded their market behavior as problem-solving action. Marketing organizations were seen as behavior systems developed to serve the market, their operations governed by principles of action that he called "functionalism." Among the concepts that Alderson infused into marketing thought were the following:

Marketing systems as input-output systems.
The normality of heterogeneity in the market.
Every firm occupying a position that is somewhat unique, and thus competing from a standpoint of differential advantage.
Negotiation as the means by which marketing systems established economic values and balance power.
Exchange as essentially the act of improving assortments held by two parties.
The domain of marketing as the process of sorting as a means of accomplishing effective matching.

Alderson introduced into marketing thought a variety of concepts from the social and physical sciences and presented an integrated theory of marketing such as had not been stated before. His ideas conceptualized some thinking then current and influenced the logic and terminology of writers in subsequent years.

Because less pretentious treatises were more common during the 1950s, "readings" relating to topics of current interest were one means by which coherence and integration were given to the new ideas relevant to marketing appearing both within and without the marketing literature. One such compilation was *Managerial Marketing: Perspectives and Viewpoints*,[41] by Eugene J. Kelley and William Lazer. Their objective was to present articles that would stimulate creative thinking about contemporary marketing problems. Their selections were made with a view toward emphasizing the consumer as the focus of marketing effort, the need for creative adaptation to change, the importance of programing or planning goal-directed marketing effort, the role of strategy in the marketing mix, and the importance of marketing communications.

Alderson presented a provocative personal theory; Kelley and Lazer presented a partially integrated structure for thought. The task remained for someone to present an acceptable integration of marketing that would serve as an introduction upon which more specialized study could be built or as a comprehensive explanation of marketing for both specialist and non-specialist in the field. While some writings on marketing management provided an integration with breadth, those works generally omitted social interpretations of marketing.

On the other hand, revisions of the former "principles" of marketing did not include much of the so-called managerial approach.

Not until 1960 and 1961 did there appear works that approximated a satisfying new general statement or explanation of marketing, embodying new concepts that had been developing and presenting the subject from the standpoints both of the firm and of society.

One was that of E. Jerome McCarthy – *Basic Marketing: A Managerial Approach*[42] – which combined the usual concepts of managerial marketing with a social and historical orientation of marketing and with an appraisal of marketing as a social institution. Although others dealing with the managerial functions in marketing had similarly treated product planning, place or channel of distribution, pricing, and promotion, McCarthy conceptualized these four factors in the marketing mix as the "Four Ps," and the management portion of his thought structure was built upon this concept.

Buskirk, in 1961, was the first writer for a number of years to present a new general book on marketing using the term "principles" in the title.[43] His approach was a managerial approach; his intent was to show nonmarketing majors how the working of the marketing system appears through managerial eyes.

1960-70 – PERIOD OF DIFFERENTIATION

During the first fifty years of its development, marketing thought came to a focus in the "general" literature. These writings were the summation of marketing thought, the integration of specialized knowledge, and constituted the nearest approximation to a statement of general marketing theory. The books of this literature served as texts in introductory marketing courses and as outlines for graduate education. They were valued for their *content* of marketing information, rather than for their conceptual framework or for the methodology which they represented. They presented the "principles" of marketing.

Beginning in the 1950s and continuing thereafter, centripetal rather than centrifugal patterns predominated as emphasis turned toward specialization and away from generalization in marketing thought. Reconception and redefinition of marketing identified challenging new areas for study and research. The subsequent explosion of knowledge expanded the entire body of thought. This expansion, however, had the character of *enlargement,* rather than *accretion,* whereby the inherent heterogeneity of the body became apparent and subject to specialized analysis. This was a process of *differentiation.*[44] It characterized the 1960s.

Differentiation consisted of the emergence of new conceptual and methodological perspectives in terms of which the marketing process was viewed. Among the new viewpoints were the following:

Management decision making
Social and behavioral patterns
Quantitative analysis
Systems structure and behavior
Environmental constraints
Comparative analysis
International markets
Physical distribution

If, as in a matrix, these viewpoints were arranged along the x axis and the commodity-functional-institutional classifications of marketing along the y axis, the intersectional cells would suggest: (1) the traditional areas into which the new perspectives were extended, and (2) the new elements which generalists must consider in presenting an overall view of marketing. Writings expounding the concepts and methods constituted new specialized literatures. The function of the general marketing literature remained that of interpreting the marketing process in terms of these new developments.

Incorporation of the new ideas into the general literature, however, was gradual, for no encompassing concept of marketing emerged to include them all in a general theory. Some preference for the traditional economic interpretation of marketing persisted. A few new books of this type were written, and revisions of older ones were made. On the other hand, readings books presented short essays on new topics, and some integrated texts presented marketing from the new standpoints.

Depending upon how one might classify some titles, at least 50 representative and significant books of a general character were published during this decade of differentiation. Their titles were varied. Some continued to be called simply *Marketing, Basic Marketing, Principles of Marketing, Essentials of Marketing,* or *Fundamentals of Marketing.* On the other hand, newer emphases were shown in such titles as *Marketing − Concepts and Strategy; Marketing − Concepts, Issues, Perspective; Marketing in a Changing Environment;* and *Introduction to Macro Marketing.*

TRADITIONAL CONTINUANCE

One evidence of changes occurring in the general literature is found in revisions during the 1960s and early 1970s of longstanding successful books of this type. Phillips and Duncan,[45] for example, in 1968 followed their usual functional-institutional format, while introducing new material on large-scale retailing, mergers and acquisitions, merchandising and product development, consumerism, franchising, physical distribution, group activities of wholesalers and retailers, and government regulation. They continued to emphasize, as they said they had through six editions, beginning an understanding of marketing with consideration of the consumer and working backward to the firm and its strategies. They continued to resist changing the title of the book to "management," for they felt one must first know the marketing structure and current developments within the social, economic, and legal environments before he can profitably study management.

The 1973 revision of the Phillips and Duncan book was made by J. M. Carman and K. P. Uhl, who, too, continued to subordinate the strictly managerial approach in preference for interpretation of systemic and environmental forces affecting the marketing system. Within the original format of the book they interjected the systems concept into the following subjects: systems of consumer behavior, retailing and wholesaling systems, structure in marketing systems, global marketing systems, marketing information systems, and promotional systems.

Similarly, the Beckman book[46] in its 1973, 9th edition, retained the format employed since 1927, while updating terminology and introducing new concepts in a subordinate way. It purported having broader social perspective, recognizing a comprehensive and cultural understanding as important as technical and managerial. It analyzed critically the totality of the marketing process, examined major marketing policies and their social implications, and explained controversial issues. Heavy emphasis was placed upon the legal environment in which marketing takes place. Increased attention was also given to concepts of value added, input-output analysis, and income-demand elasticity; to market segmentation versus market aggregation; growth of free form or conglomerates in distribution; franchising; and warehouse retailing.

Thus it appears that general thought maintained its traditional character in revisions of some earlier works. The same may be said of a few books published for the first time during the 1960s:

Taylor and Shaw, *Marketing*, 1961
Buskirk, *Principles of Marketing*, 1962
Stanton, *Fundamentals of Marketing*, 1964
Jones, *The Marketing Process*, 1965
Still and Cundiff, *Essentials of Marketing*, 1966

VARIANTS OF TRADITIONAL APPROACH

Differences between traditional literature and variants produced during the 1960s were mainly attributable to the inclusion of concepts popularized during that decade. All of the general writings had in common an intended educational use and a purpose to explain marketing as a whole. Some of the variations among them reflected interdisciplinary features; others expressed only personal differences in the explanation of marketing. The extent of their differences was apparent in the nature of their departure from the market-function-institution-commodity-government-evaluation structure.

A distinction of one group of these writings was its emphasis of environment, whereas books on environmentalism explained or conceptualized *environment;* those which could be regarded as general literature undertook to explain basic marketing *in terms of* environment. Cundiff and Still,[47] for example, overlaid an analysis of the 4 Ps of marketing with the concept that marketing is a subsystem of business, through which the business organization relates to its environment. Holloway and Hancock[48] also, first in readings and later in text, evidenced the transition from the traditional to an environmental approach. Their 1964 readings portrayed environment not unlike authors of earlier general texts, as social, anthropological, psychological, economic, legal, ethical, competitive, technological, and institutional. The first edition of their text was also conventional. But by 1969, the behavioral and economic environment was supplemented by challenging issues of the social environment: race and poverty problems, social criticism of the chemical industry, social objections to marketing, advertising wastefulness, marketing inefficiency, cigarette smoking and the public interest. The environmental concept was further expanded in their 1973 text, intended for both undergraduate and graduate use. Its theme was that the marketing system is conditioned by and responsive to environmental constraints. They amplified several concepts of environment and devoted one chapter to marketing in other national environments.

A slightly varied but similar approach was taken by Scott and Marks[49] who emphasized *change* in the environment and the adaptivity of the marketing structure. Whereas others, they thought, had dealt primarily with decision making, they were concerned with the controllable factors which exist in an uncontrollable environment. They characterized the firm as a subsystem acting within the socio-economic-political environment.

Bell took another course in carrying a general presentation into the conceptual developments of the period.[50] Half of his book was devoted to explaining concepts from allied disciplines being introduced into marketing thought in the early 1960s; the second half was devoted to the applicability of these concepts to marketing strategy. It was a somewhat static exposition of the conceptual "revolution" which he perceived taking place in marketing. The conceptual infusions he regarded as important changes in what had been considered "a maturing discipline."

Zober, in 1971, yet titling his book *Principles of Marketing,*[51] mustered quantitative, behavioral, and social concepts to explain the strategic (macro) and tactical (micro) aspects of marketing within the conventional institution-commodity-function framework. In macro dimensions, the *strategy* of marketing is to estimate marketing opportunity in consideration of the welfare of the total society. This involves understanding marketing in the context of environment. In micro dimensions, the *tactics* of marketing are the planning, identification, and assessment of the allocation of the firms resources. This involves understanding the marketing structure and alternative uses of it in performing the functions requisite for the distribution of goods. A tabulation of characteristics of Zober's book, distinguishing the traditional and newly adopted elements might be as follows:

Traditional Elements:
   History of marketing
   Demographic aspects of markets
   Economic aspects of markets
   Retailing and wholesaling structures
   New retailing developments
   Industrial marketing
   Agricultural marketing
   Functions
   Marketing mix

Newer Elements:
   Models of competition – simulation
   Market segmentation models
   Controllable and uncontrollable aspects of consumer behavior
   Foreign marketing
   Economic models applied to retailing – size of store, loss leaders, multiple
       products, profit maximization pricing
   Theory of assortment
   Physical distribution
   International marketing

Grashof and Kelman's[52] exposition of marketing presented an integration of macro and micro marketing systems, which had characterized marketing thought in early years of this century. Originally, there had been equal concern for both, but in later years interest was concentrated on micro management, with the macro only implicit. Several circumstances justified in their minds need for reintegration of these two aspects of marketing: distrust of students of the American business system; awareness of consumer and social problems; and belief that knowledge of macro marketing makes learning of micro management easier. They avoided discussing social issues *per se*, but they viewed them as vehicles for social change.

They perceived the macro environment as a narrowing progression of systems in which the marketing firm operates, each encompassing those within it and constituting the environment in which the narrower exists:

Macroscopic view of the universe
  Natural resources of the Earth
    Political, economic, and social systems
      Economy of the United States
        Marketing in the U.S. economy
          The firm in the macro-system
            Micro-macro interfaces

The market for general marketing texts is broad and wide, and in the books available there is something for everyone. Offerings range from the conservative traditional emphasis of macro economic marketing to interpretation of the same process in terms of environment, systems, or behavioral concepts. Beyond these are a number of books whose intent is less to present marketing from these points of view than to present these points of view illustrated by marketing. Such books have been discussed in the more specialized literatures.

FROM 1970 – THE PERIOD OF SOCIALIZATION

At midpoint it is difficult to characterize a decade by the literature which has already appeared. Nevertheless, there is evidence that the 1970s are distinguished by a larger social element in marketing thought. Details of this are more appropriately discussed later in the specialized literatures concerning sociological concepts in marketing, environmentalism, and marketing and society. The present interest is the degree to which social factors are incorporated into the general marketing literature and thought.

As social concepts were introduced in several ways, and as the terminology was not originally self-explanatory, the following glossary may indicate the manner, if not the degree, to which marketing thought became "socialized."

Social Behavior. From a sociological rather than an economic standpoint, behavior of participants in the marketing process was interpreted as role fulfillment in group interaction. This concept was used in explanations of consumer behavior and systems functioning. Individuals were perceived acting as social entities in a social context.

Societal Environment. This implies that the social context of action and interaction in marketing processes includes not only market role relations but also pluralistic role identification in all major institutions of the societal structure. Comparative studies have relied heavily upon this social concept for defining the total environment in which both the economy and the marketing system function.

Social Responsibility. An indication of obligation to conform to the role expectations sanctioned by society. It meant at first the responsibility to consumers implied by the Marketing Concept. Broadened, it included responsibility of management to others than consumers in the business process, and ultimately to individuals outside the marketing or business process.

Marketing and Society. Beyond the interaction of participants in marketing, there is an interface between marketing management and society in general, as the community. Being of a major and dominant institution, marketers are in a position to create or to help solve problems of social character: opportunities for the handicapped and underprivileged, pollution of the environment, the hazards of using certain marketed products, waste of resources of society, etc. These topics have evoked both positive and normative theorizing.

Social Marketing. Success in application of marketing principles to distribution of economic goods and services led to perception of possible uses of them in promoting and facilitating the exchange of values in noneconomic, nonprofit social organizations, such as hospitals, museums, churches, and the like. This is, in effect, a special case of "product" marketing, if it is to be included at all in the domain of marketing.

The quick adoption of interest in social aspects of marketing resulted from the coincidence of two factors: the introduction of social and behavioral concepts into marketing thought during the 1950s and 1960s, and the occurrence of social problems, some of which were attributed to marketing activity.

One of the general marketing books which employed social concepts, not to sharpen management skills, but to interpret the marketing institution in its context of social issues and responsibilities was that of Gist.[53] Perhaps the first introductory marketing text to emphasize societal as well as managerial perspectives, although it contained many traditional features, it approached marketing from the point of view of what marketing could contribute to society at large, to consumers as a class, and to individual buyers. The book was managerial inasmuch as it was built upon the strategy of the four Ps – Product, Place, Promotion, and Price; it was societal inasmuch as it gave emphasis to the social aspects of management in these areas. Among the social issues and problems discussed were the following: corporate policy concerning social issues, truth in advertising, deceptive selling, counter-advertising, products and society, and deceptive communications and society. In the revision, 60 short cases were included to illustrate management decision relative to issues of social concern.

A somewhat different approach to the exposition to social marketing was taken by Kotler[54] who translated basic marketing concepts into terminology presumably more familiar to the nonbusiness world, then prescribed applications of marketing management principles for the "marketing" of health services, public services, educational services, and political candidates. The format of the book is not unlike earlier ones dealing with the marketing of farm products, manufactured goods, or industrial commodities, identifying and classifying basic elements or variables of marketing: the market, processes of exchange, participant interaction, rudiments of social dynamics, market structure, product differentiation, and pricing. Its brevity also resembles that of other earlier works intended to be introductory for specialized readership. Unlike most earlier books on product marketing, however, its text is more prescriptive than descriptive of strategies appropriate for the marketing of the selected "products." Descriptive and illustrative of social marketing practice, on the other hand, are sixteen case studies concluding the book. Kotler in the book defines social marketing as "the design, implementation, and control of programs seeking to increase the acceptability of a social idea or practice in target group(s). It utilizes concepts of market segmentation, consumer research, idea configuration, communication, facilitation, incentives, and exchange theory to maximize target group response."[55]

CONTRIBUTIONS OF GENERAL LITERATURE TO MARKETING THOUGHT

Writers on the subject of general marketing have made the following contributions to marketing thought:

A. An *assortment of concepts of marketing,* ranging from simple activities to broad social and complex economic relationships:

Marketing as Technical Activities. One concept of marketing is that it consists of activities, essentially technical in nature, performed in institutional operations. This is a narrow concept; it does not embrace the interinstitutional relations of marketing organizations or the theoretical aspects of the subject. It is derived primarily from observation and is descriptive in character. The following are examples:

1. *Simple, Individual Activities.* C. S. Duncan wrote of individuals' looking at marketing from the point of view of the consumer, to whom marketing is the activity of acquiring commodities for use. Of this concept Duncan wrote: "Marketing has local and provincial meanings, illustrated by 'to go marketing,' 'to do the marketing.' " He recognized, however, that the use of the term "marketing" to convey that meaning mars "its effectiveness for the more general meaning."[56]

2. *Technical Activities.* White and Hayward, too, implied that marketing consists of the performance of activities. "When marketing is mentioned to the average business man, he immediately thinks of selling . . . . But it is doubtful whether the marketing manager of the next decade will be of the pure sales type . . . . In addition to the selling force and its machiners, executives will be required for performing other marketing activities having to do with the performing of channels of distribution."[57]

3. *Middlemen and Their Services.* A fairly complete statement of the ideas involved in the concept of marketing as activities is that made by Maynard, Weidler, and Beckman. They defined marketing as covering "all activities necessary to effect transfer in the ownership of goods and to provide for their physical distribution . . . . The various methods by which these services are rendered, together with the institutions involved and the policies adopted in the performance of such functions, are necessarily an integral part of marketing."[58]

This definition implies that, in addition to the mere performance of services or activities, marketing includes the institutions and policies involved in their performance. Two additional considerations are brought into the subject by this definition: the institutional aspects of marketing and the mental part of marketing expressed in policy formulation.

Marketing as a Process. A second concept of marketing is found in definitions that convey the idea that marketing is not merely institutional activities but a process by the performance of which the institutions are related. In accordance with this definition, a concept of the *marketing activity* replaces somewhat that of the *activities of marketing,* because the separate actions involved in the transfer of goods and titles are consolidated into a process or act. The subject is thus no longer merely described but is interpreted.

1. *A Consequential Activity.* One of the simplest definitions of marketing as a process is that it is a means to an end. Breyer expressed the idea that "the task of marketing is to get from production to consumption."[59]

In the sense in which Breyer uses the term, marketing is primarily a physical function made necessary because of the separation of production and consumption. That separation is the result of specialization in production, and the need for marketing service is a consequence of specialization. He spoke of marketing as the "price" we pay for the advantages of specialization in production and therefore as an activity that must be performed if we are to enjoy the benefits of specialization.

On the other hand, Breyer regarded marketing not only as a consequential activity but as a task that varied under different conditions. "The marketing task," he said, "varied widely from one market situation to another."[60] The logic of his concept is that, inasmuch as the marketing task is to overcome the obstacles, the nature of the task depends upon the degree to which production is specialized. Fundamental to this concept is the assumption that production is primary and distribution or marketing secondary, that production is the independent variable and marketing a dependent variable activity.

2. *Concentration, Equalization, and Dispersion.* Clark regarded marketing as the process of concentration, equalization, and dispersion. In collaboration with Weld, he wrote: "To get products from growers into the hands of distant users involves three important isolated processes which may be called concentration, equalization, and dispersion."[61] Implied in this concept are both the nature of the market in which the activity takes place and some idea of the significance of the activity. The concept of concentration and dispersion implied that producers and consumers are separated and that marketing is the process of bringing products together from numerous, widely scattered sources and of distributing them to many equally widely scattered consumers. Equalization implied that the same process is pertinent to markets separated by time. Marketing, therefore, is the process of making products available at the place, time, and price at which they are wanted.

Expressing somewhat similar ideas about the processes involved in marketing, Alderson spoke of it as the creation of value through the process of sorting, sorting out, accumulating, allocation, and assorting.[62]

3. *Process of Transfer.* Brown also employed the concept of concentration and dispersion in his study of commodity marketing, defining marketing as "the process of transferring goods through commercial channels from producer to consumer."[63] "Broadly viewed, marketing resolves itself into two complementary operations: Assembling and distributing."[64]

Marketing as an Economic Process. A third concept of marketing is one that views it as "the second of two great economic processes: production and distribution."[65] As such, it is regarded as an economic activity comparable to production, with which it is both compared and contrasted. The comparison lies in the fact that both are productive of usefulness or consumer satisfaction; the contrast lies in the kinds of utility of which each is productive. Many writers have defined marketing as an economic process, but not all of them have brought out in their analyses the full implications of this assumption.

1. *Creation of Time, Place, and Possession Utilities.* A commonly held concept of marketing is that it includes the creation of time, place, and possession utilities. That view is expressed by many of the marketing writers. Converse and Huegy said: "Marketing, in a broad sense, covers those business activities that have to do with the creation of place, time, and possession utilities."[66] They leave the creation of form utility to the realm of production in a narrower sense, as do the majority of writers.

Moriarity, thinking along somewhat similar lines, wrote: "Marketing is the essential economic element in production, for without the marketing process, material production is a technical and not an economic process . . . . When once it is clearly understood that it is the marketing process which produces the consumers' surplus, and is increased by the complexity of the market and the educational forces involved in selling, there will be less tendency to regard the marketing process as taking value which it does not create."[67]

2. *Creation of Form Utility.* Not all writers limited the economic activity of marketing to the creation of the three types of utility. Some authors have regarded it as being coterminate with production in the broad sense, embracing the creation of form utility as well as the other three. Others have expanded its scope to include in it also economic activities other than production: exchange, distribution, and consumption.

Amplifying this concept of marketing, Ryan wrote: "Recognizing the creation of form utility as an element of the marketing process does not confuse the subject. Manufacturing can still be studied as a separate subject, just as advertising, personnel, merchandising, and many other functions of marketing can be studied separately."[68] Ryan's concept of marketing as embracing the creation of form utility arises from his assumption that the marketing task and functions can be determined by observing the operation of retail institutions and from his observation that retailers often make changes in the forms of products. Consequently, from this point of view marketing includes both distribution and production. The same viewpoint is taken by some writers of the marketing of agricultural products, who include in marketing the processing that occurs in farm products between the producer and consumer.

3. *Distribution and Exchange Activity.* In the minds of some writers, marketing consists not only of productive activity but also of other types of economic activity. This is implied in Moriarity's statement: "Marketing is a specific form of economic production, and yet it is at the same time both the process by which those values of the product are determined which are to be distributed and one of the processes in the economic distribution."[69] Marketing, therefore, would include (a) a portion of all economic production, (b) all of exchange, the process of value and price determination, and (c) one of the processes of economic distribution.

4. *Demand and Supply Adjustment.* Of the economic activities other than production that are discussed in connection with marketing, exchange, or the adjusting of demand and supply, is referred to most often.

Shaw, as early as 1912, wrote of marketing: "The task is one of adjustment. The materials and forces of nature must be bent to human use."[70] A few years later he said: "The problem of distribution is to bring about an effective adjustment between demand creation and economical supply, to arouse the desired maximum of demand at a minimum of expense, and to supply without leakage the largest possible percentage of this demand."[71]

5. *Exchange of Ownership of Goods.* "The essence of marketing," wrote Vaile and Slagsvold, "is the exchange of ownership of goods . . . Marketing, in the full sense, must involve the change in ownership, physical movements merely facilitate this change or make possible the use of the commodity by the new owner."[72]

Such a concept of marketing emphasized exchange. Its significance is evident in the discussion of marketing that proceeded from it. The marketing functions growing out of that concept included all the functions of exchange. All factors affecting demand and supply are of marketing importance; all the problems involved in the adjustment of demand and supply are marketing problems. Moreover, not only is marketing essentially the transfer of ownership but the marketing structure reflects the price-making forces in competition.

6. *The Activity of Want Satisfaction.* Relatively little has been said in marketing literature concerning the relationship between marketing and the economic process of distribution; more has been said in identifying marketing with the activity of consumption. Pyle wrote: "Marketing may be thought of as that phase of business activity through which human wants are satisfied by the exchange of goods and services, on the one hand, for some valuable consideration — usually money or its equivalent — on the other."[73]

Similar emphasis of the consumer element in marketing is expressed in the following definition given by Breyer: "Marketing is not primarily a means for garnering profits for individuals. It is, in the larger, more vital sense, an economic instrument used to accomplish indispensable social ends. Under a system of division of labor there must be some vehicle to move the surplus production of specialists to deficit areas if society is to support itself. This is the social objective of marketing."[74]

Expressing both the social character of marketing and its managements aspects are these words of McCarthy: "Marketing is the performance of business activities that direct the flow of goods and service from producers to consumer or user in order to satisfy consumers and accomplish the firm's objectives."[75]

Marketing as a Social Process. A fourth concept of marketing defines it as a social, rather than merely an economic, process. This views marketing as an activity of people in their social context and setting. It is a perception of the role of the whole man, whose interests, loyalties, and responsibilities transcend and condition his behavior in the marketplace. As this concept has evolved in marketing thought since its inception in the 1950s, the breadth of its significance has become evident in an assortment of related concepts.

1. Marketing as Social Interaction. When marketing is conceived as an economic process, market behavior is deemed to be rational, hedonistic, and considerate wholly of economic values. Recognition that this interpretation of man is unrealistic contributed to perception of him in his entirety, and to explanation of his market behavior as role interaction. Having role expectations and fulfilling role responsibilities, his actions were interpreted in psychological and sociological terms. Relationships rather than individual action became the

center of interest, leading to identification of marketing structure as channels or systems for the performance of the marketing functions.

2. Marketing and Social Responsibility. The idea that marketers have responsibility to others than themselves contradicts the doctrine of caveat emptor, which dominated business of the 19th century. Gradually, and mainly through enforcement of legislation, marketers learned market expectations even before they accepted them as responsibilities. Popularization of the Marketing Concept in the 1950s identified consumers as ones to whom marketers have responsibility for ascertaining their wants and delivering their needs. This was both an economic and social responsibility.

In the late 1960s, it became apparent, however, that the consumer was not the only participant in the marketing process to whom management had a responsibility. Responsibility to resources, competitors, and distributors also became identified, as standards of fairness in economic relations became established. Such responsibilities, however, were based mainly upon economic considerations, and were due only to those who were participants in the economic — marketing — process.

3. Marketing and Society. Participants in the marketing system constitute a closed group having expectations and responsibilities among them, but they also are but a subset in the larger social order. Recognition of this increased as society identified its collective values as superior to mere economic values. Consequently, marketing has increasingly been held responsible for not only supplying consumption goods, but for doing so in ways which preserve and augment the wellbeing of people in all ways. It is expected that marketers minimize the pollution of the environment, desist from exploiting children markets, assist in the employment of minority members, protect consumers from dangerous products, make explicit dangers to health. Past marketing practices often passed to society costs which marketers themselves avoided, and often which society did not reckon with at the time. An accumulation of social problems related to marketing drew marketing into closer relation to society, and added another dimension of the concept of marketing as a social — and socially responsible — process.

B. A wide variety of *concepts* have been employed in the explanation of marketing, including the following, among others:

Advertising
Approaches to marketing
Assembly
Automatic merchandising
Blockages
Brands — private, distributors, manufacturers
Cash and carry
Channel
Commodity classifications
Comparative marketing
Consumer goods
Consumers — Household, industrial, ultimate
Consumer movement

Convenience, shopping, specialty goods
Cooperative
Credit
Direct distribution
Distribution cost
Dispersion
Environment
Exclusive distribution
Expectations
Explicit, implicit costs
Durable goods
Facilitating functions
Flows
Full-service establishments

Discounts and allowances
Holism
Horizontal integration
Interaction
International marketing
Levels of distribution
Limited-service establishment
Line of goods
Linkages
Managerialism
Merchandising
Middlemen
Market
Marketing
Marketing Concept, The
Marketing functions
Marketing institutions
Marketing channel
Marketing structure or system
Market classifications
Market segmentation
Marketing mix

Price leadership
Price or discount structure
Product differentiation
Product diversification
Resale price maintenance
Relationship
Retailing
Role relationship
Selective distribution
Services
Simplification
Social institution
Social marketing
Social process
Societal
Sorting
Standardization
System
Trade discount
Value added by marketing
Wholesaling

C. An assortment of marketing "principles," classifiable as follows:

Operational Principles. Some of the principles that pertain to business conduct and that are accepted as laws or rules to be employed in the operation of the marketing institution follow.

The leasing of departments of a department store tends to be most desirable when skill, specialized knowledge, and extreme style risks are involved in handling goods in question.

The convenience of all concerned is the foremost consideration in store layout.

The pricing policy for a store cannot be based upon the gross margin of any one profitable item. When a number of items are handled, the general policy must be composite, reflecting the nature of demand for the goods, the availability of it to the seller, competition, cost, and ease of handling.

The combination of all possible resources for the creation of one distinct impression is the best means of attracting attention and putting across the selling idea.

Principles Involving Institutional Relationships. Included in principles pertaining to the combination of institutions into marketing channels and to the competitive relations of the establishments are the following:

The outlets through which goods are distributed vary, depending upon the buying habits of consumers with respect to the goods.

In a seller's market the competition among middlemen to get the goods leads to specialization, but in a buyer's market the opposite tendency exists.

Retail price competition provides an impetus toward integration in the marketing process. The social aspects of retailing are evident in the constant tendency toward improvement in selling environment and extension of customer service. The basic economic aspect reasserts itself when competition begins to appear in pine-board stores or abandoned warehouses, but with lower prices.

When conditions demand modification in the existing marketing structure, the change will be made either by modifying existing practices or by developing new institutions.

As independents are able to increase their efficiency and meet the chains on more even ground, the comparative advantages of the chains may be reduced to a point where tax burdens will be important limiting factors in further chain expansion.

When the number of potential users of a given product is large, the market scattered, the unit of sale low, the credit standing of consumers limited, demand irregular, prompt delivery of major importance, economies in shipment possible, little or no technical sales service required, repair service essential, and relatively little sales promotional effort produces satisfactory results, then the distributor channel is the most economical means, provided, of course, that the distributor operates with a reasonable degree of efficiency.

As changes occur in the retailing structure, changes will also occur in the wholesaling system.

Principles Relating to the Marketing Task. Principles drawn from the relationship of marketing to more general social and economic phenomena are, in part, as follows.

Because personal service and convenience usually mean more to consumers than mere mechanical efficiency, the use of mechanical and automatic laborsaving devices in distribution is more limited than in production.

The enjoyment of the products of mass production depends upon the operation of a vast and complex system of distribution.

As the income of a family increases, the percentage of income expended for food and housing decreases, and the percentage expended for clothing and miscellaneous items increases.

The extent of the marketing task is dependent upon the character of production, even as the character of production is dependent upon the nature of the market and the marketing facilities.

As people and nations advance in civilization, trade increases and the structure of marketing institutions becomes more complex.

The demand for luxury goods tends to increase as wealth is concentrated in a minority of the population.

The employment of women affects the market through both the character of demand and the volume of it.

Hypothetical Principles. Among the principles that, breaking away from observation and statistical bases, project generalizations into hypothetical situations from assumed bases are the following:

So long as exchange is obstructed by a given condition, it will be a function of marketing to overcome that obstruction or difficulty.

So long as tastes vary, it will be impossible to standardize consumer goods in the same way as paving bricks or steel rails can be standardized.

So long as consumers demand and expect to obtain commodities immediately upon their decision to buy or their discovery of a need, the cost of foresight and risk will be incurred by merchants and will be included in total distribution costs.

Continuous competition in marketing, expressed in experimentation in methods of distribution, types of enterprises, arrangement of functions, and new methods of performance, evolves new patterns of distribution.

Price in the market is determined in the long run by general factors of demand and supply and in the short run by a variety of institutional pricing policies.

Because of their increasing overhead costs, department stores cannot expand their sales indefinitely without incurring proportionately higher costs of operation.

With all the modifications of the system, the general level of retail prices depends on those of goods distributed through the channels that have earned the title of "regular" because they are supposed to be made up of the types of concerns organized for the performance of the marketing functions in an orderly and economical fashion.

The seller, under conditions of pure competition, will expand his output until his marginal cost is equal to his marginal revenue.

Truisms. Some principles the truth of which is so apparent as to be obvious and the statement of which is worthwhile mainly for the attention it calls to the self-evident are:

The middleman exists because of a demand for his service.

The growth of any marketing structure is evolutionary, not revolutionary.

The costs of direct selling increase with the addition of functions to be performed.

While marketing institutions can be eliminated and functions shifted, the basic marketing functions cannot be eliminated.

Demand for certain qualities of raw materials leads to the development of standards.

Whenever a farm crop reaches a tonnage that makes it of commercial importance, middlemen or buyers appear in the local market.

ENDNOTES

[1] *Report of the Industrial Commission on the Distribution of Farm Products* (Washington, D.C.: Government Printing Office, 1901).

[2] *Ibid.,* p. 7.

[3] See Appendix A.

[4] Arch W. Shaw, *Some Problems in Market Distribution* (Cambridge, Mass.: Harvard University Press, 1915), p. 7. Republished, 1951.

[5] These ideas are drawn from Butler's books and their revisions, as follows: *Sales, Purchasing, and Shipping Methods* (1911); *Marketing Methods and Salesmanship* (1914); *Marketing Methods and Policies* (1917); *Marketing and Merchandising* (1918, rev., 1923).

[6] Louis D. H. Weld, *Studies in the Marketing of Farm Products* (Minneapolis: University of Minnesota, 1915), and *The Marketing of Farm Products* (New York: Macmillan Co., 1916; rev. with Fred E. Clark, as *Marketing Agricultural Products,* 1932).

[7] Louis D. H. Weld, *"Marketing Funcitons and Mercantile Organizations,"* American *Economic Review,* June, 1917, pp. 306-18.

[8] Paul T. Cherington, *The Elements of Marketing* (New York: Macmillan Co., 1920).

[9] C. S. Duncan, *Marketing: Its Problems and Methods* (New York: D. Appleton-Century Co., Inc., 1920).

[10] Theodore Macklin, *Efficient Marketing for Agriculture* (New York: Macmillan Co., 1921).

[11] Edmund Brown, Jr., *Marketing* (New York: Harper & Bros., 1925).

[12] Paul W. Ivey, *Principles of Marketing* New York.): Ronald Press Co., 1921).

[13] Ivey, *Principles of Marketing*, p. 5.

[14] *Ibid.*, p. iii.

[15] Paul D. Converse, *Marketing Methods and Policies* (New York: Prentice-Hall, Inc., 1921; 2d ed., 1926).

[16] Fred E. Clark, *Principles of Marketing* (New York: Macmillan Co., 1922; 2d ed., 1932; 3d ed., with Carrie P. Clark, 1942.; rev. ed., 1962 by R. D. Tousley, Eugene Clark, and F. E. Clark).

[17] Harold H. Maynard, Walter C. Weidler, and Theodore N. Beckman, *Principles of Marketing* (New York: Ronald Press Co., 1927; 2d ed., 1932; 3d ed., 1939; 4th ed., 1946; 5th ed., 1952; 6th ed., 1958, with W. R. Davidson; 7th ed., 1962; 8th ed., 1967; 9th ed., 1973 with W. W. Talarzyk).

[18] Stated by Theodore N. Beckman in correspondence with the author in 1941. See Appendix A.

[19] W. D. Moriarity, *The Economics of Marketing and Advertising* (New York: Harper & Bros., 1923).

[20] Percival White, *Scientific Marketing Management: Its Principles and Methods* (New York: Harper & Bros., 1927).

[21] Floyd L. Vaughan, *Marketing and Advertising* (Princeton, N. J.: Princeton University Press, 1928).

[22] Roland S. Vaile and Peter L. Slagsvold, *Marketing* (New York: Ronald Press Co., preliminary ed., 1929).

[23] Fred E. Clark, *Readings in Marketing* (New York: Macmillan Co., 1924; 2d ed., 1933).

[24] I. Wright and C. E. Landon, *Readings in Marketing Principles* (New York: Prentice-Hall, Inc., 1936).

[25] E. L. Rhoades, *Introductory Readings in Marketing* (New York: A. W. Shaw Co., 1927).

[26] M. P. McNair and H. L. Hensen, *Readings in Marketing* (New York: McGraw-Hill Book Co., Inc. 1949).

[27] Melvin T. Copeland, *Marketing Problems* (New York: A. W. Shaw Co., 1920; 2d ed., 1923, as *Problems in Marketing;* 3d ed., 1927; 4th ed., 1931).

[28] Ralph F. Breyer, *Commodity Marketing* (New York: McGraw-Hill Book Co., Inc., 1931).

[29] Newel H. Comish, *Marketing of Manufactured Goods,* (Boston: Stratford Co., 1935).

[30] H. E. Agnew, R. B. Jenkins, and J. C. Drury, *Outlines of Marketing* (New York: McGraw-Hill Book Co., Inc., 1936; 2d ed., 1942; 3d ed., 1950, with Harold A. Conner and William L. Doremus).

[31] C. W. Barker and N. Arshen, *Modern Marketing* (New York: McGraw-Hill Book Co., Inc., 1939).

[32] Charles F. Phillips, *Marketing* (New York: Houghton Mifflin Co., 1938); rev. with D. J. Duncan, as *Marketing: Principles and Methods* (Chicago: Richard D. Irwin, Inc., 1948; 2d ed., 1948; 3rd ed., 1956; 4th ed., 1960); 5th ed., 1964; 6th ed., 1968; 7th ed., 1973 by J. M. Carman and K. P. Uhl.

[33] R. F. Breyer, *The Marketing Institution* (New York: McGraw-Hill Book Co., Inc., 1934).

[34] H. B. Killough, *Economics of Marketing* (New York: Harper & Bros., 1933).

[35] Ralph S. Alexander, F. M. Surface, R. F. Elder, and Wroe Anderson, *Marketing* (New York: Ginn & Co., 1940; 2d ed., 1949; 3d ed., 1953).

[36] E. A. Duddy and D. A. Revzan, *Marketing, an Institutional Approach* (New York: McGraw-Hill Book Co., Inc., 1947, p. vi; 2d ed., 1953).

[37] *Ibid.*, p. 4.

[38] Roland S. Vaile, E. T. Grether, and Revis Cox, *Marketing in the American Economy* (New York: Ronald Press Co., 1952).

[39] Reavis Cox and Wroe Alderson (eds), *Theory in Marketing* (Chicago: Richard D. Irwin, Inc., 1950).

[40] Wroe Anderson, *Marketing Behavior and Executive Action* (Homewood, Ill.: Richard D. Irwin, Inc., 1957).

[41] Eugene J. Kelley and William Lazer, *Managerial Marketing: Perspectives and Viewpoints* (Homewood, Ill.: Richard D. Irwin, Inc. 1958, 1967).

[42] E. Jerome McCarthy, *Basic Marketing: A Managerial Approach* (Homewood, Ill,: Richard D. Irwin, Inc. 1960).

[43] Richard H. Burkirk, *Principles of Marketing* (New York: Holt, Rinehart and Winston, Inc., 1961).

[44] Differentiation: "Development from the one to the many, the simple to the complex, or from the homogeneous to the heterogeneous; evolution in being of any kind, as organic, inorganic, psychic, social, etc. toward the more complicated and more specialized form, structure, or the like." *Webster's New International Dictionary.* (Springfield, Mass.: G & C Merriam Company, Publishers, 1944.

[45] C. F. Phillips and D. J. Duncan, *Marketing, Principles and Methods* (Homewood, Ill.: Richard D. Irwin, Inc., 1968).

[46] T. N. Beckman, W. R. Davidson, and W. Wayne Talarzyk, *Marketing* (New York: The Ronald Press Co., 9th ed., 1973).

[47] E. W. Cundiff and R. R. Still, *Basic Marketing: Concepts, Environment, and Decision* (Englewood Cliffs, N.J.: Prentice-Hall Inc., 1964; 2d ed., 1971).

[48] R. J. Holloway and R. S. Hancock (eds.), *The Environment of Marketing Behavior* (New York: John Wiley & Sons, Inc., 1964; 2d ed., 1971); and *Marketing in a Changing Environment.* (New York: John Wiley & Sons, Inc.), 1968; 2d ed., 1973).

[49] R. A. Scott and N. E. Markes, *Marketing and Its Environment* (Belmont, Calif.: Wadsworth Publishing Company, 1968).

[50] Martin L. Bell, *Marketing: Concepts and Strategy* (Boston: Houghton Mifflin, 1966; 2d ed., 1972).

[51] Martin Zober, *Principles of Marketing* (Boston: Allyn and Bacon, 1971).

[52] J. F. Grashof and A. P. Kelman, *Introduction to Macro-Marketing* (Columbus, Ohio: Grid, Inc., 1973).

[53] Ronald R. Gist, *Marketing and Society* (New York: Holt, Rinehart & Winston, Inc. 1971; 2d ed., Hinsdale, Ill.: The Dryden Press, 1973).

Ronald R. Gist, *Readings in Marketing and Society* (New York: Holt, Rinehart & Winston, Inc., 1971; 2d ed., Hinsdale, Ill.: The Dryden Press, 1973).

[54] Philip Kotler, *Marketing for Nonprofit Organizations* (Englewood Cliffs, N.J.: Prentice-Hall, Inc., 1975).

[55] *Ibid.*, p. 283.

[56] C. S. Duncan, *Marketing: Its Problems and Methods* (New York: D. Appleton & Co., 1920), p. 1.

[57] Percival White and Walter S. Hayward, *Marketing Practice* (New York: Doubleday, Page & Co., 1924), p.2.

[58] H. H. Maynard, Walter C. Weidler, and T. N. Beckman, *Principles of Marketing* (New York: Ronald Press Co., 1927), p. 1.

[59] R. F. Breyer, *The Marketing Institution* (New York: McGraw-Hill Book Co., Inc., 1934), p. 4.

[60] *Ibid.*, p. 15.

[61] Fred E. Clark and L. D. H. Weld, *Marketing Agricultural Products* (New York: Macmillan Co., 1932), p. 13.

[62] Wroe Alderson, *Marketing Behavior and Executive Action* (Homewood, Ill.: Richard D. Irwin, Inc., 1956), p. 201.

[63] Edmund Brown, Jr., *Marketing* (New York: Harper & Bros., 1925), p. 3.

[64] *Ibid* p. 12.

[65] C. W. Barker and M. Anshen, *Modern Marketing* (New York: McGraw-Hill Book Co., Inc., 1939), p. 3.

[66] P. D. Converse and H. W. Huegy, *The Elements of Marketing* (New York: Prentice-Hall, Inc., 2d ed., 1940), p. 1.

[67] W. D. Moriarity, *The Economics of Marketing and Advertising* (New York: Harper & Bros., 1923). pp. 301-2.

[68] F. W. Ryan, "Functional Elements in Market Distribution," *Harvard Business Review,* January, 1935, p. 207.

[69] *Ibid.*, p. 22.

[70] A. W. Shaw, "Some Problems in Market Distribution," *Quarterly Journal of Economics,* August, 1912.

[71] A. W. Shaw, *An Approach to Business Problems* (Cambridge, Mass: Harvard University Press, 1916), p. 110.

[72] R. S. Vaile and P. L. Slagsvold, *Market Organization* (New York: Ronald Press Co., 1930). p. 43.

[73]J. F. Pyle, *Marketing Principles, Organization, and Policies* (New York: McGraw-Hill Book Co., Inc., 1931), p. 3.

[74]R. F. Breyer, *op cit.*, 1934, p. 192.

[75]E. J. McCarthy, *Basic Marketing: A Managerial Approach* (Homewood, Ill.: Richard D. Irwin, Inc., 1960), p. 33.

From the mid-1950s, the subject of marketing management grew rapidly to predominant proportions in academic and business circles. This emergence, however, was not sudden and without precedence, nor did the new interest appear full blown. Antecedents in marketing thought are traceable through many years, but not until the 1950s were conditions propitious to bring about a major development along this line. Those same circumstances also shaped its form during the following years.

EARLY REFERENCES TO MARKETING MANAGEMENT

So varied have been the interpretations of management in marketing that one may search their meanings for its essence. Is not all marketing intelligence useful for guidance of action? Is not all marketing practice management, varying by degree? Both questions seem to be answered in the affirmative by marketing writers and their works. At the inception of the discipline, A. W. Shaw and Ralph Starr Butler both were concerned with management practices and problems. So were such men as Paul Nystrom, Norris A. Brisco, and Leverett S. Lyon. A distinguishable element of management precept is found in all of the areas of the marketing literature already discussed: advertising, sales, credit, retailing, wholesaling, and research. And the general principles of marketing were credited as of "practical importance" in the performance of marketing.

Notwithstanding its usefulness to those who manage, marketing precepts emphasized the *marketing* element in management, and not the *management* element in marketing. At least as early as the 1930s some dissatisfaction was expressed, not so much with the management theory practiced, but with the concepts of marketing with which management dealt in its performance. These factors and others contributed in the 1950s to a new approach to and statement of marketing management. As sales management had been perhaps the broadest form of management in marketing, the new term "marketing management" was thought by some at that time to be mainly an extension of that activity. That was not to be the case, however, for more fundamental conceptual changes were to show marketing management in a new light.

CONCEPTUALIZATION OF MARKETING MANAGEMENT

Although in 1919 J. George Frederick had related sales management to the total marketing activity, and in 1926 Leverett S. Lyon employed the terms "marketing management" and "marketing strategy," new meaning was given to marketing and marketing management in the 1950s by incorporation in marketing thought of such concepts as the "Marketing Concept," "adaptive behavior," "holism," and an assortment of others derived from the behavioral sciences. Among the first to explore marketing management from this new viewpoint were Wroe Alderson, John R. Howard, E. J. Kelley and William Lazer, and E. J. McCarthy.

Whereas some broached this field with tentativeness, editing readings rather than constructing an original text, taking a first step which was later revised, or emerging gradually from the traditional format of the general marketing literature, Alderson with one sweeping stroke created a new pattern for considering marketing management.[1] He undertook to explain executive action and marketing behavior in terms of concepts drawn from psychology, sociology, anthropology, and political science, and he did not hesitate to include others from the physical, biological, and natural sciences. Thus he departed from predecessors who thought mainly in economic terms.

Alderson termed his theory "functionalism," by which he meant that management decisions are a function or derivitive of the environment, whether the environment be that of the small group in which one interacted or the larger social and economic environment. Without saying specifically what functionalism *is*, he said that it identifies some system of action and then determines how and why it works; it interprets parts in terms of the whole; it perceives function to determine structure, and groups to be continually adjusting function and structure to meet changing conditions.

In this work, Alderson introduced a number of new concepts which recast older marketing perceptions and gave marketing context to ideas more familiar in other disciplines. He saw exchange as the process of improving the "assortments" held by parties to the exchange, and the marketing process to consist of the actions of "sorting or sorting out," "accumulating," "allocating," and "assorting." Buyers were engaged in "problem solving," in improving the "potency" of their assortment. Sellers were seeking "differential advantage" for "survival and growth." Goods move through "power structures," not through supposedly neutral "marketing channels." "Negotiation" is the relating of two systems to each other and not merely the carrying out of a transaction. So viewed, both the mechanical and social aspects of marketing invite a corresponding statement of management.

Although two-thirds of his book pertains to marketing behavior, that is prelude to the last third dealing with executive actions, or the processes of management decision. It is in this last part that the work departs most from previous traditional texts and at the same time advances thought toward the elaboration of marketing management which was to follow. He made explicit the "power principle" as a guide to executive action in policies, planning, and problem solving. The role of the marketing executive is to create and direct a system of action and to reconcile its struggle for survival and growth with the broader aims of the community. In recognizing the relevance of mathematical models and other techniques, he maintained that problems should determine the methods of research and decision making and not methods of the problems. Marketing problems, moreover, he believed to be some of the most important decisions facing executives.

While Alderson exploded his new concepts, in the same year John R. Howard published a work less startling but also indicating the direction which "marketing management" would take in coming years.[2] Noting that the term "marketing manager" was fairly new, he defined this function of management as "that area of company management having to do with the broad problem of sales."[3] This included prices, advertising and other forms of promotion, sales management, and determination of the kinds of products and their channels.

"Marketing management" implied integration of marketing activities and a downward delegation of authority. The following aspects of the book were evidence of the trend of thought at that time:

1. A decision-oriented rather than research-oriented point of view
2. Incorporation of recent developments in the behavioral sciences, mainly economics, psychology, and sociology
3. Distinction between controllable elements of the business and the uncontrollable environment
4. Adaptation, as a principal task of executives
5. Uncertainty (about buyers and competitors) and probability as aspects of decision making.

Although innovative, Howard's book did not much stretch the conceptual fibers of marketing thought. The managerial portion of the book was built largely around decisions relative to products, channels, price, promotion, and location. He also gave considerable attention to competition, demand, cost, distribution structure, and the law. His handling of probability analysis was in terms of simple statistics and graphs. The book represented awareness of an oncoming movement, but it remained closely linked to the format in which the general body of marketing was still presented.

More radically departed from the conventionality which lingered in Howard's work, but still not sufficiently developed and integrated for a comprehensive text, was the book of readings edited in 1958 by Kelley and Lazer.[4] As has often been the case, in the early stage of a new development in a field, readings reflecting the advanced ideas of many people have been published prior to the achievement of a text by a single person. The articles in *Managerial Marketing* constituted collectively a managerial approach by emphasizing problem solving and decision making, by expressing interdisciplinary concepts, and by focusing on management concern with survival in a dynamic economy.

Related developments in marketing thought were evident in the author's inclusion of articles and commentary concerning the following concepts:

The Marketing Concept
The marketing mix
Product differentiation
Market Segmentation
Physical distribution
Value added
Applicability of mathematical methods to problems in marketing research and advertising
Philosophic approach to marketing thought

A unique characteristic of the book was its emphasis placed upon marketing theory. The subject at that time was in a state of uncertainty, as the body of older "principles" was being overshadowed by the newer managerial concepts. This emphasis was consistent with the increased rigor recommended for managerial decision making and with a conviction — nevertheless, debated — that marketing had the elements of a scientific discipline.

By the end of the 1950s many "general marketing" courses had been superseded by courses in marketing management, and the still extensive market for nonmanagerial instruction was left largely with the conventional Clark-Maynard-Converse approach. The inevitability of appearance of a book combining the best of the conventional and of the managerial elements was demonstrated with publication of *Basic Marketing: a Managerial Approach* by McCarthy in 1960.[5] To a waiting market it purported by show "the whole picture" of marketing. While built upon a fairly traditional format, its differences were itemized as follows: (1) approach to marketing through the manager's eyes; (2) emphasis of strategy and design in determination of the marketing mix; (3) identification of the role of management with satisfaction of the "target consumers"; (4) concern for the social efficiency of marketing management; and (5) intention to stimulate thought rather than merely to tell about marketing. However, its principal distinguishing feature, and one for which the author and the book have since been widely known, was the conceptualization of the areas of managerial concern as the four Ps: Product, Price, Place, and Promotion.

The book represented a useful integration of older and newer concepts, of textual material for undergraduate and graduate study, and of descriptive and conceptual content. It was a landmark book in the evolution of marketing management, not because it pushed out the frontiers but because it lifted the mass of students and practitioners of marketing a step higher in understanding of how marketing decisions are made.

SPECIALIZATION AND AMPLIFICATION OF MANAGEMENT THOUGHT

Having reached the point which it did by 1960, management thought could develop in two directions: it could be popularized and given a personal touch by writers who rode the crest of the wave; or it could be specialized by further research in the areas relevant to marketing management.

While of the former group, a number of works nonetheless made contributions in one way or another. Lazo and Corbin,[6] for example, as their title indicates, literally dealt with management *in* marketing, discussing first the principles of management — planning, organizing, and controlling — and then their application to production, sales, advertising, physical distribution, and channels. They mentioned the recent popularity of the "new" marketing philosophy called "marketing management," and they rejected inclusion of book references in the text because of the "hundreds" — even "thousands" — of books recently published on the subject.

It was true that many people were writing on the subject of marketing management, and of the myriad articles, Britt and Boyd[7] selected 70 for a book of readings. The book, however, dealt more with marketing than with management, viewing marketing as "a unifying agent for all activities of the business firm in the quest for profits and survival." Its content was organized under headings which had become identified with marketing management.

In quick succession, revisions of two earlier books were made, by Lazer and Kelley in 1962, and by Howard in 1963. The Lazer book was modified to keep abreast of changes occurring in marketing courses and curricula, in which the managerial emphasis was increased. As quantitative methods and models, systems thinking, and behavioral science concepts were becoming more a part of the managerial frame of reference, so they occupied a larger part in this compilation of readings. The authors continued to present a number of readings in marketing theory, showing the danger of managing from a superficial knowledge of assorted concepts. Changes in the Howard book reflected a different perception of developments of the past few years. He enlarged his analysis of demand, treated more fully the complexity of marketing channels, introduced organization theory, replaced decision with planning as the pervasive point of view, and made distinctions between short- and long-run managerial decisions. McCarthy also revised in 1964, enlarging his discussion of management at the beginning of the book.

More Specialized Books. In contrast to the new general works on management and the revisions of established books, the ensuing years brought forth a variety of specialized writings which cut more sharply and polished the facets of managerialism in marketing. They were designed to educate managers in how to think, and to what areas of marketing these forms of logic and analysis were relevant. The content of marketing management tended to parallel that of marketing research, and the earlier described works on research *not* intended for *researchers* seemed to approximate the more advanced works on marketing management. The difference of the latter was in their greater concern for *marketing* than for *technology*.

Planning and Problem Solving in Marketing, by Alderson and Green,[8] published in 1964, was such a book for managers who were *users* of research. In it Alderson reiterated some of his concepts concerning planning in organized systems, positional behavior − or the struggle of individuals to advance − strategy, and systems control. Adding to this marketing element a heavy portion of quantitative methods, Green presented such new analytical techniques as intuitive decision theory, model building, theories of decision making, Bayesian theory, sensitivity analysis, computer simulation, Markov process, multiple factors, break-even analysis, and experimentation. The relevance of all of these to marketing problems was discussed.

Going as far to the behavioral side as Green had to the quantitative, Field, Douglas, and Tarpey[9] in 1966 emphasized the need for the marketing manager to analyze reactions − of human beings within the systems of the marketing framework − before making decisions. Their behavioral emphasis urged the development of empathy in relationships. The structure of their book consisted of a kind of matrix relationship between (1) pivotal concepts in the behavioral sciences: perception, motives, groups, social stratification, reference theory, organization theory, leadership, and communication, and (2) pivotal concepts in marketing: products, price, place, and promotion. Capping their scheme of presentation, they offered for analysis several what they called "phenomenological situational episodes," − situations viewed from several points of view, in which the reader was invited to consider how each party involved would see the situation. Managers were thus encouraged similarly to view their problem situations.

Notwithstanding what had already been published, Kotler in 1967 felt that while the new quantitative and behavioral concepts had been discussed in journals and in corporate executive suites, they had not yet gotten into typical textbooks. Because variables in marketing decisions did not exhibit "neat quantitative properties," and marketing processes are "dynamic, nonlinear, lagged, stochastic, interactive, and downright difficult," he felt there was great need for more theory and analysis. Accordingly, he undertook to synthesize new marketing thought into a framework to help marketing executives.[10] With a decision orientation and taking an analytical approach, he gave heavy emphasis to concepts from the following disciplines:

Economics — for fundamental tools and concepts for seeking optimum results in the use of scarce resources

Behavioral sciences — for interpretation of buyer and executive behavior

Mathematics — for means of developing explicit statements about the relationships among variables in a problem.

Kotler's concept of the manner in which management theory is combined with marketing theory is suggested by the format of his book. Under four headings he arranged his various topics:

I. Analyzing Marketing Opportunities
   The Marketing Concept, Markets, Market Segmentation, Buyer Behavior
II. Organizing for Marketing Activity
   Goals, Planning, Decision Making, Research, Models, Creativity
III. Planning
   Theory of Marketing Programming, Product Decisions, Price, Channels, Promotion
IV. Controlling the Marketing Effort
   Marketing Control, Sales and Cost Analysis, The Marketing Audit

The literature on marketing management developed as integrative texts and specialized readings which were compilations of already published articles. Of somewhat different character was a collection edited by Sturdivant,[11] which consisted of original essays pertaining more to the substance of issues of importance to management than to methodologies for thinking about issues. Because it was felt that scholars had not dealt effectively with the social aspects of marketing, the contributors to this volume were *scholars*, well regarded as competent in the areas of interest. The lack of scholarship was attributed to a narrow context in which marketing had been held, to inadequate depth of analysis, and to failure to apply adequate methods to the full range of issues relevant to marketing. While the marketing topics analyzed were not different from those covered in other marketing management books, they were explored in depth, and they illustrated techniques of analysis and decision theory more abstractly discussed elsewhere.

By 1970, although a variety of formats continued to appear, the dimensions and content of marketing management thought were generally understood. Knowledge of four areas of consideration had come to be identified as the substance of marketing management. As illustrated by publications between 1970 and 1973, they were as follows:

1. Basic functions of management:
   Analyzing
   Planning
   Organizing
   Controlling

More illustrative of this organization of thought is the *Readings in Marketing Management,* by Kotler and Cox, published in 1972.[12] Under these headings, which constituted the body of the book, they discussed analyses of the changing social and cultural environment; organizing of competitive strategies, information systems, and marketing research; planning of product and pricing policies and coping with conflict in the channel; and controlling the marketing effort through the marketing audit.

2. Variables of the marketing process:
   Internal elements of the marketing mix: products, price, place, promotion
   External elements of the marketing mix: systems and their component relationships
   Relation of marketing to its environment

Lazer's *Marketing Management: a Systems Approach*[13] employed some of these concepts as the main framework of his exposition, approaching them through concepts from social, behavioral, and mathematical disciplines.

3. Forms of logic by which processes of management and marketing are reasoned:
   Identification of alternatives
   Designing of relationships
   Testing, measuring, and evaluating relationships

Boyd and Massy in *Marketing Management*[14] undertook to develop a systematic and comprehensive approach to marketing decision making, based upon a concept of strategic planning. The work is a high-level conceptual text, research oriented, intended to explore the many analytical approaches used in management and to identify relationships between marketing inputs and outputs.

4. Areas of application of marketing intelligence:
   Distribution of economic products
   Promotion of noneconomic propositions

With confidence and skill in marketing management, practitioners and theorists have turned attention to fields other than product distribution for the application of their understanding and to consideration of marketing responsibilities to the wider community in which the market exists. Lazer wrote of the "broader dimension of marketing," meaning its social, ethical, and international aspects. Kotler and Cox likewise were concerned with "broadening the marketing idea" to include not only soical issues and ethics in marketing research, but also marketing in low-income areas and what they termed "metamarketing." By this they implied the application of marketing management to concerns "above" and beyond its normal usage, as for example, the promotion of government programs and other noneconomic propositions.

ENDNOTES

[1] Wroe Alderson, *Marketing Behavior and Executive Action* (Homewood, Ill.: Richard D. Irwin, Inc., 1957).

[2] John R. Howard, *Marketing Management: Analysis and Decision* (Homewood, Ill.: Richard D. Irwin, Inc., 1957).

[3] *Ibid.*, p. 3.

[4] E. J. Kelley and William Lazer (eds.), *Managerial Marketing: Perspectives and Viewpoints* (Homewood, Ill.: Richard D. Irwin, Inc., 1958).

[5] E. J. McCarthy, *Basic Marketing: a Managerial Approach* (Homewood, Ill.: Richard D. Irwin, Inc., 1960).

[6] H. Lazo and A. Corbin, *Management in Marketing* (New York: McGraw-Hill Book Co., Inc., 1961).

[7] Steuart E. Britt and H. W. Boyd (eds.), *Marketing Management and Administrative Action* (New York: McGraw-Hill Book Co., Inc., 1963).

[8] Wroe Alderson and P. E. Green, *Planning and Problem Solving in Marketing* (Homewood, Ill.: Richard D. Irwin, Inc., 1964).

[9] G. A. Field, John Douglas, and L. X. Tarpey, *Marketing Management – A Behavioral Systems Approach* (Columbus, Ohio: Charles F. Merrill Books, 1966).

[10] Philip Kotler, *Marketing Management* (Englewood Cliffs, N.J.: Prentice-Hall, Inc., 1967).

[11] F. D. Sturdivant, et al. *Perspectives in Marketing Management: Readings* (Glenview, Ill.: Scott Foresman, 1971).

[12] Philip Kotler and K. K. Cox (eds.) *Readings in Marketing Management* (Englewood Cliffs, N.J.: Prentice-Hall, Inc., 1972).

[13] William Lazer, *Marketing Management: a Systems Approach* (New York: John Wiley & Sons, Inc., 1971).

[14] Harper W. Boyd and W. F. Massy, *Marketing Management* (New York: Harcourt Brace Jovanovick, 1972).

CONCEPTS FROM RELATED DISCIPLINES

12

It scarcely need be pointed out that the body of marketing thought does not consist entirely of marketing concepts. In addition, there is an abundance of factual, statistical, descriptive, narrative, and logical material filling in the conceptual structure. There are also concepts drawn from other scientific disciplines and from the general corpus of thought.

The relation of marketing to other social sciences through interdisciplination gains significance as one considers the possibility that the study of marketing may become a science. Strong claims have been made both for and against this eventuality. Proponents who see marketing as potentially a science envision the development of principles and theories stemming mainly from a mechanistic concept of marketing and embracing its economic and social influence. Concepts borrowed from other areas of thought are facilitating, contributing to the effective achievement of marketing as a function of our business system. Those disclaiming marketing as a science do so mainly on the grounds that marketing is but a formalized area of thought — a discipline — in the broader science of social behavior. In that context, interdisciplination is for the enrichment of the understanding of society and all its institutions and not merely for a technical application. Neither concept questions the possibility that the study of marketing can be carried on scientifically. The issue relates to the distinction between a discipline and a science. With respect to marketing, the distinction relates to the concept of marketing held. Viewed as a definitive area of knowledge and its application, marketing may be a "science." In this sense it would be one of the social sciences. Viewed in broader perspective, marketing, along with sociology, economics, psychology, and other studies, would be disciplines of social science or a science of society.

In the history of marketing thought, narrower rather than broader views of marketing prevailed. Emphasis has been given to the development of marketing concepts and comparatively little attention to studies being carried on in other social sciences. That condition has been a point of criticism of marketing thought and of students of marketing both by individuals engaged in this study and by other social scientists. Until about 1950, such criticism had little effect upon the development of marketing thought. So long as the traditional concept of marketing as a business activity prevailed, interdisciplination had only a technical significance. Not until marketing was conceived as a broad economic function or as a social institution did the values of interdisciplination begin to appear.

The implication of interdisciplinary study is that, in each of the major areas of social research, inquiry produces concepts and methodology peculiar to the interests of that discipline but useful also to other social scientists. One cannot work in social studies from the standpoint of his area's concepts alone. That is the reason that even during these first fifty years of the marketing literature numerous concepts from the related social sciences have accompanied those regarded as marketing concepts, by reason of their having been developed by marketing practitioners and scholars. The wonder is that with the progress made in the social sciences marketing had not sooner and more generally been more consciously interdisciplinated. That it was not may have been due to the focus of interest upon business practices and problems rather than upon people primarily. Concepts appropriated from other fields were sometimes accepted not as concepts but as unquestionable categories — as *things* instead of *thoughts*. They were tools to be used, and they were dealt with descriptively rather than conceptually. It appears also that the incorporation of concepts from other social sciences into marketing thought occurred after an appreciable time lag, when the concepts had gained some circulation in general usage. That indicates that students of marketing may not have kept currently abreast of research in related fields and did not look elsewhere for ideas that might be helpful in explaining marketing as they conceived it.

A review of the concepts in marketing thought that have originated with scientists in other fields will serve for judging the use that students of marketing made of information outside their specialization and for inferring still further the concept of marketing that they evidently were developing.

ECONOMICS

Economic theory has provided more concepts for the development of marketing thought than has any other social discipline. Whether students of marketing wrote from the standpoint of management of the individual firm or from that of broader economic aspects of marketing, economic concepts were almost indispensable for the analysis and explanation of marketing. Not every economic concept found in the literature, of course, is found in any one book. When selected and combined with marketing concepts and information, this union has given marketing thought one of its distinguishing characteristics. To the extent that certain concepts were relevant, and depending upon the point of view taken, the various marketing literatures have contained a greater or lesser number of economic concepts.

There are several reasons for the preponderance of concepts drawn from economics in the marketing literature. It must be remembered that marketing has long been regarded as a branch of economics, as an area of applied economics. Moreover, some of the earliest marketing writers were essentially economists, and others had extensive training in the field of economics with leading economists of that day. Also, at the beginning of the century the most widely held economic theories were those of classical and neoclassical economists, theories that were predicated upon an active system of trade and that contained a philosophy giving encouragement to turn-of-the-century business undertakings. Private enterprise was largely a market entrepreneurship, and the theory of the firm was an economic understanding that had wide appeal.

The interdependence of economics and marketing is illustrated by the titles of a number of the marketing books: *Economic Principles of Consumption, Economics of Retailing, Economics of Fashion* (Nystrom); *The Economics of Marketing and Advertising* (Moriarity); *The Economics of Marketing* (Killough); *The Economics of Advertising* (Vaile).

From the writings of Adam Smith were drawn concepts widely used throughout the general marketing literature as justification for the activity of marketing itself. Smith explained the advantages of *specialization* manifest in *division of labor.* Marketing, or distribution, itself one form of specialization, extended markets, creating opportunity for further specialization in production. The idea of specialization has been carried to some lengths within marketing, as between wholesale and retail levels of distribution and in the various marketing institutions and activities. From his concept of the interrelationship of mass production, distribution, and consumption has been developed the idea of the *inherence of marketing* in a specialized economy and of its particular importance when society has turned over to the mechanism of the market the supplying of its material needs. Notwithstanding the creative function of business, however, Smith conceived the end and *objective of all economic activity* to be the satisfaction of consumption. Accordingly, all marketing writers have subscribed to this end, have proclaimed the *consumer King,* and have taken the "consumers' viewpoint" in approaching the analysis of marketing. According to Smith, men have an *innate propensity to truck and barter,* thus attributing to man irresistibility to participation in the mechanism of the market. *Markets,* in turn, he defined in a manner repeated in most of the early marketing texts. In them, *price was the regulator* tending to establish *equilibrium.* The man in the market of Smith's conception was the *economic man,* bent upon the *maximization of his pleasures* and *self-interests.*

From other economicst have come still other useful concepts. From the marginalists came refinement of the concept of *utilities,* which gained some place in the explanation of consumer behavior in marketing books. Welfare economists' appraisal of marketing influenced critical writings on advertising. Institutionalism in economics focused marketing thought on some of marketing's broader implications and appeared to underlie the thinking of those writers who treated the subject from a broader than establishmental basis. From monetary theory came concepts relating to *credit;* from public finance, concepts of *taxation* in connection with chain-store growth; from the Keynesian school, theories of *governmental intervention* in marketing activities. Business cycle theory and population economics have also contributed concepts found in a few of the marketing writings.

Because most marketing writers have been dedicated to the improvement of the efficiency of marketing through management of the individual firm, they have employed liberally economists' concepts relating to the individual business enterprise. They accepted the concept of *profit as the regulator* of the market operation. With analyses of *scale of institutional operation,* they have appraised the size and number of marketing establishments and speculated on the effects of advertising on operating scales in manufacturing establishments. *Rent theory* has been interpreted in explanation of location and layout of all kinds of establishments engaged in marketing. *Price and non-price competition* has been explained in terms of marketing policy determination. The *structure of competition* has been interpreted in terms of *pure competition, monopoly, monopsony, duopoly, duopsony, oligopoly, oligopsony, and realistic competition. Product differentiation* has been fundamental to explanations of pricing, branding, advertising, and service policies. *Engle's Laws of Consumption,* as experienced in this country, have furnished concepts used in market analysis and in interpretation of consumer behavior.

The influence of economic concepts is evident throughout the marketing literature. In the general writings they have furnished the consumer viewpoint, the justification of institutional specialization, the concept of the productivity of marketing, a theory of integration and specialization in institutional management, a role of price in theory and practice, the bases of competition, and a philosophy of the relation of government to business. Following are some economic concepts found in the marketing literature: in retailing, concepts relating to location, rent, pricing, integration, and scale of operation; in advertising, to product differentiation, scale of operation, substitution costs; in wholesaling, to specialization, and price behavior; in credits, to business cycles, purchasing power, consumer spending and terms of sale.

PSYCHOLOGY

Psychology is a second discipline or branch of social science whose concepts have aided in development of marketing thought. It is concerned with the study of the mind in its various aspects, with consciousness and behavior, with the individual as a whole, especially in relation to his physical and social environment. The relevance of such knowledge to marketing is apparent, for the individual, the object of psychological study, is the party to marketing transactions. Therefore, to understand the behavior of the individual is to possess a key to effective and successful marketing.

As in economic thought, so in psychology, evolutionary processes have produced several schools of thought or explanation of human behavior. Concepts from each of these are found in the marketing literature. The first, known as "structuralism," began in 1879 by Wilhelm Wundt, conceived the human mind as composed of elementary mental states — sensations, images, and feelings. By introspection, proponents of that theory undertook to discover the physiological bases of various types of conscious experience. From their vocabularies such terms as *instincts, wants,* and *sensations* were used by marketing writers.

A second attempt to understand the human mind, begun about 1900 by John Dewey, was identified as "functionalism." Dewey was concerned with the value of mental experience in adjusting an individual to his environment. Behavior rather than consciousness became the object of study, but methods of introspection still played an important part.

About the same time that the functional idea developed in the United States, Sigmund Freud, a Viennese physician and psychiatrist, founded a third school of thought, psychoanalysis. Freud was interested in the unconscious mental processes and developed the clinical investigation that attempted to find the causes of mental disorders. His concepts and approach have been adapted in marketing thought through the development of inquiry into consumers' subconsciousness for explanation of this behavior in the market.

While those three phases of psychology were developing and attracting students throughout the world, John B. Watson proposed an explanation of behavior in terms of *stimulus* and *response, habit formation,* and *habit integration.* Discarding such concepts as sensation, perception, and imagery, in 1913 he advanced the concept of "behaviorism," based upon the premise that behavior proceeds from stimulation, which may be *learned* and habitual. According to behaviorists, man could be conditioned like any other animal and induced by proper stimuli to respond according to a plan. Like Pavlov's dog, whose salivation increased at the sound of a bell, consumers were expected to respond in pattern to sales stimuli. It is interesting that Watson's theory of behaviorism, perhaps, because it departed too far from prevailing schools of thought, did not gain wide acceptance abroad, and one might speculate as to the relation of this fact to the less frequent use of advertising and salesmanship made in even the more progressive countries outside the United States.

A fifth school of psychology is the Gestalt, the basic concept of which is that behavior is the result of integrated and inseparable physical, biological, and psychological factors.

The initial influence of psychological analysis in marketing thought resulted from the fact that some earliest writers in the marketing field were professional psychologists, such as Scott, Tipper, Hollingworth, Brewster, and others, who wrote such titles as *The Psychology of Advertising, Psychology in Advertising, Psyching the Ads, Psychology for Advertisers,* and *The New Psychology of Selling and Advertising.*

In the literature of advertising and selling are found the major use of psychological concepts, with emphasis shifting from structuralism and functionalism to behaviorism as the development of psychological thought progressed. Not only in selling and advertising, however, have psychological findings been important. They have been employed also in literature on buying, on market research, and in the general marketing writings. In the latter, a somewhat different use has been made of psychological concepts. De-emphasis has been given the influencing of individual behavior on the basis of psychological understandings, and emphasis has been placed upon broader effects and implications of human behavior, such as the Consumer Movement, increasing consumer education, and general understanding of consumer needs and wants, the satisfaction of which is the goal of marketing service.

The psychological concepts incorporated in marketing thought may be classified into several groups. One consists of concepts related to motivation and, in turn, to sales appeals. The idea of motivation itself interprets participation in the market as purposeful and suggests the possibility of determining the factors that affect market behavior. Some early marketing books discussed *instincts, wants,* and *urges* as bases of buying. Pleasure, comfort, and convenience were explained as motivations arising from sensation. Market motivation was specifically designated as "buying motives." The motives were classified as primary and selective, rational and emotional, buying and patronage, and ultimate or personal and industrial. The concept of *stimulus* was interpreted as "sales appeals" — the stimulating, want-satisfying properties of products and propositions that activated buying motivation. Unresponsiveness or indifference to supposed stimuli was regarded as "sales resistance," a condition it was believed could be overcome with proper behavior incitement. Motivation, it was also held, when based upon influences of long standing, involved *beliefs* and *attitudes.* In some of the writings, the attitudes of people in the position of consumers were explained.

A second group of psychological concepts relates to the mental functions of communication and education. An idea is admitted to consciousness through the faculty of *perception, insight,* or *intuition.* It is developed or comprehended through the faculty of *reasoning, logic,* or *association.* It is retained through the faculty of *memory* or *retention* and is subject to *recall.* It is applied through the faculty of *judgment.* Thus the concept of faculty psychology interprets the process of learning, a process of interest to marketers desirous of communicating ideas or of interpreting the success with which communication had been undertaken.

A third group of concepts relates to the pattern by which marketing ideas could be communicated effectively to the human mentality. The so-called steps in the sales process were developed, including *attention, interest, desire, conviction,* and *action.* It was recognized that under certain circumstances individuals acted on *impulse* rather than on the basis of logical inducement. The concept of *habit* in behavior expressed another type of reaction. Still other principles applied to the use of the sales procedure, including the principles of *recency, primacy, repetition,* and *intensity.*

The whole individual, who is the object of psychological analysis, is a personality. The concept of *personality* has been applied also to inanimate marketing institutions. A psychological concept more recently developed is that of *imagery,* or the imputation to products and institutions of characteristics that they can possess only by reason of a mental picture or image held in the mind of someone. Images are developed by *suggestion, education,* and *experience,* and their existence is a psychological phenomenon.

Not only concepts but also methodology have been adopted by students of marketing from psychological research. Thus methods of *observation, experimentation,* the use of *questionnaires, depth interviewing,* and *projection* have come into marketing research.

SOCIOLOGY

Sociology is a third discipline that has provided concepts useful in the development of marketing thought. It is an area concerned with understanding human behavior in groups and social settings. To the student of marketing it provided concepts increasing the effectiveness of marketing management and illuminating the institutional interpretation of marketing.

Unlike the economist, who conceives man to be mainly an "economic man," the sociologist conceives man as a member of society, as a member of a group or groups, as a representative of a civilization, or as a product of a culture embracing his time and environment. Man is seen to be conditioned not only by factors considered by psychologists but also by *customs, mores, institutions,* and *values* produced by his society and by his relation to other people in the social structure. In addition to economic self-interest, man is motivated by self-respect, affection, desire for approval, pleasure, and irrationality.

The marketing literature gives little evidence of conscious exploration and adoption of sociological concepts by students of marketing. James E. Hagerty, one of the earliest students and teachers of marketing, was a sociologist. But apart from his interest in institutional aspects of marketing, expressed in his study of mercantile credit, there is little indication that he influenced the development of marketing thought through his sociological frame of reference. The interests of sociologists have generally not coincided with those of marketing students. Sociologists did not write of marketing, and marketologists made no reference to the works of sociologists in their writings. Neither did marketing book titles contain terms relative to sociology comparable to those identifying marketing with economics and psychology.

The relative neglect of sociological concepts in marketing thought is traceable in part to the prevailing concept of marketing as a business rather than as a social institution. The dominance of a business viewpoint among students and practitioners of business obscured the cultural context in which business operates. Marketing has been regarded as a means by which *business* supplies the needs of society, rather than as a means that *society* has sanctioned for meeting its own needs. Business through marketing has strongly attempted to mold individual and social behavior, often subordinating social values to economic and commercial values. It has sometimes overlooked the deep cultural roots of behavior and the fact that utilization of sentiments is easier than modification of them.

Appreciation of the independent variability of society and the consequent dependence of marketing on it has, nevertheless, found some expression in the marketing literature. Historical interpretation of the development of marketing has generally been made in terms of *social change.* The response of marketers to such change has been referred to as the "adaptive behavior" of marketing institutions. Moreover, from whatever source derived, numerous sociological concepts have been introduced into marketing thought. They may be grouped under the following headings:

1. Social Motivation. The persistent interest that all social scientists have had in the causes of human motivation has been shared by sociologists. They emphasize, however, the interrelating influences between the individual and the group. Society fashions the *needs* and forms the standard for what may be judged *luxuries* and *necessities.* Motivation arises from the involvement in society that creates the desire for *acceptance, conformity, innovation,* or *leadership.* Some of these motivational concepts have been employed in the marketing literature without identification of their source.

2. Social Groups. Until *social structure* and *stratification* were brought to attention by sociologists, consumers were classifed primarily on an economic basis. Thus were distinguished high, middle, and low income groups. The individual, however, is recognized as affiliated, through membership, association, and inclination with many groups. One is the *family,* which is recognized as a spending unit and which acts in the market sometimes as a collective entity. The concept of *social classes* or *strata* is another grouping not limited to economic status but reflecting such factors as *ancestry, education, personality, social leadership,* and the like. There are also *work groups* aand *play groups* as well as institutional groupings of persons in such organizations as the government, the church, or the PTA. The complexity of society arises in part from the participation of individuals in a variety of groups. Groups represent *status,* the aspiration for which is a social motivation. Groups become identified by behavior and *symbols* – possessions – which become the object of demand in the market.

3. Social Interaction. The concepts of *competition* and *cooperation* signify more than merely types of business relationships. Rather, they are modes of interaction between members of society and social groups. When recognized as sociological concepts as well as economic concepts, those terms have a broader significance in marketing thought.

4. Social or Cultural Change. A fundamental interest of students of social phenomena is the question of what stimulates and directs *social change.* The object of this interest is the betterment of change through guidance, if that is possible. Experience has shown that efforts to influence society contrary to its fundamental inclinations have generally been futile, and marketers have contented themselves with such knowledge of trends as makes possible prediction and adaptation. Even sociologists have devoted much attention to describing trends and currents in society, and those descriptions have been useful in the development of marketing thought. For example, the *changing role* of women in society has been a development during the study of marketing that has altered the concept of the market. So also have been shifts in leadership in the family, the rise of children as a spending market, new personal and social values sanctioning the use of credit, the carrying of debt, the decline of abstinence, the disappearance of long-standing customs and traditions, the commercialization of social events, increased emphasis upon fashions, and greater leisure and recreational indulgence. Such factors have been described in marketing literature as influences affecting consumption. The necessity for adaptive compliance with these changes has led students of marketing to follow closely the concepts and analysis of them prepared by sociologists.

5. Ecology. Ecology deals with the spatial orientation and distribution of phenomena. Althogh some ecological concepts have geographic character, their pertinence to people and group behavior make them essentially sociological. From that area of study have come such concepts as the following: *rural* versus *urban, suburbanization, downtown areas, secondary shopping areas, shopping centers, territorial specialization, market areas,* and *trade gravitation.* Most of those concepts are found in the marketing literature in connection with store location, trade patterns, and spatial competition.

6. Population. Trends of population have been the interest of economists, but it has been mainly the sociologist who has contributed concepts of the *age composition* of the population, *geriatrics,* the *life cycle,* and *population explosion.* The introduction of those concepts into the marketing literature has occurred gradually.

MANAGEMENT

Interdisciplination includes the exchange of concepts, not only between students of business and those of other social phenomena, but also between students of marketing and those of other phases of business. The influence of developments in scientific management through the theories of Taylor, Gantt, and the Gilbreths have long been recognized. They stimulated initially the study of marketing; they inspired the concept of the "new retailing" based upon scientific principles; and they have underlain management principles and practices of the sales organization. From this area have come into marketing thought the following concepts:

1. Scientific Management. The idea of *job development, selection* and *training* of personnel, *co-ordination* of workers and supervisor, and *division of responsibility* between the manager and the managed, has been accepted in connection with the management of both marketing functions and marketing institutions.

2. The Task. The idea of building up synthetically the least wasteful and most productive *method of accomplishing a job* has been adopted in *time and duty studies* for salesmen, in routing, in setting sales quotas, and in training, compensating, stimulating, supervising, and evaluating the performance of salesmen.

3. Functionalized Management. The idea of *management functionalized* for purchasing, planning, scheduling, inspection, labor control, and maintenance in production has been adapted in a similar functionalization in management for operation of a distributive enterprise.

4. Scientific Approach. The steps of stating a problem, collecting information, and drawing conclusions have been adapted to marketing research under such terminology as situation analysis, informal investigation, planning the project, preparation for collection of data, etc.

5. Simplification. It is a management understanding that when a given volume can be obtained on fewer items made there is achieved more output per worker, less idle equipment, simpler supervision, lower raw material costs, smoother production, simpler accounting, and easier control. This same concept of simplification of product line has been accepted as a marketing technique.

6. Diversification. The multiplication of activities of product lines implied by the concept of diversification arises from an effort to meet variety in consumer demand, to maintain flexibility, to use profitably complementary processes. Where justified, it prevents waste of labor, machine time, and materials. A similar concept is applicable in marketing to meet similar problems.

7. Standardization. While applicable in production to uniformity in raw materials, tools, equipment, methods, inspection, time schedules, etc., standardization in marketing pertains to uniformity in integrated chain-store operations, to standard lines, layouts, operating procedures, and control methods, to commodity classifications, and to methods employed to unify mass production and mass merchandising.

OTHER DISCIPLINES

This survey could be extended without commensurate profit to other disciplines that have furnished concepts incorporated in marketing thought. Accounting and law are two from which many have been drawn. Social psychology and anthropology have furnished few if any concepts to the traditional body of marketing thought.

Thus it is seen that the development of marketing thought is not only the product of ideas developed by students of marketing. On the contrary, to make the maximum contribution to marketing thought, one must be conversant with other intellectual findings.

INTERDISCIPLINARY DEVELOPMENTS AFTER 1960

The development of marketing thought in the 1960s had three distinct characteristics: substantive, perspective, and formative. Its substantive development consisted of the enlargement of knowledge about elements already identified as marketing: markets, middlemen, channels, price, and the processes inherent in the distributive task. It was based upon the economic concept of marketing. Its perspective development was that by which marketing became viewed from new perspectives, namely, social perspectives, and the related concepts were derived from the behavioral disciplines. These concepts, and their corresponding theories, provided new insight into consumer behavior, motivation, social processes in business, group behavior, systemic functions, role relations and interaction, social responsibility, and culture. Its formative development consisted of the incorporation of means by which the logic of marketing thought might be made more acute. This involved employment of mathematical, statistical, and other quantitative methods whereby thought processes can be organized and conducted. Each of these developments took place in their respective literatures. Collectively they were referred to as the "interdisciplination" of marketing thought.

BEHAVIORAL DEVELOPMENT OF MARKETING

Notwithstanding the introduction of many new concepts into marketing from behavioral disciplines during the 1960s, its longstanding embodiment of concepts from other disciplines must be recognized. Because marketing was originally deemed wholly an economic activity, economic analysis and theory were liberally used from the inception of its study. As new developments occurred in the economic discipline, they were often incorporated into marketing thought. Moreover, early writings on advertising and salesmanship drew heavily upon psychology, for prominent writers in those fields were psychologists. Likewise, marketing scholars and researchers familiar with history, literature, law, accounting, and sociology drew a trickle of concepts from those fields into the growing stream of marketing thought.

Evidences of interdisciplinary inclusions may be found in the works of many marketing writers. Scott wrote of advertising from a psychological point of view as early as 1903. Nystrom had a social perspective in his writings of retailing, as did Phelps concerning credit management. Breyer used concepts from physics, sociology, and psychology. And Neifeld viewed the institution of credit as a cultural phenomenon. Nevertheless, none of these nor any others writing prior to 1950 is generally associated with the behavioral movement in marketing thought which took place after that date.

The essence of this occurrence is the conception of marketing as a social — rather than exclusively an economic — process, involving people as human beings and not merely as technicians or economic men. The tone of the concept was indicated by Duddy and Revzan in 1953: "Ours is a market society."[1] And they quote with approbation Karl Polanyi: "Normally the economic order is a function of the social order in which it is contained. Neither under tribal nor feudal, nor mercantile conditions was there . . . a separate economic system in society." However, not only humanistic concepts were obtained from the social disciplines, but also their methods of studying human behavior. These understandings were borrowed from psychology, sociology, political science, social psychology, anthropology, demography, geography, ecology, and other related areas.

Several explanations are given for the timing of this development. Most certainly it sprang from renewed vitality and inquiry in all disciplines in the post World War II resumption of scholarly pursuits. In fact, some research in human behavior had even been accelerated during the war period. Social scientists were also thinking more expansively, considering the fields of business and the marketplace as natural areas of inquiry for their disciplines. At the same time, progressive acceptance of consumer orientation in marketing management emphasized the need for better understanding of consumer behavior and motivation, and of managers' behavior relative to both consumers and others with whom they interacted in the distributive process. Thus invention of the Marketing Concept in the early 1950s, the maturing of the economy, the need for new tools to supplement those of economic analysis, and the increased interaction among social and behavioral scientists all contributed to more behavioral thinking in marketing. Also important was the encouragement given business educators to lift the level of their offerings above that based upon prior theoretical constructs. The emergent need was not only for the adoption of new concepts but for adaptation of them to the marketing medium. This undertaking was the work of marketing writers mainly during the 1960s.

Following a common pattern, writings on behavioral aspects of marketing by both marketing scholars and allied social scientists appeared first in their respective professional journals. In 1950, Cox and Alderson included in *Theory in Marketing*[2] several articles dealing with concepts from other disciplines, but it was not until 1963 that Perry Bliss published a book of readings: *Marketing and the Behavioral Sciences,*[3] and W.T. Tucker *The Social Contest of Economic Behavior.*[4] The Bliss book consisted of an assortment of essays by behavioral scientists. In short succession there appeared in 1965, *Marketing: Contributions from the Behavioral Sciences,* by Zaltman.[5] Its purpose was narrowly managerial, however, in that, with knowledge of behavioral findings, managers would improve prediction, lessen the range of alternative effects from their decisions, and thus find better ways to influence the consumer.

Evidence of the state of marketing and the behavioral sciences in the early 1960s is found in the fact that when R. L. Day published *Marketing Models – Quantitative and Behavioral*[6] in 1964, many of his selected articles had been published originally in the 1950s, and only one-third of them had been written by people identified with marketing. The behavioral portion of his book reflected the overriding interest in understanding the consumer by way of behavioral concepts, which he said provided richer, more useful models of consumers than the "economic man." The articles reported were results of empirical, not theoretical, research, thus also manifesting a turn of marketing thought toward more substantial evidence and more rigorous scientific research. In this book, Day presented a paradigm of the consumer, and he discussed social processes and structure, behavioral factors related to products, and demographic variables. This served to interpret his sense of the need for a more systematic approach to analysis of consumer actions.

Consumer motivation and behavior was indeed the principal subject of behavioral interest during the mid years of the 1960s. Advancement in understanding the consumer was immediately applicable in all areas of management. Consequently, several marketing scholars undertook not only to collate but to crystalize the new interpretations of consumers. Processes of motivation, perception, and learning were of particular interest, as well as influences of individual predisposition, personality, and attitude formation. In addition to these psychological concepts, from sociology were drawn others concerning culture, group influence, social strata, reference groups, and the family. Summation of consumers' characteristics, attributes, and behavior patterns was achieved in models of consumer motivation and behavior and in models of consumer decision processes. These were widely received as a significant breakthrough in understanding this important element in marketing and in the application to marketing of social and behavioral concepts. Foremost among the writings on the subject was the carefully researched book of Engel, Kollat, and Blackwell,[7] which not only surveyed the extant research of the period but presented a credible theory of consumer behavior.

An article by Lazer included in a group from a symposium edited by Bass, King and Pessimier[8] in 1968 may be the most comprehensive explanation of the interdisciplinary approach to marketing available at that time. He attributed the increased recourse to interdisciplinary sources to the maturing of the economy and to the need for other than economic research tools in dealing with current problems.

It was one thing to edit and publish separate papers on the behavioral context of marketing, but it was something else to introduce these ideas into the more traditional patterns of marketing thought. Such an undertaking is illustrated by the readings published by Alexis in 1969.[9] Although based upon empirical research and presented to illustrate theoretical constructs and to give meaning to abstractions, the format of the book was quite traditional, following the pattern of discussing marketing environment, systems, operations, and marketing and society. At a time when even elementary marketing courses were being made managerial, and more advanced courses were specializing in newer concerns, the amalgamation of the old and the new concepts in this manner served a need.

Persisting in the updating of his readings, Bliss in 1970 published *Marketing Management and the Behavioral Environment*,[10] in which he showed the application to marketing of specific concepts — not schools of thought nor overall theoretical frameworks — from related disciplines. His selection is more discriminating than formerly and his judgment more critical. The articles illustrated application of a concept to a *specific* marketing problem and did not attempt to develop theory therefrom. He also recognized that while borrowed concepts had often been very useful, they did not always assure success in their application.

By the date of Perry's publication, marketing thought based upon behavioral concepts had developed to the point where he could identify summarily (1) the behavioral concepts which were relevant to marketing and (2) the areas in marketing thought in which such concepts could be assimilated:

	BEHAVIORAL CONCEPTS	MARKETING THOUGHT
From anthropology — (community in entirety)	culture subculture	Comparative approach Climate for business Market research Cultural restraints Word association Communication Retailing structure

	BEHAVIORAL CONCEPTS	MARKETING THOUGHT
From Sociology (individuals in relation to other individuals)	Social class Social differentiation Status crystalization	Market segments Social class awareness New product acceptance Shopping behavior Communication Leisure
	Reference groups Informal groups Social role	Groups, products, brands Aspirations References Status conflict Personal influence
	The family Individuals Institutions	Decision making Life cycle
From Psychology (centers on the individual)	Motivation Drives Cognitive dissonance Achievement Affiliations Hierarchy of motives Perception Orientation Scope Thresholds Perceptual function Mechanics of vision Time Selective perception	Motivation Risk reduction Ego Self-image
	Classical and operant learning Serial learning "Insight" Learning of concepts Attitudes	Concept generalization Brand choice
From Political Science	Power groups and values	Trade associations Public policy

BEHAVIORAL CONTRIBUTIONS TO MARKETING THOUGHT

The principal contribution of social and behavioral disciplines to marketing thought is the variety of perspectives in which the marketing process may be viewed. Differentiation of perspective from process is an important step toward theory formation, for it represents conceptualization, increases terminology, suggests new logical relationships, and results in the development of theories. This has been the effect of perception of marketing as a social process and of the participants in this process as social entities. Thought developed along these lines has complemented prior interpretations of marketing as either a wholly economic process or a self-contained managerial function. Emergence of the social perspec-

198

tive lifted marketing thought out of a state of complacency where at mid-century it was thought that marketing had already attained maturity. The emergent thought, however, as can be seen in the earlier part of this chapter, was not without root. The developments of the 1960s expanded what some scholars had seen earlier, and they made the vision an integral part of marketing thought.

ENDNOTES

[1] Edward Duddy and David Revzan, *Marketing: An Institutional Approach,* (New York: McGraw-Hill Book Company, Inc., 1953, p. 1).

[2] Reavis Cox and Wroe Alderson (eds.). *Theory in Marketing* (Chicago: Richard D. Irwin, Inc., 1950).

[3] Perry Bliss (ed.), *Marketing and the Behavioral Sciences* (Rockleigh, N.J.: Allyn & Bacon, 1963).

[4] W. T. Tucker, *The Social Context of Economic Behavior* (New York: Holt, Rinehart and Winston, 1964).

[5] Gerald Zaltman, *Marketing: Contributions from the Behavioral Sciences* (New York: Harper & Bros., 1965).

[6] R. L. Day (ed.), *Marketing Models – Quantitative and Behavioral* (Scranton, Pa.: International Textbooks, 1964).

[7] James F. Engel, David T. Kollat, and Roger D. Blackwell, *Consumer Behavior* (New York: Holt, Rinehart, and Winston, Inc., 1968).

[8] F. M. Bass, et al. (eds.) *Applications of the Sciences in Marketing Management* (New York: John Wiley & Sons, Inc., 1968).

[9] N. Alexis, et. al (eds.), *Empirical Foundations of Marketing: Research Findings in the Behavioral and Managerial Sciences* (Chicago: Markham Publishing Co., 1969).

[10] Perry Bliss (ed.), *Marketing Management and the Behavioral Environment* (Englewood Cliffs, N.J.: Prentice-Hall, Inc., 1970).

NEWER AREAS OF MARKETING THOUGHT

13

Since 1950, traditional thought and literature has been both supplemented and complemented by thought developments which have produced a number of new literatures. That on marketing management is one. In addition, other writings may be classified as dealing with the following subjects: (1) quantitative aspects of marketing thought, (2) marketing systems, (3) environmentalism, (4) comparative marketing, (5) international marketing, (6) logistics, and (7) marketing and society. These are the subjects of the present chapter.

QUANTITATIVE ASPECTS OF MARKETING THOUGHT

However the marketing process is viewed, whether from an economic or social point of view, or even as a management process, it is presumed that thought about it has form or structure. Composition and organization are indispensible to logic and understanding. Form in marketing thought, however, prior to the 1950s, was a debatable issue. Its reputed lack of empirically researched findings, stable generalizations, and coherent theories unsettled the hope that the discipline was attaining scientific stature. A principal criticism of marketing, as of social sciences in general, was that its reasoning was based upon factors qualitative, subjective, and immeasurable. Little application was made of formal rules of logic; causality was imputed where only relationship existed; and felt dissonance was treated as exception to accepted principles. Such was the state of research and marketing theory until the movement for "quantification" gained momentum.

It cannot, of course, be said truly that marketing thought was utterly devoid of quantitative aspects. Accounting techniques had always been an integral part of management knowledge. Merchandising mathematics was standard form for thinking about inventories, pricing, and buy-sell functions. Statistical measures for averaging, dispersion, correlation, difference, time series analysis, and index numbers were common tools for research. And various numerical and graphic forms for representing economic propositions also were included. Together they served the needs of marketing thought during its first half century, but at the end of that period they too were subjected to revision through implementation of concepts derived from mathematics, advanced statistics, and econometrics.

Several circumstances accounted for this turning to more complex quantitative means of developing and expressing marketing thought. As has been said before, marketing problems were becoming increasingly complex, and decisions required control over a greater number of variables. But need alone was not all that developed about that time. There was emerging a language in the form of mathematics and a syntax in the form of model building which gave new strength to the structure of marketing thought.

This development was an outgrowth of the mathematical approach to military problems during World War II known as Operations Research. When following the war new applications of this technique were sought, business problems involving accounting, finance, and production were areas where it was successfully applied during the 1950s. Not until in the 1960s, however, were applications found for it in marketing management. Since then, employment of mathematical models for decision making gained "fad" proportions, in research, in education, and in marketing practice.

The development of expertise in the use of mathematics, however, was not an automatic process for marketing researchers in the 1950s, for their graduate education did not usually include advanced mathematics. In 1959-1960, a significant thrust was made in the interdisciplinary direction, as the Ford Foundation sponsored a program conducted at Harvard by the Institute of Basic Mathematics for Applications in Business, attended by a select group of professors of economics and business, including a number from the field of marketing. It was they who were substantially responsible for the introduction of mathematics into marketing thought.

Writing in 1964, Buzzell, one of the attendants at the Institute program, explained at some length[1] the reason for the increasing use of marketing models during the 1950s and early 1960s. He cited seven reasons: (1) efforts of Operations Researchers to find new applications for their techniques (2) perceived need for formal analysis in marketing, (3) dissatisfaction with conventional approaches to decision making in marketing, (4) increased stature of marketing research in companies, (5) the rise of marketing theory during this period, (6) the presumed competitive value of models, and (7) prestige associated with use of models. Yet even in the early 1960s little or no real use of mathematical models was being made in marketing. Its use was mainly exploratory, diagnostic, and fact determining, rather than as a basis for complete reliance.

That models should be increasingly used, on the other hand, derived from the distinctive features of marketing problems. They are essentially problems of behavioral relations. They have to do with the firm's external environment: customers, suppliers, and competitors. Behavioral relations are very difficult to measure. And many factors cannot be observed at all. Buzzell perceived possible application of models in marketing to product policy, pricing, promotion, marketing channels, credit, and physical distribution. His book presented experiences of companies using models for decision making in many of these areas.

In the same year, Day published a compilation of articles reporting research, rather than company experience, in quantitative models.[2] Crediting models with reduction of the number of variable factors to manageable proportions so that more significant relations could be identified, he presented articles dealing with Bayesian decision theory, promotional activity, simulation and programming, and models for planning and strategy formulation.

Still another effort to survey recent developments and advance research in marketing was made through scholarly papers presented at a symposium which Bass, King, and Pessemier edited and published in 1968.[3] Because the papers were written for this occasion, and not like readings being republished, special effort was made in evaluation and extension of thought. Three areas of interest were covered: consumer behavior and normative models, behavioral theories of consumer behavior, and experimental methods and simulation models in marketing management.

Because mathematical models and logic can be programmed into computers, the utilization of that mechanism in marketing decision making received special attention in Casher's *Marketing and the Computer*.[3a] Like others, he gave account of the increasing use of models and attributed it in part to the emergence of sophisticated Operations Research techniques. He showed the applicability of the computer to various marketing activities, and while avoiding technicalities of the mechanism, he related what he thought the marketing executive should know about it: the kinds of statistical techniques available, the problems on which it can be used, the data needed, the outputs obtainable, and ways of interpreting the outputs.

Actually, throughout the decade of the 1960s there was little apparent development in the substance or content of writings on the quantitative aspect of marketing. Three subjects seemed to be covered from the first: explanation and justification for introduction of quantitative techniques in marketing; second, explanation of the relevant techniques; and third, interpretation of their usefulness in marketing. Consequently, *Marketing Models: Quantitative Applications* by Day and Parsons in 1971[4] differed not a great deal from some earlier works. The topics of his format, however, indicate rather clearly the scope of quantitative techniques deemed relevant to marketing:

Deterministic Optimization Models	Regression Analysis
Stochastic Process Models	Factor and Cluster Analysis
Bayesian Decision Theory	Heuristic Problem Solving
Experimental Design	Simulation
Discriminant and Canonical Models	

CONTRIBUTIONS OF QUANTIFICATION

Contributions are made to marketing thought in terms of both *what* is thought about marketing and *how* one thinks about it. Substantive and perspective developments relate to *what* one thinks; the quantitative or formative, to *how* thought is structured and developed.

The contribution of quantitative lies in formalizing thought processes through the use of an abstract language and constructs of manipulatable variables. They are applied to the substantive concepts of marketing, whether it is viewed as economic, social, or managerial, and by them the logic of the mathematical discipline is carried to the subject matter of marketing. Through such uses of quantitative methods the following contributions to marketing thought have been made:

1. Greater precision in the differentiation and definition of marketing concepts
2. Facilitation of abstract analysis by symbolization of substantive concepts
3. Interpretation of marketing phenomena variable correlates
4. Identification and measurement of relationships among numbers of variables

5. Combination of clusters of relationships in the form of models — diagnostic, operative, or normative.
6. Improvement of theorization and the prospects of theory formation by greater innovation and precision in the statement of variable relationships
7. Facilitation of management decision making through the exposition of alternatives, measurements, and probabilities

MARKETING SYSTEMS

Another development in marketing thought during the 1960s was the conceptualization of the marketing process as "flows," and of the marketing structure as "systems." These concepts were in contrast to the idea that marketing is a movement of economic products from one distributive unit to another, and that those units act singly, more *in*dependently than *inter*dependently. The new concepts grew out of a perception that the marketing mechanism functioned *as a whole,* not as an assortment of unrelated parts. A theory based upon this interpretation of marketing was called "holism." The systems of interrelated components were of two types: economic and social. The former represented the coordinated division of the distributive task among economic specialists—middlemen and others. The latter, the interactive relationship of the people occupying the economic positions. Preponderance of economic systems analysis, but the introduction of behavioral concepts led to the study of marketing as social systems. Quantification of research, on the other hand, provided models and measurements for marketing systems.

CHANNELS AS ECONOMIC SYSTEMS

The concept of "channels" has been so inherent in marketing thought as to be regarded by some as the only concept in marketing not borrowed from another discipline. It has not, however, always represented a marketing *system* as that term has come to be defined, for the channel was perceived as a series of discrete units rather than a sequence of contiguous ones. For many years management in marketing was deemed the management of the internal operations of retail and wholesale establishments, whose external relations were principally negotiatory. Exception to this point of view, with preference for a holistic or systems concept, was expressed even while the segmented channel concept was ascendant and cresting. To early exponents of holism, however, systems were media for the performance of an economic function, not social relationships, as explained later by behaviorists. Leading contributors to the theory of channels as economic systems were Breyer, Duddy and Revzan, and Bucklin.

Ralph Breyer in 1934[5] discarded the usual cursory treatment of markets preliminary to more elaborate description of institutions and undertook to show the collective marketing institution as a synthesized unit operating under various market conditions. As a system, the marketing institution had a two-fold character: (1) affinity between channel units, and (2) indigenousness of the channel to market conditions. The relationship between units he illustrated as analogous to electric circuits whereby current flows between positive and negative poles. The essence of marketing he perceived as flows of goods, orders, payments, and title between sellers and buyers, impelled by imbalance between supply (positive poles) and demand (negative poles). Contact and negotiation established the market circuits, and transaction closed them. In this concept, it is apparent that new emphasis is given to what happens *between* units of the channel, rather than to the mere actions of the individual units. System relationships alone are discussed, with little indication given even of segmentation of the economic task among system members.

Breyer also professed taking a "social approach," proclaiming marketing to be "a social instrument designed to serve the best interests of the public at large." Thus the marketing institution was deemed a social instrument. He implied by this a social responsibility for *economic* efficiency and effectiveness. He did not, however, perceive the relations of system members as *social* relations.

Breyer's efforts made little impression upon marketing thought or practice at that time, but they were a seed which gradually grew to large proportions. Explicit in his work was the relationship of marketing to its environment, which was endemic to a later developed concept of environmentalism.

No less innovative, but no more popular at the time, was another work by Breyer published in 1949: *Quantitative Systemic Analysis and Control: Study No. 1 – Channel and Channel Group Costing.*[6] Having taught a Trade Association Course at the Wharton School of Finance and Commerce during the late 1930s, and later having done further study of vertical channels of a trade, he became convinced that "a new fundamental approach to the whole study of marketing, that somehow hinged upon the marketing channel, could be developed that would make distinct contributions to our knowledge and mastery of this field over and above all present practical and theoretical approaches." His concern was with the "complete vertical span" between producer and consumer, in contrast to the traditional enterprise analysis and the all-inclusive study of the marketing institution as a whole. A span that stretches "from producer to consumer, may be said to be of 'channel' dimension in its vertical aspect." He explored the quantitative analysis and control of channels in this sense, terming it the "Systemic Approach." He believed that the extant body of marketing "principles" should be reoriented to this pattern of systems.

Nothing in the marketing literature at that time was so deviant, so cogent, so unappreciated. Yet his work during those two unsettled decades in the development of marketing thought won for Breyer accolades from his successors who carried forward concepts of marketing systems and the marketing institution.

Contemporaries of Breyer, Duddy and Revzan too were concerned with institutional relations and processes in marketing.[7] They saw the marketing structure "as an organic whole made up of interrelated parts, subject to growth, change, and functioning in a process of distribution that is coordinated and conditioned by economic and social forces." Recognizing structure to be organization and dimension for performing functions, they identified three types of structure in the interacting marketing mechanism:

Agency — the diversity and organization of enterprises engaged in the distribution of products and services
Area — the relationship of markets resulting from cost and price factors
Price — the structure of exchange values

They regarded management and price as the coordinating forces, and not as separate subject matter somehow related to the marketing institution. In the action pattern changes wrought by these forces, some structural relations changed and some did not.

Following Duddy, Revzan and Breyer by almost two decades, Bucklin[8] reviewed the history of the channel concept and undertook to build a model of channels, to explain firm behavior and channel structure in terms of economic circumstances, and to stimulate empirical research. He defined the channel in the following ways:

As a mechanism through which the invisible hand of the private enterprise
   marketplace operates
As a creature of competitive pressures and specialization of labor
As developed by division of the marketing task
As a cooperative venture concerned with mutual adjustment
As a means by which demand for goods and goods are transmitted
As a means of directing resources

Bucklin said that while there were articles on the channel system, there was then no theory, and generalizations were rough and unbound. His own theory included a concept which he termed the principle of postponement, risk shifting, and speculation. Its thesis was that the interacting members of a channel attempted so far as possible to postpone forward movement of flows through the channel, for in this manner assumption of risk could be delayed. When circumstances seemed propitious for speculation, the delaying strategy could be reversed. He also conceived a "normative channel" as the channel status which tended to evolve in the long run. Of note too are the following ideas about channel outputs:

1. Time, place, and ownership utilities are services.
2. Service outputs are identified as holding till time of delivery, determination of desirable lot size, and decentralization of the market by delivery to a distant point.
3. The channel represents a combination of these services.
4. Variations in channel service are determined by processes of substitution.
5. Cost is a focal factor in channel construction and specialization.

It will be noted that common to the several publications representative of thought about channels prior to the mid 1960s, is the regard for them as *economic* systems functioning under the constraints of management *strategy* and environmental *circumstances* to provide for the most *effective* and *efficient* distribution of goods and services.

CHANNELS AS SOCIAL SYSTEMS

During the 1960s, the development of behavioral concepts, which were applied first to understanding consumer behavior and next to management behavior, turned the attention of systems analysts from economic to social aspects of channels. All that had been written about specialization and integration in the distributive process from an economic standpoint was sustained and extended with new conceptualization, as with Alderson's sorting, search, and transvection theory, and Aspinwall's depot and parallel systems theories. But new concepts expressing social behavior were derived from sociological theories of role and group interaction. The marketing channel was thereby perceived as a system of institutions which interact. They control, conflict, and cooperate. Power is essential and pervasive throughout.

In 1967, Mallen,[9] contending that the subject of channels had been neglected by scholars, compiled what he regarded to be the sum of existing articles dealing with the subject conceptually. His emphasis was upon social and theoretical aspects of channels. Therefore among the articles of his choice were some dealing with pluralistic competition, distributive politics, countervailing power, and organizational extension. Others dealt with simulation, Bayesian decision theory, and other quantitative aspects of channel models and measurements. Thus in a sense this was a transitional book moving from economic to social interpretation, and including concepts from the behavioral and mathematical disciplines.

Others conducting research in the same period, or writing shortly thereafter, enlarged upon the points generally incorporated in marketing systems theory, namely that:

— the marketing process consists of a variety of flows: physical products, title, orders, information, credit, payment, risk, post-sale service.
— market flows move through channels, termed systems, constituting economic specialization in the marketing process and social interaction among its members.
— marketing systems operate within the constraints of their respective environments, which may consist of the firm, the distributive group, or society at large.
— achievement of efficiency and effectiveness is gained through continual adjustment effected by management strategy and external constraints.

The contributions of several writers to development of systems theory may be briefly stated as follows.

Fisk,[10] defining marketing as a set of activities that stimulate and serve demand, regarded systems as any set of interacting variables. The social relations of system members were definable in terms of goals, organization and input, constraints, output, and efficiency and effectiveness.

Stern,[11] defining the marketing channel as a social system, regarded an economic system as a subset of the social system, even as the economy is a subset of society in general. The social system concept is expressive of relationship, interdependence, and interaction, the latter perceived in terms of role, power, conflict, and communication.

Lewis[12] identified and characterized the theoretical explanations of channels given at that time by Aspinwall (depot), Alderson (sorting and transvection), Breyer (contract), Vaile (flows), McInnes (gaps and parallel systems), and Bucklin (postponement). He saw control of channel networks gained through management strategies eliciting cooperation and resolving conflict. Lewis also briefly described marketing channels in a number of other countries.

Palamountain[13] enlarged upon the element of power in the interplay among countervailing groups in conflict over distribution practices. From analyzing conflicts in distribution during the 1930s, he undertook to show "that the economic environment enables, but does not guarantee, the creation of political groups, and that economic groups which seek to operate politically thereby enter a realm which exercises its own conditioning effects and which does far more than simply reflect the strength and drives of economic groups." He analyzed the distribution of groceries, drugs, and autos in terms of conflict created by horizontal, intertype and vertical competition. The book is an interesting combination of classical economics, group interaction and political policy.

Bucklin[14] in 1972, still decrying the lack of systems analysis in marketing literature, undertook, using literary sources and statistical analysis, to demonstrate key factors which have controlled the growth and development of middlemen. Intending to dispell myths about the role of wholesalers, about whom he said little had been written, he blended traditional history and concepts of model building and multivariate statistical analysis. Both the wholesaling and retailing structures were analyzed from the standpoints of metamorphosis, structure, and competition. The outcome was a statistically supported theory of the resiliency of these segments of the distributive system in response to management strategy and external constraints. But going beyond mere exposition of our own systems, Bucklin generalized his findings to suggest the pattern of the evolution of wholesaling in any industrialized country. His conclusions and rationale were consistent with those of the study of wholesaling in fifteen countries edited by Bartels in 1963.

CONTRIBUTIONS OF SYSTEMS THEORY

Although systems theory did not invoke a new concept of the mission of marketing, it interpreted the marketing mechanism differently and contributed to new marketing theory. Without a perception of the diversity in the unity of the marketing structure, the impact of environmental factors upon its evolution would have been less apparent. Likewise, without discernment of the social aspects of intrachannel interaction, the enrichment of marketing thought through behavioral interpretations of consumer action alone would have been minimal. Or put otherwise, through systems analysis, marketing thought has been infused with a wider dimension of management strategy, better understanding of influences shaping marketing structure as a whole, and keener appreciation of the countervailing forces playing within and around the marketing systems.

ENVIRONMENTALISM

Environmentalism generally refers to the influence of environment upon the development of systems or organisms, and in marketing it is understood particularly to refer to the relationship between environment and the practice and development of marketing.

The presence of this element in marketing thought is relatively new. In early writings it was given little attention, for the environment was the market, to be won, rather than to be compromised with. Gaining dominance over controllable factors in marketing was more engaging than the idea of compromising managerial control with environmental or uncontrollable factors. Nevertheless, with the emergency of systems theory, holism, and the concept of adaptation for survival, environmental considerations became an integral part of marketing, even an independent variable to which the marketing system and management practice responded. From the literary standpoint, the environment remained a subject merely described and classified until it was conceptualized and so made a structural component of marketing thought.

As the definition and analysis of environment progressed, several stages of its development could be identified:

1. Description of USA Environment
2. Description of Foreign Marketing Practice
3. Analysis of Advanced Marketing Technology in Underdeveloped Environments
4. Conceptualization of Environment
5. Conceptual Interpretation of Foreign Environments
6. Conceptual Interpretation of Marketing within a Foreign Environment
7. Foreign Environment Interpreted for Import Marketing

DESCRIPTION OF USA ENVIRONMENT

It would be an overstatement to say that early marketing writers considered environment *per se;* they took it for granted. Their own environment was all that they knew, and it was a variable factor only insofar as it changed. In an environment characterized as a seller's market, committed to a laissez faire philosophy, and conceived as an economic environment, the environment was little more than the market. With the increase of government regulation of the economy, the political or legal environment became recognized. And as social concepts were introduced into thought, social environment became a reality. The several aspects of environment were described, although environment was not analyzed as a separate concept. Marketers and writers were more subjective than objective about environment. They recognized a mutual impact of marketing and environment upon each other, but they did not transcend the characteristics of their *particular* environment. Such was the state of thought, in all branches of the marketing literature, until into the 1950s, when increasing travel, research, investment, and marketing in other countries brought Americans − the original developers of marketing thought − into contact with other environments.

DESCRIPTION OF FOREIGN MARKETING PRACTICE

While at first marketing abroad was described as though products and marketing strategies, and not environmental factors, were the sole determinants of marketing success, international businessmen gradually recognized that the "peculiarities" and "uniqueness" of foreign environments thwarted their successful use of practices employed at home. Articles then began to appear describing marketing practices and institutions in many countries. They usually dealt with limited subjects, were based upon more or less surface observation, and emphasized *differences* in marketing discernible throughout the world. They were intended to be informative, and thus they contributed substantially to knowledge of marketing practice. Compilations of them were made in books of readings on international or comparative marketing, such as those of Sommers and Kernan[15] and Ryans and Baker,[16] but they were always of limited scope and coverage.

Also of this exploratory period, but of larger proportions, was a book by Goldman[13] explaining marketing in the environment of the Soviet Union.

Goldman's objective, namely, was to understand Soviet marketing and therby understand ourselves better. He disclosed an insight uncommon at that time, for it implied a fundamental relationship between environment and marketing which had to be hypothesized before conceptualization of environment could take place.

The contrast between marketing in the USSR and the USA reflected the Marxian philosophy that marketing was unproductive – "parasitic." Goldman's scholarly but traditional exposition of operation of the marketing system showed the implementation of the Marxian philosophy in the planning of the distribution of consumer goods, pricing, financial control, the human element and state ownership, and distribution costs. The book was a substantial addition to knowledge and an example of how marketing practice is carried out in a different political environment.

Of similar character and, interestingly, also pertaining to marketing in the Soviet Union was a book published by Greer[18] a decade later. Based largely upon newspaper reports of the Soviet press, his intended interpretation of Soviet culture showed many of the unfortunate market consequences of the Communist marketing philosophy. He presented factual, detailed, and timely evidence of practices and problems relating to products, retail trade, advertising and communication, pricing and channels, transportation and physical distribution and Soviet international marketing.

ANALYSIS OF ADVANCED MARKETING TECHNOLOGY IN UNDERDEVELOPED ENVIRONMENTS

From the articles and books previously described, one would begin to perceive that social aspects of environment would prescribe differences in marketing practices in dissimilar countries. The *economic* conditions of dissimilar countries, on the other hand, sometimes do *not* require such alteration of marketing practices, for the economic functions of marketing are generally subject to the same laws of specialization, scale, proportions, and economy. Consequently, because during the 1960s much interest was shown in assisting economically underdeveloped nations, some marketing books relevant to this subject were written. Moyer,[19] in 1965, noting that marketing had been neglected in literature on economic development, pointed out that marketing was not parasitic but indispensible to an economy. The relevance of this to the developing concept of environmentalism is in the reciprocal relationship of marketing and environment. In the United States as in developing countries, the formative character of marketing is emphasized, and applications of marketing to smaller agricultural countries resembled the stage of marketing thought in the United States between 1900 and 1920.

A second example of marketing's formative role in developing an environment is seen in Miller's compilation of readings in Agribusiness Research.[20] Originating at the Stanford Research center, it broadly discussed marketing theory and problems in economic development, concentrating on food and fiber products, and concerned with pricing, supply, demand and management decision theory, and research and foreign economic development.

Still another book of a different character was also concerned with the contribution of marketing to developing countries. It was a collection of cases illustrating marketing management in developing countries, edited by Boyd[21] and emanating from the International Center for the Advancement of Management Education, Graduate School of Business, Stanford University. Intended to develop marketing strategies and improve decision making, it illustrated the adaptation of techniques to environment and stimulated original perception of relationships between marketing and environment.

CONCEPTUALIZATION OF ENVIRONMENT

So long as marketing studies were mononational, environment was taken for granted; but as they became multinational, although differences stood out, the *essential* aspects of environment began to appear. This raised two questions: What is *environment?* And what is *marketing?* An implicit fact was not immediately apparent, namely, that one's concept of marketing was a function of the environment in which he saw marketing performed.

As economic interpretations of marketing in the 1950s were beginning to be complemented by social interpretations, it was natural that social environment should be added to the concept of physical and economic environment and, ultimately, the culture characterizing the society. This broadening interpretation pervaded the viewpoint of the scholars surveying the conduct of wholesaling in different countries in 1961.[22] For this collaboration, Bartels, employing anthropoligical, social, economic and managerial concepts, prepared a conceptual model of environment graduated on a progressively diminishing scale. Accordingly, environment was identified by the following dimensions:

Cultural or national
Social
Economic
Market
Marketing economic and behavioral
Managerial

Each lower level of the environment is encompassed in the larger above it. Thus marketing management within a firm takes place within the context of the organizational structure, goals and resources. Marketing functions occur within the broader institution of marketing, including both its economic and social processes. Marketing in this dimension is then a function of the character of the market, its scope, forces, and constraints. The economy in turn is but one of several major social institutions, the totality of which is superior to any one of them, including the economy, and constitutes the social environment of the economy. Finally, the particular configuration of the social structure is a function of the culture or the basic values and characteristics of a people. Environmentalism is the understanding of the relation of all of these environments to the practice of marketing. The environment is a complex of uncontrollable external factors.

This conceptual framework became the pattern for many subsequent analyses of marketing, both abroad and at home. It was essential that the next progressive development in marketing thought, namely, comparative analysis, be explained later.

CONCEPTUAL INTERPRETATION OF FOREIGN ENVIRONMENTS

Many writers were simultaneously developing concepts for interpreting the marketing environment, and once this stage of theorization was reached, a variety of better and fuller analyses of marketing in other countries were made, hopefully, as one writer put it, that we might better understand ourselves.

Unlike those who were compiling readings of marketing in different environments, Carson[23] published the first solo work interpreting in terms of socioeconomic variations the marketing practices of other countries. His thesis was that marketing practice is a function of environmental variables of a country. Because his format was not unlike traditional marketing texts, his insightful interpretations based upon concepts from the social and behavioral disciplines could be better appreciated.

Scott and Marks[24] interpreted *change* in the marketing system as response to environmental change. Taking a macro point of view, they undertook to show how the individual firm — one of many firms — functions and adapts to changing environmental forces: social, psychological, cultural, economic, political, ethical, and moral. Successful marketing resulted not only from knowledge of firm strategies, but from understanding of the variables influencing the firm. Thus emphasis was shifted somewhat from management of the controllable variables to understanding of the uncontrollable ones.

Three other books also illustrated the application of a conceptual view of environment to interpretation of marketing. Anderson[25] directly applied the Bartels conceptualization to marketing in Thailand. Glade[26] developed an explanation of marketing in Peru based upon seven hypotheses — generalizations deduced from more knowledgeable studies conducted elsewhere:

1. That marketing strategy is a function of environment
2. That foreign firms in an area employ more advanced technology than local firms
3. That non-owner firms employ more advanced technology
4. That firms with high sales volume employ more advanced technology
5. That producers of consumer goods employ more advanced technology
6. That firms with heavier competition employ more advanced technology
7. That firms with low value of typical product employ more advanced technology

These propositions provided interesting insight into selective aspects of the environment of a developing nation which affect marketing practice there.

A third and particularly conceptual illustration of environmentalism is Yoshino's[27] analysis of the Japanese marketing system. Unlike contemporaries who interpreted marketing in *static* environments and underdeveloped economies, he interpreted marketing in Japan as both a developed nation and a changing economy. Thus to environmentalism he added a time dimension, speculating whether as over a period of time societies become more similar, their marketing systems would converge. The following propositions were inherent in his concept of environmentalism:

1. That marketing is a socioeconomic process, not just a mechanical process
2. That the mission of marketing is to satisfy certain human needs (consumption needs)

3. That marketing is a basic component of the social structure. Exchange is a network holding society together
4. That marketing functions in the environment
5. That the marketing system is a function of environmental variables
6. That the marketing system is a function of change
7. That the marketing system generates change

CONCEPTUAL INTERPRETATION OF MARKETING WITHIN A FOREIGN ENVIRONMENT

As knowledge of United States marketing practice spread through the academic and business world, appreciation of environmentalism soon made it clear that practices appropriate in one environment were not necessarily acceptable in another. Consequently, as scholars were capable of doing so, they wrote specialized and general works on marketing in other countries, usually using an approach and format popular in the United States. Unlike some of the already described interpretations of marketing elsewhere in terms of an environmental concept, these were intended not for edification of Americans but for educational purposes in the countries described.

Several works concerning marketing in Canada illustrated this use of the environmental concept. Mallen and Litvak[28] wrote a general treatise on marketing in Canada to stimulate more research in Canadian marketing. As there was an increased availability of higher quality published material by 1968, they revised the book, and in 1973 Mallen published another on *Marketing in the Canadian Environment*.[29] All of the books and revisions followed an approach then widely used in the United States, including analysis of the Canadian consumer and industrial markets, products, pricing, institutions, promotion and international marketing. Mallen differentiated between the external Canadian environment and internal aspects of the distributive system.

FOREIGN ENVIRONMENT INTERPRETED FOR IMPORT MARKETING

Still another version of applying environmental concepts to marketing is found in books interpreting one environment to marketers in another. Four such books are those of Wilhelms, Boddewyn, Ballon, and Bickers.

Wilhelms and Boeck[30] wrote to inform export-conscious firms in developing countries of the characteristics of the German market environment. They discussed market conditions and consumer habits, how to sell in the West German market, legal regulations, and how to obtain market information. They also presented statistical data concerning the market.

Boddewyn and collaborators[31] wrote of the environmental factors and features of the business systems of five regions of major economic interest for businessmen: Asia, Latin America, Mid-East, Sub-Sahara Africa and Western Europe. Each area was minutely analyzed in terms of economic structure, business associations, finance, legal systems, marketing, industrial relations, and political patterns.

Ballon, in *Marketing in Japan*,[32] presented a collection of articles intended for the firm going into the Japanese market. Detailed guidelines concerning TV, advertising, promotion, consumer characteristics and sizes, kitchen facilities, and typical menus were presented.

Bickers[33] interpreted market differences in Europe for strategy adaptation by firms going into the European market. For each of the countries analyzed, he presented facts and figures concerning finding financing, rules of competition, establishment of a European headquarters, staffing and labor conditions, and general trading conditions.

CONTRIBUTIONS OF ENVIRONMENTALISM

Bringing to a focus the perception that marketing occurs within an environment has made several contributions to the development of marketing thought:

1. Conceptualization of "environment" has given structure, including range of variability, to emerging marketing theory.
2. It has furnished knowledge of marketing practices and systems elsewhere, facilitating extension of marketing practices into other areas.
3. It has increased understanding of the role which marketing plays in developing economies.
4. It has shown the variety of constraints — natural, economic, and social — imposed upon marketing in different environments.
5. It has prepared the way for comparative analysis of marketing, thus making a definite contribution to the development of marketing theory.

COMPARATIVE MARKETING

Environmentalism, whereby marketing systems are related to their environment, is a short step from comparative analysis of marketing systems. But it is a conceptual step and an important one, and some of the efforts made to conceptualize environment were actually intended to take marketing thought further in the direction of theory development.

The initial tendency when foreign environments were seen, in contrast to that of the United States was to emphasize their differences. Conceptualization of environment showed that the same elements of environment were to be found in all countries but that they differed to some degree. Comparative analysis observed the degree, or extent, to which environments differed in their common respects, and therefore interpreted marketing system differences as matters of *degree*, not of *kind*. These concepts introduced into marketing brought new opportunities for postulating relationships and generalizations which are the body of theory.

Although Bartels' *Comparative Marketing: Wholesaling in Fifteen Countries* was a study of wholesaling and of environmental influence upon marketing, it was intended primarily to illustrate and to develop the process of comparative analysis. However, because the separate writers did not think in comparative terms, the comparative aspect was largely confined to interpretation of the studies. It was found that as economies become industrialized, their wholesaling system for the distribution of manufactured goods underwent stages of circumvention and renaissance; that to the extent that as some middlemen possess financial strength they tend to become captains of the channel; and that the *economic* task of the distributive system is largely independent of the *political* ideology of the nation in which it resides. Such gleamings were hints of a universality implicit in marketing thought, although not yet fully verbalized.

Undifferentiated entitlement of books as dealing with environmental or national, comparative and international marketing indicated the newness of these concepts and terminology in the mid-1960s. Nevertheless, whatever the titles, the subject of comparativism was deemed important. Reavis Cox in 1965 was credited with the perception that comparative marketing systems analysis is one of the great frontiers of marketing thought. He saw in this study the derivation of "universals," "limited generalizations," and "specific differences" concerning marketing systems and practice. Boddewyn is quoted by Sommers and Kernan as follows: "The comparative approach must be carefully distinguished from environmental studies, where the accent is on the independent explanatory variables found in the environment, rather than on the dependent ones."

The principal contribution of comparative analysis to marketing thought is a second dimension of variables which it provides for understanding marketing. Systems and performance are interpreted primarily in terms of environmental factors, but, when differences between environments as well as between systems are reduced to common sets of relationships, similarity and universality appear where before there had been difference and uniqueness. By the prospect of such generalizations as may be deduced from comparative analysis, the progress of marketing thought is carried forward.

INTERNATIONAL MARKETING

Study of *international* marketing emerged from the same circumstances which evoked comparative studies, namely, increased familiarity with and involvement in marketing within different countries — and *between* them. The diversity of points of view from which the subject was approached was evident in imprecise definition and utilization of such terms as "world marketing," "international marketing," "international trade," "foreign marketing," "domestic marketing," "national marketing," and "comparative marketing."

Most commonly referred to as "international trade," this type of selling until into the 1950s was taught in technical courses of exporting and importing, with emphasis given to documentation and sales promotion. Such courses partook little of the developing marketing thought, for marketing strategies pertained almost exclusively to domestic trade. Consequently, the Gordon-Howell recommendations for business curriculum changes did not encourage international trade courses for fear of proliferation. The dearth of courses in this area was matched by the paucity of literature dealing with the subject.

Notwithstanding this, there appeared in 1935 a book bearing the title *World Marketing*.[34] Impelled by the impass reached in world trade because of tariff structures, Collins explained the prerequisites to successful business in the complex conditions which had arisen out of the depression. He maintained the importance of being informed of the world environment and of knowing the principles and methods of gaining "consumer accessibility and consumer consciousness" for one's products abroad. In addition to discussing selling, pricing, advertising, and adaptation of products, he also told of such things as preparing for the foreign sales trip — "to the far-distant lands of Romance, Adventures, and Profit"!

Thirty years elapsed until the marketing literature on international marketing came in a steady increase. Kramer[35] caught the trend of thought moving from "international trade" to "international marketing," but his work remained colored by the older approach, which included emphasis of promotion, financing, and supporting activities in international trade.

Fayerweather,[36] on the other hand, did introduce into the subject some marketing concepts generally used in domestic marketing. Like most writers, he briefly discussed the economics of international trade and the economic, cultural and political roots of marketing systems. Against these factors, he dealt with policies concerning products, distribution, promotion, and research, and he considered the applicability of the marketing mix in the total international marketing program. Fayerweather also showed appreciation of the relevance of environmentalism to the international marketer in developing four themes:

1. The similarity of marketing problems and tasks in all countries
2. Variations arising from differences in basic systems of society
3. Forces of international economics molding international trade patterns
4. Distortion of those patterns by nationalistic government policies

In these four propositions lie the essence of international marketing theory as developed in ensuing years. Although brief, his exposition included aspects of marketing both *within* other countries and *across borders* in reaching them.

The uniqueness of *international* marketing, in constrast to national marketing within foreign borders, was not easily perceived by many writers who dwelled on environmental markets alone. Although intending to depart from the outdated export trade mechanics, Hess and Cateora[37] nevertheless expounded more upon environmental characteristics of world markets than upon trade patterns and governmental policies, mentioned by Fayerweather. Differences in marketing from country to country to them were "less conceptual than environmental."

Another addition to the literature was a book of cases and texts dealing with global marketing problems, as reported in cases developed at IMEDE, a Swiss management development institute. Leighton[38] included in it international marketing, export marketing in different environments, and marketing management in international companies. Like many "international marketing" cases written at that time, they dealt primarily with marketing by firms in many parts of the world.

The combination in one textbook of "marketing in ..." and "marketing into ..." was popular during the 1960s, for it satisfied interest in both recognized aspects of the subject. Ryans and Baker offered such a combination in *World Marketing.*[39] They demonstrated, however, that the body of thought could be cut other than along lines of the 4 Ps, and they instead perceived the structure of international marketing to include market considerations in world markets; organization, policy making and decisions; finance, research, distribution channels, and commercial policy. They also included articles on marketing in Brazil, Czechoslovakia, Japan, Turkey, Europe, Africa, and the USSR.

Throughout the decade there was a persistent effort made to differentiate between international trade and international marketing. Miracle and Albaum[40] furthered this effort, reflecting trends in thought at the time, by emphasizing management processes. They believed "international trade" to be essentially "domestic trade projected across national political boundaries," and that little has been done to treat international trade as marketing processes and activities. They intended to deal with the marketing problem in a variety of environments, emphasizing formulation of policy and making of decisions. In a word, they attempted to apply scientific American marketing principles to foreign situations.

Of environmental, comparative, and international aspects of marketing, the last has been the least contributory to the development of marketing thought. Whereas the first two were conceptual developments, international marketing was dealt with as the extension of a preconceived technical and managerial processes. If a substantial difference between domestic and international marketing is to be made, it would seem nearest to fall, as indicated by Fayerweather, along lines of economic forces shaping international trade patterns, and nationalistic government policies distorting those patterns.

LOGISTICS

The refraction of marketing which occurred during the 1960s did not necessarily magnify some aspects while minimizing others. Amplification of the human elements — consumer behavior, social systems, management decision-making, and social responsibility — was not entirely at the expense of nonhuman or economic elements. The compensatory development was a resurgent interest in the physical movement of goods from producers to consumers, which was perhaps the essence of marketing in its elemental state. This renewed areas of study became known as "logistics" or "physical distribution."[41]

Definition of marketing as the activities involved in movement of goods and transfer of their title provided a natural dichotomy of the subject and invited the development of two distinct lines of thought: the physical and the social. Separation of the two began early, as the physical process was identified with creation of time and place utilities, and immaterial processes with possession utility. Moreover, institutional specialists performing only physical functions, such as carriers and warehouses, were not regarded as *marketing* institutions, whereas those which played some part in title transfer were. The differentiation seems also implicit in the cleavage between the structure of traditional marketing thought, which emphasized title channels and promotional policies, and the less orthodox, which emphasized total systems and environmental context.

Emergence of physical distribution as a special field of study, however, occurred around 1960 in response to both environmental and conceptual developments. New marketing problems had arisen out of both the absolute and relative rise of distribution costs, the increase of inter-city freight rates, and legal rulings casting doubt on uniform delivered pricing systems, and emphasizing the importance of transfer costs. Concurrently, appreciation of the interdependence of transportation and storage and perception of the merits of an integrated approach offered hope of effecting economies in "the gray area between manufacturing and marketing." This hope was abetted by the promise held forth in application to distribution problems of Operations Research techniques, automation, and electronic data processing. Out of these circumstances germinated the new area of study, which was concerned with neither marketing research, marketing principles, nor marketing management — popular subjects of the day — but with the activities of physical supply and distribution.

In its newness, this area of interest lacked an acceptable name. Its substance was generally identifiable as including transportation and storage — place and time elements — but from any point of view these functions had both a backward and forward orientation in the channel sequence. Moreover, reservoirs of goods (inventories), rates of flow, communication lags, price variations, location of facilities, and market behavior all affected achievement of the optimal combination of factors conducive to customers' services and distributors' profits.

The diversity of terms designating this field of study resulted in part from different concepts of it, yet they were sometimes used interchangeably. A survey of representative bibliography reveals the following titles:

Physical Distribution
Physical Distribution Systems
Physical Distribution Management
Business Logistics
Business Logistics Management
Marketing Logistics
Marketing Logistics and Distribution Planning
Principles of Logistics Management
Logistical Management

Although the terms were sometimes imprecisely differentiated at first, clarity increased, and because half a dozen writers dominated the literature, frequently updating their works, consistency in usage was achieved. In general, "logistics" has been the more inclusive term. Yet even that has been used in both a macro and micro sense, referring to the logistics of the economy and the logistics of the firm. Borrowed from military usage, it meant a total flow of materials from origin to destination, the systems carrying it, and considerations given to achieving the purpose for which it was organized.[42] Such a total flow was divided into an incoming part termed Physical Supply and an outgoing termed Physical Distribution.

In earliest writings, this field of physical distribution, however termed, was linked closely with a portion of economic theory related to marketing concerning creation of utility. Heskett in 1964[43] said that logistics in the economy "concerns the translation of consumers' demand for time and place utilties into a supply of these same types of utility." Logistics in the firm facilitated the movement and coordination of demand and supply in the creation of time and place utilities. In this sense, physical distribution or logistics is directly linked to marketing thought as it had been developed up to the 1950s. Smykay,[44] however, pointed out that while earlier marketing literature had emphasized transportation and storage, the newer managerial approach included location decisions as a major part of marketing strategy. Physical distribution was regarded as inclusive of traditional marketing channels but independent of them. Further contrast with marketing was made by distinguishing between "promotion" and "physical distribution," the latter alone being the subject of the new theorizing.

The fabric of logistics thought was a mesh of distribution activities interwoven with interdisciplinary perspectives. The activities were the objective of coordination, that in the total distributive process the right goods would be at the right place at the right time. In the earlier writings, the activities or elements were few in number, identified by Smykay in 1961 as inventory control, plant location, transfer costs and distribution warehousing. As thought evolved, however, the list of manageable activities grew to include the following:

Order processing	Supply scheduling
Transportation	Packaging
Containerization	Transit insurance
Manufacturing and	Communication control
converting capacity	Customer service
Information flows	Materials handling
Storage	Movement services
Freight transportation	Order processing
Market forecasting	

Collectively, these constituted the variables which were interrelated in the physical distribution flow. The scheduling of their costs, and their influences upon costs, as a continuous, scaled function provided a quantitative basis for determining the optimal combination of controllable factors. This determination was known as the "total cost approach."

Against the warp of these activities were woven inter-disciplinary perspectives drawn from economics, marketing, mathematics, statistics, transportation economics, production management, industrial engineering, systems analysis, operations research, and electronic data processing. Thus whether the logistical problem were of commercial, industrial, agricultural, or extractive enterprises, or the public sector, the relevant variables could be fitted to appropriate model building concepts, logistical systems designed, probabilities determined and much useful information furnished upon which managerial decisions might be based.

Spawned in an era imbued with management thought and decision-making, logistics reflected this trend. Its beginning might be characterized as technical — its management strategies particularly useful to purchasing agents and shippers on an operational level. By the early 1970s, however, logistical theory was directed to executives in top levels of management. The reason given for this by Symkay in 1973[45] was the increasing recognition that physical distribution is a key element in the progress of the total corporate effort. Another apparent trend in the literature was closer integration with, rather than total segregation from, aspects of marketing from which, by definition, physical distribution had been separared, namely, the promotional aspects of marketing. Marks and Taylor[46] maintained that promotion and logistics defy separation and are interactive. They thought functions of packaging, inventory maintenance, and order processing, for example, pertained to both, and an interfunctional approach, by coordinated emphasis of functions, might result in lowest total cost. Constantin[47] also verged on the nonphysical aspects of physical distribution in emphasizing the importance of understanding the elasticity and changes in demand as a basis of management of inventory, location, and warehousing.

CONTRIBUTIONS OF LOGISTICS TO MARKETING THOUGHT

This branch of marketing thought developed under circumstances which also brought forth literature on marketing management, the systems concept, quantitative analysis and decision theory. Its beginning was regarded as pioneering, as the projection of marketing thought into new territory. After a decade, it had achieved an established state not only with relevance to marketing in the United States, but also international marketing, and marketing in other countries. In this maturing process, the following contributions were made to the development of marketing thought:

1. Recognition was given to a substantive area of marketing which had been relatively neglected, namely physical distribution, including the general functions of transportation and storage.
2. Identification of the numerous activities comprised in physical distribution, scalable and measurable variables were made available for theoretical analysis.
3. Concepts and methods from disciplines other than the social and behavioral were employed in determining such relationships as are essential to the development of theory.
4. Understanding of physical or economic systems of marketing, in contrast to its social systems, was increased. Attention was focused upon activities peculiar to the marketing of economic good and the development of strategies not readily transferable to promotion of the programs of nonprofit insitutions.
6. The concept of "customer service" in terms of measurable physical performance was added as a key element of the marketing concept. That is, the marketing concept was broadened to include physical support performance of the product or service.

MARKETING AND SOCIETY

During the 1960s a development destined to effect a major change in marketing thought began, namely, the inclusion of society in marketing theory and practice. Since 1950, several indications had been pointing in this direction. The consumer came to be regarded as a social entity, not merely an economic man. Market behavior was viewed as social interaction. Individual enterprises were associated with others in systems. The socioeconomic environment was a major independent variable to which management must adjust. "Responsibility" became the shibboleth of forward-thinking marketers. Yet none or all of these comprised the whole of the development as it moved into the 1970s.

The new element was a point of view which added substance to and required redefinition of marketing. Theretofore, the economist's or manager's point of view prevailed, holding the "business" of marketing as primary and the consequences to the market and society as secondary, although appreciable. In new perspective, marketing is viewed not merely in the context of the total market system, or even the socio-market system, but the *total social system.* As expressed by Lazer and Kelley,[48] "The result is a movement from the consideration of profits or sales only, to a consideration of the societal implications and dimensions of marketing decisions and action . . . In managerial marketing the independent variables may be such factors as the firm, profits, sales, costs, personal selling, advertising effectiveness, and related factors. In social marketing the independent variables may be society, social costs, social values, social products, and social benefits."

Although the social viewpoint gained prominence rapidly in the late 1960s, its antecedents had historic roots. Apart from administrative and judicial representation of society in conflicting private-public interests, seeds of social concern were sewn late in the 19th century.[49] Reemergence of social dominance over the economy bespoke interests of both consumers and competitors. The Consumer Movement of the 1930s, further consumer-oriented legislation and implementation of the marketing concept in the 1950s, were a prelude to expression of and acquiescence to the social demands which followed. These demands were expressed in riots, boycotting, proxy battles, consumer activism, and legislation.

There were also conceptual as well as substantive antecedents of social concern. Much of the earliest marketing literature was inspired by social criticism of marketing practices. Moreover, neither functional nor institutional literature lacked consideration of the "economic and social aspects" of its area of marketing. And behavioral concepts for marketing managers dealt further with market conflict and suggested improvements in the seller-buyer relationship.

However, when faced with the full blow of social demands in the 1960s, marketing practitioners and scholars were no better prepared to cope with this extension of marketing thought than they had previously been with others. The onrush of change constituted a challenge to marketing practice, which first had to be recorded, then analyzed, and ultimately conceptualized. Most writers recorded the attribution to marketing of defects in product quality, promotional integrity, pricing, competition, and general efficiency. Yet beyond these technical faults, other shortcomings were widely voiced:

- lack of concern for quality of life, in preference for sales volume and profits
- imbalance between producers and consumers in the marketplace
- exploitation of the poor and disadvantaged
- failure to provide opportunities for minority group members
- waste of resources
- pollution of the environment
- invasion of privacy of citizens
- deceptive advertising and promotion
- default in warranties and guarantees
- imbalance between marketing power and larger social objectives
- promotion of the dogma of materialism
- bureaucratic neglect and corporate disregard of the public.

Such circumstances abrading traditional marketing concepts might well have worn inroads sufficient to change thought and practice. In addition, such management practices coincided with new consumer and citizen expectations of the marketplace. Former President John F. Kennedy spelled out four basic "consumer rights": to have safe products, to be informed, to have a choice, and to be heard. Minority groups demanded not only opportunity but redress for their deprivations. Ecologists pointed out the social cost of private negligence. Consumer activists, more organized than ever before, wrought defiance in courts and legislatures.

Amid the smoke of battle, it became recognized that a new era had begun which demanded a metamorphosis of marketing philosophy, in theory and in practice. Such a philosophy would give higher priorities, within our capitalistic free enterprise system, to the following:

- quality of life
- community affairs
- social problems

- reduction of poverty
- opportunity for development of human capital
- provision for good health care, education, and training
- reduction of pollution
- greater consideration of one's fellow man.

Because of the urgency of the call for solution to the social problems associated directly or indirectly with marketing, scores of articles appeared in such periodicals as the *Harvard Business Review, Journal of Marketing, Quarterly Journal of Economics, Journal of Political Economy,* and the like. As in the case of other literatures relating to a new area of marketing thought, many of these articles were collected and published in books of readings. Many were reportorial; some were philosophic; others were analytical. They lacked at first, however, empirical research and a conceptual framework for what was evolving.

Writers approached the subject from a variety of viewpoints, as indicated by some twenty titles published between 1966 and 1974. Some grouped marketing problem areas functionally, as they were discussed in management-oriented texts. Others dealt with consumerism, with social issues, with marketing and society, and finally with social marketing. More familiarity with marketing history and with historical writings was shown in connection with consumerism than was evident in some other marketing literatures. Even a comparative study of the worldwide consumer movement and of government-sponsored consumer activities in nine European countries and Canada was included in one book. Originally the topics of social issues and management problems were grouped topically. As thought developed, more insight was shown in the selection and presentation of included articles, suggesting social determinism in marketing change, interface between the public sectors and marketing, business response and adaptivity, and consequent conceptualization and theorization concerning the changes taking place.[50] Virtually all books compiled were intended as supplementary reading for marketing courses with other texts.

From the outset, it was quickly apparent that marketing practice was challenged and likely to change; it was not so soon apparent, however, that marketing as a discipline was in transition toward a broader framework. This realization came gradually, and by the mid 1970s the form of the new thought had not definitively shaped up. What did seem apparent was that at this juncture, a line of thought paralleling managerial marketing would increase in importance. Advent of the social perspective introduced a new concept and definition of marketing, new variables and relationships, and consequently new theory. A subtle and unresolved issue, however, involved the question of whether marketing related the social viewpoint to the marketing of economic goods and services, or to the "marketing" of programs of all nonprofit institutions as well. The concept of marketing's relationship to society may be further refined to make this distinction.

Thus, in a short span of years, literature on marketing and society has introduced into marketing thought an unprecedented point of view and a wider sphere of thought yet to be encompassed in a general theory of marketing.

ENDNOTES

[1] Robert D. Buzzell (ed.), *Mathematical Models and Marketing Management* (Boston: Harvard University, 1964).

[2] R. L. Day (ed.), *Marketing Models – Quantitative and Behavioral* (Scranton, Pa.: International Textbooks, 1964).

[3] F. M. Bass, C. W. King, and E. A. Pessemier, *Application of the Sciences in Marketing Management* (New York: John Wiley & Sons, Inc,. 1968).

[3a] J. D. Casher, *Marketing and the Computer* (Braintree, Mass.: D. H. Mark, 1969).

[4] R. L. Day and J. Parsons (eds.), *Marketing Models: Quantitative Applications* (Scranton: Intext Educational Publishers, 1971).

[5] R. F. Breyer, *The Marketing Institution* (New York: McGraw-Hill Book Co., Inc., 1934).

[6] Ralph F. Breyer, *Quantitative Systemic Analysis and Control: Study No. 1 – Channel and Channel Group Costing* (Philadelphia: College Offset Press, 1949).

[7] E. A. Duddy and D. A. Revzan, *Marketing: An Institutional Approach* (New York: McGraw-Hill Book Co., 1947).

[8] L. P. Bucklin, *A Theory of Distribution Channel Structure* (University of California Institute of Business and Economic Research, 1966).

[9] R. E. Mallen (ed.), *The Marketing Channel* (New York: John Wiley & Sons, Inc., 1967).

[10] George Fisk (ed.), *Theories for Marketing Systems Analysis* (New York: Harper and Row, 1967).

[11] L. W. Stern (ed.), *Distribution Channels: Behavioral Dimensions* (Boston: Houghton Mifflin Company, 1969).

[12] E. H. Lewis, *Marketing Channels: Structure and Strategy* (New York: McGraw-Hill Book Company, Inc., 1968).

[13] J. C. Palamountain, *The Politics of Distribution* (Cambridge: Harvard University Press, 1955; New York: Greenwood Press, 1968).

[14] L. P. Bucklin, *Competition and Evolution in the Distributive Trades* (Englewood Cliffs, N.J.: Prentice-Hall, Inc., 1972).

[15] M. S. Sommers and J. B. Kernan (eds.), *Comparative Marketing Systems, a Cultural Approach* (New York: Appleton-Century-Crofts, 1968).

[16] J. K. Ryans and J. C. Baker (eds.), *World Marketing* (New York: John Wiley & Sons, Inc., 1967).

[17] Marshall I. Goldman, *Soviet Marketing* (New York: Macmillan Co., 1963).

[18] T. V. Greer, *Marketing in the Soviet Union* (New York: Prager, 1973).

[19] Reed Moyer, *Marketing and Economic Development* (East Lansing: Michigan State University, 1965).

[20] Clarence Miller (ed.), *Marketing and Economic Development* (University of Nebraska Press, 1967).

[21] H. W. Boyd (ed.), *Marketing Management: Cases from the Emerging Countries* (Reading, Mass.: Addison-Wesley Publishing Co., 1966).

[22] Robert Bartels (ed.), *Comparative Marketing: Wholesaling in Fifteen Countries* (Homewood, Ill.: Richard D. Irwin, Inc., 1963).

[23] David Carson, *International Marketing: A Comparative Systems Approach* (New York: John Wiley & Sons, Inc., 1967).

[24] Richard A. Scott and N. E. Marks (eds.), *Marketing and its Environment* (Belmont, Cal.: Wadsworth Publishing Co., 1968).

[25] Dole A. Anderson, *Marketing and Development, the Thailand Experience* (East Lansing: Michigan State University, 1970).

[26] William P. Glade, et al., *Marketing in a Developing Nation* (Lexington, Mass.: Heath Lexington Books, 1970).

[27] M. Y. Yoshino, *The Japanese Marketing System* (Cambridge, Mass.: The MIT Press 1971).

[28] Isaiah A. Litvak and B. E. Mallen (eds.), *Marketing: Canada* (New York: McGraw-Hill Book Co., Inc., 1964).

[29] B. E. Mallen, *Marketing in the Canadian Environment* (Scarborough, Ontario: Prentice-Hall of Canada, 1973).

[30] Christian Wilhelms and K. Boeck, *Market and Marketing in the Federal Republic of Germany* (Hamburg: Verlag Weltarchiv GMBH, 1971).

[31] Jean J. Boddewyn (ed.), *World Business Systems and Environments* (Scranton, Pa.: Intext Educational Publishers, 1972).

[32] R. J. Ballon (ed.), *Maketing in Japan* (Tokyo: Sophia University, 1973).

[33] R. L. T. Bickers, *Marketing in Europe* (London: Gower Press, 1971).

[34] V. D. Collins, *World Marketing* (Philadelphia: J. B. Lippincott, Co., 1935).

[35] Roland L. Kramer, *International Marketing* (Burlingame, California: South-Western Publishing Company, 1964).

[36] John Fayerweather, *International Marketing* (Englewood Cliffs, N.J.: Prentice-Hall, Inc., 1965).

[37] J. M. Hess and P. R. Cateora, *International Marketing* (Homewood, Ill.: Richard D. Irwin, Inc., 1966).

[38] D. S. R. Leighton, *International Marketing: Text and Cases* (New York: McGraw-Hill Book Company, Inc., 1966).

[39] J. K. Ryans and J. C. Baker (eds.), *World Marketing* (New York: John Wiley & Sons, Inc., 1967).

[40] Gordon E. Miracle and G. S. Albaum, *International Marketing Management* (Homewood, Ill.: Richard D. Irwin, Inc., 1970).

[41] Perhaps the earliest use of the term "physical distribution" in the marketing literature is in Fred E. Clark, *Readings in Marketing* (New York: The MacMillan Co., 1924, p. 464).

[42] See Graham W. Rider, *An Exploration of the Concept of Logistics: a Constitutive Approach* (Ann Arbor, Michigan; University Microfilms, 1970).

[43] J. L. Heskett, R. M. Ivie, and N. A. Glaskowsky, Jr., *Business Logistics* (New York: The Ronald Press Co., 1964).

[44] E. W. Smykay, D. J. Bowersox, and F. H. Mossman, *Physical Distribution Management* (New York: Macmillian Publishing Co., 1961, 2d ed., by Smykay, Bowersox, and Bernard J. LaLonde, 1968).

[45] E. W. Smykay, *Physical Distribution Management,* (New York: Macmillan Publishing Co., 1973).

[46] N. E. Marks and R. M. Taylor, *Marketing Logistics,* (New York: John Wiley & Sons, Inc., 1967).

[47] J. A. Constantin, *Principles of Logistics Management,* (New York: Appleton-Century-Crofts, 1966).

[48] William Lazer and Eugene J. Kelley, *Social Marketing: Perspectives and Viewpoints* (Homewood, Ill.: Richard D. Irwin, Inc., 1973, pp. 3-5).

[49] See Karl Polanyi, *The Great Transformation – Rise and Fall of Market Economy* (Chicago: The Free Press, 1960).

[50] Leonard L. Berry and James S. Hensel (eds.), *Marketing and the Social Environment* (New York: Petroceli Press, 1973).

THE MATURING OF MARKETING THOUGHT

14

As a conclusion, this chapter originally summarized the development of marketing thought from 1900 to 1960 and projected some lines for its presumed development. In its revision, it serves a double purpose. Not only does it summarize up to and since 1960, but it stands as historical evidence itself of the different perspective in which the development of thought was viewed before and after that date. The first summation, therefore, should be read with awareness of when it was written; the final summation represents a later standard of evaluation.

THE DEVELOPMENT OF THOUGHT — 1900 TO 1960

Given time and favorable circumstances, a growing body of knowledge attains successive stages of maturity. Measures of it have been taken from different standpoints: its scientific character, its usefulness, its consistency, its integration with general knowledge. Some scholars regard marketing thought as a mature body of scientific concepts and principles. Few claim that it could not be improved. Others believe that it has attained only a plateau of maturity and that further progress lies ahead.

The maturity of marketing thought is proportionate to its adequacy. If it serves the purposes for which it has been developed, it is both adequate and mature. On that basis, the traditional body of marketing thought had long been regarded as mature, for it had served well the purpose of developing marketing specialists, for which purpose it was primarily designed. In recent years, however, marketing thought has been regarded as less than mature, needing to grow along new lines as it is expected to serve new purposes: the development of marketing managers, of market-oriented general businessmen, and of competent, critical consumer citizens. Mounting recognition of this has impelled some reconception of marketing in writings, and reorganization of academic offerings. This tendency has been accelerated by claims of the inadequacy of marketing thought made by critics of the business-school curriculum. Thus, marketing thought is challenged to attain new levels of maturity and usefulness. At the moment, while new demands upon it are being interpreted and forward steps are being taken, the future shape of marketing thought is not yet clearly apparent.

In the following pages, facts presented in some detail in preceding chapters are interpreted in light of new demands being made upon marketing, and the implications of recent developments in marketing thought are appraised.

THE CHARACTER OF MARKETING THOUGHT

The adequacy or inadequacy of prevailing marketing thought is related to several characteristics of that thought as it has been developed:

1. *It is a Purposeful, Practical Body of Thought.* It was developed to solve problems of business activity—problems of functional and institutional nature. Therefore, thought has developed along lines of advertising, selling, sales management, credit, research, retailing, wholesaling, general marketing, and a miscellany of minor subjects. Thought in each area is both specialized and integrated. It has been used by businessmen and by academicians. It has served to instruct in technique and in the broader principles of marketing.

2. *It Is Based upon Definite Concepts of Marketing.* Every body of thought has its premises, and the basic assumption of marketing thought has been that marketing is a business function, a specialized, technical activity. Implicit also have been concepts of marketing as an economic process, namely, the creation of utilities, but the logic of marketing has rested upon variations of a simple mechanistic concept of marketing.

3. *It Is Scientifically Developed.* Marketing thought has been primarily a product of inductive research and analysis. Much attention has been given to describing prevailing practices and to the classification of activities and institutions. Principles, or basic generalizations, have been developed within the framework of thought based upon the accepted concept of marketing. Relatively little use has been made of theoretical analysis, of concepts from related social sciences, or of experimental hypotheses in the construction of systems of marketing thought.

4. *A Well-Integrated, Established Body of Thought Has Been Produced.* Consistency and uniformity have been more typical of it than have basically different or conflicting interpretations of marketing. In specialized areas, as in the body of general marketing thought, an almost customary analysis and interpretation have been presented. The exposition of marketing was conformed to marketing practice, and vice versa. Scholars devoting themselves to the development of marketing thought were more intent upon accuracy of reporting marketing experience than in questioning the concept of marketing that they were expounding. Consequently, development of thought consisted mainly of amplification and verification of basic ideas. Within the frame of analysis employed, a body of thought evolved that was orthodox or traditional, in that it was the standard, the accepted exposition of marketing, from which there were but few and minor deviations.

CONTRIBUTIONS OF MARKETING THOUGHT

Marketing thought has contributed measurably to business and society. Several evidences indicate that a number of wholesome circumstances have resulted from the development of that thought:

1. *It Has Furnished a Basis for Improvement of Marketing Practice.* It has resulted in better storekeepers, in more effective promotional work, in economies of operation. It has led to the development of new methods, institutions, and policies. Prediction, forecasting, and planning have been improved through the application of marketing knowledge. The marketing viewpoint has been extended to every level of management and administration. It has created in this country a distributive philosophy and system superior to any in the world for accomplishing the ends which our society has set for itself.

2. *Through the Evolution of Marketing Thought, Scientific Methodology Has Been Introduced into Distribution and Research.* Had scientific management

been confined to production, where it was employed before it was introduced into marketing, our economic progress would not have been as great as it has been. It has come into distribution through "the new retailing," based upon research, as well as through scientific salesmanship, market research, advertising, etc. The professionalization of distribution has been predicted upon scientific management methods.

3. *Marketing Thought Has Represented a New Interpretation of the Primary Service Objective in Business.* It is the means by which society is fulfilling one of its responsibilities to society—to society in the role of customers. Being an institution created by society, business has a responsibility to act so as to benefit all whom its operations touch. This attitude, new to business since the beginning of the twentieth century, has taken form in marketing, partly through laws, such as the Pure Food and Drug Act, requiring consideration of consumers; partly through the Consumer Movement, clarifying demands of the market for consumer satisfaction; and partly through application of "the marketing concept," orienting not only the marketing activity but all the functions of business to marketing considerations. The responsibility of business to customers has been epitomized by such sayings as "Consumption is the end of production and distribution," "The customer is always right," and "The consumer is King." Marketing has represented a viewpoint introduced into business that has made these concepts practical.

4. *Marketing Thought Has Contributed Concepts and Terminology to the Body of Common Thought.* Scarcely a person has not had his thinking enriched by ideas from the body of marketing thought. In this age one could not be well informed, or perform his domestic operations efficiently, without at least a rudimentary knowledge of such things as the distinction between wholesale and retail prices, the circumvention of middlemen, quantity discounts, price maintenance, discount houses, instalment credit, product differentiation, and the like. Marketing thought has contributed these concepts to the thinking of this period.

5. *Thought in Other Sciences Has Been Enriched by Ideas from Marketing Thought.* The principle of economic specialization has been illustrated by marketing itself, as well as by the variety of marketing institutions and functions. The adaptivity of marketing institutions to economic and cultural change validates the principle that functions give rise to functionaries and that institutions change or disappear when the need for them changes. Marketing studies have also amplified the concept that the functions implicit in a market situation cannot be eliminated but may be shifted to a variety of specialists in marketing.

6. *Marketing Thought Has Furnished Principles that Are Applicable beyond the Borders of Our Own Social and Political Environment for the Benefit of Mankind in General.* Marketing has been a means for advancing the economic and material welfare of our people, and it is applicable, with modifications, to the enrichment of other people as well.

UNORTHODOXY IN MARKETING THOUGHT

Notwithstanding the solidarity and uniformity of the body of marketing thought, there has not been unanimous agreement as to what the form or content of it should be. Even during the 1920s, when thought in all areas of marketing was being integrated and the pattern of its widely accepted form of statement was being set, Moriarity was giving an economic interpretation to marketing, and Vaughan was appraising marketing practices from a social rather than a managerial point of view. Throughout the succeeding decades, other men, including Breyer, Killough, Alexander, Vaile, Cox, Grether, and Alderson, also presented analyses of marketing that differed conceptually from the popular explanation of it.

The innovations introduced by those writers represented different concepts of marketing, not merely differences of terminology. They challenged the objectives for which marketing thought had been designed. They considered new problems that it might be expected to solve. They implied that the concept of marketing as "activities" was not the only important concept of the subject. Neither was the "consumer viewpoint," the only one that might be taken. They also presented marketing as a complex, interrelated system, which must be understood *as a whole*. They depicted it as an economic institution, an area of management, a social process.

CRITICISM OF MARKETING THOUGHT

Late in the 1940s, more explicit criticism of traditional marketing thought began to be expressed. That was when increasing selfconsciousness was felt concerning the stage of maturity of marketing thought, when attempts were being made to state the "principles" of marketing, and when questions were being raised whether marketing was really "a science." Optimism was expressed by adherents to the traditional exposition of marketing, who saw the lines of thought well established over a number of years, fully illustrated by experiences, and nicely interrelated through several possible "approaches" to the subject. Skepticism was expressed by others, some of whose criticisms were as follows:

> . . . We are surfeited with knowledge in the sense of isolated facts and narrow bands of factual interpretation . . . . In marketing, at present, there is no need for "pure" theory—that is, theory ranging so widely as to take the form of a logical framework with little or no relevance to reality. In marketing, rather we need various types of "applied theory," developed out of varied interests . . . .[1]

> In marketing, the devotion to the facts has been carried almost to the point of the exclusion of general theoretical interests. Marketing science must have both theory and fact-finding . . . . The development of a pure science of marketing is urgent . . . . One direction in which the science of marketing may be expected to advance . . . is by evolving a general theory which can serve as the source of hypotheses to be tested by factual investigation.[2]

> Marketing thus far has developed a plethora of individual facts and a dearth of conceptual schemes which would relate these facts in meaningful generalizations.[3]

> Students of marketing thus far have reaped from their efforts remarkably small harvests of accurate, comprehensive and significant generalizations. Marketing literature offers its readers very few true and important "principles" or "theories" . . . . Existing theories fail to satisfy students because they do not account for or take into consideration all of the relevant observed facts. In essence, this is today's situation in the study of marketing.[4]

Additional criticisms of marketing have been made. One is that marketing thought has been largely vocational. This is said particularly of the specialized literatures, but even the general literature has been designed to prepare the outlook of students for occupational careers. There is nothing wrong with vocational education, but the criticism has been made that the vocational level of marketing thought was low where techniques, operating rules, formualted thinking, and simple policy determination were involved. If that is true, it is because a narrow concept of marketing has prevailed. Marketing has long been regarded as a mechanistic performance, as a type of business function. Vocational guidance for participation in marketing, so conceived, would naturally be aimed at levels of technical performance: salesmanship, record keeping and analysis, credit decision, store layout, and the like. As the concept of marketing has expanded, thought implicit in, and stemming from, narrower concepts of marketing would be held to have shortcomings. Thus it is not necessarily the vocational character of marketing thought that is criticized but the inadequacy of much prevailing thought to meet arising needs.

Another criticism is that the concept of marketing, upon which the superstructure of thought has been built, has not kept pace with social change. Traditional marketing thought has been designed mainly for understanding and solving the distributive problems of business. It presumes marketing management to be a straight-line function, and the responsibilities of management to lie mainly within the area there defined. The social implications of marketing are increasingly coming to the fore, imposing upon management new responsibilities. Many of the demands being made cannot easily be satisfied by the structure of thought heretofore developed, for new concepts and new principles are required. Those deficiencies have exposed marketing thought to growing criticism as a vehicle for accomplishing social objectives today.

Still another criticism is that students of marketing have made insufficient use of related social sciences for concepts that would be useful in explaining marketing phenomena. Many concepts from economic theories have been incorporated into marketing thought, for marketing has been viewed primarily as a field of "applied economics." Recourse to other disciplines in the past has been for borrowing methodology for increasing the effectiveness of marketing activity. Little use has been made of such concepts as would explain marketing as a social institution rather than simply as a business system.

Finally, it has been objected that marketing thought has been based too much upon inductive research and reasoning and too little upon deductive logic and analysis. The tendency to observe, report, and describe has characterized the work of maketing students, while at the same time they were little concerned with hypotheses or assumptions implicit in their thought structures. For this reason, many writings have warranted the criticism of being descriptive rather than analytical and of falling short of the type of thought needed to solve today's marketing problems.

NEWER CONCEPTS IN MARKETING THOUGHT

Since 1950 a number of lines of thought concerning marketing, which before had appeared sporadically as unorthodox approaches and as constructive criticism, have been given fuller expression. In contrast to those writings of earlier years, these later ones have gained wide attention and in many centers have supplanted traditional expositions of marketing. The trend in the direction of dealing with marketing on a higher level of management, and from a conceptual rather than a descriptive standpoint, has been accelerated by the elevation in business of marketing to higher managerial positions and by influences brought to bear upon educators to rethink their business curricula and teaching methods. Thus into the marketing literature have come a number of new writings corresponding approximately to the "general" writings, intended to provide an introduction to the subject or to present a managerial viewpoint.

Because of the deep-rooted dedication to traditional concepts and explanations of marketing, these newer forms have been accompanied by some confusion and debate as to the nature and significance of their differences. Are they saying old ideas in new phraseology? Is anything better accomplished by their innovations? These are questions that will be answered by clearer definition of the new concepts, by recognition of the assumptions implicit in the new thought structures, and by appreciation of the many roles rather than any single conceptual role that marketing plays in our entire society.

Following are some of the concepts that have been prominent in the newer expositions of marketing:

THE MARKETING MIX

The marketing "mix" is the combination of means for achieving the marketing objective of a business firm, which are blended in varying proportions by management in consideration of prevailing circumstances. The "elements" of the mix include all promotional means under the authority of the manager of marketing activities: personal selling, advertising, credit service, product development, packaging, dealer relations, etc.

In a sense, the marketing mix is a modern version of the factors implied in the original conception of marketing by Butler, when he defined "marketing" as "everything that the promoter of a product has to do prior to his actual use of salesmen and of advertising." It is that *combination* of factors which is the promotional undertaking that has always characterized marketing that has differentiated it from trade or distribution. Whereas, formerly, marketing was a type of straight-line function, the mix management is a co-ordinative, integrated function in policy formation.

THE MARKETING CONCEPT

This term designates that viewpoint taken in business management which causes all management decisions to be oriented to market considerations. The consumer, or the customer, is assumed to be the end and object of all business effort. Sales promotion policies are not the only ones chosen to coincide with market tastes and behavior; product design, production schedules, financial budgets, personnel plans, and capital investment are also determined on the basis of the character and conditions of the market.

An earlier counterpart of this concept was that "the consumer is King." The effect of the Consumer Movement was to arouse businessmen's consciousness of their obligations to customers, but such arousing occurred mainly in selling and on the retail level. The newer application of "the marketing concept" has been adopted by producers as well.

CONCEPT OF MARKETING

Marketing is increasingly conceived not merely as a group of internal activities or functions but as ways to express other insights into the marketing task and performance. For example, marketing has been conceived as the process of sorting out, accumulating, allocating, and assorting. It has been conceived also as flows of equity, processes of negotiation, and the like.

Newer concepts tend to introduce into marketing analysis the concepts and terminology of other social sciences. They reflect new insights into the social and managerial problems involving marketing.

HOLISTIC APPROACH

Emphasis has been placed by some scholars upon viewing marketing *as a whole,* emphasizing its interrelations. Thus marketing has been explained as the complex interrelationships of products, place, promotion and price. It has also been explained as the interaction of agencies, area, and price organizations under the influence of price, management and government control. Such approaches are in contrast to earlier ones, which were concerned mainly with the separate functions, institutions, and products.

MANAGERIAL MARKETING

Marketing thought has always been developed for the purpose of guiding the formation of business policy, but in recent years emphasis has been placed upon marketing management as a decision-making process. In some recent treatises thought has been structured so as to highlight sets of variables upon which marketing policy decisions are said to be based. Consideration has also been given to the establishment of a position of "marketing manager" as a top-level position in organization structure, where, in accord with the "marketing concept," he co-operates directly in formulation of top-level policies in the integration of marketing with all other functional activities of the business.

CONSUMER PROBLEM SOLVING

Consumption has long been regarded as a passive process, with business taking the initiative in the distribution of goods and with business decisions being inherently different from consumer decisions. Consumers have more recently been regarded as engaged in problem solving, however, even as businessmen are – in evaluating multiple means for satisfying desires, in assembling assortments of goods that provide maximum realization of satisfaction in living patterns, in maintaining an inventory of products, in maintaining financial budgets, etc. Such a concept of consumer behavior has provided new insights into the task of marketing management.

PROJECTED DEVELOPMENT OF MARKETING THOUGHT

Marketing thought has unquestionably entered a new era of development. That which had evolved before 1950 was, by many evidences, mature, but changes that have occurred since then have substantially broadened the base on which an even more encompassing structure of thought will arise.

When significant alterations occur in any body of thought, three reactions may be experienced. First, ideas at variance with general beliefs are ridiculed, ignored, and rejected. That was the treatment given for many years to ideas, viewpoints, and concepts at variance with the generally accepted "theory" of marketing. Second, new ideas are embraced, and the traditional is disparaged. That reaction has been expressed in the tendency to reconstruct general marketing thought, to revise marketing curricula, and to eliminate more "technical" marketing courses. Third, innovations are assimilated and combined in proper perspective with established thought. As the meaning of new concepts in marketing, and their relevance to circumstances that impel them, are better understood, the prevailing body of marketing thought will be seen to be supplemented rather than supplanted by these new ideas. The pattern it may take is not yet clear, but it is likely that it will develop along the following lines:

Increasing Conceptualization of Marketing. Progress in the development of marketing thought will depend upon conscious dealing with the *ideas* of marketing rather than merely the *activities* of marketing. The growing concern that has been shown for theoretical considerations in recent years portends further emphasis upon ideas and respect for conceptualization as a means of advancing the understanding of marketing.

There are two ways in which this can occur. First, it will become known that the *concept* of marketing is more important than the mere *definition* of marketing. While the definition of marketing has been reduced to an already oversimplified statement, the concepts of marketing have been multiplied. Different concepts of marketing will continue to be reflected in different interpretations, and those differences will be encouraged and respected. Recognition of the conceptual rather than the definitive nature of marketing may even be shown in defining the subject so as to bring out the various *ideas* for which "marketing" stands.

Second, additional concepts within the body of marketing thought will be created, some by original and innovative marketing scholars and others by creative thinkers in related fields. Concepts comprising the body of thought are tools aiding analysis and logic and facilitating communication of ideas. The development of new concepts, whether of consumer, products, institutions, processes, or results, signifies that new insights have been achieved. They are indispensable, for new insights reveal new problems and provide the means of solving them.

Marketing as a Social Institution. One concept of marketing that may be of special significance depicts it as a social institution rather than merely as a business activity or economic process. The latter two concepts have been extensively explored throughout the marketing literature. The social character of marketing is increasingly becoming apparent. One interpretation made from that standpoint is that a marketing organization is a social group and operates by the principles of group behavior. The more important social interpretation is that the entire marketing process is a society-oriented phenomenon.

Society spawns and supports many institutions, of which the market economy is one, and marketing is a highly specialized phase of that type of economy. It is increasingly recognized that the entire business institution is a creation of society in this era and that it is molded by the values, customs, and structure of our society. The same can be said of marketing. Appreciation of this concept will lead to interpretation of marketing in terms of its environment—not only of the market but of the marketing process itself. It will be seen that marketing is society's means of providing for its material needs. Elaboration of this concept will provide new insights into the role that marketing must play and the responsibilities it must bear in our society.

Comparative Marketing Systems. A corollary of the social concept of marketing is that which recognizes existing differences among societies as social causes of different systems by which they provide for their needs—market systems and others. No consideration has been given this in marketing thought in the past, for the development of understanding of what marketing represents solely in our own society was a sufficient preoccupation. The relativity of supposedly universal principles of marketing was not seen until, with continued reduction of world space, the indigenousness of distribution systems to social structure had been perceived. The comparative aspects of markets and of marketing around the world is a subject to be developed in marketing thought in years to come.

New Economic Insights. As in the past, so in the future there will be a close relationship between economic theory and marketing thought. Not as in the past, however, is it likely that marketing thought will depend so heavily upon classical economic theory. Departures from concepts of pure competition—homogeneity of products, automaticity of market adjustments, flexibility of prices, rationality of buyers—have been introduced slowly into the body of marketing thought. The addition of concepts of product differentiation, monopolistic competition, administered pricing, and the gross national product analysis have been incorporated in marketing thought, improving the explanation of marketing. Continued close contact must be maintained with evolving economic concepts if the explanation of marketing as an economic function in the social processes is to be kept realistic.

Interdisciplination of Marketing Thought. Not only economic theory but other social disciplines will provide substance for the growing body of marketing thought. Recourse has long been had to psychology for interpretations of consumer behavior and, more recently, to sociology and statistics for analytical tools. Methodologies will continue to be borrowed from other disciplines, but it is possible that good use will be made also of substantive concepts from other fields. Historians, sociologists, anthropologists, demographers, accountants, political scientists, philosophers, and others are all producing concepts and understandings of our society that could be useful in interpreting marketing. Insights of those with other than a technical marketing viewpoint will be increasingly important as marketing is conceived of as other than merely a technical process.

Marketing Thought for Management Levels. With better balance between earlier and later types of marketing thought, a more embracing sense of the potential uses of marketing thought is becoming apparent. Whereas, previously, thought was designed for the development of functional and institutional specialists—salesmen, sales managers, credit managers, advertisers, market researchers, buyers, and retail and wholesale establishment operators—more recently it has been intended for the development of marketing managers. In this recent trend, vocational guidance in marketing on lower and intermediate levels has been overshadowed by "managerial" emphasis. Because the vast majority of the careers in marketing are to be found in "operations" rather than in "management," future development of thought must provide for all. It is a good thing that some leading educational institutions have turned to the development of marketing managers, for this meets a contemporary need that must be supplied, but it cannot be thought that that is the only purpose to which the broad array of marketing thought is to be put. Thought must be provided for various management levels, incorporating such concepts and principles as are needed on each.

New Concept of "Macro-Marketing." Distinction is made between two aspects of marketing thought which might be called "micro-marketing" and "macro-marketing." The former represents that portion of marketing thought which deals with operations of individual firms, with their objectives, processes, and problems. It represents concern for specific institutions and practices. "Macro-marketing," by contrast, relates to the over-all function of marketing, the operation of the system in the prevailing market, and the generalities of volume of goods marketed, number of persons employed, average size of institutions, and the like.

The body of marketing thought has included both, with the broad or economic aspects of the subject frequently used as introduction or background for considerations applicable to the operations of the firm. In recent years, however, with growing emphasis on management, expositions of marketing "in general" have been regarded as "descriptive" and not contributing to the immediate objectives of marketing thought. Such a view may prove to be unfortunate, both for the development of marketing thought and for the development of management talent, for management is increasingly dependent upon a workable knowledge of the marketing economy as a whole. Writers have attempted in different ways to provide this macroscopic view, as in a holistic interpretation of marketing. More conceptual and analytical explanations of marketing will provide better macro views, which will be useful to economists and businessmen alike.

Marketing and Fulfillment of Social Responsibility. It is widely recognized today that business, being a social institution, has social responsibilities—responsibilities to every category of society it touches: employees, competitors, suppliers, the trade, the community, the nation, and, last but not least, consumers. Its obligation to consumers is to conceive and supply the products and services that the market wants, or that social trends indicate that in a reasonable time they might want. Marketing is the conduct of that phase of business which is concerned with this determination and supplying of consumers' needs, and therefore it is that management operation through which business fulfills its obligations to society in the role of consumers. Where this obligation is not recognized or where the responsibility to consumers is not fulfilled, marketing, in the fullest sense, does not exist. Where it is seen, on the other hand, and fulfilled, a significant development of business in our society is taking place—in the name of marketing.

THE DEVELOPMENT OF THOUGHT SINCE 1960

When the foregoing summary and projections were written, reflecting thought in the 1950s, it was not difficult to think of marketing thought as "maturing," as attaining a fullness of development that approached completeness. Its structure had been well established for several decades. There was general acceptance of what marketing was and how one should learn and apply it. Knowledge had been reduced to its principles, although they were more implicit than explicit. And growing attention was being given to methodological and structural aspects of thought. All of these evidences were interpreted as indications of maturation, even of the probability that marketing thought had the potential of being a science.

The finality of this belief was already in jeopardy in the 1950s, however, as the concept of marketing was being split, its components differentiated, and its cohesiveness dissolved. New approaches produced new interpretations of marketing which complemented rather than supplemented the existing body of knowledge: managerialism, holism, systems analysis, and the like. Attention turned from contemplating the possiblity of a deduced *science* to validating inductively derived *theories*. Marketing was no longer monolithic; it was many things to many people. While this fragmentation was deemed progress, it lacked the essential cohesiveness and unity earlier attributed to thought. The presumed maturity then seemed to have been a plateau instead of the zenith in the development of marketing thought.

In addition to changing perceptions of marketing as a subject for theorization, marketing theorists in the 1950s became increasingly critical of the standards by which thought development should be judged. Improved evidence of both observable and unobservable phenomena was sought. Empirical research and quantitative analysis were emphasized for keeping mental constructs realistic and measurable. But it was to the logic of science and the processes of thought information that attention increasingly turned, ultimating in the appraisal of marketing in terms of metatheory. Thus while during the 1960s and 1970s, substantive knowledge of marketing increased, progress in thought development during that period was perhaps best shown in writings about the *form,* rather than the *content,* of marketing thought. The substance of those writings pertained to issues of science, of theory, and of definition.

THE ISSUE OF SCIENCE

Although earliest writers and teachers of marketing probably had no consciousness of founding a new discipline—the study at the outset even had no name—the quest for knowledge, and objective regard for the process of this quest, soon aroused interest in the scientific quality and orientation of the study.

In retrospect it is apparent that natural processes of thought development were occurring, converging on delineation of the field, particularly whether it was or could be a science. Although "science" and "theory" are often used interchangeably in the literature, neither of them appeared with any significance until after the exploration of more elemental forms of thought: concepts, definitions, categories, principles and laws.

As marketing is a process, its component elements, called functions or activities, were among the first to be identified. Shaw, Westerfield, and Weld were among the earliest writers to list marketing functions, ranging from five to eight in number. Clark, Converse, Huegy, Maynard, Weidler, Beckman, Cherington, and Breyer also attached importance to precise identification of functions and to the functional approach to understanding marketing. By 1935, Ryan[5], regarding earlier listings as "Orthodox," listed 120 functions which he perceived performed in the marketing process. Most of these listings were inductively determined, but Jones[6] in 1943 regarded any determination of functions to be dependent upon one's definition of marketing. In addition to identifying functions, writers also generally classified them. Other basic concepts, including institutions and commodities, were also identified, defined, and classified, providing a base for a higher structure of thought.

Preliminary also to any consideration of marketing as a formal body of thought was the identification of its generalizations or laws, or, as they came to be called, "principles." The existence of principles was presumed but not verified, for through the 1930s few were explicitly expressed. Bartels[7] explored the literature and found a number of implicit principles and some set forth specifically as logical generalizations. They were classified as relating to marketing operations, institutional relations, and the marketing task.

The pervasiveness of "science" in the thought of marketing scholars is further indicated by the title of an article by Converse published in 1945: "The Development of the Science of Marketing: An Exploratory Survey."[8] He perceived marketing as an area of study in its own right but having been dependent for many of its concepts upon economics, psychology, management, economic history, and accounting. He described the body of marketing thought as consisting of concepts, techniques, and groups of data, listing twenty-one, including "functions," "research," "problem method of teaching," "classification of goods," "business mortality," and "principles of marketing."

During the 1940s, the breadth and organization of marketing thought was also measured by the character and extent of its theories. The fact was that few theories could be identified, notwithstanding the fact that, as Alderson and Cox[9] observed, there was lively interest in marketing theory, enthusiastic response by members of the American Marketing Association to attend meetings on theory, and courses in marketing theory were offered in several universities. Elements of rudimentary theories of marketing were, they believed, to be found not only in the marketing literature but throughout the social sciences. To the extent that marketing study became *scientific,* it might also become a *science.*

One, and perhaps the first, of the AMA meetings devoted to discussion of the state of marketing thought was held in 1946.[10] Although addressed particularly to consideration of theory in marketing, the topics were elementary, concerned with defining the purpose of theory in marketing, the significance of different listings of functions, and the role of principles in theory formulation. Nevertheless, some areas of theory formation were tentatively identified, and confidence was expressed in the forward movement of marketing thought to higher levels of integration and statement. Association of marketing with "science" may be noted in excerpts from two talks:

> "Whether the science is eventually called economics, marketing, or market-economics; and whether we are called economists or marketeers *(sic.)* is not important. What is important is that we should welcome the opportunity to become scientists and to develop the science of market behavior rather than to remain content to describe the art of marketing, that we think in terms of basic principles, that we become scientists objectively seeking truth." (H. W. Huegy).
> "So long as the basic tasks are recognized and constant study and research are directed at devising more efficient means of performing them, the science of marketing will continue to advance." (E. S. Fullbrook).

Because claims for the scientific nature of marketing had been made mainly in the context of other discussions, none evoked the controversy which followed publication of "Can Marketing Be a Science?" in 1951.[11] Recognition was given to the impediments to recognition of "science" in social fields, but, all considered, it was felt that as marketing thought grew to embrace a number of coherent and related theories, it would warrant, on the basis of both methodology and content, being called a "science," even as economics, psychology, and sociology were social sciences. Agreement with this point of view is evident in references already quoted, in establishment of the Paul D. Converse National Award for those who have contributed significantly "to theory of marketing and toward advancement of science in marketing,"[12] and in expression of a feeling that "it would be nice to have marketing classified as a science."[13]

Strong exception was taken to this view by writers who saw marketing as an art, and not as a science. Hutchinson,[14] attributed the slow development of theory to the fact that marketing is *not* a science. He held that only teachers and marketing researchers believe that marketing is a science, because they work with the scientific method; those engaged in day-to-day distribution don't regard it as such. The rationale inherent in identification of marketing as a science, Hutchinson maintained, was based upon interpretation of dictionary definitions and upon marketing's alliance to economic theory and science. Stainton likewise argued that marketing is an art,[15] claiming that there are too many unknowns and imponderables for it to be otherwise.

For the span of almost a decade, throughout the 1950s, little more was said about marketing being a science, and attention was turned to clarification of its theoretical aspects. In 1963, Buzzell[16] summarized the contributions made to the question of science from the standpoint of the interest of management. He differentiated science and art on the basis that the *use* of *science* is an *art*. He also set for, as he saw it, the standards of a science:

- classified, systematized body of knowledge
- organized around central theories and a number of principles
- usually expressed in quantitative terms
- knowledge permitting prediction and sometimes control of future events.

Taylor,[17] in 1963, similarly contrasted science and art, associating with science the effort to know. A review of the development of marketing thought led him to believe that marketing had the potential of being a science.

By 1970, the controversy had quieted and more constructive and analytical thought was expressed concerning science and marketing. Robin[18] differentiated positive science (what is) and normative science (what ought to be), and pointed out that the efficiency standards of the positive are not always congruent with the ethical standards of the normative. The goal of marketing, he believed, should be analyzed for its "ethical desirability," and should be the goal of a normative science: to maximize total satisfaction for consumers as a group.

Dawson[19] differentiated a "normal" science from a "crisis" science, as applied to marketing, and he raised the question of whether, by concentrating on issues and knowledge within a traditional conceptual framework, marketing had missed the vital issues of society, and thereby had become an irrelevant science—a pseudo-science. He raised the question of whether relevance in marketing theory had been lost in the dedication of marketers to advance the discipline to the status of a science. He saw lack of relevance as a result of "addiction to paradigms"–generally accepted beliefs. A science structured on this basis defines its problems within its self-determined bounds and assumes solvability of problems in terms of known variables. Exceptions spur research within the framework. Such a science he termed a "normal" science. Contrariwise, a "crisis" science seeks resolution to anamoly from new approaches, wholly new insights, and new meaning. As he saw it, the marketing discipline is subjected to pressures which make for a "normal" science, namely, emulation of the physical science, emphasis on practicability, and obsession with quantifying variables. Instead, marketing should "capture the essential relationship of marketing activities to the unfolding of history and the advancement of society."[20] Notwithstanding progress in marketing, Dawson saw anamolies in marketing science (1) inability to define the field and its boundaries, (2) neglect of significant issues related to marketing, and (3) questioning of concepts long regarded basic: the marketing concept, consumer-orientation, and the marketing functions.

THE ISSUE OF THEORY

The issue of theory is the concern for the development of that form in marketing thought, beginning with wonderment whether there were marketing theories, through the proposal of identified theories, to consideration of a general theory and the metatheory by which it would be structured.

Remarks of McGarry at the 1946 AMA conference on marketing theory indicate something of the state of thought at that time:

"Any discussion of Marketing Theory must necessarily begin with the question, "What do we mean by Marketing Theory?" Some will claim that Marketing Theory and Economic Theory are one and the same thing, and that we should consider *only* the problem of Economic Theory as it applies to marketing. Others will contend, with considerable evidence to support their claim, that Economic Theory as presently constituted offers but little aid in the explanation of marketing processes, and perhaps even less aid in the solution of practical marketing problems. That there is much to be gained by the use of Economic Theory as a frame of reference for the study of marketing, no one will seriously deny. However, marketing teachers are primarily concerned with a segment of economics–albeit an important segment–to which the application of Economic Theory is often both inadequate and unrealistic."[21]

Concurrently with that conference laments were being expressed that notwithstanding almost fifty years of marketing facts accumulation, there were few identifiable marketing theories. Whatever existed were paraphrases of economic thought or disconnected generalizations about operational aspects of marketing. Alderson and Cox designated, as likely areas of theory consideration, the spatial and temporal aspects of marketing; cooperation and competition among economic entities, limitations on opportunity in economic activity, attitudes and motivations of buyers and sellers, and the development of marketing organization. Their emphasis was upon economic behavior, whereas at the same time Vaile[22] recommended use of all pertinent generalizations from any discipline in development of marketing theory, which contended should be descriptive rather than normative theory. He doubted the possibility of writing *a* theory of marketing, and he doubted that marketing had the earmarks of science.

In 1950, Cox and Alderson, leading proponents of marketing theory, from the standpoint of the increasingly visible unorthodox approach to the study of marketing, opened the dimensions of theory beyond economics to the inclusion of marketing concepts developed in other disciplines. Expanding their thoughts from the article published two years earlier to a book of papers contributed by individuals known to be active in some area of theory relative to marketing, they enlarged the perception of marketing theory to include elements of demographics, psychology, and organizational behavior, as well as economic theories relating to interregional trade, consumer actions, vertical price relations, and management of the firm.[23] They regarded marketing theory to be in its infancy, and this fact was partially evident in the miscellany of topics brought together under the title *Theory in Marketing*.

A better effort to structure theory was made by Revzan in his review of the Cox and Alderson book, which he saw as an imprecise format for expositing theory, lacking as it did a conceptual framework. His own framework of a theory of marketing included the following elements or concepts:

- An institutional approach, wherein marketing is viewed in its overall structure
- the marketing process, defined as the functioning of a system of interrelated structural units
- the organic structure of marketing related to the economy as a whole
- each unit of the marketing structure existing in its own evolutionary cycle
- group interaction
- collective action controlling individual action
- cooperation and security requiring some self-sacrifice
- institutional controls
- resolution of conflicts
- ethics in coercion and control

While thus presenting one of the earliest conceptual structures for a *theory of marketing*—not merely a marketing theory—Revzan nevertheless questioned whether marketing theory existed. He recommended that the AMA appoint a committee of interested persons, hold further conferences, and sponsor research and publication to further consider this question.

Whereas Cox and Alderson had presented incipient theories of people mainly outside the marketing group, and Revzan had proposed a framework for a rather general theory of marketing, McGarry in 1953, believing that university professors should lead in development of marketing theory, discussed theories with which four such professors became indentified.[24]

E. W. Grether — a theory of interregional trade, a wholly economic interpretation and statistical analysis of the flow of trade between regions of differential advantage.

Wroe Alderson — a theory of "searching and sorting," whereby place and time utilities are created; a sociological and psychological framework.

Reavis Cox — a theory of distribution channels, wherein the channel is conceived as an economic unit, evidencing agency cooperation in performance of the several flows inherent in the process of distribution; institutional economics.

238

E. D. McGarry — a theory of adjustments in marketing, wherein marketing
is deemed a great intermediary force in adjusting, through search and
selection, the market conditions; emphasis placed on changes in
products and psychological satisfaction, contactual relationships, and
attitudes.

McGarry believed that theory should be refined, tested, and proven. His tests of
theory were (1) logic, (2) pragmatics, and (3) expansibility.

Amidst the growing confidence concerning theory, Alderson published his
Marketing Behavior and Executive Action in 1957, unquestionably the most
fully developed theoretical exposition of marketing up to that time. Its principal
characteristics, viewed in the context of the issue of theory, were that, upon
central core concepts of "searching and sorting" and "differential advantage for
survival," it presented an integrated interpretation of marketing process and
behavior; that it embraced the marketing process in its entirety; and that it
perceived it through concepts of a number of disciplines. While Alderson's work
did not set a standard for quality in theory, it demonstrated the possibility of a
general theory of marketing embracing a number of subtheories.

Several aspects of theory were further clarified by Baumol,[25] who saw the
need for theory in that facts do not speak for themselves. He differentiated,
however, between *empirical* generalizations, which tell how things stand, and
theoretical generalizations, which tell what will happen under given conditions.
His test of theory was not whether it mirrored reality, but whether it gave
direction to decision-making and further research. He also thought that theories
of economics and sociology are not *marketing* theories, but rather elements
upon which marketing theory is built. He cited Alderson's "Functionalist
Approach to Marketing Theory" as an example of this.

Aspinwall, another marketing theorist, proposed several original theories
which not only expounded a topic but gave some indication of the *concept of
theory* which underlay them.[26] Whereas previous theorists classified goods as
convenience, shopping, and specialty goods and loosely identified distribution
of them through different channels and outlets, Aspinwall emphasized the
continuous scale of product qualities, rather than the discrete segregation of
them in distinct classes. Other variables being likewise scaled, he, perhaps
unconsciously, glimpsed a characteristic of variability later deemed essential in
marketing metatheory. His parallel systems theory explained the dependence of
channels upon the marketing characteristics of goods, giving a more conceptual
and analytical treatment of channel choice than was common. And his depot
theory of distribution, relating the movement of goods through distribution
channels to rates of flow established by ultimate consumers, was a forerunner of
theory later developed in logistics.

While some theorists, like Alderson, Cox, McGarry, and Aspinwall, advanced
marketing theory by making substantive contributions, others undertook to
clarify the form in which theory is expressed. That such parallel effort was
needed was perhaps indicated by an assessment of where theory stood in 1964[27]
and a conclusion that the field was still far from formulating such a body of
theory as existed in economics. It was held that marketing still had no central
theoretical basis, that it lacked a conceptual foundation, that it had been
considered an art in our culture, and that the major contribution of marketing as
a discipline had been to content and not to method or concept.

Implicit in most of the writings on marketing theory was the idea that the identification of variables and establishment of their relationships was the essence of theory construction, for within such relationships lay the key to explanation, prediction, and control, which are generally conceded to be the objectives of theorizing. Relatable elements vary, however, depending upon the concept and definition of marketing, for the lesser concepts are inherent in the greater. Consequently, as new views of marketing opened, new relationships were studied and new areas of theory explored. Developments occurred so extensively during the 1960s that a pattern of relationships gradually became apparent, permitting some classification of them as part of the structure of theory.

Bartels was particularly concerned with theory structure and attempted in a series of publications,[28] during the 1960s, to relate concepts of marketing to their implicit marketing concepts, variable to each other in generalized relationships, and theories to a more encompassing theory of marketing. With increasing clarity, distinction was made between economic and social aspects of marketing, between micro organizations and their macro environments, and between domestic and international marketing. Each of these areas of thought constituted a subject for a number of marketing theories, and collectively they covered the field of marketing in such a way as to suggest the possibility of a general theory of marketing.

After exploring the particular areas, Bartels attempted to integrate the structural elements in a general theory,[29] illustrating primarily the form of theory structure, and secondarily the substance of one person's theory of marketing. A more elaborate and analytical illustration of this theory interpreting a metatheory approach to theory formation was also undertaken.[30]

Considering the contrasting views held about marketing itself, not to speak of the relation of marketing to theory and science, it would be no surprise that there would be disagreement on efforts to formulate theory, particularly a general theory. On one side would be such as Alderson, who integrated a significant general theory; many theorists who have presented particular and lesser theories; and Bartels, who proposed merely the structure of an integrative theory. On the other side are those who discredit *any* theory on the grounds of inexactitude; those who deny the possiblity of *a* general theory, if by that we mean one and only one general theory appropriate for all purposes and all people; and those who disagree with the logic of particular theories presented. Of the latter group, Hunt[31] took exception to the Bartels theory, claiming that its component theories were *not* theories because they failed the test of his criteria that theories consist of (1) systematically related sets of statements, (2) lawlike generalizations, and (3) empirically testable propositions. Refutation of Hunt's contentions, on the other hand, was made by Pinson, Angelmar, and Roberto,[32] who believed that his conclusions were contradictory to his own criteria. So goes the surfaced evidence of a much deeper issue!

As theorization progressed, it was soon apparent that those who theorized were not always objectively cognizant of the requirements of good theories and that unawareness of this could retard theory development. The next step was an effort to verbalize a metatheory for marketing, or the criteria for scientific and systematic theory formation. Disparate judgments had been expressed sporadically from time to time, but in 1965 Halbert wrote at length on the subject.[33] He recognized a need to know not only about marketing phenomena but also about the methods of science. The state of marketing theory at that time he described as follows:

— preoccupation with concepts, classification of language, consolidation, systhesis
— no major theorists
— lacking major theoretical framework
— nonexistence of definite schools of thought, with the closest approximation being:
  Functionalism — Alderson
  Economic approach — Moriarity, Vaile, Grether, and Cox
  Managerialism
  Three traditional approaches: functional, institutional, commodity.

His recommendation for best developing a science of marketing included: (1) better understanding of substantive elements, especially unobservable elements; (2) imaginative methodology; and (3) interactive communication between marketing and other disciplines of research.

Halbert proposed the following criteria for theory:
1. that it consist of essential elements and their relationships
2. that it consist of both implicit and explicit theories, telling not only what things are, but also why they are and why they are important
3. that it include a statement of the operationality of the concepts in the real world
4. that it distinguish between "theories" and "theory," and that all theories be consistent with each other
5. that it reflect characteristics of the theorist as well as of the subject of his study
6. that it conform to three criteria of adequacy:
   — syntax, or the legitimacy of the logic of theory
   — semantics, or the correspondence of theoretical manipulation to manipulations possible in real phenomena
   — pragmatics, or relevance and usefulness to the solution of important problems.

Bartels also in 1970 undertook to set forth criteria for theory building in the form of seven axioms:[34]

1. Theory proceeds from a concept of its subject and should be consistent with it.
2. Theory is built upon basic concepts derived from the concept of the subject and from related scientific disciplines.
3. Basic concepts contain a range of qualities expressing their variability.
4. Variables having a range of qualities when cast in a dependent-independent relationship provide a basis for explanation or prediction.
5. Valid relationships having generality constitute a theory.
6. Diversity in theories resulting from individual and subjective aspects of theorists is normal.
7. All theories of a discipline, however diverse, should be embraceable, implicitly or explicitly in a general theory, either by grouping or by synthesis.

The continuing issue of theory is the need for more imaginative conceptualization of marketing phenomena, validation of hypothetical theories and models, and integration of subtheories into the general theory which their separate substance implies.[35]

THE ISSUE OF DEFINITION

Whether marketing is a science, and what kinds of theories comprise it, depends upon how marketing is defined. Defined that is, not simply literally as in textbooks, but actually in the minds of marketing theorists. The confusion and controversy which have made issues of the status of marketing thought have originated largely in the undelineated diversity of concepts of marketing which have been prevalent in the literature. Without clear and explicit definition of the subject, differing thought structures and controversial appraisals thereof have resulted.

Imprecision of definition has resulted to some extent from the continual broadening of the concept of marketing. So long as marketing was narrowly conceived and defined, a limited structure of thought satisfied the aspirations for completeness; when conceived multidimensionally, however, the body of thought became made up of many theories and a more complex structure. If "science" connotes the wholeness or completeness of a discipline, it is understandable how the term might have been used to characterize marketing in its early stage, *as it was then perceived.* But as enlargement occurred, the term would be appropriate only for the latter stage and no longer for the former. The terminology of marketing thought must be interpreted historically, even as the development of thought itself.

Among many definitions of marketing, two major concepts are outstanding: that marketing is an economic process, and that marketing is a social process. As a *phase of economics,* marketing has been further described as micro and macro processes, as independent and as environmentally constrained, as local and as global in its domain. In its micro, independent and local dimensions, marketing has sometimes been characterized as an art rather than as a science; its theories, if knowledge was at all so regarded, consisted of operational principles and precepts. In its larger dimensions, economic-based marketing thought was regarded as having characteristics of the economic science. Conceived as a *social process,* on the other hand, personal rather than economic elements are predominant and theories relate to such matters as role identification and interaction; groups and social environment; culture, expectations, and responsibility.

When marketing thought is so outlined, it is apparent that progress in its development has consisted of enlargement of the concept of marketing as a whole, and of differentiation and magnification of its component elements. Contemplation of whether its future development will continue along these lines provides opportunity for interesting specualtion. It will surely be affected by the prevailing concept of marketing, of which two alternatives are critical: (1) that marketing consists of explicated processes, which from time to time may be supplemented by conceptual additions, or (2) that marketing is a pervasive but yet unfully conceived process, which is proximated by our progressive enlargement of marketing thought. The former implies that marketing is relative, a function of descriptions made of it; the latter, that marketing is an absolute concept and that definitions and theories are a relative approximation of the

242

absolute. The former implies a progression of knowledge from percepts to concepts to body of thought; the latter, progression from concepts to body of thought to application and perception of evidence. The former holds theory to be nonexistent until explicitly set forth. The latter regards theory as implicit in a concept of marketing, to be discovered, not invented, by marketing theorists.

However marketing is conceived in the future, the relation of definition to theory will be the same. Historically, the evolution of marketing thought has progressed from the narrower concept to the broader, from the predative action to the serviceful, from self-interest to social consideration, from economic to social determinism, from action to interaction, from the provincial to the global. Is there some orderly progression implicit in these contrasts in what marketing should be understood to be? Has the fullest interpretation of the role of marketing in human affairs yet been stated? Will progress ultimate the maturation? How these questions are answered will much affect the nature of marketing theory and whatever larger proportions marketing thought assumes.

ENDNOTES

[1] E. T. Grether, "A Theoretical Approach to the Analysis of Marketing," in *Theory in Marketing* Reavis Cox and Wroe Alderson, eds. (Chicago: Richard D. Irwin, Inc., 1949), pp. 113, 114.

[2] Wroe Alderson, "Progress in the Theory of Marketing" in *Changing Perspectives in Marketing* Hugh G. Wales, ed. (Urbana: University of Illinois Press, 1951), pp. 79-83.

[3] E. D. McGarry, "Some New Viewpoints in Marketing," *Journal of Marketing* (July, 1953), p. 33.

[4] Wroe Alderson and Reavis Cox, "Towards a Theory of Marketing" *Journal of Marketing, XIII* (October, 1948). p. 139.

[5] F. W. Ryan, "Functional Elements of Market Distribution," *Harvard Business Review* XIII (January, 1935), p. 205.

[6] F. M. Jones, "A New Interpretation of Marketing Functions," *Journal of Marketing* VII (January, 1943), p. 256.

[7] Robert Bartels, "Marketing Principles," *Journal of Marketing* IX (October, 1944), p. 151.

[8] P. D. Converse, "The Development of the Science of Marketing: An Exploratory Survey," *Journal of Marketing* X (July, 1945), p. 14.

[9] Wrote Alderson and Reavis Cox, "Towards a Theory of Marketing," *Journal of Marketing* XIII (October, 1948), p. 137.

[10] See *Proceedings of the Christmas Meeting of the Academic Division of the American Marketing Association* (Pittsburgh: University of Pittsburg, 1946).

[11] Robert Bartels, "Can Marketing be a Science?", *Journal of Marketing* XV (January, 1951), p. 319.

[12] For papers presented at the first Awards conference, 1949, see Hugh G. Wales, ed., *"Changing Perspectives in Marketing* (Urbana: University of Illinois Press, 1951). Initial recipiants of the awards were R. S. Butler, M. T. Copeland, C. S. Duncan, Herbert Hoover, P. H. Nystrom, W. D. Scott, A. W. Shaw, W. H. S. Stevenson, P. T. Cherington, F. E. Clark, L. D. H. Weld.

[13] S. F. Otteson, ed., *Marketing: Current Problems and Theories* (Indiana Business Report No. 16, Bloomington: Indiana University, 1952).

[14] H. D. Hutchinson, "Marketing as a Science: An Appraisal," *Journal of Marketing* XVI (January, 1952), p. 119.

[15] R.S. Stainton, "Science in Marketing," *Journal of Marketing* VII (July, 1952), p. 64.

[16] Robert Buzzell, "Is Marketing a Science?" *Harvard Business Review* (January-February, 1963), p. 32.

[17] W.J. Taylor, "Is Marketing a Science? Revisited" *Journal of Marketing* XXIX (July, 1965), p. 49.

[18] Donald P. Robin, "Toward a Normative Science in Marketing" *Journal of Marketing* XXXIV (October, 1970), p. 73.

[19] Leslie M. Dawson, "Marketing Science in the Age of Aquarius," *Journal of Marketing* XXXV (July, 1971), p. 66.

[20] *Ibid.,* p. 71.

[21] *Proceedings of AMA Conference, op. cit.,* p. 1.

[22] R. S. Vaile, "Towards a Theory of Marketing: A Comment," *Journal of Marketing* XIII (April, 1949), p. 520.

[23] Reavis Cox and Wroe Alderson, eds., *Theory in Marketing* (Chicago: Richard D. Irwin, Inc., 1950).

[24] E. D. McGarry, "Some New Viewpoints in Marketing," *Journal of Marketing* VIII (July, 1953), p. 33.

[25] William J. Baumol, "On the Role of Marketing Theory," *Journal of Marketing* XXI (April, 1957), p. 413.

[26] William Lazer and E. J. Kelley, (eds.), *Managerial Marketing: Perspectives and Viewpoints,* Revised ed., 1962 (Homewood, Illinois: Richard D. Irwin, Inc.; Leo V. Aspinwall, "The Characteristics of Goods Theory," p. 633; "The Depot Theory of Distribution," p. 652; "The Parallel Systems Theory," p. 644.

[27] Reavis Cox, Wroe Alderson, and Stanley J. Shapiro, eds., *Theory in Marketing* (Homewood, Ill.: Richard D. Irwin Inc., 1964).

[28] Robert Bartels, "Sociologists and Marketologists," *Journal of Marketing* XXIV (October, 1959), p. 37; "Marketing as a Social and Political Tool," *Marketing: A Maturing Discipline* (Chicago: American Marketing Association, 1961), p. 210; "The Dimensions of Marketing Thought," in *Managerial Marketing: Perspectives and Viewpoints* by William Lazer and E. J. Kelley, eds., rev. ed. (Homewood, Ill.: Richard D. Irwin, Inc., 1962), p. 578; "A Methodological Framework for Comparative Marketing Study," *Toward Scientific Marketing, Proceedings of the Winter Conference of the American Marketing Association* Stephen A. Greyer, ed., (Chicago: American Marketing Association, 1964), p. 383; "Marketing Technology, Tasks, and Relationships," *Journal of Marketing* XXIX (January, 1965), p. 45; "A Model for Ethics in Marketing," *Journal of Marketing* XXXI (January, 1967), p. 20; "Are Domestic and International Marketing Dissimilar?" *Journal of Marketing* XXXII (July, 1968), p. 56. These articles are reprinted in Robert Bartels, *Marketing Theory and Metatheory* (Homewood, Ill.: Richard D. Irwin, Inc., 1970), pages 138, 146, 195, 205, 213, and 231, respectively.

[29] Robert Bartels, "Marketing," *Lincoln Library* 25th ed., (Columbus, Ohio: The Frontier Press Company, 1961), p. 1235; "The General Theory of Marketing," *Journal of Marketing* XXXII (January, 1968), p. 29. These articles are reprinted in *Marketing Theory and Metatheory* pages 155 and 243, respectively.

[30] Robert Bartels, "A Metatheory for World Marketing," *Marketing Theory and Metatheory* (Homewood, Ill.: Richard D. Irwin, Inc., 1970), p. 254.

[31] Shelby D. Hunt, "The Morphology of Theory and the General Theory of Marketing," *Journal of Marketing* XXXV (July, 1971), p. 65.

[32] Christian R. A. Pinson, Reinhard Angelmar, and Eduardo L. Roberto, "An Evaluation of the General Theory of Marketing," *Journal of Marketing* XXXVI (July, 1972), p. 66.

[33] Michael H. Halbert, *The Meaning and Sources of Marketing Theory* (McGraw-Hill Book Co., Inc., 1965); also "The Requirements for Theory in Marketing," in *Theory in Marketing,* Reavis Cox, Wroe Alderson, and Stanley J. Shapiro, (eds.), (Homewood, Ill.: Richard D. Irwin, Inc., 1964), p. 17.

[34] Robert Bartels, *Marketing Theory and Metatheory* (Homewood, Illinois,: Richard D. Irwin, Inc., 1970), p. 4.

[35] For criteria of theory formation see also: Perry Bliss, "How We Can 'Know' More About Marketing," in *Theory in Marketing* by Reavis Cox, Wroe Alderson, and Stanley J. Shapiro, eds., (Homewood, Ill.: Richard D. Irwin, Inc., 1964, p. 84), and Gerald Zaltman, Christian R. A. Pinson, and Reinhard Anglemar, *Metatheory and Consumer Research* (New York: Holt, Rinehart and Winston, Inc., 1973).

INFLUENCES ON THE DEVELOPMENT OF MARKETING THOUGHT, 1950–1987

15

INTRODUCTION

The reason for reviewing the history of marketing thought today is the same as fifty years ago: to consider whether there is a "whole" of marketing that is greater than the sum of its parts, and whether marketing thought is expressive of that wholeness, or only of its parts.

A "whole" of marketing must be the effort of society to satisfy, in the economy, particular basic needs, which effort scholarship attempts to conceptualize. The extent to which these objectives are achieved indicates the effectiveness of the economy and the adequacy of marketing thought. However, if society's expectations are not perceived, marketing theories may lack breadth and embody only narrower concepts. Whichever is the case, scholars' concepts of the need to be fulfilled by marketing are products of influences upon their thinking. It is the purpose of this study to present, as reported by marketing scholars themselves, subjective influences which they believe shaped their thoughts about marketing, their writings, and the body of marketing thought in this century.

Throughout this century, economic circumstances and standards of scholarship have changed. This has produced a varying body of thought. The environmental context was initially an economy in transition from sellers' to buyers' markets. The broadening of markets, the rise of new distributive institutions, market urbanization and affluence, and rising material and ethical expectations stimulated unprecedented interest in trade early in this century. This led to development of a literature for educational purposes written from the viewpoints of economists, psychologists, industrial organizationists, and educators responsible for developing and communicating a new intelligence. The initial concepts and definitions of "marketing" continued to be acceptable until mid-century.

Subsequently, new viewpoints, as well as new circumstances, changed the definition of marketing and the concept of its social role and professional responsibility. Theories from other social and behavioral disciplines were introduced into the subject. Research technology became more refined, and areas of interest became specialized. These changes were attributable to new viewpoints of theorists more than to changes in the subject with which they were concerned. The conceptualizing character and capability of marketing scholars have been of prime importance in defining marketing, and consequently in proclaiming not only what it is *presumed* to be, but, by implication, what it is *expected* to be.

The significance of subjective factors in the conception and development of marketing thought was realized in the late 1930s. Contact was made in 1940 and 1941 with the same twenty principal contributors to the marketing literature since 1900, to ascertain what had induced them to engage in this new field of research, and what education and experiences had led them to think as they did about the subject. Those were scholars who developed the functional/institutional, or so-called "traditional" concept of marketing. With backgrounds as economists, businessmen, teachers, and graduate students they developed an understanding of marketing which served business, educators, and public administrators alike. Their writings are reviewed in *The History of Marketing Thought,*[1] and their accounts of what motivated and influenced them are presented in the appendix of this book.

With the belief that similar influence patterns were repeated in recent years, inquiry was made in 1987 of some thirty leading contributors to marketing since 1950. They were asked to relate (a) what subjective factors and personal experiences had influenced their creativity in marketing scholarship, (b) how this had taken form in their writings, and (c) how they had affected or fitted into the developing stream of marketing thought. Selection was made from recommendations of peers by leading scholars themselves. Not all who were contacted responded, but those who did were the following:

Richard P. Bagozzi	Robert J. Holloway
Robert Bartels	John A. Howard
Frank M. Bass	Shelby D. Hunt
James R. Bettman	Harold H. Kassarjian
Donald J. Bowersox	Philip Kotler
Robert D. Buzzell	William Lazer
Gilbert A. Churchill	Theodore Levitt
Joel B. Cohen	Sidney J. Levy
James F. Engel	William J. Stanton
Stanley C. Hollander	Louis W. Stern

The changes in marketing thought which resulted from these and other writers since 1950 have been characterized as follows:

Holism	Consumerism
Functionalism	Internationalism
Managerialism	Comparativism
Environmentalism	Physical distributionism
Interdisciplinism	Futurism

In the following pages, trends in marketing thought are related to the changing frames of reference which scholars brought to the discipline. Intellectual breakthroughs from significant new insights were particularly sought. Where important contributers have not fully disclosed the foundations of their thinking, their place in the stream of thought is credited as well as possible. Personal records not included in the text are included in the appendix, as seemed appropriate.

EARLY INFLUENCES

For better perspective on changes to come later, it will be helpful to review some of the factors which induced and influenced writing in the early years of marketing.

The earliest inducement to thinking and writing about marketing or "distributive trade," as it was called, seemed to have arisen from the introduction of college courses in the subject, offered independently in five universities between 1902 and 1905. Without precedent or conference, teachers in preparing their offerings drew upon their respective thought references: Simon Litman (California), from writings of German economists; James E. Hagerty (Ohio), from mercantile credit study as graduate research; B. H. Hibbard (Wisconsin), from problems of farm products marketing. What writers thought about marketing reflected their experiences. The earliest marketing publication to which reference was made was Vol. 6 of the *Industrial Commission Reports*, published in 1905. Within a few years, experience in business, too, began to influence writers.

RALPH STARR BUTLER

Ralph Starr Butler wrote of his having developed correspondence courses in business at the University of Wisconsin in 1910:

> My experience as eastern sales manager with Proctor and Gamble had convinced me that a manufacturer seeking to market a product had to consider and solve a large number of problems before he ever gave expression to the selling idea by sending a salesman on the road or inserting an advertisement in a publication.

> I surveyed the very meager literature of business which was available at that time and was astonished to find that the particular field that I have briefly described above had never been treated by any writer. I decided to prepare a correspondence course covering this phase of business activity.[2]

Butler regarded this perception as a new concept and gave it the name "marketing."

ARCH W. SHAW

Arch W. Shaw similarly conceptualized his perception of business practices and problems in different companies. He wrote:

> Isolate any phase of business, strike into it anywhere, and the invariable essential element will be found to be application of motion to materials. This may be stated, if you will, as the simplest general concept to which all the activities of manufacturing, selling, finance, and management can ultimately be reduced.[3]

L.D.H. WELD

L.D.H. Weld conceived marketing activities structurally, classifying and designating them as "functions." Paul T. Cherington saw advertising as a "business force" and wrote the *Elements of Marketing*. Fred E. Clark, Paul D. Converse, Harold H. Maynard, Walter C. Weidler, and Theodore N. Beckman dignified their textbooks and studied generalizations as "principles." This illustrates the manner in which perceptions became conceptions, reflecting in some degree how individuality differences became expressed in marketing writings.

Notwithstanding different experiences and other subjective factors, consensus gradually formed as to how marketing was to be defined and how it was to be represented intellectually. That conceptualization remained the standard for more than thirty years. Its prolongation was due largely to the education then common to students of business. At the beginning of the century, the intellectual roots of most marketing teachers were in classical and institutional economics, with doctrines of Commons, Ely, Scott, Taylor, and Taussig, at Harvard and Wisconsin, prominent. By the early 1920s there was a second generation of marketing students, taught by those who had been taught by economists. In the 1920s, students were crediting the marketing pioneers—Cherington, Nystrom, Butler, Shaw, and Weld—as the wellsprings of their professional inspiration. Progressively, Clark, Converse, and the Maynard-Weidler-Beckman triumverate were the authorities for marketing education. This consensus later caused the new discipline to be regarded as having been a single "school of thought."

As cited by those men, the subjective and personal influences upon their scholarship were: academic assignments, business experiences, family interests and occupations, educational programs and associates, and natural curiosity.

Because of the commonality of their educational experiences, early writers produced a uniform body of thought and literature. It listed the marketing functions, discussed marketing issues and public policy, described the marketing of farm products, and gave attention to psychological aspects of the consumer market. As marketing developed, it became increasingly devoted to the marketing of manufactured consumer products, with emphasis on exchange functions rather than those of physical supply. Selling, sales management, and advertising were the most considered functions, and wholesaling and retailing establishments in consumer goods distribution were of primary interest. Study of the marketing of agricultural products gravitated to colleges of agriculture. The functions of buying, transportation, and storage became secondary. Those changes evidenced the influence of diversifying subjective factors beginning to alter marketing thought as it developed in the 1920s.

BEGINNINGS OF CONCEPTUAL CHANGE

The acceptance of marketing thought which had developed between 1900 and 1940, based upon economic concepts and current marketing research, was not without reservations and criticism. Dissent was mild at first, but by the mid-1950s new concepts of marketing appeared which led eventually to unimagined alteration of the structure and focus of the discipline. The change to come was due to new interests and perspectives of marketing scholars, as well as to changes in the environment.

RALPH F. BREYER

Ralph F. Breyer, rejecting the prevailing concept of marketing, expounded during the 1930s an integrated and holistic concept of it. He was one of the first but not the only one to do this. And although commodity marketing was then subordinate to functional and institutional analyses, Breyer gave it particular attention, regarding it as a springboard for his further integration of the subject. Of this he wrote:

> Shortly after (writing *Commodity Marketing*) I began thinking about methods of integrating the subject of marketing. (Because the N.R.A. and A.A.A.) had such tremendous import for marketing . . . I incorporated these new developments, along with some of my ideas on integration in the volume, *The Marketing Institution*. . . .I think that my natural aptitude for seeking the wholeness and order in marketing phenomena, and other phenomena for that matter, along with my serious impairment of hearing, . . . have in large part influenced my point of view in marketing.[4]

Breyer's interpretation of marketing channels as analogous to the electric flow in the field *between* magnetic poles was an innovative concept in the late 1930s. It directed attention away from *individual* institutions, which had been the principal object of consideration. At the same time, David R. Revzan explored the "linkages and blockages" in marketing channels, also focusing attention on the relations *between* channel institutions, rather than on activities within them. E.T. Grether presented a larger view of marketing in his analyses of *regional* rather than local marketing. Grether, along with Roland S. Vaile and Reavis Cox, in *Marketing in the American Economy* also enlarged the view of marketing as a phenomenon in the total economy.

COX AND ALDERSON

Not all of the departure from established marketing thought, however, was found in books showing differing viewpoints. Outright criticism was also made of the traditional function-institution interpretation of marketing. When confidence was felt that marketing thought had attained a maturity that justified calling its generalizations "principles," the word principle fell into disrepute. It was claimed by Reavis Cox and Wroe Alderson that marketing had achieved only "a plethora of facts and a paucity of theory." It was argued that marketing was not a science, and doubt was expressed as to whether it ever could be. These contrasting interpretations arose from new viewpoints from which scholars were regarding the subject. The meaning of marketing and the role of its application were in transition.

The transition became evident in substance as well as in form, as other new concepts appeared: the "marketing mix" by Neil H. Borden and the "product life cycle" by Joel Dean (1950); "brand image" by Sidney J. Levy (1955); "market segmentation" by Wendell Smith (1956); the "marketing concept" by John B. McKitterick (1957); the "marketing audit" by Abe Shuchman (1969); and the "4 Ps" by E. Jerome McCarthy (1960).[5] Titles including "Principles" continued to appear, but the new perspective employed such words as "managerial," "management," and "behavior," as in *Marketing Behavior and Executive Action,* by Wroe Alderson (1957); *Managerial Marketing: Perspectives and Viewpoints* by Eugene J. Kelley and William Lazer (1958); and *Basic Marketing: A Managerial Approach,* by E. Jerome McCarthy (1960).

REEVALUATION IN THE 1950S

The general satisfaction with marketing thought felt prior to 1950 was, during the following decade, shaken with criticism and mixed with doubt for many who had enjoyed that satisfaction. This was due in part to the fact that new ideas were surfacing, but most of the marketing faculty had been educated in concepts inherent in the earlier thought. Marketing literature was likewise oriented. Older academics were not impervious to change, but their courses and writings often carried marks of an era regarded by some as passing. Some adapted, but because their intellectual framework was rooted in precedent, they did not conceptualize as did their differently educated successors. The following observations of several of the contributors of that period indicate the turbulence then in marketing thought.

WILLIAM J. STANTON

William J. Stanton is one who has attributed his perspective largely to studying and working with marketing scholars eminent prior to 1950:

> Two Northwestern University professors who had an inestimable influence on my career were Delbert Duncan and Fred Clark. Duncan served as mentor, counselor, sounding board, and good friend for many, many years.[6]

He paid high tribute to renowned marketing scholars holding traditional concepts, even with whom he had not studied:

> I never studied under Harold H. Maynard or Theodore N. Beckman, but their work shaped some of my efforts. Maynard's work in sales management guided me. And Ted Beckman's famous seminar in basic marketing . . . was something that I later adopted at the University of Colorado. Through the years as I recruited faculty, I always was certain that any Beckman-trained doctoral student really knew marketing.

However, Stanton was also influenced by others of the period, particularly those with whom he interacted in the Marketing Theory Seminar held annually alternately in Colorado and Vermont: Wroe Alderson, Ed McGarry, Leo Aspinwall, Reavis Cox, Paul Converse, and Harvey (Hix) Huegy. Seminar participants discussed new marketing ideas that were on the threshold of wider acceptance.

The mix of old and new influences effected in Stanton a conflict which others also experienced. Acquaintance with new viewpoints cast the old in a dimmer light, but like many who were grounded in the older concepts and methodology he did not move far into the newer trends of thought. His awareness of the change in process was expressed in the following evaluation of the status of thought at that time:

> As a student and during my early teaching years, the principles of marketing books typically were macro oriented. They followed the combined institutional-functional approach as they described the role of marketing in our economy. Unfortunately, students felt that the course was dull. . . . The text approach in those days was not useful to graduates going into the

marketing (then called sales) department of a company. So I wanted to write a book that reflected the planning and operation of a marketing program in an individual organization—business or non-business—marketing products or services, domestic or international.

Stanton's principal publications: *Management of the Sales Force* and *Fundamentals of Marketing,* continued into their 7th and 8th editions, respectively.

STANLEY C. HOLLANDER

Stanley C. Hollander was another whose introduction and entrance into marketing occurred during the transition years of the 1940s and 1950s. His work has been identified with individuals and interests of conventional thought, but his creativity and resourcefulness carried him creditably into the reconceptualization of marketing.

An anomaly of that period was that, while some clung to old concepts, not seeing what was ahead, others modified the old by embracing the new. Hollander wrote of an experience in 1956 as follows:

A postdoctoral seminar at Carnegie Tech with Herbert Simon reinforced much of the institutional thinking to which I had been exposed. Here again, it became evident that organizations were power systems and that they involved complex, and often sub-optimizing, internal relationships. This has influenced my teaching more than my writing. Incidentally, I went to the seminar to plan to exploit thoughts on the channel as an organization, but Simon was so self-deprecatory about his ideas . . . and other participants were so convincing that organizations were self-contained that I abandoned the idea.[7]

Much of Hollander's work experience was in retailing, but, although his education had been largely of pre-1950 books and teachers, his insights into retailing were fresh and advanced, notwithstanding the fact that retailing was one of the courses then much disparaged. He perceived retailing as

. . . a complex and significant institution in both economic and social life, a fact that was well recognized in the writings of such major teachers as Paul Nystrom, Malcolm McNair and Delbert Duncan, but that had at times been given insufficient attention in retail education."

He maintained that

. . . retailing could, and should be studied at a deeper, more conceptual and, if you will, more theoretical level than was generally popular at the time. A major outlet for this view came through editing a book of readings, *Explorations in Retailing* (1959). No commercial publisher wanted to touch this book because they considered it far too advanced for the market . . . .

A characteristic of Hollander has been his devotion to the development of ideas. A course in History of Economic Thought with Dr. Howard Piquet, he said, taught him that "people could be interested in ideas as well as in facts and techniques." Later, intellectual stimulation and "reinforcement of the idea that ideas count" was derived from work with E.D. McGarry, who took a "very eclectic and interdisplinary view toward marketing . . . and he strongly influenced the types of interdisciplinary things I tried to do with *Explorations in Retailing."* Also

> Working with or under Reavis Cox was a major experience. He continued McGarry's questioning and interdisciplinary mode, but with somewhat more rigor. He had more interest in the problem of measurement of marketing performance and he imparted that interest to us. He encouraged me to do historical work. I believe I developed an interest in doing a dissertation on discount retailing on my own, but Cox championed that interest against the recommendations of other faculty who felt it was too unorthodox a topic.

Hollander's work has kept abreast of the times as his interest has enlarged to include multinational retailing, marketing in developing countries, public policy toward retailing, and the social and ethical impacts of problems of marketing and retailing.

WILLIAM LAZER

William Lazer was another whose career in marketing began during the years of transition. Following a liberal and interdisciplinary beginning at the University of Chicago, and after familiarization with "the basic books in retailing, advertising, sales management, marketing research, etc." through teaching, Lazer enrolled for doctoral work, completed in 1956, at The Ohio State University. Of that period he wrote:

> It was there that I really delved into marketing. Those were very important years in my development. I am sure you recall the History of Marketing Thought Seminar that you taught as well as the section taught by Harold Maynard. That stimulated my interest in the historical aspects of the discipline which are with me to date. . . . Theodore N. Beckman, my advisor, forced me to investigate marketing very intensively. We went through the basic marketing book with a fine tooth comb, providing invaluable grounding. In fact, I think the very emphasis on description, which so many of our younger scholars seem to avoid and hold in low esteem provided an invaluable background.[8]

Lazer's career attests the merit which others also have found in a knowledge of rudimentary marketing, when supplemented by newer concepts and thought development. Deprecation of basic principles during the 1950s, however, led to specializations which have tended to fragment the field.

JOHN A. HOWARD

John A. Howard presents still another view of the thought transition which was in process in the 1950s. In choosing a career path and having found economics to be exciting, he was advised by the head of Public Utilities at the Harvard Business School to "go across the river to the Harvard Economics Department and 'get a good degree,' " the type of statement, Howard has said, that "could have been made about any business school at that time." Such a statement not only could have been made but was made, generally enough to cause the Ford Foundation to make a comprehensive review of teaching and research in marketing in American business schools. Howard was asked to make this review. Of his observations, he wrote:

> The courses in disrepute in the 1950s were the highly specialized functional field courses and, in marketing, retailing was viewed as one such course. The Ford Foundation's philosophy was to increase the discipline courses (economics, other behavioral sciences and mathematics and statistics). It was felt that these would encourage the building of intellectual content in the functional fields which should be the heart of a professional business school.[9]

Concerning the allegation that at that time there was not much further to be learned in the study of marketing, Howard recalled:

> Quite the contrary, . . . there was no question but that much could be learned in marketing . . . . As you know, only in the past few years has economics contributed much to even the competitive side of marketing and this was where microeconomics was by far the strongest compared to the consumer area.

Notwithstanding that marketing programs could be improved, and that there was still much to be learned in marketing, out of his Ford Foundation work came in 1963 his book, *Marketing: Executive and Buyer Behavior* and "a clear conclusion on my part that consumer research was ready to move." This was but one evidence that the field of marketing was about to become many things to many people.

E. JEROME McCARTHY

Although many persons were involved in the transition of thought during the 1950s, culmination of the development toward managerialism in marketing occurred in the work of E. Jerome McCarthy, whose *Basic Marketing: A Managerial Approach* (1960) by 1987 had nine published editions. So widely adopted was his concept "the '4 P' strategy planning framework," that the term became a generic concept in basic marketing instruction. The challenge of the period was to usefully combine macro and micro perspectives—the earlier and the then-developing approaches to marketing. Of his effort to effect that combination McCarthy has said:

> Any exiting theories and techniques that would help beginning students analyze and/or develop better market-oriented strategies were integrated into *Basic Marketing: A Managerial Approach*. This included not only material from the business press, but also ideas from the academic literature—often refocused to emphasize the managerial implications, e.g., goods classes defined by how customers see them rather than their physical characteristics. I also incorporated the micro and macro implications from Vaile-Grether-Cox and Alderson thinking re markets, marketing institutions, channels and market structure; economics; and managerial accounting. Both micro and macro perspectives were maintained, so that managerial emphasis did not wipe out a macro view.[10]

254

McCarthy's work was pervaded by a strong dual sense of the importance of "the bottom line," and of the importance to "saving mankind" and "helping people get a better deal." These two interests were basic to his micro and macro emphases.

My 'bottom-line' mentality applied a criterion of "Will this be useful" to every possible inclusion (in the book). It was not to be a dictionary of "buzzwords." Many terms had to be defined so students would have a meaningful "technical language" to aid effective communication. (Inasmuch as) the marketing language then, as now, was very imprecise, *Basic Marketing* language was used very carefully and logically to weave an integrated whole, in order that students could handle and leave the course—and college—with a good grasp of the 4 Ps, segmenting markets, and market-oriented strategy plannings. New terms and frameworks have been added over the years—to refine and tighten the 4 P strategy planning framework—to make it more useful for serious "how-to-do-it" students. This attention to useful details and logical organization gained more and more adopters—and the 'Managerial Approach' became *the* approach of the first course.

NEW CONCEPTS APPEARING

Although traditional perspectives continued into and beyond the 1950s, new concepts effected profound changes in marketing thought and literature. Marketing itself was reconceived and redefined, not as distributive activity, but as the function of management in distributive activity, especially of manufacturers marketing consumer goods. This was evidenced in a number of ways, including new terms and their connotations: the "marketing concept" implied an integrated intraorganizational viewpoint; the "4 Ps" suggested the interrelatedness of manageable marketing variables; "marketing management" succeeded sales management; "channel management" contrasted with institution management; "modeling" patterned management decision making; and buyers' and sellers' behavior was perceived in multidisciplinary terms. These new views instituted a turning point in marketing thought.

The concept of marketing management had been suggested by some scholars years before, as, for example, by Leverett S. Lyon in 1926, but the times and the state of scholarship were not receptive to it. The breakthrough is sometimes identified with Wroe Alderson, a person of business experience, marketing education, and ranging familiarity with philosophy and the natural and social sciences. He saw marketing as management behavior in institutional and environmental context. His book *Marketing Behavior and Executive Action* (1957) introduced a deeper sense of managerialism and a broader sense of the economic, social, and political environment in which management occurred. His place in thought development, however, is not covered in this study, which is based not upon literature, per se, but upon the self-perceptions of men who have created it. Nothing would be more interesting than a depth interview with Alderson, to probe the subjectivity of his creativity., if that were possible.

Since 1960, marketing thought has undergone further change, as some scholars have extended it while others have carried it to new depths of specialization and analysis. In the following pages, some of these developments are taken up from the standpoints of *individuals* and of the *areas* in which their contributions have been made.

PHILIP KOTLER

Philip Kotler has been a provocative contributor to marketing thought, having, since 1960, redefined marketing several times, as his perception of it changed from economic to social to generic. He exemplifies scholarship which broke with tradition, yet refused confinement to narrow research which engaged many during the same period. He cites the following as basic values and attitudes which have shaped his perspective:

The assumption that "progress" is possible, even in the face of much contradictory evidence.

Interest in wanting to fight conditions that lead to human suffering and lost human potential.

Enjoyment in working on new ideas and solutions more than staying with existing ones and digging deeper. My comparative advantage lies in the former[11]

After studying economics with Milton Friedman at Chicago and Paul Samuelson at M.I.T., he left economics for he felt that that was "the only way to reduce the felt dissonance level" between "free enterprise" and "Keynesianism." He then

. . . spent 1959–1960 at Harvard in a special one-year-long Ford Foundation-sponsored program designed to train professors in higher mathematics. This workshop was the direct result of the Gordon and Howell report on making business schools better. (There) I became friendly with several marketing professors in the program, including Frank Bass, Bob Buzzell, William Lazer, Jerome McCarthy, and Ed Pessemier. All of us became convinced that the future of marketing lay partly in model building and statistical analysis.

In 1962, Kotler joined the faculty of Northwestern University, where he was told that "the marketing field needed 'help.' " There he became associated with a faculty ". . . of such stars as Harper Boyd, Richard Clewett, Sidney Levy, and Ralph Westfall. . . . They were systematizing the fields of marketing research, marketing management, channel management and consumer behavior. Their example had a great influence on me."

Management. Like others at that time, Kotler thought that the "help" that marketing needed was to be found in the managerial approach to it. Its inadequacy he felt lay in want of scientific rigor.

In examining the existing marketing textbooks, I felt that they lacked the tight analytical quality of the economics textbooks. They contained many lists (such as the advantages and disadvantages of wholesalers, etc.) and hardly any theory. Little was reported in the way of research findings and methodologies from the social, economic, and quantitative sciences. As a result, I decided around 1964 to write my own marketing textbook. The original draft was highly quantitative and my publisher advised me to "tone down the math" and "beef up the prose and stories." The result was *Marketing Management* published in 1967. I saved the "expurgated material" and extended and published it in 1971 as *Marketing Decision Models. A Model-Building Approach.* The University of Chicago liked the advanced treatment so much that they used it in their introductory marketing course.

During these early years, the work of two marketing scholars had the most impact on my thinking. One was Wroe Alderson (Wharton) who, in my mind, is the discipline's most original theorist. He synthesized ideas from the emerging fields of managerial economics, organizational behavior, human ecology, communication theory, and psychology into a highly original theory of markets and marketing behavior. The other scholar is John A. Howard (Pittsburgh, Columbia) who brought into the marketing discipline major insights from economic theory, psychological learning theory, and organizational theory. His *Theory of Buyer Behavior* represents a major effort to build and test theories of consumer buying behavior.

The Broadening Concept. In 1969, Kotler and Sidney Levy began to explore the limits of marketing. Conventionally, marketing had been held as a business subject but, as a result of Levy's research in consumer behavior in a number of nonprofit contexts, it became clear to both that

> . . . all organizations have marketing problems and do marketing. . . . We wrote 'Broadening the Concept of Marketing'. . . . In a poll of professors two years later, the vast majority said nonprofit organization marketing was a legitimate domain of marketing.

Social Marketing. In the early 1970s, Kotler was influenced by events of social protest and countercultural experimentation.

> I felt that marketing could be applied to furthering worthwhile social causes. This view was shared by Gerald Zaltman on our faculty, and we published "Social Marketing: An Approach to Planned Social Change." Today social marketing is being endorsed by international agencies such as U.S. AID, World Health Organization, and the World Bank as a highly effective management technology for social change.

Megamarketing. Apart from the business or social institutions availing themselves of marketing tools for the direct promotion of their cause, Kotler saw also an indirect utilization of those tools for opening environmental barriers.

> (It was) recognized that entry into many markets is blocked by political, legal, and economic barriers. Therefore I have argued that marketing executives need to acquire skills and understandings of political and public opinion forces in their efforts to enter and/or operate in markets characterized by "gatekeeper power." This concept was named "mega-marketing."

Demarketing In the early 1970s, still another idea grew out of changing business and economic conditions:

> Levy and I researched another "new idea," namely that of "demarketing."

We had observed some organizations (hotels, restaurants, etc.) discourage certain customers either because these organizations faced excess demand, or wanted a certain type of clientele, etc. We argued that marketers need to be as skilled in "demarketing" as in "marketing." Demarketing called for using all the marketing tools in reverse.

Generic.   In 1971, Kotler conceptualized marketing even more broadly as he sought to identify its core meaning.

As I probed deeper into marketing, I asked myself "What is the core concept of marketing?" The fundamental concept of economics is *scarcity;* politics, *power;* sociology, the *group;* anthropology, *culture.* I became increasingly convinced that the core concept of marketing is *exchange.* If marketers pretended to know anything, it was the conditions under which two or more parties decided whether to trade some things of value between them. I developed a comprehensive set of axioms that defined the domain of marketing in a 1971 article entitled "The Generic Concept of Marketing."

With Kotler's work the inventory of significant marketing concepts—and concepts of marketing—has been enlarged. This reflected infusion of organizational, behavioral, social, political, and global concepts into his frame of reference and vocabulary. Basically, his varied dimensions of marketing all derive from the central theme of his conviction, namely, that marketing is exchange in different contexts.

UPGRADING THROUGH QUANTIFICATION

Claims made during the 1950s that marketing was neither a science nor scientific were generally based upon allegations that it was factual and not theoretical, descriptive and not explanatory, derived for specific and not general understanding, and logical but not replicable. For these reasons classes and textbooks were deemed dull, repetitive, and of low intellectual demand. The Ford and Carnegie Foundations' reports confirmed this, and in order to provide a remedy the Ford Foundation sponsored a year of higher mathematical study at Harvard for a group of selected marketing professors. The outcome was the infusion of mathematical formulas, models, and tests into many aspects of marketing but, more importantly, the introduction of a new viewpoint into the study of marketing.

Varying with professorial interests, application of quantitative technology ranged from minimum to maximum, sometimes with form of analysis overshadowing significance of content. Whichever, the body of marketing thought acquired more scientific credibility, judged by standards of the social sciences. Some scholars strove for reliability of findings; others for refinement of research methodology. Two who have shaped marketing thought through quantification of research are Frank M. Bass and Robert D. Buzzell.

FRANK M. BASS

Frank M. Bass, reflecting in 1986 upon the qualitative changes in marketing thought during the previous 30 years,[12] saw progress resulting from new technologies employed in the discipline:

As a young Ph.D. student of Paul D. Converse at the University of Illinois (1951–1954), I often heard the question: Is marketing a science? The answer to this question at that time was far from clear, but I was inclined to think that it was not. . . . There were all sorts of interesting questions and issues about which very little was known and there was the potential to apply powerful methods then emerging in statistics and mathematics in a search for answers. . . . Since then, scientific inquiry in marketing has exploded. . . . If marketing was not a science, it is now possible to mount a strong argument that, as a result of the explosion of scientific inquiry, it has become one.

In 1950, however, the state-of-the-art in marketing was not a mere impersonal fact of the discipline for Bass. It became a determining factor in his choice of career and an experience in stochastic choice, of which he later became a leading exponent in the quantification of marketing behavior. Having developed an interest in economics as an undergraduate, he sought advice for directions in graduate study.

Dejected (from a previous interview), I wandered somewhat aimlessly over to the business school building. . . . I spotted a professor sitting in his office. . . . He recommended that I take as many courses (for an M.B.A. degree) in economics as the program allowed because there was not much to be learned about marketing anyway. . . . This unplaned encounter . . . and other random-like events undoubtedly helped shape my views about the stochastic nature of choice.[13]

After completing his Ph.D., still desiring to learn more about mathematics and statistics, Bass attended the 1959 Ford Foundation-sponsored Institute of Basic Mathematics for Application to Business. The experience provided the foundation for a career focused on the development of mathematical and statistical models in marketing.

The question of choice became a prepossessing interest as he noted with increasing disagreement that even late in the 1950s ". . . the preconceptions and theories in the social sciences toward choice behavior were deterministic in character. The notion of 'choice probability' was foreign." In 1974 he wrote:

Although it is heresy, in some circles, honesty compels one to question the fundamental premise that all behavior is caused. If there is a *stochastic element in the brain* which influences choice, then it is not possible, even in principle, to predict or to understand completely the choice behavior of individual consumers. Moreover, even if behavior is caused but the bulk of the explanation lies in a multitude of variables which occur with unpredictable frequency, then, in practice, the process is stochastic.

Along another line, Bass became interested in the importance of new ideas and in their diffusion through a relevant population. Thoughts of this type led him to develop a diffusion theory model of innovations (1969). This has become known as "the Bass model."

ROBERT BUZZELL

Robert Buzzell was a different product of exposure to rigorous training in traditional marketing of the early 1950s, later supplemented by the Ford year of mathematics. Of both he has said:

At OSU, Ted Beckman was undoubtedly the biggest influence on me. . . . His seminar was an intensive learning experience. . . . Some of his questions seemed to me to be nit-picking ones. One that I recall was: "What is the difference between Marketing Functions and the Functions of Marketing?" I still can't give a good answer to it. But wrestling with questions like this was useful: it instilled a kind of mental discipline: define terms precisely; be sure that you use them consistently; classify things into well-defined categories. He didn't phrase it this way, but he insisted on what mathematicians call "mutually exclusive, collectively exhaustive" taxonomies.

The Harvard-Ford year of 1959–1960 brought other viewpoints:

This year affected me greatly. For one thing, I learned a lot about math and statistics. By the standards of the 1980s it wasn't much, but by the standards of the day it was "state-of-the-art". . . . The program gave me a "quantitative view" of the world that I'll never lose. The program also exposed me to a group of bright young faculty people from a variety of fields—finance, control, economics, and so forth. Our common interest was management. I stopped thinking of marketing as a separate specialized function. I started thinking of it as one element or dimension of an integrated process. . . .[14]

Another experience that affected my thinking and my interests was the time I spent as a Visiting Professor at INSEAD in 1967. It gave me a much wider point of view about marketing and about life in general. Today everyone talks about "global competition," and it seems obvious that managers and academics must consider customers, competition, and marketing practices on a worldwide scale. Twenty years ago it wasn't obvious, and it was quite a revelation to me.

Several criticisms of marketing thought prior to and during the 1950s have been cited above. Marketing was not entirely absolved of its weaknesses by new technologies thereafter introduced. A comment to this effect has also been made by Buzzell. Having early learned the merit of avoiding being pompous, he said in 1987:

These values make me impatient with much of the work that is done in marketing today. When I skim through the *JM* or the *JMR*, at least half of the articles strike me as pompous. Considerably more than half, in my view, deal with unimportant questions. I find myself asking, "Who could care about the results? Does it really matter?" I try to keep these reactions to myself, but I don't always succeed.

CONSUMER BEHAVIOR

The most imposing substantive change in marketing in the post-1950 decades has been the rise of research and writing on consumer behavior. The consumer had been a subject of interest in marketing texts before the 1930s, and in the late 1940s courses on "the consumer" were offered in marketing departments. Also, the consumer was partially the object of concern in market research courses, albeit quantitative aspects of the market were emphasized. In the late 1950s, however, the term "the consumer" began to assume a different meaning.

The new "consumer" was a creature born of the belief that in mathematical and multidisciplinary concepts were the solution to the needed revitalization of marketing. The need, however, was not to be supplied by those who had brought the study of marketing up to that point. A new viewpoint was to be provided by some who understood the application of higher mathematics to business problems, and by others who came as experts from the social disciplines, although they knew little if anything about marketing. Acceptance into the marketing coterie was not instant, nor were articles on new views of the consumer readily accepted by marketing publications. Nevertheless, with conventional marketing on the wane and new research technologies ascendent, for twenty-five years, consumer behavior, along with marketing management, become one of the two leading contenders for identification as "marketing."

The genealogy of leaders in the field has furnished an interesting example of the diffusion of an innovation. Almost of necessity, seeds of the new subject germinated in marketing faculties. Doctoral majors in marketing found support and inspiration among colleagues who were glimpsing the light of new meanings. Peer support and collaboration produced leaders who had mastered or were developing relevant analytical technologies. Much-quoted and long-lasting books were written. The Association for Consumer Research was founded. Experts in behavioral analysis were imported from allied social and behavioral disciplines, with or without interest either in the development of marketing theory or in the application of their findings in business practice. The field became heady with popularity; new ideas occurred less frequently; leaders retired from the field; and a dilution of interest spread as it had over conventional marketing thirty years earlier.

In the following pages are recounted, in words of those who developed this area of marketing thought, the inspiration which motivated them, the expertise which they undertook to develop, and their ultimate appraisal of the state of the subject. Although many eminent contributors to the field of consumer behavior could have been included in this review, for reason only of their cooperation in this survey, the following are represented: Harold H. Kassarjian, James F. Engel, Sidney J. Levy, James R. Bettman, Joel B. Cohen, and Richard P. Bagozzi.

HAROLD H. KASSARJIAN

Harold H. Kassarjian has said: ". . . in many ways my growth and development parallels the development of the growth of the field of consumer behavior." That could possibly be said by others who began the integration of a behavioral background with marketing in the early 1960s. With a doctoral degree in social psychology and brief experience with a marketing research firm, in 1961 he joined the marketing department of University of California at Los Angeles.

I joined the marketing department soon after the publication of the Carnegie and Ford Foundation reports which were critical of business schools. . . . The reports recommended hiring people from mathematics and social sciences for their inputs into business. . . . I suspect that those reports were one of the reasons I was hired. At the same time people like Engel were being hired at Ohio State, Levy at Northwestern, Newman at Stanford, Wells at Rutgers, Green at Wharton, Kuehn at Carnegie, and Frank and Massy at Penn State.

It seems to me that about that time marketing departments were becoming stale. Those trained in the structural approach . . . had contributed what they could. Marketing teachers were getting older, often past the productive post doctorate decade. And business schools were training only their own kind.

Into that melieu stepped psychologists, statisticians, and mathematicians, not the least interested in marketing. . . . Our salvation was Marketing Management for there one did not need (structural) details or even economic theory. We could substitute models and psychological theory.[15]

UCLA was willing to take a chance—willing to hire a psychologist who did not know the difference between a rack jobber and a drop shipper. . . . Assigned to teach a course in advertising, it soon became obvious to me that I knew a lot about human behavior that economists and marketing professors did not seem to know—personality, dissonance, experimental design, communications research, attitude research, etc.—topics that later were to become the field of consumer behavior. . . . Soon other non-traditional academics were added to the department: Al Silk, and George Haines. . . . It was there, working with those colleagues, that I gained the needed confidence that my work was indeed relevant. . . . Marketing need not be merely a way station back to psychology. . . .[16] I realized . . . that statistics, psychology, and sociology were the new wave in marketing. The older generation was moving on and we were coming into our own. . . . Little wonder that consumer behavior began wagging the marketing dog. We had it all, the better students, apparently the more interesting subject matter, and a growing group that was alive with excitement.

Besides replacing the technical competence of the former marketing faculty, the newer incumbents were also to change the intended use of marketing intelligence. They did not regard themselves "handmaidens of industry," nor "handmaidens of the establishment, the munitions makers, and the war mongers." Instead, during the late 1960s, those interested in consumer behavior claimed their interest to be the protection, rather than the manipulation, of the consumer.

At that time, behavioral, or for that matter modeling, type papers were unacceptable to marketing publications and the AMA conference was a closed shop run by the "old boy" network. Getting our work published was tough indeed until Bob Ferber began the *Journal of Marketing Research* and was receptive to behavioral work. That was the real beginning both for myself and for the field of consumer research, for now we had a medium that would accept our work and we did not have to create imagined "marketing implications."

By the mid-1960s the term consumer behavior began to emerge in full force although the term had been around in earlier publications by Clark and by Newman. Suddenly classes were being taught in several universities on the topic with no real text material that could fit a college course. Perry Bliss had a behaviorally oriented book of readings published, and McNeal we knew was working on some sort of compendium. Hence Tom Robertson and I put together our book of readings, *Perspectives in Consumer*

Behavior. It emerged about the same time that the Engel, Kollat, and Blackwell text had its debut, Myers' paperback, and Newman and Britt's compendia. The field began to blossom.

Kassarjian during ensuing years published innovatively and extensively. Among the papers that he "liked best" are the following:

- A 1965 *Journal of Marketing Research* article introducing Riesman's theory to the consumer behavior community.
- A 1971 JMR piece reviewing the work in personality.
- The cognitive dissonance paper coauthored with then doctoral student, Joel Cohen, in the *California Management Review*.
- The 1977 presidential address to the Association for Consumer Research.
- The original book of readings, *Perspectives in Consumer Behavior*.

As others have reported who have ridden the wave of consumer behavior to its crest, Kassarjian has observed:

By the 1980s, conditions had changed. The times had become more conservative. Management science people started to become more important. Suddenly, the tables were turned, it was the original consumer behavior folks that started turning grey. The excitement of the new venture was gone, the consumer behavior organizations and journals were the establishment. Now the marketing management and the quantitative types started to come to the forefront and the rallying cry was Marketing Strategy. . . . Consumer Behavior is fine and I love it, but it has become old hat to me and the students are much better trained. I can't present stuff I learned in the 1950s as new fresh material. . . . I now prefer teaching law.

JAMES F. ENGEL

James F. Engel, unlike Kassarjian who started with social psychology and worked into marketing, started with marketing and worked into technologies of the social disciplines. While being instructed in traditional marketing as an undergraduate at Drake University (1956), his advisor, Marty Zober, foreseeing that ". . . there was going to be a behavioral integration into the field of marketing," urged him to take a minor in behavioral science. At the University of Illinois (1960), projective and nonprojective techniques, information processing, selective perception, and the integration into economics of the underlying principles and postulates of social psychology began to form his views of the consumer. Concerned with ". . . how we should think about the consumer," he felt that marketing history showed how barren were the theories of rational versus emotional motives. "That motivated me all the more to do something about it."

In 1960, Joe Klapper published his book on communication and . . . what we know about people and their selective response. . . . During the reading of that book things fell into place. I saw clearly that marketing had to start with the consumer. . . . I proposed a session at the American Marketing Association annual meetings in 1962. Don Cox, Ray Bauer, and others joined me on that panel. That's when I published the paper focusing on the selective perception in marketing. . . . I also became known quite early from my papers on cognitive dissonance.[17]

Of special interest is the turn which occurred in Engel's career and productivity with his moving to Ohio State University in 1963. With the hiring of Roger Blackwell and David Kollat the following year, a team was formed which was to have notable impact upon the development of the field of consumer behavior. Kollat brought a perspective that focused on extended problem solving behavior; Blackwell brought orientation in learning theory and cultural anthropology. The three offered the first course any of them had given on the field of consumer behavior.

The seminar was built upon Theodore Newcomb's Social Psychology and Krech and Krutchfield's book on social psychology. . . . But that seminar was to be something which would later shape the field. Those who participated in it, and its successor the next year, included Larry Light, Brian Sternthal, and Sam Craig, all of whom went on to be major leaders in the field.

In that seminar, the students were to come up with a model of consumer behavior. . . . One stood out—the input of Larry Light. The Engel, Kollat, Blackwell model is an extension of the foundation laid by Larry Light. Light, of course, built on the input we gave in the seminar. . . . In 1967, at a three-day seminar at Purdue, I gave a paper on cognitive dissonance which expanded the model that Larry came up with, and which then appeared in the *Consumer Behavior* book in 1968.

Of the first edition of *Consumer Behavior,* Kollat was, in many ways, the backbone, looking particularly at the purchase process; I centered on information processing and attitude change; Blackwell contributed macro perspective and learning. . . . A whole generation of marketing faculty was educated using the EKB book.

We three had an idea to convene a meeting focusing just on the field of consumer behavior and to do this at Ohio State. I worked through the American Marketing Association and had official sanction for the 1969 workshop which was to lead to the formation of the Association for Consumer Research . . . Spearheading an effort, I was joined by Harold Kassarjian and Joel Cohen to put together a constitution. . . . Then, in 1970 our first meeting was held at the University of Massachusetts. . . . That was the launch of the ACR. . . . When in 1981, for the book and the formation of the ACR, I was designated along with John Howard as Fellow in Consumer Behavior by the Association for Consumer Research, I gave the glory where it belongs—to the Lord Jesus Christ for the purpose he's given me and the motivation in my own life.

Another facet of the subject of consumer behavior is the interest—or the disinterest—which its proponents have had concerning its practical application. Scholars from other disciplines have been interested in the behavior of people as people, of people as consumers, or of consumers in contrast to business. Important as consumer behavior has been in the marketing camp and curriculum, such indifference to its usefulness has affected the character of the marketing objective.

At a point in his career, Engel faced this issue unexpectedly and experienced a reedirection of his work in the field. It was brought to his attention that his perspective ". . . was highly academic and not always really actionable or practical from the perspective of marketing action." He and Blackwell put on "dog and pony show" seminars for business executives.

> I began to realize that much of what I had done in my career had impacted the academic field profoundly but it had very little influence on the field of marketing action. That was devastating to me, because it caused me to question the whole validity of my premise: that my best reference group is my academic peers. I began to see that if we haven't influenced marketing practice, then what have we done? . . . Greater involvement with the business world . . . led to a diminishing of my publications. . . . My concern was to see things applied meaningfully in the field.

In 1972, the EKB team split up. Engel went from Ohio State to Wheaton College. The move, for personal reasons, he said,

> . . . represented the leading of the Lord in my life to come to Wheaton where I have pioneered the application of marketing thinking to the whole field of Christian communication. My publications here are an extension of the EKB efforts. I have published a model of conversion process behavior which is used throughout the world and has shaped this field as well. . . . In 1981, I founded a consulting organization with two others which is known as Management Development Associates. We are a leading marketing consulting firm focusing on all aspects of ministry effectiveness. . . . I suppose my involvement in marketing now is similar to that of many senior faculty who are tempted to find their greatest gratifications outside the academic arena. My interests have gone distinctly to the world.

The perspective which Engel has in 1987 concerning the thirty-year history of consumer behavior must resemble that of marketing pioneers at mid-century when their work was being reevaluated. His concluding observations are therefore thought-provoking.

> Maybe a few observations on the whole field of consumer behavior are in order to conclude this. I think the field has settled down remarkably from where it began. You will see great flux in the early editions of our book reflecting new developments. There seem to be few quantum leaps now, but we do grow each year in understanding the variables a bit more. Yet, I feel that the field has degenerated to a substantial amount of number crunching over trivial issues. Much of the literature is irrelevant and does not find its way into our books. I don't think this is a salutary development. I think it reflects a field which has gotten decidedly academic in its perspective and loses the fact that ultimately we are teachers and diffusers of knowledge in a discipline which is closer to engineering than it is a pure science. If we can restore this perspective we might have some hope.

> Today, there are tons of consumer behavior books. I don't see a whole lot of difference between the top three or four. Therefore, no one stands out today as a great contributor. Now there are many. It's interesting that one doesn't see people who you would now call leaders anymore. I believe it was easy for those of us from the generation of the thirties because there were so few of us. Now there are many people who are making reasonably

good contributions. I wonder if this will be the last book you write or anyone writes on leaders in marketing?

SIDNEY J. LEVY

Sidney J. Levy was educated in interdisciplinary thought and analysis in the Committee on Human Development at the University of Chicago, between 1946 and 1956, where the aim was to understand "how people come to be, grow up, and die. That meant learning not to be a sociologist or psychologist defending one's disciplinary territory, but rather how to use anthropological, sociological, psychological, and biological ideas to study the phenomena of human growth"[18] Integration, rather than multiplication, of disciplinary concepts has given Levy a holistic interpretation of human behavior, at Social Research, Inc. since 1948, and at Northwestern University since 1961. In collaborative research and writing at the latter, he has carried the interdisciplinary viewpoint deeply into marketing thought.

The development of his own perspective benefitted from association with a number of leading social scientists, among whom were W. Lloyd Warner, who saw the social system as a symbol system, and understood the significance and effects of hierarchy in social life upon human behavior; William E. Henry, authority on the Thematic Appreciation Technique and on personality projection in story telling; Burleigh B. Gardner, anthropologist-author; Harriett Bruce Moore, a model of how to think dynamically and deeply, and how to be free and brave in having and expressing one's thought

> In 1955, through the encouragement of Joe Newman, I wrote (with Burleigh Gardner) 'The Product and the Brand' (*HBR,* M-A, 1955), launching the concept of brand imagery into the business world, a concept that stressed the role of perception, directing attention to the importance of symbolic configurations in consumer behavior. This idea was extended in 'Symbols for Sale' (*HBR,* J-A, 1959). Joe's conference at Stanford University in 1964, *On Knowing the Consumer,* led me to prepare 'Social Class and Consumer Behavior.'

In his affiliation with the Northwestern University faculty, Levy's interdisciplinary orientation found new application through considering how marketing problems related to contemporary and changing culture, how social stratification disclosed the effects of social class upon market behavior; how the nature of social subgroups or segments tease out the central psychological/dynamics, etc. Reviewing some of the anthropological perspectives in marketing led to writing "Interpreting Consumer Mythology: A Structural Approach to Consumer Behavior" (*JM,* 1981).

> Much depends on exploring reminiscence and self-report, to learn how reality is being construed. The role of fantasy is central, and the telling of stories—whether called scientific analysis, reports of consumption behavior, or dreamy tales—is the main human activity. . . . Marketing research and research into marketing are ways of investigating these fantasies, soliciting them, organizing and analyzing them, putting them into another fantastic form, one that we call theorizing. . . . I look forward to learning more about the forever provocative field to which all of us are devoted.

JAMES R. BETTMAN

James R. Bettman has brought to the marketing/consumer behavior field special attention to how people process information. Neither his interest nor education initially pertained to marketing. Rather, theory of consumer choice had his attention as early as his 1961 freshman year at Yale, when he perceived the incompleteness of such existing theory. Standard utility theory in economics seemed inadequate. But "A Behavioral Model of Rational Choice" by Herbert Simon gave confidence that choice could be modeled. This set his future agenda. As he said, he was hooked!

His gravitation toward identification of information processing technology with marketing problems came gradually through discovery that real choices by consumers could be modeled in detail. When the realization was gained that information processing ideas might be relevant to consumer policy issues, many possible applications were perceived. This realization led to the thinking behind his book: *An Information Processing Theory of Consumer Choice.*

> Overall, I would say that I was one of the first (along with George Haines), and certainly probably the most persistent, to try to get consumer researchers to think about how people process information. Selling the idea that one should examine the real details of choice processes was not easy initially. However, I remained with this basic stream of research and eventually the climate was right (the Zeitgeist became favorable, as psychology also went in the direction of more detailed cognitive models). It also became easier when people saw how this could be related to marketing and policy concerns.[19]

JOEL B. COHEN

Joel B. Cohen's interest in consumer behavior did not stem from marketing nor did it extend primarily to the solution of marketing problems. Nor did it lie in pursuit to an ultimate resolution of some narrow methodological tool or concept. Rather, his concern was with the development of a multidisciplinary behavioral perspective describing the "whole" individual. Whereas Levy emphasized integration of disparate disciplinary views of the consumer, Cohen sought through diverse perspectives to understand man as a complex but integrated actor.

> I looked upon consumer behavior, which was then (in the early 1960s) in its infancy as a serious academic research domain, as having the potential to "force" inquiry to a useful level of integration, since it seemed to be an assumption of most people who were becoming interested in the topic that the field should focus on why and how people behave as they do in a complex domain. There seemed an opportunity to break down some artificial barriers (e.g., between those concerned exclusively with learning or cognitive processes and others concerned exclusively with motivational or personality variables) and in the process establish consumer behavior as an area of inquiry that would have broad appeal within the social sciences.

> This orientation to consumer behavior has influenced everything I have done as an educator and researcher. When I began in the field, this orientation was not popular or even well understood. I have worked to

establish it as one of the principal views of consumer behavior if not *the* overriding orientation to the subject.[20]

Twenty years later as professor/researcher, and ten years later as Director of the Center for Consumer Research, Cohen made the following observation:

> As I look at the field at this point in its development I continue to feel that two goals for the study of consumer behavior are paramount (1) to more adequately describe and understand all aspects of consumers' behavior (from the acquisition of basic tastes and preferences through the search for information to the outcome of choice processes) and (2) to contribute as a social science to the better understanding of human behavior by directing particular attention to how personal, social, and contextual factors combine to impact on human behavior in complex settings. Certainly, I am encouraged by the formation of the Association for Consumer Research and the development of the *Journal of Consumer Research,* both of which reflect a good deal of the orientation I have described above. At the same time I am often discouraged by the research performance of consumer researchers, many of whom appear to be simply duplicating the work of other behavioral and social scientists without either contributing to a better understanding of consumer behavior or placing their research in a more integrative context. But the field is still quite young, and I am forever an optimist!

RICHARD P. BAGOZZI

Richard P. Bagozzi represents a second generation of behaviorist, a type late-come not as refuge from traditional marketing, nor bearer from other disciplines of solutions for marketing problems. Those entering into marketing in 1970s were under the tutilage of those who had earlier established themselves as discoverers and creators of the "new" marketing. It was this new vision of marketing as "a broad subject matter, marked with diverse points of view" that gave the impression that marketing was then "in the formative growth stages.[21] It was the beginning of a period when, as noted above, some of the creativity and originality of consumer behavior research was waning and marketing was on the threshhold of a new era, not yet defined.

NEW DIMENSIONS

Concurrent after 1950 with the infusion of managerialism, quantification, social psychology, and the subject of consumer behavior into marketing, other trends developed, both broadening the subject and deepening investigation along earlier functional and institutional lines. *Broadening* depicted marketing in its larger business environment, in its historic setting, in its theoretical capabilities, and in its philosophic foundation. Some writers interpreted marketing along those lines. Others gave new interpretations and applications of marketing. Still others appealed for higher professionalism in marketing scholarship. Among the contributors identified with these trends are Theodore Levitt, William Lazer, Shelby D. Hunt, and Robert Bartels.

THEODORE LEVITT

Theodore Levitt is one whose works are known by their spirit and style as well as for their substance. His nine books published since 1951 have been mainly concerned with marketing, but his articles, averaging four for each of thirty-three years, have dealt with economic and social as well as of marketing issues. His provocative style is in attention-catching titles and phrases; his spirit in magnification of the relevant but unseen; his substance in the wide periphery of ideas encircling his central themes. Not narrowing his focus by deeper probing of selected topics, he opened vistas for practitioners and academics in works translated into nine languages.

Levitt's perspective is attributable to somewhat unorthodox factors. To begin with, his university training was in the liberal arts and economics. No formal study of marketing was included, nor of the social sciences to the extent sought by behaviorists. After completing his doctoral study in economics at Ohio State University, until he joined the Harvard Business School faculty in 1959, he taught economics for four years at the University of North Dakota. Prior to 1959, his writings were almost entirely on economic issues: labor; unionism, inflation, taxation, capitalism, and irrigation in North Dakota, the exception being, in 1958, an article titled "Are Advertising and Marketing Corrupting Society?" The year after going to Harvard he wrote his classic article "Marketing Myopia," and in 1962 his book *Innovation in Marketing*. These facts evidence subjective influences uncommon among marketing writers. But what are the reasons for Levitt's eclectic point of view, his mastery of the well-turned phrase, his urgency for practicality?

Levitt attributes much of his outlook to early upbringing and self-initiative in education. His practicality grew out of necessity. Of his childhood, he has written:[22]

> Rural childhood life . . . instilled (in him and his brother) curiosity about what made things work—also awareness of the burdens and benefits of direct labor. Thereby came a great respect for efficiency, economy, and value. Finding simpler, faster, easier, cheaper ways to get things done seemed common-sense sensible, especially when parents put much store in such matters and were observed practicing what they preached . . .

> Preaching was mostly explaining how things worked, and especially, with the rudimation of a grade-school education, how the polity and the economy worked; and it was nightly reading of cautionary fiction to the gathered family. Then there were the chores, which seemed ordinary parts of ordinary life.

> Later transported in extremis foreign into distant urbandom, everything instantly changed except what a decade (age 10) had so firmly fixed. Curiosity became resourcefulness, economy enterprise, efficiency advantage, value good judgment, direct labor responsibility and attentiveness, political economy justice, and stories imagination. All these in retrospective reconstruction surfaced as life's new requirements in the new foreign urban land. . . . The need to management became early need to achieve and master, and then to have impact and influence.

In the city, youthful inventiveness led to commercial self-education and entrepreneurship, knowledge of how the world works, advantage in developing "street smarts." Early teen-aged summer days included long bicycle explorations of the city, hanging out in second-hand magazine stores, a paper route, an outdoor co-ed boys' club summer swimming pool, and discovery of the public library.

> The library was "explored more intensely each day after every previous day's new exhilirating discoveries. . . . Martha Foley's collection of Best Short Stories of the year led to imitative attempts at Best-Short-Stories-of-the-Year writing. Then (the discovery of) American Plays. . . , leading somehow to Hemingway, H. H. Monroe, Chekhov, E. W. White, and James Thurber. . . . Everything mingled omniverously with everything else—a great continuous stream of exhiliration and discovery.

College experience opened the vision of an academic career:

> . . . an occupation at once stimulating, noble, and letting you order your own time, more or less. Economics was the field that beckoned, especially after learning to know Karl Marx, John Maynard Keynes, Joseph Schumpeter, and Thorstein Veblen, whose very variations, perversities, and attendant social commentaries made the field precisely that much more appealing. To see the world through different lenses generated a constant wish to see and understand more, to question and ruminate, all this facilitated by enormously learned and committed professors in all fields, especially astronomy, geology, physics, philosophy, literature, and, of course, the social sciences.

> In time the gaze landed professionally on the economics of petroleum pricing, which led serendipitously without formal training to marketing. Help came via Peter Drucker's *The Concept of the Corporation,* and, fortuitously from Malcolm McNair's "The Wheel of Retailing."

> Always the outsider, . . .but always conditioned by the experience that responsibility cannot be evaded or action avoided by flight into rhetoric.

Experience, practicality, and perspective! These are ingredients which have characterized and distinguished Levitt's contribution to marketing thought. When pressed further concerning his manner of research, he wrote:

> In 1946 I started a card file of handwritten excerpts (often long ones) from a wide range of authors, going back to undergraduate days. These were in either my or my wife's handwriting. . . . Once a week I'd file them, years later often spending long hours arranging and rearranging the file categories. . . . During our Chicago commuting days, on the train I read lots of novels and an eclectic mix of magazines, never the newspaper. . . . I was curious, interested, and ragpicker enough to want to save certain things I'd read; the range of subjects was not narrow, but included no business subjects or business disciplines; somehow I was constantly drawn back to arrange and re-arrange the file while adding to it over the years. . . . I stopped adding to it a few years ago, having earlier started three others—one a 3" x 5" file of short thoughts or ideas, of interesting or apt or colorful phrases, two, a file drawer of clippings, reprints, excerpts, and citations on marketing matters; and a third similar one on other business subjects, titles, and disciples.

What's now interesting is that I so often re-arranged the original 3″ x 5″ file. Surely the fact of this activity is in some way connected with what Bob Bartels is looking for. It reminds me also that over the years I've often re-read certain undergraduate and graduate school notes.

From this, ". . . a few connections dimly emerge:

Almost all my marketing writings reflect a consciousness of how technology unfolds and influences everything.

A belief that if things can't be understood in simple clear constructions they probably have not been visualized properly.

That feelings are more important than hard data or concrete artifacts.

That thinking things through is more productive than adding things up, but that, in human affairs, thinking that's not rooted in experience or close familiarity with conditions and events is probably wasteful and wrong.

That if things are worth saying they're better said with some attentiveness to easy communicability and to crafting for impact.

Among Levitt's most influential writings, in addition to "Marketing Myopia," are his books: *Innovation in Marketing* (1962), *Marketing: A Contemporary Analysis* (1964, 1972), *The Marketing Mode: Pathways to Corporate Growth* (1969), *Marketing for Business Growth* (1974), and *The Marketing Imagination* (1983, 1986).

WILLIAM LAZER

William Lazer is a scholar whose marketing career has had extraordinary breadth, whose interests have spanned the developmental stages of marketing thought, and whose writings have reflected academic, business, social, and governmental marketing interests. His competence has been founded in scholastic and practical, private and public, educational and administrative experience. His writings have been individual and collaborative, philosophic and technical. He has not confined himself to one point of view nor to a limited subject, but has moved innovatively on a broad front through thirty years of the development of marketing thought. He has been a Renaissance type in marketing.

Broad scholastic preparation enabled him to relate and contribute to the changing concepts and viewpoints which have evolved since 1950. Liberal arts undergraduate education at the University of Manitoba furnished an introductory appreciation of the social and behavioral sciences. That was followed by study at the University of Chicago, where the relevance of the interdisciplinary viewpoint to marketing was seen, in use of the Alderson and Cox book on marketing theory. There, too, he was introduced to statistical analysis, marketing research, marketing history, and the economics of pricing. Returning to Manitoba, he taught from traditional functional and institutional texts such courses as retailing, advertising, sales management, and marketing research.

He credits doctoral study at The Ohio State University, completed in 1956, with reinforcing his understanding of the basics of marketing, and with introducing him to its legal aspects, cost analysis, and its historic and philosophic aspects. Subsequently, at Michigan State University he became interested in business ethics and marketing management. Thus by the end of the 1950s Lazer had been oriented in the traditional and the transitional aspects of then-current marketing thought.

Further enrichment of his capability was added by his attendance at the Ford Foundation program at Harvard (1959–1960). He followed this with additional courses at M.S.U., including Systems Engineering and Stochastic Processes. Although he published some articles on mathematical models and operations research, quantitative considerations never replaced other interests in marketing.

In the early 1960s, new lines of thought opened. Contacts with Japanese professors started his interest in international marketing. Also, as a result of offering a course and presenting a paper on sales forecasting, consulting opportunities opened, confirming his conviction that his real interest was in "solving unstructured problems—major problems of the real world." An opportunity, in 1970, to project the conditions of living and marketing in 1985 started interest in futurism. This was repeated fifteen years later, solidifying his interest in demography, lifestyles, and the mature market.

Professional service also directed his endeavors. As President of the American Marketing Association, he undertook to establish relations with associations in other countries and to further consideration of certification and professionalism. Early in the 1970s, as Vice President for Education for the AMA, he became interested in consumerism and cochaired White House conferences on government-business relations, inflation, and trade negotiations.

Lazer's writings have been as diverse as the talents which produced them. Some of the principal ones, along with commentary,[23] are as follows:

Managerial Marketing: Perspectives and Viewpoints (with E. J. Kelley, 1958, 1962, 1967).
Accepting a position at Michigan State University got me into the area of marketing management. Gene Kelley and I got hooked up and developed our book of readings. . . . It started out as an investigation of literature reflecting the interdisciplinary approach—readings for our students—and it ended up being a book. This encouraged us to develop and publish articles on *Interdisciplinary Contributions to Marketing Management* (1959).

"Sales Forecasting: Key to Integrated Management," *Business Horizons,* Fall 1959.
I became interested in sales forecasting through teaching a course in the subject. . . . As the antecedent to strategic planning, and the role of marketing and sales forecasting in it, this article highlighted the importance of the sales forecasting process and indeed marketing and market environments as the key to planning a total business system.

"Systems Approach to Transportation," *Managerial Marketing* and *Distribution Age* (with E. J. Kelley, September 1960)
Early in my career I became interested in the systems approach to marketing . . . and this article on the distribution mix was one of the outcomes. According to Don Bowersox, this was a seminal article in physical distribution. . . . (In it) Gene Kelley and I may have helped lay some of the groundwork for the development of the 4 P's approach, breaking the marketing mix into three integrated areas: product and service mix, communications mix, and distribution mix, utilizing a systems approach.

Social Marketing: Perspectives and Viewpoints (with E. J. Kelley 1973).
I tend to disagree with some others [and probably have lost the case] on
how social marketing is defined. I think that social marketing is a discipline
like social anthropology or social psychology. Others have perceived social
marketing as the marketing of social programs. . . . My conception is that
there are different *approaches* to marketing, i.e., a managerial approach, a
social approach, a historical approach, etc.

The following are other titles in his production line:
Interdisciplinary Contributions to Marketing Management (1959).
"Philosophic Aspects of the Marketing Discipline" (late 1950s).
The Knowledge Industry: Research Consultants (1965).
Marketing Management: A Systems Approach (1971).
Marketing Management: Policies, Strategies, and Decisions (1973).
Myths and Reality in the Coming Decade (1980).
Marketing Management: Foundations and Practices (1983).
American Marketing Demographics (1987).

SHELBY D. HUNT

Shelby D. Hunt is known for his writings on franchising and macromarketing
but he is perhaps best known for his contributions concerning marketing theory
and the philosophy of marketing science. That he should be interested in
franchising would have been normal during the late 1960s and early 1970s, when
new specialized topics were being explored. It was equally normal at that time to
be responsive to the broadening concept of marketing, narrowed by some by
emphasis on marketing management and consumer behavior. Macromarketing
also became the area of breadth that interested him. It was also not unlikely that
he should have found interest in consideration of theory in marketing, as a result
of discussion given this topic during the previous decade.

Having majored in mechanical engineering as an undergraduate (1962), and in
business administration for his doctorate (1969), several conventional lines of
professional development were open to him; mathematical modeling, industrial
marketing, or consumer behavior. He himself has questioned why he did not
follow those directions and concluded that other circumstances became the
"drum" to which he marched. Three specific experiences became "critical
incidents that stimulated and channeled (his) thinking and research efforts. Each
was highly serendipitous.[24] He has related their occurrence.

While in a doctoral seminar in marketing theory taught by B. J. (Bud)
LaLonde at Michigan State University in 1966, he became concerned that the
students often seemed to "talk past" each other rather than engage in truly
productive interaction.

At that time, a neighbor, who was working on a Ph.D. in the Philosophy of
Science, . . . seemed to be able to critically analyze the issues debated in our
marketing theory class even though he knew nothing about "marketing."
He showed me that a major reason our class discussion was unproductive
was that we were failing to separate substantive disagreements from those
of a semantical nature. In short, as long as the discussants were using terms
and concepts in radically different ways, the communication process was
unlikely to resolve whatever *substantive* disagreements might have existed.

He introduced me to the intellectual tool kit of modern analytical philosophy, exemplified by the works of Richard Rudner and Carl Hempel. The works of these authors and others with a similar orientation substantially affected all of my future efforts in the area of marketing theory. Their approach to philosophy of science emphasized the importance of the twin values of *logic* and *clarity.* These values became central to me.

The second critical incident, he relates, occurred after joining the faculty of the University of Wisconsin—Madison—in 1969. An invitation from the Small Business Administration for submission of a research proposal to study the economic effects of franchising as a system of distribution in the United States was passed among the faculty and landed on his desk.

Urban Ozanne and I prepared the winning proposal and immediately immersed ourselves (for two years) in franchising. We put our other research efforts "temporarily" on hold, including my work on consumer behavior. . . . The project culminated in a monograph entitled *"The Economic Effects of Franchising"* (1971), and spawned a succession of publications and other research projects on franchising and channels of distribution.

A third critical incident, in 1976—equally unplanned—led to Hunt's interest and writing on macromarketing.

In July 1976, the *Journal of Marketing* published my article, "The Nature and Scope of Marketing." (presenting) my views on the nature of marketing, the nature of science, and what has come to be called the "Three Dichotomies Model." The following month, after attending an AMA Educators' Conference, Charles C. "Chuck" Slater (Colorado), who had read the article, called urgently inviting me to attend a special conference at the University of Colorado on the topic of macromarketing, which started that very evening. He persuaded me that missing this conference would be a serious professional lapse on my part, and I agreed to catch the "red-eye special" for Denver the next morning.

I had always believed that, although issues in marketing management were very important, the marketing discipline had a special obligation to devote more time to macromarketing topics.

Because of the success of that initial symposium, the original attendees decided to hold a macromarketing conference each year. Eventually these meetings culminated in the launching of the *Journal of Macromarketing*

These three serendipitous . . . incidents served to stimulate and channel my research efforts. Further, four values have guided my research: (1) logic, (2) clarity, (3) objectivity, and (4) the belief that marketing should devote more attention to the broader societal issues that have come to be called "macromarketing."

ROBERT BARTELS

Robert Bartels is best known in the marketing literature for his *History of Marketing Thought* (1976),[25] although his concern for form as well as substance of thought is expressed in *Marketing Theory and Metatheory* (1970). His published articles, many reprinted in the latter, span a forty-year period beginning in 1942. They express a progressive conceptualization of new frontiers of marketing thought and a continuing effort to search and state the broader meaning of marketing.

Such a natural interest grew out of receptivity to ideas, rather than out of an interest in marketing or business, per se. Proper nurturing fed this predilection.

During undergraduate study of marketing at Ohio State University (1935), two books lastingly influenced the perspective: *Man the Unknown,* by Alexis Carrel, showed man viewed as a whole—in his entirety; and *One Increasing Purpose,* by Francis Stocking, introduces a vision of a determined progression for betterment in human affairs. This has based the effort to see marketing in its enlarging wholeness, to state the "bigger" idea of what it represents. It has also been consistent with his scholastic effort to discern the causal laws or principles of marketing.

Graduate study at Northwestern University and at The Ohio State University added to the traditional rudiments of marketing, under Fred Clark and Harold Maynard, a concept taught by Horace Secrist: that research findings are determined, first, by the technologies one applies, and, second, by the subjective factors which determine his choice of both subject and methods.

Because the discipline of marketing was then scarcely forty years old, a seminar with Maynard introducing early writers, combined with the Secrist principle, led to correspondence with thirty-five leading marketing writers to ascertain what factors induced them to study marketing. This served as the basis for a dissertation, *Marketing Literature: Development and Appraisal* (1941), which ultimately became the *History of Marketing Thought.*

Imbued in the early 1940s with the gathering conviction that marketing had reached such a stage of maturity that its 'principles' could be postulated, he wrote for the *Journal of Marketing* during the period 1942–1968 articles relating to principles, marketing science, and general marketing. These appeared during the period when marketing was moving from macro to micro, from economic to social, and from verbal to quantitative. The challenge was, always, not to freeze a concept and periphery of marketing, but rather to seek the conceptual cohesion of the subject which would counter its increasing fragmentation and define its raison d'etre.

Not attracted to the managerial, quantitative, or consumer aspects of marketing, I exploited other areas to which interest and experience led. Early European travel and professional observation (1952) disclosed the relationship between mass production and mass marketing. An article concerning this was published in *Dun's Review and Modern Industry* (October 1954) and later in London and Paris.

A year's teaching and research in Greece (1954–55) was followed by collaboration with others in the AMA in publication of *Comparative Marketing: Wholesaling in Fifteen Countries* (ed.) (1963). Teaching a seminar in business and society yielded articles defining marketing as a social rather than merely a business institution. Reading Karl Polany's *Trade and Market in the Early Empires* inspired distinguishing domestic and foreign marketing systems on a cultural or anthropological basis. Confusion at the 1976 conference on macromarketing as to what the concept and term should mean led to the article "Macromarketing," judged the best *JM* article on marketing theory in 1979. Around-the-world teaching on the Semester-at-Sea ship was followed by *Global Development and Marketing* (1981).

In the context of the 1960s and 1970s, these topics were frontier probes of the heart and core of marketing, calling for an integration of the subject and a statement of whether marketing was for business or society, for the domestic or foreign market, for consumers or for people. Equivocation on these questions impelled writing "The Identity Crisis in Marketing," *JM,* (October 1974). The question still remains and it underlies this present effort to ascertain what and how leading academics think of the subject.

SPECIAL-INTEREST AREAS

Neither criticism of conventional marketing in the 1950s, nor incorporation of interdisciplinary concepts into marketing thought in the 1960s eliminated functional and institutional considerations from ongoing development of marketing thought. It did for a while reduce course offerings in salesmanship and credit management as marketing functions. It shifted sales management into marketing management, wholesaling into industrial distribution, institutions into channels, and advertising into promotion or marketing communications. Because these activities are indigenous to the marketing process, search for higher levels of research and theorization concerning them was inevitable. In some instances, this resulted in reconceptualization of the subject; in others, in application of interdisciplinary concepts to the specialized areas, as it had been to general management and study of consumer behavior. Four specialized areas in which new insights have enriched marketing thought are: physical distribution, sales management, international marketing, and marketing channels.

DONALD J. BOWERSOX

Donald J. Bowersox has been foremost among several who contributed to the development of physical distribution theory as a part of marketing thought. The activity and management of the physical distribution of products had been of disinterest to marketing scholars, as attention was given the negotiatory and promotional functions. It was discounted, too, because management was considered to be related to internal rather than to external activities. Moreover, transportation agencies were not considered as marketing institutions, and inventories were storage rather than investment. Of his introduction to this field, Bowersox has said:

I was involved in doctoral training at a point in time that the physical distribution concept was initially evolving. I had opportunity to work and socialize with young professors who were trying very hard to crystallize some basic concepts. . . . This opportunity provided the motivation for me to expend substantial effort to prove that I could carry my weight. The result was the publication of the first text in the field *Physical Distribution Management* (1960).[26]

The result of this experience was a fundamental change in my basic interests in the marketing discipline. I began to favor aspects of marketing that dealt with the physical side of product movement and storage. . . . From the initial work in basic cost relationships, theoretical development has been directed to channel concepts and interorganizational behavior. A second stream of development has been conceived with the strategic dimensions of integrating the total materials logistics management process.

Because of his insight into the relation of physical distribution to marketing Bowersox was pressed to answer further some specific questions.

1. What basic concepts were the "young professors" struggling with, and what in your frame of reference contributed to them and began to grow into what it did?

Two basic concepts were emerging in the literature at the time we began working in physical distribution. . . . The first was the concept of total cost. The second concerned systems analyses. The systems approach to problem solving gained prominence during World War II . . . but it did not receive extensive application to business until the early 1950s . . . I had had some experience with the concept in a military setting, and its extension and application to business appeared extremely appropriate.

At the time of this early work a prime dissatisfaction with marketing served as a motivating force, namely, the general neglect of the competitive impact of such physical distribution created factors as customer service performance. It appeared to many of us that marketing had seriously neglected the physical dimensions of performance. In fact, Professor Converse's *Other Half of Marketing* was a focal point of a great deal of dispute at that particular time. I would have to conclude that during the early 1950s management talent was not being effectively applied to physical distribution.

2. What perception of opportunities ahead confirmed the wisdom of your predilection for physical distribution?

At that time, as well as today, I continue to believe that physical distribution opportunities represent one of the most fertile areas for improving business productivity. It is not yet clear that the costs of physical distribution . . . represent only a portion of the total cost of logistics when purchasing, operations management, and physical distribution are combined.

Over the years, the gap between physical distribution and marketing has not narrowed. . . . As the behavioral dimensions of marketing became more sophisticated the field began to fragmentize, which, of course, is in direct contradiction to the basic notion of the marketing concept. Fragmentation as contrasted to further integration seemed to become the by-word of the 1960s and 1970s.

3. What internal growth led to your transition from basic cost relationships to channel concepts and interorganizational behavior, and then to PD management strategy?.

One of the primary motivations to thinking in terms of channel concepts was an increasing awareness that physical distribution performance occurred in a channel setting which involved many institutions other than those performing physical distribution activities.

My initial approach to this dilemma was to build upon concepts of specialization of labor. In fact, I was an early advocate of a concept known as channel separation. This concept advocates that institutions be bundled with respect to their role in the channel setting.

In other words, we began to specify that physical distribution intermediaries should be selected on their capabilities to perform physical distribution functions with a high degree of efficiency as a result of specialization. The most effective and efficient arrangement of physical distribution intermediaries might well be different than those selected for marketing competency.

When this concept evolved it became increasingly clear to me that the glue that held the channel together was in fact the behavioral dimensions of what I came to call in most of my writing from the 1970s forward the *interorganizational behavior issues* (IOB). IOB as contrasted to OB, was primarily centered on the behavioral relationships *between* channel members. To this date, I feel one of my more positive contributions to the literature is Chapter 5 in *Management in Marketing Channels* that deals with marketing negotiation.

In summary, my interest in the behavioral dimensions of channel was a result of a matured understanding of what makes channels work. I might add that my interest in behavior is not conflict resolution motivated, as is that of many other marketers. I believe that the prevailing state of a channel is cooperation and in fact channel solidarity is fundamentally the result of cooperative perceptions and reward sharing.

4. What new perceptions and conceptions were provided by your extensive business consultations?

This question hits at the essence of what I consider to be the major part of my career. . . . The discipline of physical distribution has been very fortunate in that over most of the last 30 years the field has had a hand-in-hand relationship with business in the practical implementation of theoretical concepts being propagated on the campuses. During the development period the academic community has been in a position to be somewhat prescriptive to the business community. For example, concepts of integrated organization, customer service measurement, functional distribution costing, system design concepts, location models, and planning procedures are concepts that in part evolved from campus research often completed in cooperation with major corporations. From concept to corporate implementation has been a process with a lot of give and take between a generation of professional managers who have been forging new roads in the industrial environment and the commitment of a select few universities to conducting research and developing physical distribution.

5. What reaction might you have had to comments that the field of PD has been descriptive rather than theoretical?

The criticism is in part based on the fact that a great deal of physical distribution research has been closely coordinated with business practitioners. . . . The final judge of theory is whether or not it has practical application. . . . I think this has been a problem of the marketing discipline overall and is best illustrated by the content of many marketing books that talk extensively about concepts and ideas that have little relevancy to real marketing practice and more often than not have never been empirically tested. . . . I agree that physical distribution literature and research has been highly descriptive; but, not at the neglect of theory generating activity.

6. How did your work break off from and probably exceed that of the other "young professors"?

My work eventually broke off from my contemporaries because of differences in areas of interest and the degree of funding that became available to pursue particular kinds of research effort.

7. How have these developments helped shape general marketing theory, if they have; and why not if they haven't?

This is a capstone question. I still have considerable concern that in reality the contribution of physical distribution toward shaping a general marketing theory has been minimal. I believe this can be directly traced to the separation of the disciplines which I have discussed earlier and a general desire among marketing people not to pursue integration. I have found the structure and the direction of the American Marketing Association to be prohibitive to integration. Without such an integration, it is difficult to comprehend furthering the theory of an arms length discipline. I am presently quite encouraged by the potential that is coming from the leaders of the Academy of Marketing Sciences to foster such integration. As such I am devoting what energies I can to encourage integration with marketing through the Academy. However, at this point I am more concerned with developing the general strategic theory of business which integrates across disciplines.

GILBERT A. CHURCHILL, JR.

Gilbert A. Churchill, Jr. specialized in another area whose roots were in early-in-this-century marketing thought: salesmanship and sales management, now often referred to as sales force performance and sales force management. So long as salesmanship was a "born" and not a "learned" talent, rules of thumb were applied and taught. Sales management was responsibility for recruiting, training, scheduling, etc. Those were the kinds of offerings deemed questionably worthy of university credit when business programs were reviewed in the 1950s. As management became an integration of marketing with other business functions, and as behavioral concepts were introduced into interpersonal relations, these two subjects assumed different meaning. Churchill was one of several who effected the reconceptualization.

After obtaining his MBA degree, Churchill worked as a sales engineer, where competition was intense, customers' needs according to specifications, opportunities for customer service minimal, and prices negotiable. Requests to management for price flexibility to meet competition, however, often "fell upon deaf ears."[27]

> After completing my doctoral degree, I commented to two colleagues on my sales experience and the frustration of having the sales manager's orders countermanded by executives at higher corporate levels. Orville Walker suggested that I suffered role conflict and role ambiguity. I was surprised that there were scientific names for the dilemma! . . . Up to that time, I had done no research that focused specifically on the question of salesperson productivity.

> Orville Walker, Neil Ford, and I thought the problem worthy of consideration, and we systematically began to explore the literature on salesperson performance and related literature that dealt with role conflict and role ambiguity as related to individual productivity. . . . We felt that the subject had research potential, and we initiated a program that became a commitment for each of us for more than 15 years.

In the process of sounding out their initial convictions, however, they experienced the discouragement which others also have found in disagreement between old and new points of view when thought is in a state of change. Referring to a conversation with colleagues, Churchill wrote:

> It occurred at the University of Chicago during a conference addressing multivariate models in marketing. A group of us were sitting around a table one evening at the close of the day's session discussing our current research interests. When I mentioned that mine was understanding the factors that impact a salesperson's performance, the unanimous response of those around the table was "Why bother with a nonsense topic like that" when there were so many interesting things happening in consumer behavior, models, promotion, pricing, and a number of other topics that were "hot" at that time. I am not sure if many people can appreciate how devastating a comment like that can be, particularly to someone at an early stage in his career.

After that conversation, the three of them, while recognizing that it was a high-risk topic, none the less decided to go ahead because they were personally interested in the subject, and they felt that it was extremely important.

To a considerable extent, works speak for themselves, but Churchill has also cited impressive objective evidence of the impact of their work upon the field:

1. One of our articles won the William O'Dell award for the outstanding article appearing in the *Journal of Marketing Research* in a given year.
2. Among those attending the doctoral consortium, before 1980 practically no one did a dissertation in the area of salesperson performance. Since then, approximately eight percent of those attending the consortium have had some aspect of salesperson behavior and/or performance as the central focus of their dissertation.

3. During the mid-1970s it was virtually impossible to put together a session on sales force management at one of the national AMA conferences. Today many more people in the discipline seem to be interested in the subject.

4. In our development of measures, we put together a set of measures by which we could assess the key constructs in our investigations. We had several of the instruments copyrighted and currently receive 15–25 requests per year to use one or more of them, suggesting that at least this many people are interested in the topic.

5. Of 116 articles on sales force performance published since 1918, over one-fourth of them seem to be traceable to our work, as judged by their positioning statements and literature references.

6. Churchill received the Distinguished Educator of the Year award from the AMA, with the following comment made in the anonymous nominating papers: "In sales management, Churchill and his colleagues did much more than simply add to the body of knowledge in an accepted area of marketing—they legitimized sales management as an arena for serious academic research."

ROBERT J. HOLLOWAY

Robert J. Holloway has combined an eclectic academic perspective, attributable to study with Roland S. Vaile, and familiarity with diverse world cultures, to make a contribution in the name of environmentalism and international marketing. This was a facet of marketing which emerged during his professional years (1950–1987) but which has been tardily assimilated into marketing thought. Evidence of this is in imposition of a requirement by the AACSB that business students be exposed to internationalism in their curricula. Holloway has commented on the evolution of marketing thought relative to the two influences which have so motivated and characterized his work: eclecticism and internationalism:

> Because of the eclectic influence, I was never very impressed with principles of marketing, for they usually turned out to be principles of psychology, economics, or something else. . . . In early years we had a great deal of economics (not today's economics) that was the basis for much of marketing. Vaile, Grether, and Cox exemplified that. My feeling is that we have gone too far in the direction of management and away from economics. As we move into the 'thinner' atmosphere, we get further away from substance. To emphasize marketing management is to deemphasize marketing.[28]

Eclecticism has been closely related to environmentalism in Holloway's work, often in collaboration with Bob Hancock, and in his writings on environmental influence he has made his most important contribution to the field of marketing. However, in recent years he has become interested more in international marketing, which he also interprets in terms of environmentalism and eclecticism.

> To move to international marketing management is to move well beyond the basics. . . . The international situation necessitates dealing with

environments—that is, what is different from nation to nation. If marketing is different it is because the environment is different. We should be studying environments, but little of that has been done.

I think that this area is poorly developed in marketing. International marketing is really national marketing—marketing in different countries. What is different is the culture or environment that casts its shadow on marketing. We are miles behind in this area. . . . Developments in international marketing have come from business. Our articles on multinational corporations came long after they existed. Our attention to bartering, matrix organizations, sourcing, etc. have all come long after the fact. We have not led. . . . We teach marketing as if the U.S. model were the only one in the world. . . . Business is far ahead of academia in international matters.

Domestic, foreign, international, and comparative marketing are concepts like social, societal, organizational, and interorganizational which have been used ambiguously in marketing thought and parlance. But as they represent substantial and not merely semantical categories, clear deliniation of them is essential in the general structure of marketing. Until the integration of international marketing with basic marketing is more fully achieved, this may continue as one of the specialized or fragmented areas of marketing.

LOUIS P. BUCKLIN

Louis P. Bucklin was another who in the late 1950s conceived new models where such had not existed, and the evolution of his thought in channel function and structure illustrates the manner in which strategies have been lifted to a level of theorization, to the enhancement and enrichment of the marketing literature. Personal, environmental, and academic influences all contributed to the formation of his frame of reference, but it was the creative process of conceptualization that gave new direction to his thought and to the marketing discipline. He has said:[29]

Throughout my career, the marketing topics of greatest interest to me have centered upon the vertical organization of markets and the efficiency of those markets. The origin of these interests lies in my doctoral student days at Northwestern in the late 1950s. There, one of my most exciting areas of study was that of the economic structure of markets under Richard Heflebower, a noted industrial organization theorist of the times. There, I met a conceptual framework which provided a rationale as to why markets were organized as they were, and the impact of organization upon the behavior of the firm and consumer welfare.

Simultaneously, I was intrigued by the absence of any comparable theoretical framework to explain the rationale behind vertical market structures. The literature of distribution channels was largely of an institutional and descriptive character. Although certainly the best of this work, as represented in the writings of E. T. Grether, Wroe Alderson, Reavis Cox, Richard M. Clewett, David Revzan, and Delbert Duncan, was rich in provocative ideas concerning the determinants of channel structure, there was no clear, simple set of principles. Ideas concerning flows, functions, and especially Alderson's notions of sorting, offered important and illuminating insights into the underlying activities to be found in channels, but provided no normative or predictive framework. To a hopeful, young doctoral student, this looked like fertile ground.

The first tangible outcome of this view was my doctoral dissertation. In this I endeavored to lay out a methodology by which the structure of the channel could be explained through an analysis of how marketing functions were linked together to obtain maximum efficiency. While in retrospect the dissertation served to advance my thinking, it did not advance the cause of model building in channels to any great degree. Influenced by the previous work, it carried with it a large element of description and institutionalism.

Not until the middle of the 1960s was further progress made on this topic. Perhaps more by accident than by design, I had initiated a number of research projects dealing with a different problem, that of consumer shopping behavior. In an early classroom encounter with some inquisitive undergraduates, I encountered difficulty defending some of the traditional concepts that had evolved in the classification of goods. One consequence was an attempt to put together a better framework for this classification. This resulted in the article "Retail Strategy and the Classification of Consumer Goods," in *The Journal of Marketing* in 1963 and reprinted often since that time. In this piece I endeavored to clarify the importance of consumer shopping needs, the determinants of these needs, and how varying determinants resulted in the choice of different types of retail facilities. This paper was subsequently followed by a number of empirical studies which endeavored to measure consumer shopping search activity, especially in the context of choice of shopping facility.

These conceptual and empirical studies suggested that consumer needs, and the resultant impact of these needs upon shopping behavior, was an important factor driving channel structure. Different retailers were essentially providers of specific types of services, services that offered buyers the opportunity to reduce their investment in shopping time and transport in exchange for a higher price. That is to say, the consumer had the choice of performing these services himself or purchasing the products with these services bundled into a higher price for the product. The selection of retailer was formed from this basic tradeoff.

The key to my work in channel theory was the gradual recognition that channel structures could be systematically linked to this tradeoff. Higher levels of service typically evoked the need for a longer, and more elaborate, set of channel institutions. In a developed economy, with economies of scale in manufacturing, it could be shown that lengthier distribution systems were more efficient at providing these services. The spanning of significant expanses of time and space by direct, or other short channels, where consumers need few services, e.g. they could buy in large quantities, was less efficient.

The initial perceptions having been made and classified, the fitting together of ideas in Bucklin's thought, as also related by others, occurred in that process of integration and generalization which is the essence of theory building. He continues:

The combination of these two ideas, e.g. the tradeoff in services/price between the channel and the consumer and the relationship between channels structure and services provided, provided the basis for my channel theory. The initial dawning of these insights was a moment of considerable excitement. I can still recall the day, sitting in my office at Berkeley, when the idea emerged that a longer channel was more efficient in providing extensive services than a shorter channel. I had been doodling with some diagrams of cost for different channel structures and their relationship to delivery time. The sudden insight of superimposing a cost function to represent the relation of consumer buying costs to different service levels supplied by the channel provided the impetus. From this eventually came my theorem that, under competitive conditions, channel structures would gravitate to those which would minimize total service costs to the consumer, where total costs included those incurred by the consumer as well as the members of the commercial channel. These ideas were subsequently published in a number of places, including *A Theory of Distribution Channel Structure* from Berkeley and *Vertical Marketing Systems* from Scott, Foresman.

Underlying this concept of a normative channel was the more central notion that many marketing phenomena may be understood from the balancing of opposing economic forces. This view played a central role in my thinking and work since this point of time. It appeared in my theoretical study of organizational processes in distribution, "A Theory of Distribution Channel Control." Here, I was concerned about conceptualizing the costs and benefits of control. It also played a major role with much of the work I undertook with regard to measuring and understanding productivity in marketing.

My concerns with productivity in marketing arose quite naturally from the study of distribution channels. If one examines the cost of marketing, the great bulk of the cost may be attributed to the operation of middleman type operations. Consequently, if substantial savings are to be obtained in the cost of providing goods and services to consumers, the great bulk of these must fall within the distribution sector.

Many key issues in the study of productivity in marketing revolve around the problem of changing levels of channel service. Reductions in the level of service, such as those occurring from the increasing use of self service, can give the appearance of productivity improvements in marketing. Consequently the empirical study of productivity change in marketing requires the development of mechanisms whereby variations in service levels can be controlled. The understanding of the concept of the normative structure of distribution channels, reflecting the tradeoffs between channel service and self service are helpful in developing these controls. My monograph, *Productivity in Marketing,* published by the American Marketing Association in 1979, represented the culmination of that work and served to stimulate numerous other studies of a similar genre.

During the 1980s, this concern with efficiency has manifested itself in research projects oriented to both macro and micro problems. At the macro level, a major public policy question is the maintenance of competitive conditions in markets where concentration is growing through larger establishments and mergers across evolving retail systems. In another vein, a study of gray market channels and their differential effect upon consumer versus manufacturer welfare has been instituted.

A third research stream, at the micro level, involves the modeling of strategic planning in distribution channels by producers and others. Again we see here a situation where there is a great deal of description of alternative strategic practices, but little general theory available to tie the various parts together. In particular, there again appear to be a number of tradeoffs facing the firm. The resolution of the costs and benefits of these tradeoffs may provide the channel strategists with fresh insight for decisions and, with some luck, the researcher with a better than average probability of making significant contributions to the literature.

LOUIS W. STERN

Louis W. Stern has been a leading interpreter of the marketing channels concept. Initially, a channel was a sequence of institutions through which products and/or title passed. Then it was seen that services and other "flows" established their own sequence of agencies. Usually, channels were interpreted in economic terms, and with the availability of Census of Distribution data in the 1930s they were conceived as bookkeeping or accounting structures. Managers of channels—"channel captains"—were differentiated from managers of institutions. And eventually, through behavioral concepts, interpersonal and interorganizational relations were deemed the essence of the channel. It has been in this latter interpretation that Stern has been eminent. In 1986 he wrote:[30]

> It is amazing that the study of marketing channels seems to be coming of age as a truly scholarly pursuit. . . . Despite the work of wonderful thinkers as Grether (1939), Cox (1962), Alderson (1957), Breyer (1934), and others, the study of marketing channels remained, in the minds of most marketing scholars . . . downright anti-intellectual.

> The turnaround has been slow and tortuous, and I'd be the first to admit that we're not "there" yet. (I suspect "there" is where the study of consumer behavior is or where the development of marketing models of advertising and promotion is.) But we're getting better.

> What is fascinating about this year's award symposium is that the recipients of the awards had a great deal to do with the "awakening" of channels. Pete Bucklin's work on channel structure, focusing on service output levels and normative channels (1966), was a motivating force to those of us, in later years, who took his work and popularized it. . . . Frank Bass would probably be astonished to hear someone say that he had anything to do with the "awakening" of channels. But it's true! . . . As editor of the *Journal of Marketing Research,* he accepted an article entitled 'Power Measurement in the Distribution Channel' written by Adel El-Ansary and me and published in February, 1972.

> Shelby Hunt played a critical role in the process as well. His May 1974, *JMR* article "Power in a Channel of Distribution: Sources and Consequences"

with Jack Nevin, building on the article by Adel and me, served as a catalyst to all sorts of future work.

Stern's account of how his interest and insight into channel management developed may serve to encourage others in a formative stage of creativity:

> My original attraction to the channels area was through a course I had in industrial organization economics as an undergraduate at Harvard. . . . It became clear to me that the industrial organization economics orientation was not going to lead to major new insights for me, primarily because my training in economics was relatively superficial. I had never been forced to learn the mathematics that has become so central to economics. I also became increasingly aware that economics is a very myopic discipline. Due to its heavy reliance on the price mechanism to explain almost all human behavior, it seemed to be missing some of the blood and guts of marketplace and particularly institutional interactions.

> The "thunderbolt" clapped on a warm spring evening in 1966 as I sat on Jim Heskett's front porch in Columbus, Ohio. Jim, a colleague of mine at Ohio State, turned to me as we were chatting about research interests and said, "Lou, have you ever thought about looking at marketing channels from an interorganizational behavior perspective?" The earth shook, angels appeared on the lawn and sang Bach's B Minor Mass, and horns could be heard from as far away as Jericho! It dawned on me that if I adopted such a perspective, it would permit me to get into all sorts of literature that were exciting to me, from such fields as sociology, political science, and psychology, while at the same time freeing me from the tyranny of studying the 27 functions of merchant wholesalers. Jim's inspirational question led to a proceedings paper, published by the AMA in 1966, entitled "Channel Control and Inter-Organization Management." That was the beginning.

Along with the flash of inspiration which comes usually only after a lot of searching thought looking for the "light," there also often come doubts and discouragements concerning a new idea before it begins to grow. Stern tells of three such discouragements along the way.

1. When, in 1967, Heskitt and I finished the first draft of a paper, I gave the paper to Theodore N. Beckman (an early winner of the Converse Award) to obtain his comments. He walked into my office several weeks later, handed me the paper, said "What you've written sounds like sophistry to me," and walked out. I spent the rest of the day at Forest Lawn Cemetery in an effort to pick up my spirits!

2. At various stages of my career, I have been fortunate to interact with and be supported by the Marketing Science Institute. In the early 1970s, I again approached the MSI, asking the then executive director (Bob Buzzell, of whom I am very fond) whether MSI would be interested in working with me on other projects I might conjure up. In a phone conversation he said, "Sure, we'd like to work with you, Lou, but please don't send us any of that power and conflict crap."

3. In 1975, Harper Boyd, editor of *JMR,* asked me whether I would be willing to write a review paper for him on the marketing channels area. . . Four years later, after losing two collaborators, and after countless drafts and long, exhausting comments on reviewers' comments, Jerry Wind, then editor of the *Journal of Marketing,* made the unilateral decision to publish the paper, entitled "Distribution Channels as Political Economies: A Framework for Comparative Analysis." It was published in 1980 and was the recipient of the Harold H. Maynard Award the year after it was published.

The message is a simple one. If you give up after receiving a few lumps, you probably don't deserve the loving cup!

Stern also wrote of the state of the arts in channel analysis. He perceives that the study of marketing channels is at a critical point, and that there are several paths that may need to be traveled before the area can reach maturity.

First, while I believe that taking a political economy perspective to the study of channels is the "right" way to go, perspective merely provides a framework. It is not a theory. Economic and behavioral variables must be wedded in some holistic manner in order to understand and map channel interactions. . . . My orientation is that of a prospector, continuously searching the basic disciplines. . . . I have borrowed heavily from transaction cost economics, decision theory, attribution theory, and information economics, including principal-agent theory.

Most studies in the channels area have been descriptive. . . . It is time to move on to predictions of processes and outcomes. . . . One reason for slowness to mature is that we are still wrestling with our methodologies. . . . We're ready to look for significant relationships among critical variables and to build some important predictive models using the excellent theories available to us.

Second, we must get more analytical without losing sight of management realities. We're dealing with interorganizational, not interpersonal, phenomena. . . . I'm not sure that mathematical economics will be helpful here. . . . There is danger of becoming too sterile when applying game theoretic paradigms. . . . Our research should lead us to managerial suggestions for improved performance.

Third, and most important, there are those who argue that, because of the "squishiness" of such constructs as power and conflict, we ought to abandon them. . . . I cannot be sympathetic with any call to walk away. . . . If we can't get a handle on them now, we will eventually. . . . Our measurement techniques are not appropriate to the task. We've got to try harder, that's all.

CONCLUSIONS

A survey of marketing thought and of writers' subjective influences was made in 1939, and a similar survey was again made in 1987. It might have been expected that a century of scholarly work had evolved a comprehensive or general theory of marketing. Evidence from the latter survey, which could not have been known from the earlier alone, is that while marketing thought has increased in scope and changed in composition, according to those who developed it, it has not evolved into a cohesive whole. Hence the question: Is there a *whole* of marketing that is greater than the sum of its *parts?* The scholars surveyed have here expressed their views concerning this. Their assessment may evoke further discussion. All that is needed here is the perspective which a brief summary might provide. A few significant contrasts might be pointed out.

1. Implicit in the diversity of subjects constituting "parts" of marketing is quest for understanding what marketing *is,* what it is really about, how it should be defined. It has been defined as a process, as institutional activity, a realm of management; as an economic institution and as a process of exchange common to many types of interaction; as private and public enterprise; as provincial and global; as particular and universal. No integrating concept has been advanced upon which could be based a comprehensive theory, defining marketing, for example, as the institutional means of society for meeting its consumption needs, at home and abroad, in all types of market situations.

2. Fragmentation rather than integration is said to characterize the discipline. Earlier in this century, there was a general concept of marketing comprising functions and institutions. These were specialized areas of research and practice. Subsequently, the central concept was restated and functions and institutions were given consideration somewhat apart from more general marketing. In recent years, some specializations have constituted almost the whole of marketing to those concerned with them. Consumer behavior, management technology, research methodology, physical distribution, and international marketing are areas of thought which have not been integrated into a cohesive general theory.

3. Marketing thought development is shown to have followed a pattern of successive waves of acceptance, popularity, dissatisfaction, and decline. Illustrative was the traditional concept of marketing held from 1900 to 1950. After its structure had been standardized, it was the sole framework for understanding marketing until the managerial concepts superceded it, students found the subject boring and impractical, and business school curriculum studies found it intellectually undemanding. This was followed by management decision making, and by consumer behavior, which it is reported here have also declined somewhat from their peak of interest. Innovation results from infusion of new concepts; declines from the lack of new conceptual discoveries and from retirement of leaders who have espoused and developed them. A succession of concepts of marketing have been left unintegrated.

4. Constructive appraisal has been expressed by some of the more mature contributors to marketing thought, possibly because they see in historical context its mission and potential which a short-run viewpoint does not reveal. The role of the American Marketing Association and the character of the professional journals have been faulted for giving no inducement to integration and for publishing articles too technical for general readership

or of research too untested to be of practical significance. Such indictments are inseparable from prevailing academic standards of graduate programs, peer esteem, recruitment criteria, and tenure and promotion requirements. They also reflect prevailing relations of business and academia. In its first formative stage, marketing thought was developed by university scholars; rarely did men in business conceptualize and construct theory. More recently, it is claimed that research in business is ahead of that reported in universities. Accordingly, some scholars have reported here the high priority they place upon maintaining close contacts with business in their discipline.

As the marketing discipline approaches the beginning of its second century, new assessments will be made of the role which marketing should play in business and in society. Significant in determination of the assessment which scholars make, and of their contributions which follow, will be the subjective influences upon their thinking: their education, experiences, personal influences, private convictions, peer and professional pressures, and awareness of the expection which society holds of marketing.

ENDNOTES

[1] Robert Bartels, *The History of Marketing Thought,* 2d ed. (Columbus, OH: Grid, Inc., 1976); see pp. 245–259.

[2] *Op. cit.,* p. 249.

[3] *Op cit.* p. 257.

[4] *Op.cit.,* p. 248.

[5] Cited in an address by Philip Kotler, 1987.

[6] Letter dated April 15, 1987.

[7] Letter dated December 17, 1986.

[8] Letter dated February 26, 1987.

[9] Letter dated April 29, 1987.

[10] Letter dated July 21, 1987.

[11] Letter dated May 27, 1987.

[12] "Marketing Science and Organizational Behavior," from a paper presented at the 1986 Paul D. Converse Awards Conference.

[13] Letter dated March 27, 1987.

[14] Letter dated April 13, 1987.

[15] Letter dated April 15, 1987.

[16] Letter dated March 21, 1987.

[17] Letter dated March 30, 1987.

[18] Sidney J. Levy, "Interdisciplinary Marketing Study," 1982, with letter dated March 4, 1987.

[19] Letter dated April 13, 1987.

[20] Letter dated March 16, 1987.

[21] Letter dated April 28, 1987.

[22] Letters dated February 3 and March 10, 1987.

[23] Letters dated February 26 and March 27, 1987.

[24] Letter dated March 27, 1987.

[25] Initially published as *Development of Marketing Thought* (Homewood, Ill: Richard D. Irwin, Inc., 1962).

[26] Letter dated April 26, 1987.

[27] Letter dated February 26, 1987.

[28] Letter dated May 13, 1987.

[29] Letter dated August 17, 1987.

[30] "Vanity Fair Trade: Reflections of a Channels Person," A Paper Delivered at the Paul D. Converse Awards Symposium, University of Illinois at Urbana-Champaign, May 18, 1986.

PIONEERS IN
MARKETING THOUGHT

A

Appendix A consists of excerpts from correspondence carried on with pioneers in marketing thought in 1940 and 1941. Each was asked to recall the influences that had contributed to shaping his interest in and outlook upon marketing. Their replies are here presented.

HUGH E. AGNEW

My first venture in the marketing field was in my father's store in Kunkle, Ohio. He kept what is known as a "general store," and I worked in that store. Also, during that time I rode horseback through the country peddling *The Life of Barnum.* Afterwards, the family moved to Hillsdale, Michigan, which was a larger city, and there I worked on the college paper as a typesetter. Now, I realize that these do not exactly correspond to the "eminent thinkers who may have influenced me," but they were real influences, nevertheless.

I bought a country newspaper soon after leaving the University of Michigan. This was in part because of a natural flair for writing and editorial work, partly because of the modest success I had had with college publications, and partly because it seemed to be the only avenue open to me at that time to get into editorial work. Naturally, I became very much interested in advertising. This was stimulated by the fact that in order to build up a larger printing business, I used direct mail advertising for soliciting printing in two or three narrowly specialized fields. This was quite successful and gave me a little of the "feel" of what could be actually done with advertising.

In 1912, I received a bid from a man in Canton, Illinois, who wanted to start a much larger newspaper than I had had before, and I went there as manager, staying about a year. This enlarged my contact, particularly with foreign advertising. Because of some strong feeling I had about the unbusinesslike way in which advertising was handled, I wrote several articles in publications which corresponded to the advertising publications of today. I got into some controversies which encouraged me in writing more than I had done previously.

In 1913, I had an opportunity to go to the University of Washington as instructor in Journalism, primarily devoting my time to advertising. By this time, some very able books had appeared, notably Scott's *Psychology of Advertising* and *The Theory and Practice of Advertising.* Also Earnest Elmo Calkins had brought out his *Modern Advertising,* and Cherington, the first book on marketing. He called it *Advertising as a Business Force,* which was not a good title for it, as it was really a book on marketing.

These books influenced my teaching, and I began writing to other teachers in regard to the work that we were trying to do. The president of the university, Mr. Suzzalo, thought that I was getting too much interested in outside activities and invited me to disassociate myself from the university. Naturally, I accepted the invitation.

Next year, I went to A. Schilling and Company to work in their advertising department, and as the war soon came on, I was promoted to sales manager; that is, I had charge of the hiring and firing of their sales force. As I recall, I did not actually have the title of sales manager at the time. As the war became more severe and interfered more and more with routine business, I soon found that another field would be more inviting, and I joined *Western Advertising,* which was just getting ready to start, as their editor. There I continued writing, and I also wrote a considerable amount for other magazines, such as in the grocery and trade journals.

In 1920, I was asked to come to New York University, and about the same time received an invitation from *Printers' Ink* to do editorial work for them. As the two could be combined, I jumped at the opportunity. For about two years, I continued writing regularly for *Printers' Ink,* along with my university work.

1940

THEODORE N. BECKMAN

The most important contribution to my experience and training has probably come from the many and varied contacts I have enjoyed over the years with business groups and business individuals. My varied contacts with leaders in the fields of marketing, economics, and statistics have also played their part in enriching my background and contributing to my thinking on marketing subjects.

When I studied marketing in 1919, I was impressed by the misunderstandings of the wholesaler's position in the field of distribution and the lack of sympathy in the treatment of that institution in the few books then available. As I recall, all of our discussion of the wholesaler centered about the question of going around him. It happened that I had had some contacts with wholesalers prior to that time.

From my limited experience I felt that the treatment of the wholesaler was entirely erroneous. I, therefore, set out in 1920, when I began to do my graduate work, to find out who was right about the wholesaler. It was nothing but a matter of sheer curiosity on my part. I had absolutely no axe to grind. That is how I came to take as subject for my Master's thesis "The Wholesale Trades of Columbus, Ohio."

For this purpose I studied intensively several wholesale concerns operating in the grocery business, in dry goods, and in hardware. The results of this study convinced me more than ever that the few writers on marketing at that time knew practically nothing about the subject. My appetite was thus whetted and I continued with my investigations, with the idea of making some contribution to the subject of marketing by exploring a field that was practically unknown. This task required much more time than I anticipated, since most of the material had to be gathered at first hand from various wholesale houses located in different parts of the United States except the Pacific Coast.

I finally succeeded, after six years of constant research, in preparing the manuscript for my book on *Wholesaling,* which was published in 1926. It may thus be said that this book resulted from sheer curiosity to explore a relatively unknown area of our marketing structure. When I say unknown, I mean unknown to academicians.

Early in 1921 the dean of our College of Commerce, Dr. J. E. Hagerty, urged me to become instructor of the Columbus chapter of the Institute on Credit of the National Association of Credit Men. Never having had any courses on the subject, for credits and collections were at that time taught by very few schools, and having no familiarity whatsoever with existing literature in the field, I hesitated to accept the appointment. The urging, however, persisted and I succumbed to the pressure, largely out of deference to and respect for Dr.

Hagerty. My class in credits and collections consisted of businessmen, some of whom had had as high as fifteen years of practical experience. It became necessary, therefore, for me to study the subject both intensively and extensively to gain as much practical knowledge as possible. To accomplish the latter purpose, I spent a great deal of my time during the first year in the credit offices of the various concerns in Columbus, Ohio.

When the course was introduced at the University in the summer of 1922, I found the literature inadequate and completely out of date. Our readings, therefore, had to be supplemented with lectures based upon my studies of the practical operations of credit departments. The more familiar I became with credit and collection management problems and techniques and with the underlying theory, the more dissatisfied I was with the existing textbook material and other miscellaneous readings. It was thus purely a matter of necessity to provide adequate material for my teaching that I started out deliberately in 1922 to prepare a book on credits and collections. This book was published in 1924 and is now in its fourth edition.

Our textbook *Principles of Marketing* also resulted largely from an experience similar to that described above. It was a matter of supplying suitable text material for our classes in marketing. We felt that our points of view were somewhat different from all but one of the existing textbooks. Our organization seemed more teachable, and we thought that we had had more practical experience than some of the writers, and therefore could enrich the material with many more useful illustrations. As time advanced, our ideas became more crystallized and we have tended to put more and more emphasis on principles and relatively less on practical illustrative material.

1941

NEIL H. BORDEN

I came to Harvard after taking my undergraduate work at the University of Colorado. Here I came under the influence of the case approach and the training that I received as a student, followed by subsequent work in case collection and association with men such as Professor M. T. Copeland, guided pretty much my thinking regarding marketing.

Following my graduation in 1922, I served as a case collector in the Harvard Bureau of Business Research. In 1923-24 I acted as an instructor in marketing, under Professor Copeland, teaching his *Problems in Marketing.* I also assisted Professor Daniel Starch in his advertising course. Starch's interest in advertising had come from his training as a psychologist, and his teaching method was different, although he made some use of cases. When he left the School, I was put in charge of Advertising, and I immediately set about putting the course on a case basis. Out of this effort came my original volume, *Problems in Advertising,* which has been followed by two subsequent editions. The case approach was also used in Volume II of the Harvard Business Reports on "Cooperative Advertising by Trade Associations." I also collaborated with Professor Copeland in Volume 6, Harvard Business Reports, "Industrial Marketing."

In monograph "Determination of Confusion in Trade-Mark Conflict Cases," grew out of a consulting job. My work in marketing and advertising had led me into fields of market research and I had also become very much interested in brand problems. When attorneys for the Stetson Hat Company put to me the problem of determining the confusion of consumers between their trade-mark and that of a competitor, I was interested in the task and took on the job with the understanding that I might subsequently publish my findings.

The monograph on "A Test on the Consumer Jury Method of Ranking

294

Advertisements" naturally grew out of my work in advertising. In this study, Mr. Osgood S. Lovekin, as associate, collaborated.

The study of "Marketing Policies of the California Walnut Growers Association" developed as the result of a request of the United States Farm Credit Administration that I act as consultant in marketing.

The monograph "Merchandise Testing as a Guide to Consumer Buying," written by Mrs. M. T. Gragg, with whom I collaborated, is part of an extensive research which was undertaken as the result of a gift from Mrs. A. W. Erickson for a study of the economics of advertising. I am now completing the manuscript of this study and hope to publish it in the spring. It represents by far the most extensive research writing effort that I have undertaken. In this work I have departed from the straight business administrative approach to advertising and have attempted an appraisal of advertising effects, not only from a business standpoint but from a social standpoint as well.

1940

RALPH F. BREYER

I think that my undergraduate and graduate education at the Wharton School, Univeristy of Pennsylvania, has been one of the significant contributions to my knowledge of marketing. The usual personal contacts with men in the field that one makes while teaching the subject at a large university in a metropolitan center have also added considerably to my knowledge of this field. A few research projects have done likewise.

I think that I probably turned to the teaching of marketing, rather than some other subject, partly through natural predilection for the subject and partly by accident. My father was a retail food merchant, so that I was brought up in the retail end of marketing. Immediately after graduating from the Wharton School I took a position in the selling field. Shortly thereafter I was offered the opportunity of returning to the Wharton School and teaching in the Commerce and Transportation Department. Of the courses I was asked to teach, one dealt with marketing. This course was taught largely on a commodity basis. I finally inherited the lectureship of this course, and, in order to improve the reading assignments and also to fill what I thought to be a serious gap in our marketing literature at that time, I wrote *Commodity Marketing*. Shortly after this was published I began thinking about methods of integrating the study of marketing. I started a manuscript on this subject when the N.R.A. and A.A.A. were established. These latter had such tremendous import for marketing that they induced me to reduce my original manuscript and incorporate these new developments, along with some of my ideas on integration in the volume, *The Marketing Institution.*

I rather think that my natural aptitude for seeking the wholeness and order in marketing phenomena, and other phenomena for that matter, along with my serious impairment of hearing, which has made it impossible for me to establish the practical contacts that may have turned my work in that direction, have in large part influenced my point of view in marketing.

1940

RALPH STARR BUTLER

I have, perhaps, a unique story to tell because, as far as I am aware, I wrote the first book on the marketing of manufactured products. The story is as follows:

After graduating from the University of Michigan in 1904, I taught commercial subjects for a year and a half in a high school in Racine, Wisconsin, and then came to New York to run the New York office of a Chicago teachers' agency. After a few months I left that work and actively began my business career with the Herring-Hall-Marvin Safe Company in New York. In 1907 I went to Cincinnati to serve as assistant to the eastern sales manager of the Proctor and Gamble Company. Here I had my first experience in the field which we now know as Marketing.

In 1910, I left the Proctor and Gamble Company and went to the University of Wisconsin as Assistant Professor of Business Administration, with the assignment of developing correspondence study courses in business in the University Extension Division. Most of the courses that were scheduled dealt with specific business activities such as bookkeeping, retail salesmanship, advertising, commercial law, and similar subjects, which had even prior to that time been taught in schools and colleges.

In considering the whole field of selling, I developed the idea that personal salesmanship and advertising had to do simply with the final expression of the selling idea. My experience with the Procter and Gamble Company had convinced me that a manufacturer seeking to market a product had to consider and solve a large number of problems before he ever gave expression to the selling idea by sending a salesman on the road or inserting an advertisement in a publication.

I surveyed the very meager literature of business which was available at that time and was astonished to find that the particular field that I have briefly described above had never been treated by any writer. I decided to prepare a correspondence course covering this phase of business activity.

In brief, the subject matter that I intended to treat was to include a study of everything that the promoter of a product has to do prior to his actual use of salesmen and of advertising. A name was needed for this field of business activity. I remember the difficulties I had in finding a suitable name, but I finally decided on the phrase "Marketing Methods," Under this name a course consisting of six printed pamphlets was published by the University in the fall of 1910.

In 1911, I revised this same material for use by the Alexander Hamilton Institute, and it was published by the Institute as part of the fourth volume of their first series of textbooks, with the title "Selling and Buying." This title was changed after a year or two, with a further revision of the material, to "Marketing." For several years this Alexander Hamilton Institute textbook was the only available book on the subject, and I know it was rather widely used in schools and colleges.

In the fall of 1911, I expanded my material and began to give this course to resident students in the course in commerce at the University of Wisconsin. I do not think that my course either in correspondence or in residence was the first one in which this subject was treated. I believe Paul Cherington covered approximately the same material at Harvard as early as 1909, and I understand that a similar course was given even prior to that at Ohio State. I do know, however, that none of these earlier courses used the title "Marketing," and I have never heard of any textbook covering this subject or using this title which was available prior to the appearance of my own material.

Although I have written occasionally on other phases of marketing, my original material, with the revisions and expansions above referred to, is all that I have put in book form on this subject.

1940

296

FRED E. CLARK

My first important marketing experience was the usual high school and college experience, namely, selling books, atlases (Rand McNally), and Wearever Aluminum Ware, all from house to house. Following my graduation from college, there was a few months' experience in a sales promotion job for the Fireless Cooker Company in their Detroit offices. Also in my younger days, I had considerable contact with relatives and friends of the family who were businessmen. And finally, through my teaching experience, there has been a good deal of consulting work with busienss firms, trade associations, and work for, and consulting assistance with, governmental agencies, including three code authorities under the A.A.A., and a summer spent investigating the Market News Service for the Department of Agriculture.

The subject of my Master's thesis was the "Cooperative Grain Elevator Movement in Illinois." At the University of Illinois, where I majored in economics, I worked closely with the School of Commerce, and this resulted in giving me an interest in the business ("practical") point of view both on public questions and on problems of private administration. Professor David Kinley was then head of the Department of Economics, guiding the School of Commerce, and dean of the Graduate School—later president of the University. He was very active in the graduate work of the Department of Economics when I was there and I think had considerable influence on the students at the time. He was a man with a particularly keen mind, very able as a theoretical economist, but also greatly interested in business and business problems. He had as fine a combination of the practical and theoretical understanding of economic problems as anyone I have ever known.

My interest in agricultural marketing has been aided and abetted by three things: my early life on a farm, my later experience in operating a farm from the business end, and my contact with Chicago's great central agricultural market since 1918.

Like all early students of marketing, I was undoubtedly influenced by the work of such pioneers as L. D. H. Weld, Paul H. Nystrom, Ralph Starr Butler, Sparling of the University of Wisconsin, and A. W. Shaw. I was greatly infleunced and encouraged to write by my first "boss" (this was after taking my Ph.D.) Professor Henry Carter Adams, head of the Economics Department at the University of Michigan where I taught marketing in 1916-17 and 1918-19. The first draft of my text *Principles of Marketing* was used at Michigan in mimeographed form in 1918-19, and at the University of Michigan, University of Minnesota, and Northwestern University in 1919-20.

In coming to Northwestern in the fall of 1919 to join the School of Commerce faculty, I found Dean Heilman particularly sympathetic to, and helpful with, the completion of the first edition of the *Principles.* Incidentally, Homer B. Vanderblue, the present dean of the School of Commerce, was my colleague here at the time and read the mimeographed editions of the text critically, and our conversations of many of the points involved were most helpful.

1940

N. H. COMISH

Both my undergraduate and graduate work were along broad lines. As an undergraduate, while majoring at Utah State College in business and economics, I had courses in all the natural sciences and mathematics. As a graduate, I majored in economics which encompassed marketing, and minored in sociology and education. Likewise, I had considerable work in history and political science and philosophy. From all these fields, I have drawn for my writings when I could wisely do so.

My graduate work was done at the University of Chicago and the University of Wisconsin. But all my work in marketing was taken at the University of Wisconsin where I came in close touch with the men in that field. Hibbard and Macklin had considerable influence on me; but so also have other writers as I have given courses in marketing since 1915. In doing so, I have used many texts and references in the field.

I have been extremely close to practical fields. I was reared on the farm and have owned two farms since 1913. Besides, I have organized some cooperatives and have advised several.

In the business field, I have been a salesman in stores and on the road; helped organize two stores. For 12 years I was adviser to one and for 14 years on the board of Directors of the other.

As to my books, before beginning to write each, I read practically everything I could find in the field and made some original investigations on points that I felt needed more light.

All my works are taken up from the viewpoint of particular classes. *"The Standards of Living"* considers marketing and other topics from the standpoint of the consumer. *The Cooperative Marketing of Agricultural Products* was written from the viewpoint of the farmer, *The Marketing of Manufactured Goods* from the angle of the manufacturer, and my magazine articles on retailing from the point of view of the merchant. It is my belief that books written from the viewpoint of a particular class are more readable than those written from the point of view of that indefinite thing we call society. Yet I think books from both viewpoints are good.

1940

P. D. CONVERSE

I recall a conversation that I recently had with Professor Patterson of the University of Pennsylvania. He said that he had asked his graduate class how two men like Carver and Hobson could come to such different views as to merits of the present economic system. After discussing the question for a long time they came to the conclusion that Carver was born poor and had made a success of his life. He was a big man with rugged health and a good digestion. Hobson on the other side was born well-to-do but with a poor stomach. His digestion was bad, and he didn't seem to progress beyond the point where his father started him in life. Hence these two men looked at society through entirely different eyes.

As for my own environment:

1. Home environment: my father was a well educated Presbyterian minister who became much interested in social reform. He was a single taxer but disagreed with Henry George. His writing had placed his name in *Who's Who* (although too poor to buy a copy) and in the leading religious encyclopedia. He was so sincere that food and clothing were unimportant matters. This started me off with a social slant on economics.

2. Education: My teachers of economics were largely of the Wisconsin School trained under Ely, Commons, etc., in the day when Wisconsin was considered radical. They taught sound money, were very critical of the ethics of business, perhaps did not believe that the profit motive always produced the most desirable ends, but they were not socialists. They believed in private property, profit, and individual initiative.

3. I was then thrown into an urban university in a large industrial city. I found that the labor unions instead of being the ideal institutions as represented in the textbooks were just as crooked as the employers; they resorted to the same methods and were actuated by the same motives.

4. As a young man I became an examiner for the Federal Trade Commission and had to contact many businessmen. I found many very fine men personally whose actions in business were not the most desirable socially. However, I found an economic system that worked. It had defects, but it seemed that these defects could be mitigated by policing and that businessmen could be induced to practice fair competition by appeals to ethical and profit considerations. In other words, the economic system had worked to produce the highest standard of living for millions of people of any system known to the world. It could be made to do better, but human nature is inherently selfish. Indolence, laziness, greed, meanness, are always to be combated. The weapons are: incentive for gain (profit, wages, etc.), religious teachings, and policemen. This leads to the belief in the government as a policeman rather than an operator or minute regulator of economic activities.

As nearly as I can analyze the matter, these are the influences that worked on me in my formative years. Since that time "I have been on my own" in my thinking. If I differ from others it may be largely that I have remained an academic man with an outside and detached point of view and yet I contact many businessmen every year. I find that this world is still full of opportunities for young men (even if they don't think so).

In regard to approach to marketing, my first course was a very short course under Ralph Starr Butler in which he gave me some of the material which later appeared in his *Marketing Methods and Policies.* Then I started teaching marketing in a school with a strong vocational slant. There was no textbook, so I had the students buy Nystrom's *Economics of Retailing.* Next in market studies for the government, the approach was very direct and practical. For these reasons, I used largely the middlemen or institutional approach to the subject in my first book.

After coming to the University of Illinois, I saw that the marketing of farm products was much more important than the subject had appeared when in an urban university. This led to the increased use of functions in my teaching. Another and, perhaps, a more important cause was the difference in the point of view of the two schools. The University of Illinois is located outside of any metropolitan area and has no evening school students. It lays emphasis on a sound training in fundamentals rather than vocational training. I therefore developed the functional approach more than formerly.

In conclusion, I started life with a rugged constitution and have enjoyed good health most of the time. I have had reasonably good digestion and have enjoyed my food. This fact may be more important than all of the foregoing in evaluating my point of view on economic society.

1940

MELVIN T. COPELAND

After graduating from Bowdoin College, I entered the Harvard Graduate School of Arts and Sciences as a student of economics in the autumn of 1906. I undertook some seminar work with Professor Taussig in my first year, choosing the cotton industry as my field. I had no particular reason for selecting that industry rather than another. After considerable library work on the tariff, technical developments, and the like, I went out to visit numerous textile concerns in New England and in the South. During the course of those inquiries,

I became interested in the marketing aspects of the industry, and the results are apparent in my first book, *The Cottom Manufacturing Industry of the United States.*

Another factor which had some influence, the exact degree of which it is impossible to determine, is that in 1907-8, I became assistant to Professor Edwin F. Gay in his course in Economic History in Harvard College. In the spring of that year, Mr. Gay was appointed dean of the new Graduate School of Business Administration. Consequently, I may have picked up there, perhaps, some suggestions that may have had a bearing on my later work.

In 1909-10, I gave a little half-year course in the Business School in Economic Resources of Europe. The following year I spent in Europe as a Traveling Fellow, giving attention primarily to the cotton manufacturing industry. After my return, I taught for a year at New York University. There I taught all the courses in economics and sociology in the College of Arts and Sciences, and also a course in the School of Commerce on European trade. In the fall of 1912, I returned to the Harvard Business School as an instructor. One of my assignments was to start a course in business statistics. The other was to take part in the instruction in a course known as "Commercial Organization." Two years later we changed the name of the course and introduced the title of "Marketing." That culminated a gradual evolution.

In the summer of 1913, I went out as a field agent of our newly established Bureau of Business Research, gathering figures on the cost of doing business in retail shoe stores. The next year it was decided to start a similar investigation in the retail grocery trade and I took charge of that. In the summer of 1916 I was appointed director of the Bureau of Business Research in charge of the various studies of operating expenses in several retail and wholesale trades.

In April, 1917, I went to Washington as secretary of the Commercial Economic Board of the Counsel of National Defense. In 1918, our Board became the Conservation Division of the War Industries Board. I was the executive secretary. That brought me into contact with a great many different businesses.

In 1919, I returned to the School, teaching marketing and, for a couple years, business policy.

When the Business School was started, Dean Gay decided that instruction, in so far as possible, should be by the discussion of problems rather than lecturing. He impressed that upon me, particularly when I returned to the School in 1912. All my teaching from the start was by classroom discussion rather than by lecturing. When Mr. Donham became Dean of the Business School in November, 1919, one of his first requests of me was that I should undertake to get out a case book. This resulted in the first edition of my *Marketing Problems.* I wrote all that book myself from situations that I had run across in my varied contacts with businessmen, experiences in Washington, and my reading. In 1920, at Dean Donham's request, we undertook to organize a collection of cases for other courses in the Bureau of Business Research, of which I was still director. Presently the revision of the marketing book resulted, which incorporated cases that our field agents had obtained. My continued research work and contacts with business led to my *Principles of Merchandising,* published in 1924.

In 1928, I participated in a study conducted by the National Bureau of Economic Research and contributed the chapter on marketing published in that Bureau's two-volume work, *Recent Economic Changes.* Out of that presently grew an inquiry into hand-to-mouth buying, merchandise stocks, raw material stocks, and commodity prices. The results have been presented in a series of research bulletins, the last of which was *A Raw Commodity Revolution.*

During the last twenty years I have done a considerable amount of consulting work with business concerns. This work has always been subordinated to my teaching and research activities but has served as a very valuable laboratory experience for me. My first work was with one of the advertising agencies in New York City. Subsequently, I worked with several textile manufacturing companies, a glass manufacturing company, a radio accessory company, a sugar refining company, a drug manufacturer, several grocery manufacturers, a small stationery manufacturer, and others.

The most significant single influence, I suppose, has been the constant contact with industry since the early days of research on my doctoral thesis. This has served to keep before me constantly the realities of life.

1940

C. S. DUNCAN

As I look back now, it seems to me that my original interest grew out of the fact that for some time as a youngster I clerked in the general merchandise store in a small town of less than 700 inhabitants. Being of a somewhat philosophical turn of mind, I was wondering constantly about such things as the origin of prices of the numerous things I had to sell, about where they came from and how they happened to be what they were. For example, calico prints—where did the patterns come from? The same was true of wallpaper. I wondered, too, why some things sold on the dozen basis, some by the pound or yard, and whether this was the proper way to sell.

It is a fact, also, that I had an uncle who ran a drugstore in the same small town. There were more different articles in that store than I could count. I wondered how he kept them all supplied, where they came from. These were mysteries to me. I also had an uncle who each year for a brief period became a grain commission merchant. Some way he was able to quote a price the origin of which I did not know. For some time also I worked on a farm that had a large apple orchard. We picked the apples and sorted them, and boxed the best and shipped them to Danville, Illinois. The name of the man to whom we shipped them I recall to this day, a Mr. Breen. I wondered how it could be that we could ship these apples off to him on trust, not knowing what he did with them, what he really sold them for, or whether he gave us the full return. These returns were very little above the commission and freight.

All this was in the background when I took a course one summer at the University of Chicago under Professor Paul T. Cherington. To me it was a most illuminating course and I am quite sure that the influence of that course is very apparent in what I have written on the subject. At any rate, it showed me the possibilities of a study in this field with which I had been so dimly acquainted and about which I had such wonderment.

1941

B. H. HIBBARD

As to the reasons I went into the subject of marketing, I suspect they were rather incidental than fundamental. I had lived in the northwestern part of Iowa and had noticed that as the years went by the farmer sold his produce at a very low figure, whereas the same products went on the market a little later much augmented in price.

Next, at the Iowa State College I found myself in a very small department of agriculture and economics with no research funds. In casting about for something that I could do in the way of research with almost no support, I hit upon the quesiton of grain marketing. I did not get very far in this subject, but being one of the first, attracted a very modest bit of notice.

After a few years, the University of Wisconsin was looking for a man to take charge of marketing studies and research. Being acquainted at the University of Wisconsin, I was asked whether or not I could be induced to move from Ames to Madison. This I did and probably gave the first organized course in co-operative marketing in agricultural products for the country.

After working for several years at marketing, writing a few bulletins, particularly on the subject of marketing dairy products, the personnel of the department underwent a considerable change, and it became necessary for someone to take charge of the more central field. This fell to my lot, and I have been working at theoretical analysis and the like as applied to agriculture ever since.

Thus, it seems that I got into the various lines more or less by accident, although my leading interests have been: first, marketing, then land economics and taxation.

1941

THEODORE MACKLIN

During the year September 1, 1911, to August 31, 1912, my work under P. G. Holdren, Director of Extension, Iowa State College, took me throughout Iowa and gave intensive observation of farmers doing a fine job of marketing. This led to my search for opportunity to learn about marketing, which took me to the University of Wisconsin, where I studied to the bottom of the question both through postgraduate courses and by means of research and investigations over a wide range of commodities and conditions.

Contacts with eminent thinkers: this runs to rather an extensive list—a few of whom, selected on the moment, and with whom I was intimately associated as student and colleague are:

Dr. Richard T. Ely—noted economist
Dr. B. H. Hibbard—agricultural economist
Dr. H. C. Taylor—agricultural economist
Dr. E. A. Ross—sociologist
Dr. John R. Commons—economist
Dr. H. L. Russell—bacteriologist and Dean of Agriculture College, University of Wisconsin
Dr. P. G. Holden—Director of Extension Service, Iowa State College

1941

H. H. MAYNARD

Doubtless, my early years on an Iowa farm have given me an appreciation of the importance of, as well as the difficulty of, the process involved in marketing farm products. For example, I maintain that no course in principles of marketing can be thought of as properly organized if it overlooks procedures in agricultural marketing. This is in contrast to the point of view of certain men in metropolitan cities who find it difficult, or impossible, to interest their students in farm marketing.

Similarly, my doctoral investigation in the marketing of boxed apples has probably been reflected in certain parts of my writing in *Principles of Marketing.* My experience as a college debater led to certain abilities to speak in public before many types of sales conventions, all of which have intensified my interest in the sales field and its techniques. This has led to my continuing interest in that area of instruction and to what writings I have done in the field of sales management. I was brought to The Ohio State University in 1923 to organize

302

our course, "Introduction to Business," a fact which early led to the first edition
of our book in business management.

1941

PAUL H. NYSTROM

My first book, *Retail Selling and Store Management,* started in manuscript
and mimeographed form in 1911, had to be done in order to give extension
classes in the University of Wisconsin something to study in preparation for the
weekly class meetings that we held in those days. This material was published in
book form about 1914 by the University Extension Division of the University of
Wisconsin.

My second book, *The Economics of Retailing,* served the purpose of
satisfying the requirements of the University of Wisconsin as a Ph.D.
dissertation. This book following publication served as a textbook in the many
schools that instituted classes in retailing. It has been revised in part several
times, and fully revised three times.

My next book, *The Economics of Fashion,* grew out of my experiences as the
head of a resident buying office here in New York City for seven years. I was
impressed by my observations that buyers of fashion goods had no idea of the
real significance of fashion underlying the saleability of the goods they were
handling. Indeed, they had no idea of the difference between style and fashion.
It was my intention in the *Economics of Fashion* to explain the significance of
fashion. This book, first written in 1928, has served rather widely as a college
textbook.

When I returned to university teaching here at Columbia in 1926, one of the
subjects that I decided to offer was "Economics of Consumption." I had
pondered over and gathered material on this subject for a number of years. The
book *The Economics of Consumption,* first published in 1929, represented an
urge to get this subject off my chest.

1940

ARCH W. SHAW

(Written by Joseph C. Seibert)

In the early 1900s Mr. Shaw and Mr. Walker were partners in the office
equipment business which still flourishes under the same name, and under the
same management. This business dealing in supplies for offices naturally
confronted its managers with possible systems for office and business
management. Mr. Shaw's intellectual curiosity led him to devote a great deal of
his time to the discovery of these systems and brought him conferences with
leaders of many different types of industries. The outstanding discovery from
these meetings, to Mr. Shaw, appeared to be the uniformity of procedures in
spite of the variety of products produced and the outward differences of the
separate organizations. Furthermore in spite of the similarity of procedures there
was an appalling lack of interchange of ideas, and what appeared to Mr. Shaw a
consequent retardation of business progress.

It was to this problem that Mr. Shaw devoted his energies, which led to the
publication of the "System" magazine and to the marketing works which bear
his name. For a time he lectured on "Business Policy" at Harvard University,
advancing these notions which grew out of his contacts and experiences. He
considered his publication as a clearing house for the exchange of ideas. To him
the breaking down of the barriers to the exchange of ideas was one of the most
wonderful things which happened in business during the first quarter of the
present century.

Such a background of experience indicates and adds meaning to his major concept, which is expressed in the first page of his *Approach to Business Problems:*

"Isolate any phase of business, strike into it anywhere, and the invariable essential element will be found to be the application of motion to materials. This may be stated, if you will, as the simplest general concept to which all the activities of manufacturing, selling, finance, and management can ultimately be reduced."

1941

ROLAND S. VAILE

The fact that my immediate post-college work was in economic entomology and related aspects of agriculture accounts in no small measure for some of the points of view that I have held ever since. Moreover, the fact that I grew up closely associated with the co-operative movement as it was developing in the formation of irrigation companies and marketing associations in southern California was influential. As a matter of fact, as a young man just out of college, I was one of the minor influences that persuaded C. C. Teague to give up his private sales agency and join the California Fruit Growers Exchange. I was working for him on the Limoneria Ranch in charge of pest control at the time he made the change.

I also believe the fact that for at least five generations back of me some members of my immediate ancestry were either ministers or lawyers left its effect. My paternal grandfather was graduated from Amherst shortly after 1830 and almost immediately moved with his young bride, who was the daughter of a Massachusetts clergyman, to Indianapolis. My father was graduated in '78 from Oberlin and in '80 from Andover Theological and moved immediately to California. After some twenty years of active ministry in California, he joined the group of early co-operators in the citrus industry and from the late 1900's on I have heard about and lived with that movement.

Among the teachers who particularly influenced me should be mentioned the following: Professor A. J. Cook and Charles Baker in the Biological Science Department at Pomona College; George S. Sumner, professor of economics also at Pomona College; H. J. Weber, director of the citrus experiment station at Riverside; and my associates, Leon D. Bathelor and H. S. Fawcett of the citrus experiment station; T. N. Carver, F. W. Taussig, and E. E. Day of Harvard.

1940

W. C. WEIDLER

It is almost impossible for me to select those experiences which have been particularly definitive insofar as my marketing viewpoint is concerned ... Perhaps a summary statement of my occupational and educational experience will be of some help as may also a statement of the occupational backgrounds of those who were close to me in my early years.

I was born and raised in Columbus, Ohio, and it so happened that a number of relatives, also close family friends, were engaged in the distributive fields. Most of these individuals were manufacturers' and wholesalers' sales representatives. My older brother traveled for a manufacturing firm, selling to the wholesale dry goods trade. I was, therefore, brought into early contact with discussions of sales and distributive problems.

Upon my graduation from high school, I served an apprenticeship in the Sheldon Dry Goods Company, the second largest local wholesaler in this field.

Beginning as a stock boy, I was gradually given increased responsibilities until I was devoting a part of my time to house sales. It was my ambition at that time to secure a traveling sales position with the company, and I had hopes that at a later date I might secure a more advantageous sales connection with a manufacturing enterprise.

Subsequently, I developed ambitions for a college education and resigned my position with the Sheldon Company and entered The Ohio State University. Throughout most of my undergraduate years, I worked as a salesman and floor manager for the old A. E. Pitts Shoe Company, at that time the largest retail shoe store in central Ohio.

I also sold life insurance for the Massachusetts Mutual Life Insurance Company, on a part-time basis, during a part of my undergraduate years.

My major interest in my undergraduate years and in the earlier part of my graduate experience was in the field of economic theory. Indeed, my first staff appointment in The Ohio State University was that of Teaching Fellow in Economics. Subsequently, I was appointed to an Austin Scholarship in Economics at Harvard University. Much of my earlier teaching was done in the field of economic theory in both elementary and advanced areas. I am sure that this interest in economic theory and a leaning toward the philosophical approach is reflected in my writing in the marketing field. I suppose that it is also true that my general environmental and work experiences have contributed to an interest in the more practical phases or what might be termed the managerial aspects of marketing.

1940

L. D. H. WELD

I went to the University of Minnesota as an instructor in 1912 and spent the first year in the Economics Department on the main campus. In 1913 I was shifted to the College of Agriculture, which was very anxious to develop a knowledge of how Minnesota products were marketed. There was a great demand among farmers for information on this subject, and on the general question of co-operative marketing.

Fortunately, I was supposed to spend most of my time in research work to find out what became of Minnesota farm products after they left the farmer. I had to teach only one course; and that was on the marketing of farm products.. The word "marketing" appeared in the name of the course–undoubtedly the first time that this word had been used in connection with a course on the marketing of farm products. Taylor and Hibbard were using some material on marketing in their courses in farm management at the University of Wisconsin at the time.

When I began to teach marketing in the fall of 1913, there was practically no literature on the subject. I had to go out and dig up my own information. I studied at first hand the movement of grain through the use of future trading in the Minneapolis Chamber of Commerce. I wrote a report on this subject for the Bureau of Markets in Washington, but this material was never published because it put future trading and its economic functions in too favorable a light! I was also called before a legislative investigating committee in Minnesota, which tried to prove that I had been instructed by the trustees of the University to teach my dangerous doctrines about the efficiency of grain marketing through the Minneapolis Chamber of Commerce and the functions of future trading!

I personally followed shipments of butter and eggs and other commodities from the country shipper in Minnesota through the wholesalers, jobbers, and retailers to New York, Chicago, and other cities. I analyzed each item of expense involved in this passage through the channels of trade.

I studied the methods of determining price quotations, the operations of butter and egg exchanges, and the auction markets in eastern cities. I also studied at first hand the operations of the co-operative shipping associations of Minnesota and issued bulletins on this subject.

As a result, I was not only able to give my students firsthand information that had never before been collected, but was able at the same time to develop in my own mind some general fundamental principles about marketing, including the functions of middlemen, the factors affecting the cost of marketing, etc.

By the end of two years of this work I had written my book, *The Marketing of Farm Products,* in which I could refer to very few printed sources of material. This book was finished in 1915 but was not actually published until early in 1916, after I had gone to Yale.

In the meantime I had had a chance in 1914 to read a paper before the American Economic Association on "Market Distribution." This was the first scientific presentation of the subject of marketing, as we know it today, before that Association. Shortly after this I was offered a professorship in the Sheffield Scientific School at Yale, where I continued to teach marketing, and where I kept up my research work in this field, mainly in the marketing of manufactured goods.

From then on, courses in marketing began to develop in various universities and articles on marketing methods and costs gradually began to appear. But these courses were few and far between for several years. After two years at Yale, I had joined Swift and Company, and in 1918 at a meeting of the American Economic Association in Richmond I was able to scrape together five or six men who were interested in marketing, and we had dinner together. This group, which I assembled yearly at subsequent meetings of the American Economic Association, grew fairly rapidly, and was soon important enough to get a place on the Economic Association's program for round table discussions of marketing. This was the first associative effort among men interested in marketing as we know it today, and it formed the nucleus out of which developed the Association of Teachers of Marketing.

1941

CONTRIBUTORS TO MARKETING THOUGHT, 1950-1987

B

Writers were requested to submit letters stating their self-perception of subjective factors which influenced their involvement and creativity in the marketing discipline. It was presumed that personal nature, environment, education, relationships, etc. would have conditioned their outlook, and therefore their perception and interpretation of marketing. The effects of these factors upon their writings are told in the text, but additional significant and relevant personal information is also given here, the subjects being listed alphabetically.

RICHARD P. BAGOZZI

"One of the biggest influences on me was the experiences I had as a first-generation American, . . . part of an extended family of Trentini people . . . from a section of the Alps known as the Dolomites. . . . Their history includes reference to being the first in Europe to achieve freedom for serfs, grant the right to vote to women, etc. . . . I mention these things to give a flavor for why the *value of individual freedom* . . . is at the center of everything I do.

"Along with freedom, my family emphasized an appreciation for history and education. As a consequence, I have tended to devote more time than the norm to the foundations of the field in my studies.

"The meaning of freedom was instrumental in my choice of a doctoral program. . . . I saw marketing as a field where I could pursue both behavioral and quantitative directions, more or less in my own way. Most other academic fields require a greater conformity to established views. . . . Marketing has a broad subject matter, is marked by diverse points of view, and is in the formative growth stages. In short, marketing is tailor-made for my inclinations.

"My approach to marketing was shaped much by experiences I had. Ferdinand Mauser (Wayne State University) introduced me to marketing in a very positive way. At Northwestern, Richard Clewett taught me an appreciation of marketing thought. Philip Kotler was a stimulus for expanding my knowledge into how and where marketing is done. Sidney Levy, both an inspiration and role model, provided the freedom, encouragement, and feedback to explore the basic disciplines and their relation to marketing. . . . Human contact with these individuals, rather than their articles, was the real vehicle for learning and motivation.

"I have also been influenced greatly by work in the philosophy of science.The Zaltman, Pinson, and Angelmar 1973 book was my first exposure to the subject and got me started with a nice foundation and enthusiasm for the conceptual foundations of the field. . . . This affected my outlook and approach to research and has influenced my choice of topics for study, methodology, etc.

"A final determinant of my values and attitude was the interactions I had with doctoral students when I was a student. . . . I mention these things because many faculty you survey may not have had similar experiences or have forgotten how important such interactions were in shaping one's ideas and values."

(1987).

ROBERT BARTELS

"Initially aspiring to a career in the performing arts, I was parentally encouraged toward more practicality during the Depression years, and choice, interest, and unending pursuit of the idea of marketing became my life-long professional activity.

"Certain innate and cultivated values shaped my research and writings: a conviction of determinism, first temporal and later spiritual, in human affairs; preference to reasoning from principle, or the broad general conception, in theoretical research; willingness to grapple with an unformulated idea and carry it to expression; a historical orientation of contemporary affairs; and an irrepressible propensity to teach.

"My principle mentors were Theodore N. Beckman, Harold H. Maynard (The Ohio State University), and Fred Clark and Horace Secrist (Northwestern University). Perspective-determining books were *Man the Unkown*, by Alexis Carrel; *One Increasing Purpose*, by Francis Stocking, *Trade and Market in the Early Empires* and *The Great Transformation*, by Karl Polanyi; and *Revelation*, by John (The Bible). Traveling, teaching, lecturing, and studying in other countries furnished a broader outlook on marketing.

"Among the subjects which were frontier areas of marketing thought in my own mind when I wrote of them were the following: history of marketing thought, marketing theory and metatheory, comparative marketing, marketing as a societal institution, macromarketing, marketing in economic development, and global principles of marketing."

(1987).

FRANK M. BASS

"Toward the end of my rather undistinguished career as an undergraduate student at Southwestern University. . . . I developed an interest in economics. I made arrangements to discuss the possibility of graduate study in economics with the Chairman of the Economics Department at the University of Texas in Austin. My conversation with him was, from my viewpoint, entirely unsatisfactory. . . . Dejected, I wandered somewhat aimlessly over to the business school building. It was late in the afternoon and the building was almost deserted. However, I did spot a professor sitting in his office. . . . It turned out to be a marketing professor, Alfred L. Seelye. He explained to me that I could obtain an M.B.A. degree in one year, specializing in marketing. He recommended that I take as many courses in economics as the program allowed because there was not much to be learned about marketing anyway.

"This unplanned encounter and other random-like events in my youth had profound influence on my career. They helped shape my views about the stochastic nature of choice.

"As a young Ph.D. student at the University of Illinois in the early 1950s I read, among other things, Keynes' *The General Theory of Employment, Interest, and Money*. Along with others, I was captivated by the sheer audacity of this book. There is no greater marketing challenge, I think, than to attempt to overturn strongly entrenched ways of looking at something than to attempt to do so with mere ideas and arguments. . . . Althought much of what Keynes wrote was wrong . . . it did demonstrate the importance of new ideas. . . . New ideas, like other innovations, diffuse through a relevant population. . . . Thought of this type led me to develop a diffusion theory model of innovations . . . . I developed a differential equation model, . . .since termed by others "the Bass model" . . . a mathematical model of the diffusion of innovations.

"At Illinois I came into contact with. . .Paul D. Converse . . .who had a strong sense of history and fully understood the then-primitive state of marketing as a topic of serious study. . . . I learned from Harvey W. Huegy the possibility of modeling relationships among marketing variables. And Robert Ferber was an effective, generous, and patient tutor for me in statistics. In 1959, I was selected by the Ford Foundation to attend the year-long program at Harvard, the 'Institute of Basic Mathematics for Application to Business.' This experience provided the foundation for a career focused on the development of mathematical and statistical models in marketing."

(1987).

JAMES R. BETTMAN

"I first became interested in the problem of consumer choice as a freshman at Yale in 1961. I took the introductory economics course, with its obligatory dose of Samuelson, and found consumer theory fascinating but incomplete. In my senior year (1965), I switched my major to a combined major in mathematics and economics . . . I still found the standard utility treatment lacking. . . . I also took a course from a visiting professor from Columbia, Dr. Ruth Mack, who taught using several readings, one of which was by Herbert Simon, an article entitled "A Behavioral Model of Rational Choice" that set my future agenda. . . . It attempted to model how choice 'really' worked. I was hooked! . . . I then started graduate school. In Administrative Behavioral Gaming and Simulation, I learned that one could model real choices in detail. I decided to apply this approach to the area of consumer choice.

"Yale had no marketing area, or even any marketing courses, so I saw my work as being a study of decision making by consumers, not as marketing. Even my first job at UCLA was not really a marketing job.

"My dissertation applied information-processing ideas to consumer choice. I tried to understand the detailed processes underlying choice. I espoused process-tracing methodologies that would enable one to get at such details. I pursued this type of research not because of applications, but because I was interested in it. I didn't really care if it could be applied at that time.

"Later, it occured to me that information-processing ideas might have a lot to say about consumer policy issues. . . . This realization that information processing work had important implications, and my struggles to introduce motivation into my models led to the thinking behind my book, *An Information Processing Theory of Consumer Choice* (1979). Overall, I would say that I was one of the first (along with George Haines), and certainly probably the most persistent, to try to get consumer researchers to think about how people process information. Selling the idea that one should examine the real details of choice processes was not easy. . . . It became easier when people saw how this could be related to marketing and policy concerns. . . ."

(1987).

DONALD J. BOWERSOX

"I was involved in doctoral training at a point in time that the physical distribution concept was initially evolving. I had an opportunity to work and socialize with young professors who were trying very hard to crystallize some basic concepts. Their attitudes and values were such that they were very happy to include a doctoral student as a full partner provided the 'return-on-investment' was satisfactory. This opportunity was unique and provided the motivation for me to expend substantial effort to prove that I could carry my weight. The result was the publication of the first text in the field *Physical Distribution Management* (1960).

"The result of this experience was a fundamental change in my basic interests in the marketing discipline. I began to favor aspects of marketing that dealt with the physical side of product movement and storage. This basic experience has influenced my research and writing over the past twenty-five years. From the initial work in basic cost relationships, theoretical development has been directed to channel concepts and interorganizational behavior. A second stream of development has been conceived with the strategic dimensions of integrating the total materials logistics management process." Further information is included in the text.

(1987).

LOUIS P. BUCKLIN

Louis P. Bucklin's response has been included in the text.

ROBERT D. BUZZELL

"My parents were important influences on me. My mother . . . taught me to read when I was 3 years old . . . My father taught me two things: to avoid being pompous and to pay attention to things that matter. These values make me impatient with much of the work that is done in marketing today. When I skim through the *JM* or the *JMR,* at least half of the articles strike me as pompous. I find myself asking, 'Who would care about the results? Does it really matter?'

"My teachers have influenced me also. The first of them in Marketing was Gordon Barnewall, not a disciplined scholar, but he persuaded me that marketing is fun—it deals with people, with motivations, with action, with creativity. . . . At Illinois I studied with Paul Converse, a down-home country boy with a keen mind and boundless curiosity. . . . At OSU, Ted Beckman was undoubtedly the biggest influence on me. He was not the easiest person in the world to work with, but his seminar was an intensive learning experience. . . . His wrestling with questions instilled a kind of mental discipline: define terms precisely; be sure that you use them consistently, classify things into well-defined categories. He didn't phrase it this way, but Ted insisted on what mathematicians call 'mutually exclusive, collectively exhausting' taxonomies. He also taught me the importance of being thorough and introduced me to the world of 'commercial academic activity'—that you could actually be paid to do interesting work!

"In 1959-60, I came to Harvard to spend a year at the Ford Foundation 'Institute for Basic Mathematics for Application to Business.' . . . This program gave me a 'quantitative view' of the world that I'll never lose. It also exposed me to a group of bright young faculty people from a variety of fields—finance, control, economics, and so forth. Our common interest was *management*. I stopped thinking of marketing as a separate, specialized, function. I started thinking of it as one element or dimension of an integrated process.

"In 1961, I came back to HBS as a faculty member. . . . My colleagues, and the general 'culture' of HBS, have influenced my thinking greatly. The case method forces all of us to see problems in their real-world contexts. . . . Another experience that affected my thinking and my interests was the time I spent as a Visiting Professor at INSEAD in 1967. It was my first experience with foreign travel. It gave me a much wider point of view about marketing and about life in general. Today everyone talks about 'global competition,' and it seems obvious that managers and academics must consider customers, competition, and marketing practices on a worldwide scale. Twenty years ago it wasn't obvious. and it was quite a revelation to me."

(1987).

GILBERT A. CHURCHILL

"I was struck by the fortuitous nature of many of the circumstances that had a profound impact on my career. Upon graduating with my MBA degree, I took a job as a sales engineer. The training for the job included several years as inside salesperson before being assigned to one's own territory. . . . During the time I worked as an inside sales engineer, the economy was in a recession. Given the few orders being placed, competition was very intense. We would periodically receive exhortations from the branch manager to be more aggressive, to work harder, to sell more. . . . Interestingly, we were somewhat limited in what we could do to sell more. . . . Yet, our requests for some price flexibility to meet, not beat, competitor prices most often fell on deaf ears.

"After completing the work for my doctoral degree, I happened to comment to Neil Ford and Orville Walker on my sales experience, and pointed out how frustrating and dysfunctional those exhortations and subsequent inaction from corporate headquarters were. Orv suggested that I had suffered role conflict and role ambiguity. I countered: "They even had a scientific name for it." We discussed the idea of doing research in the sales force area. . . . Up to that time, I had not done any research that focused specifically on the question of salesperson productivity.

"We systematically began to explore the literature on salesperson performance and related literature that dealt specifically with the issue of the impact of role conflict and role ambiguity on an individual's productivity. . . . The inadequacy of measures available in the literature forced us to develop our own measures. . . . That experience triggered an interest in measurement issues that I have maintained since." See text for additional information.

(1987).

JOEL B. COHEN

"While a graduate student at UCLA in the early 1960's, I became fascinated with the idea of study now known as 'consumer behavior'. . . . My perspective was then and now quite different from most people in marketing. It did not stem from a basic interest in marketing, and therefore I had never adopted the orientation of looking at consumers as 'targets' or a means to some marketing or corporate end. Nor have I felt I have an obligation to help marketers persuade consumers to buy their products. I have always been interested in understanding why it is people do the things they do and what factors might have made a real difference in their behavior. I had become frustrated by the tendencies of the social and behavioral sciences (particularly psychology) to build what I saw as artificial and often rather narrow walls around selected interest areas—thus largely ignoring the dynamic interplay of forces on the 'whole' individual.

"I felt that there had been limited progress toward the development of more integrative theory and that among the consequences of this was an inability to assess the importance of these various domain-relevant factors on individual judgments, decisions, and actions. . . . I looked upon consumer behavior as having the potential to 'force' inquiry to a useful level of integration. . . . There seemed an opportunity to break down some artificial barriers (between those concerned exclusively with learning or cognitive processes and others concerned exclusively with motivational or personality variables) and in the process establish consumer behavior as an area of inquiry that would have broad appeal within social sciences. . . . . This orientation to consumer behavior has influenced everything I have done as an educator and researcher.

"I continue to feel that two goals for the study of consumer behavior are paramount: (1) to more adequately describe and understand all aspects of consumers' behavior and (2) to contribute as a social science to a better understanding of human behavior by directing particular attention to how personal, social, and contextual factors combine to impact on human behavior in complex settings. . . . At times I am often discouraged by the research performance of consumer researchers, many of whom appear to be simply duplicating the work of other behavioral and social scientists without either contributing to a better understanding of consumer behavior or placing their research in a more integrative context."

(1987).

JAMES F. ENGEL

"My interest in marketing began when I was a student at Drake University in 1956, advised to take a minor in behavioral sciences by my advisor, Martin

Zober, who saw even then that there was going to be a behavioral integration into the field of marketing. . . . At that point my focus was strictly methodological. . . . My mentor at the University of Illinois was Hugh Wales, who also was trying to integrate behavioral sciences into marketing. . . . I was also strongly influenced by Ivan Steiner and Fred Fiedler, on the faculty of psychology. I really got my roots down in social psychology and began to see the truth of today's emphasis on information processing. . . . This began to form my views about the consumer. . . . In another course, an assignment was to compare the basic underlying principles and primacies from one of the related disciplines as compared with economics. . . . I investigated the principles and postulates of social psychology and did a careful integration into economics.

"At Michigan, Jim Scott was trying to integrate behavioral viewpoints into the field of promotion. . . . Jim Morgan did a great deal to help me think through how we could come up with a systematic model of consumer behavior. . . . Other things, too, showed me that marketing had to start with the consumer. . . . After proposing a session on selective perception at an AMA annual meeting, I published a paper on selective perception in marketing. I began also to think seriously about the consumer from the perspective of dissonance.

"In 1963 I moved to Ohio State. That was the beginning of an auspicious team with David Kollat and Roger Blackwell, who added knowledge of problem-solving behavior, learning theory, and cultural anthropology. We taught a seminar which did much to shape the field. In it were Larry Light, Brian Sternthal, and Sam Craig, all of whom went on to become major leaders in the field.

"Then came the first edition of *Consumer Behavior* (1968) on which a whole generation of marketing faculty was educated. In 1969, a workshop on consumer behavior was held which led to the formation of the Association for Consumer Research in 1970. . . . For the contributions of this book and the formation of the ACR, in 1981 I was designated along with John Howard as Fellow in Consumer Behavior by the Association of Consumer Research. I gave the glory where it belongs—to the Lord Jesus Christ for the purpose he's given me and the motivation in my own life.

"About 1968, however, I underwent one of the major factors which was to shape my career: I came to see that my own perspective was highly academic and not always really actionable or practical from the perspective of marketing action. This led me to rethink the field of cognitive dissonance and to say "forget it." I turned towards a more consulting viewpoint. . . . Greater involvement with the business world led to a diminishing of my own publications.

"In 1972 our team split up and I came to Wheaton College, where I have pioneered the application of marketing thinking to the whole field of Christian communication. I have published a model of conversion process behavior which is used throughout the world.

"Maybe a few observations on the whole field of consumer behavior are in order to conclude this. I think the field has settled down remarkably from where it began. You will see great flux in the early editions of our book reflecting new developments. There seem to be few quantum leaps now, but we do grow each year in understanding the variables a bit more. Yet, I feel that the field has degenerated to a substantial amount of number crunchings over trivial issues. Much of the literature is irrelevant and does not find its way into our books. I don't think this is a salutary development. I think it reflects a field which has gotten decidedly academic in its perspective and loses the fact that ultimately we are teachers and diffusers of knowledge in a discipline which is closer to engineering than it is a pure science. . . . Today, there are tons of books. No one stands out as a great contributor. One doesn't see people who you would now call leaders anymore."

(1987).

STANLEY C. HOLLANDER

"I wonder if a single event, or course of study, is a sufficient cause for change or whether it mainly triggers potential and latent tendencies. Nevertheless, here are some of the academic and other influences on my work.

"Pre-1937 (and thereafter): Family influences suggested a marketing career.

"1937–41: Undergraduate education at New York University School of Commerce with a retailing major, marketing minor taught me: that I very much enjoyed spending time at the university and in the libraries, even though I had no thoughts of becoming a professor; that the idea later expressed as the 'marketing concept' permeated the marketing and retailing courses. . . . Businesses were seen as pursuing enlightened long-run self-interest.

"1943–46: Working in the Office of Price Administration, I learned that business was more complex than indicated by the neoclassical model we studied in school.

1. The first course I took, History of Economic Thought . . . taught me that people could be interested in ideas as well as in facts and techniques.

2. Industrial organization with Corwin Edwards demonstrated that(a) business was influenced by custom and arbitrary rules of behavior, and (b) businesspeople were not adverse to trying to use government regulation to further their own interests. A good deal of my interest in retail price legislation and in restraints on retail competition was stimulated by this course and by Saul Nelson's course on price behavior.

"1947: Explicit self-conscious interest in a university teaching career went from zero to intense as a result of advice from friend and former professor Elmer Schaller.

"1947–49: University of Buffalo. Again, reinforcement of the idea that ideas count. E. D. McGarry took a very eclectic and interdisciplinary view toward marketing. . . . He taught us to question assumptions and values. I believe he strongly influenced the types of interdisciplinary things I tried to do with *Explorations in Retailing*. (No commercial publisher wanted to touch this book because they considered it far too advanced for the market, but it has quite respectable sales for an unpromoted book when published by our Bureau of Business and Economic Research.) He encouraged me to visit England. Contact with the large British retailers and trade press exposed me to trends in retail conglomeration and internationalization, both of which developed in Britain before the United States, and led to several papers and *Multinational Retailing*.

"1949–54: University of Pennsylvania. Working with Reavis Cox continued the interdisciplinary mode, but with somewhat more rigor. He imparted to me interest in the problem of measurement of marketing performance and in doing historical work. I developed an interest in doing a dissertation on discount retailing on my own, but Cox championed that interest against the recommendations of other faculty who felt it was too unorthodox a topic. Much of my interest in macromarketing and public policy history is attributable to Cox and McGarry.

"1956: A postdoctoral seminar at Carnegie Tech with Herbert Simon reinforced much of the institutional thinking to which I had been exposed. Here again, it became evident that organizations were power systems and that they involved complex, and often suboptimizing, internal relationships. I went to the seminar to plan to exploit thoughts on the channel as an organization, but Simon was so self-deprecatory about his ideas and the other participants were so convincing that organizations were self-contained that I abandoned the idea.

"Since 1958 at Michigan State: MSU's strong international program and particularly its involvement with LDCs has made me want to know more about marketing and economic development. Charles Slater, Donald Taylor, and many others have exemplified that area of concern and made me excited about participating with Reed Moyer in preparing *Markets and Marketing in Developing Countries* for the AMA.

"1960: The article on 'Wheel of Retailing' developed out of responding to class questions when teaching as a visiting faculty member at UCLA and then further developed by discussion at the old Marketing Theory Seminar (Alderson, Cox, Aspinwall, McGarry) at Boulder, Colorado.

"1966: A research trip to Europe and Turkey produced the book *Multinational Retailing* and also increased my interest in comparative work.

"1970: Lecturing at a rather intellectual retailers' meeting in Zurich made me realize how much students could gain from contacts with such executives.

"During the last six years or so, the Social Reports issued by the Migros Federation of Swiss Cooperatives have nurtured an interest in the externalities of retailing. So has participation in several of the Macromarketing Theory Conferences.

"One of the advantages of studying marketing for fifty years is the ability to be impressed with present developments without forgetting that there were bright people around half a century ago."

(1986–87).

ROBERT J. HOLLOWAY

"Looking back over my years in marketing, 1950–87, I find that there have been several important influences:

1. Roland S. Vaile taught me about the eclectic nature of marketing.
2. Contacts I had with people in the AMA taught me much about techniques and the value of research.
3. My overseas experiences gave me an international orientation.

"Because of the eclectic influence, I never got very impressed with principles of marketing for they usually turned out to be principles of psychology, economics, or something else.

"My work with Bob Hancock (environmental) relates closely to the eclecticism. Environmental influences on marketing seem to me to be the most important part of marketing today. It is in this area that I have made my most important contribution to the field of marketing.

"In recent years I have become more interested in international marketing. This area is extremely poorly developed as a field of marketing.

"As a general comment about marketing, I might say that I feel it has gone too far in the direction of management and away from economics. To emphasize management is to deemphasize marketing, in many ways. Also, there is a need to move more into international marketing. To date, most of the developments in this area have come from business. . . . Why should we teach marketing from the standpoint of the United States when we are now competing in world markets."

(1987).

JOHN A. HOWARD

"In grade school and high school I read voraciously about our industrial leaders: the Harrimans, Hills, Vanderbilts, Carnegies, etc. They were my heroes.

"Dean C. M. Thompson, an intellectual foster father, encouraged this interest at the University of Illinois and further graduate work. He showed me the excitement of economic research and wrote about me to Professor Ruggles, head of the Public Utilities at the Harvard Business School. Professor Ruggles agreed it was a good idea for me to do graduate work but that I should go across the river to the Harvard Economics Department and 'get a good degree,' the type of statement that could have been made about any business school at that time.

"At Harvard I worked in industrial organization (anti-trust) under Dean Edward S. Mason. This required a major shift in values, but Joseph A. Schumpeter later gave me a broader perspective and relieved the value tensions. Also, it was helpful to spend a summer at Oxford University reviewing the British attempt to develop a monopolies act in the House of Commons.

"Eight years on the faculty at the University of Chicago provided the opportunity to attempt to reconcile the Harvard and Chicago views of the industrial world. I was finding that the demand side of economics was insufficiently developed for what I wanted to do in marketing. Professor Harold J. Leavitt, then a colleague there, introduced me to psychology. Later, at Columbia, I was to work closely with Professor William J. McGuire, now of the Yale University Psychology Department.

"Soon afterward the Ford Foundation asked me to review the teaching and research in marketing in American business schools; at the same time it asked Ezra Solomon to do the field of finance. Out of that came *Marketing: Executive and Buyer Behavior* (Columbia Press, 1963) and a clear conclusion on my part that consumer research was ready to move. Parallel with this Ford Foundation project I had come to know Herbert A. Simon as we were both consultants to the Foundation's effort to improve business schools. His influence was very important in opening for me new intellectual vistas.

"Finally, Columbia University, and especially Dean Courtney C. Brown, provided the opportunity and encouragement to build a group of scholars devoted to basic research in marketing." See text for additional information.

(1987).

SHELBY D. HUNT

Shelby D. Hunt's response has been incorporated in the text.

HAROLD H. KASSARJIAN

"That a college education was essential was always a part of my value system inculcated by my parents. . . . Hence in 1948 I matriculated at UCLA with majors in pre-med and mathematics. By my senior year I had become a psychology major for it seemed more interesting and I could get better grades. As an undergraduate I had my first two publications. . . . Doing research and seeing it published was a true joy. . . . Upon discharge from the military after the Korean War, I entered the graduate program in social psychology at UCLA. During those years I met my wife, also a graduate student in social psychology. She, along with my doctoral committee chairman had profound influence in developing my academic values, and in my early research and publications.

"Upon finishing the degree in 1960, it became obvious that jobs in major universities were not easily found, not in Social Psychology. Hence, a major milestone in my career: I got a job as a project director with the marketing research firm that years before had hired me as an interviewer. . . . After the 1960 election, . . . I went back into the academic job market but this time included marketing departments, for now I could try to sell myself as an expert in marketing research.

"Fortunately, Bill Brown, chairman of the marketing department at UCLA, was willing to take a chance. Here was a marketing department, populated with economists, which was willing to hire a psychologist. Here, it soon became obvious to me that I knew a lot about human behavior that economists and marketing professors did not seem to know—personality, dissonance, experimental design, communications research, attitude research, etc.—topics that later were to become the field of consumer behavior. Soon, other nontraditional academics were added to the department: Al Silk and George Haines. Working with these colleagues, I gained the needed confidence that my work was indeed relevant, and that a career in marketing was a distinct possibility.

"At that time, behavioral, or for that matter modeling, type papers were unacceptable to marketing publications and the AMA conference was a closed shop run by the 'old boy' network. Getting our work published was tough indeed until Bob Ferber began the *Journal of Marketing Research* and was receptive to behavioral work. That was the real beginning both for myself and for the field of consumer research.

"My entire academic career has been at UCLA, starting almost 40 years ago. However, I have been fortunate to have the opportunity for several visiting professorships. . . . Each had an important impact on my thinking at various stages in my career. . . . A most important year was 1973, when I was hired as a full-time consultant to the Federal Trade Commission, for, like many others who were to follow us, it changed our career path at least temporarily; exciting interests in public policy and the law. Today, my favorite course is not consumer behavior, or mass communications or marketing, but rather a course I teach in Marketing Law."

(1987).

PHILIP KOTLER

Philip Kotler's response has been incorporated in the text.

WILLIAM LAZER

William Lazer's response has been incorporated in the text.

THEODORE LEVITT

Theodore Levitt's response has been incorporated in the text.

SIDNEY J. LEVY

"Having pursued a somewhat maverick vein of work for many years, I did not regard myself as in the mainstream of consumer research.

"An interdisciplinary approach to the study of consumer behavior gets a certain amount of lip service. One sees the idea exemplified in the sequence of topics in textbooks on consumer behavior, in the diagram of consumers at the center of a series of concentric circles representing the behavioral disciplines. Having this idea also permits scholars to focus where they wish—on deep motives, on situations, on attitude change, on sociological groupings, on cultural characteristics, etc. Nevertheless, the results are often piecemeal, multi-rather than interdisciplinary as each person works on preferred variables, processes, or level of conceptualization.

"Achieving greater integration requires a holistic orientation that builds into an inquiry the varied perspectives and concepts of several behavioral modes of thought. . . I was indoctrinated into the interdisciplinary viewpoint by my education in the Committee on Human Development at the University of Chicago. . . One of the people whose influence was especially important to me was W. Lloyd Warner . . . William E. Henry was also an early mentor.

"As a graduate student, I went to work at Social Research, Inc., developing these social and psychological foundations, and connecting them with problems of the marketplace. . . . Others with whom I worked were Burleigh B. Gardner, Harriett Bruce Moore, Lee Rainwater, Richard Coleman, Gerald Handel and others. We theorized, probed, and lived the psychological analysis of marketplace behavior. . . . Through the encouragement of Joe Newman, I wrote (with Burleigh Gardner) 'The Product and the Brand' for the *Harvard Business Review* (1955), launching the concept of brand imagery into the business world.

"Wooed by Harper Boyd to Northwestern University's Department of Marketing. . . . I was stirred to ruminations about marketing, its meaning, and its domain. Phil Kotler and I wrote 'Broadening the Concept of Marketing,' (*Journal of Marketing,* 1969), creating some entertaining controversy. . . . I suggested that we call the scholarly study of marketing Marcology to distinguish it from the activity called marketing; so far that's gone nowhere." (Remarks prepared when Levy was named Fellow of the Association for Consumer Behavior.)

E. JEROME McCARTHY

"I was raised as a 'bottom-line,' 'survival-oriented,' 'inner-city' kid who also had some 'save mankind' feelings. As I see it now, I had a bundle of micro and macro objectives—and still do!

"After some undergrad engineering and business training, and sales and purchasing experience, I was not willing to follow a career in large company bureaucracies which were using narrow functional management. In fact, I was repulsed by the prospect and eventually chose an academic career. I went to the University of Minnesota in Labor Economics and Industrial Engineering to 'help people get a better deal.'

"My M.S. Thesis was a study of the extremely high worker incomes at Geo. A. Hormel (a large meat packer). It showed that the high incomes were due to paternalistic management distributing the profits from successful *'marketing'*—not from more efficient labor or production methods. So I shifted to marketing. This program leaned toward macro-functional-cause and effect-economics-accounting-industrial engineering training which has served me well. The 'marketing' part was based on the thinking of Alderson and Vaile-Grether-Cox, as well as sales and cost analysis which assumed that marketing costs *were* incurred for a meaningful managerial purpose.

"I earned a B.S. in Business Administration (1950) at Northwestern University, an M.A. in Labor Economics (1954) and a Ph.D. in Business Administration (1958) at the University of Minnesota. Post-doctoral study included the Ford Foundation study of applied mathematics at Harvard (1959–60), and a Ford Foundation Fellowship to study the role of marketing in economic development (1963–64).

"In 1956, I went to the University of Notre Dame to teach a freshman course in 'management-oriented marketing' with several case-oriented Harvard Business School people. Here, my past experience, academic training, and 'bottom-line' mentality began to come together. But I felt the students needed a textbook—cases alone were not enough—and existing texts did not have the managerial emphasis we wanted. Frustration and various patchwork efforts followed.

"In 1958–59, while struggling to develop and assemble course materials, several book publishers' representatives encouraged me to turn those efforts into a book. Eventually, I agreed to sign with Richard D. Irwin, Inc. and began to organize a text around 'marketing strategy planning' as it should be done by the marketing manager (or any market-oriented top manager) of a business. The 4 Ps in a marketing mix aimed at a target market became the organizing structure. The outcome was publication of *Basic Marketing: A Managerial Approach* in 1960. A shorter version of this text, *Essentials of Marketing,* was published in 1985.

"I deliberately brought in a co-author, W. D. Perreault, 'early' for *Basic Marketing,* (9th edition, 1987), to ensure that this market will continue to receive the best managerially oriented teaching materials it is possible to supply. This 'passing of the baton' also enables me to devote more time to (1) training top management teams to use the same principles and techniques in their strategy planning (to improve *micro*marketing activity), and (2) research on the operation of our *macro*marketing system—with the objective of improving that too."

(1987).

WILLIAM J. STANTON

William J. Stanton's response has been incorporated in the text.

LOUIS W. STERN

Louis W. Stern's response has been incorporated in the text.

When this book was first published, the bibliography represented a fairly complete listing of books then regarded as the body of marketing literature. They were classified as follows:

Conception and Development of Marketing Thought
Advertising
Credit
Sales and Salesmanship
Sales Management
Marketing Research
Retailing
Wholesaling
General Marketing

Inasmuch as in recent years the volume of publications has increased greatly and new areas of thought have appeared in the literature, a selection of works has been necessary. Those included are books which have made appreciable contributions to marketing thought and others which indicate the trend and character of its development.

The present classification includes:

The Beginnings of Marketing Thought
Advertising
Credit
Selling and Salesmanship
Sales Management
Retailing
Wholesaling
Marketing Research
General Marketing
Marketing Management
Social and Behavioral Aspects of Marketing
Quantitative Aspects of Marketing
Marketing Systems
Environmentalism and Comparative Marketing
International Marketing
Logistics
Marketing and Society
Conceptual Development of Marketing Theory

Within each category, titles are arranged chronologically, according to the date of original publications, and alphabetically within the date groups.

Revisions and subsequent editions are shown with the title of their first publication.

THE BEGINNINGS OF MARKETING THOUGHT

1936 HAGERTY, JAMES E. "Experiences of Our Early Marketing Teachers," *Journal of Marketing.* I, July, 1936, p. 20.
1938 MAYNARD, H. H. "Training Teachers of Marketing and Research Workers," *Journal of Marketing.* II, April, 1938, p. 282.
1941 AGNEW, H. E. "The History of the American Marketing Association," *Journal of Marketing.* V, April, 1941, p. 374.
   MAYNARD, H. H. "Marketing Courses Prior to 1910," *Journal of Marketing.* V, April, 1941, p. 382.
   WELD, L. D. H. "Early Experiences in Teaching Courses in Marketing," *Journal of Marketing.* V, April, 1941, p. 380.
1942 MAYNARD, H. H. "Early Teachers of Marketing," *Journal of Marketing.* VII, October, 1942, p. 158.
1945 CONVERSE, PAUL D. "Fred Clark's Bibliography as of the Early 1920's," *Journal of Marketing.* X, July, 1945, p. 54.
1950 LITMAN, SIMON. "The Beginnings of Teaching Marketing in American Universities," *Journal of Marketing.* XV, October, 1950, p. 220.
1951 BARTELS, ROBERT, "Influences on the Development of Marketing Thought," *Journal of Marketing.* XVI, July, 1951, p. 1.
1952 CONVERSE, P. D. "Notes on Origin of the American Marketing Association," *Journal of Marketing,* XVII, July, 1952, p. 65.
1955 REVZAN, DAVID A. *A Comprehensive Classified Marketing Bibliography,* Parts I and II. Berkeley: University of California, 1955.
1958 THOMPSON, RALPH B. *Selected and Annotated Bibliography of Marketing Theory.* Bureau of Business Research Bibliography Series, No. 14, Austin: University of Texas, 1958.
1959 CONVERSE, P. D. *The Beginning of Marketing Thought in the United States, with Reminiscences of Some of the Pioneer Scholars.* Bureau of Business Research Studies in Marketing, No. 3. Austin: University of Texas, 1959.
1960 COOLSEN, FRANK G. *Marketing Thought in the United States in the Late Nineteenth Century.* Lubbock, Texas: Texas Tech Press, 1960.

ADVERTISING

1903 SCOTT, W. D. *The Theory of Advertising.* Boston: Small, Maynard & Co., 1903.
1905 CALKINS, E. E., and R. HOLDEN. *Modern Advertising.* New York: D. Appleton-Century Co., Inc. 1905; rev. by CALKINS, 1913, as *The Business of Advertising.*
   POWELL, G. H. *Powell's Practical Advertiser.* New York: G. H. Powell, 1905.
1908 DeWEESE, T. A. *The Principles of Practical Publicity.* 3d ed., Philadelphia: G. W. Jacobs & Co., 1908.
   SCOTT, W. D. *The Psychology of Advertising.* Boston: Small, Maynard & Co., 1908; 2d ed., 1921; 3d ed., 1931.
1910 BRIDGEWATER, H. *Advertising.* New York: I. Pitman & Sons, 1910.

1912 PARSONS, F. A. *The Principles of Advertising Arrangement.* New York: Prang Co., 1912.

SCHRYER, W. A. *Analytical Advertising.* Detroit: Business Service Corporation, 1912.

1913 CHERINGTON, PAUL T. *Advertising as a Business Force.* Garden City, N.Y.: Doubleday, Page & Co., 1913.

HOLLINGWORTH, H. L. *Advertising and Selling.* New York: D. Appleton-Century Co., Inc. 1913; 2d ed., 1925.

MacDONALD, J. A. *Successful Retail Advertising.* Chicago: Dry Goods Reporter Co., 1913.

1914 HAWKINS, G. H. E. *Newspaper Advertising.* Chicago: Advertisers Publishing Co., 1914.

LEWIS, E. St. E. *Preliminaries to Efficient Advertising.* New York: Alexander Hamilton Institute, 1914.

1915 HALL, S. R. *Writing an Advertisement.* Boston: Houghton Mifflin Co., 1915.

HESS, H. W. *Productive Advertising.* Philadelphia: J. B. Lippincott, 1915; rev. ed., 1931, as *Advertising: Its Economics, Philosophy, and Technique.*

TIPPER, HARRY, H. L. HOLLINGWORTH, G. R. HOTCHKISS, and F. A. PARSONS. *Advertising: Its Principles and Practices.* New York: Ronald Press Co., 1915.

1916 ADAMS, HENRY F. *Advertising and Its Mental Laws.* New York: Macmillan Co., 1916.

MacFARLANE, C. A. *Principles and Practice of Direct Advertising.* 2d ed., Hamilton, Ohio: Beckett Paper Co., 1916.

1917 DeBOWER, HERBERT F. *Advertising Principles.* New York: Alexander Hamilton Institute, 1917.

1918 KASTOR, E. H. *Advertising.* Chicago: LaSalle Extension University, 1918.

OPDYCKE, J. B. *Advertising and Selling Practice.* Chicago: A. W. Shaw Co., 1918.

1919 SANGER, J. W. *Advertising Methods in Chile, Peru, and Bolivia.* Washington, D.C.: U.S. Government Printing Office, 1919.

1920 SANGER, J. W. *Advertising Methods in Argentina, Uruguay, and Brazil.* Washington, D.C.: U.S. Government Printing Office, 1920.

SLOAN, C. A., and J. D. MOONEY. *Advertising the Technical Product.* New York: McGraw-Hill Book Co., Inc., 1920.

1921 DURSTINE, ROY S. *Making Advertisements and Making Them Pay.* New York: Charles Scribner's Sons, 1921.

HALL, S. R. *The Advertising Handbook.* New York: McGraw-Hill Book Co., Inc., 1921; 2d ed., 1930.

1923 BURDICK, RUPERT L. *Advertising to Retailers.* New York: Ronald Press Co., 1923.

HERROLD, L. D. *Advertising for the Retailer.* New York: D. Appleton-Century Co., Inc., 1923.

PROPSON, C. F. *Export Advertising Practice.* New York: Prentice-Hall, Inc., 1923.

STARCH, D. *Principles of Advertising.* New York: A. W. Shaw Co., 1923.

1924 BREWSTER, A. J., and H. H. PALMER. *Introduction to Advertising.* New York: A. W. Shaw Co., 1924; 2d ed., 1931; 3d ed., 1933; 4th ed., 1941; 5th ed., 1947; 6th ed., 1954, with ROBERT G. INGRAHAM.

DONAVAN, H. McC., *Advertising Response.* Philadelphia: J. B. Lippincott, 1924.

HALL, S. R., *Retail Advertising and Selling.* New York: McGraw-Hill Book Co., Inc., 1925.

HOTCHKISS, G. G. *Advertising Copy.* New York: Harper & Bros., 1924; rev. ed., 1937; 3d ed., 1949.

NAMM, B. J. *Advertising the Retail Store.* New York: U.P.C. Book Co., Inc., 1924; Scientific Book Corp. 1926.

ROLPH, INEW K. *Cooperative Retail Advertising.* Washington, D.C.: U.S. Government Printing Office, 1924.

1925 KLEPPNER, OTTO. *Advertising Procedure,* New York: Prentice-Hall, Inc., 1925; 2d ed., 1933; 3d ed., 1941; 4th ed., 1950; 5th ed., 1966; 6th ed., 1973.

POFFENBERGER, A. T. *Psychology in Advertising.* New York: A. W. Shaw Co., 1925.

SHELDON, GEORGE H. *Advertising Elements and Principles.* New York: Harcourt, Brace & Co., 1925.

TIPPER, HARRY, and GEORGE FRENCH. *Advertising Campaign.* New York: D. Van Nostrand Co., 1925.

1926 AGNEW, H. E. *Cooperative Advertising by Competitors.* New York: Harper & Bros., 1926.

BREWSTER, A. J. *An Introduction to Retail Advertising.* New York: A. W. Shaw Co., 1926.

HALL, S. R. *Theory and Practice of Advertising.* New York: McGraw-Hill Book Co., Inc., 1926.

HERROLD, L. D. *Advertising Copy.* New York: A. W. Shaw Co., 1926.

LICHTENBERG, BERNARD, and BRUCE BARTON. *Advertising Campaigns.* New York: Alexander Hamilton Institute, 1926.

METZGER, G. P. *Copy.* Garden City, N.Y.: Doubleday, Page & Co., 1926.

POFFENBERGER, ALBERT T. *Psychology in Advertising.* Chicago: A. W. Shaw Co., 1926; 2d ed., 1932.

WOOLF, J. D. *Writing Advertising.* New York: Ronald Press Co., 1926.

1927 AGNEW, H. E., and G. B. HOTCHKISS. *Advertising Principles.* New York: Alexander Hamilton Institute, 1927.

BORDEN, NEIL H. *Problems in Advertising.* New York: A. W. Shaw Co., 1927; 2d ed., 1932; 3d ed., 1937.

CRUM, W. L. *Advertising Fluctuations.* New York: A. W. Shaw Co., 1927.

GOODE, K. M. and H. POWELL, Jr., *What about Advertising?* New York: Harper & Bros., 1927.

LEWIS, NORMAN. *How To Become an Advertising Man.* New York: Ronald Press Co., 1927.

NAMM, BENJAMIN H. *Advertising the Retail Stores.* New York: Scientific Book Corp., 1927.

PARRISH, AMOS. *Advertising.* New York: Alexander Hamilton Institute, 1927.

PICKEN, J. H. *Advertising.* New York: System Magazine, 1927.
. *Principles of Window Display.* New York: A. W. Shaw Co., 1927.

STARCH, DANIEL. *Advertising Principles.* New York: A. W. Shaw Co., 1927.

VAILE, R. S. *Economics of Advertising.* New York: Ronald Press Co., 1927.

1928 CALKINS, E. E. *Business, the Civilizer.* Boston: Little, Brown & Co., 1928.

CHERINGTON, PAUL T. *The Consumer Looks at Advertising.* New York: Harper & Bros., 1928.

DURSTINE, ROY S. *This Advertising Business.* New York: Charles Scribner's Sons, 1928.

DWIGGINS, W. A. *Layout in Advertising.* New York: Harper & Bros., 1928; rev. ed., 1948.

NAETHER, CARL G. *Advertising to Women.* New York: Prentice-Hall, Inc., 1928.

PERCY, CARL. *Window Display Advertising.* New York: John Day Co., 1928.

VAUGHAN, F. L. *Marketing and Advertising.* Princeton, N.J.: Princeton University Press, 1928.

YOUNG, F.A. *Advertising Layout.* New York: Convici, 1928.

1929 DIPPY, A. W. *Advertising Production Methods.* New York: McGraw-Hill Book Co., Inc., 1929.

LOCKWOOD, R. B. *Industrial Advertising Copy.* New York: McGraw-Hill Book Co., Inc., 1929.

PRESBERY, F. S. *The History and Development of Advertising.* New York: Doubleday, Doran & Co., 1929.

RHEINSTROM, CARROL. *Psyching the Ads; the Case Book of Advertising.* New York: Covici, 1929.

1930 *The Ethical Problems of Modern Advertising.* New York: Ronald Press Co., 1930.

HERROLD, L. D. *Advertising Copy, Principles, and Practice.* New York: McGraw-Hill Book Co., Inc., 1930.

LUCAS, D. E. *Psychology for Advertisers.* New York: Harper & Bros., 1930.

TOBIAS, M. E. *Profitable Retail Advertising.* New York: Harper & Bros., 1930.

1931 GARDNER, E. H. *The Economics of Advertising.* Chicago: E. H. Gardner, 1931.

GREER, C. R. *Advertising and Its Mechanical Production.* Hamilton, Ohio: Beckett Paper Co., 1931; 2d ed., 1948.

GUNDLACK, E. T. *Facts and Fetishes in Advertising.* Chicago: Consolidated Book Publishers, Inc., 1931.

HAASE, A. E. *The Advertising Appropriation.* New York: Harper & Bros., 1931.

1932 AGNEW, H. E. *Advertising Media.* New York: D. Van Nostrand Co., 1932., 2d ed. with WARREN B. BYGERT. New York: McGraw-Hill Book Co., Inc., 1938.

COLLINS, KENNETH R. *The Road to Good Advertising.* New York: Greenberg, 1932.

LINK, H. C. *The New Psychology of Selling and Advertising.* New York: Macmillan Co., 1932.

LYONS, L. S. *Advertising Allowances.* Washington, D.C.: The Brookings Institution, 1932.

1933 ARNOLD, FRANK A. *Broadcast Advertising.* New York: John Wiley & Sons, Inc., 1933.

HETTINGER, H. S. *A Decade of Radio Advertising.* Chicago: University of Chicago Press, 1933.

HOTCHKISS, G. B. *An Outline of Advertising: Its Philosophy, Science, Art, and Strategy.* New York: Macmillan Co., 1933; 2d ed., 1940; 3d ed., 1950.

KING, H. F. *Practical Advertising.* New York: D. Appleton-Century Co., Inc., 1933.

1934 FIRTH, L. E. *Testing Advertisements*. New York: McGraw-Hill Book Co., Inc., 1934.

HAASE, A. E., L. C. LOCKLEY, and I. W. DIGGES. *Advertising Agency Compensation*. New York: National Process Co., 1934.

RORTY, JAMES. *Our Master's Voice: Advertising*. New York: John Day Co., 1934.

TAYLOR, F. W. *The Economics of Advertising*. London: G. Allen & Unwin, Ltd., 1934.

1935 DeLEPATICKI, E. *Advertising Layout and Typography*. New York: Ronald Press Co., 1935.

DUFFY, B. *Advertising Media and Markets*. New York: Prentice-Hall, Inc., 1935; 2d ed., 1951.

HANLON, WALTER. *Breaking into Advertising*. New York: National Library Press, 1935.

MATTHEWS, J. B. *Partners in Plunder*. New York: Covici, 1935.

STANLEY, T. B. *A Manual of Advertising Typography*. New York: Prentice-Hall, Inc., 1935.

1936 CAPLES, JOHN. *Advertising for Immediate Sales*. New York: Harper & Bros., 1936.

GROSS, M. *Dealer Display Advertising*. New York: Ronald Press Co., 1936.

KENNER, H. J. *The Fight for Truth in Advertising*. New York: Round Table Press, 1936.

REED, V. D. *Advertising and Selling Industrial Goods*. New York: Ronald Press Co., 1936.

SANDAGE, C. H. *Advertising Theory and Practice*. Chicago: Business Publications, Inc., 1936; 2d ed., Richard D. Irwin, Inc., 1939; 3d ed., 1948; 4th ed., 1953, with VERNON FRYBURGER.; 5th ed., 1958; 6th ed., 1963; 7th ed., 1967; 8th ed., 1971.

1937 EDWARDS, C. M., JR. *Retail Advertising and Sales Promotion*. New York: Prentice-Hall, Inc., 1937; 2d ed., 1950, with W. H. HOWARD; 3d ed., 1959, with R. A. BROWN.

HOWARD, K. S. *How To Write Advertisements*. New York: McGraw-Hill Book Co., Inc., 1937.

NIXON, H. K. *Principles of Advertising*. New York: McGraw-Hill Book Co., Inc., 1937.

O'DEA, MARK. *A Preface to Advertising*. New York: McGraw-Hill Book Co., Inc., 1937.

Scientific Space Selection. Chicago: Audit Bureau of Circulations, 1937.

1938 AGNEW, H. E. *Outdoor Advertising*. New York: McGraw-Hill Book Co., Inc., 1938.

BURTT, H. E. *Psychology of Advertising*. New York: Houghton Mifflin Co., 1938.

CAPLES, JOHN. *Advertising Ideas*. New York: McGraw-Hill Book Co., Inc., 1938.

WEISS, E. B. *The Handbook of Advertising*. New York: McGraw-Hill Book Co., Inc., 1938.

1939 DURRY, BEN. *Advertising Media and Markets*. New York: Prentice-Hall, Inc., 1939.

GOODE, K. M., and Z. KAUFMAN. *Showmanship in Business*. New York: Harper & Bros., 1939; 2d ed., 1947.

1940 APPEL, JOSEPH H. *Growing Up with Advertising*. New York: Business Bourse, 1940.

EGNER, FRANK, and L. R. WALTER. *Direct-Mail Advertising and Selling.* New York: Harper & Bros., 1940.

STANLEY, T. B. *The Technique of Advertising Production.* New York: Prentice-Hall, Inc., 1940; 2d ed., 1954.

1941 HEPNER, H. W. *Effective Advertising.* New York: McGraw-Hill Book Co., Inc., 1941; 2d ed., 1949; 3d ed., 1956, as *Modern Advertising.*

1942 BORDEN, N. H. *The Economic Effects of Advertising.* Chicago: Richard D. Irwin, Inc., 1942.

WISEMAN, MARK. *The Anatomy of Advertising.* New York: Harper & Bros., 1942.

1943 CLOYES, CARRIE. *Advertising and Its Role in War and Peace.* Washington, D. C.: U. S. Government Printing Office, 1943.

1945 BORDEN, N. H. *Advertising in Our Econommy.* Chicago: Richard D. Irwin, Inc., 1945.

ROPER, B. W. *State Advertising Legislation.* New York: Printers' Ink Publishing Co., Inc., 1945.

1946 BELL, H. A. *Getting the Right Start in Direct Advertising.* New York: Graphic Books, 1946.

DALGIN, BEN. *Advertising Production.* New York: McGraw-Hill Book Co., Inc., 1946.

1947 CAPLES, JOHN. *Tested Advertising Methods.* New York: Harper & Bros., 1947.

DOREMUS, W. L. *Advertising for Profit.* New York: Pitman Publishing Corp., 1947.

FREY, A. W. *Advertising.* New York: Ronald Press Co., 1947; 2d ed., 1953; 3d ed., 1961.

LUND, J. V. *Newspaper Advertising.* New York: Prentice-Hall, Inc., 1947.

MANVILLE, RICHARD. *How To Create and Select Winning Advertisements.* New York: Harper & Bros., 1947.

RUDOLPH, H. J. *Attention and Interest Factors in Advertising.* New York: Funk and Wagnalls Co., 1947.

1948 MAYTHAM, T. E. *Introduction to Advertising Principles and Practice.* New York: Harper & Bros., 1948.

1949 BORDEN, N. H. *Advertising: Text and Cases.* Chicago: Richard D. Irwin, Inc., 1949; rev. ed., 1959, as *Advertising Management, Text and Cases,* with M. V. MARSHALL, rev. ed., 1965.

BRIDGE, H. P. *Practical Advertising.* New York: Rinehart, 1949.

BURTON, PHILIP W. and G. BOWMAN KREER. *Advertising Copywriting.* Englewood Cliffs, N. J.: Prentice-Hall, Inc., 1949; 2d ed., 1962; 3d ed., 1974.

1950 BARTON, ROGER, *et al. Advertising Handbook.* New York: Prentice-Hall, Inc., 1950.

HATTWICK, M. S. *How To Use Psychology for Better Advertising.* New York: Prentice-Hall, Inc., 1950.

HYMES, D. G. *Production in Advertising.* New York: Colton Press, 1950.

LUCAS, D. B. *Advertising Psychology.* New York: McGraw-Hill Book Co., Inc., 1950.

SCOTT, JAMES D. *Advertising Principles and Problems.* New York: Prentice-Hall, Inc., 1950; 1953.

1951 *Advertising Idea Book.* New York: Funk and Wagnalls, 1951.

BRENNAN, ED. *Advertising Media.* New York: McGraw-Hill Book Co., Inc., 1951.

328

BURTON, P. W. *Retail Advertising for the Small Store.* New York: Prentice-Hall, Inc., 1951.

SEEHAFER, G. F., and J. W. LAEMMAR. *Successful Radio and Television Advertising.* New York: McGraw-Hill Book Co., Inc., 1951.

RAMEN, J. R., and D. F. BLANKERTZ. *Profitable Retail Advertising.* New York: Ronald Press Co., 1951.

1952   *Advertising and Marketing.* Chicago: La Salle Extension University, 1952.

GRAHAM, IRVIN. *Encyclopedia of Advertising.* New York: Fairchild Publications, 1952.

————. *Advertising Agency Practice.* New York: Harper & Bros., 1952.

GROHMANN, H. VICTOR. *Advertising Terminology.* New York: Needham and Grohmann, 1952.

HOTCHKISS, G. B. *Advertising.* New York: Alexander Hamilton Institute, 1952.

1953   BOONE, J. (ed.). *Industrial Advertising Handbook.* New York: McGraw-Hill Book Co., Inc., 1953.

HUTCHINES, M. S. *Cooperative Advertising.* New York: Ronald Press Co., 1953.

1955   BURTON, PHILIP W. *Principles of Advertising.* New York: Prentice-Hall, Inc., 1955.

DAVIS, DONALD W. *Basic Text in Advertising.* Pleasantville, N.Y.: Printers' Ink Books, 1955.

FREY, A. W. *How Many Dollars for Advertising.* New York: Ronald Press Co., 1955.

WHITTIER, CHARLES L. *Creative Advertising.* New York: Henry Holt & Co., 1955.

1956   DE VOE, MERRILL. *Effective Advertising Copy.* New York: Macmillan Co., 1956.

DIX, W. R. *Industrial Advertising for Profit and Prestige.* Pleasantville, N.Y.: Printers' Ink Books, 1956.

1957   BROWN, L. O., R. S. LESSLER, and W. M. WEILBACHER. *Advertising Media.* New York: Ronald Press Co., 1957.

MARTINEAU, PIERRE. *Motivation in Advertising.* New York: McGraw-Hill Book Co., Inc., 1957.

PACKARD, V. O. *The Hidden Persuaders.* New York: D. McKay Co., 1957.

SMITH, R. B. *Advertising to Business.* Homewood, Ill.: Richard D. Irwin, Co., 1957.

1958   *The Advertising Agency Business around the World.* New York: American Association of Advertising Agencies, 1958.

CRISP, R. D. *How To Increase Advertising Effectiveness.* New York: McGraw-Hill Book Co., Inc., 1958.

FREY, A. W., and K. R. DAVIS. *The Advertising Industry.* New York: Association of National Advertisers, Inc., 1958.

GROESBECK, K. *Advertising Agency Success.* New York: Harper & Bros., 1958.

LOOK, AL. *Advertising or Retail.* Denver: Golden Bell Press, 1958.

MAYER, MARTIN. *Madison Avenue, U. S. A.* New York: Harper & Bros., 1958.

WALES, H. G., P. L. GENTRY, and M. WALES. *Advertising Copy, Layout, and Typography.* New York: Ronald Press Co., 1958.

WOOD, J. P. *The Story of Advertising.* New York: Ronald Press Co., 1958.

1959 BORDEN, Neil H. and MARTIN V. MARSHALL. *Advertising Management.* Homewood, Ill.: Richard D. Irwin, Inc. 1959.

BURTON, P. W. *The Profitable Sciences of Making Media Work.* New London, Conn.: Printers' Ink Books, 1959.

CLARKE, G. T. *Copywriting.* New York: Harper & Bros., 1959.

KIRKPATRICK, C. A. *Advertising: Mass Communication in Marketing.* Boston: Houghton Mifflin, 1959; 2d ed., 1964; 3d ed. with J. E. LITTLEFIELD, 1970.

SEEHAFER, G. F. and J. W. LAEMMAR. *Successful Television and Radio Advertising.* New York: McGraw-Hill Book Co., Inc., 1959.

WISEMAN, M. *The New Anatomy of Advertising.* New York: Harper & Bros., 1951.

1960 ARNOLD, E. C. *Profitable Newspaper Advertising.* New York: Harper & Bros., 1960.

CAPLES, J. *Tested Advertising Methods.* New York: Harper & Bros., 1960.

CRAWFORD, J. W. *Advertising: Communications for Management.* Boston: Allyn and Bacon, 1960.

DIRKSEN, C. J., and A. KROEGER. *Advertising Principles and Problems.* Homewood, Ill.: Richard D. Irwin, Inc., 1960; rev. ed., 1964; 3d ed., 1968; 4th ed., 1973.

SANDAGE, C. H. and V. R. FRYBURGER. *The Role of Advertising.* Homewood, Ill.: Richard D. Irwin, Inc., 1960.

WEIR, W. *On the Writing of Advertising.* New York: McGraw-Hill Book Co., Inc., 1960.

1961 AXELFOD, JOEL N. *Choosing the Best Advertising Alternative.* New York: Association of National Advertisers, Inc., 1961.

GAW, WALTER A. *Advertising: Methods and Media.* San Francisco: Wadsworth Publishing Co., 1961.

ZACHER, ROBERT V. *Advertising Techniques and Management.* Homewood, Ill.: Richard D. Irwin, Inc., 1961; rev. ed., 1967.

1962 SCHWAB, VICTOR O. *How to Write a Good Advertisement.* New York: Harper & Row, 1962.

WEDDING, C. NUGENT and RICHARD S. LESSLER. *Advertising Management.* New York: Ronald Press Co., 1962.

WRIGHT, JOHN S. and D. S. WARNER. *Advertising.* New York: McGraw-Hill Book Co., Inc., 1962; 2d ed., 1966; 3d ed., with W. H. WINTER, Jr., 1971.

1963 BRINK, EDWARD L. and WILLIAM T. KELLEY. *The Management of Promotion.* Englewood Cliffs, N.J.: Prentice-Hall, Inc., 1963.

CHESTER, GIRAUD, *et al. Television and Radio.* New York: Appleton-Century-Crofts, 3d ed., 1963.

FERGUSON, JAMES. *The Advertising Rate Structure in the Daily Newspaper Industry.* Englewood Cliffs, N.J.: Prentice-Hall, Inc., 1963.

LUCAS, DARREL B. and STEUART H. BRITT. *Measuring Advertising Effectiveness.* New York: McGraw-Hill Book Co., Inc., 1963.

MESSNER, FRED R. *Industrial Advertising.* New York: McGraw-Hill Book Co., Inc., 1963.

WIRSIG, WOODROW (ed.). *Principles of Advertising.* New York: Pittman Publishing Co., 1963.

1964 BURTON, ROGER. *Media in Advertising.* New York: McGraw-Hill Book Co., Inc., 1964.

McCLURE, LESLIE W. and PAUL C. FULTON. *Advertising in the Printed Media.* New York: Macmillan Co., 1964.

OGILVY, DAVID. *Confessions of an Advertising Man.* New York: Atheneum Publishers, 1964.

PALDA, KRISTIAN S. *The Measurement of Cumulative Advertising Effects.* Englewood Cliffs, N.J.: Prentice-Hall, Inc., 1964.

STEWART, JOHN B. *Repetitive Advertising in Newspapers.* Boston: Harvard University Graduate School of Business Administration, 1964.

TOWNSEND, DEREK. *Advertising and Public Relations.* London: A. Redman, 1964.

1965   BOYD, HARPER W., JR. and JOSEPH W. NEWMAN (eds.). *Advertising Management.* Homewood, Ill.: Richard D. Irwin, Inc., 1965.

COLLEY, RUSSELL H. *Defining Advertising Goals for Measured Advertising Results.* New York: Association of National Advertisers, Inc., 1965.

CRANE, E. *Marketing Communications.* New York: John Wiley & Sons, Inc., 1965.

HIGGINS, DENIS. *The Art of Writing Advertising.* Chicago: Advertising Publications, Inc., 1965.

1966   MIRACLE, G. E. *Management of International Advertising.* Ann Arbor: University of Michigan Bureau of Business Research, 1966.

NORINS, HANLEY. *The Complete Copywriter.* New York: McGraw-Hill Book Co. Inc., 1966.

RICE, CRAIG S. *How To Plan and Execute the Marketing Campaign.* Chicago: Dartnell Corp., 1966.

WOLFE, H. D., *et al, Evaluating Media.* New York: National Industrial Conference Board, Inc., 1966.

1967   BACKMAN, JULES. *Advertising and Competition.* New York: New York University Press, 1967.

BOGART, LEO. *Strategy in Advertising.* New York: Harcourt, Brace & World, Inc., 1967.

BOYD, H. W. and S. J. LEVY, *Promotion: A Behavioral View.* Englewood Cliffs, N.J.: Prentice-Hall, Inc., 1967.

DURKEE, BURTON R. *How to Make Advertising Work.* New York: McGraw-Hill Book Co., Inc., 1967.

ENGEL, J.F., HUGH G. WALES, and MARTIN WARSHAW. *Promotional Strategy.* Homewood, Illinois: Richard D. Irwin, Inc., 1967, rev. ed., 1971.

SAMSON, HARLAND E. *Advertising and Displaying Merchandise.* Cincinnati: South-Western Publishing Co., 1967.

1968   BAUER, RAYMOND A. and STEPHEN A. GREYSER. *Advertising in America: The Consumer View.* Cambridge, Mass.: Harvard Business School Division of Research, 1968.

COWAN, D. S. and R. W. JONES. *Advertising in the 21st Century.* London: Hutchinson, 1968.

MANDELL, MAURICE I. *Advertising.* Englewood Cliffs, N.J.: Prentice-Hall, Inc., 1968; 2d ed., 1974.

NODAR, MANUEL V. *Advertising Department Management.* Serial 6788A (ed. 1) Scranton: International Correspondence Schools, 1968.

ROBINSON, PATRICK J. (ed.). *Advertising Measurement and Decision Making.* Boston: Allyn & Bacon, 1968.

TILLMAN, ROLLIE and C. A. KIRKPATRICK. *Production.* Homewood, Ill., Richard D. Irvin, Inc., 1968.

1969   American Association of Advertising Agencies. *A Handbook for the Advertising Agency Account Executive.* Reading, Mass.: Addison-Wesley Publishing Company, Inc., 1969.

BACKUS, H. WILLIAM. *Advertising Graphics.* New York: Macmillan Co., 1969.

CODDINGTON, ROBERT H. *Modern Radio Broadcasting.* Blue Ridge Summit, Pa.: Tab Books, 1969.

OBERMEYER, HENRY. *Successful Advertising Management.* New York: McGraw-Hill Book Co., Inc., 1969.

OLIVER, ROBERT E. *Advertising.* Toronto, New York: Gregg Division, McGraw-Hill Co. Inc. of Canada, 1969.

STANSFIELD, RICHARD H. *The Dartnell Advertising Manager's Handbook.* Chicago: Dartnell Corp., 1969.

1970   BARTON, ROGER. *The Handbook of Advertising Management.* New York: McGraw-Hill Co., Inc., 1970.

BURTON, PHILIP W. and J. ROBERT MILLER. *Advertising Fundamentals.* Scranton: International Textbook Co., 1970.

GAW, WALTER A. *Specialty Advertising.* Chicago: Specialty Advertising Associaiton, 2d. ed., 1970.

GLATZER, HAROLD. *The New Advertising.* New York: The Citadel Press, 1970.

KLEPPNER, OTTO and IRVING SETTEL (eds.). *Exploring Advertising.* Englewood Cliffs, N. J.: Prentice-Hall, Inc., 1970.

SIMON, JULIAN L. *Issues in the Economics of Advertising.* University of Illinois Press, Urbana, Ill., 1970.

1971   Marketing Science Institute. *Appraising the Economic and Social Effects of Advertising.* Cambridge, Mass., 1971.

1972   GREYSER, STEPHEN A. *Cases in Advertising and Communications.* Englewood Cliffs, N.J.: Prentice-Hall, Inc., 1972.

HERPEL, GEORGE I. and R. A. COLLINS. *Specialty Advertising in Marketing.* Homewood. Ill.. Dow Jones – Irsin, 1972.

JACOBS, LAURENCE WILE. *Advertising and Promotion for Retailing: Text and Cases.* Glenview, Ill.: Scott, Foresman, 1972.

MAYER, MARTIN. *About Television.* New York: Harper & Row Publishers, 1972.

1973   HOWARD, JOHN A. and JAMES HULBERT. *Advertising and the Public Interest.* Chicago: Crain Co., 1973.

RESO, OVID. *Advertising Cost Control Handbook.* New York: Van Nostrand Reinhold Co., 1973.

CREDIT

1906   PRENDERGAST, W. A. *Credit and Its Uses,* New York: D. Appleton-Century Co., Inc., 1906; 2d ed., 1931, with W. H. STEINER.

1907   ZIMMERMAN, T. J. *Credits and Collections.* Chicago: System Co., 1907.

1912   CHURCH, FRANK P. *Modern Credit Methods.* Detroit: Modern Methods Publishing Co., 1912.

GALLOWAY, L., and R. S. BUTLER. *Advertising, Selling and Credits.* New York: Alexander Hamilton Institute, 3d ed., 1912.

1913   HAGERTY, JAMES E. *Mercantile Credit.* New York: Henry Holt & Co., 1913.

1914   *Credits, Collections, and Finance.* New York: A. W. Shaw Co., 1914.

KALLMAN, M. MARTIN, *et al. Mercantile Credits.* New York: Ronald Press Co., 1914.

332

1915 BLANTON, B. H. *Credit: Its Principles and Practices.* New York: Ronald Press Co., 1915.

1916 SKINNER, ED M., R. S. WHITE, and H. E. KRAMER. *Credits and Collections.* Chicago: LaSalle Extension University, 1916.

1917 ETTINGER, R. P., and D. E. GOLIEB. *Credits and Collections.* New York: Prentice-Hall, Inc., 1917; 2d ed., 1926, 1937; 3d ed., 1949; 4th ed., 1956; 5th ed., 1962

1918 *Credits and Collections.* New York: A. W. Shaw Co., 1918.

1919 BEEBE, DWIGHT E. *Retail Credits and Collections: Modern Principles and Practices.* New York: Harper & Bros., 1919.

_____.C.W. GERSTENBERG, W.S. JOHNSON, and P.P. WAKESTED. *Credit and the Credit Man.* New York: Alexander Hamilton Institute, 1919.

MEYER, CHARLES A. *Mercantile Credits.* New York: Macmillan Co., 1919.

1922 EDWARDS, G. W. *Foreign Commercial Credits.* New York: McGraw-Hill Book Co., Inc., 1922.

GARDNER, ED H. *New Collection Methods.* New York: Ronald Press Co., 1922.

McADOW, F. H. *Mercantile Credits.* New York: Ronald Press Co., 1922.

STEINER, W. H. *The Mechanism of Commercial Credit.* New York: D. Appleton-Century Co., Inc., 1922.

WALTER, FREDERICK W. *The Retail Charge Account.* New York: Ronald Press Co., 1922.

WHITNEY, EDSON L. *Cooperative Credit Societies.* Washington, D. C.: U. S. Government Printing Office, 1922.

1923 BREWSTER, STANELY F. *Legal Aspects of Credit.* New York: Ronald Press Co., 1923.

GRIFFIN, BRYANT W. *Instalment Sales and Collections.* New York: Prentice-Hall, Inc., 1923.

POOLE, GORDON C. *Export Credits and Collections.* New York: Prentice-Hall, Inc., 1923.

1924 BECKMAN, THEODORE N. *Credits and Collections in Theory and Practice.* New York: McGraw-Hill Book Co., Inc., 1924; 2d ed., 1930; 3d ed., 1938; 4th ed., 1939; 5th ed., 1949, with ROBERT BARTELS; 6th ed., 1955; 7th ed., 1962, by T. H. BECKMAN; 8th ed., 1969, with RONALD S. FOSTER, as *Credits and Collections, Management and Theory.*

1925 GRIMES, W. A. *Financing Automobile Sales.* New York: A. W. Shaw Co., 1925.

MUNN, G. G. *Bank Credit.* New York: McGraw-Hill Book Co., Inc., 1925.

OLSON, E. E. and J. W. HALLMAN. *Credit Management.* New York: Ronald Press Co., 1925.

SCHULTER, W. C. *Credit Analysis.* New York: Prentice-Hall, Inc., 1925.

1926 SELIGMAN, E. R. A. *The Economics of Instalment Selling.* 2 vols. New York: Harper & Bros., 1926.

1927 BEEBE, D. E., G. S. CHILDS, and G. L. COURTNEY. *Credits, Collections, and Correspondence.* New York: Alexander Hamilton Institute, 1927.

PICKEN, JAMES H. *Credits and Collections.* New York: System Magazine, 1927.

TRUESDALE, T. R. *Credit Bureau Management.* New York: Prentice-Hall, Inc., 1927.

YOUNG, ROBERT. *Industrial Credits.* New York: Harper & Bros., 1927.

1928 BARTLETT, JOHN T., and CHARLES M. REED. *Retail Credit Practice.*
New York: Harper & Bros., 1928.
PICKEN, J. H. *Credit and Collection Correspondence.* New York: A. W.
Shaw Co., 1929.
1929 BRISCO, NORRIS A. *Retail Credit Procedure.* New York: Prentice-Hall,
Inc., 1929.
CHAPIN, A. F. *Credit and Collection Principles and Practices.* New York:
McGraw-Hill Book Co., Inc., 1929; 2d ed., 1935; 3d ed., 1940;
4th ed., 1941; 5th ed., 1947; 6th ed., 1953; 7th ed., 1960, with
G. E. HASSETT.
1930 MARKS, MORRIS. *How To Correct Credit Abuses.* New York: Harper &
Bros., 1930.
1932 BARTLETT, JOHN T., and CHARLES M. REED. *Credit Department
Salesmanship and Collection Psychology.* New York: Harper &
Bros., 1932.
GARDNER, ED M. *Effective Collection Methods.* New York: Ronald
Press Co., 1932.
1933 GUGGENHEIM, SAMUEL W. *How To Collect Instalment Accounts.*
Rochester, N.Y.: Credit. 1933.
NEIFELD, M. R. *The Personal Finance Business.* New York: Harper &
Bros., 1933.
1936 BLUMBERG, HYMAN. *Successful Credit Store Operation.* New York:
Harper & Bros., 1936.
GRIFFIN, BRYANT W. *Instalment Credits and Collections.* New York:
Prentice-Hall, Inc., 1936.
NEIFELD, M. R. *Cooperative Consumer Credit.* New York: Harper &
Bros., 1936.
STEINER, W. H. *Mercantile Credit.* New York: Longmans, Green & Co.,
1936.
1938 BABSON, R. W. *The Folly of Instalment Buying.* New York: Frederick
A. Stokes Co., 1938.
HARDY, C. O., *et al. Consumer Credit and Its Uses.* New York:
Prentice-Hall, Inc., 1938.
PHELPS, C. W. *Retail Credit Fundamentals.* St. Louis: National Retail
Credit Association, 1938; 2d ed., 1947; 3d ed., 1952; 4th ed.,
1963.
WHITE, W. L., and DUDLEY CATES. *Economic Effects of Instalment
Credit.* New York: American Management Association, 1938.
1939 FOSTER, W. T. *Public Supervision of Consumer Credit.* Newton, Mass.:
Pollack Foundation, 1939.
FOULKE, ROY A., and H. V. PROCHNOW. *Practical Bank Credit.* New
York: Prentice-Hall, Inc., 1939; 2d ed., 1950.
NEIFELD, M. R. *Personal Finance Comes of Age.* New York: Harper &
Bros., 1939.
NUGENT, ROLF. *Consumer Credit and Economic Stability.* New York:
Russell Sage Foundation, 1939.
1940 BERNSTEIN, BLANCHE. *The Pattern of Consumer Debt.* New York:
National Bureau of Economic Research, 1940.
CHAPMAN, JOHN M., *et al. Commercial Bank and Consumer Instalment
Credit.* New York: National Bureau of Economic Research, 1940.
HOLTHAUSEN, D. McC., MALCOLM L. MERRIAM, and ROLF
NUGENT. *The Volume of Consumer Instalment Credit.* New
York: National Bureau of Economic Research, 1940.

334

PLUMMER, W. C., and R. A. YOUNG. *Sales Finance Companies and Their Practices.* New York: National Bureau of Economic Research, 1940.

1941 CRAGG, ALLISTON. *Do You Need Some Money?* New York: Harper & Bros., 1941.

FOULKE, ROY A. *The Sinews of American Commerce.* New York: Dun and Bradstreet, Inc., 1941.

PHELPS, C. W. *Accounts Receivable System for Small Stores.* Chicago: Household Finance Corp., 1941.

____. *Bookkeeping for Credit Control.* Household Finance Corp., 1941.

ROLLER, JOHN R. *Retail Credit Office Expenses in Ohio Department Stores.* Columbus, Ohio: Bureau of Business Research, Ohio State University, 1941.

1942 BRISCO, NORRIS A., and R. M. SEVERA. *Retail Credit.* New York: Prentice-Hall, Inc., 1942.

FOULKE, ROY A. *Credit Problems in a War Economy.* New York: Dun and Bradstreet, Inc., 1942.

IRONS, W. H. *Commercial Credit and Collection Practice.* New York: Ronald Press Co., 1942; 2d ed., 1957, with D. H. BELLMORE.

1943 GEE, ED F. *Evaluation of Receivables and Inventories.* Cambridge, Mass.: Banker Publishing Co., 1943.

MERGENDAHL, CHARLES N., and LeBARON R. FOSTER. *One Hundred Problems in Consumer Credit.* Newton, Mass.: Pollack Foundation, 1943.

SAULNIER, R. J. *Accounts Receivable Financing.* New York: National Bureau of Economic Research, 1943.

SPRAGUE, J. R. *The Romance of Credit.* New York: D. Appleton–Century Co., Inc., 1943.

1945 FOSTER, LeBARON R. *Credit for Consumers.* New York: Public Affairs Co., Inc., 1945.

1946 AYRES, MILAN V. *Instalment Mathematics Handbook.* New York: Ronald Press Co., 1946.

BUTTERFIELD, WILLIAM H. *How To Write Good Credit Letters.* St. Louis: National Retail Credit Assocaition, 1946.

1947 PHELPS, C. W. *Important Steps in Retail Credit Operation.* St. Louis: National Retail Credit Association, 1947.

____. *Retail Credit Fundamentals.* New York: McGraw-Hill Book Co., Inc., 1947.

SHULTZ, W. J. *Credit and Collection Management.* New York: Prentice-Hall, Inc., 1947; 2d ed., 1954, with H. REINHARDT; 3d ed., 1962.

1948 COX, REAVIS. *The Economics of Instalment Buying.* New York: Ronald Press Co., 1948.

1949 BECKMAN, THEODORE N., and S. F. OTTESON. *Cases in Credits and Collections.* New York: McGraw-Hill Book Co., Inc., 1949.

PHELPS, C. W. *Retail Credit Management.* St. Louis: National Retail Credit Association, 1949.

1950 DAKINS, JOHN GORDON. *Retail Credit Manual.* New York: National Retail Dry Goods Association, 1950.

SCHULTZ, W. J., and H. REINHARDT. *Problems in Credits and Collections.* New York: Prentice-Hall, Inc., 1950.

1952 PHELPS, C. W. *The Role of the Sales Finance Companies in the American Economy.* Baltimore: Commercial Credit Co., 1952.

1953   *Analysis and Evaluation of Credit Management Functions.* New York:
       Credit Research Foundation, 1953.
       LITTLE, J. D. *Complete Credit and Collection Letters.* New York:
       Prentice-Hall, Inc., 1953.
       PHELPS, C. W. *Instalment Sales Financing: Its Service to the Dealer.*
       Baltimore: Commercial Credit Co., 1953.
       SCHWARTZ, ROBERT J., and ALLYN M. SCHIFFER. *Credit and
       Collection Know-How.* New York: Fairchild, 1953.
1954   FLANAGAN, GEORGE A. *Secrets of Successful Collections by Mail.*
       New York: New Voices Publishing Co., 1954.
       PHELPS, C. W. *Financing the Instalment Purchases of the American
       Family.* Baltimore: Commercial Credit Co., 1954.
       WOOD, JOSEPH L. *Better Sales through Credit.* New York: Vantage
       Press, 1954.
1955   STURGES, WESLEY ALBA. *Cases and Materials on the Law of Credit
       Transactions.* St. Paul, Minn.: West, 1955, 4th ed.
       WINCHESTER, JAMES P. *Consumer Installment Loan Losses and
       Valuation Reserves.* Boston: Bankers Publishing Co., 1955.
1956   BRAYER, H. O. *Tested Credit and Collection Letters.* Chicago: Dartnell,
       1956.
       PHELPS, C. W. *The Role of Factoring in Modern Business Finance.*
       Baltimore: Commercial Credit Co., 1956.
1957   D'ANDREA, M. T. *Constructive Credit Management.* New York: 1957.
       PHELPS, C. W. *Accounts Receivable Financing as a Method of Business
       Finance.* Baltimore: Commercial Credit Co., 1957.
1958   *Credit Management Handbook.* Homewood, Ill.: Richard D. Irwin, Inc.,
       1958; 2d ed., 1965.
       CURTIS, EDWARD T. *Credit Department Organization and Operation.*
       New York: American Management Association, 1958.
1960   COLE, R. N., and R. S. HANCOCK. *Consumer and Commercial Credit
       Management.* Homewood, Ill.: Richard D. Irwin, Inc., 1960; 2d ed
       1964; 3d ed., 1968; 4th ed., 1972, by R. H. Cole.
       LEVI, ARTHUR. *Credit Insurance.* Baltimore: American Credit
       Indemnity Co. of New York, 1960.
       WALLACE, H. A. *Starting and Managing a Small Credit Bureau and
       Collection Agency.* Washington, D. C.: Small Business
       Administration, 1960.
1961   NEIFELD, M. R. *Neifeld's Manual on Consumer Credit.* Easton, Pa.:
       Mack Publishing Co., 1961.
       PHELPS, C. W. *Commercial Credit Insurance as a Management Tool.*
       Baltimore: Commercial Credit Co., 1961.
1966   LOISEAUX, PIERRE R. *Cases on Creditors' Remedies.* Indianapolis:
       Bobbs Merrill, 1966.
1967   BARTELS, ROBERT. *Credit Management.* New York: The Ronald Press
       Co., 1967.
       Credit Card and Revolving Credit Survey. New York: American Bankers
       Association, 1967.
1968   FRANCIS, KENT W. *Credit Union Dynamics.* Madison, Wisc.: CUNA
       International, 1968.
       KOHN, D. P. *Credit and Collections.* Cincinnati: South-Western
       Publishing Co., 1968.
       PARRY, RICHARD L. *The Credit Reporting Industry in Transition.*
       Unpublished Ohio State University Ph.D. dissertation, 1968.

1969 FRANCIS, KENT W. *Credit Unions are People.* Madison, Wisc.: CUNA
      International, 1969.
      Trends in Cash Application and Control of Accounts Receivable. Lake
      Success, N.Y.: Credit Research Foundation, Inc., 1969.
1970 *Credit Limits Established by Formula and Computer.* Lake Success,
      N.Y.: Credit Research Foundation, Inc., 1970.
1971 DUBLIN, JACK. *Credit Unions.* Detroit: Wayne State University Press,
      1971.
      GRIFFIN, AL. *The Credit Jungle.* Chicago: H. Remnery Co., 1971.
      JAFFEE, DWIGHT M. *Credit Rationing and the Commercial Loan
      Market.* N.Y.: Wiley, 1971.
      MEYER, MARTIN J. *Credit-cardsmanship.* Lynbrook, N.Y.: Farnsworth
      Publishing Co., 1971.
      MOODY, J. CARROLL. *The Credit Union Movement.* Lincoln:
      University of Nebraska Press, 1971.
1973 SMALLEY, ORANGE A. *The Credit Merchants.* Carbondale: Southern
      Illinois University Press, 1973.

SELLING AND SALESMANSHIP

1904 ESTABROOK, P. L. *Science of Salesmanship.* Dallas: University
      Textbook Co., 1904.
1909 HIRSCHLER, D. *The Art of Retail Selling.* New York: New York
      Institute of Mercantile Training, 1909.
1910 ATKINSON, W. W. *Psychology of Salesmanship.* Chicago: Progress Co.,
      1910.
      READ, H. E. *Read's Lessons in Salesmanship.* New York: J. A. Lyons &
      Co., 1910; rev. eds., 1915 and 1930.
      RUSSELL, T. H. *Salesmanship: Theory and Practice.* Minneapolis:
      International Law and Business Institute, 1910.
      WELD, L. D. H. *Practical Salesmanship.* New York: Universal Business
      Institute, 1910.
1911 SCOTT, W. D. *Influencing Men in Business.* New York: Ronald Press Co.,
      1911; 2d ed., 1916; 3d ed., 1928.
1913 COLLINS, C. A. *Productive Sales Methods.* New York: Collin Armstrong,
      Inc., 1913.
      GOFFE, W. T. *Problems in Retail Selling, Analyzed.* Racine, Wis.:
      Western Printing and Lithographing Co., 1913.
      HOLLINGWORTH, H. L. *Advertising and Selling.* New York: D.
      Appleton-Century Co., Inc., 1913.
      MAXWELL, WILLIAM. *Salesmanship.* Boston: Houghton Mifflin Co.,
      1913.
1914 BUTLER, R. S., H. DeBOWER, and J. G. JONES. *Marketing Methods
      and Salesmanship.* New York: Alexander Hamilton Institute,
      1914.
      LEICHTER, ELSA. *Successful Selling.* New York: Funk and Wagnalls
      Co., 1914.
      NYSTROM, PAUL H. *Retail Selling and Store Management.* New York:
      D. Appleton—Century Co., Inc., 1914.
      RUST, T. D. *ABC of Salesmanship.* New York: R. F. Fenno & Co., 1914.
1916 BRISCO, N. A. *Fundamentals of Salesmannship.* New York: D.
      Appleton-Century Co., Inc., 1916.
      FISK, J. W. *Retail Selling.* New York: Harper & Bros., 1916.

HOOVER, S. R. *Science and Art of Salesmanship.* New York: Macmillan Co., 1916.

1917 WHITEHEAD, H. *Principles of Salesmanship.* New York: Ronald Press Co., 1917; 2d ed., 1923.

BARRETT, H. J. *How To Sell More Goods.* New York: Harper & Bros., 1918.

FARRINGTON, FRANK. *The Successful Salesman.* Chicago: Laird and Lee, 1918.

HAWKINS, N. A. *The Selling Process.* Detroit: N. A. Hawkins, 1918.

JONES, J. R., and RAYMOND J. COMYNS. *Salesmanship and Sales Management.* New York: Alexander Hamilton Institute, 1918.

1919 DOUGLAS, A. W. *Traveling Salesmanship.* New York: Macmillan Co., 1919.

NORTON, H. R. *Textbook of Retail Selling.* New York: Ginn & Co., 1919; 2d ed., 1924.

1920 BRISCO, N. A. *Retail Salesmanship.* New York: Ronald Press Co., 1920.

1921 KITSON, H. D. *The Mind of the Buyer.* New York: Macmillan Co., 1921.

KNOX, JAMES S. *The Science and Art of Selling.* Cleveland: Knox Business Books Co., 1921.

LEIGH, RUTH. *The Human Side of Retail Selling.* New York: D. Appleton-Century Co., Inc., 1921.

RUSSELL, T. H. *Salesmanship and Advertising.* Chicago: Lincoln Institute of Business, 1921.

1922 CHARTERS, W. W. *How To Sell at Retail.* New York: Houghton Mifflin Co., 1924.

1923 BAER, LAURA. *Retail Selling Methods.* New York: McGraw-Hill Book Co., Inc., 1922.

FERRIS, E. E. *Developing a Sales Personality.* New York: Prentice-Hall, Inc., 1923.

HESS, H. W. *Creative Salesmanship.* Philadelphia: J. B. Lippincott Co., 1923.

IVEY, PAUL W. *Elements of Retail Salesmanship.* New York: Macmillan Co., 1923.

STEVENSON, J. A. *Constructive Salesmanship: Principles and Practices.* New York: Harper & Bros., 1923.

1924 FERRIS, E. E., and G. R. COLLINS. *Salesmanship.* New York: Ronald Press Co., 1924; 2d ed., 1930; 3d ed., 1939; 4th ed., 1941.

HALL, R. S. *Retail Advertising and Selling.* New York: McGraw-Hill Book Co., Inc., 1924.

RUSSELL, F. A. *The Textbook of Salesmanship.* New York: McGraw-Hill Book Co., Inc., 1924; 2d ed., 1933, with F. H. BEACH; 3d ed., 1941; 4th ed., 1949; 5th ed., 1955; 6th ed., 1959.

1925 BITTNER, G. E. *Planning Salesmen's Territories.* Washington, D.C.: U.S. Government Printing Office, 1925.

IVEY, PAUL W. *Salesmanship Applied.* New York: A. W. Shaw Co., 1925; 2d ed., 1937.

TOSDAL, H. R. *Principles of Personal Selling.* New York: A. W. Shaw Co., 1925; rev. and abridged, 1927, as *Principles of Personal Salesmanship.*

1926 FERNALD, C. H. *Salesmanship.* New York: Prentice-Hall, Inc., 1926; 2d ed., 1935; 3d ed., 1942.

KNOX, J. S. *Salesmanship and Business Efficiency.* Oak Park, Ill.: Knox Business Book Co., 1926.

PELZ, V. H. *Selling at Retail.* New York: McGraw-Hill Book Co., Inc., 1926.

1927 COMYNS, R. J., and J. G. JONES. *Selling.* New York: Alexander Hamilton Institute, 1927.

PICKEN, J. H. *Salesmanship.* New York: System Magazine, 1927.

TOSDAL, H. R. *Principles of Personal Salesmanship.* New York: A. W. Shaw Co., 1927.

1928 FREDERICK, J. G. *Selling by Telephone.* New York: The Business Course, 1928.

WALTERS, R. G. *Fundamentals of Salesmanship.* Cincinnati: South-Western Publishing Co., 1928; 2d ed., 1932; 3d 3d., 1937, as *Fundamentals of Selling;* 4th ed., 1942, with J. W. WINGATE; 5th ed., 1944; 6th ed., 1953.

1931 NIXON, H. K. *Principles of Selling.* New York: McGraw-Hill Book Co., Inc., 1931; 2d ed., 1942.

1932 LINK, H. C. *The New Psychology of Selling and Advertising.* New York: Macmillan Co., 1932.

ROBINSON, O. PRESTON, *et al. Store Salesmanship.* Englewood Cliffs, N.J.: Prentice-Hall, Inc., 1932; 2d ed., 1941; 3d ed., 1947; 4th ed., 1953; 5th ed., 1959; 6th ed., 1966.

1933 BENNETT, CHARLES. *Scientific Salesmanship.* St. Louis: American Efficiency Bureau, 1933.

1934 IVEY, PAUL W. *Getting Results in Selling.* New York: Macmillan Co., 1934.

1936 NYSTROM, P. H. *Elements of Retail Selling.* New York: Ronald Press Co., 1936.

1937 IVEY, P. W. and W. HORVATH. *Successful Salesmanship.* Englewood Cliffs, N.J.: Prentice-Hall, Inc., 1937; 2d ed., 1947; 3d ed., 1953; 4th ed., 1961; with WAYLAND A. TONNING.

1938 COLCORD, D. H. *You, Too, Can Sell.* Charlottesville, Va.: Business Book House, 1938.

HARDY, R. M. *How To Succeed in Retail Selling.* New York: Harper & Bros., 1938.

REICH, E. *Selling to the Consumer.* Cincinnati: American Book Co., 1938.

1939 BAKER, B. F. *Effective Retail Selling.* Chicago: American Technical Society, 1939.

BEACH, F. H. *Salesmanship Manual.* Champaign, Ill.: Stipes Publishing Co., 1939.

DOUBMAN, J. RUSSELL. *Salesmanship and Types of Selling.* New York: Appleton-Century-Crofts, Inc., 1939.

GOODE, K. M., and Z. KAUFMAN. *Profitable Showmanship.* New York: Prentice-Hall, Inc., 1939.

____. *Showmanship in Business.* New York: Harper & Bros., 1939; 2d ed., 1947.

HAAS, H. M. *A Short Course in Salesmanship.* New York: Prentice-Hall, Inc., 1939.

HAYTER, E. F. *Retail Selling Simplified.* New York: Harper & Bros., 1939.

SIMMONS, H. *A Practical Course in Successful Selling.* New York: Harper & Bros., 1939.

1940 CANFIELD, B. R. *Salesmanship Practices and Problems.* New York: McGraw-Hill Book Co., Inc., 1940; 2d ed., 1947; 3d ed., 1958.

1941 BRISCO, N. A., G. GRIFFITH, and O. P. ROBINSON. *Store Salesmanship*. New York: Prentice-Hall, Inc., 1941.

WELCH, R. H. W. *The Road to Salesmanship*. New York: Ronald Press Co., 1941.

WHEELER, E. *Tested Retail Selling*. New York: Prentice-Hall, Inc., 1941.

1942 BLACKSTONE, EARL G., *et al. Selling*. New York: D. C. Heath & Co., 1942.

KNEELAND, NATALIE, LOUISE BERNARD, and GERALD B. TALLMAN, *Selling to Today's Customer*. New York: Ginn & Co., 1942.

ROBINSON, O.P., and C. H. ROBINSON. *Successful Retail Salesmanship*. New York: Prentice-Hall, Inc., 1942; 2d ed., 1950.

STRAND, C. B. *Salesmanship*. New York: McGraw-Hill Book Co., Inc., 1942; 2d ed., 1949, as *Salesmanship: For Vocational and Personal Use*.

1944 IVEY, PAUL W. *Successful Salesmanship*. New York: Prentice-Hall, Inc., 1944; 2d ed., 1947; 3d ed., 1953, with W. HORVATH; 4th ed., 1961, with W. A. TONNING.

1945 LEWIS, C. W. (ed.). *Essentials of Selling*. New York: Prentice-Hall, Inc., 1945; 2d ed., 1952.

1947 MORAN, E. B. *The Credit Side of Selling*. Chicago: Dartnell Corp., 1947.

ROTH, C.B. *The Handbook of Selling*. New York: Prentice-Hall, Inc., 1947.

SMITH, P. E., and G. E. BREEN. *Selling in Stores*. New York: Harper & Bros., 1947.

1949 ROTH, C. B., *Professional Salesmanship*. New York: McGraw-Hill Book Co., Inc., 1949.

1950 LESTER, B. *Sales Engineering*. New York: John Wiley & Sons, Inc., 1950.

1951 KIRKPATRICK, C.A. *Salesmanship*. Cincinnati: South-Western Publishing Co., 1951; 2d ed., 1956; 3d ed.; 4th ed., 1966; 5th ed., 1971.

MOORE, ROBERT E. *The Human Side of Selling*. New York: Harper & Bros., 1951.

PEDERSON, C. A., and M. D. WRIGHT. *Salesmanship*. Homewood, Ill.: Richard D. Irwin, Inc., 1951; 2d ed., 1955; 3d ed., 1961; 4th ed., 1966; 5th ed., 1971.

1952 GROSS, A. *Salesmanship: Principles and Methods of Effective Selling*. New York: Ronald Press Co., 1952; 2d ed., 1959.

SMALL, R. L. *Salesmanship*. New York: Macmillan Co., 1952.

1953 HOBART, D. M., and J. P. WOOD. *Selling Forces*. New York: Ronald Press Co., 1953.

1954 ERNEST, JOHN W. *Salesmanship Fundamentals*. New York: McGraw-Hill Book Co., Inc., 1954; 2d ed., 1959; 3d ed., 1965; 4th ed., 1973, with Richard Ashmun.

HORVATH, WALTER. *How To Overcome Objections in Selling*. New York: Prentice-Hall, Inc., 1954.

ROBINSON, O. P., and WILLIAM R. BLACKLER. *Store Salesmanship*. 4th ed. New York: Prentice-Hall, Inc., 1954; 5th ed., 1959, with J. R. HALES.

SIMMONS, HARRY. *How To Develop Your Sales Ability*. New York: Prentice-Hall, Inc., 1954.

1955 BROOKS, P. P. *How Power Selling Brought Me Success in Six Hours*. New York: Prentice-Hall, Inc., 1955.

340

ENGLESMAN, RALPH G., and N. L. ENGLESMAN. *Keys to Modern Selling.* New York: McKay Co., 1955.

FEHLMAN, F. E. *Anyone Can Sell.* New York: Printers' Ink Publishing Co., 1955.

ROTH, C. B. *Successful Sales Presentations.* Englewood Cliffs, N.J.: Prentice-Hall, Inc., 1955.

SELTZ, D. *Successful Industrial Selling.* Englewood Cliffs, N.J.: Prentice-Hall, Inc., 1956.

1956 BROWN, HARRY N. *Salesmen in the Making.* New York: Mycroft, 1956.

DeVOE, MERRILL. *Effective Self Management in Selling.* New York: Prentice-Hall, Inc., 1956.

BELL, H. S. *How To Be a Winner in Selling.* Englewood Cliffs, N.J.: Prentice-Hall, Inc., 1957.

LAPP, C. L. *Successful Selling Strategies.* New York: McGraw-Hill Book Co., Inc., 1957.

TOSDAL, H. R. *Selling in Our Economy.* Homewood, Ill.: Richard D. Irwin, Inc., 1957.

1958 GREIF, E.C. *Modern Salesmanship.* Englewood Cliffs, N.J.: Prentice-Hall, Inc., 1958.

HAAS, K. B., and E. C. PERRY. *Sales Horizons.* Englewood Cliffs, N.J.: Prentice-Hall, Inc., 1958.

JENKS, E. E., and E. J. BENGE. *Salesmanship.* New York: Alexander Hamilton Institute, 1958.

1959 BELL, H. S. *Championship Selling.* Englewood Cliffs, N.J.: Prentice-Hall, Inc., 1959.

LEWIS, W. K. *How To Make Yourself a Born Salesman.* New York: Hawthorn Books, 1959.

1960 HATTWICK, N. S. *The New Psychology of Selling.* New York: McGraw-Hill Book Co., Inc., 1960.

LOHSE, C. F. *Creative Selling.* New York: Charles Scribner's Sons, 1960.

MELOAN, T. W., and J. M. RATHMELL (eds.). *Selling: Its Broader Dimensions.* New York: Macmillan Co., 1960.

MONAGHAN, P. C. *How To Sell Appliances at Retail.* New York: Fairchild Publications, 1960.

NEWMAN, B. N. *Handbook of Successful Sales Meetings.* Englewood Cliffs, N.J.: Prentice-Hall, Inc., 1960.

SHAW, S. J., and J. W. THOMPSON (eds). *Salesmanship.* New York: Henry Holt & Co., 1960.

1961 BENDER, J. F. *How To Sell Well.* New York: McGraw-Hill Book Co., Inc., 1961.

LEE, R. E. *The Mental Dynamics of Selling.* New York: Exposition Press, 1961.

1962 HAAS, K. B. *Professional Salesmanship.* New York: Holt, Rinehart and Winston, 1962.

WEISS, E. B. *The Vanishing Salesman.* New York: McGraw-Hill Book Co., Inc., 1962.

1963 DAY, RALPH L. *Salesmen in the Field.* Homewood, Ill.: Richard D. Irwin, Inc., 1963.

1966 BAKER, R. M. and G. PHIFER. *Salesmanship.* Boston, Allyn & Bacon, 1966.

JOHNSON, H. W. *Creative Selling.* Cincinnati: South-Western Publishing Co., 1966.

STROH, T. F. *Salesmanship.* Homewood, Ill.: Richard D. Irwin, Inc., 1966.

THOMPSON, J. W. *Selling: a Behavioral Science Approach*. New York: McGraw-Hill Book Co., Inc., 1966; 2d ed., 1973.

1967 BOYD, HARPER W. and S. J. LEVY. *Promotion: a Behavioral View*. Englewood Cliffs, N.J.: Prentice-Hall, Inc., 1967.

ROBINSON, PATRICK J. and BENT STIDSEN. *Personal Selling in a Modern Perspective*. Boston: Allyn & Bacon, 1967.

1968 MARTIN, HOWARD J. *Blueprint for Success in Selling*. West Nyack, N.Y.: Parker Publishing Co., 1968.

1969 CRISSY, W. J. E. and R. M. KAPLAN. *Salesmanship*. New York: John Wiley & Sons, Inc., 1969.

1970 BLAKE, R. R. and J. S. MOUTON. *The Grid for Sales Excellence*. New York: McGraw-Hill Book Co., Inc., 1970.

CHRISTENSEN, N. C. *The Art of Persuasion in Selling*. West Nyack, N.Y.: Parker Publishing Co., 1970.

STEINKAMP, W. E. *How to Sell and Market Industrial Products*. Philadelphia: Chilton Book Co., 1970.

WOOLMAN, L. H. *Salesmanship Concepts and Strategies*. Belmont, Calif.: Wadsworth Publishing Co., 1970.

1971 FISHER' JAMES R. *Confident Selling*. West Nyack, N.Y.: Parker Publishing Co., 1971.

MICALI, PAUL J. *The Lacy Techniques of Salesmanship*. Homewood, Ill.: Dow Jones – Irwin, Inc., 1971.

1972 BAER, EARL E. *Salesmanship*. New York: McGraw-Hill Book Co., Inc., 1972.

BUZZOTTA, V. R., *et al. Effective Selling Through Psychology*. New York: Wiley Interscience, 1972.

HARRISON, J. F. *Profitable Self-Management for Salesmen*. Englewood Cliffs, N.J.: Prentice-Hall, Inc., 1972.

WARREN, HAROLD P. *Computerized Salesmanship; the New Last Frontier*. New York: Vantage Press, 1972.

1973 BLACK, GEORGE. *Sales Engineering*. Houston: Gulf Publishing Co., 1973.

HANAN, MACK. *Consultative Selling*. New York: AMACOM, 1973.

MORTELL, ARTHUR. *Anatomy of a Successful Salesman*. Rockville Center, N.Y.: Farnsworth Publishing Co., 1973.

SUSSER, SAMUEL C. *The Truth About Selling*. New York: Paul S. Eriksson, Inc., 1973.

SALES MANAGEMENT

1913 HOYT, C. W. *Scientific Sales Management*. New Haven, Conn.: G. B. Woolson & Co., 1913.

1914 BUTLER, R.S., H. DeBOWER, and J. G. JONES. *Marketing Methods and Salesmanship*. New York: Alexander Hamilton Institute, 1914.

1916 SCOTT, W. D. *Aids in Selecting Salesmen*. Pittsburgh, Pa.: Carnegie Institute of Technology, 1916.

1918 JONES, J. G. *Salesmanship and Sales Management*. New York: Alexander Hamilton Institute, 1918.

1919 ASPLEY, J. C. *Modern Sales Management Practices*. Chicago: The Dartnell Corp., 1919.

1919 FREDERICK, J. G. *Modern Sales Management*. New York: D. Appleton– Century Co., Inc., 1919.

1921 TOSDAL, H. R. *Problems in Sales Management*. New York: A. W. Shaw Co., 1921; 2d ed., 1925; 3d ed., 1933; 4th ed., 1939.

342

1922 RUSSELL, F. A. *The Management of the Sales Organization.* New York: McGraw-Hill Book Co., Inc., 1922.
1924 HALL, R. S. *The Handbook of Sales Management.* New York: McGraw-Hill Book Co., Inc., 1924.
1925 KENAGY, H. G., and C. S. YOAKUM. *The Selection and Training of Salesmen.* New York: McGraw-Hill Book Co., Inc., 1925.
1926 HAYWARD, W. S. *Sales Administration: A Study of the Manufacturer's Marketing Problems.* New York: Harper & Bros., 1926.
     LYON, L. S. *Salesmen in Marketing Strategy.* New York: Macmillan Co., 1926.
1927 TOSDAL, H. R. *Sales Organization and Operation.* New York: System Magazine, 1927.
1929 ASPLEY, J. C. *Intensive Sales Management.* Chicago: Dartnell Corp., 1929.
     HAY, R. C. *Sales Management Fundamentals.* New York: Harper & Bros., 1929.
     WHITE, PERCIVAL. *Sales Quotas.* New York: Harper & Bros., 1929.
1933 TOSDAL, H. R. *Introduction to Sales Management.* New York: McGraw-Hill Book Co., Inc., 1933; 2d ed., 1940; 3d ed., 1950; 4th ed., 1957.
1934 ASPLEY, J. C. *The Sales Manager's Handbook.* Chicago: Dartnell Corp., 1934; rev. eds., 1937, 1940, 1945, 1947, 1950, 1956.
1937 DOUBMAN, J. R. *Fundamentals of Sales Management.* New York: F. S. Crofts & Co., 1937.
     FOX, W. M. *Profitable Control of Salesmen's Activities.* New York: McGraw-Hill Book Co., Inc., 1937.
1938 COWAN, D. R. G. *Sales Analysis from the Management Standpoint.* Chicago: University of Chicago Press, 1938.
1939 CANFIELD, B. R. *Sales Administration: Principles and Problems.* New York: Prentice-Hall, Inc., 1939; 2d ed., 1947; 3d ed., 1954; 4th ed., 1961.
1940 EASTWOOD, R. P. *Sales Control by Quantitative Methods.* New York: Columbia University Press, 1940.
     LESTER, BERNARD. *Sales Engineering.* New York: John Wiley & Sons, Inc., 1940.
     NOLEN, H. C., and H. H. MAYNARD. *Sales Management.* New York: Ronald Press Co., 1940; 2d ed., 1950, by H. H. MAYNARD and H. C. NOLEN; 3d ed., 1957, by H. H. MAYNARD and J. H. DAVIS.
1942 DILLON, JOHN H. *How To Train Salespeople.* Chicago: American Technical Society, 1942.
     TOSDAL, H. R., and ROSS CUNNINGHAM. *What Salesmen Think of Their Sales Managers.* Boston: Chamber of Commerce, 1942.
1944 ROSENSTEIN, J. L. *The Scientific Selection of Salesmen.* New York: McGraw-Hill Book Co., Inc., 1944.
1945 DYNNER, E. *Successful Sales Training.* Chicago: Advertising Publications, 1945.
     LaCLEVE, F. *Basic Problems of Sales Management.* New York: McGraw-Hill Book Co., Inc., 1945.
1946 RADOS, W. *How To Select Better Salesmen.* New York: Prentice-Hall, Inc., 1946.
     SIMMONS, H. *Practical Sales Management.* New York: Prentice-Hall, Inc., 1946.

1947   HAGERTY, E. J. *Building a Sales Training Plan*. New York: McGraw-Hill
       Book Co., Inc., 1947.
       ____. *How To Run a Meeting*. New York: McGraw-Hill Book Co., Inc.,
       1947.
       POLIAK, S. *Rebuilding the Sales Staff*. New York: McGraw-Hill Book
       Co., Inc., 1947.
1948   DAVIS, J. H. *Increasing Wholesale Drug Salesmen's Effectiveness*.
       Columbus, Ohio: Bureau of Business Research, Ohio State
       University, 1948.
       ROTH, C. B. *Stimulating Salesmen Successfully*. New York:
       Prentice-Hall, Inc., 1948.
       TOSDAL, H. R., and ROSS CUNNINGHAM. *Sales Organization and
       Compensation of the Sales Executive*. New York: National
       Industrial Conference Board, 1948.
1949   DeARMOND, F., and C. M. GRAF. *Route Sales Management*. New York:
       Moon Publishing Co., 1949.
1950   ASPLEY, J. C. *The Sales Promotion Handbook*. Chicago: Dartnell, 1950;
       2d ed., 1953.
       SIMMONS, HARRY, *et al. Sales Executives Handbook*. New York:
       Prentice-Hall, Inc., 1950.
       ____. *Successful Sales Promotion*. New York: Prentice-Hall, Inc., 1950.
       Whitehead, N. *Administration of Marketing and Selling*. New York:
       Pitman Publishing Corp., 1950.
       WILSON, G. L. *Marketing and Traffic Management*. Washington: Traffic
       Service Corporation, 1950.
1951   DAVIS, J. H. *Sales Meetings That Pay Off*. New York: National
       Wholesale Druggists Association, 1951.
       PHELPS, D.M. *Sales Management: Policies and Procedures*. Homewood,
       Ill.: Richard D. Irwin, Inc., 1951; rev. ed., as *Marketing
       Management*, 1960, with J. H. Westing; 3d ed., 1968.
1952   SIMMONS, HARRY. *Successful Sales Management*. New York:
       Prentice-Hall, Inc., 1952.
1954   *Handbook of Sales Training*. National Society of Sales Training
       Executives. New York: Prentice-Hall, Inc., 1954.
1955   GOPEL, R. A. *Managing Salesmen*. Pleasantville, N.Y.: Printers' Ink
       Books, 1955.
       HEPPNER, H. W. *Modern Marketing Dynamics and Management*. New
       York: McGraw-Hill Book Co., Inc., 1955.
       MANDELL, MILTON M. *A Company Guide to the Selection of
       Salesmen*. New York: American Management Association, 1955.
1956   BECKHARD, RICHARD. *Planning Effective Meetings*. Chicago: Dartnell
       Corp., 1956.
       TOSDAL, HARRY R., and WALLER CARSON, JR. *Salesmen's
       Compensation*. 2 vols. Boston: Harvard Business School, 1956.
       WELD, C. M. *Compensation of Salesmen*. Chicago: Dartnell Corp., 1956.
1957   DeVOE, M. *The How of Successful Sales Management*. Englewood Cliffs,
       N.J.: Prentice-Hall, Inc., 1957.
1957   HOWARD, J. D. *Marketing Management*. Homewood, Ill.: Richard D.
       Irwin, Inc., 1957.
       HASS, K. B. *How To Develop Successful Salesmen*. New York:
       McGraw-Hill Book Co., Inc., 1957.
       JOHNSON, L. K. *Sales and Marketing Management*. (Text and Cases.)
       Boston: Allyn and Bacon, 1957.
       SIMMONS, H. *Profitable Sales Promotion*. Englewood Cliffs, N.J.:
       Prentice-Hall, Inc., 1957.

1958   DeVOE, M. *How To Be an Effective Sales Manager.* Englewood Cliffs, N.J.: Prentice-Hall, Inc., 1958; rev. ed., *The Effective Sales Manager,* Lexington, Ky: EMD Publication, 1968.

JONES, J. G., and W. L. DOREMUS. *Sales Management.* New York: Alexander Hamilton Institute, 1958.

SIMMONS, H. *New Techniques in Marketing Management.* Englewood Cliffs, N.J.: Prentice-Hall, 1958.

STILL, R. R., and E. W. CUNDIFF. *Sales Management.* Englewood Cliffs, N.J.: Prentice-Hall, Inc., 1958; 2d ed., 1969.

1959   SHUBIK, M. *Strategy and Market Structures.* New York: John Wiley & Sons Co., 1959.

STANTON, W. J., and R. H. BUSKIRK. *Management of the Sales Force.* Homewood, Ill.: Richard D. Irwin, Inc., 1959; rev. ed., 1964; 3d ed., 1969.

TURNER, H. M. *Sales Promotion That Gets Results.* New York: McGraw-Hill Book Co., Inc., 1959.

1960   LAPP, C. L. *Training and Supervising Salesmen.* Englewood Cliffs, N.J.: Prentice-Hall, Inc., 1960.

NEWGARDEN, A. (ed.). *The Field Sales Manager.* New York: American Management Association, 1960.

ROTH, C. B. *How To Manage and Help Salesmen.* Englewood Cliffs, N.J.: Prentice-Hall, Inc., 1960.

SEETZ, D. D. *Sales Contests and Incentive Programs.* Englewood Cliffs, N.J.: Prentice-Hall, Inc., 1960.

1961   BIGELOW, B. *The Human Side of Sales Management.* New Haven: Yale University Press, 1961.

1965   ALEXANDER, MILTON and E. M. MAZZE (eds.). *Sales Management: Theory and Practice.* New York: Pitman Publishing Co., 1965.

1967   TRUETT, F. M. *The Arithmetic of Sales Management.* New York: American Management Association, 1967.

1968   BROWN, RONALD. *From Selling to Managing.* New York: American Management Association, 1968.

DAVIS, K. R. and F. E. WEBSTER. *Sales Force Management.* New York: The Ronald Press Co., 1968.

_____. *Readings in Sales Force Management.* New York: The Ronald Press Co., 1968.

DUNN, A. H. *Creative Selling and Sales Management.* New York: Sales and Marketing Executives-International, 1968.

1969   DOWNING, G. D. *Sales Management.* New York: John Wiley & Sons, Inc., 1969.

ELSBY, F. H. *Marketing and the Sales Manager.* Oxford, N.Y.: Pergamon Press, 1969.

SEGAL, MENDEL. *Sales Management for the Small and Mid-size Businesses.* West Nyack, N.Y.: Parker Publishing Co., 1969.

1970   BARNHILL, J. ALLISON (ed.). *Sales Management: Contemporary Perspectives.* Glenview, Ill.: Scott, Foresman, 1970.

BOYD, HARPER W. and R. T. DAVIS (eds). *Readings in Sales Management.* Homewood, Ill.: Richard D. Irwin, Inc., 1970.

NEWTON, D. A. *Cases in Sales Force Management.* Homewood, Ill.: Richard D. Irwin, Inc., 1970.

1971   BURSK, E. C. and G. SCOTT HUTCHINSON. *Salesmanship and Sales Force Management.* Cambridge, Mass., Harvard University Press, 1971.

CHRISTENSEN, N. C. *The Art of Persuasion for Sales Managers.* West Nyack, N.Y.: Parker Publishing Co., 1971.

GOODMAN, C. S. *Management of the Personal Selling Function.* New York: Holt, Rinehart & Winston, 1971.

WATZUBA, THOMAS R. *Sales Management.* New York: Holt, Rinehart & Winston, 1971.

1972 BOONE, LOUIS E. and D. L. KURLY. *The Sales Management Game.* Morristown, N.J.: General Learning Press, 1972.

BUZZOTTA, V. R. and M. SHERBERG. *Effective Sales and Sales Management Strategies.*

DODGE, H. R. *Field Sales Management: Text and Cases.* Dallas: Business Publications, 1973.

RETAILING

1911 APPEL, J. H. *Golden Book of the Wanamaker Stores; Jubilee Year, 1861–1911.* New York: J. Wanamaker, 1911.

1913 NYSTROM, PAUL H. *Retail Selling and Store Management.* New York: D. Appleton-Century Co., Inc., 1913; repub., 1917, as *Retail Store Management.*

1914 COLLINS, H. S. *Retail Store Management.* New York: Alexander Hamilton Institute, 1914.

1915 HOTCHKIN, W. R. *The Manual of Successful Storekeeping.* Garden City, N.Y.: Doubleday, Page & Co., 1915.

NYSTROM, PAUL H. *The Economics of Retailing.* Vols. 1 and 2. New York: Ronald Press Co., 1915; 2d ed., 1919; 3d ed., 1930, Vols. 1 and 2; rev. ed., 1932, Vol. 2 only; 4th ed., 1937, as *Retail Store Operation.*

1916 FISK, JAMES W. *Retail Selling: A Guide to the Best Modern Practice.* New York: Harper & Bros., 1916.

1917 FIELD, C. C. *Retail Buying: Modern Principles and Practices.* New York: Harper & Bros., 1917.

NYSTROM, PAUL H. *Retail Store Management.* Chicago: LaSalle Extension University, 1917.

SWINNEY, J. B. *Merchandising of Fashion.* New York: Alexander Hamilton Institute, 1917.

1918 DOUGLAS, A. W. *Merchandising.* New York: Macmillan Co., 1918.

1920 CARTHAGE, PHILIP L. *Retail Organization and Accounting Control.* New York: D. Appleton & Co., 1920.

1921 WHITEHEAD, HAROLD. *How To Run a Store.* New York: Crowell Publishing Co., 1921.

1922 DAVID, DONALD KIRK. *Retail Store Management Problems.* Chicago: A. W. Shaw Co., 1922.

1923 BAER, LAURA. *Retail Selling Methods.* New York: McGraw-Hill Book Co., Inc., 1923.

1924 BUSH, ADA L. *Retail Store Planning.* Washington: Government Printing Office, 1924.

CHARTERS, W. W. (ed.). *Merchandise Manuals for Retail Salespeople.* New York: A. W. Shaw Co., 1924-25.

COPELAND, M. T. *Principles of Merchandising.* Chicago and N.Y.: A. W. Shaw Co., 1924.

GREENE, J. H. *Principles and Methods of Retailing.* New York: McGraw-Hill Book Co., Inc., 1924.

HAHN, LEW and PERCIVAL WHITE (eds.). *The Merchant's Manual.* New York: McGraw-Hill Book Co., Inc., 1924.

HALL, S. R. *Retail Advertising and Selling.* New York: McGraw-Hill Book Co., Inc. 1924.

HAYWARD, W. S. *The Retail Handbook,* N.Y.: McGraw-Hill Book Co., Inc., 1924.

NAMM, B. H. *Advertising in Retail Stores.* New York: U.P.C. Book Co., 1924.

1925 BRISCO, N. A., and J. W. WINGATE. *Retail Buying.* New York: Prentice-Hall, Inc., 1925.

DAVID, D. K., and M. P. McNAIR. *Problems in Retailing.* Chicago: A. W. Shaw Co., 1925; 2d ed., 1931.

FILENE, E. A. *More Profits from Merchandising.* New York: A. W. Shaw Co., 1925.

FRI, JAMES L. *Retail Merchandising, Planning, and Control.* New York: Prentice-Hall, Inc., 1925.

HODGE, ALBERT C. *Retail Accounting and Control.* Chicago: Univ. of Chicago Press, 1925.

McNAIR, M. P. *The Retail Method of Inventory.* Chicago: A. W. Shaw Co., 1925.

WESS, H. B. *Merchandise Control.* New York: Dry Goods Economist, 1925.

1926 BREWSTER, ARTHUR J. *An Introduction to Retail Advertising.* Chicago and N.Y.: A. W. Shaw Co., 1926.

1927 BRISCO, N. A. *Principles of Retailing.* New York: Prentice-Hall, Inc., 1927; 2d ed., 1935, as *Retailing;* 2d ed., 1947, by NORRIS B. BRISCO; 3d ed., 1957, with PEARCE C. KELLEY.

DOUBMAN, J. R., and J. R. WHITAKER. *Organization and Operation of Department Stores.* New York: John Wiley & Sons, Inc., 1927.

FREY, ALBERT W., and PAUL H. NYSTROM. *Merchandise Control.* New York: Alexander Hamilton Institute, 1927.

MAZUR, PAUL M. *Principles of Organization Applied to Modern Retailing.* New York: Harper & Bros., 1927.

MURPHY, J. A., and JOHN BLOCK. *Buying.* New York: Alexander Hamilton Institute, 1927.

1928 BITTNER, G. E. *Retail Profits through Stock Control* Washington, D.C.: U.S. Government Printing Office. 1928.

NYSTROM, PAUL H. *Economics of Fashion.* New York: Ronald Press Co., 1928.

1929 BRISCO, N. A. *Retail Credit Procedure.* New York: Prentice-Hall, Inc., 1929; rev., 1942, as *Retail Credit,* with R. W. SEVERA.

GUERNSEY, JOHN. *Retailing Tomorrow.* New York: Dry Goods Economist, 1929.

KOCH, W. E. *Methods of Retail Management.* New York: McGraw-Hill Book Co., Inc., 1929.

NYSTROM, PAUL H. *Economic Principles of Consumption.* New York: Ronald Press Co., 1929, 1931.

1930 BLOOMFIELD, DANIEL. *Selected Articles on Trends in Retail Distribution.* New York: H. W. Wilson Co., 1930.

DAMERON, KENNETH. *Men's Wear Merchandising.* New York: Ronald Press Co., 1930.

EMMET, BORIS. *Department Stores, Recent Policies, Costs, and Profits.* Stanford, Calif.: Stanford University Press, 1930.

FILENE, E. A. *The Model Stock Plan.* New York: McGraw-Hill Book Co., Inc., 1930.

FRI, JAMES L. (ed.). *The Buyer's Manual.* New York: National Retail
Dry Goods Association, 1930; 2d ed., 1937; 3d ed., 1957.

GODLEY, E. A., and ALEXANDER KAYLIN. *Control of Retail Store
Operations.* New York: Ronald Press Co. 1930.

McNAIR, M. P., and C. J. GRAGG. *Problems in Retail Distribution.* New
York: McGraw-Hill Book Co., Inc., 1930.

SHACTER, H. W. *Profitable Department Store Management.* New York:
Harper & Bros., 1930.

WHITE, WILFORD L. *Cooperative Retail Buying Associations.* New
York: McGraw-Hill Book Co., Inc., 1930.

1931 BEDELL, CLYDE. *The Seven Keys to Retail Profits.* New York:
McGraw-Hill Book Co., Inc., 1931.

McNAIR, M. P., and C. I. GRAGG. *Problems in Retail Store
Management.* New York: McGraw-Hill Book Co., Inc., 1931.

REILLY, WILLIAM J. *The Law of Retail Gravitation.* New York:
William J. Reilly Co., 1931; 2d ed., New York: Pilsbury
Publishers, 1953.

WALTERS, R. G., and E. J. ROWSE. *Fundamentals of Retail Selling.*
Cincinnati: South-Western Publishing Co., 1931; 2d ed., 1938, as
Fundamentals of Retailing; 3d ed., 1943, as *Retail Merchandising,*
with J. W. WINGATE 4th ed., 1951, by R. G. WALTERS, J. W.
WINGATE, and J. D. WEINER; 5th ed., 1957, by J. W.
WINGATE and J. D. Weiner.

WESS, HAROLD B. *Profit Principles of Retailing.* New York: Mc-
Graw-Hill Book Co., Inc., 1931.

WINGATE, JOHN W. *Manual of Retail Terms.* New York: Prentice-Hall,
Inc., 1931.

WINGATE, J. W., and E. O. SCHALLER. *Problems in Retail
Merchandising.* New York: Prentice-Hall, Inc., 1931; 2d ed., 1937;
3d ed., 1944, with I. GOLDENTHAL; 4th ed., 1952; 5th ed.,
1961; 6th ed., 1973.

1932 HART, ERNEST R. *Retail Management.* Chicago: Bureau of Business
Practice, 1932.

NYSTROM, PAUL H. *Fashion Merchandising.* New York: Ronald Press
Co., 1932.

1933 NEAL, LAWRENCE E. *Retailing and the Public.* London: G. Allen &
Unwin, 1933.

SECRIST, HORACE. *The Triumph of Mediocrity in Business.* Evanston,
Ill.: Northwestern University, 1933.

WINGATE, J. W. *Retail Merchandise Control.* New York: Prentice-Hall,
Inc., 1933; 2d ed., 1938; 3d ed., 1950; 4th ed., 1956 as
Techniques of Retail Merchandising.

1934 LYANS, C. K., and N. A. BRISCO. *Retail Accounting.* New York:
Prentice-Hall, Inc., 1934.

1935 BARKER, C. W., and I. D. ANDERSON. *Principles of Retailing.* New
York: McGraw-Hill Book Co., Inc., 1935; 2d ed., 1941; 3d ed.,
1956, with J. DONALD BUTTERWORTH.

CASSADY, RALPH and H. J. OSTLUND. *The Retail Distribution
Structure of the Small City.* Minneapolis: University of Minnesota
Press, 1935.

1936 BELL, HERMON F. *Retail Merchandise Accounting.* New York: Ronald
Press Co., 1936; 2d ed., 1956; 3d ed., 1961.

348

DOUBMAN, J. RUSSELL. *Principles of Retail Merchandising.* New York: Longmans, Green & Co., 1936; rev. ed., as *Retail Merchandising: Principles and Practice.* New York: Littlefield, Adams, 1949.

EDWARDS, C. M., JR., and W. H. HOWARD. *Retail Advertising and Sales Promotion.* New York: Prentice-Hall, Inc., 1936; 2d ed., 1943.

LEIGH, RUTH. *Elements of Retailing.* rev. ed., New York: D. Appleton-Century Co., Inc., 1936.

NYSTROM, PAUL H. *Elements of Retail Selling.* New York: Ronald Press Co., 1936.

1937 DeSCHWEINITZ, DOROTHEA. *Occupations in Retail Stores.* Scranton, Pa.: International Textbook Co., 1937.

EDWARDS, C. M. JR. and W. H. HOWARD. *Retail Advertising and Sales Promotion.* New York: Prentice-Hall, Inc., 1937; rev. ed., 1943; 3d ed., 1959 by C. M. Edwards and R. H. Brown.

FILENE, E. A., WARNER K. GABLER, and PERCY S. BROWN. *Next Steps Forward in Retailing.* Boston: E. A. Filene, 1937.

1937 LAZO, H. *Retailer Cooperatives: How to Run Them.* New York: Harper & Bros., 1937.

McNAIR, M. P., C. I. GRAGG, and S. F. TEELE. *Problems in Retailing.* New York: McGraw-Hill Book Co., Inc., 1937.

NYSTROM, PAUL H. *Retail Store Operation.* New York: Ronald Press Co., 1937; 4th ed., of *The Economics of Retailing;* rev. ed., 1940.

WINGATE, J. W. and N. A. BRISCO. *Buying for Retail Stores.* New York: Prentice-Hall, Inc., 1937; 2d ed., 1946; 3d ed., 1953, by J. W. Wingate; rev. ed., 1963, as *The Management of Retail Buying,* by J. W. Wingate and J. S. Friedlander.

1938 BECKMAN, T. N., and H. C. NOLEN. *The Chain Store Problem.* New York: McGraw-Hill Book Co., Inc., 1938.

MAYNARD, H. H., K. DAMERON, and C. J. SEIGLER. *Retail Marketing and Merchandising.* New York: Ginn & Co., 1938

PHELPS, C. W. *Retail Credit Fundamentals.* St. Louis, Mo.: National Retail Credit Association, 1938; 2d ed., 1947; 3d ed., 1952; 4th ed., 1963.

RICHART, G. D. *Retailing: Principles and Practices of Retail Buying, Advertising, Selling and Management.* New York: Gregg Publishing Co., 1938; 2d ed., 1947; 3d ed., 1954; 4th ed., 1962; 5th ed., 1968 with W. G. MEYER and P. G. HAINES.

ROBINSON, O. P., and N. B. BRISCO. *Retail Store Organization and Management.* New York: Prentice-Hall, Inc., 1938; rev. ed., 1949, as *Store Organization and Operation;* 2d ed., 1957, by O. P. ROBINSON, J. G. ROBINSON, M. P. MATTHEWS.

WINGATE, J. W., and N. A. BRISCO. *Elements of Retail Merchandising.* New York: Prentice-Hall, Inc., 1938.

1939 BAKER, B. F. *Effective Retail Selling.* Chicago: American Technical Society, 1939.

BAKER, HAROLD A. *Principles of Retail Merchandising.* New York: McGraw-Hill Book Co., Inc., 1939.

BURLEY, O. E. *The Consumer Cooperative as a Distributive Agency.* New York: McGraw-Hill Book Co., Inc., 1939.

MAYER, JOSEPH. *The Revolution in Merchandising.* New York Greenberg Publishing Co., 1939.

WINGATE, J. W., E. O. SCHALLER, and F. GORDENTHAL. *A Workbook for Retail Buying and Marketing.* New York: Prentice-Hall, Inc., 1939.

1940 LESTER, HELENA MARSH. *Retail Training in Principle and Practice.* New York: Harper & Bros., 1940.

MITCHELL, WALTER LeROY. *Standard Ratios for Retailing.* New York: Dun & Bradstreet, Inc., 1940.

ROBINSON, O. P. *Retail Personnel Relations.* New York: Prentice-Hall, Inc., 1940.

1941 DUNCAN, D. J. and C. F. PHILLIPS. *Retailing: Principles and Methods.* Chicago: Richard D. Irwin, Inc., 1941; 2d ed., 1947; 3d ed., 1951; 4th ed., 1955; 5th ed., 1959; 6th ed., 1964; 7th ed., 1967; 8th ed., 1972 with S. C. HOLLANDER, as *Modern Retailing Management – Basic Concepts and Practices.*

1942 BRISCO, N. A., and LEON ARNOWITT. *Introduction to Modern Retailing.* New York: Prentice-Hall, Inc., 1942.

BRISCO, N. A. and R. W. Severa. *Retail Credit.* New York: Prentice-Hall, Inc., 1942.

HEGADONE, EDWINA B., and D. K. BECKLEY. *Merchandising Techniques.* New York: McGraw-Hill Book Co., Inc., 1942.

McNAIR, M. P. *Problems in Merchandise Distribution.* New York: McGraw Hill Book Co., Inc., 1942.

ROBINSON, O. P., and C. H. ROBINSON. *Successful Retail Salesmanship.* New York: Prentice-Hall, Inc., 1942; 2d ed., 1950; 4th ed., 1954, with W. R. BLACKER, as *Store Salesmanship;* 5th ed., 1959, with W. B. LOGAN; 6th ed., 1966.

SWINNEY, J. B. *Merchandising of Fashions.* New York: Ronald Press Co., 1942.

1945 BRADFORD, J. *Retail Merchandiser's Handbook.* Boston: Bruce Humphries, Inc., 1945.

1946 COMISH, NEWEL H. *Small Scale Retailing.* Portland, Ore.: Binsford and Mort, 1946; 2d ed., 1948.

JOHNSON, ROBERT H. *Retail Policies.* Washington: U.S. Government Printing Office, 1946.

1947 FOWLER, B. B. *The Co-Operative Challenge.* Boston: Little, Brown & Co., 1947.

1948 BECKLEY, DONALD K., and WILLIAM B. LOGAN. *The Retail Salesperson at Work.* New York: McGraw-Hill Book Co., Inc., 1948.

1949 GRAHAM, IRVIN. *How To Sell Through Mail-Order.* New York: McGraw-Hill Book Co., Inc., 1949.

JONES, FRED M. *Principles of Retailing.* New York: Pitman & Co., 1949.

MAYFIELD, F. M. *The Department Store Story.* New York: Fairchild, 1949.

ROBINSON, O.P., and N. B. BRISCO. *Store Organization and Operation.* New York: Prentice-Hall, Inc., 1949; 2d ed., 1957, by O. P. ROBINSON, J. E. ROBINSON, and M. P. MATTHEWS.

1950 BECKLEY, DONALD K., and JOHN W. ERNEST. *Modern Retailing.* New York: McGraw-Hill Book Co., Inc., 1950.

DOLVA, W. R. and DONALD K. BECKLEY. *The Retailer.* New York: Prentice-Hall, Inc., 1950.

WINGATE, J. W. and E. O. SCHALLER. *Techniques in Retail Merchandising.* New York: Prentice-Hall, Inc., 1950; 2d ed., 1956; 3d ed., 1972, with F. L. MILLER.

BURTON, P. W. *Retail Advertising for the Small Store.* New York: Prentice-Hall, Inc., 1951.

PACKER, H. Q., and M. E. WATERMAN. *Basic Retailing.* New York: Prentice-Hall, Inc., 1951.

SPRIEGEL, WILLIAM R. and J. W. TOWLE. *Retail Organization and Accounting Control.* New York: McGraw-Hill Book Co., Inc., 1951.

1952 BROWN, PAUL L., and W. R. DAVIDSON. *Retailing: Principles and Practices.* New York: Ronald Press Co., 1952; 2d ed., 1960; as *Retailing;* 3d ed., 1966 as *Retailing Management,* by W. R. DAVIDSON and A. F. DOODY.

HAHN, Lew. *Stores, Merchants, and Customers.* New York: Fairchild Publications, 1952.

McNAIR, M. P. *The Retail Inventory Method and Lifo.* New York: McGraw-Hill Book Co., Inc., 1952.

1953 McGREGOR, C. M. *Retail Management Problems.* Homewood, Ill.: Richard D. Irwin, Inc., 1953; 2d ed., 1957; 3d ed., 1962; 4th ed., 1970.

1954 *Dynamic Retailing in the Modern Economy.* National Retail Dry Goods Assn., 1954.

Expense Center Accounting Manual. New York: National Retail Dry Goods Assn., 1954.

1955 COMMITTEE OR RETAILING. *Principles of Retailing.* New York: Pitman & Co., 1955.

JONASSEN, C. T. *The Shopping Center versus Downtown.* Columbus: Bureau of Business Research, Ohio State University, 1955.

MAHONEY, T. *The Great Merchants.* New York: Harper & Bros., 1955.

1956 FAVILLE, DAVID E. *Selected Case Problems in Retailing.* New York: Prentice-Hall, Inc., 1956.

MONGLON, I. F. *Merchandising: The Small Store.* New York: NRDGA, 1956.

WINGATE, J. W. and A. CORBIN. *Changing Patterns in Retailing.* Homewood, Ill.: Richard D. Irwin, Inc., 1956.

1957 JONES, F. M. *Retail Merchandising.* Homewood, Ill.: Richard D. Irwin, Inc., 1957; rev. ed., 1967 as *Retail Management.*

McNAIR, M. P., ELIZABETH A. BURNHAM, and ANITA C. HERSUM. *Cases in Retail Management.* New York: McGraw-Hill Book Co., Inc., 1957.

1959 *Careers for Women in Retailing.* Washington: U.S. Department of Labor, 1959.

HOLLANDER, S. C. *Explorations in Retailing.* East Lansing: Bureau of Business and Economic Research, Michigan State University, 1959.

SCOTT, W. E. *Everyday Consumer Business.* Englewood Cliffs, N.J.: Prentice-Hall, Inc., 1959.

1960 REICH, EDWARD, *et. al. Basic Retailing.* New York: Pitman, 1960; 2d ed., 1970 as *Basic Retailing and Distribution.*

HOLDREN, B. R. *The Structure of a Retail Market, and the Market Behavior of Retail Units.* Englewood Cliffs, N.J.: Prentice-Hall, Inc., 1960.

REICH, E. and Others. *Basic Retailing.* New York: Pitman Publishing Company, 1960.

1961 WEISS, E. B. *Merchandising for Tomorrow.* New York: McGraw-Hill Book Co., Inc., 1961.

1962 HARRINGTON, M. *The Retail Clerks.* New York: John Wiley & Sons, Inc., 1962.
JEFFREYS, J. B. and D. KNEE. *Retailing in Europe: Present Structure and Future Trends.* London: Macmillan Co., 1962.
Retail Accounting Manual. New York: National Retail Merchants Association, 1962.
1963 PHILPOTT, W. J. *Retail Business Administration.* New York: Pitman Publishing Company, 1963.
RACHMAN, DAVID J. *Retail Management Cases.* Englewood Cliffs, N.J.: Prentice-Hall, Inc., 1963.
1964 FIBER, ALAN. *The Independent Retailer.* London: Heinemann, 1964.
SIMMONS, J. W. *The Changing Patterns of Retail Location.* Chicago: University of Chicago, 1964.
1966 CROWN, P. *What You Should Know About Retail Merchandising.* Dobbs Ferry, N.Y.: Oceana Publications, 1966.
DALRYMPLE, D.J. *Merchandising Decision Models for Department Stores.* East Lansing, Michigan: Bureau of Business and Administration Research, Michigan State University, 1966.
ENTENBERG, R.D. *Effective Retail and Market Distribution.* Cleveland: The World Publishing Company, 1966.
MAHONEY, T. *The Great Merchants.* New York: Harper & Bros., 1966.
REILLY, PHILIP J. *Old Masters of Retailing.* New York: Fairchild Publications, 1966.
1967 COX, ELI P. and L. G. ERICKSON. *Retail Decentralization.* East Lansing: Bureau of Business and Economic Research, Michigan State University, 1967.
GIST, R. R. *Management Perspectives in Retailing.* New York: John Wiley & Sons, Inc., 1967.
Management By Objectives in Retailing. New York: National Retail Merchants Association, 1967.
MATHIAS, PETER. *Retailing Revolution.* London: Longmans, 1967.
McNAIR, M. P. and M. BERMAN (eds.). *Marketing Through Retailers.* New York: American Management Association, 1967.
WEISS, E. B. *Retail Trends That Will Shape Tomorrow's Marketing.* New York: Doyle Dane Bernbach, 1967.
1968 GABER, HAROLD. *Retail Merchandising and Management with Electronic Data Processing.* New York: National Retail Merchants Association., 1968.
GIST, R.R. *Retailing: Concepts and Decisions.* New York: John Wiley & Sons, Inc., 1968.
LUICK, J. F. and W. L. ZIEGLER. *Sales Promotion and Modern Merchandising.* New York: McGraw-Hill Book Co., Inc., 1968.
PFAHL, P. B. *The Retail Florist Business.* Danville, Ill.: Interstate Printers and Publishers, 1968.
1969 BACHMAN, D. J. *Retail Strategy and Structure.* Englewood Cliffs, N.J.: Prentice-Hall, Inc., 1969.
DALRYMPLE, D. J. and D. L. THOMPSON. *Retailing: an Economic View.* New York: Free Press, 1969.
THOMPSON, D. and D. J. DALRYMPLE. *Retail Management Cases.* New York: Free Press, 1969.
WELCH, D. T. *Budgetary Control and Cost Reduction for Retail Companies.* London: MacDonald, 1969.
WILLIAMS, E.D. *Training for Retailing.* London: MacDonald, 1969.
1970 ALEXANDER, DAVIS. *Retailing in England During the Industrial Revolution.* London: Athlone Press, 1970.

DREW-BEAR, ROBERT. *Mass Merchandising: Revolution and Evolution.* New York: Fairchild Publications, 1970.

GILLESPIE, K. R. and J. C. HECHT. *Retail Business Management.* New York: McGraw-Hill Book Co., Inc., 1970.

HOLLANDER, S. C. *Multinational Retailing.* East Lansing: Michigan State University, 1970.

RYANS, JOHN K. *et al. New Dimensions in Retailing.* Belmont, California: Wadsworth Publishing Co., 1970

1971 GIST, R. R. *Basic Retailing: Text and Cases.* New York: John Wiley & Sons, Inc., 1971.

MARKIN, R. J. *Retailing: Concepts, Institutions, and Management.* New York: Macmillan Co., 1971.

Retailing Management: A Systems Approach. New York: Macmillan Co., 1971.

OCKO, J. Y. *Retail Advertising Copy.* New York: National Retail Merchants Association, 1971.

PINTEL, G. *Retailing.* Englewood Cliffs, N.J.: Prentice-Hall, Inc., 1971.

1972 BODDEWYN, JEAN J. and S. C. HOLLANDER (eds.). *Public Policy and Retailing.* Lexington, Mass.: Lexington Books, 1972.

1973 BUTCHER, B. C. *Fundamentals of Retailing.* New York: Macmillan Co., 1973.

POWERS, J.T., *et al. Executive Compensation in Retailing.* New York: National Retail Merchants Association, 1973.

WILL, RALPH and R. W. HASTY. *Retailing: a Mid-Management Approach.* San Francisco, Canfield Press, 1973.

1974 KNEIDER, ALBERT P. *Mathematics of Merchandising.* Englewood Cliffs, N.J.: Prentice-Hall, Inc., 1974.

WHOLESALING

1920 *Wholesale Marketing of Foods.* Washington, D.C.: U.S. Government Printing Office, 1920.

1926 BECKMAN, THEODORE N. *Wholesaling.* New York: Ronald Press Co., 1926; rev. ed., 1937, with N. H. ENGLE, as *Wholesaling: Principles and Practice;* 2d ed., 1949; 3d ed., 1959, with R. D. BUZZELL.

1928 MILLARD, JAMES W. *The Wholesale Grocer's Problems.* Washington, D.C.: U.S. Government Printing Office, 1928.

193- CAVES, W. T. *The Wholesaler and His Functions.* New York: Wholesale Dry Goods Institute, 193-.

1934 SANDBERG, LARS J. *Truck Selling.* Boston: Harvard Business School, 1934.

FREDERICK, J. H. *Industrial Marketing.* New York: Prentice-Hall, Inc., 1934.

1935 ELDER, R. F. *Fundamentals of Industrial Marketing.* New York: McGraw-Hill Book Co., Inc., 1935.

HECKERT, J. B., and I. J. STONE. *Wholesale Accounting and Control.* New York: McGraw-Hill Book Co., Inc., 1935.

LESTER, B. *Marketing Industrial Equipment.* New York: McGraw-Hill Book Co., Inc., 1935.

1936 REED, V. D. *Advertising and Selling Industrial Goods.* New York: Ronald Press Co., 1936.

1937 WEISS, E. B., C. B. LARRABEE, and PETER BALL. *How To Sell through Wholesalers.* New York: Harper & Bros., 1937.

1939 DEUPREE, R. G. *The Wholesale Marketing of Fruits and Vegetables in Baltimore.* Baltimore: Johns Hopkins Press, 1939.
      TAGGERT, H. F. *Distribution Cost Accounting for Wholesaling.* Washington, D.C.: U.S. Government Printing Office, 1939.
1940 BLANKERTZ, D. F. *Marketing Cooperatives.* New York: Ronald Press Co., 1940.
1941 MESEROLE, W. H. H., and C. H. SEVIN. *Effective Grocery Wholesaling.* Washington, D. C.: U.S. Government Printing Office, 1941.
1948 FISHER, A. B. *Warehouse Operations of Service Wholesale Druggists.* New York: National Wholesale Druggists Association. 1948.
      WEISS, E. B. *How to Sell to and through Department Stores.* New York: McGraw-Hill Book Co., Inc., 1948.
1949 CASSADY, R., and W. L. JONES. *Changing Competitive Structure in Wholesaling Grocery Trade.* Berkeley: University of California Press, 1949.
      MITCHELL, HARRY A. *Wholesale Buying Centers for Retailers in the Deep South.* Baton Rouge, La.: Tulane University, 1949.
1952 LEWIS, EDWIN H. *Wholesaling in the Twin Cities.* Minneapolis: University of Minnesota Press, 1952.
1956 ALEXANDER, R. S., J. S. CROSS, and R. M. CUNNINGHAM. *Industrial Marketing.* Homewood, Ill.: Richard D. Irwin, Inc., 1956; rev. ed., 1961.
1958 HILL, RICHARD M. *Improving the Competitive Position of the Independent Wholesaler.* Urbana; Bureau of Business Management, University of Illinois, 1958.
1959 BOUMA, J. C. and MARTIN KRIESBERG. *Views of Independent Grocers on Wholesaler-Retailer Relations.* Washington: U.S. Department of Agriculture, 1959.
      CASSIDY, P. J. and P. WISCHKAEMPER. *Policies and Practices of Some Leading Institutional Wholesale Grocers.* Washington, D.C.: U. S. Government Printing Office, 1959.
1960 *Wholesale Merchandising.* Washington: Office of Industrial Resources, International Cooperation Administration, 1960.
1961 REVZAN, D. A. *Wholesaling in Marketing Organization.* New York: John Wiley & Sons, Inc., 1961.
      STILL, R. R. and H. R. GREEN. *Distribution of Industrial Goods.* Syracuse, N.Y.: Syracuse University Business Research Center, 1961.
      WARSHAW, M. R. *Effective Selling Through Wholesalers.* Ann Arbor: University of Michigan Press, 1961.
1962 COREY, E. R. *Industrial Marketing.* Englewood Cliffs, N.J.: Prentice-Hall, Inc., 1962.
      HILL, RICHARD M. *Techniques of Measuring Market Potentials for Wholesalers.* Urbana: Bureau of Business Management, University of Illinois, 1962.
      HIRSCH, LEON V. *Wholesaling in India's Economy.* (n.p.) United Research, 1942.
1963 BARTELS, ROBERT. *Comparative Marketing: Wholesaling in Fifteen Countries.* Homewood, Ill.: Richard D. Irwin, Inc., 1963.
      DIAMOND, W. M. *Distribution Channels for Industrial Goods.* Columbus, O.: Ohio State University Bureau of Business Research, 1963.
      HILL, RICHARD M. *Wholesaling Management: Text and Cases.* Homewood, Ill.: Richard D. Irwin, Inc., 1963.

1964 MANCHESTER, ALDEN COE. *The Organization of Wholesale Fruit and Vegetable Markets.* Washington: U. S. Department of Agriculture, 1964.

1965 BECKMAN, T. N. and A. F. DOODY. *Wholesaling.* Washington: Small Business Administration, 1965.

BRION, JOHN M. *Marketing Through Wholesaler/Distributor Channel.* Chicago: American Marketing Association, 1965.

1966 REVZAN, D. A. *The Marketing Significance of Geographical Variations in Wholesale/Retail Sales Ratios.* Berkeley: Institute of Business and Economic Research, University of California, 1966; 2d ed., 1972.

1967 ROBINSON, P. J. and C. W. FARIS. *Industrial Buying and Creative Marketing.* Boston: Allyn & Bacon, 1967.

1968 DENING, JAMES (ed.). *Marketing Industrial Goods.* London: Business Publications, 1968.

WILMOT, CHARLES A. *Retailer Attitudes Toward Wholesaler-Retailer Integration.* Ann Arbor: University Microfilms, 1968.

1970 BROWN, MILTON P. *et al. Strategy Problems of Mass Retailers and Wholesalers.* Homewood, Ill.: Richard D. Irwin, Inc. 1970.

ERTEL, K and E. DORR. *Wholesaling.* New York: McGraw-Hill Book Co., Inc., 1970.

VANCE, JAMES E. *Merchant's World: The Geography of Wholesaling.* Englewood Cliffs, N.J.: Prentice-Hall, Inc., 1970.

1971 PADBERG, DANIEL I. *Today's Food Broker.* New York: Chain Store Age Books, 1971.

1972 BUCKLIN, LOUIS P. *Competition and Evolution in the Distributive Trades..* Englewood Cliffs, N.J.: Prentice-Hall, Inc., 1972.

MARKETING RESEARCH

1916 SHAW, A. W. *An Approach to Business Problems.* Cambridge: Harvard University Press, 1916.

1919 DUNCAN, C. S. *Commercial Research.* New York: Macmillan Co., 1919.

1920 FREDERICK, GEORGE J. *Business Research and Statistics.* New York: D. Appleton-Century Co., Inc., 1920.

1921 WHITE, PERCIVAL. *Market Analysis: Its Principles and Methods.* New York: McGraw-Hill Book Co., Inc., 1921. 2d ed., 1925.

1926 EIGELBERNER, J. *Investigation of Business Problems.* Chicago: A. W. Shaw Co., 1926.

1927 WHITE, PERCIVAL. *Advertising Research.* New York: D. Appleton-Century Co., Inc., 1927.

1928 DICKINSON, CLARK Z. *Industrial and Commercial Research.* Ann Arbor: University of Michigan Press, 1928.

1929 CARROLL, JEAN F. *Standards of Research.* New York: Meredith Publishing Co., 1929.

REED, VIRGIL D. *Planned Marketing.* New York: Ronald Press Co., 1929.

REILLY, W. J. *Marketing Investigations.* New York: Ronald Press Co., 1929.

WHITE, PERCIVAL. *Sales Quotas.* New York: Harper & Bros., 1929.

1931 WHITE, PERCIVAL. *Marketing Research Technique.* New York: Harper & Bros., 1931.

1935 COUTANT, FRANK R., and J. RUSSELL DOUBMAN. *Simplified Market Research.* Philadelphia: Walther Printing House, 1935.

1937 BROWN, LYNDON O. *Market Research and Analysis*. New York: Ronald Press Co., 1937; 2d ed., 1949, as *Marketing and Distribution Research;* 3d ed., 1955; 4th ed., 1969 with L. L. BEIK.

PHELPS, D. M. *Marketing Research: Its Function, Scope and Method*. Ann Arbor: University of Michigan Bureau of Business Research, Business Studies, Vol. 8, No. 2.

WHEELER, FERDINAND C. *The Technique of Markeing Research*. New York: McGraw-Hill Book Co., Inc., 1937.

1938 COWAN, DONALD R. G. *Sales Analysis from the Management Standpoint* Chicago: University of Chicago Press, 1938.

1940 EASTWOOD, R. PARKER. *Sales Control by Quantitative Methods*. New York: Columbia University Press, 1940.

HECKERT, J. B. *Distribution Costs*. New York: Ronald Press Co., 1940; 2d ed., 1953, with R. B. MINER.

1943 BLANKENSHIP, A. B. *Consumer and Opinion Research*. New York: Harper & Bros., 1943.

1946 BLANKENSHIP, A. B. (ed.). *How To Conduct Consumer and Opinion Research*. New York: Harper & Bros., 1946.

1947 HEIDINGSFIELD, M. S., and A. B. BLANKENSHIP. *Market and Marketing Analysis*. New York: Henry Holt & Co., 1947.

PEATMAN, D. M. *Descriptive and Sampling Techniques*. New York: Harper & Bros., 1947.

STOCKTON, J. R. *An Introduction to Business Statistics*. 2d ed. New York: D. C. Heath, 1947.

ZEISEL, HANS. *Say It with Figures*. New York: Harper & Bros., 1947.

1948 FREEMAN, H. A. (ed.). *Sampling Inspection*. New York: McGraw-Hill Book Co., Inc., 1948.

1949 FERBER, ROBERT. *Statistical Techniques in Market Research*. New York: McGraw-Hill Book Co., Inc., 1949; rev. ed., 1963 as *Market Research.*

1950 DELINS, A. H. R. *Principles of Market Research*. London: Lockwood, 1950.

FOX, W. M. *How To Use Market Research for Profit*. New York: Prentice-Hall, Inc., 1950.

GEE, WILSON *Social Science Research Methods*. New York: Appleton-Century-Crofts Co., 1950.

GOODMAN, O. R. *Forecasting Methods Used in Sales Planning*. Madison, Wis., 1953.

HOBART, D. M. (ed.). *Marketing Research Practice*. New York: Ronald Press Co., 1950.

LUCAS, DARRELL BLAINE, and S. H. BRITT *Advertising Psychology and Research*. New York: McGraw-Hill Book Co., Inc., 1950.

1951 BRADFORD, E. S. *Marketing Research*. New York: McGraw-Hill Book Co., Inc., 1951.

FERBER, ROBERT. *Problem Manual for Statistical Techniques in Market Research*. (n.p.): Author, 1951.

LORIE, J.H., and HARRY V. ROBERTS. *Basic Methods of Marketing Research*. New York: McGraw-Hill Book Co., Inc., 1951.

1952 LUCK, D. G., and WALES, H. G. *Marketing Research*. New York: Prentice-Hall Inc., 1952; 2d ed., 1962 with D. A. TAYLOR; 3d ed., 1970.

1954 BLANKERTZ, D. F., ROBERT FERBER, and HUGH G. WALES. *Cases and Problems in Marketing Research*. New York: Ronald Press Co., 1954.

356

SMITH, G. H. *Motivation Research in Advertising and Marketing.* New York: McGraw-Hill Book Co., Inc., 1954.

1955 BRENNER, HENRY (ed.). *Marketing Research Pays Off.* Pleasantville, N.Y.: Printers' Ink Books, 1955.

LEONARD, DIETZ L. *Consumer Research and Projective Techniques.* (n.p.): Ajax, 1955.

LONGMAN, D. R., and M. SCHIFF. *Practical Distribution Cost Analysis.* Homewood, Ill.: Richard D. Irwin, Inc., 1955.

1956 BOYD, H. W., JR. and RALPH WESTFALL. *Marketing Research.* Homewood, Ill.: Richard D. Irwin, Inc., 1956; rev. ed., 1964; 3d ed., 1972.

WALES, HUGH G. and ROBERT FERBER, (eds.). *A Basic Bibliography on Marketing Research.* Chicago: American Marketing Assn., 1956; 2d ed., 1963.

1957 ADLER, M. *Modern Market Research.* New York: Philosophical Library, 1957.

CRISP, R. D. *Marketing Research.* New York: McGraw-Hill Book Co., Inc., 1957.

1958 FERBER, R., and H. G. WALES. *Motivation and Market Behavior.* Homewood, Ill.: Richard D. Irwin, Inc., 1958.

1959 ALEVIZOS, J. P. *Marketing Research.* Englewood Cliffs, N.J.: Prentice-Hall, Inc., 1959.

1960 HOLMES, P.M. *Marketing Research.* Cincinnati: South-Western Publishing Co., Inc., 1970; 2d ed., 1966.

1961 BASS, F.M., *et al. Mathematical Models and Methods in Marketing.* Homewood, Ill.: Richard D. Irwin, Inc., 1961.

HOLLOWAY, R. J. *Marketing Research and Market Planning for the Small Manufacturer.* Minneapolis: University of Minnesota, 1961.

1962 BALDERSTON, F. E. and A. C. HOGGATE. *Simulation in Market Processes.* Berkeley: Institute of Business and Economic Research, University of California, 1962.

BUZZELL, R. D. *A Basic Bibliography on Mathematical Methods in Marketing.* Chicago: American Marketing Assn., 1962.

FRANK, R. E., *et al* (eds.). *Quantitative Techniques in Marketing Analysis.* Homewood, Ill.: Richard D. Irwin, Inc., 1962.

HEIDINGSFIELD, M. S. and F. H. EBY. *Marketing and Business Research.* New York: Holt, Rinehart and Winston, Inc., 1962.

1963 ALDERSON, W. and S. J. SHAPIRO. *Marketing and the Computer.* Englewood Cliffs, N.J.: Prentice-Hall, Inc., 1963.

BARKSDALE, H. C. *Problems in Marketing Research; in-Basket Simulation.* New York: Holt, Rinehart and Winston, 1963.

FERBER, R. *Market Research.* New York: McGraw-Hill Book Inc., 1963.

SCHREIER, F. T. *Modern Marketing Research.* Belmont, California: Wadsworth Publishing Company, Inc., 1963.

1964 FERBER, R. and others. *Marketing Research.* New York: The Ronald Press Company, 1964.

GREENLAW, P.S. and F. W. KNIFFIN. *Markim; A Marketing Decision Simulation.* Scranton: International Textbook Co., 1964.

WASSON, C. R. *The Strategy of Marketing Research.* New York: Appleton-Century-Crofts, Inc., 1964.

1965 BANKS, SEYMOUR. *Experimentation in Marketing.* New York: McGraw-Hill Book Co., Inc., 1965.

BLANKENSHIP, A. B. and J. B. DOYLE. *Marketing Research Management.* Chicago: American Marketing Association, 1965.

CRESPI, I. *Attitude Research.* Chicago: American Marketing Association, 1965.

1966   BARKSDALE, H. C. and W. M. WEILBACHER (eds.). *Marketing Research: Selected Readings and Analytical Commentaries.* New York: The Ronald Press Co., 1966.

GREEN, P. E. and D. S. TULL. *Research for Marketing Decisions.* Englewood Cliffs, N.J.: Prentice-Hall, Inc., 1966; 2d ed., 1970; 3d ed., 1975.

KONRAD, E. and R. ERICKSON (eds.). *Marketing Research: A Management Overview.* Chicago: American Marketing Association, 1966.

1967   COX, K. K. (ed.) *Readings in Market Research.* New York: Appleton-Century-Crofts, Inc., 1967.

FRANK, R. E. and P. E. GREEN. *Quantitative Methods in Marketing.* Englewood Cliffs, N.J.: Prentice-Hall, Inc., 1967.

GREEN, P. E. and R. E. FRANK. *A Manager's Guide to Marketing Research.* New York: John Wiley & Sons, Inc., 1967.

KING, W. R. *Quantitative Analysis for Marketing Management.* New York: McGraw-Hill Book Co., Inc., 1967.

LEONHARD, DIETZ L. *The Human Equation in Marketing Research.* New York: American Management Association, 1967.

1968   ENGEL, J. F., D. T. KOLLAT, and R. D. BLACKWELL. *Consumer Behavior.* New York: Holt, Rinehart and Winston, 1968; 2d ed., 1972.

1969   BLACKWELL, R. D., D. T. KOLLAT, and J. F. ENGEL. *Cases in Consumer Behavior.* New York: Holt, Rinehart and Winston, 1969.

BOGART, L. (ed.). *Current Controversies in Marketing Research.* Chicago: Markham Co., 1969.

BUZZELL, R. D., D. F. COX, and R. V. BROWN. *Marketing Research and Information Systems: Text and Cases.* New York: McGraw-Hill Book Co., Inc., 1969.

COX, K. K. and B. M. ENIS. *Experimentation for Marketing Decisions.* Scranton, Pa.: International Textbook Co., 1969.

HARDER, THEODORE. *Introduction to Mathematical Models in Market and Opinion Research.* N.Y.: Gordon and Breach Science Publishers, 1969.

1970   DAVIS, D. J. *Experimental Marketing.* New York: American Management Association, 1970.

GREEN, P. E. *et al. Multidimensional Scaling and Related Techniques in Marketing Analysis.* Boston: Allyn & Bacon, 1970.

KOLLAT, D. T., R. D. BLACKWELL, and J. F. ENGEL (eds.). *Research in Consumer Behavior.* New York: Holt, Rinehart and Winston, 1970.

1971   ENIS, B. M. and C. L. BROOME. *Marketing Decisions: A Bayesian Approach.* Scranton: Intext Educational Publishers, 1971.

KRAEMAR, J.Z. *Marketing Research in the Developing Countries.* New York: Praeger Publications, 1971.

1972   COX, K. K. and B. M. ENIS. *The Marketing Research Processs.* Pacific Palisades, Calif.: Goodyear Publishing Co., Inc., 1972.

JENKINS, J. R. G. *Marketing and Customer Behavior.* Oxford, N.Y.: Pergamon Press, 1972.

WORCESTER, R. M. (ed.). *Consumer Market Research Handbook.* New York: McGraw-Hill Book Co., Inc., 1972.

WENTZ, W. B. *Marketing Research: Management and Methods.* New York: Harper & Row, 1972

1973 CHESNALL, P. M. *Marketing Research: Analysis and Measurement.* New York: McGraw-Hill Book Co., Inc., 1973.

COX, KEITH K and B. M ENIS. *Readings in the Marketing Research Process.* Pacific Palisades, Calif.: Goodyear Publishing Co., Inc., 1973.

GREEN, P. E. and YOREM WIND. *Multiattribute Decisions in Marketing: A Measurement Approach.* Hindsdale, Ill.: Dryden Press, 1973.

1974 FERBER, ROBERT (ed.). *Handbook of Marketing Research.* New York: McGraw-Hill Book Co., Inc., 1974.

GENERAL MARKETING

1901 *Report of the Industrial Commission on the Distribution of Farm Products, Vol. VI.* Washington, D.C.: Government Printing Office, 1901.

1906 SPARLING, SAMUEL E. *Business Organization.* New York: Macmillan Co., 1906.

1911 BUTLER, R. S. *Selling, Buying, and Shipping Methods.* New York: Alexander Hamilton Institute, 1911; rev. ed., 1917, as *Marketing Methods and Policies.*

1912 SHAW, A.W. "Some Problems in Market Distribution," *Quarterly Journal of Economics,* August, 1912; published in book form, 1915, same title. Cambridge: Harvard University Press, 1951.

1913 BRISCO, N. A. *Economics of Business.* New York: Macmillan Co., 1913.

1914 BUTLER, R.S., H. DeBOWER, and J. G. JONES. *Marketing Methods and Salesmanship.* New York: Alexander Hamilton Institute, 1914.

1915 WELD, L. D. H. *Studies in the Marketing of Farm Products.* Minneapolis: University of Minnesota, 1915.

1916 WELD, L. D. H. *The Marketing of Farm Products.* New York: Macmillan Co., 1916; rev. with FRED E. CLARK, as *Marketing Agricultural Products,* 1932.

1917 BUTLER, R. S. *Marketing Methods.* New York: Alexander Hamilton Institute, 1917.

WELD, L. D. H. "Marketing Agencies between Manufacturer and Jobber," *Quarterly Journal of Economics,* August, 1917.

_____. "Marketing Functions and Mercantile Organizations," *American Economic Review,* June, 1917.

1918 BUTLER, R.S., and J.B. SWINNEY. *Marketing and Merchandising.* New York: Alexander Hamilton Institute, 1918.

DOUGLAS, A. W. *Merchandising.* New York: Macmillan Co., 1918.

1920 CHERINGTON, PAUL T. *The Elements of Marketing.* New York: Macmillan Co., 1920.

COPELAND, M. T. *Marketing Problems.* New York: A. W. Shaw Co., 1920; 2d ed., 1923, as *Problems in Marketing;* 3d ed., 1930; 4th ed., 1931.

DUNCAN, C. S. *Marketing: Its Problems and Methods.* New York: D. Appleton-Century Co., Inc., 1920.

1921 CONVERSE, PAUL D. *Marketing: Methods and Policies.* New York: Prentice-Hall, Inc., 1921; 2d ed., 1926.

HIBBARD, B. H. *Marketing Agriculture Products.* New York: D. Appleton-Century Co., Inc., 1921.

IVEY, PAUL W. *Principles of Marketing.* New York: Ronald Press Co., 1921.

MACKLIN, T. *Efficient Marketing for Agriculture.* New York: Macmillan Co., 1921.

1922 CLARK, FRED. *Principles of Marketing.* New York: Macmillan Co., 1922; 2d ed., 1932; 3d ed., 1942 with CARRIE P. CLARK; rev. ed., 1962 by R.D. TOUSLEY, EUGENE CLARK and F.E. CLARK.

1923 BUTLER, R. S. *Marketing and Merchandising.* New York: Alexander Hamilton Institute, 1923.

MORIARITY, W. D. *The Economics of Marketing and Advertising.* New York: Harper & Bros., 1923.

1924 CLARK, FRED E. *Readings in Marketing.* New York: Macmillan Co., 1924.

COPELAND, M. T. *Principles of Merchandising.* New York: A. W. Shaw Co., 1924.

SIMONDS, E. N. *Marketing the Technical Product.* London: Emmott & Co., Ltd., 1924.

WHITE, P., and W. S. HAYWARD. *Marketing Practice.* New York: Doubleday, Page & Co., 1924.

1925 BROWN, E., JR. *Marketing.* New York: Harper & Bros., 1925.

1926 ELBOURNE, E. T. *The Marketing Problem: How It Is Being Tackled in the U.S.A.,* London: Longmans, Green & Co., 1926.

MARTIN, P. W. *The Limited Market.* London: G. Allen and Unwin, Ltd., 1926.

McNAIR, M. P., and D. K. DAVID. *Problems in Retailing.* New York: McGraw-Hill Book Co., Inc., 1926.

WRIGHT, I., and C. E. LANDON. *Readings in Marketing Principles.* New York: Prentice-Hall, Inc., 1926.

1927 CONVERSE, PAUL D. *Selling Policies.* New York: Prentice-Hall, Inc., 1927.

BARSODI, R. *The Distribution Age.* New York: D. Appleton-Century and Co., Inc., 1927.

MAYNARD, H.H., W.C. WEIDLER, and T.N. BECKMAN, *Principles of Marketing.* New York: Ronald Press Co., 1927; 2d ed., 1932; 3d ed., 1939; 4th ed., 1946; 5th ed., 1954; 6th ed., 1958 with W. R. DAVIDSON; 7th ed., 1962 by BECKMAN and DAVIDSON; 8th ed., 1967, with J. F. ENGEL; 9th ed., 1973, by BECKMAN, DAVIDSON, and W. WAYNE TALARZYK.

RHOADES, E. L. *Introductory Readings in Marketing.* New York: A. W. Shaw Co., 1927.

TOSDAL, H. R. *Market Planning.* New York: System Magazine, 1927.

WHITE, P. *Scientific Marketing Management: Its Principles and Methods.* New York: Harper & Bros., 1927.

1928 VAUGHAN, F. L. *Marketing and Advertising.* Princeton, N.J.: Princeton University Press, 1928.

1929 VAILE, R. S., and P. L. SLAGSVOLD. *Marketing.* New York: Ronald Press Co. (preliminary edition), 1929.

1930 VAILE, R. S., and P. L. SLAGSVOLD. *Market Organization.* New York: Ronald Press Co., 1930.

1930 CONVERSE, PAUL D. *Elements of Marketing.* New York: Prentice-Hall, Inc., 1930; rev. ed., 1935, with H. W. HUEGY; 2d ed., 1940; 3d ed., 1947; 5th ed., 1952, with ROBERT V. MITCHELL; 6th ed., 1958; 7th ed., 1965.

1931   BREYER, R. F. *Commodity Marketing.* New York: McGraw-Hill Book Co., Inc., 1931.

DuPLESSIS, A. F. *The Marketing of Wool.* London: Sir I. Pitman & Sons, Ltd., 1931.

PYLE, J.F. *Marketing Principles, Organization, and Policies.* New York: McGraw-Hill Book Co., Inc., 1931; 2d ed., 1936.

1932   BECKMAN, T. N. (ed.). *Channels of Distribution for Manufactured Goods, by Industries.* Columbus, Ohio, 1932.

1933   KILLOUGH, H. B. *The Economics of Marketing.* New York: Harper & Bros., 1933.

ROST, O. F. *Distribution Today.* New York: McGraw-Hill Book Co., Inc., 1933.

SIMMAT, R. *The Principles and Practice of Marketing.* New York: Pitman Publishing Co., 1933.

1934   BREYER, R. F. *The Marketing Institution.* New York: McGraw-Hill Book Co., Inc., 1934.

FREDERICK, J. H. *Industrial Marketing.* New York: Prentice-Hall, Inc., 1934.

1935   COMISH, N. H. *Marketing Manufactured Goods.* Boston: Stratford Co., 1935.

ELDER, R. F. *Fundamentals of Industrial Marketing.* New York: McGraw-Hill Book Co., Inc., 1935.

HOLTZCLAW, H. F. *Principles of Marketing.* New York: Thomas Y. Crowell Co., 1935.

LESTER, B. *Marketing Industrial Equipment.* New York: McGraw-Hill Book Co., Inc., 1935.

1936   AGNEW, H. E., R. B. JENKINS, and J. C. DRURY. *Outlines of Marketing.* New York: McGraw-Hill Book Co., Inc., 1936; 2d ed., 1942; 3d ed., 1950, with HAROLD A. CONNER and WILLIAM L. DOREMUS.

CONVERSE, P. D. *Essentials of Distribution.* New York: Prentice-Hall, Inc., 1936.

1938   COX, R. *The Marketing of Textiles.* Washington: Textile Foundation, 1938.

EASTMAN, R. O. *Marketing Geography.* New York: Alexander Hamilton Institute, 1938.

HOTCHKISS, G. B. *Milestones of Marketing.* Macmillan Co., 1938.

PHILLIPS, C. F. *Marketing.* New York: Houghton Mifflin Co.,; 1938; rev. ed. with D. J. DUNCAN, as *Marketing, Principles and Methods.* Chicago: Richard D. Irwin Inc., 1948; 2d ed., 1948; 3d ed., 1956; 4th ed., 1960; 5th ed., 1964; 6th ed., 1968; 7th ed., 1973 by J. M. CARMAN and K. P. UHL.

WALTER, L. R. *Effective Marketing.* New York: McGraw-Hill Book Co., Inc., 1938.

1939   BARKER, C. W., and M. ANSHEN. *Modern Marketing.* New York: McGraw-Hill Book Co., Inc., 1939.

SHIRK, A. U. *Marketing through Food Brokers.* New York: McGraw-Hill Book Co., Inc., 1939.

1940   ALEXANDER, R. S., F. M. SURFACE, R. F. ELDER, and W. ALDERSON. *Marketing.* New York: Ginn & Co., 1940; 2d ed., 1949; 3d ed., 1953.

McKEE, JANE (ed.). *Marketing Organization and Technique.* Toronto: University of Toronto Press, 1940.

1941   AGNEW, H. E. *Marketing Policies.* New York: McGraw-Hill Book Co., Inc., 1941; 2d ed., 1951, with DALE HOUGHTON.

1942 McNAIR, M. P., E. P. LEARNED, and S. F. TEELE. *Problems in Merchandise Distribution.* New York: McGraw-Hill Book Co., Inc., 1942.

PYLE, J. F. *Marketing Management.* Ypsilanti, Mich.: University Litho-printers. 1942.

VAUGHAN, F. *Marketing: Functions, Mediums, Practices, Variations, Appraisal.* New York: Farrar and Rinehart, Inc., 1942.

1946 ENGLE, N. H. *Marketing in the West.* New York: Ronald Press Co., 1946.

PHILLIPS, C. F. *Marketing by Manufacturers.* Chicago: Richard D. Irwin, Inc., 1946.

SHEPHERD, G. W. *Marketing Farm Products.* Ames: Iowa State College Press, 1946.

1947 DUDDY, E. A., and D. A. REVZAN. *Marketing: An Institutional Approach.* New York: McGraw-Hill Book Co., Inc., 1947; 2d ed., 1953.

STOCKING, S. B. *Management in Marketing.* Toronto: University of Toronto Press, 1947.

1948 CONVERSE, PAUL D., and F. M. JONES. *Introduction to Marketing: Principles of Wholesale and Retail Distribution.* New York: Prentice-Hall, Inc., 1948.

NYSTROM, P. H., *et al. Marketing Handbook.* New York: Ronald Press Co., 1948.

1949 BREYER, R. F. *Quantitative Systemic Analysis and Control, Study No. 1: Channel and Channel Group Costing.* Philadelphia: College Offset Press, 1949.

McNAIR, M. P., and H. L. HANSEN. *Problems in Marketing.* New York: McGraw-Hill Book Co., Inc., 1949; 2d ed., 1957.

_____. *Readings in Marketing.* New York: McGraw-Hill Book Co., Inc., 1949; 2d ed., 1956.

1950 COX, REAVIS, and WROE ALDERSON (eds.). *Theory in Marketing.* Chicago: Richard D. Irwin, Inc., 1950.

LAZO, HECTOR. *Case Histories of Successful Marketing.* New York: Funk and Wagnalls, 1950.

TERRY, G. R. *Marketing and Selected Case Problems.* New York: Prentice-Hall, Inc., 1950.

1951 WALES, H. G. (ed.). *Changing Perspectives in Marketing.* Urbana: University of Illinois Press, 1951.

1952 COLE, R. H. *et al. Vertical Integration in Marketing.* Urbana: University of Illinois., 1952.

OTTESON, S. F. (ed.). *Marketing: Current Problems and Theories.* Indiana Business Report No. 16. Bloomington: Indiana University, 1952.

VAILE, R. S., E. F. GRETHER, and REAVIS COX. *Marketing in the American Economy.* New York: Ronald Press Co., 1952.

1953 BAKKEN, H. H. *Theory of Markets and Marketing.* Madison: University of Wisconsin, 1953.

BLANKENSHIP, A. B., and MYRON S. HEIDINGSFIELD. *Marketing: An Introduction.* New York: Barnes and Noble, 1953; rev. ed., 1957.

CANNON, J. T., and J. A. WICHERT. *Marketing.* New York: McGraw-Hill Book Co., Inc., 1953.

WESTING, J. H. (ed.). *Readings in Marketing.* New York: Prentice-Hall, Inc., 1953.

WILSON, J. H. *Merchandising Primer.* New York: McGraw-Hill Book Co., Inc., 1953.

1954 CLEWETT, RICHARD M. (ed.). *Marketing Channels.* Homewood, Ill.: Richard D. Irwin, Inc., 1954.

FREY, GEORGE F., and RAYMOND D. BUREUX. *Current Readings in Marketing.* New York: Printers' Ink Publishing Co., 1954; rev. ed., 1957.

LOCKLEY, L. C., and CHARLES J. DIRKSEN. *Cases in Marketing.* Allyn and Bacon, 1954; 2d ed., 1959.

1955 HEPNER, H. W. *Modern Marketing: Dynamics and Management.* New York: McGraw-Hill Book Co., Inc., 1955.

1956 ALEXANDER, R.S. *et. al., Industrial Marketing.* Homewood, Ill.: Richard D. Irwin, Inc., 1956; 2d ed., 1961; 3d ed., 1967.

COLLINS, G. R. *Marketing.* New York: Alexander Hamilton Institute, 1956.

HANSEN, HARRY L. *Marketing: Text, Cases, Readings.* Homewood, Ill.: Richard D. Irwin, Inc., 1956; rev. ed., 1961; 3d ed., 1967.

SHULTZ, WILLIAM J. *Outline of Marketing.* New York: Littlefield, Adams, 1956.

1957 BANNING, D. *Techniques for Marketing New Products.* New York: McGraw-Hill Book Co., Inc., 1957.

BOYD, H.W. (ed.). *Contemporary American Marketing.* Homewood, Ill.: Richard D. Irwin, Inc., 1957; rev. ed., 1962.

A New Approach to Marketing Theory. Bloomington: Indiana University, 1957.

1958 EWING, D. W. *Effective Marketing Action.* New York: American Marketing Association, 1959.

SEELYE, A. L. *Marketing in Transition.* New York: Harper & Bros., 1958.

1960 HILL, RICHARD M. (ed.). *Marketing Concepts in Changing Times.* Chicago: American Marketing Association, 1960.

McCARTHY, E. J. *Basic Marketing: a Managerial Approach.* Homewood, Ill.: Richard D. Irwin, Inc., 1960.

1961 BUSKIRK, R. H. *Principles of Marketing.* New York: Holt, Rinehart, and Winston, 1961; rev. ed., 1966.

SHULTZ, W. J. *American Marketing.* San Francisco: Wadsworth Publishing Co., Inc., 1961.

TAYLOR, W. J. and R. T. SHAW. *Marketing: An Integrated Analytical Approach.* Cincinnati: South-Western Publishing Company. 1961; 2d ed., 1969.

1962 BURSK, E. C. *Text and Cases in Marketing: A Scientific Approach.* Englewood Cliffs, N.J.: Prentice-Hall, Inc., 1962.

WALTERS, S. G. and others. *READINGS in MARKETING.* Cincinnati: South-Western Publishing Company, 1962.

1963 ANDERSON, R. C. and P. R. CATEORA (eds.). *Marketing Insights.* New York: Appleton-Century-Crofts, Inc., 1963; 2d ed., 1968.

DIRKSEN, C. J. (ed.) *Readings in Marketing.* Homewood, Ill.: Richard D. Irwin, Inc., 1963, rev. ed., 1968.

HOLLOWAY, R.J. and R.S. HANCOCK. *Marketing in a Changing Environment.* New York: John Wiley & Sons, Inc., 1963.

HOLMES, P. M. and others (eds.) *Readings in Marketing.* Columbus, Ohio: Charles E. Merrill Books, Inc., 1963.

1964 BUZZELL, R.D. *et al. Marketing an Introductory Analysis.* New York: McGraw-Hill Book Co., Inc., 1964; 2d ed., as *Marketing: A Contemporary Analysis,* 1972.

CUNDIFF, E. W. and R. R. STILL. *Basic Marketing: Concepts, Environment, and Design.* Englewood Cliffs, N.J.: Prentice-Hall, Inc., 1964; 2d ed., 1971.

HEIDINGSFELD, M. S. and A. B. BLANKENSHIP. *Marketing.* New York: Barnes & Noble, 1964, 2d ed., 1968.

HOLLOWAY, R. J. and R. S. HANCOCK (eds.). *The Environment of Marketing Behavior.* New York: John Wiley & Sons, Inc., 1964; 2d ed., 1969.

MATTHEWS, J. B. and Others. *Marketing.* New York: McGraw-Hill Book Co., Inc., 1964.

OTTESON, S. F. and Others. *Marketing: the Firm's Viewpoint.* New York: MacMillan Co., 1964.

STANTON, W.J. *Fundamentals of Marketing.* New York: McGraw-Hill Book Co., Inc., 1964; 2d ed., 1967; 3d ed., 1971.

WESTING, J.H. and G. ALBAUM (eds.). *Modern Marketing Thought.* New York: MacMillan Co., 1964; 2d ed., 1970.

1965   COX, REAVIS, *et al. Distribution in a High-level Economy.* Englewood Cliffs, N.J.: Prentice-Hall, Inc., 1965.

JONES, M.H. *The Marketing Process, An Introduction.* New York: Harper and Row, 1965.

1966   BELL, MARTIN L. *Marketing: Concepts and Strategy.* Boston: Houghton Mifflin, 1966; 2d ed., 1972.

STILL, R. R. and E. W. CUNDIFF. *Essentials of Marketing.* Englewood Cliffs, N.J.: Prentice-Hall, Inc., 1966. New York: Harper & Bros., 1966.

1967   RAYMOND, R. S. *Basic Marketing: Programmed Text and Cases.* Cleveland: World Publishing Co., 1967.

1968   DAY, R. L. *Concepts for Modern Marketing.* Scranton: International Textbook Company, 1968.

HEIDINGSFELD, M. S. *Changing Patterns in Marketing.* Boston: Allyn & Bacon, 1968.

HOLLOWAY, R. J. and R. S. HANCOCK (eds.). *Marketing in a Changing Environment.* New York: John Wiley & Sons, Inc., 1968; 2d ed., 1973.

MASON, R. E. and P. N. RATH. *Marketing and Distribution.* New York: McGraw-Hill Book Co., Inc., 1968.

REVZAN, D. A. *A Geography of Marketing: Integrative Statement.* Berkeley, California: University of California, 1968.

SCOTT, R. A. and N. E. MARKS. *Marketing and Its Environment.* Belmont, California: Wadsworth Publishing Company, 1968.

SHAPIRO, S. J. and A. F. DOODY (comps.). *Readings in the History of American Marketing: Settlement to Civil War.* Homewood, Ill.: Richard D. Irwin, Inc., 1968.

1969   CRAWFORD, C. Merle. *The Future Environment for Marketing.* Ann Arbor, Bureau of Business Research, University of Michigan, 1969.

ELLING, K. A. *Introduction to Modern Marketing.* New York: Macmillan Co., 1969.

ENIS, B. M. and K. K. COX (comps.). *Marketing Classics.* Boston: Allyn & Bacon, Inc., 1969.

LYNN, R. A. *Marketing Principles and Market Action.* New York: McGraw-Hill Book Co., Inc., 1969.

1970   BUELL, VICTOR P. (ed.). *Handbook of Modern Marketing.* New York: McGraw-Hill Book Co., Inc., 1970.

WENTZ, W. B. and G. I. EYRICH. *Marketing: Theory and Application.* New York: Harcourt, Brace and World, 1970.

1971 GIST, R. R. *Marketing and Society.* New York: Holt, Rinehart & Winston, Inc., 1971; 2d ed., 1974.

GIST, R. R. (ed.). *Readings in Marketing and Society.* New York: Holt, Rinehart & Winston, Inc., 1971; 2d ed., 1974.

GRAYSON, R. A. and R. A. OLSEN. *Introduction to Marketing: a Practical Approach.* New York: Appleton-Century-Crofts, 1971.

NARVER, J. C. and R. SAVITT. *The Marketing Economy: an Analytical Approach.* New York: Holt, Rinehart and Winston, 1971.

REVZAN, D. A. *A Marketing View of Spatial Competition.* Berkeley, California: University of California, 1971.

ZOBER, MARTIN. *Principles of Marketing.* Boston: Allyn and Bacon, 1971.

1972 BUCKLIN, LOUIS P. *Competition and Evolution in the Distributive Trades.* Englewood Cliffs, N.J.: Prentice-Hall, Inc., 1972.

FRANK, R. E. and YOREM WIND. *Market Segmentation.* Englewood Cliffs, N.J.: Prentice-Hall, Inc., 1972.

HANAN, MACK. *Life-Styled Marketing.* New York: American Management Association, 1972.

1973 CUNDIFF, E. W., R. R. STALL, and N. A. P. Govoni. *Fundamentals of Modern Marketing.* Englewood Cliffs, N.J.: Prentice-Hall, Inc., 1973.

FRYE, R. W. *Introduction to the Marketing System.* San Francisco: Canfield Press, 1973.

GRASHOF, J. F. and A. P. KELMAN. *Introduction to Macro-Marketing.* Columbus, Ohio: Grid, Inc., 1973.

1975 KOTLER, PHILIP. *Marketing for Nonprofit Organizations.* Englewood Cliffs, N.J.: Prentice-Hall, Inc., 1975.

MARKETING MANAGEMENT

1948 CULLITON, JAMES W. *The Management of Marketing Costs.* Boston: Harvard University, Graduate School of Business Administration, 1948.

1953 PHELPS, D. M. *Marketing Management:* Homewood, Ill.: Richard D. Irwin, Inc., 1953; rev. ed., 1960 with J. H. Westing; 3d ed., 1968.

1957 ALDERSON, W. *Marketing Behavior and Executive Action.* Homewood, Ill.: Richard D. Irwin, Inc., 1957.

HOWARD, J. R. *Marketing Management: Analysis and Decision.* Homewood, Ill.: Richard D. Irwin, Inc., 1957; rev. ed., 1963; 3d ed., 1973.

1958 KELLEY, E. J. and W. LAZER (eds.). *Managerial Marketing: Perspectives and Viewpoints.* Homewood, Ill.: Richard D. Irwin, Inc., 1958; rev. ed., 1962; 3d ed., 1967.

1960 McCARTHY, E. J. *Basic Marketing: a Managerial Approach.* Homewood, Ill.: Richard D. Irwin, Inc., 1960; rev. ed., 1964; 3d ed., 1968; 4th ed., 1971.

1961 DAVIS, K. R. *Marketing Management.* New York: The Ronald Press Company, 1961; 2d ed., 1966; 3d ed., 1972.

FAVILLE, D. E. *Selected Cases in Marketing Management.* Englewood Cliffs, N.J.: Prentice-Hall, Inc., 1961.

LAZO, H. and A. CORBIN. *Management in Marketing.* New York: McGraw-Hill Book Co., Inc., 1961.

MAUSER, F.F. *Modern Marketing Management*. New York: McGraw-Hill Book Co., Inc., 1961; 2d ed., 1973.

1962 BURSK, E. C. *Text and Cases in Marketing: a Scientific Approach*. Englewood Cliffs, N.J.: Prentice-Hall, Inc., 1962.

LEVITT, THEODORE. *Innovation in Marketing*. New York: McGraw-Hill Book Co., Inc., 1962.

1963 BERG, T. L. and A. SCHUCHMAN (eds.). *Product Strategy and Management*. New York: Holt, Rinehart and Winston, 1963.

BRITT, S.H. and H.W. BOYD (eds.). *Marketing Management and Administrative Action*. New York: McGraw-Hill Book Co., Inc., 1963, rev. ed., 1968; 3d ed., 1973.

1964 ALDERSON, W. and P. E. GREEN. *Planning and Problem Solving in Marketing*. Homewood, Ill., Richard D. Irwin, Inc., 1964.

BURSK, E. C. *et al.* (eds.). *Modern Marketing Strategy*. Cambridge: Harvard University Press, 1964.

CHARVAT, F. J. and W. T. WHITMAN. *Marketing Management*. New York: Simmons-Boardman Publishing Co., 1964.

GENTRY, D. L. and D. L. SHAWYER. *Fundamentals of Managerial Marketing*. New York: Simmons-Boardman Publishing Co., 1964.

JONES, FRED M. *Introduction to Marketing Management*. New York: Appleton-Century-Crofts, 1964.

ZOBER, M. *Marketing Management*. New York: John Wiley & Sons, Inc., 1964.

1965 ALDERSON, W. *Dynamic Marketing Behavior*. Homewood, Ill.: Richard D. Irwin, Inc., 1965.

ALEXANDER, R. S. and T. L. BERG. *Dynamic Management in Marketing*. Homewood, Ill.: Richard D. Irwin, Inc., 1965.

BURSK, E. C. *Cases in Marketing Management*. Englewood Cliffs, N.J.: Prentice-Hall, Inc., 1965.

KELLEY, E. J. *Marketing: Strategy and Functions*. Englewood Cliffs, N.J.: Prentice-Hall, Inc., 1965.

STAUDT, T. A. and D. A. TAYLOR. *A Managerial Introduction to Marketing*. Englewood Cliffs, N.J.: Prentice-Hall, Inc., 1965; 2d ed., 1970.

1966 BUELL, V. P. *Marketing Management in Action*. New York: McGraw-Hill Book Co., Inc., 1966.

FIELD, G.A., JOHN DOUGLAS, L.X. TARPEY. *Marketing Management – A Behavioral Systems Approach*. Columbus, Ohio: Charles F. Merrill Books, 1966.

1967 BRION, J. M. *Corporate Marketing Planning*. New York: John Wiley & Sons, Inc., 1967.

KOTLER, PHILIP. *Marketing Management*. Englewood Cliffs, N.J.: Prentice-Hall, Inc., 1967; 2d ed., 1972.

MYERS, J. H. and W. H. REYNOLDS. *Consumer Behavior and Marketing Management*. Boston: Houghton Mifflin Company, 1967.

NEWMAN, J. W. *Marketing Management and Information*. Homewood, Illinois: Richard D. Irwin, Inc., 1967.

1968 COX, K. K. *Analytical Viewpoints in Marketing Management*. Englewood Cliffs, N.J.: Prentice-Hall, Inc., 1968.

LUCK, D. J. and A. E. PRELL. *Marketing Strategy*. New York: Appleton-Century-Crofts, Inc., 1968.

MORSE, S. *The Practical Approach to Marketing Management*. New York: McGraw-Hill Book Co., Inc., 1968.

OTTESON, S. F. *et al. Marketing: the Firm's Viewpoint.* New York: Macmillan Co., 1968.

1969 COX, K. K. and K. KEITH. *Experimentation for Marketing Decision.* Scranton: International Textbook Company, 1969.

MONTGOMERY, D. B. and G. L. URBAN. *Management Science in Marketing.* Englewood Cliffs, N.J.: Prentice-Hall, Inc., 1969.

RATHMELL, J. M. *Managing the Marketing Functions.* New York: John Wiley & Sons, Inc., 1969.

1970 STURDIVANT, F. D., *et al. Managerial Analysis in Marketing.* Glenview, Ill.: Scott, Foresman and Company, 1970.

1971 KOTLER, PHILIP. *Marketing Decision Making: a Model Building Approach.* New York: Holt, Rinehart and Winston, 1971.

LAZER, WILLIAM. *Marketing Management: a Systems Approach.* New York: John Wiley & Sons, Inc., 1971.

LIPSON, H. A. and J. R. DARLING. *Introduction to Marketing: an Administrative Approach.* New York: John Wiley & Sons, Inc., 1971.

STURDIVANT, F. D. *et. al. Perspectives in Marketing Management: Readings.* Glenview Ill.: Scott Foresman, 1971.

BOYD, H. W. and W. F. MASSY. *Marketing Management:* New York: Harcourt, Brace & Jovanovick. 1972.

HARTLEY, R. F. *Marketing: Management and Social Change.* Scranton: Intext Educational Publishers, 1972.

KOLLAT, D. T., R. G. BLACKWELL, J. F. ROBESON. *Strategic Marketing.* New York: Holt, Rinehart and Winston, 1972.

KOTLER, P. and K. K. COX. *Readings in Modern Management.* Englewood Cliffs, N.J.: Prentice-Hall, Inc., 1972.

SOCIAL AND BEHAVIORAL
ASPECTS OF MARKETING

1955 CLARK, LINCOLN (ed.). *The Life Cycle and Consumer Behavior.* New York: New York University Press, 1955.

LOMBARD, GEORGE. *Behavior in a Selling Group.* Boston: Harvard University, 1955.

1956 HICKMAN, C. S. and M. KUHN. *Individuals, Groups, and Economic Behavior.* New York: Dryden Press, Inc., 1956.

1957 CLEWETT, ROBERT L. *Marketing's Role in Scientific Management.* Chicago: American Marketing Association,

MARTINEAU, PIERRE. *Motivation in Advertising.* New York: McGraw-Hill Book Co., Inc., 1957.

NEWMAN, JOSEPH. *Motivation Research and Marketing Management.* Boston: Harvard University, 1957.

1958 CLARK, LINCOLN (ed.). *Consumer Behavior: Research on Consumer Reactions.* New York: Harper & Brothers, 1958.

FERBER, ROBERT and HUGH WALES. *Motivation and Market Behavior.* Homewood, Ill.: Richard D. Irwin, Inc., 1958.

1960 KATONA, GEORGE. *The Powerful Consumer.* New York: McGraw-Hill Book Co., Inc., 1960.

1961 FOOTE, NELSON (ed.). *Household Decision Making.* New York: N.Y. University Press, 1961.

1962 DECKER, WILLAIM S. (ed.). *Emerging Concepts in Marketing.* Chicago: American Marketing Association, 1962.

ROGERS, EVERETT M. *Diffusion of Innovation.* New York: The Free Press of Glencoe, 1962.

1963 BLISS, PERRY (ed.). *Marketing and the Behavioral Sciences.* Rockleigh, N. J.: Allyn & Bacon, Inc., 1963; 2d ed., 1967.

CYERT, RICHARD M. and JAMES G. MARCH. *A Behavioral Theory of the Firm.* Englewood Cliffs, N.J.: Prentice-Hall, Inc., 1963.

1964 DAY, R. L. (ed.). *Marketing Models – Quantitative and Behavioral.* Scranton, Pa.: International Textbooks, 1964.

SMITH, GEORGE L. *Reflections on Progress in Marketing.* Chicago: American Marketing Assn., 1964.

TUCKER, W. T. *The Social Context of Economic Behavior.* New York: Holt, Rinehart and Winston, 1964.

1965 OPPENHEIM, IRENE. *The Family as Consumers.* New York: Macmillan Co., 1965.

ZALTMAN, GERALD. *Marketing: Contributions from the Behavioral Sciences.* New York: Harper & Bros., 1965.

1966 BRITT, STEUART H. (ed.). *Consumer Behavior and the Social Sciences.* New York: John Wiley & Sons, Inc., 1966.

FIELD, G. A., J. DOUGLAS, and L. X. TARPEY. *Marketing Management: A Behavioral Systems Approach.* Columbus, Ohio: C. E. Merrill Books, 1966.

1967 LAZER, WILLAIM. "The Interdisciplinary Approach to Marketing: A Management Overview."

TUCKER, W. T. *Marketing: A Behavioral Approach* New York: Holt, Rinehart, and Winston, 1967.

1968 ENGEL, JAMES F., DAVID T. KOLLAT, and ROGER D. BLACKWELL. *Consumer Behavior.* Holt, Rinehart, and Winston, 1968.

1969 ALEXIS, N., *et. al. Empirical Foundations of Marketing; Research Findings in the Behavioral and Managerial Sciences.* Chicago: Markham Publishing Co., 1969.

HOLLOWAY, R. J., R. A. MITTELSTAEDT, and M. VENKATESAN (eds.). *Consumer Behavior: Contemporary Research in Action.* New York: Free Press, 1969; 2d ed., Boston: Houghton-Mifflin Co., 1971.

1970 BLISS, PERRY (ed.). *Marketing Management and The Behavioral Environment.* Englewood Cliffs, N.J.: Prentice-Hall, Inc., 1970.

1971 DAY, R. L. and T. E. Ness (eds.). *Marketing Models: Behavioral Science Application.* Scanton: Intext Educational Publishers, 1971.

QUANTITATIVE ASPECTS OF MARKETING

1964 BUZZELL, ROBERT D. (ed.) *Mathematical Models and Marketing Management.* Boston: Harvard University, 1964.

DAY, R. L. (ed.). *Marketing Models – Quantitative and Behavioral.* Scranton, Pa.: International Textbooks, 1964.

1965 LANGHOFF, P. *Models, Measurement and Marketing.* Englewood Cliffs, N.J.: Prentice-Hall, Inc., 1965.

1967 CATEORA, P. R. and L. RICHARDSON (eds.). *Readings in Marketing: the Qualitative and Quantitative Areas.* New York: Appleton-Century-Crofts, 1967.

FRANK, R. E. and P. E. GREEN. *Quantitative Methods in Marketing.* Englewood Cliffs, N.J.: Prentice-Hall, Inc., 1967.

KING, W. R. *Quantitative Analysis for Marketing Management.* New York: McGraw-Hill Book Co., Inc., 1967.

1968 BASS, F. M., C. W. KING and E. A. PESSEMIER. *Application of the Sciences in Marketing Management.* New York: John Wiley & Sons, Inc., 1968.

DAY, R. L. *Marketing in Action, a Decision Game.* Homewood, Ill.: Richard D. Irwin, Inc., rev. ed., 1968.

1969 CASHER, J. D. *Marketing and the Computer.* Braintree, Mass.: D. H. Mark, 1969.

1971 DAY, R. L. and J. PARSONS (eds.). *Marketing Models: Quantitative Applications.* Scranton: Intext Educational Publishers, 1971.

KOTLER, P. *Marketing Decision Making: a Model Building Approach.* New York, Holt, Rinehart and Winston, 1971.

1973 JOLSON, M. A. *et al. Quantitative Techniques for Marketing.* New York: Macmillan Co., 1973.

MARKETING SYSTEMS

1923 MORIARITY, W. D. *The Economics of Marketing and Advertising.* New York: Harper & Bros., 1923.

1929 VAILE, R. S. and P. L. SLAGSVOLD. *Marketing.* New York: Ronald Press Co. (preliminary edition), 1929.

1930 VAILE R. S. and P. L. SLAGSVOLD. *Market Organization.* New York: Ronald Press Co., 1930.

1934 BREYER, R. F. *The Marketing Institution.* New York: McGraw-Hill Book Co., Inc., 1934.

1947 DUDDY, E. A. and D. A. REVZAN. *Marketing: An Institutional Approach.* New York: McGraw-Hill Book Co., 1947; 2d ed., 1953.

1949 BREYER, RALPH F. *Quantitative Systemic Analysis and Control: Study No. 1 – Channel and Channel Group Costing.* Philadelphia: College Offset Press, 1949.

1954 CLEWETT, RICHARD M. (ed.). *Marketing Channels for Manufactured Goods.* Homewood, Ill.: Richard D. Irwin, Inc., 1954.

1955 PALAMOUNTAIN, J. C. *The Politics of Distribution.* Cambridge: Harvard University Press, 1955; New York: Greenwood Press, 1968.

1966 BUCKLIN, L. P. *A Theory of Distribution Channel Structure.* University of California Institute of Business and Economic Research, 1966.

1967 BALIGH, H. R. and L. RICHARTY. *Vertical Marketing Structure.* Boston: Allyn & Bacon, Inc., 1967.

FISK, G. *Marketing Systems.* New York: Harper & Row, 1967.

FISK, G. (ed.). *Theories for Marketing Systems Analysis.* New York: Harper and Row, 1967.

MALLEN, R. E. (ed.). *The Marketing Channel.* New York: John Wiley & Sons, Inc., 1967.

1968 LEWIS, E. H. *Marketing Channels: Structure and Strategy.* New York: McGraw-Hill Book Co., Inc., 1968.

1969 STERN, L. W. (ed.). *Distribution Channels: Behavioral Dimensions.* Boston: Houghton Mifflin Company, 1969.

1971 MOLLER, W. G. *Marketing Channels: a Systems Viewpoint.* Homewood, Ill.: Richard D. Irwin, Inc., 1971.

THOMPSON, D. W. *Contractual Marketing Systems.* Lexington, Mass.: Heath Lexington Books, 1971.

1972 ANDERSEN, R.C. (ed.). *Distribution Systems.* New York: Appleton-Century-Crofts, 1972.

BUCKLIN, L. P. *Competition and Evolution in the Distributive Trades.* Englewood Cliffs, N.J.: Prentice-Hall, Inc., 1972.

STASCH, S. F. *Systems Analysis for Marketing Planning and Control.* Glenview, Ill.: Scott Foresman, 1972.

1973 WALKER, B. J. and J. B. HAYNES (eds.). *Marketing Channels.* Columbus, Ohio: Grid, Inc., 1973.

ENVIRONMENTALISM AND COMPARATIVE MARKETING

1963 BARTELS, ROBERT (ed.). *Comparative Marketing: Wholesaling in Fifteen Countries.* Homewood, Ill.: Richard D. Irwin, Inc., 1963.

GOLDMAN, M. I. *Soviet Marketing.* New York: Macmillan Co., 1963.

1964 B. E. MALLEN and I. A. LITVAK, (eds.). *Marketing: Canada.* New York: McGraw-Hill Book Co., Inc., 1964; 2d ed., 1968.

1965 BENNETT, P. D. (ed.). *Marketing and Economic Development.* Chicago: Proceedings of American Marketing Association, 1965.

MOYER, REED. *Marketing and Economic Development.* East Lansing: Michigan State University, 1965.

1966 BOYD, H. W. (ed.). *Marketing Management: Cases from the Emerging Countries.* Reading, Mass.: Addison-Wesley Publishing Co., Inc., 1966.

1967 CARSON, DAVID. *International Marketing: A Comparative Systems Approach.* New York: John Wiley & Sons, Inc., 1967.

MILLER, CLARENCE (ed.). *Marketing and Economic Development.* University of Nebraska Press, 1967.

1968 MOYER, REED and S. C. HOLLANDER (eds.). *Markets and Marketing in Developing Countries.* Homewood, Ill.: Richard D. Irwin, Inc., 1968.

SCOTT, RICHARD A. and N. E. MARKS. (eds.). *Marketing and its Environment.* Belmont, Cal.: Wadsworth Publishing Co., 1968.

SOMMERS, M. S. and J. B. KERNAN (eds.). *Comparative Marketing Systems, a Cultural Approach.* New York: Appleton-Century-Crofts, 1968.

1969 ARCHER, M. and W. J. L. CLARK. *Canadian Marketing.* Toronto: McGraw-Hill Company of Canada Limited, 1969.

BODDEWYN, JEAN J. (ed.). *Comparative Management and Marketing: Text and Readings.* Glenview, Ill.: Scott Foresman, 1969.

1970 ANDERSON, DOLE A. *Marketing and Development, the Thailand Experience.* East Lansing: Michigan State University, 1970.

GLADE, WILLIAM P., *et. al. Marketing in a Developing Nation.* Lexington, Mass.: Heath Lexington Books, 1970.

1971 BICKERS, R. L. T. *Marketing in Europe.* London: Gower Press, 1971.

WILHELMS, CHRISTIAN and K. BOECK. *Market and Marketing in the Federal Republic of Germany.* Hamburg: Verlag Weltarchiv GMBH, 1971.

YOSHINO, M. Y. *The Japanese Marketing System.* Cambridge, Mass.: The MIT Press, 1971.

1972 BODDEWYN, JEAN J. (ed.). *World Business Systems and Environments.* Scranton, Pa.: Intext Educational Publishers, 1972.

1973 BALLON, R. J. (ed.). *Marketing in Japan.* Tokyo: Sophia University, 1973.

BERRY, LEONARD L. and JAMES S. HENSEL (eds.). *Marketing and the Social Environment.* New York: Petroceli Press, 1973.

DESCHAMPSNEUFS, HENRY. *Marketing in the Common Market.* London: Pan Books, 1 Ltd., 1973.

GREER, T. V. *Marketing in the Soviet Union.* New York: Prager, 1973.

MALLEN, B. E. *Marketing in the Canadian Environment.* Scarborough, Ontario: Prentice-Hall job Canada, 1973.

THOMPSON, D. N. and D. S. R. LEIGHTON (ed.). *Canadian Marketing.* Toronto: Wiley Publishers of Canada, 1973.

INTERNATIONAL MARKETING

1935 COLLINS, V. D. *World Marketing.* Philadelphia: J. B. Lippincott, Co. 1935.

1963 STANLEY, A. O., (ed.) *Handbook of International Marketing.* New York: McGraw-Hill Book Co., Inc., 1963.

1964 KRAMER, R. L. *International Marketing.* Burlingame, California: South-Western Publishing Co., 1964; 3d ed., 1970.

1965 FAYERWEATHER, J. *International Marketing.* Englewood Cliffs, N.J.: Prentice-Hall, Inc., 1965.

1966 HESS, J. M. and P. R. CATEORA. *International Marketing.* Homewood, Ill. Richard D. Irwin, Inc., 1966; Rev. ed., 1971.

LEIGHTON, D. S. R. *International Marketing: Text and Cases.* New York: McGraw-Hill Book Co., Inc., 1966.

1967 RYANS, J. K. and J. C. BAKER (eds.). *World Marketing.* New York: John Wiley & Sons, Inc., 1967.

1969 PATTY, C. ROBERT and H. L. VREDENBURG. *Readings in Global Marketing Management.* New York: Appleton-Century-Crofts, 1969.

THOMAS, M. J. (ed.). *International Marketing Management.* Boston: Houghton Mifflin Co., 1969.

1970 MIRACLE, G. E. and G. S. ALBAUM. *International Marketing Management.* Homewood, Ill.: Richard D. Irwin, Inc., 1970.

1971 GRUB, P.D. and M. KASKIMIES (eds.). *International Marketing in Perspective.* Helsinki, Finland; S. Kirja Cy, 1971.

1972 TERPSTRA, VERN. *International Marketing.* New York: Holt, Rinehart and Winston, Inc., 1972.

1973 THORELLI, H. B. (ed.). *International Marketing Strategy: Selected Readings.* Harmondsworth, England: Penguin Books, 1973.

LOGISTICS

1955 TAFF, CHARLES A. *Management of Physical Distribution and Transportation.* Homewood, Ill.: Richard D. Irwin, Inc., 1955; 2d ed. 1959; 3d ed., 1964; 4th ed., 1968; 5th ed. 1972.

1961 SMYKAY, E. W., D. J. BOWERSOX, and F. H. MOSSMAN. *Physical Distribution Management.* New York: Macmillan Co., 1961; 2d ed., by D. J. BOWERSOX, E. W. SMYKAY, and B. J. LaLONDE, 1968; 3d ed., by E. W. SMYKAY, 1973.

1964 HESKETT, J.L., R.M. IVIE, and N. A. GLASKOWSKY, JR. *Business Logistics.* New York: The Ronald Press Co., 1964; 2d ed., 1973.

1965 MOSSMAN, F. H. and N. MORTON. *Logistics of Distributive Systems.* Boston: Allyn and Bacon, 1965.

1966   BARTLETT, H. C. (ed.). *Readings in Physical Distribution.* Danville, Ill.:
          Interstate Printers and Publishers, 1966; rev. ed., 1970.
       CONSTANTIN, J. A. *Principles of Logistics Management.* New York:
          Appleton-Century-Crofts, 1966.
1967   ARBURY, J. N. and others. *A New Approach to Physical Distribution.*
          New York: American Management Assn., 1967.
       MAGEE, J. F. *Physical Distribution Systems.* New York: McGraw-Hill
          Book Co., Inc., 1967.
       MARKS, N. E. and R. M. TYALOR. *Marketing Logistics.* New York:
          John Wiley & Sons, Inc., 1967.
       MARTIN, N. E. *Marketing Logistics.* New York: John Wiley & Sons, Inc.,
          1967.
       SMYKAY, E. W. and B. J. LaLONDE. *Physical Distribution.* Chicago:
          The Dartnell Corp., 1967.
1968   BOWERSOX, D. J. and others. *Physical Distribution Management.* New
          York: Macmillan Co., 1968.
1969   DANIEL, N. E. and J. R. JONES (eds.). *Business Logistics, Concepts and
          Viewpoints.* Boston: Allyn and Bacon, Inc., 1969.
       SCHORR, J. *et al.* (eds.). *Logistics in Marketing.* New York: Pitman
          Publishing Corp., 1969.
1972   CHRISTOPHER, M. and GORDON WILLS. *Marketing Logistics and
          Distribution Planning.* New York: John Wiley & Sons, Inc., 1972.
1973   BALLOU, RONALD H. *Business Logistics Management.* Englewood
          Cliffs, N.J.: Prentice-Hall, Inc., 1973.
       HESKETT, J. L., L. M. SCHNEIDER, and N. A. GLASKOWSKY, JR.
          Case Problems in Business Logistics, New York: The Ronald Press
          Co., 1973.
1974   BOWERSOX, D. R. *Logistical Management.* New York: Macmillan Co.,
          1974.

MARKETING AND SOCIETY

1962   STEVENS, WILLIAM J. (ed.). *The Social Responsibilities of Marketing.*
          Chicago: American Marketing Assn., 1962.
1966   GRETHER, E. T. *Marketing and Public Policy.* Englewood Cliffs, N.J.:
          Prentice-Hall, Inc., 1966.
1968   MAGNUSON, WARREN G. and JEAN CARPER. *The Dark Side of the
          Marketplace.* Englewood Cliffs, N.J.: Prentice-Hall, Inc., 1968.
       PRESTON, LEE E. (ed.). *Social Issues in Marketing.* Glenview, Ill.: Scott,
          Foresman Publishing Co., 1968.
1969   LAVIDGE, R. J. and R. J. HOLLOWAY. (eds.). *Marketing and Society:
          the Challenge.* Homewood, Ill.: Richard D. Irwin, Inc., 1969.
       STURDIVANT, FREDERICK D. (ed.). *The Ghetto Marketplace.* New
          York: The Free Press, 1969.
1971   AAKER, DAVID A. and GEORGE S. Day. (eds.). *Consumerism – Search
          for the Consumer Interest.* New York: The Free Press, 1971; 2d
          ed., 1974.
       FURUHASHI, Y. HUGH and E. J. McCARTHY. *Social Issues of
          Marketing in the American Economy.* Columbus, Ohio: Grid, Inc.,
          1971.
       WISH, J. R. and S. H. GAMBLE (eds.). *Marketing and Social Issues.* New
          York: John Wiley & Sons, Inc., 1971.
1972   KANGUN, N. (ed.). *Society and Marketing.* New York: Harper and Row,
          1972.

ANDREASEN, ALAN R. (ed.). *Improving Inner-City Marketing.* Chicago: American Marketing Association, 1972.

GAEDEKE, RALPH M. and WARREN W. ETCHESON. (eds.). *Consumerism.* San Francisco: Canfield Press, 1972.

MOYER, REED. *Macro Marketing: a Social Perspective.* New York: John Wiley & Sons, Inc., 1972.

1973 ALLVINE, FRED C. (ed.). *Public Policy and Marketing Practices.* Chicago: American Marketing Association, 1973.

BERENSON, CONRAD and HENRY EILBIRT. (eds.). *The Social Dynamics of Marketing.* New York: Random House, 1973.

KELLEY, WILLAIM T. (ed.). *New Consumerism: Selected Readings.* Columbus, Ohio: Grid, Inc., 1973.

LAZER, WILLIAM and EUGENE J. KELLEY. (eds.). *Social Marketing.* Homewood, Ill.: Richard D. Irwin, Inc., 1973.

CONCEPTUAL DEVELOPMENT OF MARKETING THEORY

1935 RYAN, F. W. "Functional Elements of Market Distribution," *Harvard Business Review.* XIII, January, 1935, p. 205.

1943 JONES, F. M. "A New Interpretation of Marketing Functions," *Journal of Marketing.* VII, January, 1943, p. 256.

1944 BARTELS, ROBERT. "Marketing Principles," *Journal of Marketing.* IX, October, 1944, p. 151.

1945 CONVERSE, P. D. "The Development of the Science of Marketing; "An Exploratory Survey." *Journal of Marketing.* X, July, 1945, pp. 14-23.

1946 BARTELS, ROBERT. "Marketing Theory: Its Essential Nature," *Proceedings of the Christmas Meetings of the American Marketing Association.* Pittsburgh, 1946.

1948 ALDERSON, WROE, and REAVIS COX. "Towards a Theory of Marketing," *Journal of Marketing.* XIII, October, 1948, p. 137.

BROWN, LYNDON C. "Toward a Profession of Marketing," *Journal of Marketing.* XIII, July, 1948, p. 27.

1949 VAILE, R. S. "Towards a Theory of Marketing: A Comment," *Journal of Marketing.* XIII, April, 1949, p. 520.

1950 COX, REAVIS, and WROE ALDERSON (eds.). *Theory in Marketing.* Chicago: Richard D. Irwin, Inc., 1950.

REVZAN, DAVID A. "A Framework of a Theory of Marketing," in a review of *Theory in Marketing* by Reavis Cox and Wroe Alderson. *Journal of Marketing.* XV, July, 1950, pp. 101-109.

1951 BARTELS, ROBERT. "Can Marketing be a Science?" *Journal of Marketing.* XV, January, 1951, p. 319.

_____. "The Role of Theory in the Teaching of Marketing," *Proceedings of the Christmas Meetings of the American Marketing Association, 1950.* Atlanta: University of Georgia, 1951.

McGARRY, E. D. "The Contractual Function in Marketing," *Journal of Business* April, 1951, p. 96.

WALES, HUGH G. (ed.). *Changing Perspectives in Marekting.* Urbana: University of Illinois Press, 1951.

1952 ALDERSON, WROE. "Psychology for Marketing and Economics," *Journal of Marketing.* XVII, October, 1952, p. 119.

HUTCHINSON, K. D. "Marketing as a Science: An Appraisal," *Journal of Marketing.* XVI, January, 1952, p. 286.

OTTESON, S. F. (ed.). *Marketing: Current Problems and Theories.* Indiana Business Report No. 16, Bloomington: Indiana University, 1952.

STAINTON, R. S. "Science in Marketing," *Journal of Marketing.* XVII, July, 1952, p. 64.

1953 JEUCK, JOHN H. "Marketing Research – Milestone or Millstone?". *Journal of Marketing.* XIII, April, 1953, p. 382.

McGARRY, E. D. "Some New Viewpoints in Marketing," *Journal of Marketing.* XVIII, July, 1953, p. 33.

1954 McINNES, WILLIAM C. "A General Theory of Marketing," unpublished Ph.D. dissertation. New York University, 1954.

1957 BAUMOL, WILLIAM J. "On the Role of Marketing Theory," *Journal of Marketing.* XXI, April, 1957, pp. 413-418.

1959 BARTELS, ROBERT. "Sociologists and Marketologists," *Journal of Marketing.* XXIV, October, 1959, pp. 37-40.

1961 ASPINWALL, LEO V. *Four Marketing Theories.* Commemorative collection produced for the 1961 Colorado Marketing Conference, Boulder, Colorado: Bureau of Business Research, University of Colorado (papers first published in 1956 in Alderson & Sessions, *Cost and Profit Outlook).*

BARTELS, ROBERT. "Marketing as a Social and Political Tool," *Marketing: A Maturing Discipline.* Chicago: American Marketing Association, 1961, pp. 210-216.

_____. "Marketing," *Lincoln Library.* 25th ed., Columbus, Ohio: The Frontier Press Company, 1961, pp. 1235-45.

MILLS, HARLAN D. "Marketing as a Science," *Harvard Business Review,* 39, September-October, 1961, pp. 137-142.

1962 ASPINWALL, LEO V. "The Characteristics of Goods Theory," in *Managerial Marketing: Perspectives and Viewpoints.* rev. ed., William Lazer and Eugene J. Kelley (eds.). Homewood, Illinois: Richard D. Irwin, Inc., 1962, pp. 633-643.

_____. "The Depot Theory of Distribution," in *Managerial Marketing: Perspectives and Viewpoints.* rev. ed., by William Lazer and Eugene J. Kelley (eds.). Homewood, Illinois: Richard D. Irwin, Inc., 1962, pp. 652-659.

_____. "The Parallel Systems Theory," in *Managerial Marketing: Perspectives and Viewpoints.* rev. ed., by William Lazer and Eugene J. Kelley (eds.). Homewood, Illinois: Richard D. Irwin, Inc., 1962, pp. 644-652.

BARTELS, ROBERT. *The Development of Marketing Thought,* Homewood, Ill.: Richard D. Irwin, Inc., 1962. Also published in Spanish in Mexico: *El Desarrollo del Pensamiento en Mercadotecnia,* Mexico, D.F.: Compania Editorial Contenental, S.A., 1964. 2nd ed., *The History of Marketing Thought.* Columbus, Ohio, Grid, Inc., 1976. Japanese ed. 1979. "The Dimensions of Marketing Thought," in *Managerial Marketing: Perspectives and Viewpoints* by William Lazer and Eugene J. Kelley (eds.), rev. ed. Homewood, Illinois: Richard D. Irwin, Inc., 1962, pp. 578-585.

DECKER, WILLAIM S. (ed.). *Emerging Concepts in Marketing. Proceedings of the National Conference of the American Marketing Association.* Chicago, Ill.: American Marketing Assn., 1962.

374

LAZER, WILLIAM. "The Role of Models in Marketing," *Journal of Marketing.* XXVI, 2, April, 1962, pp. 9-14.

WEISS, E. B. "Will Marketing Ever Become a Science?" *Advertising Age.* August 20, 1962, pp. 64-65.

1963 BUZZELL, ROBERT. "Is Marketing a Science?" *Harvard Business Review.* 41, January-February, 1963, pp. 32-34; 36; 40; 166; 168; and 170.

HUEGY, H. W. (ed.). *The Conceptual Framework for a Science of Marketing.* Urbana: University of Illinois, 1963.

SCHWARTZ, GEORGE. *Development of Marketing Theory.* Cincinnati: South-Western Publishing Company, 1963.

1964 ASPINWALL, LEO V. "Consumer Acceptance Theory," in *Theory in Marketing* by Reavis Cox, Wroe Alderson, Stanley J. Shapiro (eds.), 2d series. Homewood, Illinois: Richard D. Irwin, Inc., 1964, pp. 247-253.

BARTELS, ROBERT. "A Methodological Framework for Comparative Marketing Study," *Toward Scientific Marketing, Proceedings of the Winter Conference of the American Marketing Association.* Stephen A. Greyser (ed.). Chicago: American Marketing Association, 1964, pp. 383-92.

COX, REAVIS, WROE ALDERSON, and STANLEY J. SHAPIRO (eds.). *Theory in Marketing.* Homewood, Illinois: Richard D. Irwin, 1964.

STARR, MARTIN K. "Management Science and Marketing Science," *Management Science.* X, 1964, pp. 557-673.

1965 ALDERSON, WROE, and MILES W. MARTIN, "Toward A Formal Theory of Transactions and Transvections," *Journal of Marketing Research.* II, May, 1965, pp. 117-27.

BARTELS, ROBERT. "Marketing Technology, Tasks, and Relationships," *Journal of Marketing.* XXIX, January, 1965, pp. 45-48.

HALBERT, M. *The Meaning and Sources of Marketing Theory.* New York: McGraw-Hill Book Co., Inc., 1965.

HOWARD, JOHN A. *Marketing Theory.* Boston: Allyn and Bacon, 1965.

LEE, CHARLES E. "Measurement and the Development of Science and Marketing," *Journal of Marketing Research.* II, February, 1965, pp. 20-25.

SCHWARTZ, G. (ed.). *Science in Marketing.* New York: John Wiley and Sons, Inc., 1965.

TAYLOR, W. J. "Is Marketing a Science? Revisited," *Journal of Marketing.* XXIX, July, 1965, pp. 49-53.

ZALTMAN, GERALD. *Marketing: Contributions from the Behavioral Sciences.* New York: Harcourt, Brace and World, 1965.

1967 BARTELS, ROBERT. "A Model for Ethics in Marketing," *Journal of Marketing.* XXXI, January, 1967, pp. 20-26.

LAZER, WILLIAM. "Some Observations of the 'State of the Art' of Marketing Theory," in *Managerial Marketing: Perspectives and Viewpoints.* Eugene J. Kelley and William Lazer (eds.), 3d ed., Homewood, Illinois: Richard D. Irwin, Inc., 1967, pp. 707-17.

1968 BARTELS, ROBERT. "Are Domestic and International Marketing Dissimilar?" *Journal of Marketing.* XXXII, July, 1968, pp. 56-61.

——. "The General Theory of Marketing," *Journal of Marketing.* XXXII, January, 1968, pp. 29-33.

KERNAN, J. B. and M. S. Sommers (eds.). *Perspectives in Marketing Theory.* New York: Appleton-Century-Crofts, Inc., 1968.

1969 HOWARD, JOHN and J. N. SHETH. *The Theory of Buyer Behavior.* New York: John Wiley and Sons, Inc., 1969.

KOTLER, PHILIP and SIDNEY J. LEVY. "Broadening the Concept of Marketing," *Journal of Marketing.* XXXIII, January, 1969, p. 10.

____. "A new Form of Marketing Myopia: Rejoinder to Professor Luck," *Journal of Marketing,* XXXIII, July, 1969, p. 55.

LAZER, WILLIAM. "Marketing's Changing Social Relationships," *Journal of Marketing,* XXXIII, January, 1969, p. 3.

LEWIS, RICHARD J. and LEO G. ERICKSON, "Marketing Functions and Marketing Systems: A Synthesis," *Journal of Marketing.* XXXIII, July, 1969, pp. 10-14.

LUCK, DAVID J. "Broadening the Concept of Marketing–Too Far," *Journal of Marketing.* XXXIII, July, 1969, p. 53.

MARTINELLI, PATRICK A. "Can Marketing Theory Be Developed Through The Study of Social Institutions?," *Journal of Marketing.* XXXIII, April, 1969, p. 60.

1970 BARTELS, ROBERT. *Marketing Theory and Metatheory.* Homewood, Illinois: Richard D. Irwin, Inc., 1970.

ROBIN, DONALD P. "Toward a Normative Science in Marketing," *Journal of Marketing.* XXXIV, October, 1970, p. 73.

ZALTMAN, GERALD. "Marketing Inference in the Behavioral Sciences," *Journal of Marketing.* XXXIV, July, 1970, p. 27-32.

1971 DAWSON, LESLIE M. "Marketing Science in the Age of Aquarius," *Journal of Marketing.* XXXV, July, 1971, p. 66.

EHRENBERG, A. S. C. "Laws in Marketing: A Tailpiece," in *New Essays in Marketing Theory* by George Fisk. Boston: Allyn and Bacon, 1971, pp. 28-40.

FISK, GEORGE. *New Essays in Marketing Theory.* Boston: Allyn and Bacon, 1971.

HUNT, SHELBY D. "The Morphology of Theory and the General Theory of Marketing," *Journal of Marketing.* XXXV, April, 1971, p. 65.

KOTLER, PHILIP and GERALD ZALTMAN. "Social Marketing: An Approach to Planned Social Change," *Journal of Marketing.* XXXV, July, 1971, p. 3.

1972 KOTLER, PHILIP. "A Generic Concept of Marketing," *Journal of Marketing.* XXXVI, April, 1972, p. 46.

PINSON, CHRISTIAN R. A., REINHARD ANGELMAR, and EDUARDO L. ROBERTO. "An Evaluation of the General Theory of Marketing," *Journal of Marketing.* XXXVI, July, 1972, p. 66.

STIDSON, BENT and THOMAS F. SCHUTTE. "Marketing as a Communication System: The Marketing Concept Revisited," *Journal of Marketing.* XXXVI, October, 1972, p. 22.

SWEENEY, DANIEL J. "Marketing: Management Technology or Social Process?," *Journal of Marketing.* XXXVI, October, 1972, p. 3.

1973 BARTELS, ROBERT and BRUCE E. MacNAB. "Marketing Theory and Practice," *Marketing Handbook.* Steuart H. Britt (ed.). 1973.

ENIS, BEN M. "Deepening the Concept of Marketing," *Journal of Marketing.* October, 1973, p. 57.

HUNT, SHELBY D. "Lawlike Generalizations and Marketing Theory," *Journal of Marketing.* July, 1973, p. 69.

ZALTMAN, GERALD, CHRISTIAN P. A. PINSON, and REINHARD ANGELMAR. *Metatheory and Consumer Research.* New York: Holt, Rinehart and Winston, Inc., 1973.

376

1974 BARTELS, ROBERT. "The Identity Crisis in Marketing," *Journal of Marketing*. October, 1974, p. 73.

LUCK, DAVID J. "Social Marketing: Confusion Compounded," *Journal of Marketing*. October, 1974, p. 65.

TAKAS, ANDREW. "Societal Marketing: A Businessman's Perspective," *Journal of Marketing*. October, 1974, p. 2.

TUCKER, W. T. "Future Directions in Marketing Theory," *Journal of Marketing*. April, 1974, p. 30.

LEADING CONTRIBUTORS TO MARKETING LITERATURE, CLASSIFIED INDEX

THE BEGINNINGS OF MARKETING THOUGHT

Agnew
Bartels
Converse
Hagerty
Litman
Maynard
Weld

ADVERTISING

Agnew
Borden
Boyd
Burton
Cherington
Dirksen
Engel
Hollingworth
Hotchkiss
Kirkpatrick
Kleppner
Miracle
Namm
Nixon
Sandage
Scott
Starch
Vaughn
Wales
Warshaw
Wright

CREDIT

Bartels
Beckman
Brisco
Chapin
Cole
Dakins
Ettinger
Foulke
Golieb
Hagerty
Hancock
Neifeld
Phelps
Picken
Prendergast
Seligman
Shultz
Steiner

SELLING

Black
Boyd
Brisco
Buzzotta
Canfield
Crissy
Douglas
Ernest
Estabrook
Fernald
Hanan
Ivey
Kirkpatrick
Lapp
Leigh
Nixon
Nystrom
Pederson
Robinson
Russell, T. H.
Russell, F. A.
Tosdal
Weld
Whitehead
Wright

SALES MANAGEMENT

Churchill
Cowan
Davis
Doubman
Eastwood
Frederick
Hoyt
Lyon
Maynard
Nolen
Phelps
Russell
Scott
Tosdal
Webster

RETAILING

Anderson	Duncan	McNair	Whitehead
Barker	Filene	Nystrom	Wingate
Bedell	Fisk	Phillips	
Brisco	Fri	Robinson	
Charters	Gist	Rowse	
Dalrymple	Hollander	Wess	
Davidson	Leigh	White	
Doody			

WHOLESALING

Alexander	Bucklin	Reed
Bartels	Elder	Revzan
Beckman	Hill	

MARKETING RESEARCH

Alderson	Cox	Kollat
Bass	Duncan	Luck
Blackwell	Eastwood	Reed
Blankenship	Engel	Shaw
Brown, L.O.	Enis	Wales
Buzzell	Ferber	Westfall
Boyd	Green	Wheeler
Cowan	Heckert	White

GENERAL MARKETING

Agnew	Clark	Killough	Stanton
Alexander	Converse	Matthews	Still
Anshen	Copeland	Maynard	Tosdal
Barker	Cundiff	McCarthy	Weidler
Beckman	Duncan	McNair	Weld
Bell	Hancock	Phillips	
Butler	Holloway	Pyle	
Cherington	Ivey	Shaw	

MARKETING READINGS

Alderson	Enis	Otteson
Bliss	Hancock	Roades
Boyd	Hansen	Shapiro
Clark	Holloway	Wales
Clewett	Kelley	Walters
Cox	Lazer	Westing
Doody	Landon	Wright

MARKETING MANAGEMENT

Alderson	Field	Lyon
Bell	Green	Phelps
Boyd	Howard	Pyle
Butler	Kelley	Tarpey
Davis	Kotler	White
Douglas	Lazer	

SOCIAL AND BEHAVIORAL ASPECTS OF MARKETING

Alderson	Blackwell	Kollat
Bagozzi	Cohen	Lazer
Bass	Cox	Levy
Bell	Day	Palamountain
Bettman	Engel	Shapiro
Bliss	Kassarjian	Tucker
Britt	Kelley	Zaltman

QUANTITATIVE ASPECTS OF MARKETING

Bass	King
Buzzell	Kotler
Day	Pessemier
Green	

MARKETING SYSTEMS

Andersen	Cox	Mallen
Baligh	Duddy	Revzan
Breyer	Fisk	Richarty
Bucklin	Grether	Stern
Clewett	Lewis	

ENVIRONMENTALISM AND COMPARATIVE MARKETING

Ballon	Hancock	Mallen	Sommers
Bartels	Hollander	Marks	Yoshino
Boddewyn	Holloway	Moyer	
Boyd	Kernan	Preston	
Goldman	Litvak	Scott	

INTERNATIONAL MARKETING

Albaum	Hess	Ryans
Baker	Holloway	Terpstra
Cateora	Kramer	Thomas
Collins	Leighton	
Fayerweather	Miracle	

LOGISTICS

Ballou	Heskett	Marks
Bauersox	Ivie	Mossman
Constantin	LaLonde	Smykay
Glaskowsky	Magee	Taylor

MARKETING AND SOCIETY

Allvine	Lavidge	Preston
Gamble	Lazer	Sturdivant
Holloway	Moyer	Wish

CONCEPTUAL DEVELOPMENT OF MARKETING THEORY

Alderson	Halbert	Luck	Sweeney
Aspinwall	Howard	McGarry	Tucker
Bartels	Hunt	Revzan	Vaile
Cox	Kotler	Robin	Zaltman
Enis	Lazer	Schwartz	
Fisk	Levitt	Shapiro	

NAME INDEX

Adams, H.F., 36
Agnew, H.E., 25, 27, 41, 42, 153, 291
Albaum, G.S., 214
Alderson, W. 156, 157, 177, 178, 181, 195, 234, 236, 237, 238, 249
Alexander, R.S., 25, 27, 117, 156
Alexis, N., 196
Anderson, D.A., 210
Anderson, I.D., 99
Angelmar, R., 239
Anshen, N., 154
Aspinwall, L., 238
Atkinson, E., 30
Ayers, M.V., 35

Bagozzi, R.P., 246, 267, 307
Baker, J.C., 207, 214
Ballon,, R.J., 211
Barker, C.W., 25, 99, 154
Bartels, R., 61, 62, 64, 119, 208, 212, 234, 239, 240, 246, 273, 308
Bartlett, J.T., 57
Barton, B., 42
Bass, F.M., 135, 196, 200, 246, 257, 308
Baumol, W.J., 238
Beckman, T.N., 25, 26, 57, 58, 61, 114, 147, 150, 160, 292
Beik, L.L., 136
Bell, M.L., 162
Bernstein, B., 60
Berry, L.L., 222
Bettman, J.R., 246, 266, 309
Bickers, R.L.T., 211
Black, G., 78
Blackwell, R.D., 196
Blankenship, A.B., 132
Blanton, B.H., 55
Bliss, P., 195, 196, 243
Boddweyn, J.J., 106, 211
Boeck, K., 211
Borden, N.H., 25, 26, 35, 43, 46, 293
Bowersox, D.J., 222, 246, 275, 310
Boyd, H.W., 134, 180, 193, 208
Brewster, A.J., 35, 39
Breyer, R.F., 25, 153, 154, 202, 295
Brisco, N.A., 27, 57, 74, 94, 96, 97, 178
Brisco, N.B., 94
Britt, S.E., 180
Brown, E., Jr., 147
Brown, L.O., 45, 130, 135
Brown, P.L., 100

Bucklin, L.P., 120, 202, 204, 206, 281, 310
Burton, P.W., 49
Bush, I., 75
Buskirk, R.H., 83, 159, 161
Butler, R.S., 24, 25, 26, 80, 124, 143, 178, 247, 294
Buzzell, R.D., 121, 200, 235, 246, 258, 310
Buzzotta, V.R., 79

Calkins, E.E., 37
Canfield, B.R., 76, 82
Carman, J.M., 160, 173
Carson, D., 210
Casher, J.D., 201
Casson, H.N., 75
Cateora, P.R., 214
Chapin, A.F., 58, 62
Charters, W.W., 75, 95
Cherington, P.T., 22, 26, 35, 38, 143, 146
Churchill, G.A., 246, 278, 311
Clark, E., 173
Clark, F.E., 25, 26, 30, 147, 149, 152, 222, 250, 296
Cohen, J.B., 246, 266, 312
Cole, R.H., 62, 64
Collins, G.R., 75
Collins, V.D., 213
Comish, N.H., 25, 26, 153, 296
Comyns, R.J., 73
Constantin, J.A., 217
Converse, P.D., 25, 26, 147, 149, 234, 251, 297
Coolsen, F.G., 34
Copeland, M.T., 25, 26, 152, 298
Corbin, A., 84, 180
Corey, E.R., 119
Cowan, D.R.G., 131
Cox, E.P., 105
Cox, K.K., 183
Cox, R., 60, 156, 157, 195, 234, 236, 237, 243, 249
Craig, S., 263
Cross, J.S., 117
Crowell, J.F., 142
Cundiff, E.W., 85, 161
Cunningham, R.M., 117

Dakins, J.G., 59
Dalrymple, D.J., 105
David, D.K., 110
Davidson, W.R., 100, 105, 173, 174

SUBJECT INDEX

3